FIFTH EDITION

POETRY

An Introduction

FIFTH EDITION

POETRY

An Introduction

Michael Meyer

University of Connecticut

BEDFORD / ST. MARTIN'S   Boston ◆ New York

For Bedford/St. Martin's

Executive Editor: Stephen A. Scipione
Senior Developmental Editor: Ellen Thibault
Senior Production Editor: Lori Chong Roncka
Production Supervisor: Andrew Ensor
Executive Marketing Manager: Jenna Bookin Barry
Marketing Manager: Adrienne Petsick
Associate Developmental Editor: Christina Gerogiannis
Production Assistants: Kristen Merrill, Amy Derjue, Katherine Caruana
Copyeditor: Mary Lou Wilshaw-Watts
Text Design: Claire Seng-Niemoeller
Cover Design: Donna Lee Dennison
Cover Art: Peter Kalkhof, *Constellation-Horizon (night-day)*, 2001, acrylic on canvas, 250 × 200 cm. Courtesy Annely Juda Fine Art, London.
Composition: Stratford Publishing Services, Inc.
Printing and Binding: Haddon Craftsmen, Inc., an R. R. Donnelley & Sons Company

President: Joan E. Feinberg
Editorial Director: Denise B. Wydra
Editor in Chief: Karen S. Henry
Director of Marketing: Karen Melton Soeltz
Director of Editing, Design, and Production: Marcia Cohen
Managing Editor: Elizabeth M. Schaaf

Library of Congress Control Number: 2006926010

Manufactured in the United States of America.

1 0 9 8
f e d c

For information, write: Bedford/St. Martin's
75 Arlington Street, Boston, MA 02116
(617-399-4000)

ISBN-10: 0-312-45051-6
ISBN-13: 978-0-312-45051-9

Acknowledgments

Fleur Adcock. "The Video" from *Poems 1960–2000* by Fleur Adcock (Bloodaxe Books, 2000). Copyright © 2000 by Fleur Adcock. Reprinted by permission of Bloodaxe Books Ltd.

Anna Akhmatova. "Lot's Wife" from *Anna Akhmatova, Selected Poems*, translated by Richard McKane (Bloodaxe Books, 1989). Copyright © 1967 by Richard McKane. Reprinted by permission of Bloodaxe Books Ltd.

Claribel Alegría. "I Am Mirror" from *Sobrevivo* by Claribel Alegría. Reprinted by permission of the author.

Sherman Alexie. "On the Amtrak from Boston to New York City" from *First Indian on the Moon*, copyright © 1993 by Sherman Alexie, reprinted by permission of Hanging Loose Press.

Acknowledgments and copyrights are continued at the back of the book on pages 758–66, which constitute an extension of the copyright page. It is a violation of the law to reproduce these selections by any means whatsoever without the written permission of the copyright holder.

For My Wife
Regina Barreca

About Michael Meyer

Michael Meyer has taught writing and literature courses for more than thirty years — since 1981 at the University of Connecticut and before that at the University of North Carolina at Charlotte and the College of William and Mary. In addition to being an experienced teacher, Meyer is a highly regarded literary scholar. His scholarly articles have appeared in distinguished journals such as *American Literature, Studies in the American Renaissance,* and *Virginia Quarterly Review.* An internationally recognized authority on Henry David Thoreau, Meyer is a former president of the Thoreau Society and coauthor (with Walter Harding) of *The New Thoreau Handbook,* a standard reference source. His first book, *Several More Lives to Live: Thoreau's Political Reputation in America,* was awarded the Ralph Henry Gabriel Prize by the American Studies Association. He is also the editor of *Frederick Douglass: The Narrative and Selected Writings* and the author of *The Little, Brown Guide to Writing Research Papers,* Third Edition. His other books for Bedford/St. Martin's include *The Bedford Introduction to Literature,* Seventh Edition and *Thinking and Writing about Literature,* Second Edition.

Preface for Instructors

Like its predecessors, this fifth edition of *Poetry: An Introduction* assumes that reading and understanding literature offer valuable means of apprehending life in its richness and diversity. This book also reflects the hope that its selections will inspire students to become lifelong readers of imaginative literature as well as more thoughtful and skillful writers.

This text is flexibly organized into four parts that may be taught consecutively or in any order you prefer. Part One — the first eleven chapters — is devoted to the elements of poetry; Part Two consists of ten chapters that feature a variety of approaches to poetry; Part Three is a collection of poems that includes albums of world and contemporary literature; and Part Four discusses strategies for critical thinking, reading, and writing about literature that can be assigned selectively throughout the course. Sample student papers and more than one thousand assignments appear in the text, offering students the support they need to write about poetry.

Poetry: An Introduction accommodates many teaching styles and addresses the needs of today's poetry classrooms. Among the features of the fifth edition are new sample close readings, new thematic case studies, a new in-depth chapter on the contemporary poet Julia Alvarez, and a new CD-ROM that offers instructors more options for teaching and students even more help for exploring, enjoying, and writing about literature.

FEATURES OF *POETRY: AN INTRODUCTION,* FIFTH EDITION

Following is a description of the features and contents that have long made *Poetry: An Introduction* a favorite of students and teachers. What is new to this edition is described starting on page x. (For a description of the *LiterActive* CD-ROM, see p. xiii of this preface.)

Teachable poems your students will want to read

Chosen for their appeal to students, *Poetry*'s rich and diverse selections range from the classic to the contemporary and include such gems as Gary Soto's "Mexicans Begin Jogging," Janice Mirikitani's "Recipe," and Billy Collins's "Introduction to Poetry." The poems represent a variety of periods, nationalities, cultures, styles, and voices — from the serious to the humorous and from the canonical to very recent works. As in previous editions, classic works by John Donne, Robert Frost, Elizabeth Bishop, Langston Hughes, and others are generously represented. In addition, there are many contemporary selections from writers such as Thomas Lux, Cathy Song, Susan Minot, and Sherman Alexie. Recent selections appear throughout the anthology and are also conveniently collected in Chapter 22, "An Album of Contemporary Poems."

Many options for teaching, learning — and enjoying

Over five editions, in its continuing effort to make literature come to life for students and the course a pleasure to teach for instructors, *Poetry: An Introduction* has developed and refined these innovative features:

A CLEAR, LIVELY DISCUSSION OF THE ELEMENTS OF POETRY.   The first ten chapters are devoted to the elements of poetry — diction, tone, images, figures of speech, symbols, sounds, rhythm, and poetic forms. Each begins with a focused, student-friendly discussion of the element interspersed with lively examples that show students how that element contributes to the meanings of a poem. At the end of each of these chapters is a mini-anthology of poems for further study, each accompanied by questions for critical thinking and writing.

ENRICHING PERSPECTIVES AND VISUALS.   Intriguing documents and images — including personal journals, letters, critical essays, interviews, photographs, and paintings — appear throughout the book to stimulate class discussion and writing. A visual portfolio titled "Encountering Poetry: Images of Poetry in Popular Culture" (p. 8) opens students' eyes to the presence of poetry in their lives.

USEFUL CONNECTIONS BETWEEN POPULAR AND LITERARY CULTURE.   *Poetry* draws carefully on examples from popular culture to explain the elements of poetry, inviting students to relate to literature through what they already know. Writing questions that help students draw connections between popular culture and more canonical works appear after each example. The examples include greeting-card verse and contemporary song lyrics, such as Bruce Springsteen's "You're Missing" and S. Pearl Sharp's "It's the Law: A Rap Poem."

POETS — AND POEMS — IN DEPTH AND THEMATIC CASE STUDIES.   In-depth chapters on Emily Dickinson, Robert Frost, Langston Hughes, and now Julia Alvarez, provide multiple works by each poet along with letters, interviews, draft manuscript pages, photos, and other contextual materials that enhance the study of these authors and their works. Case study chapters on specific poems — T. S. Eliot's "The Love Song of J. Alfred Prufrock" and Louise Erdrich's "Dear John Wayne" — invite students to respond to critical and cultural approaches to poetry; and the book's thematic chapters, including case studies on love and longing and on teaching and learning, connect students to literature through universal human experience.

ACCESSIBLE COVERAGE OF LITERARY THEORY.   For instructors who wish to incorporate literary theory into their courses, Chapter 25, "Critical Strategies for Reading" introduces students to a variety of critical strategies, ranging from formalism to cultural criticism. In brief examples, the approaches are applied in analyzing Robert Frost's "Mending Wall" and other works so that students will have a sense of how to use these strategies in their own reading and writing.

Plenty of help with reading and writing about poetry

SEVEN CHAPTERS ON READING AND WRITING ABOUT POETRY ensure that students get the help they need, beginning — in the book's introduction and first chapter — with how to approach a poem and think critically about it. Chapters 2 and 11 take students through every step of the writing process, from generating topics to documenting sources — while eight sample papers throughout the book model the results. (See the "Resources for Reading and Writing about Poetry" chart at the back of the book on p. 804.) For students who need help with researched writing, Chapter 27, "The Literary Research Paper," offers detailed advice for finding, evaluating, and incorporating print and electronic sources in a paper. It also includes the most current MLA documentation guidelines.

MORE THAN 1,500 QUESTIONS AND ASSIGNMENTS — First Response prompts, Considerations for Critical Thinking and Writing questions, Connections to Other Selections questions, Critical Strategies questions, and Creative Response questions — give students many opportunities for thinking and writing. In addition, these helpful checklists offer questions and suggestions for reading and writing about poetry:

- Suggestions for Approaching Poetry (Ch. 1, p. 40)
- Questions for Responsive Reading and Writing (Ch. 2, p. 61)
- Suggestions for Scanning a Poem (Ch. 8, p. 220)
- Questions for Writing about an Author in Depth (Ch. 12, p. 342)
- Questions for Revising and Editing (Ch. 26, p. 693)
- Questions for Incorporating Secondary Sources (Ch. 27, p. 728)

NEW TO THIS EDITION

105 new poems

These new poems represent canonical, multicultural, contemporary, and popular literature. Complementing the addition of several classic works that have long made classroom discussion come alive are numerous works not frequently anthologized, such as Carolina Hospital's "The Hyphenated Man" and Billie Bolton's "Memorandum." Featuring many of the most engaging poets of the twenty-first century, *Poetry* includes plenty of humorous poems on daily life and contemporary issues, including:

- Tony Hoagland's "America" (on a country walled in by "RadioShacks, Burger Kings, and MTV episodes")
- Richard Hague's "Directions for Resisting the SAT" (on avoiding life and its tests)
- Tom Wayman's "Did I Miss Anything?" (an ode to a student who has skipped class)

New annotated sample close readings

New annotated versions of several poems — William Hathaway's humorous "Oh, Oh," Elizabeth Bishop's widely taught "Manners," and John Donne's classic sonnet "Death Be Not Proud" — model for students the kind of critical reading that leads to excellent writing about poetry.

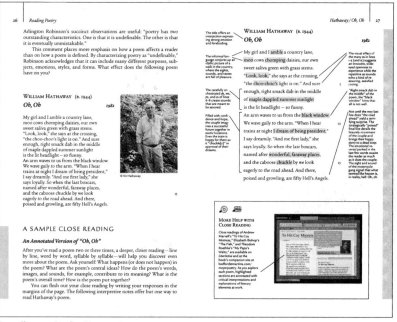

From Chapter 1: Reading Poetry

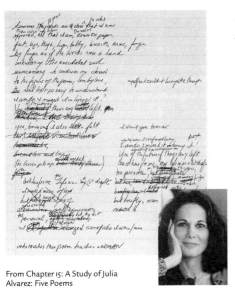

An inspiring new case study on Julia Alvarez

Developed in collaboration with the poet herself, Chapter 15 includes five of Julia Alvarez's favorite poems, her personal insights on these works—written expressly for this anthology—and contextual images, including many draft manuscript pages that showcase her remarkable writing and editing process.

From Chapter 15: A Study of Julia Alvarez: Five Poems

Two new thematic case studies

Chapter 21, *Poetry*'s new **border crossings** chapter, pairs seven poems—by writers such as Chitra Banerjee Divakaruni and Wole Soyinka—with visual texts on themes central to human experience: the crossing of racial, class-based, and geographic borders. The new Chapter 20, on **humor and satire**, offers literature that is rich in wit—with such works as Peter Schmitt's "Friends with Numbers" (about math, love, and loneliness) and Thomas Lux's "Commercial Leech Farming Today" (on the intersection of vanity, capitalism, and a humble blood-sucking parasite).

From Chapter 21: A Thematic Case Study: Border Crossings

Pablo Neruda

An interesting look at translation

In addition to four different translations of a poem by Sappho, a new section in Chapter 3, "Word Choice, Word Order, and Tone," features a short poem by **Pablo Neruda**. The poem, "Verbo," appears in the original Spanish and in three very different English versions that expose students to the issues and questions surrounding the translation of literature.

An emphasis on the visual that brings poetry to life

New visual contexts in the case studies include two illustrated letters and a recently discovered portrait of her in the chapter on Emily Dickinson; in the chapter on Langston Hughes, the original cover of *The Weary Blues* and photos of the Harlem Renaissance; and in the chapter on T. S. Eliot's "The Love Song of J. Alfred Prufrock," a photo of Eliot from the time when he wrote the poem, remarkably, at age twenty-three.

From Chapter 12: A Study of Emily Dickinson

Innovative multimedia tools for reading and writing

The fifth edition of *Poetry* offers an unparalleled set of multimedia tools to help students read, enjoy, think about, and write about poetry. Cross-references throughout the book direct students and instructors to the following resources.

The book's companion site — at *bedfordstmartins.com/meyerpoetry* — offers a generous array of resources including:

- The *VirtuaLit Interactive Poetry Tutorial*, offering in-depth readings with coverage of literary elements, cultural contexts, and critical approaches for:
  - Elizabeth Bishop's "The Fish"
  - Theodore Roethke's "My Papa's Waltz"
  - Andrew Marvell's "To His Coy Mistress"
- *Annotated LitLinks* that offer biographical information on the poets in the anthology and provide students with a starting point for their research

Book companion site

- *LitQuizzes* on the elements of poetry and a gradebook for instructors
- *LitGloss*, a glossary that offers quick access to hundreds of literary terms
- A PDF version of the Instructor's Manual: *Resources for Teaching* POETRY: AN INTRODUCTION

LiterActive CD-ROM

This groundbreaking resource is packed with contextual materials, activities for exploring poetry, and help with research and documentation. In addition to the VirtuaLit tutorials described above, LiterActive offers:

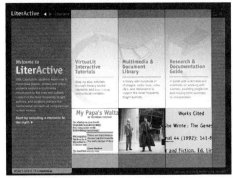

- A *Multimedia and Documents Gallery* stocked with hundreds of images, audio and video clips, and contextual documents supporting forty-three authors
- A *Research and Documentation Guide* with advice for students on how to find, evaluate, summarize, interpret, and document sources

LiterActive CD-ROM

This CD-ROM, a $10 value, is **available free** when packaged with *Poetry*; to order the two together, use ISBN-13: 978-0-312-46110-2 / ISBN-10: 0-312-46110-0.

Course Management Content

A variety of student and instructor resources developed for *Poetry: An Introduction*, Fifth Edition, are ready for use in course-management systems such as WebCT and Blackboard. For more information, visit bedfordstmartins.com/cms.

Literature Aloud, two-CD set

(ISBN-10: 0-312-43011-6 / ISBN-13: 978-0-312-43011-5)
These enriching audio recordings feature celebrated writers and actors reading stories, poems, and selected scenes included in Michael Meyer's anthologies. Poetry highlights include E. E. Cummings, T. S. Eliot, Robert Frost, Sylvia Plath, Langston Hughes, and other major authors reading their own works. This resource is free to instructors who adopt the text.

ANCILLARIES

Print Resources

Instructor's Manual: *Resources for Teaching* POETRY: AN INTRODUCTION, FIFTH EDITION

ISBN-10: 0-312-45062-1/ISBN-13: 978-0-312-45062-5

This comprehensive manual supports every selection, offering helpful resources for new and experienced instructors alike. Resources include commentaries, biographical information, and writing assignments, as well as teaching tips from instructors who have taught with the book, additional suggestions for connections among the selections, and thematic groupings with questions for discussion and writing. An online version of the manual is available at bedfordstmartins.com/meyerpoetry.

Literary Reprints

Titles in the Case Studies in Contemporary Criticism series, Bedford Cultural Editions series, and the Bedford Shakespeare series are available for instructors who wish to teach longer works in conjunction with the anthology. (For a complete list of titles, see the Instructor's Manual or consult bedfordstmartins.com/meyerpoetry.)

TradeUp Program

TradeUp

Get 50% off all trade titles when packaged with your textbook!

Add more value and choice to your students' learning experiences by packaging their Bedford/St. Martin's textbook with one of a thousand titles from our sister publishers such as Farrar, Straus and Giroux and St. Martin's Press — at a discount of 50% off the regular price.

New Media Resources

For information on the multimedia resources available with *Poetry*, see page xii of this preface.

ACKNOWLEDGMENTS

This book has benefited from the ideas, suggestions, and corrections of scores of careful readers who helped transform various stages of an evolving manuscript into a finished book and into subsequent editions. I remain grateful to those I have thanked in prefaces of *The Bedford Introduction to Literature*, particularly to the late Robert Wallace of Case Western Reserve University. I would also like to give special thanks to Ronald Wallace of the University of Wisconsin and William Henry Louis of Mary Washington College. In addition, many instructors who have used *Poetry: An Introduction* responded to a questionnaire on the book. For their valuable comments and advice I am grateful to Michael Bibby, Shippensburg University; Tina Blue, University of Kansas; Heather Bouwman, University of St. Thomas; John D. Boyd, University of Georgia; Juniper Ellis, Loyola College; Richard Frohock, Oklahoma State University; Charlie Geer, College of Charleston; Leslie J. Henson, Butte College; Allan Johnston, DePaul University/Columbia College; Michael Kaffer, Spring Hill College; Adam Katz, Quinnipiac University; Raffi Kevorkian, Loyola Marymount University; David Killoran, Loyola Marymount University; Erika H. Kreger, University of California at Berkeley; Seema Kurup, William Rainey Harper College; Karen P. Liebhaber, Black River Technical College; Heidi Ann Marshall, Florida State University; Elizabeth McLagan, Portland Community College; Mary Sadler, College of Charleston; Nancy A. Shaffer, University of Texas at El Paso; Ravi Shankar, Central Connecticut State University; LeAnn Smith, Eastern Illinois University; Barbara Foster Tribble, University of St. Thomas; Amy Watkin, University of North Dakota; Lucy A. Wilson, Loyola Marymount University.

I am also indebted to those who cheerfully answered questions and generously provided miscellaneous bits of information. What might have seemed to them like inconsequential conversations turned out to be important leads. Among these friends and colleagues are Raymond Anselment, Barbara Campbell, Ann Charters, Irving Cummings, William Curtin, Margaret Higonnet, Patrick Hogan, Lee Jacobus, Greta Little, George Monteiro, Brenda Murphy, Joel Myerson, Thomas Recchio, William Sheidley, Milton Stern, Kenneth Wilson, and the dedicated reference librarians at the Homer Babbidge Library, University of Connecticut.

I continue to be grateful for what I have learned from teaching my students and for the many student papers I have received over the years that I have used in various forms to serve as good and accessible models of student writing. I am particularly indebted to Stefanie Wortman for her excellent work on the fifth edition of *Resources for Teaching* POETRY: AN INTRODUCTION.

At Bedford/St. Martin's, my debts once again require more time to acknowledge than the deadline allows. Charles H. Christensen and Joan Feinberg initiated this project and launched it with their intelligence, energy, and sound advice. Karen Henry, Kathy Retan, Alanya Harter, and

Aron Keesbury tirelessly steered earlier editions through rough as well as becalmed moments; their work was as first-rate as it was essential. As developmental editor for the fifth edition, Ellen Thibault, once again, navigated the book swiftly, smoothly, and (so it seemed) effortlessly to its happy conclusion; her valuable contributions richly remind me how fortunate I am to be a Bedford/St. Martin's author. Christina Gerogiannis gracefully handled a variety of editorial tasks and developed the book's instructor's manual. Permissions were deftly arranged by Arthur Johnson and Jason Reblando. The difficult tasks of production were skillfully managed by Lori Chong Roncka. Mary Lou Wilshaw-Watts provided careful copyediting, and Janet Cocker and Jeannine Thibodeau did more-than-meticulous proofreading. I thank all of the people at Bedford — including Donna Dennison, who designed the cover, and Adrienne Petsick and Jenna Bookin Barry, the marketing managers — who helped make this formidable project a manageable one.

Finally, I am grateful to my sons Timothy and Matthew for all kinds of help, but mostly I'm just grateful they're my sons. And for making all the difference, I thank my wife, Regina Barreca.

Brief Contents

AN ANTHOLOGY OF POEMS   553

CRITICAL THINKING AND WRITING ABOUT POETRY   641

Contents

THE ELEMENTS OF POETRY   19

There is no happiness like mine. I have been eating poetry.
— MARK STRAND

2. Writing about Poetry 60

3. Word Choice, Word Order, and Tone 68

A poet has a duty to words . . . words can do wonderful things.

— GWENDOLYN BROOKS

A Note on Reading Translations 102

4. Images 109

Poetry's Appeal to the Senses 109

Poems for Further Study 118

Between my finger and my thumb / The squat pen rests. / I'll dig with it.

— SEAMUS HEANEY

5. Figures of Speech   133

Simile and Metaphor   135

Other Figures   138

Poems for Further Study   143

*Like a piece of
ice on a hot
stove the poem
must ride on its
own melting.*
— ROBERT FROST

6. Symbol, Allegory, and Irony 156

Literature is the apparatus through which the world tries to keep intact its important ideas and feelings.

— MARY OLIVER

7. Sounds 183

*I would define,
in brief, the
Poetry of words
as the Rhythmi-
cal Creation of
Beauty. Its sole
arbiter is Taste.*
— EDGAR ALLAN POE

9. Poetic Forms   237

Some Common Poetic Forms   238

Sonnet   240

A short poem need not be small.
— MARVIN BELL

Villanelle   247

Sestina   249

Epigram   251

Limerick   253

In poetry you have a form looking for a subject and a subject looking for a form. When they come together successfully you have a poem.

—W. H. AUDEN

APPROACHES TO POETRY   299

My business is circumference.

—EMILY DICKINSON

*A cartoon from a
letter from Emily
Dickinson to
William Cowper
Dickinson.*

A poem . . . begins as a lump in the throat, a sense of wrong, a homesickness, a love-sickness . . .

— ROBERT FROST

A manuscript page from "Neither Out Far nor In Deep."

14. A Study of Langston Hughes   388

A Brief Biography   390

I believe that poetry should be direct, comprehensible, and the epitome of simplicity.

— LANGSTON HUGHES

An Introduction to His Work   394

A couple on West 127th St., New York, during the Harlem Renaissance.

15. A Study of Julia Alvarez: Five Poems   425

A Brief Biography   426

An Introduction to Her Work   428

When I'm asked what made me into a writer, I point to the watershed experience of coming to this country. Not understanding the language, I had to pay close attention to each word— great training for a writer.

— JULIA ALVAREZ

16. A Critical Case Study: T. S. Eliot's "The Love Song of J. Alfred Prufrock" 453

Genuine poetry can communicate before it is understood

—T. S. ELIOT

17. A Cultural Case Study: Louise Erdrich's "Dear John Wayne" 472

18. A Thematic Case Study: Love and Longing   489

For a man to become a poet . . . he must be in love or miserable.

— LORD BYRON

19. A Thematic Case Study: Teaching and Learning   501

20. A Thematic Case Study: Humor and Satire   516

21. A Thematic Case Study: Border Crossings   *534*

Transcendence and Borders   *535*

Race and Borders   *538*

Identity and Borders   *540*

Immigration and Borders   *542*

Expectations and Borders   *544*

Beauty and Borders   *547*

Freedom and Borders   *549*

AN ANTHOLOGY OF POEMS 553

Poetry has become a kind of tool for knowing the world in a particular way.
— JANE HIRSHFIELD

If there were no poetry on any day in the world, poetry would be invented that day. For there would be an intolerable hunger.
— MURIEL RUKEYSER

— LUCILLE CLIFTON

— WILLIAM WORDSWORTH

CRITICAL THINKING AND WRITING ABOUT POETRY · 641

Great literature is simply language charged with meaning to the utmost possible degree.

— EZRA POUND

The answers you get from literature depend upon the questions you pose.

— MARGARET ATWOOD

I can't write five words but that I change seven.
— DOROTHY PARKER

Thematic Contents

Ordinary Objects and the Everyday

Identity and Culture

Gender

Home and Family

Animals

Health and Sickness

Love and Longing

Sexuality

Humor and Satire

(Note: The following list includes poems from Chapter 20, A Thematic Case Study:

Immigration

Postcolonial Works

Teaching and Learning

(Note: The following list includes poems from Chapter 19, A Thematic Case Study: Teaching and Learning, as well as other poems in the text that fit within this theme.)

Creativity and the Creative Process

Language and Literature

Science and Technology

Religion

Spirituality and Immortality

Mortality

FIFTH EDITION

POETRY

An Introduction

Reading
Imaginative Literature

Poetry does not need to be defended,
any more than air or food needs to be
defended.
— LANGSTON HUGHES[1]

THE NATURE OF LITERATURE

Literature does not lend itself to a single tidy definition because the making of it over the centuries has been as complex, unwieldy, and natural as life itself. Is literature everything that has been written, from ancient prayers to graffiti? Does it include songs and stories that were not written down until many years after they were recited? Does literature include the television scripts from *The Sopranos* as well as Shakespeare's *King Lear*? Is literature only writing that has permanent value and continues to move people? Must literature be true or beautiful or moral? Should it be socially useful?

Although these kinds of questions are not conclusively answered in this book, they are implicitly raised by the poems included here. No definition

[1]Photograph © copyright of the Estate of Carl Van Vechten; Gravure and Compilation © copyright of the Eakins Press
Foundation.

of literature, particularly a brief one, is likely to satisfy everyone because definitions tend to weaken and require qualification when confronted by the uniqueness of individual works. In this context it is worth recalling Herman Melville's humorous use of a definition of a whale in *Moby-Dick* (1851). In the course of the novel Melville presents his imaginative and symbolic whale as inscrutable, but he begins with a quotation from Georges Cuvier, a French naturalist who defines a whale in his nineteenth-century study *The Animal Kingdom* this way: "The whale is a mammiferous animal without hind feet." Cuvier's description is technically correct, of course, but there is little wisdom in it. Melville understood that the reality of the whale (which he describes as the "ungraspable phantom of life") cannot be caught by isolated facts. If the full meaning of the whale is to be understood, it must be sought on the open sea of experience, where the whale itself is, rather than in exclusionary definitions. Although they may be helpful, facts and definitions do not always reveal the whole truth.

Despite Melville's reminder that a definition can be too limiting and even comical, it is useful for our purposes to describe literature as a fiction consisting of carefully arranged words designed to stir the imagination. Stories, poems, and plays are fictional. They are made up — imagined — even when based on actual historic events. Such imaginative writing differs from other kinds of writing because its purpose is not primarily to transmit facts or ideas. Imaginative literature is a source more of pleasure than of information, and we read it for basically the same reasons we listen to music or view a dance: enjoyment, delight, and satisfaction. Like other art forms, imaginative literature offers pleasure and usually attempts to convey a perspective, mood, feeling, or experience. Writers transform the facts the world provides — people, places, and objects — into experiences that suggest meanings.

Consider, for example, the difference between the following factual description of a snake and a poem on the same subject. Here is the *Webster's Eleventh New Collegiate Dictionary* definition:

> any of numerous limbless scaled reptiles (suborder Serpentes or Ophidia) with a long tapering body and with salivary glands often modified to produce venom which is injected through grooved or tubular fangs.

Contrast this matter-of-fact definition with Emily Dickinson's poetic evocation of a snake in "A narrow Fellow in the Grass":

A narrow Fellow in the Grass
Occasionally rides —
You may have met Him — did you not
His notice sudden is —

The Grass divides as with a Comb —   5
A spotted shaft is seen —
And then it closes at your feet
And opens further on —

He likes a Boggy Acre
A floor too cool for Corn —   10
Yet when a Boy, and Barefoot —
I more than once at Noon
Have passed, I thought, a Whip lash
Unbraiding in the Sun
When stooping to secure it   15
It wrinkled, and was gone —

Several of Nature's People
I know, and they know me —
I feel for them a transport
Of cordiality —   20

But never met this Fellow
Attended, or alone
Without a tighter breathing
And Zero at the Bone —

The dictionary provides a succinct, anatomical description of what a snake is, whereas Dickinson's poem suggests what a snake can mean. The definition offers facts; the poem offers an experience. The dictionary description would probably allow someone who had never seen a snake to sketch one with reasonable accuracy. The poem also provides some vivid subjective descriptions — for example, the snake dividing the grass "as with a Comb" — yet it offers more than a picture of serpentine movements. The poem conveys the ambivalence many people have about snakes — the kind of feeling, for example, so evident on the faces of visitors viewing the snakes at a zoo. In the poem there is both a fascination with and a horror of what might be called snakehood; this combination of feelings has been coiled in most of us since Adam and Eve.

That "narrow Fellow" so cordially introduced by way of a riddle (the word *snake* is never used in the poem) is, by the final stanza, revealed as a snake in the grass. In between, Dickinson uses language expressively to convey her meaning. For instance, in the line "His notice sudden is," listen to the *s* sound in each word and note how the verb *is* unexpectedly appears at the end, making the snake's hissing presence all the more "sudden." And anyone who has ever been surprised by a snake knows the "tighter breathing / And Zero at the Bone" that Dickinson evokes so successfully by the rhythm of her word choices and line breaks. Perhaps even more significant, Dickinson's poem allows those who have never encountered a snake to imagine such an experience.

A good deal more could be said about the numbing fear that undercuts the affection for nature at the beginning of this poem, but the point here is that imaginative literature gives us not so much the full, factual proportions of the world as some of its experiences and meanings. Instead of defining the world, literature encourages us to try it out in our imaginations.

THE VALUE OF LITERATURE

Mark Twain once shrewdly observed that a person who chooses not to read has no advantage over a person who is unable to read. In industrialized societies today, however, the question is not who reads, because nearly everyone can and does, but what is read. Why should anyone spend precious time with literature when there is so much reading material available that provides useful information about everything from the daily news to personal computers? Why should a literary artist's imagination compete for attention that could be spent on the firm realities that constitute everyday life? In fact, national best-seller lists much less often include collections of stories, poems, or plays than they do cookbooks and, not surprisingly, diet books. Although such fare may be filling, it doesn't stay with you. Most people have other appetites, too.

Certainly one of the most important values of literature is that it nourishes our emotional lives. An effective literary work may seem to speak directly to us, especially if we are ripe for it. The inner life that good writers reveal in their characters often gives us glimpses of some portion of ourselves. We can be moved to laugh, cry, tremble, dream, ponder, shriek, or rage with a character by simply turning a page instead of turning our lives upside down. Although the experience itself is imagined, the emotion is real. That's why the final chapters of a good adventure novel can make a reader's heart race as much as a 100-yard dash or why the repressed love of Hester Prynne in Nathaniel Hawthorne's *The Scarlet Letter* is painful to a sympathetic reader. Human emotions speak a universal language regardless of when or where a work was written.

In addition to appealing to our emotions, literature broadens our perspectives on the world. Most of the people we meet are pretty much like ourselves, and what we can see of the world even in a lifetime is astonishingly limited. Literature allows us to move beyond the inevitable boundaries of our own lives and culture because it introduces us to people different from ourselves, places remote from our neighborhoods, and times other than our own. Reading makes us more aware of life's possibilities as well as its subtleties and ambiguities. Put simply, people who read literature experience more life and have a keener sense of a common human identity than those who do not. It is true, of course, that many people go through life without reading imaginative literature, but that is a loss rather than a gain. They may find themselves troubled by the same kinds of questions that reveal Daisy Buchanan's restless, vague discontentment in F. Scott Fitzgerald's *The Great Gatsby:* "What'll we do with ourselves this afternoon?" cried Daisy, "and the day after that, and the next thirty years?"

Sometimes students mistakenly associate literature more with school than with life. Accustomed to reading it in order to write a paper or pass an examination, students may perceive such reading as a chore instead of a pleasurable opportunity, something considerably less important than studying for the "practical" courses that prepare them for a career. The study of literature, however, is also practical because it engages you in the kinds of problem solving important in a variety of fields, from philosophy to science and technology. The interpretation of literary texts requires you to deal with uncertainties, value judgments, and emotions; these are unavoidable aspects of life.

People who make the most significant contributions to their professions — whether in business, engineering, teaching, or some other area — tend to be challenged rather than threatened by multiple possibilities. Instead of retreating to the way things have always been done, they bring freshness and creativity to their work. F. Scott Fitzgerald once astutely described the "test of a first-rate intelligence" as "the ability to hold two opposed ideas in the mind at the same time, and still retain the ability to function." People with such intelligence know how to read situations, shape questions, interpret details, and evaluate competing points of view. Equipped with a healthy respect for facts, they also understand the value of pursuing hunches and exercising their imaginations. Reading literature encourages a suppleness of mind that is helpful in any discipline or work.

Once the requirements for your degree are completed, what ultimately matters are not the courses listed on your transcript but the sensibilities and habits of mind that you bring to your work, friends, family, and, indeed, the rest of your life. A healthy economy changes and grows with the times; people do, too, if they are prepared for more than simply filling a job description. The range and variety of life that literature affords can help you to interpret your own experiences and the world in which you live.

To discover the insights that literature reveals requires careful reading and sensitivity. One of the purposes of a college literature class is to cultivate the analytic skills necessary for reading well. Class discussions often help establish a dialogue with a work that perhaps otherwise would not speak to you. Analytic skills can also be developed by writing about what you read. Writing is an effective means of clarifying your responses and ideas because it requires you to account for the author's use of language as well as your own. This book is based on two premises: that reading literature is pleasurable and that reading and understanding a work sensitively by thinking, talking, or writing about it increase the pleasure of the experience of it.

Understanding its basic elements — such as point of view, symbol, theme, tone, and irony — is a prerequisite to an informed appreciation of literature. This kind of understanding allows you to perceive more in a literary work in much the same way that a spectator at a tennis match sees more if he or she understands the rules and conventions of the game. But literature is not simply a spectator sport. The analytic skills that open up literature also have their uses when you watch a television program or film and, more important, when you attempt to sort out the significance of the people, places, and events that constitute your own life. Literature enhances and sharpens your perceptions. What could be more lastingly practical as well as satisfying?

THE CHANGING LITERARY CANON

Perhaps the best reading creates some kind of change in us: we see more clearly; we're alert to nuances; we ask questions that previously didn't occur to us. Henry David Thoreau had that sort of reading in mind when he remarked in *Walden* that the books he valued most were those that caused him to date "a new era in his life from the reading." Readers are sometimes changed by literature, but it is also worth noting that the life of a literary work can also be affected by its readers. Melville's *Moby-Dick,* for example, was not valued as a classic until the 1920s, when critics rescued the novel from the obscurity of being cataloged in many libraries (including Yale's) not under fiction but under cetology, the study of whales. Indeed, many writers contemporary to Melville who were important and popular in the nineteenth century—William Cullen Bryant, Henry Wadsworth Longfellow, and James Russell Lowell, to name a few—are now mostly unread; their names appear more often on elementary schools built early in the twentieth century than in anthologies. Clearly, literary reputations and what is valued as great literature change over time and in the eyes of readers.

Such changes have accelerated during the past forty years as the literary *canon*—those works considered by scholars, critics, and teachers to be the most important to read and study—has undergone a significant series of shifts. Writers who previously were overlooked, undervalued, neglected, or studiously ignored have been brought into focus in an effort to create a more diverse literary canon, one that recognizes the contributions of the many cultures that make up American society. Since the 1960s, for example, some critics have reassessed writings by women who had been left out of the standard literary traditions dominated by male writers. Many more female writers are now read alongside the male writers who traditionally populated literary history. This kind of enlargement of the canon also resulted from another reform movement of the 1960s. The civil rights movement sensitized literary critics to the political, moral, and esthetic necessity of rediscovering African American literature, and more recently Asian and Hispanic writers have been making their way into the canon. Moreover, on a broader scale the canon is being revised and enlarged to include the works of writers from parts of the world other than the West—a development that reflects the changing values, concerns, and complexities of the past several decades or so, when literary landscapes have shifted as dramatically as the political boundaries of Eastern Europe and the former Soviet Union.

. . .

No semester's reading list—or anthology—can adequately or accurately echo all of the new voices competing to be heard as part of the mainstream literary canon, but recent efforts to open up the canon attempt to sensitize readers to the voices of women, minorities, and writers from all over the world. This development has not occurred without its urgent advocates or passionate dissenters. It's no surprise that issues about race, gender, and class often get people off the fence and on their feet (these controversies are discussed further in Chapter 25, "Critical Strategies for Reading"). Although what we regard as literature—whether it's called great, classic, or canonical—continues to generate debate, there is no question that such controversy will continue to reflect readers' values as well as the writers they admire.

ENCOUNTERING POETRY:
IMAGES OF POETRY
IN POPULAR CULTURE

Although poets may find it painful to acknowledge, poetry is not nearly as popular as prose among contemporary readers. A quick prowl through almost any bookstore reveals many more shelves devoted to novels or biographies, for example, than the meager space allotted to poetry. Moreover, few poems are made into films (although there have been some exceptions, such as Alfred, Lord Tennyson's "The Charge of the Light Brigade" [p. 231]), and few collections of poetry have earned their authors extraordinary wealth or celebrity status.

Despite these facts, however, there is plenty of poetry being produced that saturates our culture and suggests just how essential it is to our lives. When in 2001 Billy Collins was named the poet laureate of the United States, he shrewdly observed that "we should notice that there is no *prose* laureate." What Collins implicitly acknowledges here is the importance of poetry. He acknowledges the idea that poetry is central to any literature, because it is the art closest to language itself; its emphasis on getting each word just right speaks to us and for us. The audience for poetry may be relatively modest in comparison to the readership of prose, but there is nothing shy about poetry's presence in contemporary life. Indeed, a particularly observant person might find it difficult to reach the end of a day without encountering poetry in some shape or form.

You may, for instance, read yet again that magnetic poem composed on your refrigerator door as you reach for your breakfast juice, or perhaps you'll be surprised by some poetic lines while riding the bus or subway, where you might encounter a Poetry in Motion poster, featuring the work of a local poet or well-known author such as Dorothy Parker. What the poems have in common is the celebration of language as a means of surprising, delighting, provoking, or inspiring their readers. There's no obligation and no quiz. The poems are for the taking: all for pleasure.

The following portfolio of images — including provocative posters, a humorous cartoon, poetry-related art in public spaces, and vibrant photographs from the poetry slam scene — illustrate the significance of poetry in our culture. These images recognize the importance not only of such canonical authors as Carl Sandburg, Philip Levine, and T. S. Eliot, but also of aspiring poets — spoken word performers or Magnetic Poetry authors, for example — whose works reflect the growth of poetry as a popular form of expression.

Perhaps the largest, most recent explosion of poetry can be found on the Internet. For example, following the attacks of September 11, 2001, the International Library of Poetry reported a posting of nearly 40,000 poetic tributes at poetry.com. As Poetry Portal (poetry-portal.com) indicates, the number of poetry sites is staggering; these include sites that provide poems, audio readings, e-zines, reviews, criticism, festivals, slams, conferences, workshops, and even collaborative poetry writing in real time. This growth in poetry on the Internet is significant because it reflects an energy and vitality about the poetic activity in our daily lives. Poetry may not be rich and famous, but it is certainly alive and well. Consider, for example, the following images of poetry that can be found in contemporary life. What do they suggest to you about the nature of poetry and its audience?

DOROTHY PARKER, *Unfortunate Coincidence*

Begun in New York City in 1992, the Poetry in Motion program has spread from coast to coast on buses and subways. Offering works ranging from ancient Chinese poetry to contemporary poetry, Poetry in Motion posters give riders more to read than their own reflections in the window. In this example, Dorothy Parker, a poet known for her sharp wit, becomes a presence on a New York subway car.

This poster was part of the New York City Poetry in Motion® program which is a registered trademark of MTA/New York City Transit and the Poetry Society of America. "Unfortunate Coincidence," copyright 1926, renewed © 1954 by Dorothy Parker, from *The Portable Dorothy Parker* by Dorothy Parker, edited by Brendan Gill. Used by permission of Viking Penguin, a division of Penguin Group (USA) Inc.

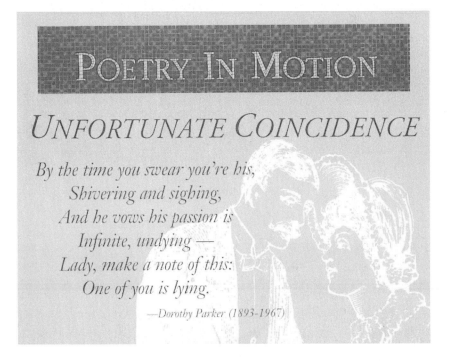

POETRY IN MOTION

UNFORTUNATE COINCIDENCE

By the time you swear you're his,
Shivering and sighing,
And he vows his passion is
Infinite, undying —
Lady, make a note of this:
One of you is lying.

—Dorothy Parker (1893–1967)

CONSIDERATIONS FOR CRITICAL THINKING AND WRITING

1. How does the unromantic nature of this poem seem especially appropriate for New York City subway riders?

2. What kinds of poetry do you find on billboards or public transportation in your own environment? If there is none, what poem would you choose to post on a bus or train in your area?

CARL SANDBURG, *Window*

This mural, painted on a station wall of the Chicago El, features the poem "Window," from a collection of poems by Carl Sandburg titled *Chicago*. This work transforms the evening commute into an encounter with a vivid image.

CONSIDERATIONS FOR CRITICAL THINKING AND WRITING

1. Discuss the effectiveness of the images in these two lines.
2. Try writing two lines of vivid imagery that capture the movement seen from a quickly moving automobile during daylight.

They said I had a head for business
They said to get ahead
I had to lose my head.
They said
be concrete
& I became
concrete.
They said,
go, my son,
multiply,
divide, conquer.

PHILIP LEVINE AND TERRY ALLEN, *Corporate Head*

Located in the Los Angeles business district, "Corporate Head" is the product of a collaboration between poet Philip Levine (b. 1928) and sculptor Terry Allen (b. 1943). The poem, embedded in the sidewalk and enlarged here, clearly complements the visual pun and extends its satirical thrust.

CONSIDERATIONS FOR CRITICAL THINKING AND WRITING

1. What sort of commentary is made about corporate life in the sculpture and the poem?

2. Write your own poem to accompany the sculpture, but make a different point than Philip Levine's poem does.

ROZ CHAST, *The Love Song of J. Alfred Crew*

This *New Yorker* cartoon by Roz Chast (b. 1954) updates lines from T. S. Eliot's "The Love Song of J. Alfred Prufrock" (page 456, lines 120–24) with the kind of language used in the popular J. Crew clothing catalog. Though published in 1917, Eliot's poem clearly remains fashionable.

CONSIDERATIONS FOR CRITICAL THINKING AND WRITING

1. Read "The Love Song of J. Alfred Prufrock" (p. 456) and compare the speaker's personality to the kind of image associated with the typical J. Crew customer. How does this comparison serve to explain the humor in the cartoon?

2. Explain why you think the J. Crew company would be flattered or annoyed to have its image treated this way in a cartoon.

TIM TAYLOR, *I shake the delicate apparatus*

Magnetic Poetry™ kits are available in a number of languages, including Yiddish, Norwegian, and sign language, along with a variety of thematic versions such as those dedicated to cats, love, art, rock and roll, college, and Shakespeare. This poem by Tim Taylor (b. 1957) graces his Manhattan apartment refrigerator and is but one example of the creative expression that poetry magnets inspire in kitchens around the world.

Reprinted by permission of Tim Taylor (poem) and Pelle Cass (image).

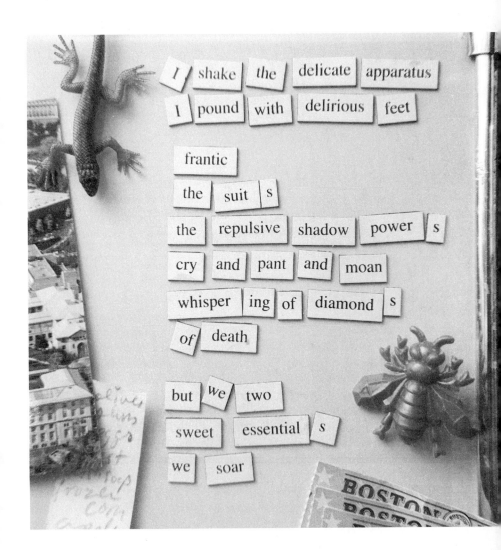

CONSIDERATIONS FOR CRITICAL THINKING AND WRITING

1. Write a paragraph that describes what you think is the essential meaning of this poem.
2. How do you explain the enormous popularity of Magnetic Poetry?

© David Huang/poeticdream.com. Reprinted with permission.

At a poetry slam, poets perform their own work and are judged by the audience — not only on what they say but on how they say it. As a poet performs, the audience cheers, snaps fingers, stomps feet, and sometimes boos the poet off the stage. Judged on a scale from one to ten, the poet with the most points at the end of the night wins a cash prize. The roots of the poetry slam trace to Chicago 1984, when construction worker and writer Marc Smith broke format at an "open mike" night by performing his poetry at an event traditionally slated for music. Shown here are a poster advertising an annual event hosted by Poetry Slam, Inc. (poetryslam.com) and an image from a poetry slam held in San Francisco.

Considerations for Critical Thinking and Writing

1. What sorts of poetry events occur on your campus or in your community?

2. If possible, attend a slam and comment on the kinds of performances you see. Explain whether you think the performance and audience participation add to or detract from the experience of hearing spoken poetry.

Reprinted by permission of Eric Dunn (designer/copywriter) and Mike Wigton (copywriter).

Poetry-portal.com

Poetry Portal (poetry-portal.com), offering access to databases of poems and a cornucopia of online resources about poetry, is an excellent site to begin an exploration of poetry on the Internet.

Reprinted by permission of poetry-portal.com and Colin John Holcombe.

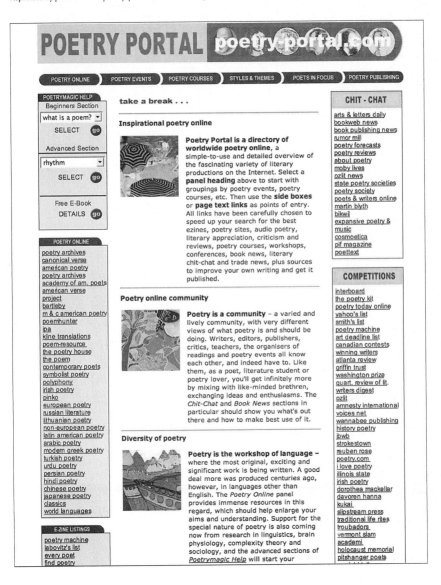

CONSIDERATIONS FOR CRITICAL THINKING AND WRITING

1. Log on to the home page of poetry-portal.com and explore some of the online sites listed there. Describe three sites that you found particularly interesting. Any surprises?

2. In what sense does the Poetry Portal demonstrate that poetry is, indeed, a "community"?

AMERICAN LIFE IN POETRY

A FREE COLUMN FOR NEWSPAPERS BY TED KOOSER, THE POET LAUREATE OF THE UNITED STATES

HOME

PROJECT DESCRIPTION

PERMISSIONS & TERMS OF USE

Ted Kooser, U.S. Poet Laureate Photo © Sarah Greer

CURRENT COLUMN

COLUMN ARCHIVE

KOOSER BIO & PHOTOS

SPONSORS

The Poetry Foundation

Library of Congress

University of Nebraska at Lincoln

American Life in Poetry provides newspapers and online publications with a free weekly column featuring contemporary American poems. The sole mission of this project is to promote poetry: America Life in Poetry seeks to create a vigorous presence for poetry in our culture. There are no costs for reprinting the columns; we do require that you register your publication here and that the text of the column be reproduced without alteration.

The poem in each column is brief and will be enjoyable and enlightening to readers of newspapers and online publications. Each week, a new column will be posted. Registered publications will receive new columns by email. Our archive of previous columns is also available for publication.

American Life in Poetry: Column 060

Most of us have taken at least a moment or two to reflect upon what we have learned from our mothers. Through a catalog of meaningful actions that range from spiritual to domestic, Pennsylvanian Julia Kasdorf evokes the imprint of her mother's life on her own. As the poem closes, the speaker invites us to learn these actions of compassion.

Read the column >>

EMAIL SIGN-UP

Register here to receive American Life in Poetry via weekly email.

Register Today >>

American Life in Poetry (americanlifeinpoetry.org) is a weekly newspaper column featuring a contemporary poem and brief introduction. Initiated by Ted Kooser, a poet laureate of the United States, and supported by the Poetry Foundation in partnership with the Library of Congress, this popular source is distributed free to newspapers and online publications. The site provides countless readers with a wide variety of high-quality, accessible poems. The reprint from the Detroit *Metro Times* (*opposite page*), featuring a poem by David Allan Evans, offers an engaging example of the weekly column.

DAVID ALLAN EVANS, *Neighbors*

metrotimes

April 6-12, 2005

detroit's weekly alternative   www.metrotimes.com • free

ART BAR

POETRY FOR THE PEOPLE: New Pulitzer-winner Ted Kooser, America's 13th poet laureate, gets us. He's no suit sitting in an office consulting ancient texts. For 35 years, he worked in the insurance business. "I wrote each morning ... and I often took my fresh drafts of poems and showed them to my secretary. ... If she didn't understand them, I went home and worked to make them more clear."

Kooser received funding as poet laureate and founded "American Life In Poetry," a free weekly newspaper column. *Metro Times* readers love to be talked to straight up, so we've signed up. Here's our and Kooser's premiere. If we don't have room in print, find it faithfully on our Web site. Kooser is excited *MT* signed on — "This is wonderful news! ... REALLY a start!"

Reprinted from Train Windows, *Ohio University Press, 1976, by permission of the author, whose most recent book is* The Bull Rider's Advice: New and Selected Poems. *This weekly column is supported by The Poetry Foundation, The Library of Congress, and the department of English at the University of Nebraska, Lincoln.*

AMERICAN LIFE IN POETRY
by Ted Kooser,
U.S. poet laureate
We all know that the manner in which people behave toward one another can tell us a lot about their private lives. In this amusing poem by David Allan Evans, poet laureate of South Dakota, we learn something about a marriage by being shown a couple as they take on an ordinary household task.

Neighbors

They live alone
together,

she with her wide hind
and bird face,
he with his hung belly
and crewcut.

They never talk
but keep busy.

Today they are
washing windows
(each window together)
she on the inside,
he on the outside.
He squirts Windex
at her face,
she squirts Windex
at his face.

Now they are waving
to each other
with rags,

not smiling.

Courtesy of the Detroit *Metro Times*, the Poetry Foundation, and David Allan Evans.

Considerations for Critical Thinking and Writing

1. Put together a cluster of images that reflect your encounters with poetry. Where do you find poetry? How is it used? What do these images suggest to you about the state of poetry in contemporary culture?

2. Surely not all manifestations of poetry in popular culture represent good poetry. Does bad poetry undercut good poetry? Does it cheapen its value? At this point in your study of poetry — the beginning — how do you define a good poem or a bad poem?

3. What is your favorite poem? Where did you first encounter it? Why is it important to you? Alternatively, if you can't come up with a favorite poem, why can't you?

The Elements
of Poetry

1

Reading Poetry

© Lilo Raymond.

Ink runs from the corners of my mouth.
There is no happiness like mine.
I have been eating poetry.
— MARK STRAND

READING POETRY RESPONSIVELY

Perhaps the best way to begin reading poetry responsively is not to allow yourself to be intimidated by it. Come to it, initially at least, the way you might listen to a song on the radio. You probably listen to a song several times before you hear it all, before you have a sense of how it works, where it's going, and how it gets there. You don't worry about analyzing a song when you listen to it, even though after repeated experiences with it you know and anticipate a favorite part and know, on some level, why it works for you. Give yourself a chance to respond to poetry. The hardest work has already been done by the poet, so all you need to do at the start is listen for the pleasure produced by the poet's arrangement of words.

Try reading the following poem aloud. Read it aloud before you read it silently. You may stumble once or twice, but you'll make sense of it if you pay attention to its punctuation and don't stop at the end of every line where there is no punctuation. The title gives you an initial sense of what the poem is about.

Marge Piercy (b. 1936)

The Secretary Chant

1973

My hips are a desk.
From my ears hang
chains of paper clips.
Rubber bands form my hair.
My breasts are wells of mimeograph ink.   5
My feet bear casters.
Buzz. Click.
My head is a badly organized file.
My head is a switchboard
where crossed lines crackle.   10
Press my fingers
and in my eyes appear
credit and debit.
Zing. Tinkle.
My navel is a reject button.   15
From my mouth issue canceled reams.
Swollen, heavy, rectangular
I am about to be delivered
of a baby
Xerox machine.   20
File me under W
because I wonce
was
a woman.

What is your response to this secretary's chant? The point is simple
enough — she feels dehumanized by her office functions — but the pleas-
ures are manifold. Piercy makes the speaker's voice sound mechanical by
using short bursts of sound and by having her make repetitive, flat, matter-
of-fact statements ("My breasts . . . My feet . . . My head . . . My navel").
"The Secretary Chant" makes a serious statement about how such women
are reduced to functionaries. The point is made, however, with humor, as
we are asked to visualize the misappropriation of the secretary's body — her
identity — as it is transformed into little more than a piece of office equip-
ment, which seems to be breaking down in the final lines, when we learn
that she "wonce / was / a woman." Is there the slightest hint of something
subversive in this misspelling of "wonce"? Maybe so, but the humor is clear
enough, particularly if you try to make a drawing of what this dehuman-
ized secretary has become.

The next poem creates a different kind of mood. Think about the title,
"Those Winter Sundays," before you begin reading the poem. What associ-
ations do you have with winter Sundays? What emotions does the phrase
evoke in you?

ROBERT HAYDEN (1913–1980)

Those Winter Sundays   *1962*

Sundays too my father got up early
and put his clothes on in the blueblack cold,
then with cracked hands that ached
from labor in the weekday weather made
banked fires blaze. No one ever thanked him.   5

I'd wake and hear the cold splintering, breaking.
When the rooms were warm, he'd call,
and slowly I would rise and dress,
fearing the chronic angers of that house,

Speaking indifferently to him,   10
who had driven out the cold
and polished my good shoes as well.
What did I know, what did I know
of love's austere and lonely offices?

    Does the poem match the feelings you have about winter Sundays? Either way, your response can be useful in reading the poem. For most of us, Sundays are days at home; they might be cozy and pleasant experiences or they might be dull and depressing. Whatever they are, Sundays are more evocative than, say, Tuesdays. Hayden uses that response to call forth a sense of missed opportunity in the poem. The person who reflects on those winter Sundays didn't know until much later how much he had to thank his father for "love's austere and lonely offices." This is a poem about a cold past and a present reverence for his father — elements brought together by the phrase "Winter Sundays." *His* father? You may have noticed that the poem doesn't use a masculine pronoun; hence the voice could be a woman's. Does the gender of the voice make any difference to your reading? Would it make any difference about which details are included or what language is used?

    What is most important about your initial readings of a poem is that you ask questions. If you read responsively, you'll find yourself asking all kinds of questions about the words, descriptions, sounds, and structure of a poem. The specifics of those questions will be generated by the particular poem. We don't, for example, ask how humor is achieved in "Those Winter Sundays" because there is none, but it is worth asking what kind of tone is established by the description of "the chronic angers of that house." The remaining chapters in this part will help you to formulate and answer questions about a variety of specific elements in poetry, such as speaker, image, metaphor, symbol, rhyme, and rhythm. For the moment, however, read the following poem several times and note your response at different points in the poem. Then write down a half-dozen or so questions about what produces your response to the poem. To answer questions, it's best to know first what the questions are, and that's what the rest of this chapter is about.

JOHN UPDIKE (B. 1932)

Dog's Death

1969

She must have been kicked unseen or brushed by a car.
Too young to know much, she was beginning to learn
To use the newspapers spread on the kitchen floor
And to win, wetting there, the words, "Good dog! Good dog!"

We thought her shy malaise was a shot reaction.   5
The autopsy disclosed a rupture in her liver.
As we teased her with play, blood was filling her skin
And her heart was learning to lie down forever.

Monday morning, as the children were noisily fed
And sent to school, she crawled beneath the youngest's bed.   10
We found her twisted and limp but still alive.
In the car to the vet's, on my lap, she tried

To bite my hand and died. I stroked her warm fur
And my wife called in a voice imperious with tears.
Though surrounded by love that would have upheld her,   15
Nevertheless she sank and, stiffening, disappeared.

Back home, we found that in the night her frame,
Drawing near to dissolution, had endured the shame
Of diarrhoea and had dragged across the floor
To a newspaper carelessly left there. *Good dog.*   20

Here's a simple question to get started with your own questions: What would the poem's effect have been if Updike had titled it "Good Dog" instead of "Dog's Death"?

THE PLEASURE OF WORDS

The impulse to create and appreciate poetry is as basic to human experience as language itself. Although no one can point to the precise origins of poetry, it is one of the most ancient of the arts, because it has existed ever since human beings discovered pleasure in language. The tribal ceremonies of peoples without written languages suggest that the earliest primitive cultures incorporated rhythmic patterns of words into their rituals. These chants, very likely accompanied by the music of a simple beat and the dance of a measured step, expressed what people regarded as significant and memorable in their lives. They echoed the concerns of the chanters and the listeners by chronicling acts of bravery, fearsome foes, natural disasters, mysterious events, births, deaths, and whatever else brought people pain or pleasure, bewilderment or revelation. Later cultures, such as the ancient Greeks, made poetry an integral part of religion.

Thus, from its very beginnings, poetry has been associated with what has mattered most to people. These concerns — whether natural or supernatural — can, of course, be expressed without vivid images, rhythmic patterns, and pleasing sounds, but human beings have always sensed a magic in words that goes beyond rational, logical understanding. Poetry is not simply a method of communication; it is a unique experience in itself.

What is special about poetry? What makes it valuable? Why should we read it? How is reading it different from reading prose? To begin with, poetry pervades our world in a variety of forms, ranging from advertising jingles to song lyrics. These may seem to be a long way from the chants heard around a primitive campfire, but they serve some of the same purposes. Like poems printed in a magazine or book, primitive chants, catchy jingles, and popular songs attempt to stir the imagination through the carefully measured use of words.

Although reading poetry usually makes more demands than does the kind of reading we use to skim a magazine or newspaper, the appreciation of poetry comes naturally enough to anyone who enjoys playing with words. Play is an important element of poetry. Consider, for example, how the following words appeal to the children who gleefully chant them in playgrounds:

> I scream, you scream
> We all scream
> For ice cream.

These lines are an exuberant evocation of the joy of ice cream. Indeed, chanting the words turns out to be as pleasurable as eating ice cream. In poetry, the expression of the idea is as important as the idea expressed.

But is "I scream . . ." poetry? Some poets and literary critics would say that it certainly is one kind of poem because the children who chant it experience some of the pleasures of poetry in its measured beat and repeated sounds. However, other poets and critics would define poetry more narrowly and insist, for a variety of reasons, that this isn't true poetry but merely **doggerel**, a term used for lines whose subject matter is trite and whose rhythm and sounds are monotonously heavy-handed.

Although probably no one would argue that "I scream . . ." is a great poem, it does contain some poetic elements that appeal, at the very least, to children. Does that make it poetry? The answer depends on one's definition, but poetry has a way of breaking loose from definitions. Because there are nearly as many definitions of poetry as there are poets, Edwin

Arlington Robinson's succinct observations are useful: "poetry has two outstanding characteristics. One is that it is undefinable. The other is that it is eventually unmistakable."

This comment places more emphasis on how a poem affects a reader than on how a poem is defined. By characterizing poetry as "undefinable," Robinson acknowledges that it can include many different purposes, subjects, emotions, styles, and forms. What effect does the following poem have on you?

WILLIAM HATHAWAY (B. 1944)

Oh, Oh   *1982*

My girl and I amble a country lane,
moo cows chomping daisies, our own
sweet saliva green with grass stems.
"Look, look," she says at the crossing,
"the choo-choo's light is on." And sure
enough, right smack dab in the middle
of maple dappled summer sunlight
is the lit headlight — so funny.
An arm waves to us from the black window.
We wave gaily to the arm. "When I hear
trains at night I dream of being president,"
I say dreamily. "And me first lady," she
says loyally. So when the last boxcars,
named after wonderful, faraway places,
and the caboose chuckle by we look
eagerly to the road ahead. And there,
poised and growling, are fifty Hell's Angels.

© Kit Hathaway.

15

A SAMPLE CLOSE READING

An Annotated Version of "Oh, Oh"

After you've read a poem two or three times, a deeper, closer reading — line by line, word by word, syllable by syllable — will help you discover even more about the poem. Ask yourself: What happens (or does not happen) in the poem? What are the poem's central ideas? How do the poem's words, images, and sounds, for example, contribute to its meaning? What is the poem's overall tone? How is the poem put together?

You can flesh out your close reading by writing your responses in the margins of the page. The following interpretive notes offer but one way to read Hathaway's poem.

WILLIAM HATHAWAY (B. 1944)

Oh, Oh

1982

e title offers an
erjection express-
g strong emotion
d foreboding.

My girl and I amble a country lane,
moo cows chomping daisies, our own
sweet saliva green with grass stems.

e informal lan-
age conjures up an
llic picture of a
lk in the country,
ere the sights,
unds, and tastes
full of pleasure.

"Look, look," she says at the crossing,
"the choo-choo's light is on." And sure   5

The visual effect of
the many os in lines
1–5 (and 15) suggests
an innocent, wide-
eyed openness to
experience while the
repetitive *oo* sounds
echo a kind of re-
assuring, satisfied
cooing.

e carefully or-
estrated *d*s, *m*s,
, and *ss* of lines
8 create sounds
at are meant to
savored.

enough, right smack dab in the middle
of maple dappled summer sunlight
is the lit headlight — so funny.

"Right smack dab in
the middle" of the
poem, the "black
window" hints that
all is not well.

led with confi-
nce and hope,
e couple imag-
es a successful
ture together in
otic locations.
en the train is
ppy for them as
"chuckle[s]" in
proval of their
eams.

An arm waves to us from the black window.
We wave gaily to the arm. "When I hear   10
trains at night I dream of being president,"
I say dreamily. "And me first lady," she
says loyally. So when the last boxcars,
named after wonderful, faraway places,
and the caboose chuckle by we look   15
eagerly to the road ahead. And there,
poised and growling, are fifty Hell's Angels.

Not until the very last
line does "the road
ahead" yield a terri-
fying surprise. The
strategically "poised"
final line derails the
leisurely movement
of the couple and
brings their happy
story to a dead stop.
The emotional re-
versal parked in the
last few words awaits
the reader as much
as it does the couple.
The sight and sound
of the motorcycle
gang signal that what
seemed like heaven is,
in reality, hell: Oh, oh.

MORE HELP WITH CLOSE READING

Close readings of Andrew
Marvell's "To His Coy
Mistress," Elizabeth Bishop's
"The Fish," and Theodore
Roethke's "My Papa's
Waltz," are available on
LiterActive and at the
book's companion site at
bedfordstmartins.com/
meyerpoetry. As you explore
each poem, highlighted
sections are annotated with
critical interpretations and
explanations of literary
elements at work.

Hathaway's poem serves as a convenient reminder that poetry can be full of surprises. Full of confidence, this couple, like the reader, is unprepared for the shock to come. When we see those "fifty Hell's Angels," we are confronted with something like a bucket of cold water in the face.

But even though our expectations are abruptly and powerfully reversed, we are finally invited to view the entire episode from a safe distance — the distance provided by the delightful humor in this poem. After all, how seriously can we take a poem that is titled "Oh, Oh"? The poet has his way with us, but we are brought in on the joke, too. The terror takes on comic proportions as the innocent couple is confronted by no fewer than *fifty* Hell's Angels. This is the kind of raucous overkill that informs a short animated film produced some years ago titled *Bambi Meets Godzilla*: you might not have seen it, but you know how it ends. The poem's good humor comes through when we realize how pathetically inadequate the response of "Oh, Oh" is to the circumstances.

As you can see, reading a description of what happens in a poem is not the same as experiencing a poem. The exuberance of "I scream . . ." and the surprise of Hathaway's "Oh, Oh" are in the hearing or reading rather than in the retelling. A ***paraphrase*** is a prose restatement of the central ideas of a poem in your own language. Consider the difference between the following poem and the paraphrase that follows it. What is missing from the paraphrase?

Robert Francis (1901–1987)

Catch   1950

Two boys uncoached are tossing a poem together,
Overhand, underhand, backhand, sleight of hand, every hand,
Teasing with attitudes, latitudes, interludes, altitudes,
High, make him fly off the ground for it, low, make him stoop,
Make him scoop it up, make him as-almost-as-possible miss it,   5
Fast, let him sting from it, now, now fool him slowly,
Anything, everything tricky, risky, nonchalant,
Anything under the sun to outwit the prosy,
Over the tree and the long sweet cadence down,
Over his head, make him scramble to pick up the meaning,   10
And now, like a posy, a pretty one plump in his hands.

Paraphrase: A poet's relationship to a reader is similar to a game of catch. The poem, like a ball, should be pitched in a variety of ways to challenge and create interest. Boredom and predictability must be avoided if the game is to be engaging and satisfying.

. . .

A paraphrase can help us achieve a clearer understanding of a poem, but, unlike a poem, it misses all of the sport and fun. It is the poem that "outwit[s] the prosy" because the poem serves as an example of what it suggests poetry should be. Moreover, the two players — the poet and the reader — are "uncoached." They know how the game is played, but their expectations do not preclude spontaneity and creativity or their ability to surprise and be surprised. The solid pleasure of the workout — of reading poetry — is the satisfaction derived from exercising your imagination and intellect.

That pleasure is worth emphasizing. Poetry uses language to move and delight even when it includes a cast of fifty Hell's Angels. The pleasure is in having the poem work its spell on us. For that to happen, it is best to relax and enjoy poetry rather than worry about definitions of it. Pay attention to what the poet throws you. We read poems for emotional and intellectual discovery — to feel and to experience something about the world and ourselves. The ideas in poetry — what can be paraphrased in prose — are important, but the real value of a poem consists in the words that work their magic by allowing us to feel, see, and be more than we were before. Perhaps the best way to approach a poem is similar to what Francis's "Catch" implies: expect to be surprised, stay on your toes, and concentrate on the delivery.

A SAMPLE STUDENT ANALYSIS

Tossing Metaphors Together in "Catch"

The following sample paper on Robert Francis's "Catch" was written in response to an assignment that asked students to discuss the use of metaphor in the poem. Notice that Chris Leggett's paper is clearly focused and well organized. His discussion of the use of metaphor in the poem stays on track from beginning to end without any detours concerning unrelated topics (for a definition of **metaphor,** see p. 135). His title draws on the central metaphor of the poem, and he organizes the paper around four key words used in the poem: "attitudes, latitudes, interludes, altitudes." These constitute the heart of the paper's four substantive paragraphs, and they are effectively framed by introductory and concluding paragraphs. Moreover, the transitions between paragraphs clearly indicate that the author was not merely tossing a paper together.

Chris Leggett

Professor Lyles

English 203-1

November 9, 2006

Exploration of the meaning of the word *catch*.

Tossing Metaphors Together in "Catch"

The word "catch" is an attention getter. It usually means something is

Thesis statement identifying purpose of poem's metaphors.

about to be hurled at someone and that he or she is expected to catch it. "Catch" can also signal a challenge to another player if the toss is purposefully difficult. Robert Francis, in his poem "Catch," uses the extended metaphor of two boys playing catch to explore the considerations a poet makes when

Reference to specific language in poem, around which the paper is organized.

"tossing a poem together." Line 3 of "Catch" enumerates these considerations metaphorically as "attitudes, latitudes, interludes, [and] altitudes." While regular prose is typically straightforward and easily understood, poetry usually takes great effort to understand and appreciate. To exemplify this, Francis presents the reader not with a normal game of catch with the ball flying back and forth in a

Introductory analysis of the poem's purpose.

repetitive and predictable fashion, but with a physically challenging game in which one must concentrate, scramble, and exert oneself to catch the ball, as one must stretch the intellect to truly grasp a poem.

Analysis of the meaning of *attitude* in the poem.

The first consideration mentioned by Francis is attitude. Attitude, when applied to the game of catch, indicates the ball's pitch in flight, upward, downward, or straight. It could also describe the players' attitudes toward each other or toward the game in general. Below this literal level lies attitude's meaning in

Discussion of how the attitude metaphor contributes to poem's tone.

relation to poetry. Attitude in this case represents a poem's tone. A poet may "teas[e] with attitude" by experimenting with different tones to achieve the desired mood. The underlying tone of "Catch" is a playful one, set and reinforced by the use of a game. This playfulness is further reinforced by such words and phrases as "teasing," "outwit," and "fool him."

Analysis of the meaning of *latitude* in the poem.

Considered also in the metaphorical game of catch is latitude, which, when applied to the game, suggests the range the object may be thrown--how high, how low, or how far. Poetic latitude, along similar lines, concerns a poem's breadth, or the scope of topic. Taken one level further, latitude suggests freedom from normal restraints or limitations, indicating the ability to go outside the norm to find originality of expression. The entire game of catch described in Francis's poem reaches outside the normal expectations of something being merely tossed back and forth in a predictable manner. The ball is thrown in almost every conceivable fashion, "overhand, underhand . . . every hand." Other terms describing the throws--such as "tricky," "risky," "fast," "slowly," and "Anything under the sun"--express endless latitude for avoiding predictability in Francis's game of catch and metaphorically in writing poetry.

Discussion of how the latitude metaphor contributes to the poem's scope and message.

During a game of catch the ball may be thrown at different intervals, establishing a steady rhythm or a broken, irregular one. Other intervening features, such as the field being played on or the weather, could also affect the game. These features of the game are alluded to in the poem by the use of the word "interludes." "Interlude" in the poetic sense represents the poem's form, which can similarly establish or diminish rhythm or enhance meaning. Lines 6 and 9, respectively, show a broken and a flowing rhythm. Line 6 begins rapidly as a hard toss that stings the catcher's hand is described. The rhythm of the line is immediately slowed, however, by the word "now" followed by a comma, followed by the rest of the line. In contrast, line 9 flows smoothly as the reader visualizes the ball flying over the tree and sailing downward. The words chosen for this line function perfectly. The phrase "the long sweet cadence down" establishes a sweet rhythm that reads smoothly and rolls off the tongue easily. The choice of diction not only affects the poem's rhythmic flow but also establishes through connotative language the various levels at which the poem can be understood, represented in "Catch" as altitude.

Analysis of the meaning of *interlude* in the poem.

Discussion of how the interlude metaphor contributes to the poem's form and rhythm.

While "altitudes" when referring to the game of catch means how high an object is thrown, in poetry it could refer to the level of diction, lofty or down-to-earth, formal or informal. It suggests also the levels at which a poem can be comprehended, the literal as well as the interpretive. In Francis's game of catch, the ball is thrown high to make the player reach, low to make him stoop, or over his head to make him scramble, implying that the player should have to exert himself to catch it. So too, then, should the reader of poetry put great effort into understanding the full meaning of a poem. Francis exemplifies this consideration in writing poetry by giving "Catch" not only an enjoyable literal meaning

Analysis of the meaning of *altitudes* in the poem.

Discussion of how the altitude metaphor contributes to the poem's literal and symbolic meanings, with references to specific language.

concerning the game of catch, but also a rich metaphorical meaning--reflecting the process of writing poetry. Francis uses several phrases and words with multiple meanings. The phrase "tossing a poem together" can be understood as tossing something back and forth or the process of constructing a poem. While "prosy" suggests prose itself, it also means the mundane or the ordinary. In the poem's final line the word "posy" of course represents a flower, while it is also a variant of the word "poesy," meaning poetry, or the practice of composing poetry.

Conclusion summarizing ideas explored in paper.

Francis effectively describes several considerations to be taken in writing poetry in order to "outwit the prosy." His use of the extended metaphor in "Catch" shows that a poem must be unique, able to be comprehended on multiple levels, and a challenge to the reader. The various rhythms in the lines of "Catch" exemplify the ideas they express. While achieving an enjoyable poem on the literal level, Francis has also achieved a rich metaphorical meaning. The poem offers a good workout both physically and intellectually.

Before beginning your own writing assignment on poetry, you should review Chapter 2, "Writing about Poetry," and Chapter 26, "Reading and Writing," which provides a step-by-step overview of how to choose a topic, develop a thesis, and organize various types of writing assignments. If you are using outside sources in your paper, you should make sure that you are familiar with the conventional documentation procedures described in Chapter 27, "The Literary Research Paper."

Poets often remind us that beauty can be found in unexpected places. What is it that Elizabeth Bishop finds so beautiful about the "battered" fish she describes in the following poem?

Web Explore contexts for Elizabeth Bishop and approaches to this poem on *LiterActive* and at bedfordstmartins .com/meyerpoetry.

ELIZABETH BISHOP (1911–1979)

The Fish

1946

I caught a tremendous fish
and held him beside the boat
half out of water, with my hook
fast in a corner of his mouth.

He didn't fight.   5
He hadn't fought at all.
He hung a grunting weight,
battered and venerable
and homely. Here and there
his brown skin hung in strips   10
like ancient wall-paper,
and its pattern of darker brown
was like wall-paper:
shapes like full-blown roses
stained and lost through age.   15
He was speckled with barnacles,
fine rosettes of lime,
and infested
with tiny white sea-lice,
and underneath two or three   20
rags of green weed hung down.
While his gills were breathing in
the terrible oxygen
— the frightening gills,
fresh and crisp with blood,   25
that can cut so badly —
I thought of the coarse white flesh
packed in like feathers,
the big bones and the little bones,
the dramatic reds and blacks   30
of his shiny entrails,
and the pink swim-bladder
like a big peony.
I looked into his eyes
which were far larger than mine   35
but shallower, and yellowed,
the irises backed and packed
with tarnished tinfoil
seen through the lenses
of old scratched isinglass.   40
They shifted a little, but not
to return my stare.
— It was more like the tipping
of an object toward the light.
I admired his sullen face,   45
the mechanism of his jaw,
and then I saw
that from his lower lip
— if you could call it a lip —
grim, wet, and weapon-like,   50
hung five old pieces of fish-line,
or four and a wire leader
with the swivel still attached,
with all their five big hooks
grown firmly in his mouth.   55

A green line, frayed at the end
where he broke it, two heavier lines,
and a fine black thread
still crimped from the strain and snap
when it broke and he got away.   60
Like medals with their ribbons
frayed and wavering,
a five-haired beard of wisdom
trailing from his aching jaw.
I stared and stared   65
and victory filled up
the little rented boat,
from the pool of bilge
where oil had spread a rainbow
around the rusted engine   70
to the bailer rusted orange,
the sun-cracked thwarts,
the oarlocks on their strings,
the gunnels — until everything
was rainbow, rainbow, rainbow!   75
And I let the fish go.

CONSIDERATIONS FOR CRITICAL THINKING AND WRITING

1. **FIRST RESPONSE.** Which lines in this poem provide especially vivid details of the fish? What makes these descriptions effective?

2. How is the fish characterized? Is it simply a weak victim because it "didn't fight"?

3. Comment on lines 65–76. In what sense has "victory filled up" the boat, given that the speaker finally lets the fish go?

The speaker in Bishop's "The Fish" ends on a triumphantly joyful note. The *speaker* is the voice used by the author in the poem; like the narrator in a work of fiction, the speaker is often a created identity rather than the author's actual self. The two should not automatically be equated. Contrast the attitude toward life of the speaker in "The Fish" with that of the speaker in the following poem.

PHILIP LARKIN (1922–1985)

A Study of Reading Habits   1964

When getting my nose in a book
Cured most things short of school,
It was worth ruining my eyes
To know I could still keep cool,
And deal out the old right hook   5
To dirty dogs twice my size.

Later, with inch-thick specs,
Evil was just my lark:
Me and my cloak and fangs
Had ripping times in the dark.   10
The women I clubbed with sex!
I broke them up like meringues.

Don't read much now: the dude
Who lets the girl down before
The hero arrives, the chap   15
Who's yellow and keeps the store,
Seem far too familiar. Get stewed:
Books are a load of crap.

What the speaker sees and describes in "The Fish" is close if not identical to Bishop's own vision and voice. The joyful response to the fish is clearly shared by the speaker and the poet, between whom there is little or no distance. In "A Study of Reading Habits," however, Larkin distances himself from a speaker whose sensibilities he does not wholly share. The poet—and many readers—might identify with the reading habits described by the speaker in the first twelve lines, but Larkin uses the last six lines to criticize the speaker's attitude toward life as well as reading. The speaker recalls in lines 1-6 how as a schoolboy he identified with the hero, whose virtuous strength always triumphed over "dirty dogs," and in lines 7-12 he recounts how his schoolboy fantasies were transformed by adolescence into a fascination with violence and sex. This description of early reading habits is pleasantly amusing, because many readers of popular fiction will probably recall having moved through similar stages, but at the end of the poem the speaker provides more information about himself than he intends to.

As an adult the speaker has lost interest in reading because it is no longer an escape from his own disappointed life. Instead of identifying with heroes or villains, he finds himself identifying with minor characters who are irresponsible and cowardly. Reading is now a reminder of his failures, so he turns to alcohol. His solution, to "Get stewed" because "Books are a load of crap," is obviously self-destructive. The speaker is ultimately exposed by Larkin as someone who never grew beyond fantasies. Getting drunk is consistent with the speaker's immature reading habits. Unlike the speaker, the poet understands that life is often distorted by escapist fantasies, whether through a steady diet of popular fiction or through alcohol. The speaker in this poem, then, is not Larkin but a created identity whose voice is filled with disillusionment and delusion.

The problem with Larkin's speaker is that he misreads books as well as his own life. Reading means nothing to him unless it serves as an escape from himself. It is not surprising that Larkin has him read fiction rather than poetry because poetry places an especially heavy emphasis on language. Fiction, indeed any kind of writing, including essays and drama, relies on carefully chosen and arranged words, but poetry does so to an even greater extent. Notice, for example, how Larkin's deft use of trite expressions and slang characterizes the speaker so that his language reveals nearly as much about his dreary life as what he says. Larkin's speaker would have no use for poetry.

What is "unmistakable" in poetry (to use Robinson's term again) is its intense, concentrated use of language — its emphasis on individual words to convey meanings, experiences, emotions, and effects. Poets never simply process words; they savor them. Words in poems frequently create their own tastes, textures, scents, sounds, and shapes. They often seem more sensuous than ordinary language, and readers usually sense that a word has been hefted before making its way into a poem. Although poems are crafted differently from the ways a painting, sculpture, or musical composition is created, in each form of art the creator delights in the medium. Poetry is carefully orchestrated so that the words work together as elements in a structure to sustain close, repeated readings. The words are chosen to interact with one another to create the maximum desired effect, whether the purpose is to capture a mood or feeling, create a vivid experience, express a point of view, narrate a story, or portray a character.

Here is a poem that looks quite different from most *verse,* a term used for lines composed in a measured rhythmical pattern, which are often, but not necessarily, rhymed.

Robert Morgan (b. 1944)
Mountain Graveyard   *1979*

for the author of "Slow Owls"

Spore Prose

stone	notes
slate	tales
sacred	cedars
heart	earth
asleep	please
hated	death

Though unconventional in its appearance, this is unmistakably poetry because of its concentrated use of language. The poem demonstrates how serious play with words can lead to some remarkable discoveries. At first glance "Mountain Graveyard" may seem intimidating. What, after all, does this list of words add up to? How is it in any sense a poetic use of language? But if the words are examined closely, it is not difficult to see how they

a serious subject chronicling heroic deeds and important events. Among the most famous epics are Homer's *Iliad* and *Odyssey,* the Old English *Beowulf,* Dante's *Divine Comedy,* and John Milton's *Paradise Lost.* More typically, however, narrative poems are considerably shorter, as is the case with the following poem, which tells the story of a child's memory of her father.

REGINA BARRECA (B. 1957)

Nighttime Fires 1986

Courtesy of Robert Benson, © 2004.

When I was five in Louisville
we drove to see nighttime fires. Piled seven of us,
all pajamas and running noses, into the Olds,
drove fast toward smoke. It was after my father
lost his job, so not getting up in the morning
gave him time: awake past midnight, he read old
       newspapers
with no news, tried crosswords until he split the
       pencil
between his teeth, mad. When he heard
the wolf whine of the siren, he woke my mother,
and she pushed and shoved   10
us all into waking. Once roused we longed for burnt wood
and a smell of flames high into the pines. My old man liked
driving to rich neighborhoods best, swearing in a good mood
as he followed fire engines that snaked like dragons
and split the silent streets. It was festival, carnival.   15

If there were a Cadillac or any car
in a curved driveway, my father smiled a smile
from a secret, brittle heart.
His face lit up in the heat given off by destruction
like something was being made, or was being set right.   20
I bent my head back to see where sparks
ate up the sky. My father who never held us
would take my hand and point to falling cinders that
covered the ground like snow, or, excited, show us
the swollen collapse of a staircase. My mother   25
watched my father, not the house. She was happy
only when we were ready to go, when it was finally over
and nothing else could burn.
Driving home, she would sleep in the front seat
as we huddled behind. I could see his quiet face in the   30
rearview mirror, eyes like hallways filled with smoke.

This narrative poem could have been a short story if the poet had wanted to say more about the "brittle heart" of this unemployed man whose daughter so vividly remembers the desperate pleasure he took in watching fire consume other people's property. Indeed, a reading of William Faulkner's famous short story "Barn Burning" suggests how such a character can be further developed and how his child responds to him. The similarities between Faulkner's angry character and the poem's father, whose "eyes [are] like hallways filled with smoke," are coincidental, but the characters' sense of "something . . . being set right" by flames is worth comparing. Although we do not know everything about this man and his family, we have a much firmer sense of their story than we do of the story of the couple in "Western Wind."

Although narrative poetry is still written, short stories and novels have largely replaced the long narrative poem. Lyric poems tend to be the predominant type of poetry today. Regardless of whether a poem is a narrative or a lyric, however, the strategies for reading it are somewhat different from those for reading prose. Try these suggestions for approaching poetry.

Suggestions for Approaching Poetry

1. Assume that it will be necessary to read a poem more than once. Give yourself a chance to become familiar with what the poem has to offer. Like a piece of music, a poem becomes more pleasurable with each encounter.

2. Pay attention to the title; it will often provide a helpful context for the poem and serve as an introduction to it. Larkin's "A Study of Reading Habits" is precisely what its title describes.

3. As you read the poem for the first time, avoid becoming entangled in words or lines that you don't understand. Instead, give yourself a chance to take in the entire poem before attempting to resolve problems encountered along the way.

4. On a second reading, identify any words or passages that you don't understand. Look up words you don't know; these might include names, places, historical and mythical references, or anything else that is unfamiliar to you.

5. Read the poem aloud (or perhaps have a friend read it to you). You'll probably discover that some puzzling passages suddenly fall into place when you hear them. You'll find that nothing helps, though, if the poem is read in an artificial, exaggerated manner. Read in as natural a voice as possible, with slight pauses at line breaks. Silent reading is preferable to imposing a te-tumpty-te-tum reading on a good poem.

6. Read the punctuation. Poems use punctuation marks — in addition to the space on the page — as signals for readers. Be especially careful not to assume that the end of a line marks the end of a sentence, unless it is concluded by punctuation. Consider, for example, the opening lines of Hathaway's "Oh, Oh":

   > My girl and I amble a country lane,
   > moo cows chomping daisies, our own
   > sweet saliva green with grass stems.

Line 2 makes little or no sense if a reader stops after "own." Keeping track of the subjects and verbs will help you find your way among the sentences.

7. Paraphrase the poem to determine whether you understand what happens in it. As you work through each line of the poem, a paraphrase will help you to see which words or passages need further attention.

8. Try to get a sense of who is speaking and what the setting or situation is. Don't assume that the speaker is the author; often it is a created character.

9. Assume that each element in the poem has a purpose. Try to explain how the elements of the poem work together.

10. Be generous. Be willing to entertain perspectives, values, experiences, and subjects that you might not agree with or approve of. Even if baseball bores you, you should be able to comprehend its imaginative use in Francis's "Catch."

11. Try developing a coherent approach to the poem that helps you to shape a discussion of the text. See Chapter 25, "Critical Strategies for Reading," to review formalist, biographical, historical, psychological, feminist, and other possible critical approaches.

12. Don't expect to produce a definitive reading. Many poems do not resolve all of the ideas, issues, or tensions in them, and so it is not always possible to drive their meaning into an absolute corner. Your reading will explore rather than define the poem. Poems are not trophies to be stuffed and mounted. They're usually more elusive. And don't be afraid that a close reading will damage the poem. Poems aren't hurt when we analyze them; instead, they come alive as we experience them and put into words what we discover through them.

A list of more specific questions using the literary terms and concepts discussed in the following chapters begins on page 61. That list, like the suggestions just made, raises issues and questions that can help you to read just about any poem closely. These strategies should be a useful means for getting inside poems to understand how they work. Furthermore, because reading poetry inevitably increases sensitivity to language, you're likely to find yourself a better reader of words in any form—whether in a novel, a newspaper editorial, an advertisement, a political speech, or a conversation—after having studied poetry. In short, many of the reading skills that make poetry accessible also open up the world you inhabit.

You'll probably find some poems amusing or sad, some fierce or tender, and some fascinating or dull. You may find, too, some poems that will get inside you. Their kinds of insights—the poet's and yours—are what Emily Dickinson had in mind when she defined poetry this way: "If I read a book and it makes my whole body so cold no fire can ever warm me, I know that it is poetry. If I feel physically as if the top of my head were taken off, I know that it is poetry." Dickinson's response may be more intense than most — poetry was, after all, at the center of her life — but you, too, might find yourself moved by poems in unexpected ways. In any case, as Edwin Arlington Robinson knew, poetry is, to an alert and sensitive reader, "eventually unmistakable."

BILLY COLLINS (B. 1941)

Introduction to Poetry   *1988*

I ask them to take a poem
and hold it up to the light
like a color slide

or press an ear against its hive.

I say drop a mouse into a poem   5
and watch him probe his way out,

or walk inside the poem's room
and feel the walls for a light switch.

I want them to water-ski
across the surface of a poem   10
waving at the author's name on the shore.

But all they want to do
is tie the poem to a chair with rope
and torture a confession out of it.

They begin beating it with a hose   15
to find out what it really means.

CONSIDERATIONS FOR CRITICAL THINKING AND WRITING

1. **FIRST RESPONSE.** In what sense does this poem offer suggestions for approaching poetry? What kinds of advice does the speaker provide in lines 1–11?

2. How does the mood of the poem change beginning in line 12? What do you make of the shift from "them" to "they"?

3. Paraphrase the poem. How is your paraphrase different from what is included in the poem?

POETRY IN POPULAR FORMS

Before you try out these strategies for reading on a few more poems, it is worth acknowledging that the verse that enjoys the widest readership appears not in collections, magazines, or even anthologies for students, but in greeting cards. A significant amount of the personal daily mail delivered in the United States consists of greeting cards. That represents millions of lines of verse going by us on the street and in planes over our heads. These verses share some similarities with the poetry included in this anthology, but there are also important differences that indicate the need for reading serious poetry closely rather than casually.

The popularity of greeting cards is easy to explain: just as many of us have neither the time nor the talent to make gifts for birthdays, weddings, anniversaries, graduations, Valentine's Day, Mother's Day, and other holidays, we are unlikely to write personal messages when cards conveniently say them for us. Although impersonal, cards are efficient and convey an important message no matter what the occasion for them: I care. These greetings are rarely serious poetry; they are not written to be. Nevertheless, they demonstrate the impulse in our culture to generate and receive poetry.

In a handbook for greeting-card freelancers, a writer and past editor of such verse began with this advice:

> Once you determine what you want to say — and in this regard it is best to stick to one basic idea — you must choose your words to do several things at the same time:
>
> 1. Your idea must be expressed as a complete idea; it must have a beginning, a middle, and an end.
>
> 2. There must be coherence in your verse. Every line must be linked logically and smoothly with its neighbors.
>
> 3. Your expressions . . . must be conversational. High-flown language rarely comes off successfully in greeting-card writing.
>
> 4. You must write with emphasis — and something else: enthusiasm. It's necessary to create interest in that all-important first line. From that point on, writing your verse is a matter of developing your idea and bringing it to a peak of emphasis in the last line. Occasionally you will find that you have shot your wad too early in the verse, and whatever you say after that point sounds like an afterthought.
>
> 5. You must do all of the above and at the same time make everything come out right in the meter-and-rhyme department.[1]

This advice is followed by a list of approximately fifty of the most frequently used rhyme sounds accompanied by rhyming words, such as *love, of, above* for the sound *uv.* The point of these prescriptions is that the verse must be written so that it is immediately accessible — consumable — by

---

[1] Chris Fitzgerald, "Conventional Verse: The Sentimental Favorite," *The Greeting Card Writer's Handbook,* ed. H. Joseph Chadwick (Cincinnati: Writer's Digest, 1975), 13, 17.

both the buyer and the recipient. Writers of these cards are expected to avoid any complexity.

Compare the following greeting-card verse with the poem that comes after it. "Magic of Love," by Helen Farries, has been a longtime favorite in a major greeting-card company's "wedding line"; with different endings it has been used also in valentines and friendship cards.

HELEN FARRIES

Magic of Love
date unknown

There's a wonderful gift that can give you a lift,
It's a blessing from heaven above!
It can comfort and bless, it can bring happiness —
It's the wonderful MAGIC OF LOVE!

Like a star in the night, it can keep your faith bright,   5
Like the sun, it can warm your hearts, too —
It's a gift you can give every day that you live,
And when given, it comes back to you!

When love lights the way, there is joy in the day
And all troubles are lighter to bear,   10
Love is gentle and kind, and through love you will find
There's an answer to your every prayer!

May it never depart from your two loving hearts,
May you treasure this gift from above —
You will find if you do, all your dreams will come true,   15
In the wonderful MAGIC OF LOVE!

JOHN FREDERICK NIMS (1913–1999)

Love Poem
1947

My clumsiest dear, whose hands shipwreck vases,
At whose quick touch all glasses chip and ring,
Whose palms are bulls in china, burs in linen,
And have no cunning with any soft thing

Except all ill-at-ease fidgeting people: 5
The refugee uncertain at the door
You make at home; deftly you steady
The drunk clambering on his undulant floor.

Unpredictable dear, the taxi drivers' terror,
Shrinking from far headlights pale as a dime   10
Yet leaping before red apoplectic streetcars —
Misfit in any space. And never on time.

A wrench in clocks and the solar system. Only
With words and people and love you move at ease.
In traffic of wit expertly maneuver   15
And keep us, all devotion, at your knees.

Forgetting your coffee spreading on our flannel,
Your lipstick grinning on our coat,
So gaily in love's unbreakable heaven
Our souls on glory of spilt bourbon float.   20

Be with me, darling, early and late. Smash glasses —
I will study wry music for your sake.
For should your hands drop white and empty
All the toys of the world would break.

CONSIDERATIONS FOR CRITICAL THINKING AND WRITING

1. **FIRST RESPONSE.** Read these two works aloud. How are they different? How
   the same?
2. To what extent does the advice to would-be greeting-card writers apply to
   each work?
3. Compare the two speakers. Which do you find more appealing? Why?
4. How does Nims's description of love differ from Farries's?

In contrast to poetry, which transfigures and expresses an emotion or
experience through an original use of language, the verse in "Magic of
Love" relies on *clichés* — ideas or expressions that have become tired and
trite from overuse, such as describing love as "a blessing from heaven
above." Clichés anesthetize readers instead of alerting them to the possi-
bility of fresh perceptions. They are used to draw out **stock responses** —
predictable, conventional reactions to language, characters, symbols, or
situations; God, heaven, the flag, motherhood, hearts, puppies, and peace
are some often-used objects of stock responses. Advertisers manufacture
careers from this sort of business.

Clichés and stock responses are two of the major ingredients of senti-
mentality in literature. **Sentimentality** exploits the reader by inducing re-
sponses that exceed what the situation warrants. This pejorative term
should not be confused with *sentiment,* which is synonymous with *emotion*
or *feeling.* Sentimentality cons readers into falling for the mass murderer
who is devoted to stray cats, and it requires that we not think twice about
what we're feeling because those tears shed for the little old lady, the rage
aimed at the vicious enemy soldier, and the longing for the simple virtues
of poverty might disappear under the slightest scrutiny. The experience of
sentimentality is not unlike biting into a swirl of cotton candy; it's mo-
mentarily sweet but wholly insubstantial.

Clichés, stock responses, and sentimentality are generally the hallmarks
of weak writing. Poetry — the kind that is unmistakable — achieves fresh-
ness, vitality, and genuine emotion that sharpen our perceptions of life.

Although the most widely read verse is found in greeting cards, the most widely *heard* poetry appears in song lyrics. Not all songs are poetic, but a good many share the same effects and qualities as poems. Consider these lyrics by Bruce Springsteen about the attack on the World Trade Center on September 11, 2001.

BRUCE SPRINGSTEEN (B. 1949)

You're Missing   *2002*

Shirts in the closet, shoes in the hall
Mama's in the kitchen, baby and all
Everything is everything
Everything is everything
But you're missing   5

Coffee cups on the counter, jackets on the chair
Papers on the doorstep, you're not there
Everything is everything
Everything is everything
But you're missing   10

Pictures on the nightstand, TV's on in the den
Your house is waiting, your house is waiting
For you to walk in, for you to walk in
But you're missing, you're missing
You're missing when I shut out the lights   15
You're missing when I close my eyes
You're missing when I see the sun rise
You're missing

Children are asking if it's alright
Will you be in our arms tonight?   20

Morning is morning, the evening falls I have
Too much room in my bed, too many phone calls
How's everything, everything?
Everything, everything
You're missing, you're missing   25

God's drifting in heaven, devil's in the mailbox
I got dust on my shoes, nothing but teardrops

CONSIDERATIONS FOR CRITICAL THINKING AND WRITING

1. **FIRST RESPONSE.** How do the descriptions of home and the phrases that are repeated evoke a particular kind of mood in this song?

2. Explain whether you think this song can be accurately called a narrative poem. How would you describe its theme?

3. How does your experience of reading "You're Missing" compare with listening to Springsteen singing the song (available on *The Rising*)?

S. Pearl Sharp (b. 1942)

It's the Law: A Rap Poem   *1991*

You can learn about the state of the U.S.A.
By the laws we have on the books today.
The rules we break are the laws we make
The things that we fear, we legislate.

We got laws designed to keep folks in line   5
Laws for what happens when you lose your mind
Laws against stealing, laws against feeling,
The laws we have are a definite sign
That our vision of love is going blind.
(They probably got a law against this rhyme.)   10
Unh-hunh . . . . .

We got laws for cool cats & laws for dirty dogs
Laws about where you can park your hog
Laws against your mama and your papa, too
Even got a law to make the laws come true.   15

It's against the law to hurt an ol' lady,
It's against the law to steal a little baby,
The laws we make are what we do to each other
There is no law to make brother love brother
Hmmm   20

Now this respect thang is hard for some folks to do
They don't respect themselves so they can't respect you
This is the word we should get around —
These are the rules: we gonna run 'em on down.
Listen up!:   25

It ain't enough to be cute,
It ain't enough to be tough
You gotta walk tall
You gotta strut your stuff

You gotta learn to read, you gotta learn to write.   30
Get the tools you need to win this fight
Get your common sense down off the shelf
Start in the mirror . . . . Respect your Self!

When you respect yourself you keep your body clean
You walk tall, walk gentle, don't have to be mean   35
You keep your mind well fed, you keep a clear head
And you think 'bout who you let in your bed —
Unh-hunh . . . . . .

When you respect yourself you come to understand
That your body is a temple for a natural plan,   40
It's against that plan to use drugs or dope —
Use your heart and your mind when you need to cope . . .
It's the law!

We got laws that got started in '86
And laws made back when the Indians got kicked   45
If we want these laws to go out of favor
Then we've got to change our behavior

Change what!? you say, well let's take a look
How did the laws get on the books? Yeah.
I said it up front but let's get tougher   50
The laws we make are what we do to each other

If you never shoot at me then I don't need
A law to keep you from shooting at me, do you see?
There's a universal law that's tried and true
Says Don't do to me —   55
What you don't want done to you
Unh-hunh!
Don't do to me —
What you don't want done to you
It's the law!   60

Considerations for Critical Thinking and Writing

1. **First Response.** According to this rap poem, what do laws reveal "about the state of the U.S.A."?

2. How are the "laws" different from the "rules" prescribed in the middle stanzas of the poem?

3. What is the theme of this rap poem?

Perspective

ROBERT FRANCIS (1901–1987)

On "Hard" Poetry   *1965*

When Robert Frost said he liked poems hard he could scarcely have meant he liked them difficult. If he had meant difficult he would have said he didn't like them easy. What he said was that he didn't like them soft.

Poems can be soft in several ways. They can be soft in form (invertebrate). They can be soft in thought and feeling (sentimental). They can be soft with excess verbiage. Frost used to advise [writers] to squeeze the water out of a poem. He liked poems dry. What is dry tends to be hard, and what is hard is always dry, except perhaps on the outside.

Yet though hardness here does not mean difficulty, some difficulty naturally goes with hardness. A hard poem may not be hard to read but is hard to write. Not too hard, preferably. Not so hard to write that there is no flow in the writer. But hard enough for the growing poem to meet with some healthy resistance. Frost often found this healthy resistance in a tight rhyme scheme and strict meter. There are other ways of getting good resistance, of course.

And in the reader too, a hard poem will bring some difficulty. Preferably not too much. Not enough difficulty to completely baffle him. Ideally a hard poem should not be too hard to make sense of, but hard to exhaust its meaning and its beauty.

"What I care about is the hardness of the poems. I don't like them soft, I want them to be little pebbles, but placed where they won't dislodge easily. And I'd like them to be little pebbles of precious stone—precious, or semiprecious" (interview with John Ciardi, *Saturday Review,* March 21, 1959).

Here is hard prose talking about hard poetry. Frost was never shrewder or more illuminating. Here, as well as in anything else he ever said, is his flavor.

What contemporary of his can you imagine saying this or anything like it?

In 1843 Emerson jotted in his journal: "Hard clouds and hard expressions, and hard manners, I love."

From *The Satirical Rogue on Poetry*

CONSIDERATIONS FOR CRITICAL THINKING AND WRITING

1. What is the distinction between "hard" and "soft" poetry?
2. Given Francis's brief essay and his poem "Catch" (p. 28), write a review of Helen Farries's "Magic of Love" (p. 44) as you think Francis would.
3. Explain whether you would characterize Bruce Springsteen's "You're Missing" (p. 46) as hard or soft.

POEMS FOR FURTHER STUDY

RUDYARD KIPLING (1865–1936)

If—
1910

If you can keep your head when all about you
    Are losing theirs and blaming it on you,
If you can trust yourself when all men doubt you,
    But make allowance for their doubting too;
If you can wait and not be tired by waiting,   5
    Or being lied about, don't deal in lies,
Or being hated, don't give way to hating,
    And yet don't look too good, nor talk too wise:

If you can dream—and not make dreams your master;
    If you can think—and not make thoughts your aim;   10
If you can meet with Triumph and Disaster
    And treat those two impostors just the same;
If you can bear to hear the truth you've spoken
    Twisted by knaves to make a trap for fools,
Or watch the things you gave your life to, broken,   15
    And stoop and build 'em up with worn-out tools:

If you can make one heap of all your winnings
    And risk it in one turn of pitch-and-toss,°   *pitching coins*
And lose, and start again at your beginnings

And never breathe a word about your loss; 20
If you can force your heart and nerve and sinew
    To serve your turn long after they are gone,
And so hold on when there is nothing in you
    Except the Will which says to them: "Hold on!"

If you can talk with crowds and keep your virtue, 25
    Or walk with Kings — nor lose the common touch,
If neither foes nor loving friends can hurt you,
    If all men count with you, but none too much;
If you can fill the unforgiving minute
    With sixty seconds' worth of distance run, 30
Yours is the Earth and everything that's in it,
    And — which is more — you'll be a Man, my son!

CONSIDERATIONS FOR CRITICAL THINKING AND WRITING

1. **FIRST RESPONSE.** Though the poem is addressed to the speaker's son, could the speaker's advice apply to a daughter as well? Explain why or why not.

2. What is meant by Kipling's capitalization of "Man" in the poem's last line? Is this speaker defining masculinity or something else? Do these definitions seem dated to you? Why or why not?

3. Read the poem aloud and comment on the effects of the rhymes and rhythms.

CONNECTION TO ANOTHER SELECTION

1. Discuss Kipling's treatment of what a man is in contrast to Marge Piercy's description of what a woman is in "The Secretary Chant" (p. 22). What significant differences do you find in their definitions?

MARY OLIVER (B. 1935)

Mindful

2004

Every day
    I see or I hear
        something
            that more or less

kills me 5
    with delight,
        that leaves me
            like a needle

in the haystack
    of light. 10
        It is what I was born for —
            to look, to listen,

to lose myself
    inside this soft world —

to instruct myself
    over and over
15

in joy,
    and acclamation.
        Nor am I talking
           about the exceptional,
20

the fearful, the dreadful,
    the very extravagant —
        but of the ordinary,
           the common, the very drab,

the daily presentations.
    Oh, good scholar,
        I say to myself,
           how can you help
25

but grow wise
    with such teachings
        as these —
           the untrimmable light
30

of the world,
    the ocean's shine,
        the prayers that are made
           out of grass?
35

CONSIDERATIONS FOR CRITICAL THINKING AND WRITING

1. **FIRST RESPONSE.** How are the "ordinary, / the common, the very drab" given new meaning in Oliver's description of them?

2. Write out the first three stanzas as you would standard prose sentences and then compare that to Oliver's line breaks. How do the line breaks affect your reading?

3. Discuss the possible meanings of the title. Would you read the poem any differently if the title were "Attentive" or "Heedful" rather than "Mindful"?

CONNECTION TO ANOTHER SELECTION

1. Explain why you think this poem and John Frederick Nims's "Love Poem" (p. 44) are sentimental or not.

LISA PARKER (B. 1972)

Snapping Beans

1998

For Fay Whitt

I snapped beans into the silver bowl
that sat on the splintering slats
of the porchswing between my grandma and me.
I was home for the weekend,

from school, from the North,   5
Grandma hummed "What A Friend We Have In Jesus"
as the sun rose, pushing its pink spikes
through the slant of cornstalks,
through the fly-eyed mesh of the screen.
We didn't speak until the sun overcame   10
the feathered tips of the cornfield
and Grandma stopped humming. I could feel
the soft gray of her stare
against the side of my face
when she asked, *How's school a-goin'*?   15
I wanted to tell her about my classes,
the revelations by book and lecture,
as real as any shout of faith
and potent as a swig of strychnine.
She reached the leather of her hand   20
over the bowl and cupped
my quivering chin; the slick smooth of her palm
held my face the way she held tomatoes
under the spigot, careful not to drop them,
and I wanted to tell her   25
about the nights I cried into the familiar
heartsick panels of the quilt she made me,
wishing myself home on the evening star.
I wanted to tell her
the evening star was a planet,   30
that my friends wore noserings and wrote poetry
about sex, about alcoholism, about Buddha.
I wanted to tell her how my stomach burned
acidic holes at the thought of speaking in class,
speaking in an accent, speaking out of turn,   35
how I was tearing, splitting myself apart
with the slow-simmering guilt of being happy
despite it all.
I said, *School's fine.*
We snapped beans into the silver bowl between us   40
and when a hickory leaf, still summer green,
skidded onto the porchfront,
Grandma said,
It's funny how things blow loose like that.

CONSIDERATIONS FOR CRITICAL THINKING AND WRITING

1. **FIRST RESPONSE.** Describe the speaker's feelings about starting a life at college. How do those feelings compare with your own experiences?

2. How does the grandmother's world differ from the speaker's at school? What details especially reveal those differences?

3. Given that the poem is about how "school['s] a-goin'," why do you think the title is "Snapping Beans"?

4. Discuss the significance of the grandmother's response to the hickory leaf in line 44. How do you read the last line?

CONNECTION TO ANOTHER SELECTION

1. Discuss the treatment of the grandmother in this poem and in "Behind Grandma's House" by Gary Soto (p. 181).

ALBERTO RÍOS (B. 1952)
Seniors   1985

Courtesy of Alberto Ríos.

William cut a hole in his Levi's pocket
so he could flop himself out in class
behind the girls so the other guys
could see and shit what guts we all said.
All Konga wanted to do over and over   5
was the rubber band trick, but he showed
everyone how, so nobody wanted to see
anymore and one day he cried, just cried
until his parents took him away forever.
Maya had a Hotpoint refrigerator standing   10
in his living room, just for his family to show
anybody who came that they could afford it.

Me, I got a French kiss, finally, in the catholic
darkness, my tongue's farthest half vacationing
loudly in another mouth like a man in Bermudas,   15
and my body jumped against a flagstone wall,
I could feel it through her thin, almost
nonexistent body: I had, at that moment, that moment,
a hot girl on a summer night, the best of all
the things we tried to do. Well, she   20
let me kiss her, anyway, all over.

Or it was just a flagstone wall
with a flaw in the stone, an understanding cavity
for burning young men with smooth dreams —
the true circumstance is gone, the true   25
circumstances about us all then
are gone. But when I kissed her, all water,
she would close her eyes, and they into somewhere
would disappear. Whether she was there
or not, I remember her, clearly, and she moves   30
around the room, sometimes, until I sleep.

I have lain on the desert in watch
low in the back of a pick-up truck
for nothing in particular, for stars, for

the things behind stars, and nothing comes   35
more than the moment: always now, here in a truck,
the moment again to dream of making love and sweat,
this time to a woman, or even to all of them
in some allowable way, to those boys, then,
who couldn't cry, to the girls before they were   40
women, to friends, me on my back, the sky over me
pressing its simple weight into her body
on me, into the bodies of them all, on me.

CONSIDERATIONS FOR CRITICAL THINKING AND WRITING

1. **FIRST RESPONSE.** Comment on the use of slang in the poem. Does it surprise you? How does it characterize the speaker?

2. How does the language of the final stanza differ from that of the first stanza? To what purpose?

3. Write an essay that discusses the speaker's attitudes toward sex and life. How are they related?

CONNECTIONS TO OTHER SELECTIONS

1. Compare the treatment of sex in this poem with that in Sharon Olds's "Sex without Love" (p. 93).

2. Think about "Seniors" as a kind of love poem and compare the speaker's voice here with the one in T. S. Eliot's "The Love Song of J. Alfred Prufrock" (p. 456). How are these two voices used to evoke different cultures? Of what value is love in these cultures?

PHILLIS LEVIN (B. 1954)
End of April   *1996*

Under a cherry tree
I found a robin's egg,
broken, but not shattered.

I had been thinking of you,
and was kneeling in the grass   5
among fallen blossoms

when I saw it: a blue scrap,
a delicate toy, as light
as confetti.

It didn't seem real,   10
but nature will do such things
from time to time.

I looked inside:
it was glistening, hollow,
a perfect shell   15

except for the missing crown,
which made it possible
to look inside.

What had been there
is gone now   20
and lives in my heart

where, periodically,
it opens up its wings,
tearing me apart.

CONSIDERATIONS FOR CRITICAL THINKING AND WRITING

1. **FIRST RESPONSE.** Describe the effect of the final line. How does it alter your reading of the rest of the poem?

2. Comment on the appropriateness of line 10. How does the line pivot between what comes before and after it?

3. Discuss Levin's use of rhyme in the final two stanzas. How does the rhyme reinforce the poem's meanings?

CONNECTION TO ANOTHER SELECTION

1. Explain how the descriptive details in "End of April" and in Robert Hass's "A Story about the Body" (p. 278) reveal the emotions of each speaker.

ALFRED, LORD TENNYSON (1809–1892)

Crossing the Bar   *1889*

Sunset and evening star,
   And one clear call for me!
And may there be no moaning of the bar,°   sandbar
   When I put out to sea,

But such a tide as moving seems asleep,   5
   Too full for sound and foam,
When that which drew from out the boundless deep
   Turns again home.

Twilight and evening bell,
   And after that the dark!   10
And may there be no sadness of farewell,
   When I embark;

For tho' from out our bourne of Time and Place
   The flood may bear me far,
I hope to see my Pilot face to face   15
   When I have crost the bar.

1. **FIRST RESPONSE.** How does Tennyson make clear that this poem is about more than a sea journey?

2. Why do you think Tennyson indicated to his publishers that "Crossing the Bar" be placed as the last poem in all collections of his poetry?

3. Discuss the purpose of the punctuation (or its absence) at the end of each line.

CONNECTION TO ANOTHER SELECTION

1. Compare the speaker's mood in "Crossing the Bar" with that in Dylan Thomas's "Do Not Go Gentle into That Good Night" (p. 247).

LI HO (791–817)

A Beautiful Girl Combs Her Hair   *date unknown*

TRANSLATED BY DAVID YOUNG

Awake at dawn
she's dreaming
by cool silk curtains

fragrance of spilling hair
half sandalwood, half aloes   5

windlass creaking at the well
singing jade

the lotus blossom wakes, refreshed

her mirror
two phoenixes   10
a pool of autumn light

standing on the ivory bed
loosening her hair
watching the mirror

one long coil, aromatic silk   15
a cloud down to the floor

drop the jade comb — no sound

delicate fingers
pushing the coils into place
color of raven feathers   20

shining blue-black stuff
the jewelled comb will hardly hold it

spring wind makes me restless
her slovenly beauty upsets me

eighteen and her hair's so thick   25
she wears herself out fixing it!

she's finished now
the whole arrangement in place

in a cloud-patterned skirt
she walks with even steps   30
a wild goose on the sand

turns away without a word
where is she off to?

down the steps to break a spray of
    cherry blossoms   35

CONSIDERATIONS FOR CRITICAL THINKING AND WRITING

1. **FIRST RESPONSE.** Try to paraphrase the poem. What is lost by rewording?
2. How does the speaker use sensuous language to create a vivid picture of the girl?
3. What are the speaker's feelings toward the girl? Do they remain the same throughout the poem?

CONNECTIONS TO OTHER SELECTIONS

1. Compare the description of hair in this poem with that in Cathy Song's "The White Porch" (p. 129). What significant similarities do you find?
2. Write an essay that explores the differing portraits in this poem and in Sylvia Plath's "Mirror" (p. 145). Which portrait is more interesting to you? Explain why.

LUISA LOPEZ (B. 1957)
Junior Year Abroad   *2002*

We were amateurs, that winter in Paris.

The summer before we agreed:
he would come over to keep me company at Christmas.
But the shelf life of my promise expired
before the date on his airline ticket.   5
So we ended up together under a French muslin sky.

Together alone.

Certainly I was alone, inside dark hair, inside foreign blankets,
against white sheets swirling like a cocoon,
covering my bare skin,   10
keeping me apart.
The invited man snored beside me not knowing
I didn't love him anymore.

At first I tried,
perky as a circus pony waiting at the airport gate   15
to be again as I once had been.
But even during the first night
betrayal, the snake under the evergreen,
threw me into nightmares
of floods and dying birds.   20

You see, a new boy just last month
had raised my shy hand to his warm mouth
and kissed the inside of my palm.
I thought "this is impossible,
too close to Christmas, too soon, too dangerous."   25

In Paris I concede:
deceiving my old lover, the one now stirring in his sleep
is even more dangerous.
See him opening his eyes, looking at my face,
dropping his eyes to my breasts and smiling   30
as if he were seeing two old friends? Dangerous.

When I move away and hold the sheet against
myself he,
sensing what this means,
refuses, adamant yet polite,   35
to traffic in the currency of my rejection.

He made a journey. I offered a welcome.
Why should he give me up?

CONSIDERATIONS FOR CRITICAL THINKING AND WRITING

1. **FIRST RESPONSE.** This poem is about strength and dominance as much as it is about love and attraction. Discuss the ways in which the two characters are vying for control.

2. Why is the setting important? How might the sense of the poem be different if this were happening during a typical school year as opposed to "Junior Year Abroad"?

3. Do you think the girl has the right to reject her old boyfriend under these circumstances? Does the old boyfriend have the right to expect a "welcome" since he was invited to visit?

4. The girl is wrapped in sheets that are like a "cocoon." What does this suggest about the changes she is experiencing during this encounter?

THOMAS LUX (B. 1946)   *Title part of poem*

The Voice You Hear When You Read Silently   1997

Why italics? / emphasis

is not silent, it is a speaking-
out-loud voice in your head; it is *spoken*,
a voice is *saying* it
as you read. It's the writer's words,

Speaker = a poet

of course, in a literary sense
his or her *voice*, but the sound
of that voice is the sound of your voice.
Not the sound your friends know
or the sound of a tape played back
but your voice
caught in the dark cathedral
of your skull, your voice heard
by an internal ear informed by internal abstracts
and what you know by feeling,
having felt. It is your voice
saying, for example, the word barn
that the writer wrote
but the barn you say
is a barn you know or knew. The voice
in your head, speaking as you read,
never says anything neutrally — some people
hated the barn they knew,
some people love the barn they know
so you hear the word loaded
and a sensory constellation
is lit: horse-gnawed stalls,
hayloft, black heat tape wrapping
a water pipe, a slippery
spilled chirr of oats from a split sack,
the bony, filthy haunches of cows. . . .
And barn is only a noun — no verb
or subject has entered into the sentence yet!
The voice you hear when you read to yourself
is the clearest voice: you speak it
speaking to you.

[Handwritten margin notes: "Merging: writer's words / reader's voice / distinction in voices"; "5"; "Why does skull = cathedral?"; "10"; "What we hear = based on what we know + what we've already felt"; "15"; "20"; "loaded words = full of associations"; "25"; "30"; "It's just one word!"; "silently (title)"; "no longer / sense of sound"; "35"; "What issues are raised about poetry?"]

CONSIDERATIONS FOR CRITICAL THINKING AND WRITING

1. **FIRST RESPONSE.** Describe the voice you hear when you read silently. How does it differ from your own speaking voice?

2. What do you think is the speaker's main point about how readers experience and interpret a writer's work?

3. Discuss Lux's choice of words in the phrase about the voice "caught in the dark cathedral / of your skull." Consider the difference between this phrase and "what you hear in your head."

4. **CREATIVE RESPONSE.** Choose a word that has the same evocative power for you as *barn* does for the poem's speaker, and write down a "sensory constellation" of images that captures the word's meanings for you.

[Web] Research the poets in this chapter at bedfordstmartins.com/ meyerpoetry.

[Handwritten note at bottom: "What does it mean to a poet when the same word means different things to different people? (what happens to the wheelbarrow + the chicken?)"]

[Handwritten note left margin: "lk at:"]

2

Writing about Poetry

Poems reveal secrets when they are analyzed. The poet's pleasure in finding ingenious ways to enclose her secrets should be matched by the reader's pleasure in unlocking and revealing secrets.

— DIANE WAKOSKI

© Robert Turney.

FROM READING TO WRITING

Writing about poetry can be a rigorous means of testing the validity of your own reading of a poem. Anyone who has been asked to write several pages about a fourteen-line poem knows how intellectually challenging this exercise is, because it means paying close attention to language. Such scrutiny of words, however, sensitizes you not only to the poet's use of language but also to your own use of language. At first you may feel intimidated by having to compose a paper that is longer than the poem you're writing about, but a careful reading will reveal that there's plenty to write about what the poem says and how it says it. Keep in mind that your job is not to produce a definitive reading of the poem—even Carl Sandburg once confessed that "I've written some poetry I don't understand myself." It is enough to develop an interesting thesis and to present it clearly and persuasively.

An interesting thesis will come to you if you read and reread, take notes, annotate the text, and generate ideas (for a discussion of this process see Chapter 26, "Reading and Writing"). Although it requires energy to read closely and to write convincingly about the charged language found in poetry, there is nothing mysterious about such reading and writing. This chapter provides a set of questions designed to sharpen your reading and writing about poetry. Following these questions is a sample paper that offers a clear and well-developed thesis concerning Elizabeth Bishop's "Manners."

Questions for Responsive Reading and Writing

The following questions can help you respond to important elements that reveal a poem's effects and meanings. The questions are general, so not all of them will necessarily be relevant to a particular poem. Many, however, should prove useful for thinking, talking, and writing about each poem in this collection. If you are uncertain about the meaning of a term used in a question, consult the Glossary of Literary Terms beginning on page 741.

Before addressing these questions, read the poem you are studying in its entirety. Don't worry about interpretation on a first reading; allow yourself the pleasure of enjoying whatever makes itself apparent to you. Then on subsequent readings, use the questions to understand and appreciate how the poem works.

1. Who is the speaker? Is it possible to determine the speaker's age, sex, sensibilities, level of awareness, and values?
2. Is the speaker addressing anyone in particular?
3. How do you respond to the speaker? Favorably? Negatively? What is the situation? Are there any special circumstances that inform what the speaker says?
4. Is there a specific setting of time and place?
5. Does reading the poem aloud help you to understand it?
6. Does a paraphrase reveal the basic purpose of the poem?
7. What does the title emphasize?
8. Is the theme presented directly or indirectly?
9. Do any allusions enrich the poem's meaning?
10. How does the diction reveal meaning? Are any words repeated? Do any carry evocative connotative meanings? Are there any puns or other forms of verbal wit?
11. Are figures of speech used? How does the figurative language contribute to the poem's vividness and meaning?

(continued)

12. Do any objects, persons, places, events, or actions have allegorical or symbolic meanings? What other details in the poem support your interpretation?

13. Is irony used? Are there any examples of situational irony, verbal irony, or dramatic irony? Is understatement or paradox used?

14. What is the tone of the poem? Is the tone consistent?

15. Does the poem use onomatopoeia, assonance, consonance, or alliteration? How do these sounds affect you?

16. What sounds are repeated? If there are rhymes, what is their effect? Do they seem forced or natural? Is there a rhyme scheme? Do the rhymes contribute to the poem's meaning?

17. Do the lines have a regular meter? What is the predominant meter? Are there significant variations? Does the rhythm seem appropriate for the poem's tone?

18. Does the poem's form — its overall structure — follow an established pattern? Do you think the form is a suitable vehicle for the poem's meaning and effects?

19. Is the language of the poem intense and concentrated? Do you think it warrants more than one or two close readings?

20. Did you enjoy the poem? What, specifically, pleased or displeased you about what was expressed and how it was expressed?

21. Is there a particular critical approach that seems especially appropriate for this poem? (See Chapter 25, "Critical Strategies for Reading.")

22. How might biographical information about the author help to determine the poem's central concerns?

23. How might historical information about the poem provide a useful context for interpretation?

24. To what extent do your own experiences, values, beliefs, and assumptions inform your interpretation?

25. What kinds of evidence from the poem are you focusing on to support your interpretation? Does your interpretation leave out any important elements that might undercut or qualify your interpretation?

26. Given that there are a variety of ways to interpret the poem, which one seems the most useful to you?

Elizabeth Bishop (1911–1979)

Manners   *1965*

for a Child of 1918

My grandfather said to me
as we sat on the wagon seat,
"Be sure to remember to always
speak to everyone you meet."

 Explore
contexts for Elizabeth
Bishop and approaches
to this poem on
LiterActive and at
bedfordstmartins
.com/meyerpoetry.

We met a stranger on foot.
My grandfather's whip tapped his hat.
"Good day, sir. Good day. A fine day."
And I said it and bowed where I sat.

Then we overtook a boy we knew
with his big pet crow on his shoulder.
"Always offer everyone a ride;
don't forget that when you get older,"

my grandfather said. So Willy
climbed up with us, but the crow
gave a "Caw!" and flew off. I was worried.
How would he know where to go?

But he flew a little way at a time
from fence post to fence post, ahead;
and when Willy whistled he answered.
"A fine bird," my grandfather said,   20

"and he's well brought up. See, he answers
nicely when he's spoken to.
Man or beast, that's good manners.
Be sure that you both always do."

When automobiles went by,   25
the dust hid the people's faces,
but we shouted "Good day! Good day!
Fine day!" at the top of our voices.

When we came to Hustler Hill,
he said that the mare was tired,   30
so we all got down and walked,
as our good manners required.

© Bettmann/CORBIS.

A SAMPLE CLOSE READING

An Annotated Version of "Manners"

The following annotations represent insights about the relationship of various elements at work in the poem gleaned only after several close readings. Don't expect to be able to produce these kinds of interpretive notes on a first reading because such perceptions will not be apparent until you've read the poem and then gone back to the beginning to discover how each word, line, and stanza contributes to the overall effect. Writing your responses in the margins of the page can be a useful means of recording your impressions as well as discovering new insights as you read the text closely.

Elizabeth Bishop (1911–1979)

Manners   *1965*

Title refers to what is socially correct, polite and/or decent behavior.

for a Child of 1918

WWI ended in 1918 and denotes a shift in values and manners that often follows rapid social changes brought about by war.

My grandfather said to me
as we sat on the wagon seat,
"Be sure to remember to always
speak to everyone you meet."

Wagon seat suggests a simpl[e] past—as does simple language and informal diction of the child speaker.

We met a stranger on foot.   5
My grandfather's whip tapped his hat.
"Good day, sir. Good day. A fine day."
And I said it and bowed where I sat.

Grandfather seems kind, but also carries a wh[ip] that reinforces h[is] authoritative voice.

Idea that values "always" transcend time is emphasized by the grandfather's urging: "don't forget."

Then we overtook a boy we knew
with his big pet crow on his shoulder.   10
"Always offer everyone a ride;
don't forget that when you get older,"

"My grandfather," repeated four times in first five stanzas, reflects the child's affection and a sense of belonging in his world. The crow, however, worries the child and indicates an uncertain future.

my grandfather said. So Willy
climbed up with us, but the crow
gave a "Caw!" and flew off. I was worried.   15
How would he know where to go?

But he flew a little way at a time
from fence post to fence post, ahead;
and when Willy whistled he answered.
"A fine bird," my grandfather said,   20

Predictable quatrains and *abcb* rhyme scheme throughout the poem take the worry out of where they—an[d] the crow—are headed.

"and he's well brought up. See, he answers
nicely when he's spoken to.
Man or beast, that's good manners.
Be sure that you both always do."

Third time the grandfather says "always." This and the inverted syntax of line 24 call attention, again, to idea that good manners are forever important.

When automobiles went by,   25
the dust hid the people's faces,

The modern symbolic automobile races by raising dust tha[t] obscures everyone's vision and forces them to shout. Rhymes [in] lines 26 and 28 a[re] off (unlike all th[e] other rhymes) j[ust] enough to sugg[est] the dissonant future that will supercede the calm wagon rid[e].

but we shouted "Good day! Good day!
Fine day!" at the top of our voices.

> The horse, like the simple past it symbolizes, is weakened by the hustle of modern life, but even so, "our" good manners prevail, internalized from the grandfather's values.

When we came to Hustler Hill,
he said that the mare was tired,   30
so we all got down and walked,
as our good manners required.

MORE HELP WITH CLOSE READING

Close readings of Andrew Marvell's "To His Coy Mistress," Elizabeth Bishop's "The Fish," and Theodore Roethke's "My Papa's Waltz," are available on *LiterActive* and at the book's companion site at bedfordstmartins.com/meyerpoetry. As you explore each poem, highlighted sections are annotated with critical interpretations and explanations of literary elements at work.

A SAMPLE STUDENT ANALYSIS

Memory in Elizabeth Bishop's "Manners"

The following sample paper on Elizabeth Bishop's "Manners" was written in response to an assignment that called for a 750-word discussion of the ways in which at least five of the following elements work to develop and reinforce the poem's themes:

diction and tone	irony	form
images	sound and rhyme	speaker
figures of speech	rhythm and meter	setting and situation
symbols		

In her paper, Debra Epstein discusses the ways in which a number of these elements contribute to what she sees as a central theme of "Manners": the loss of a way of life that Bishop associates with the end of World War I. Not all of the elements of poetry are covered equally in Epstein's paper because some, such as the speaker and setting, are more important to her argument than others. Notice how rather than merely listing each of the elements, Epstein mentions them in her discussion as she needs to in order to develop the thesis that she clearly and succinctly expresses in her opening paragraph.

Web Research the poets in this chapter at bedfordstmartins.com/ meyerpoetry.

Epstein 1

Debra Epstein

Professor Brown

English 210

May 2, 2006

Memory in Elizabeth Bishop's "Manners"

Thesis providing interpretation of poem.

The subject of Elizabeth Bishop's "Manners" has to do with behaving well, but the theme of the poem has more to do with a way of life than with etiquette. The poem suggests that modern society has lost something important--a friendly openness, a generosity of spirit, a sense of decency and consideration--in its race toward progress. Although the narrative is simply told, Bishop enriches this

Statement of elements in poem to be discussed in paper.

poem about manners by developing an implicit theme through her subtle use of such elements of poetry as speaker, setting, rhyme, meter, symbol, and images.

Summary of poem's narrative and introduction to discussion of elements.

The dedication suggests that the speaker is "a Child of 1918" who accompanies his or her grandfather on a wagon ride and who is urged to practice good manners by greeting people, offering everyone a ride, and speaking when spoken to by anyone. During the ride they say hello to a stranger, give a ride to a boy with a pet crow, shout greetings to a passing automobile, and get down from the wagon when they reach a hill because the horse is tired. They walk because "good manners required" (line 32) such consideration, even for a horse. This summary indicates what goes on in the poem but not its significance. That requires a closer look at some of the poem's elements.

Analysis of speaker in poem.

Given the speaker's simple language (there are no metaphors or similes and only a few words out of thirty-two lines are more than two syllables), it seems likely that he or she is a fairly young child, rather than an adult reminiscing. (It is interesting to note that Bishop herself, though not identical with the speaker, would have been seven in 1918.) Because the speaker is a young child who uses

Epstein 2

simple diction, Bishop has to show us the ride's significance indirectly rather
than having the speaker explicitly state it.

The setting for the speaker's narrative is important because 1918 was the
year World War I ended, and it marked the beginning of a new era of technology
that was the result of rapid industrialization during the war. Horses and wagons
would soon be put out to pasture. The grandfather's manners emphasize a time
gone by; the child must be told to "remember" what the grandfather says be-
cause he or she will take that advice into a new and very different world.

Analysis of poem's setting.

The grandfather's world of the horse and wagon is uncomplicated, and this
is reflected in both the simple quatrains that move predictably along in an abcb
rhyme scheme and the frequent anapestic meter (ăs wĕ sát ŏn thĕ wágŏn [2])
that pulls the lines rapidly and lightly. The one moment Bishop breaks the set
rhyme scheme is in the seventh stanza when the automobile (the single four-
syllable word in the poem) rushes by in a cloud of dust so that people cannot
see or hear each other. The only off rhymes in the poem--"faces" (26) and
"voices" (28)--are also in this stanza, which suggests that the automobile and
the people in it are somehow off or out of sync with what goes on in the other
stanzas. The automobile is a symbol of a way of life in which people--their faces
hidden--and manners take a back seat to speed and noise. The people in the car
don't wave, don't offer a ride, and don't speak when spoken to.

Analysis of rhyme scheme and meter.

Analysis of symbols.

Maybe the image of the crow's noisy cawing and flying from post to post is
a foreshadowing that should prepare readers for the automobile. The speaker
feels "worried" about the crow's apparent directionlessness: "How would he know
where to go?" (16). However, neither the child nor the grandfather (nor the
reader on a first reading) clearly sees the two worlds that Bishop contrasts in
the final stanza.

Analysis of images.

"Hustler Hill" is the perfect name for what finally tires out the mare. There
is no hurry for the grandfather and child, but there is for those people in the car
and the postwar hustle and bustle they represent. The fast-paced future over-
takes the tired symbol of the past in the poem. The pace slows as the wagon
passengers get down to walk, but the reader recognizes that the grandfather's
way has been lost to a world in which good manners are not required.

Conclusion supporting thesis on poem's theme.

3

Word Choice, Word Order, and Tone

I still feel that a poet has a duty to words, and that words can do wonderful things. And it's too bad to just let them lie there without doing anything with and for them.

— GWENDOLYN BROOKS

By permission of The Granger Collection, New York.

WORD CHOICE

Diction

Like all good writers, poets are keenly aware of **diction,** their choice of words. Poets, however, choose words especially carefully because the words in poems call attention to themselves. Characters, actions, settings, and symbols may appear in a poem, but in the foreground, before all else, is the poem's language. Also, poems are usually briefer than other forms of writing. A few inappropriate words in a 200-page novel (which would have about 100,000 words) create fewer problems than they would in a 100-word poem. Functioning in a compressed atmosphere, the words in a poem must convey meanings gracefully and economically. Readers therefore have to be alert to the ways in which those meanings are released.

Web Explore the poetic elements in this chapter on *LiterActive* and at bedfordstmartins .com/meyerpoetry.

Although poetic language is often more intensely charged than ordinary speech, the words used in poetry are not necessarily different from everyday speech. Inexperienced readers may sometimes assume that language must be high-flown and out of date to be included in a poem: instead of reading about a boy "enjoying a swim," they expect to read about a boy "disporting with pliant arm o'er a glassy wave." During the eighteenth century this kind of *poetic diction* — the use of elevated language over ordinary language — was highly valued in English poetry, but since the nineteenth century poets have generally overridden the distinctions that were once made between words used in everyday speech and those used in poetry. Today all levels of diction can be found in poetry.

A poet, like any writer, has several levels of diction from which to choose; they range from formal to middle to informal. *Formal diction* consists of a dignified, impersonal, and elevated use of language. Notice, for example, the formality of Thomas Hardy's description of the sunken luxury liner *Titanic* in this stanza from "The Convergence of the Twain" (the entire poem appears on p. 89):

> In a solitude of the sea
> Deep from human vanity,
> And the Pride of Life that planned her, stilly couches she.

There is nothing casual or relaxed about these lines. Hardy's use of "stilly," meaning "quietly" or "calmly," is purely literary; the word rarely, if ever, turns up in everyday English.

The language used in Richard Wilbur's "A Late Aubade" (p. 84) represents a less formal level of diction; the speaker uses a *middle diction* spoken by most educated people. Consider how Wilbur's speaker tells his lover what she might be doing instead of being with him:

> You could be sitting now in a carrel
> Turning some liver-spotted page,
> Or rising in an elevator-cage
> Toward Ladies' Apparel.

The speaker elegantly enumerates his lover's unattractive alternatives to being with him — reading old books in a library or shopping in a department store — but the wit of his description lessens its formality.

Informal diction is evident in Philip Larkin's "A Study of Reading Habits" (p. 34). The speaker's account of his early reading is presented *colloquially,* in a conversational manner that in this instance includes slang expressions not used by the culture at large:

> When getting my nose in a book
> Cured most things short of school,
> It was worth ruining my eyes
> To know I could still keep cool,
> And deal out the old right hook
> To dirty dogs twice my size.

This level of diction is clearly not that of Hardy's or Wilbur's speakers.

Poets may also draw on another form of informal diction, called *di-alect*. Dialects are spoken by definable groups of people from a particular geographic region, economic group, or social class. New England dialects are often heard in Robert Frost's poems, for example. Gwendolyn Brooks uses a black dialect in "We Real Cool" (p. 98) to characterize a group of pool players. Another form of diction related to particular groups is *jargon*, a category of language defined by a trade or profession. Sociologists, photographers, carpenters, baseball players, and dentists, for example, all use words that are specific to their fields. E. E. Cummings manages to get quite a lot of mileage out of automobile jargon in "she being Brand" (p. 73).

Many levels of diction are available to poets. The variety of diction to be found in poetry is enormous, and that is how it should be. No language is foreign to poetry because it is possible to imagine any human voice as the speaker of a poem. When we say a poem is formal, informal, or somewhere in between, we are making a descriptive statement rather than an evaluative one. What matters in a poem is not only which words are used but how they are used.

Denotations and Connotations

One important way that the meaning of a word is communicated in a poem is through sound: snakes *hiss*, saws *buzz*. This and other matters related to sound are discussed in Chapter 7. Individual words also convey meanings through denotations and connotations. *Denotations* are the literal, dictionary meanings of a word. For example, *bird* denotes a feathered animal with wings (other denotations for the same word include a shuttle-cock, an airplane, or an odd person), but in addition to its denotative meanings, *bird* also carries *connotations* — associations and implications that go beyond a word's literal meanings. Connotations derive from how the word has been used and the associations people make with it. Therefore, the connotations of *bird* might include fragility, vulnerability, altitude, the sky, or freedom, depending on the context in which the word is used. Consider also how different the connotations are for the following types of birds: hawk, dove, penguin, pigeon, chicken, peacock, duck, crow, turkey, gull, owl, goose, coot, and vulture. These words have long been used to refer to types of people as well as birds. They are rich in connotative meanings.

Connotations derive their resonance from a person's experiences with a word. Those experiences may not always be the same, especially when the people having them are in different times and places. *Theater,* for instance, was once associated with depravity, disease, and sin, whereas today the word usually evokes some sense of high culture and perhaps visions of elegant opulence. In several ethnic communities in the United States many people would find *squid* appetizing, but elsewhere the word is likely to produce negative connotations. Readers must recognize, then, that words written in other times and places may have unexpected connotations. Annotations usually help in these matters, which is why it makes sense to pay attention to them when they are available.

Ordinarily, though, the language of poetry is accessible, even when the circumstances of the reader and the poet are different. Although connotative language may be used subtly, it mostly draws on associations experienced by many people. Poets rely on widely shared associations rather than the idiosyncratic response that an individual might have to a word. Someone who has received a severe burn from a fireplace accident may associate the word *hearth* with intense pain instead of home and family life, but that reader must not allow a personal experience to undermine the response the poet intends to evoke. Connotative meanings are usually public meanings.

Perhaps this can be seen most clearly in advertising, where language is also used primarily to convey moods and feelings rather than information. For instance, nearly three decades of increasing interest in nutrition and general fitness have created a collective consciousness that advertisers have capitalized on successfully. Knowing that we want to be slender or lean or slim (not *spare* or *scrawny* and certainly not *gaunt*), advertisers have created a new word to describe beers, wines, sodas, cheeses, canned fruits, and other products that tend to overload what used to be called sweatclothes and sneakers. The word is *lite.* The assumed denotative meaning of *lite* is "low in calories," but as close readers of ingredient labels know, some *lites* are heavier than regularly prepared products. There can be no doubt about the connotative meaning of *lite,* however. Whatever is *lite* cannot hurt you; less is more. Even the word is lighter than *light;* there is no unnecessary droopy *g* or plump *h. Lite* is a brilliantly manufactured use of connotation.

Connotative meanings are valuable because they allow poets to be economical and suggestive simultaneously. In this way emotions and attitudes are carefully woven into the texture of the poem's language. Read the following poem and pay close attention to the connotative meanings of its words.

RANDALL JARRELL (1914–1965)

The Death of the Ball Turret Gunner   1945

From my mother's sleep I fell into the State
And I hunched in its belly till my wet fur froze.
Six miles from earth, loosed from its dream of life,
I woke to black flack and the nightmare fighters.
When I died they washed me out of the turret with a hose.

The title of this poem establishes the setting and the speaker's situation. Like the setting of a short story, the setting of a poem is important when the time and place influence what happens. "The Death of the Ball

Turret Gunner" is set in the midst of a war and, more specifically, in a ball turret—a Plexiglas sphere housing machine guns on the underside of a bomber. The speaker's situation obviously places him in extreme danger; indeed, his fate is announced in the title.

Although the poem is written in the first-person singular, its speaker is clearly not the poet. Jarrell uses a **persona,** a speaker created by the poet. In this poem the persona is a disembodied voice that makes the gunner's story all the more powerful. What is his story? A paraphrase might read something like this:

> After I was born, I grew up to find myself at war, cramped into the turret of a bomber's belly some 31,000 feet above the ground. Below me were exploding shells from antiaircraft guns and attacking fighter planes. I was killed, but the bomber returned to base, where my remains were cleaned out of the turret so the next man could take my place.

This paraphrase is accurate, but its language is much less suggestive than the poem's. The first line of the poem has the speaker emerge from his "mother's sleep," the anesthetized sleep of her giving birth. The phrase also suggests the comfort, warmth, and security he knew as a child. This safety was left behind when he "fell," a verb that evokes the danger and involuntary movement associated with his subsequent "State" (*fell* also echoes, perhaps, the fall from innocence to experience related in the Bible).

Several dictionary definitions appear for the noun *state;* it can denote a territorial unit, the power and authority of a government, a person's social status, or a person's emotional or physical condition. The context provided by the rest of the poem makes clear that "State" has several denotative meanings here: because it is capitalized, it certainly refers to the violent world of a government at war, but it also refers to the gunner's vulnerable status as well as his physical and emotional condition. By having "State" carry more than one meaning, Jarrell has created an intentional ambiguity. **Ambiguity** allows for two or more simultaneous interpretations of a word, phrase, action, or situation, all of which can be supported by the context of a work. Through his ambiguous use of "State," Jarrell connects the horrors of war not just to bombers and gunners but to the governments that control them.

Related to this ambiguity is the connotative meaning of "State" in the poem. The context demands that the word be read with a negative charge. The word is not used with patriotic pride but to suggest an anonymous, impersonal "State" that kills rather than nurtures the life in its "belly." The state's "belly" is a bomber, and the gunner is "hunched" like a fetus in the cramped turret, where, in contrast to the warmth of his mother's womb, everything is frozen, even the "wet fur" of his flight jacket (newborn infants have wet fur too). The gunner is not just 31,000 feet from the ground but "Six miles from earth." *Six miles* has roughly the same denotative meaning as 31,000 feet, but Jarrell knew that the connotative meaning of *six miles* makes the speaker's position seem even more remote and frightening.

When the gunner is born into the violent world of war, he finds himself waking up to a "nightmare" that is all too real. The poem's final line is grimly understated, but it hits the reader with the force of an exploding shell: what the State-bomber-turret gives birth to is a gruesome death that is merely one of an endless series. It may be tempting to reduce the theme of this poem to the idea that "war is hell," but Jarrell's target is more specific. He implicates the "State," which routinely executes such violence, and he does so without preaching or hysterical denunciations. Instead, his use of language conveys his theme subtly and powerfully. Consider how this next poem uses connotative meanings to express its theme.

Explore contexts
for E. E. Cummings
on *LiterActive*.

E. E. CUMMINGS (1894–1962)

she being Brand   *1926*

she being Brand

-new;and you
know consequently a
little stiff i was
careful of her and(having   5

thoroughly oiled the universal
joint tested my gas felt of
her radiator made sure her springs were O.

K.)i went right to it flooded-the-carburetor cranked her

up,slipped the   10
clutch(and then somehow got into reverse she
kicked what
the hell)next
minute i was back in neutral tried and

again slo-wly;bare,ly nudg. ing (my   15

lev-er Right-
oh and her gears being in
A 1 shape passed
from low through
second-in-to-high like   20
greasedlightning)just as we turned the corner of Divinity

avenue i touched the accelerator and give

her the juice,good

            (it

was the first ride and believe i we was   25
happy to see how nice she acted right up to

the last minute coming back down by the Public
Gardens i slammed on

the
internalexpanding   30
&
externalcontracting
brakes Bothatonce and

brought allofher tremB
-ling   35
to a:dead.

stand-
;Still)

Considerations for Critical Thinking and Writing

1. **FIRST RESPONSE.** How does Cummings's arrangement of the words on the page help you to read this poem aloud? What does the poem describe?

2. What ambiguities in language does the poem ride on? At what point were you first aware of these double meanings?

3. Explain why you think the poem is primarily serious or humorous.

4. Find some advertisements for convertibles or sports cars in magazines and read them closely. What similarities do you find in the use of connotative language in them and in Cummings's poem? Write a brief essay explaining how language is used to convey the theme of one of the advertisements and the poem.

5. **CREATIVE RESPONSE.** Using Cummings's arrangement of words on the page as your inspiration, try reorganizing the words and lines in Robert Francis's "Catch" (p. 28) so that they look as if Cummings wrote the poem.

WORD ORDER

Meanings in poems are conveyed not only by denotations and connotations but also by the poet's arrangement of words into phrases, clauses, and sentences to achieve particular effects. The ordering of words into meaningful verbal patterns is called *syntax.* A poet can manipulate the syntax of a line to place emphasis on a word; this is especially apparent when a poet varies normal word order. In Emily Dickinson's "A narrow Fellow in the Grass" (p. 2), for example, the speaker says about the snake that "His notice sudden is." Ordinarily, that would be expressed as "his notice is sudden." By placing the verb *is* unexpectedly at the end of the line, Dickinson creates the sense of surprise we feel when we suddenly come upon a snake. Dickinson's inversion of the standard word order also makes the final sound of the line a hissing *is.*

Cummings uses one long sentence in "she being Brand" to take the reader on a ride that begins with a false start but accelerates quickly before

CONSIDERATIONS FOR CRITICAL THINKING AND WRITING

1. **FIRST RESPONSE.** Compare the difference between the title and its slightly revised version as it appears in line 25. How does that difference reveal the theme?

2. At what point does the tone of the poem shift from chuckles to something else?

3. What is the effect of the rhymes in lines 25 and 28? How do the rhymes serve to reinforce the poem's theme?

CONNECTION TO ANOTHER SELECTION

1. Discuss the tone of this poem and that of Gwendolyn Brooks's "We Real Cool" (p. 98).

The next work is a ***dramatic monologue,*** a type of poem in which a character — the speaker — addresses a silent audience in such a way as to reveal unintentionally some aspect of his or her temperament or personality. What tone is created by Machan's use of a persona?

KATHARYN HOWD MACHAN (B. 1952)

Hazel Tells LaVerne   *1976*

```
last night
im cleanin out my
howard johnsons ladies room
when all of a sudden
up pops this frog                                    5
musta come from the sewer
swimmin aroun an tryin ta
climb up the sida the bowl
so i goes ta flushm down
but sohelpmegod he starts talkin                    10
bout a golden ball
an how i can be a princess
me a princess
well my mouth drops
all the way to the floor                            15
an he says
kiss me just kiss me
once on the nose
well i screams
ya little green pervert                             20
an i hitsm with my mop
an has ta flush
the toilet down three times
me
a princess                                         25
```

CONSIDERATIONS FOR CRITICAL THINKING AND WRITING

1. **FIRST RESPONSE.** What do you imagine the situation and setting are for this poem? Do you like this revision of the fairy tale "The Frog Prince"?

2. What creates the poem's humor? How does Hazel's use of language reveal her personality? Is her treatment of the frog consistent with her character?

3. Although it has no punctuation, this poem is easy to follow. How does the arrangement of the lines organize Hazel's speech for clarity and emphasis?

4. What is the theme? Is it conveyed through denotative or connotative language?

5. **CREATIVE RESPONSE.** Write what you think might be LaVerne's reply to Hazel. First, write LaVerne's response as a series of ordinary sentences, and then try editing and organizing them into poetic lines.

CONNECTION TO ANOTHER SELECTION

1. Although Robert Browning's "My Last Duchess" (p. 177) is a more complex poem than Machan's, both use dramatic monologues to reveal character. How are the strategies in each poem similar?

MARTÍN ESPADA (B. 1957)

Latin Night at the Pawnshop   *1987*

Chelsea, Massachusetts
Christmas, 1987

The apparition of a salsa band
gleaming in the Liberty Loan
pawnshop window:

Golden trumpet,
silver trombone,
congas, maracas, tambourine,   5
all with price tags dangling
like the city morgue ticket
on a dead man's toe.

CONSIDERATIONS FOR CRITICAL THINKING AND WRITING

1. **FIRST RESPONSE.** What is "Latin" about this night at the pawnshop?

2. What kind of tone is created by the poet's word choice and by the poem's rhythm?

3. Does it matter that this apparition occurs on Christmas night? Why or why not?

4. What do you think is the central point of this poem?

How do the speaker's attitude and tone change during the course of this next poem?

PAUL LAURENCE DUNBAR (1872–1906)

To a Captious Critic

1903

Dear critic, who my lightness so deplores,
Would I might study to be prince of bores,
Right wisely would I rule that dull estate —
But, sir, I may not; till you abdicate.

CONSIDERATIONS FOR CRITICAL THINKING AND WRITING

1. **FIRST RESPONSE.** How do Dunbar's vocabulary and syntax signal the level of diction used in the poem?

2. Describe the speaker's tone. How does it characterize the speaker as well as the critic?

3. **CREATIVE RESPONSE.** Using "To a Captious Critic" as a model, try writing a four-line witty reply to someone in your own life — perhaps a roommate, coach, teacher, waiter, dentist, or anyone else who provokes a strong response in you.

DICTION AND TONE IN FOUR LOVE POEMS

The first three of these love poems share the same basic situation and theme: a male speaker addresses a female (in the first poem it is a type of female) urging that love should not be delayed because time is short. This theme is as familiar in poetry as it is in life. In Latin this tradition is known as *carpe diem,* "seize the day." Notice how the poets' diction helps create a distinctive tone in each poem, even though the subject matter and central ideas are similar (although not identical) in all three.

ROBERT HERRICK (1591–1674)

To the Virgins, to Make Much of Time

1648

Gather ye rose-buds while ye may,
   Old Time is still a-flying;
And this same flower that smiles today,
   Tomorrow will be dying.

The glorious lamp of heaven, the sun,
   The higher he's a-getting,
The sooner will his race be run,
   And nearer he's to setting.

Courtesy of the National Portrait Gallery, London.

That age is best which is the first,
 When youth and blood are warmer;   10
But being spent, the worse, and worst
 Times still succeed the former.

Then be not coy, but use your time,
 And while ye may, go marry;
For having lost but once your prime,   15
 You may for ever tarry.

CONSIDERATIONS FOR CRITICAL THINKING AND WRITING

1. **FIRST RESPONSE.** Would there be any change in meaning if the title of this poem were "To Young Women, to Make Much of Time"? Do you think the poem can apply to young men, too?

2. What do the virgins have in common with the flowers (lines 1–4) and the course of the day (5–8)?

3. How does the speaker develop his argument? What will happen to the virgins if they don't "marry"? Paraphrase the poem.

4. What is the tone of the speaker's advice?

The next poem was also written in the seventeenth century, but it includes some words that have changed in usage and meaning over the past three hundred years. The title of Andrew Marvell's "To His Coy Mistress" requires some explanation. "Mistress" does not refer to a married man's illicit lover but to a woman who is loved and courted — a sweetheart. Marvell uses "coy" to describe a woman who is reserved and shy rather than coquettish or flirtatious. Often such shifts in meanings over time are explained in the notes that accompany reprintings of poems. You should keep in mind, however, that it is helpful to have a reasonably thick dictionary available when you are reading poetry. The most thorough is the *Oxford English Dictionary (OED)*, which provides histories of words. The *OED* is a multivolume leviathan, but there are other useful unabridged dictionaries and desk dictionaries.

Knowing its original meaning can also enrich your understanding of why a contemporary poet chooses a particular word. Elizabeth Bishop begins "The Fish" (p. 32) this way: "I caught a tremendous fish." We know immediately in this context that "tremendous" means very large. In addition, given that the speaker clearly admires the fish in the lines that follow, we might even understand "tremendous" in the colloquial sense of wonderful and extraordinary. But a dictionary gives us some further relevant insights. Because, by the end of the poem, we see the speaker thoroughly moved as a result of the encounter with the fish ("everything / was rainbow, rainbow, rainbow!"), the dictionary's additional information about the history of *tremendous* shows why it is the perfect adjective to introduce the fish. The word comes from the Latin *tremere* (to tremble) and therefore once meant "such as to make

Explore contexts for Andrew Marvell and approaches to this poem on *LiterActive* and at bedfordstmartins .com/meyerpoetry.

one tremble." That is precisely how the speaker is at the end of the poem: deeply affected and trembling. Knowing the origin of *tremendous* gives us the full heft of the poet's word choice.

Although some of the language in "To His Coy Mistress" requires annotations for the modern reader, this poem continues to serve as a powerful reminder that time is a formidable foe, even for lovers.

Courtesy of the National Portrait Gallery, London.

ANDREW MARVELL (1621–1678)

To His Coy Mistress 1681

Had we but world enough, and time,
This coyness, lady, were no crime.
We would sit down, and think which way
To walk, and pass our long love's day.
Thou by the Indian Ganges'° side
Shouldst rubies find; I by the tide
Of Humber° would complain.° I would   *write love songs*
Love you ten years before the Flood,
And you should, if you please, refuse
Till the conversion of the Jews.   10
My vegetable love should grow°
Vaster than empires, and more slow;
An hundred years should go to praise
Thine eyes and on thy forehead gaze,
Two hundred to adore each breast,   15
But thirty thousand to the rest:
An age at least to every part,
And the last age should show your heart.
For, lady, you deserve this state,
Nor would I love at lower rate.   20
    But at my back I always hear
Time's wingèd chariot hurrying near;
And yonder all before us lie
Deserts of vast eternity.
Thy beauty shall no more be found,   25
Nor in thy marble vault shall sound
My echoing song; then worms shall try
That long preserved virginity,
And your quaint honor turn to dust,
And into ashes all my lust.   30
The grave's a fine and private place,
But none, I think, do there embrace.

---

5 *Ganges:* A river in India sacred to the Hindus.   7 *Humber:* A river that flows through Marvell's native town, Hull.   11 *My vegetable love . . . grow:* A slow, unconscious growth.

Now, therefore, while the youthful hue
Sits on thy skin like morning dew,
And while thy willing soul transpires°   *breathes forth*   35
At every pore with instant fires,
Now let us sport us while we may,
And now, like amorous birds of prey,
Rather at once our time devour
Than languish in his slow-chapped° power.   *slow-jawed*   40
Let us roll all our strength and all
Our sweetness up into one ball,
And tear our pleasures with rough strife
Thorough° the iron gates of life.   *through*
Thus, though we cannot make our sun   45
Stand still, yet we will make him run.

Considerations for Critical Thinking and Writing

1. **FIRST RESPONSE.** Do you think this *carpe diem* poem is hopelessly dated, or does it speak to our contemporary concerns?

2. This poem is divided into a three-part argument. Briefly summarize each section: if (lines 1–20), but (21–32), therefore (33–46).

3. What is the speaker's tone in lines 1–20? How much time would he spend adoring his mistress? Is he sincere? How does he expect his mistress to respond to these lines?

4. How does the speaker's tone change beginning with line 21? What is his view of time in lines 21–32? What does this description do to the lush and leisurely sense of time in lines 1–20? How do you think his mistress would react to lines 21–32?

5. In the final lines of Herrick's "To the Virgins, to Make Much of Time" (p. 79), the speaker urges the virgins to "go marry." What does Marvell's speaker urge in lines 33–46? How is the pace of these lines (notice the verbs) different from that of the first twenty lines of the poem?

6. This poem is sometimes read as a vigorous but simple celebration of flesh. Is there more to the theme than that?

Perspective

Bernard Duyfhuizen (b. 1953)

"To His Coy Mistress": On How a Female Might Respond   *1988*

Clearly a female reader of "To His Coy Mistress" might have trouble identifying with the poem's speaker; therefore, her first response would be to identify with the listener-in-the-poem, the eternally silent Coy Mistress. In such a reading she is likely to recognize that she has heard this kind of line before although maybe not with the same intensity and insistence. Moreover, she is likely to (re)experience the unsettling emotions that such an egoistic assault on her virginal autonomy would provoke. She will also see differently, even by contemporary standards, the plot beyond closure, the possible consequences — both physical and social — that the Mistress will encounter. Lastly, she is likely to be angered by this poem, by her marginalization in an argument that seeks to overpower the core of her being.

From "Textual Harassment of Marvell's Coy Mistress:
The Institutionalization of Masculine Criticism,"
College English, April 1988

Considerations for Critical Thinking and Writing

1. Explain whether you find convincing Duyfhuizen's description of a female's potential response to the poem. How does his description compare with your own response?

2. Characterize the silent mistress of the poem. How do you think the speaker treats her? What do his language and tone suggest about his relationship to her?

3. Does the fact that this description of a female response is written by a man make any difference in your assessment of it? Explain why or why not.

The third in this series of *carpe diem* poems is a twentieth-century work. The language of Richard Wilbur's "A Late Aubade" is more immediately accessible than that of Marvell's "To His Coy Mistress"; a dictionary will quickly identify any words unfamiliar to a reader, including the allusion to Arnold Schoenberg, the composer, in line 11. An **allusion** is a brief reference to a person, place, thing, event, or idea in history or literature. Allusive words, like connotative words, are both suggestive and economical; poets use allusions to conjure up biblical authority, scenes from Shakespeare's plays, historic figures, wars, great love stories, and anything else that might serve to deepen and enrich their own work. The speaker in "A Late Aubade" makes an allusion that an ordinary dictionary won't explain. He tells his lover: "I need not rehearse / The rosebuds-theme of centuries of verse." True to his word, he says no more about this for her or the reader. The lines refer, of course, to the *carpe diem* theme as found familiarly in Herrick's "To the Virgins, to Make Much of Time." Wilbur assumes that his reader will understand the allusion.

Allusions imply reading and cultural experiences shared by the poet and reader. Literate audiences once had more in common than they do today because more people had similar economic, social, and educational backgrounds. But a judicious use of specialized dictionaries, encyclopedias, and other reference tools can help you decipher allusions that grow out of this body of experience. (See page 715 for a list of useful reference works for students of literature.) As you read more, you'll be able to make connections based on your own experiences with literature. In a sense, allusions make available what other human beings have deemed worth remembering, and that is certainly an economical way of supplementing and enhancing your own experience.

Wilbur's version of the *carpe diem* theme follows. What strikes you as particularly modern about it?

RICHARD WILBUR (B. 1921)

A Late Aubade

1968

You could be sitting now in a carrel
Turning some liver-spotted page,
Or rising in an elevator-cage
Toward Ladies' Apparel.

You could be planting a raucous bed   5
Of salvia, in rubber gloves,
Or lunching through a screed of someone's loves
With pitying head,

Or making some unhappy setter
Heel, or listening to a bleak   10
Lecture on Schoenberg's serial technique.
Isn't this better?

Think of all the time you are not
Wasting, and would not care to waste,
Such things, thank God, not being to your taste.   15
Think what a lot

Of time, by woman's reckoning,
You've saved, and so may spend on this,
You who had rather lie in bed and kiss
Than anything.   20

It's almost noon, you say? If so,
Time flies, and I need not rehearse
The rosebuds-theme of centuries of verse.
If you *must* go,

Wait for a while, then slip downstairs   25
And bring us up some chilled white wine,
And some blue cheese, and crackers, and some fine
Ruddy-skinned pears.

CONSIDERATIONS FOR CRITICAL THINKING AND WRITING

1. **FIRST RESPONSE.** Explain whether or not you find the speaker appealing.
2. An *aubade* is a song about lovers parting at dawn, but in this "late aubade," "It's almost noon." Is there another way of reading the adjective *late* in the title?

3. How does the speaker's diction characterize both him and his lover? What sort of lives do they live? What does the casual allusion to Herrick's poem (line 23) reveal about them?

4. What is the effect of using "liver-spotted page," "elevator-cage," "raucous bed," "screed," "unhappy setter," and "bleak / Lecture" to describe the woman's activities?

CONNECTIONS TO OTHER SELECTIONS

1. How does the man's argument in "A Late Aubade" differ from the speakers' in Herrick's and Marvell's poems? Which of the three arguments do you find most convincing?

2. Explain how the tone of each poem is suited to its theme.

This fourth love poem is by a woman. Listen to the speaker's voice. Does it sound different from the way the men speak in the previous three poems?

SHARON OLDS (B. 1942)

Last Night   1996

The next day, I am almost afraid.
Love? It was more like dragonflies
in the sun, 100 degrees at noon,
the ends of their abdomens stuck together, I
close my eyes when I remember. I hardly   5
knew myself, like something twisting and
twisting out of a chrysalis,
enormous, without language, all
head, all shut eyes, and the humming
like madness, the way they writhe away,   10
and do not leave, back, back,
away, back. Did I know you? No kiss,
no tenderness — more like killing, death-grip
holding to life, genitals
like violent hands clasped tight   15
barely moving, more like being closed
in a great jaw and eaten, and the screaming
I groan to remember it, and when we started
to die, then I refuse to remember,
the way a drunkard forgets. After,   20
you held my hands extremely hard as my
body moved in shudders like the ferry when its
axle is loosed past engagement, you kept me
sealed exactly against you, our hairlines
wet as the arc of a gateway after   25

a cloudburst, you secured me in your arms till I slept —
that was love, and we woke in the morning
clasped, fragrant, buoyant, that was
the morning after love.

CONSIDERATIONS FOR CRITICAL THINKING AND WRITING

1. **FIRST RESPONSE.** How is your response to this poem affected by the fact that the speaker is female? Explain why this is or isn't a *carpe diem* poem.

2. Comment on the descriptive passages of "Last Night." Which images seem especially vivid to you? How do they contribute to the poem's meaning?

3. Explain how the poem's tone changes from beginning to end.

CONNECTIONS TO OTHER SELECTIONS

1. How does the speaker's description of intimacy compare with Herrick's and Marvell's?

2. Compare the speaker's voice in Olds's poem with the voice you imagine for the coy mistress in Marvell's poem.

3. **CRITICAL STRATEGIES.** Read the section on formalist criticism (pp. 648–50) in Chapter 25, "Critical Strategies for Reading," and compare the themes in Olds's poem and Philip Larkin's "A Study of Reading Habits" (p. 34) the way you think a feminist critic might analyze them.

POEMS FOR FURTHER STUDY

MARGARET ATWOOD (B. 1939)

Bored

1995

All those times I was bored
out of my mind. Holding the log
while he sawed it. Holding
the string while he measured, boards,
distances between things, or pounded   5
stakes into the ground for rows and rows
of lettuces and beets, which I then (bored)
weeded. Or sat in the back
of the car, or sat still in boats,
sat, sat, while at the prow, stern, wheel   10
he drove, steered, paddled. It
wasn't even boredom, it was looking,
looking hard and up close at the small
details. Myopia. The worn gunwales,
the intricate twill of the seat   15
cover. The acid crumbs of loam, the granular

pink rock, its igneous veins, the sea-fans
of dry moss, the blackish and then the greying
bristles on the back of his neck.
Sometimes he would whistle, sometimes   20
I would. The boring rhythm of doing
things over and over, carrying
the wood, drying
the dishes. Such minutiae. It's what
the animals spend most of their time at,   25
ferrying the sand, grain by grain, from their tunnels,
shuffling the leaves in their burrows. He pointed
such things out, and I would look
at the whorled texture of his square finger, earth under
the nail. Why do I remember it as sunnier   30
all the time then, although it more often
rained, and more birdsong?
I could hardly wait to get
the hell out of there to
anywhere else. Perhaps though   35
boredom is happier. It is for dogs or
groundhogs. Now I wouldn't be bored.
Now I would know too much.
Now I would know.

CONSIDERATIONS FOR CRITICAL THINKING AND WRITING

1. **FIRST RESPONSE.** Atwood has described this poem as one of several about her father and his death. Is it possible to determine that "he" is the speaker's father from the details of the poem? Explain whether or not you think it matters who "he" is.

2. Play with the possible meanings of the word *bored* and its variations in the poem. What function does the repetition of the word serve?

3. What does the speaker "know" at the end of the poem that she didn't before?

CONNECTION TO ANOTHER SELECTION

1. Write an essay on the speaker's attitude toward the father in this poem and in Robert Hayden's "Those Winter Sundays" (p. 23).

BARBARA HAMBY (B. 1929)

Ode to American English   *2004*

I was sitting in Paris one day missing English, American, really,
    with its pill-popping Hungarian goulash of everything
from Anglo-Saxon to Zulu, because British English
    is not the same, if the paperback dictionary I bought

at Brentano's on the Avenue de l'Opéra is any indication,   5
      too cultured by half. Oh, the English know their delphiniums,
but what about doowop, donuts, Dick Tracy, Tricky Dick?
      With their elegant Oxfordian accents, how could they
understand my yearning for the hotrod, hotdog, hot flash
      vocabulary of the U.S. of A., the fragmented fandango   10
of Dagwood's everyday flattening of Mr. Beasley on the sidewalk,
      fetuses floating on billboards, drive-by monster
hip-hop stereos shaking the windows of my dining room
      like a 7.5 earthquake, Ebonics, Spanglish, "you know"
used as a comma and period, the inability of 90% of the population   15
      to get the past perfect. *I have went, I have saw,*
I have tooken Jesus into my heart, the battle cry of the Bible Belt,
      but no one uses the King James anymore, only plain-speak
versions, in which Jesus, raising Lazarus from the dead, says,
      "Dude, wake up," and the L-man bolts up like a B-movie   20
mummy. "Whoa, I was toasted." Yes, ma'am, I miss the mongrel
      plenitude of American English, its fall-guy, rat-terrier,
dog-pound neologisms, the bomb of it all, the rushing River Jordan
      backwoods mutability of it, the low-rider, boom-box cruise of it,
from New Joisey to Ha-wah-ya with its sly dog, malasada-scarfing   25
      beach blanket lingo to the ubiquitous Valley Girl's
like-like stuttering, shopaholic rant. I miss its quotidian beauty,
      its querulous back-biting righteous indignation, its preening
rotgut flag-waving cowardice. *Suffering Succotash,* sputters
      Sylvester the Cat; *sine die,*° say the pork-bellied legislators   30
of the swamps and plains. I miss all those guys, their Tweety-bird
      resilience, their Doris Day optimism, the candid unguent
of utter unhappiness on every channel, the midnight televangelist
      euphoric stew, the junk mail-voice mail vernacular.
On every *boulevard* and *rue* I miss the Tarzan cry of Johnny   35
      Weismueller, Johnny Cash, Johnny B. Goode,
and all the smart-talking, gum-snapping hard-girl dialogue,
      finger-popping x-rated street talk, sports babble,
Cheetoes, Cheerios, chili-dog diatribes. Yeah, I miss 'em all,
      sitting here on my sidewalk throne sipping champagne,   40
verses lined up like hearses, metaphors juking, nouns zipping
      in my head like Corvettes on dexedrine, French verbs
slitting my throat, yearning for James Dean to jump my curb.

CONSIDERATIONS FOR CRITICAL THINKING AND WRITING

1. **FIRST RESPONSE.** Consult the Glossary of Literary Terms (p. 741) for the defi-
   nition of *ode*. How does this poem constitute an ode to American English?

2. Explain how the diction of this poem is vital to its meaning. What is it
   about American English that causes the speaker to admire it so much?

3. What kind of characterization of American life is presented by the varieties
   of English cataloged in the poem?

---

30 *sine die:* Latin for without a day; indefinitely.

Connections to Other Selections

1. Discuss the strategic use of American phrasing in this poem and in Florence Cassen Mayers's "All-American Sestina" (p. 250), and compare the tone of each poem.

2. Write an essay comparing the themes of Hamby's poem and Lydia Huntley Sigourney's "Indian Names" (p. 622). Compare how the diction of each controls its tone.

Thomas Hardy (1840–1928)

The Convergence of the Twain   *1912*

Lines on the Loss of the "Titanic"°

I

  In a solitude of the sea
   Deep from human vanity,
And the Pride of Life that planned her, stilly couches she.

II

  Steel chambers, late the pyres
   Of her salamandrine fires,°   5
Cold currents thrid,° and turn to rhythmic tidal lyres.   *thread*

III

  Over the mirrors meant
   To glass the opulent
The sea-worm crawls — grotesque, slimed, dumb, indifferent.

IV

  Jewels in joy designed   10
   To ravish the sensuous mind
Lie lightless, all their sparkles bleared and black and blind.

V

  Dim moon-eyed fishes near
   Gaze at the gilded gear
And query: "What does this vaingloriousness down here?"   15

"Titanic": A luxurious ocean liner, reputed to be unsinkable, which sank after hitting an iceberg on its maiden voyage in 1912. Only a third of the 2,200 passengers survived. 5 *salamandrine fires:* Salamanders were, according to legend, able to survive fire; hence the ship's fires burned even though under water.

VI

Well: while was fashioning
This creature of cleaving wing,
The Immanent Will that stirs and urges everything

VII

Prepared a sinister mate
For her — so gaily great —   20
A Shape of Ice, for the time far and dissociate.

VIII

And as the smart ship grew
In stature, grace, and hue,
In shadowy silent distance grew the Iceberg too.

IX

Alien they seemed to be: 25
No mortal eye could see
The intimate welding of their later history,

X

Or sign that they were bent
By paths coincident
On being anon twin halves of one august event,   30

XI

Till the Spinner of the Years
Said "Now!" And each one hears,
And consummation comes, and jars two hemispheres.

Considerations for Critical Thinking and Writing

1. **FIRST RESPONSE.** Describe a contemporary disaster comparable to the sinking of the *Titanic*. How was your response to it similar to or different from the speaker's response to the fate of the *Titanic*?

2. How do the words used to describe the ship in this poem reveal the speaker's attitude toward the *Titanic*?

3. The diction of the poem suggests that the *Titanic* and the iceberg participate in something like an arranged marriage. What specific words imply this?

4. Who or what causes the disaster? Does the speaker assign responsibility?

sarcastic jokes, the snarky dialogue
of British films eludes him, phone calls   10
cast him adrift in that cochlear maze
that thrums and bristles even now, when
it doesn't have to: an unnecessary kind
of elegance, the vestige of a sense

no longer obligated to transmit   15
the crack of thawing ice that fills the yard's
wide dip in winter, or the scrape of his
dull rake in spring, its prongs' vibration thrilled
by grass and peat moss. Imagine his desires
released like saffron pistils in the wind;   20
mark their trace against the cords of wood

he spent the summer splitting. See his quiet
flicker like a film, a Super-8
projected on the wall, and all of us
there, laughing on the porch without a sound.   25
No noisome cruelty, no baffled rage,
no aging children sullen in their lack.
Love hurts much less in this serenity.

CONSIDERATIONS FOR CRITICAL THINKING AND WRITING

1. **FIRST RESPONSE.** Why does the speaker prefer the word *deaf* to the phrase "abled differently" as a means of describing her father? Which description do you prefer? Why?

2. Explain how sound and silence move through the poem from beginning to end.

3. Choose a single word from each stanza that strikes you as particularly effective, and explain why you think Diaz chose it over other possibilities.

4. What do you make of the poem's final line? How does it relate to the tone of the rest of the poem?

CONNECTIONS TO OTHER SELECTIONS

1. Discuss the relationship between love and pain in "On My Father's Loss of Hearing" and in the Meinke poem that precedes it.

2. Compare the speakers' attitudes toward the fathers in Diaz's poem and in Margaret Atwood's "Bored" (p. 86).

SHARON OLDS (B. 1942)

Sex without Love   *1984*

How do they do it, the ones who make love
without love? Beautiful as dancers,
gliding over each other like ice skaters
over the ice, fingers hooked

inside each other's bodies, faces   5
red as steak, wine, wet as the
children at birth whose mothers are going to
give them away. How do they come to the
come to the   come to the   God   come to the
still waters, and not love   10
the one who came there with them, light
rising slowly as steam off their joined
skin? These are the true religious,
the purists, the pros, the ones who will not
accept a false Messiah, love the   15
priest instead of the God. They do not
mistake the lover for their own pleasure,
they are like great runners: they know they are alone
with the road surface, the cold, the wind,
the fit of their shoes, their over-all cardio-   20
vascular health — just factors, like the partner
in the bed, and not the truth, which is the
single body alone in the universe
against its own best time.

CONSIDERATIONS FOR CRITICAL THINKING AND WRITING

1. **FIRST RESPONSE.** What is the nature of the question asked by the speaker in the poem's first two lines? What is being asked here?

2. What is the effect of describing the lovers as athletes? How do these descriptions and phrases reveal the speaker's tone toward the lovers?

3. To what extent does the title suggest the central meaning of this poem? Try to compose some alternative titles that are equally descriptive.

CONNECTIONS TO OTHER SELECTIONS

1. How does the treatment of sex and love in Olds's poem compare with that in Cummings's "she being Brand" (p. 73)?

2. Just as Olds describes sex without love, she implies a definition of love in this poem. Consider whether the lovers in Wilbur's "A Late Aubade" (p. 84) fall within Olds's definition.

CATHY SONG (B. 1955)

The Youngest Daughter   *1983*

The sky has been dark
for many years.
My skin has become as damp
and pale as rice paper
and feels the way   5
mother's used to before the drying sun
parched it out there in the fields.

 Lately, when I touch myself,
my hands react as if
I had just touched something   10
hot enough to burn.
My skin, aspirin-colored,
tingles with migraine. Mother
has been massaging the left side of my face
especially in the evenings   15
when it flares up.

This morning
her breathing was graveled,
her voice gruff with affection
when I took her into the bath.   20
She was in good humor,
making jokes about her great breasts,
floating in the milky water
like two walruses,
flaccid and whiskered around the nipples.   25
I scrubbed them with a sour taste
in my mouth, thinking:
six children and an old man
have sucked from these brown nipples.

I was almost tender   30
when I came to the blue bruises
that freckle her body,
places where she has been injecting insulin
for thirty years, ever since
I can remember. I soaped her slowly,   35
she sighed deeply, her eyes closed.

In the afternoons
when she has rested,
she prepares our ritual of tea and rice,
garnished with a shred of gingered fish,   40
a slice of pickled turnip
a token for my white body.
We eat in the familiar silence.
She knows I am not to be trusted,
even now planning my escape.   45
As I toast to her health
with the tea she has poured,
a thousand cranes curtain the window,
fly up in a sudden breeze.

Considerations for Critical Thinking and Writing

1. **FIRST RESPONSE.** Though the speaker is the youngest daughter in the family, how old do you think she is based on the description of her in the poem? What, specifically, makes you think so?

2. How would you characterize the relationship between mother and daughter? How are lines 44–45 ("She knows I am not to be trusted, / even now planning my escape") particularly revealing of the nature of the relationship?

3. Interpret the final four lines of the poem. Why do you think it ends with this image?

JOHN KEATS (1795–1821)

Ode on a Grecian Urn   *1819*

I

Explore contexts for John Keats on *LiterActive*.

Thou still unravished bride of quietness,
    Thou foster-child of silence and slow time,
Sylvan° historian, who canst thus express
    A flowery tale more sweetly than our rhyme:
What leaf-fringed legend haunts about thy shape   5
    Of deities or mortals, or of both,
        In Tempe or the dales of Arcady?°
What men or gods are these? What maidens loath?
    What mad pursuit? What struggle to escape?
        What pipes and timbrels? What wild ecstasy?   10

II

Heard melodies are sweet, but those unheard
    Are sweeter; therefore, ye soft pipes, play on;
Not to the sensual ear, but, more endeared,
    Pipe to the spirit ditties of no tone:
Fair youth, beneath the trees, thou canst not leave   15
    Thy song, nor ever can those trees be bare;
        Bold Lover, never, never canst thou kiss,
Though winning near the goal — yet, do not grieve;
    She cannot fade, though thou hast not thy bliss,
        For ever wilt thou love, and she be fair!   20

III

Ah, happy, happy boughs! that cannot shed
    Your leaves, nor ever bid the Spring adieu;
And, happy melodist, unwearièd,
    For ever piping songs for ever new;
More happy love! more happy, happy love!   25
    For ever warm and still to be enjoyed,
        For ever panting, and for ever young;

---

3 *Sylvan:* Rustic. The urn is decorated with a forest scene.   7 *Tempe, Arcady:* Beautiful rural valleys in Greece.

Nose

is tuberous, rootlike, with subsoil
affinities, has its own mossy   10
aromas, feels bulbous as corms or
crimped as rhizomes but, even so,
stands graced with little wings above
the harbored nostrils.

The nose   15

sunders the face in symmetry,
bisects us in hemispheres where selves
negotiate along the boundary lines
of smiles or scowls.

All night,   20

in the snug bed of the face,
the nose exults.

CONSIDERATIONS FOR CRITICAL THINKING AND WRITING

1. **FIRST RESPONSE.** What do you think is the speaker's attitude toward the nose?

2. In what ways is the nose "antithetical"?

3. Discuss the speaker's diction and its effect on your reading of the poem. What words or phrases are particularly effective? How?

4. Look up *exults* in the dictionary. Why is it just right in the final line?

CONNECTION TO ANOTHER SELECTION

1. Compare the central idea of "Nose" with "The Larynx," the next poem by Alice Jones. Which poem do you prefer? Why?

ALICE JONES (B. 1949)

The Larynx   *1993*

Under the epiglottic flap
the long-ringed tube sinks
its shaft down to the bronchial
fork, divides from two
to four then infinite branches,   5
each ending finally in a clump
of transparent sacs knit
with small vessels into a mesh
that sponge-like soaks up breath
and gives it off with a push   10
from the diaphragm's muscular wall,
forces wind out of the lungs'
wide tree, up through this organ's

single pipe, through the puzzle
box of gristle, where resonant   15
    plates of cartilage fold
into shield, horns, bows,
    bound by odd half-spirals
of muscles that modulate air
as it rises through this empty place   20
    at our core, where lip-like
folds stretch across the vestibule,
    small and tough, they flutter,
    bend like birds' wings finding
        just the right angle to stay   25
    airborne; here the cords arch
in the hollow of this ancient instrument,
curve and vibrate to make a song.

CONSIDERATIONS FOR CRITICAL THINKING AND WRITING

1. **FIRST RESPONSE.** What is the effect of having this poem written as one long sentence? How does the length of the sentence contribute to the poem's meaning?

2. Make a list of words and phrases from the poem that strike you as scientific, and compare those with a list of words that seem poetic. How do they compete or complement each other in terms of how they affect your reading?

3. Comment on the final three lines. How would your interpretation of this poem change if it ended before the semicolon in line 26?

CONNECTION TO ANOTHER SELECTION

1. Compare the diction and the ending in "The Larynx" with those of "The Foot" (p. 222), another poem by Jones.

LOUIS SIMPSON (B. 1923)

In the Suburbs   1963

There's no way out.
You were born to waste your life.
You were born to this middleclass life

As others before you
Were born to walk in procession
To the temple, singing.

CONSIDERATIONS FOR CRITICAL THINKING AND WRITING

1. **FIRST RESPONSE.** Is the title of this poem especially significant? What images does it conjure up for you?

2. What does the repetition in lines 2–3 suggest?

3. Discuss the possible connotative meanings of lines 5 and 6. Who are the "others before you"?

CONNECTION TO ANOTHER SELECTION

1. Write an essay on suburban life based on this poem and John Ciardi's "Suburban" (p. 518).

JANE YOLEN (B. 1939)

Fat Is Not a Fairy Tale   2000

I am thinking of a fairy tale,
Cinder Elephant,
Sleeping Tubby,
Snow Weight,
where the princess is not   5
anorexic, wasp-waisted;
flinging herself down the stairs.

I am thinking of a fairy tale,
Hansel and Great,
Repoundsel,   10
Bounty and the Beast,
where the beauty
has a pillowed breast,
and fingers plump as sausage.

I am thinking of a fairy tale   15
that is not yet written,
for a teller not yet born,
for a listener not yet conceived,
for a world not yet won,
where everything round is good: 20
the sun, wheels, cookies, and the princess.

CONSIDERATIONS FOR CRITICAL THINKING AND WRITING

1. **FIRST RESPONSE.** What do you think is Yolen's purpose in renaming classic fairy tales?

2. Why do you think that the speaker can imagine in the final stanza only "a fairy tale / that is not yet written"?

3. Comment on the appropriateness of the word order in line 21.

A NOTE ON READING TRANSLATIONS

Sometimes translation can inadvertently be a comic business. Consider, for example, the discovery made by John Steinbeck's wife, Elaine, when in a Yokohama bookstore she asked for a copy of her husband's famous novel *The Grapes of Wrath* and learned that it had been translated into Japanese as *Angry Raisins*. Close but no cigar (perhaps translated as: Nearby, yet no smoke). As amusing as that *Angry Raisins* title is, it teaches an important lesson about the significance of a poet's or a translator's choices when crafting a poem: a powerful piece moves us through diction and tone, both built word by careful word. Translations are frequently regarded as merely vehicular, a way to arrive at the original work. It is, of course, the original work — its spirit, style, and meaning — that most readers expect to find in a translation. Even so, it is important to understand that a translation is *by nature* different from the original — and that despite that difference, a fine translation can be an important part of the journey and become part of the literary landscape itself. Reading a translation of a poem is not the same as reading the original, but neither is watching two different performances of *Hamlet*. The translator provides a reading of the poem in much the same way that a director shapes the play. Each interprets the text from a unique perspective.

Basically, there are two distinct approaches to translation: literal translations and adaptations. A literal translation sets out to create a word-for-word equivalent that is absolutely faithful to the original. As simple and direct as this method may sound, literal translations are nearly impossible over extended passages because of the structural differences between languages. Moreover, the meaning of a single word in one language may not exist in another language, or it may require a phrase, clause, or entire sentence to capture its implications. Adaptations of works offer broader, more open-ended approaches to translation. Unlike a literal translation, an adaptation moves beyond denotative meanings in an attempt to capture the spirit of a work so that its idioms, dialects, slang, and other conventions are re-created in the language of the translation.

The question we ask of an adaptation should not be "Is this exactly how the original reads?" Instead, we ask "Is this an insightful, graceful rendering worth reading?" To translate poetry it is not enough to know the language of the original; it is also necessary that the translator be a poet. A translated poem is more than a collation of decisions based on dictionaries and grammars; it must also be poetry. However undefinable poetry may be, it is unmistakable in its intense use of language. Poems are not merely translated; they are savored.

Four Translations of a Poem by Sappho

Sappho, born about 630 B.C. and a native of the Greek island of Lesbos, is the author of a hymn to Aphrodite, the goddess of love and beauty in Greek myth. The four translations that follow suggest how widely translations can differ from one another. The first, by Henry T. Wharton, is intended to be a literal prose translation of the original Greek.

SAPPHO (CA. 630 B.C.–CA. 570 B.C.)
Immortal Aphrodite of the broidered throne   *date unknown*
TRANSLATED BY HENRY T. WHARTON (1885)

© Bettmann/CORBIS.

Immortal Aphrodite of the broidered throne, daughter of Zeus, weaver of wiles, I pray thee break not my spirit with anguish and distress, O Queen. But come hither, if ever before thou didst hear my voice afar, and listen, and leaving thy father's golden house camest with chariot yoked, and fair fleet sparrows drew thee, flapping fast their wings around the dark earth, from heaven through mid sky. Quickly arrived they; and thou, blessed one, smiling with immortal countenance, didst ask What now is befallen me, and Why now I call, and What I in my mad heart most desire to see. "What Beauty now wouldst thou draw to love thee? Who wrongs thee, Sappho? For even if she flies she shall soon follow, and if she rejects gifts shall yet give, and if she loves not shall soon love, however loth." Come, I pray thee, now too, and release me from cruel cares; and all that my heart desires to accomplish, accomplish thou, and be thyself my ally.

Beautiful-throned, immortal Aphrodite
TRANSLATED BY THOMAS WENTWORTH HIGGINSON (1871)

Beautiful-throned, immortal Aphrodite,
Daughter of Zeus, beguiler, I implore thee,
Weigh me not down with weariness and anguish
      O Thou most holy!

Come to me now, if ever thou in kindness   5
Hearkenedst my words, — and often hast thou hearkened —
Heeding, and coming from the mansions golden
      Of thy great Father,

Yoking thy chariot, borne by the most lovely
Consecrated birds, with dusky-tinted pinions,   10
Waving swift wings from utmost heights of heaven
      Through the mid-ether;

Swiftly they vanished, leaving thee, O goddess,
Smiling, with face immortal in its beauty,
Asking why I grieved, and why in utter longing   15
      I had dared call thee;

Asking what I sought, thus hopeless in desiring,
Wildered in brain, and spreading nets of passion —
Alas, for whom? and saidst thou, "Who has harmed thee?
            "O my poor Sappho!   20

"Though now he flies, ere long he shall pursue thee;
"Fearing thy gifts, he too in turn shall bring them;
"Loveless to-day, to-morrow he shall woo thee,
            "Though thou shouldst spurn him."

Thus seek me now, O holy Aphrodite!   25
Save me from anguish; give me all I ask for,
Gifts at thy hand; and thine shall be the glory,
            Sacred protector!

Prayer to my lady of Paphos

TRANSLATED BY MARY BARNARD (1958)

Dapple-throned Aphrodite,
eternal daughter of God,
snare-knitter! Don't, I beg you,

cow my heart with grief! Come,
as once when you heard my far-   5
off cry and, listening, stepped

from your father's house to your
gold car, to yoke the pair whose
beautiful thick-feathered wings

oaring down mid-air from heaven   10
carried you to light swiftly
on dark earth; then, blissful one,

smiling your immortal smile
you asked, What ailed me now that
made me call you again? What   15

was it that my distracted
heart most wanted? "Whom has
Persuasion to bring round now

"to your love? Who, Sappho, is
unfair to you? For, let her   20
run, she will soon run after;

"if she won't accept gifts, she
will one day give them; and if
she won't love you — she soon will

"love, although unwillingly...."   25
If ever — come now! Relieve
this intolerable pain!

What my heart most hopes will
happen, make happen; you your-
self join forces on my side!   30

Artfully adorned Aphrodite, deathless

TRANSLATED BY JIM POWELL (1993)

Artfully adorned Aphrodite, deathless
child of Zeus and weaver of wiles I beg you
please don't hurt me, don't overcome my spirit,
    goddess, with longing,

but come here, if ever at other moments   5
hearing these my words from afar you listened
and responded: leaving your father's house, all
    golden, you came then,

hitching up your chariot: lovely sparrows
drew you quickly over the dark earth, whirling   10
on fine beating wings from the heights of heaven
    down through the sky and

instantly arrived — and then O my blessed
goddess with a smile on your deathless face you
asked me what the matter was *this* time, what I   15
    called you for this time,

what I now most wanted to happen in my
raving heart: "Whom *this* time should I persuade to
lead you back again to her love? Who *now*, oh
    Sappho, who wrongs you?   20

If she flees you now, she will soon pursue you;
if she won't accept what you give, she'll give it;
if she doesn't love you, she'll love you soon now,
    even unwilling."

Come to me again, and release me from this   25
want past bearing. All that my heart desires to
happen — make it happen. And stand beside me,
    goddess, my ally.

CONSIDERATIONS FOR CRITICAL THINKING AND WRITING

1. **FIRST RESPONSE.** Try rewriting Wharton's prose version in contemporary language. How does your prose version differ in tone from Wharton's?
2. Explain which translation seems closest to Wharton's prose version.
3. Discuss the images and metaphors in Higginson's and Barnard's versions. Which version is more appealing to you? Explain why.
4. Explain which version seems to you to be the most contemporary in its use of language.

Three Translations of a Poem by Pablo Neruda

The following poem by the Chilean Nobel Prize–winner Pablo Neruda is in its original Spanish. By using a substantial Spanish/English dictionary, you might be able to translate it into English even if you are unfamiliar with Spanish. Following the poem are three translations that offer some subtle and intriguing differences in their approaches to the poem.

© Luis Poirot.

PABLO NERUDA (1904–1973)

Verbo

1968

Voy a arrugar esta palabra,
voy a torcerla,
sí,
es demasiado lisa,
es como si un gran perro o un gran río   5
le hubíera repasado lengua o agua
durante muchos años.

Quiero que en la palabra
se vea la aspereza,
la sal ferruginosa,   10
la fuerza desdentada
de la tierra,
la sangre
de los que hablaron y de los que no hablaron.

Quiero ver la sed   15
adentro de las sílabas:
quiero tocar el fuego
en el sonido:
quiero sentir la oscuridad
del grito. Quiero   20
palabras ásperas
como piedras vírgenes.

Word

TRANSLATED BY BEN BELITT (1974)

I'm going to crumple this word,
to twist it,
yes,
it's too slick
like a big dog or a river   5
had been lapping it down with its tongue, or water
had worn it away with the years.

I want gravel
to show in the word,
the ferruginous salt,   10
the gap-toothed power
of the soil.
There must be a blood-letting
for talker and non-talker alike.

I want to see thirst   15
in the syllables,
touch fire
in the sound;
feel through the dark
for the scream. Let   20
my words be acrid
as virginal stone.

Word

TRANSLATED BY KRISTIN LINKLATER (1992)

I'm going to crumple this word,
I'm going to twist it,
yes,
it's too smooth,
it's as though a big dog or a big river   5
had been licking it over and over with tongue or water
for many years.

I want the word
to reveal the roughness,
the ferruginous salt,   10
the toothless strength
of the earth,
the blood
of those who talked and of those who did not talk.

I want to see the thirst   15
inside the syllables,

I want to touch the fire
in the sound:
I want to feel the darkness
of the scream. I want   20
rough words,
like virgin rocks.

Verb

TRANSLATED BY ILAN STAVANS (2003)

I'm going to wrinkle this word,
twist it,
yes,
it's too smooth,
as if the tongue   5
of a big dog or a big river's water
had washed it
for years and years.

I want to see
roughness in the word,   10
ironlike salt,
earth's
toothless strength,
the blood
of those who spoke out and those who didn't.   15

I want to see thirst
deep in its syllables.
I want to touch fire
in the sound.
I want to feel   20
the darkness of a scream.
I want rough words
like virginal stones.

CONSIDERATIONS FOR CRITICAL THINKING AND WRITING

1. **FIRST RESPONSE.** Discuss whether or not all three translations convey the same essential themes.

2. What are the major differences that you see in diction, syntax, and tone among the translations?

3. Explain why you think "Word" or "Verb" is the better title. Does the Spanish/English dictionary affect your opinion, or is your response based solely on the poem?

4. Which translation do you think is the most effective? Explain why you prefer one translation over another.

Web) Research the poets in this chapter on LitLinks at bedfordstmartins .com/meyerpoetry.

JEANNETTE BARNES (B. 1956)

Battle-Piece
1999

Confederate monument, Ocean Pond, Olustee, Florida, 1864

Picknickers sojourn here an hour,
get their fill, get gone.
Seldom, they quickstep as far downhill
as this bivouac; they miss sting, snap,

grit in clenched teeth, carbine, cartridge,   5
cap, *hurrah boys*. Cannon-cracks
the peal, the clap of doom.

Into the billows, white, filthy,
choked by smoke, Clem, Eustace, Willy —
it would be useless to name names or call them all.   10

Anyway, that's done already. Every fall
sons of sons and reverent veterans' wives
lay wreaths, a prize of plastic daisies,

everlasting. Nobody calls this lazy.
It's August, and it's late, it's afternoon,   15
heat-mist glistens on slick granite, sun

fingers through sleek pines, their edges cropped
like the clipped elegant grass. It is a shock
to see a caisson blown

to flinders; a horse shrieks,   20
the mortar-shell zooms, spiral-
ripping tender belly. Oh, yes, here

are raked paths, cindered, sweet trees
and cool water. That whimper
you do not hear now was the doves,   25
spooning. Evening calls you all, eager

as spruce-gum-chewing, apple-filching boys
to pull one long last gulp of switchel
as if, now, somebody's sons had almost done

haying. Keen to victual, nearly home, feature the sharp   30
surprise when, smooth as oiled stone
stroking the clean edge of a scythe, these boys achieved
each his marble pillow, astonished by the sky.

CONSIDERATIONS FOR CRITICAL THINKING AND WRITING

1. **FIRST RESPONSE.** Contrast the images used to describe the present moment at the battle site with the images used to describe the actual battle.

2. Describe the speaker's tone. What do the images reveal about the speaker's emotions?

3. Analyze the diction and images of the final stanza. What makes it so powerful?

What mood is established in this next poem's view of Civil War troops moving across a river?

Explore contexts for Walt Whitman on *LiterActive*.

WALT WHITMAN (1819–1892)

Cavalry Crossing a Ford   1865

A line in long array where they wind betwixt green islands,
They take a serpentine course, their arms flash in the sun — hark to the
    musical clank,
Behold the silvery river, in it the splashing horses loitering stop to drink,
Behold the brown-faced men, each group, each person, a picture, the
    negligent rest on the saddles,
Some emerge on the opposite bank, others are just entering the ford — while,
Scarlet and blue and snowy white,
The guidon flags flutter gaily in the wind.

CONSIDERATIONS FOR CRITICAL THINKING AND WRITING

1. **FIRST RESPONSE.** Do the colors and sounds establish the mood of this poem? What *is* the mood?
2. How would the poem's mood have been changed if Whitman had used "look" or "see" instead of "behold" (lines 3–4)?
3. Where is the speaker as he observes this troop movement?
4. Does "serpentine" in line 2 have an evil connotation in this poem? Explain your answer.

Whitman seems to capture momentarily all of the troop's actions, and through carefully chosen, suggestive details — really very few — he succeeds in making "each group, each person, a picture." Specific details, even when few are provided, give us the impression that we see the entire picture; it is as if those are the details we would remember if we had viewed the scene ourselves. Notice, too, that the movement of the "line in long array" is emphasized by the continuous winding syntax of the poem's lengthy lines.

Movement is also central to the next poem, in which action and motion are created through carefully chosen verbs.

DAVID SOLWAY (B. 1941)

Windsurfing   1993

It rides upon the wrinkled hide
of water, like the upturned hull
of a small canoe or kayak
waiting to be righted — yet its law

JIMMY SANTIAGO BACA (B. 1952)

Green Chile   *1989*

I prefer red chile over my eggs
and potatoes for breakfast.
Red chile *ristras*° decorate my door,   *a braided string of peppers*
dry on my roof, and hang from eaves.
They lend open-air vegetable stands   5
historical grandeur, and gently swing
with an air of festive welcome.
I can hear them talking in the wind,
haggard, yellowing, crisp, rasping
tongues of old men, licking the breeze.   10

       But grandmother loves green chile.
When I visit her,
she holds the green chile pepper
in her wrinkled hands.
Ah, voluptuous, masculine,   15
an air of authority and youth simmers
from its swan-neck stem, tapering to a flowery
collar, fermenting resinous spice.
A well-dressed gentleman at the door
my grandmother takes sensuously in her hand,   20
rubbing its firm glossed sides,
caressing the oily rubbery serpent,
with mouth-watering fulfillment,
fondling its curves with gentle fingers.
Its bearing magnificent and taut   25
as flanks of a tiger in mid-leap,
she thrusts her blade into
and cuts it open, with lust
on her hot mouth, sweating over the stove,
bandanna round her forehead,   30
mysterious passion on her face
and she serves me green chile con carne
between soft warm leaves of corn tortillas,
with beans and rice — her sacrifice
to her little prince.   35
I slurp from my plate
with last bit of tortilla, my mouth burns
and I hiss and drink a tall glass of cold water.

All over New Mexico, sunburned men and women
drive rickety trucks stuffed with gunny-sacks   40
of green chile, from Belen, Veguita, Willard, Estancia,
San Antonio y Socorro, from fields
to roadside stands, you see them roasting green chile
in screen-sided homemade barrels, and for a dollar a bag,
we relive this old, beautiful ritual again and again.   45

CONSIDERATIONS FOR CRITICAL THINKING AND WRITING

1. **FIRST RESPONSE.** What's the difference between red and green chiles in this poem? Find the different images the speaker uses to distinguish between the two.

2. What kinds of images are used to describe the grandmother's preparation of green chile? What is the effect of those images?

3. **CREATIVE RESPONSE.** Try writing a description—in poetry or prose—that uses vivid images to evoke a powerful response (either positive or negative) to a particular food.

POEMS FOR FURTHER STUDY

AMY LOWELL (1874–1925)

The Pond   *1919*

Cold, wet leaves
Floating on moss-colored water,
And the croaking of frogs—
Cracked bell-notes in the twilight.

CONSIDERATIONS FOR CRITICAL THINKING AND WRITING

1. **FIRST RESPONSE.** This poem is not a complete sentence. What is missing? Does it matter in terms of understanding what is described by the images?

2. What senses are stimulated by the images? Which sense seems to be the most dominant in the poem? Why?

3. **CREATIVE RESPONSE.** Is the title of the poem necessary to convey its meaning? Choose an appropriate alternate title and explain how it subtly suggests something different from "The Pond."

H. D. (HILDA DOOLITTLE/1886–1961)

Heat   *1916*

O wind, rend open the heat,
cut apart the heat,
rend it to tatters.

Fruit cannot drop
through this thick air—
fruit cannot fall into heat   5
that presses up and blunts
the points of pears
and rounds the grapes.

Cut the heat—   10
plough through it,
turning it on either side
of your path.

CONSIDERATIONS FOR CRITICAL THINKING AND WRITING

1. **FIRST RESPONSE.** Is this poem more about heat or fruit? Explain your an-
   swer.
2. What physical properties are associated with heat in this poem?
3. Explain the effect of the description of fruit in lines 4–9.
4. Why is the image of the cutting plow especially effective in lines 10–13?

SHEILA WINGFIELD (1906–1992)

A Bird   *1983*

Unexplained
In the salt meadow
Lay the dead bird.
The wind
Was fluttering its wings.

CONSIDERATIONS FOR CRITICAL THINKING AND WRITING

1. **FIRST RESPONSE.** How does each line of this poem contribute to the overall
   tone?
2. What is the effect of the last line?
3. **CREATIVE RESPONSE.** Try writing a five-line poem—using Wingfield's as a
   model—that establishes a light, optimistic tone about a bird by way of
   vivid images.

MARY ROBINSON (1758–1800)

London's Summer Morning   *1806*

Who has not wak'd to list° the busy sounds   *listen to*
Of summer's morning, in the sultry smoke
Of noisy London? On the pavement hot
The sooty chimney-boy, with dingy face
And tatter'd covering, shrilly bawls his trade,   5
Rousing the sleepy housemaid. At the door
The milk-pail rattles, and the tinkling bell
Proclaims the dustman's office; while the street
Is lost in clouds impervious. Now begins

The din of hackney-coaches, waggons, carts;   10
While tinmen's shops, and noisy trunk-makers,
Knife-grinders, coopers, squeaking cork-cutters,
Fruit-barrows, and the hunger-giving cries
Of vegetable venders, fill the air.
Now ev'ry shop displays its varied trade,   15
And the fresh-sprinkled pavement cools the feet
Of early walkers. At the private door
The ruddy housemaid twirls the busy mop,
Annoying the smart 'prentice, or neat girl,
Tripping with band-box° lightly. Now the sun   *hat box*   20
Darts burning splendour on the glitt'ring pane,
Save where the canvas awning throws a shade
On the gay merchandize. Now, spruce and trim,
In shops (where beauty smiles with industry,)
Sits the smart damsel; while the passenger   25
Peeps thro' the window, watching ev'ry charm.
Now pastry dainties catch the eye minute
Of humming insects, while the limy snare
Waits to enthral them. Now the lamp-lighter
Mounts the tall ladder, nimbly vent'rous,   30
To trim the half-fill'd lamp; while at his feet
The pot-boy° yells discordant! All along   *drink server*
The sultry pavement, the old-clothes-man cries
In tones monotonous, and side-long views
The area for his traffic: now the bag   35
Is slily open'd, and the half-worn suit
(Sometimes the pilfer'd treasure of the base
Domestic spoiler), for one half its worth,
Sinks in the green abyss. The porter now
Bears his huge load along the burning way;   40
And the poor poet wakes from busy dreams,
To paint the summer morning.

CONSIDERATIONS FOR CRITICAL THINKING AND WRITING

1. **FIRST RESPONSE.** How effective is this picture of a London summer morn-
   ing in 1806? Which images do you find particularly effective?

2. How does the end of the poem bring us full circle to its beginning? What
   effect does this structure have on your understanding of the poem?

3. **CREATIVE RESPONSE.** Try writing about the start of your own day—in the
   dormitory, at home, the start of a class—using a series of images that pro-
   vide a vivid sense of what happens and how you experience it.

CONNECTION TO ANOTHER SELECTION

1. How does Robinson's description of London differ from William Blake's
   "London," the next poem? What would you say is the essential difference in
   purpose between the two poems?

WILLIAM BLAKE (1757–1827)

London   *1794*

I wander through each chartered° street,   *defined by law*
Near where the chartered Thames does flow,
And mark in every face I meet
Marks of weakness, marks of woe.   Explore contexts
                                                            for William Blake
In every cry of every man,   on *LiterActive*.   5
In every Infant's cry of fear,
In every voice, in every ban,
The mind-forged manacles I hear.

How the Chimney-sweeper's cry
Every black'ning Church appalls;   10
And the hapless Soldier's sigh
Runs in blood down Palace walls.

But most through midnight streets I hear
How the youthful Harlot's curse
Blasts the new-born Infant's tear,   15
And blights with plagues the Marriage hearse.

CONSIDERATIONS FOR CRITICAL THINKING AND WRITING

1. **FIRST RESPONSE.** What feelings do the visual images in this poem suggest to you?

2. What is the predominant sound heard in the poem?

3. What is the meaning of line 8? What is the cause of the problems that the speaker sees and hears in London? Does the speaker suggest additional causes?

4. The image in lines 11 and 12 cannot be read literally. Comment on its effectiveness.

5. How does Blake's use of denotative and connotative language enrich this poem's meaning?

6. An earlier version of Blake's last stanza appeared this way:

   But most the midnight harlot's curse
   From every dismal street I hear,
   Weaves around the marriage hearse
   And blasts the new-born infant's tear.

Examine carefully the differences between the two versions. How do Blake's revisions affect his picture of London life? Which version do you think is more effective? Why?

WILFRED OWEN (1893–1918)

Dulce et Decorum Est

1920

Bent double, like old beggars under sacks,
Knock-kneed, coughing like hags, we cursed through
    sludge,
Till on the haunting flares we turned our backs,
And towards our distant rest began to trudge.

Explore contexts for Wilfred Owen on *LiterActive*.

Men marched asleep. Many had lost their boots,   5
But limped on, blood-shod. All went lame, all blind;
Drunk with fatigue; deaf even to the hoots
Of gas-shells dropping softly behind.

Gas! GAS! Quick, boys! — An ecstasy of fumbling,
Fitting the clumsy helmets just in time,   10
But someone still was yelling out and stumbling
And flound'ring like a man in fire or lime. —
Dim through the misty panes and thick green light,
As under a green sea, I saw him drowning.

In all my dreams before my helpless sight   15
He plunges at me, guttering, choking, drowning.

If in some smothering dreams, you too could pace
Behind the wagon that we flung him in,
And watch the white eyes writhing in his face,
His hanging face, like a devil's sick of sin,   20
If you could hear, at every jolt, the blood
Come gargling from the froth-corrupted lungs
Bitter as the cud
Obscene as cancer,
Of vile, incurable sores on innocent tongues, —   25
My friend, you would not tell with such high zest
To children ardent for some desperate glory,
The old lie: *Dulce et decorum est
Pro patria mori.*

CONSIDERATIONS FOR CRITICAL THINKING AND WRITING

1. **FIRST RESPONSE.** The Latin quotation in lines 27 and 28 is from Horace: "It is sweet and fitting to die for one's country." Owen served as a British soldier during World War I and was killed. Is this poem unpatriotic? What is its purpose?

2. Which images in the poem are most vivid? To which senses do they speak?

3. Describe the speaker's tone. What is his relationship to his audience?

4. How are the images of the soldiers in this poem different from the images that typically appear in recruiting posters?

PATRICIA SMITH (B. 1955)

What It's Like to Be a Black Girl
(for Those of You Who Aren't)

1991

First of all, it's being 9 years old and
feeling like you're not finished, like your
edges are wild, like there's something,
everything, wrong. it's dropping food coloring
in your eyes to make them blue and suffering   5
their burn in silence. it's popping a bleached
white mophead over the kinks of your hair and
primping in front of the mirrors that deny your
reflection. it's finding a space between your
legs, a disturbance at your chest, and not knowing   10
what to do with the whistles. it's jumping
double dutch until your legs pop, it's sweat
and vaseline and bullets, it's growing tall and
wearing a lot of white, it's smelling blood in
your breakfast, it's learning to say fuck with   15
grace but learning to fuck without it, it's
flame and fists and life according to motown,
it's finally having a man reach out for you
then caving in
around his fingers.   20

CONSIDERATIONS FOR CRITICAL THINKING AND WRITING

1. **FIRST RESPONSE.** Describe the speaker's tone. What images in particular
   contribute to it? How do you account for the selected tone?

2. How does the speaker characterize her life? On which elements of it does
   she focus?

3. Discuss the poem's final image. What sort of emotions does it elicit in you?

CHARLES SIMIC (B. 1938)

To the One Upstairs

1999

Boss of all bosses of the universe.
Mr know-it-all, wheeler-dealer, wire-puller,
And whatever else you're good at.
Go ahead, shuffle your zeros tonight.
Dip in ink the comets' tails.   5
Staple the night with starlight.

You'd be better off reading coffee dregs,
Thumbing the pages of the Farmer's Almanac.
But no! You love to put on airs,
And cultivate your famous serenity   10

While you sit behind your big desk
With zilch in your in-tray, zilch
In your out-tray,
And all of eternity around you.

Doesn't it give you the creeps   15
To hear them begging you on their knees,
Sputtering endearments,
As if you were an inflatable, life-size doll?
Tell them to button up and go to bed.
Stop pretending you're too busy to notice.   20

Your hands are empty and so are your eyes.
There's nothing to put your signature to,
Even if you knew your own name,
Or believed the ones I keep inventing,
As I scribble this note to you in the dark.   25

CONSIDERATIONS FOR CRITICAL THINKING AND WRITING

1. **FIRST RESPONSE.** Describe the speaker's relationship to the "Boss of all bosses." What do you think of that relationship?
2. What images are associated with God in the poem? Describe the sort of character and personality that the speaker attributes to God.
3. How do the final two lines affect your reading of the poem?

CONNECTION TO ANOTHER SELECTION

1. Discuss the themes in Simic's poem and in Emily Dickinson's "I know that He exists" (p. 344).

RAINER MARIA RILKE (1875–1926)

The Panther   1927

TRANSLATED BY STEPHEN MITCHELL

His vision, from the constantly passing bars,
has grown so weary that it cannot hold
anything else. It seems to him there are
a thousand bars; and behind the bars, no world.

As he paces in cramped circles, over and over,   5
the movement of his powerful soft strides
is like a ritual dance around a center
in which a mighty will stands paralyzed.

Only at times, the curtain of the pupils
lifts, quietly — . An image enters in,   10
rushes down through the tensed, arrested muscles,
plunges into the heart and is gone.

1. **FIRST RESPONSE.** Why do you think Rilke chooses a panther rather than, say, a lion as the subject of the poem's images?

2. What kind of "image enters in" the heart of the panther in the final stanza?

3. How are images of confinement achieved in the poem? Why doesn't Rilke describe the final image in lines 10–12?

CONNECTION TO ANOTHER SELECTION

1. Write an essay explaining how a sense of movement is achieved by the images and rhythms in this poem and in Dickinson's "A Bird came down the Walk —" (p. 187).

JANE KENYON (1947–1995)

The Blue Bowl   *1990*

Like primitives we buried the cat
with his bowl. Bare-handed
we scraped sand and gravel
back into the hole.
        They fell with a hiss   5

and thud on his side,
on his long red fur, the white feathers
between his toes, and his
long, not to say aquiline, nose.

We stood and brushed each other off.   10
There are sorrows keener than these.

Silent the rest of the day, we worked,
ate, stared, and slept. It stormed
all night; now it clears, and a robin
burbles from a dripping bush   15
like the neighbor who means well
but always says the wrong thing.

CONSIDERATIONS FOR CRITICAL THINKING AND WRITING

1. **FIRST RESPONSE.** How do the descriptions of the cat — "the white feathers / between his toes" — affect your reading of the poem?

2. Why do you think Kenyon titles the poem "The Blue Bowl" rather than, perhaps, "The Cat's Bowl"?

3. What is the effect of being reminded that "There are sorrows keener than these"?

4. Why is the robin's song "the wrong thing"?

1. Write an essay comparing the death of this cat with the death of the dog in John Updike's "Dog's Death" (p. 24). Which poem draws a more powerful response from you? Explain why.

SALLY CROFT (B. 1935)
Home-Baked Bread   *1981*

Nothing gives a household a greater sense of stability and common comfort than the aroma of cooling bread. Begin, if you like, with a loaf of whole wheat, which requires neither sifting nor kneading, and go on from there to more cunning triumphs.
— *The Joy of Cooking*

What is it she is not saying?
Cunning triumphs. It rings
of insinuation. Step into my kitchen,
I have prepared a cunning triumph
for you. Spices and herbs   5
sealed in this porcelain jar,

a treasure of my great-aunt
who sat up past midnight
in her Massachusetts bedroom
when the moon was dark. Come,   10
rest your feet. I'll make
you tea with honey and slices

of warm bread spread with peach butter.
I picked the fruit this morning
still fresh with dew. The fragrance   15
is seductive? I hoped you would say that.
See how the heat rises
when the bread opens. Come,

we'll eat together, the small flakes
have scarcely any flavor. What cunning   20
triumphs we can discover in my upstairs room
where peach trees breathe their sweetness
beside the open window and
sun lies like honey on the floor.

1. **FIRST RESPONSE.** Why does the speaker in this poem seize on the phrase "cunning triumphs" from the *Joy of Cooking* excerpt?
2. Distinguish between the voice we hear in lines 1–3 and the second voice in lines 3–24. Who is the "you" in the poem?
3. Why is the word "insinuation" an especially appropriate choice in line 3?

4. How do the images in lines 20–24 bring together all of the senses evoked in the preceding lines?

5. **CREATIVE RESPONSE.** Write a paragraph — or stanza — that describes the sensuous (and perhaps sensual) qualities of a food you enjoy.

JOHN KEATS (1795–1821)

To Autumn   *1819*

I

Season of mists and mellow fruitfulness,
   Close bosom-friend of the maturing sun;
Conspiring with him how to load and bless
   With fruit the vines that round the thatch-eves run;
To bend with apples the mossed cottage-trees,   5
   And fill all fruit with ripeness to the core;
     To swell the gourd, and plump the hazel shells
   With a sweet kernel; to set budding more,
And still more, later flowers for the bees,
Until they think warm days will never cease,   10
   For summer has o'er-brimmed their clammy cells.

II

Who hath not seen thee oft amid thy store?
   Sometimes whoever seeks abroad may find
Thee sitting careless on a granary floor,
   Thy hair soft-lifted by the winnowing wind;   15
Or on a half-reaped furrow sound asleep,
   Drowsed with the fume of poppies, while thy hook°   *scythe*
     Spares the next swath and all its twinèd flowers:
And sometimes like a gleaner thou dost keep
   Steady thy laden head across a brook;   20
   Or by a cider-press, with patient look,
     Thou watchest the last oozings hours by hours.

III

Where are the songs of spring? Ay, where are they?
   Think not of them, thou hast thy music too —
While barred clouds bloom the soft-dying day,   25
   And touch the stubble-plains with rosy hue;
Then in a wailful choir the small gnats mourn
   Among the river swallows,° borne aloft   *willows*
     Or sinking as the light wind lives or dies;
And full-grown lambs loud bleat from hilly bourn;°   *territory*   30

Explore contexts
for John Keats
on *LiterActive*.

Hedge-crickets sing; and now with treble soft
The redbreast whistles from a garden-croft,
    And gathering swallows twitter in the skies.

CONSIDERATIONS FOR CRITICAL THINKING AND WRITING

1. **FIRST RESPONSE.** How is autumn made to seem like a person in each stanza of this ode?
2. Which senses are most emphasized in each stanza?
3. How is the progression of time expressed in the ode?
4. How does the imagery convey tone? Which words have particularly strong connotative values?
5. What is the speaker's view of death?

CONNECTIONS TO OTHER SELECTIONS

1. Compare this poem's tone and perspective on death with those of Robert Frost's "After Apple-Picking" (p. 364).
2. Write an essay comparing the significance of this poem's images of "mellow fruitfulness" (line 1) with that of the images of ripeness in Theodore Roethke's "Root Cellar" (p. 114). Explain how the images in each poem lead to very different feelings about the same phenomenon.

KATE CLANCHY (B. 1965)

Spell   *1999*

If, at your desk, you push aside your work,
take down a book, turn to this verse
and read that I kneel there, pressing
my ear where on your chest the muscles
arch as great books part, in seagull curves,   5
bridging the seasounds of your heart,

and that your hands run through my hair,
draw the wayward mass to strands
as flat as scarlet silk-thread bookmarks,
and stroke my cheeks as if smoothing   10
back the tissue leaves from chilly,
plated pages, and pull me near

to read my eyes alone, then you shall see,
silvered and monochrome, yourself,
sitting at your desk, taking down a book,   15
turning to this verse, and then, my love,
you shall not know which one of us is reading
now, which writing, and which written.

CONSIDERATIONS FOR CRITICAL THINKING AND WRITING

1. **FIRST RESPONSE.** How does Clanchy cast a kind of spell through her use of images as she describes the relationship between these two lovers?
2. Trace how images of books are used in each stanza. Which image do you find to be the most strikingly effective?
3. Discuss the significance of the final two lines.

CONNECTIONS TO ANOTHER SELECTION

1. Compare "Spell" and Dickinson's "There is no Frigate like a Book" (p. 330) on the act of reading. Which poem do you think is more demanding on the reader? Explain why.

EZRA POUND (1885–1972)

In a Station of the Metro°

1913

The apparition of these faces in the crowd;
Petals on a wet, black bough.

Metro: Underground railroad in Paris.

CONSIDERATIONS FOR CRITICAL THINKING AND WRITING

1. **FIRST RESPONSE.** Why is the title essential for this poem?
2. What kind of mood does the image in the second line convey?
3. Why is "apparition" a better word choice than, say, "appearance" or "sight"?
4. **CREATIVE RESPONSE.** Write a two-line vivid image for a poem titled "At a Desk in the Library."

CATHY SONG (B. 1955)

The White Porch

1983

I wrap the blue towel
after washing,
around the damp
weight of hair, bulky
as a sleeping cat,   5
and sit out on the porch.
Still dripping water,
it'll be dry by supper,
by the time the dust

settles off your shoes,   10
though it's only five
past noon. Think
of the luxury: how to use
the afternoon like the stretch
of lawn spread before me.   15
There's the laundry,
sun-warm clothes at twilight,
and the mountain of beans
in my lap. Each one,
I'll break and snap   20
thoughtfully in half.

But there is this slow arousal.
The small buttons
of my cotton blouse
are pulling away from my body.   25
I feel the strain of threads,
the swollen magnolias
heavy as a flock of birds
in the tree. Already,
the orange sponge cake   30
is rising in the oven.
I know you'll say it makes
your mouth dry
and I'll watch you
drench your slice of it   35
in canned peaches
and lick the plate clean.

So much hair, my mother
used to say, grabbing
the thick braided rope   40
in her hands while we washed
the breakfast dishes, discussing
dresses and pastries.
My mind often elsewhere
as we did the morning chores together.   45
Sometimes, a few strands
would catch in her gold ring.
I worked hard then,
anticipating the hour
when I would let the rope down   50
at night, strips of sheets,
knotted and tied,
while she slept in tight blankets.
My hair, freshly washed
like a measure of wealth,   55
like a bridal veil.
Crouching in the grass,

you would wait for the signal,
for the movement of curtains
before releasing yourself   60
from the shadow of moths.
Cloth, hair and hands,
smuggling you in.

CONSIDERATIONS FOR CRITICAL THINKING AND WRITING

1. **FIRST RESPONSE.** How is hair made erotic in this poem? Discuss the images
   that you deem especially effective.

2. Who is the "you" to whom the speaker refers in each stanza?

3. What role does the mother play in this poem about desire?

4. Why do you think the poem is titled "The White Porch"?

CONNECTIONS TO OTHER SELECTIONS

1. Compare the images used to describe the speaker's "slow arousal" (line 22)
   in this poem with Sally Croft's images in "Home-Baked Bread" (p. 126).
   What similarities do you see? What makes each description so effective?

2. Write an essay comparing the images of sensuality in this poem with those
   in Li Ho's "A Beautiful Girl Combs Her Hair" (p. 56). Which poem seems
   more erotic to you? Why?

Perspective

T. E. HULME (1883–1917)

On the Differences between Poetry and Prose   *1924*

In prose as in algebra concrete things are embodied in signs or counters which
are moved about according to rules, without being visualized at all in the
process. There are in prose certain type situations and arrangements of words,
which move as automatically into certain other arrangements as do functions
in algebra. One only changes the X's and the Y's back into physical things at
the end of the process. Poetry, in one aspect at any rate, may be considered as
an effort to avoid this characteristic of prose. It is not a counter language, but
a visual concrete one. It is a compromise for a language of intuition which
would hand over sensations bodily. It always endeavors to arrest you, and to
make you continuously see a physical thing, to prevent you gliding through an
abstract process. It chooses fresh epithets and fresh metaphors, not so much
because they are new, and we are tired of the old, but because the old cease to
convey a physical thing and become abstract counters. A poet says a ship
"coursed the seas" to get a physical image, instead of the counter word "sailed."
Visual meanings can only be transferred by the new bowl of metaphor; prose is
an old pot that lets them leak out. Images in verse are not mere decoration, but

the very essence of an intuitive language. Verse is a pedestrian taking you over the ground, prose — a train which delivers you at a destination.

From "Romanticism and Classicism," in *Speculations*,
edited by Herbert Read

CONSIDERATIONS FOR CRITICAL THINKING AND WRITING

1. What distinctions does Hulme make between poetry and prose? Which seems to be the most important difference?

2. Write an essay that discusses Hulme's claim that poetry "is a compromise for a language of intuition which would hand over sensations bodily."

Web Research the poets in this chapter at bedfordstmartins.com/ meyerpoetry.

5

Figures of Speech

Like a piece of ice on a hot stove the poem must ride on its own melting.
— ROBERT FROST

Figures of speech are broadly defined as a way of saying one thing in terms of something else. An overeager funeral director might, for example, be described as a vulture. Although figures of speech are indirect, they are designed to clarify, not obscure, our understanding of what they describe. Poets frequently use them because, as Emily Dickinson said, the poet's work is to "tell all the Truth but tell it slant" to capture the reader's interest and imagination. But figures of speech are not limited to poetry. Hearing them, reading them, or using them is as natural as using language itself.

Suppose that in the middle of a class discussion concerning the economic causes of World War II your history instructor introduces a series of statistics by saying, "Let's get down to brass tacks." Would anyone be likely to expect a display of brass tacks for students to examine? Of course not. To interpret the statement literally would be to wholly misunderstand the instructor's point that the time has come for a close look at the economic circumstances leading to the war. A literal response transforms the statement into the sort of hilariously bizarre material often found in a sketch by Woody Allen.

The class does not look for brass tacks because, in a nutshell, they understand that the instructor is speaking figuratively. They would understand, too, that in the preceding sentence "in a nutshell" refers to brevity and conciseness rather than to the covering of a kernel of a nut. Figurative language makes its way into our everyday speech and writing as well as into literature because it is a means of achieving color, vividness, and intensity.

Consider the difference, for example, between these two statements:

Literal: The diner strongly expressed anger at the waiter.
Figurative: The diner leaped from his table and roared at the waiter.

The second statement is more vivid because it creates a picture of ferocious anger by likening the diner to some kind of wild animal, such as a lion or tiger. By comparison, "strongly expressed anger" is neither especially strong nor especially expressive; it is flat. Not all figurative language avoids this kind of flatness, however. Figures of speech such as "getting down to brass tacks" and "in a nutshell" are clichés because they lack originality and freshness. Still, they suggest how these devices are commonly used to give language some color, even if that color is sometimes a bit faded.

There is nothing weak about William Shakespeare's use of figurative language in the following passage from *Macbeth*. Macbeth has just learned that his wife is dead, and he laments her loss as well as the course of his own life.

WILLIAM SHAKESPEARE (1564–1616)

From Macbeth *(Act V, Scene v)*   1605–1606

Tomorrow, and tomorrow, and tomorrow
Creeps in this petty pace from day to day
To the last syllable of recorded time;
And all our yesterdays have lighted fools
The way to dusty death. Out, out, brief candle!   5
Life's but a walking shadow, a poor player,
That struts and frets his hour upon the stage,
And then is heard no more. It is a tale
Told by an idiot, full of sound and fury,
Signifying nothing.   10

This passage might be summarized as "life has no meaning," but such a brief paraphrase does not take into account the figurative language that reveals the depth of Macbeth's despair and his view of the absolute meaninglessness of life. By comparing life to a "brief candle," Macbeth emphasizes the darkness and death that surround human beings. The light of life is too brief and unpredictable to be of any comfort. Indeed, life for Macbeth is a "walking shadow," futilely playing a role that is more farcical than dramatic, because life is, ultimately, a desperate story filled with pain and devoid of significance. What the figurative language provides, then, is the emotional force of Macbeth's assertion; his comparisons are disturbing because they are so apt.

The remainder of this chapter discusses some of the most important figures of speech used in poetry. A familiarity with them will help you to understand how poetry achieves its effects.

SIMILE AND METAPHOR

The two most common figures of speech are simile and metaphor. Both compare things that are ordinarily considered unlike each other. A *simile* makes an explicit comparison between two things by using words such as *like, as, than, appears,* or *seems:* "A sip of Mrs. Cook's coffee is like a punch in the stomach." The force of the simile is created by the differences between the two things compared. There would be no simile if the comparison were stated this way: "Mrs. Cook's coffee is as strong as the cafeteria's coffee." This is a literal comparison because Mrs. Cook's coffee is compared with something like it, another kind of coffee. Consider how simile is used in this poem.

Web Explore the poetic elements in this chapter on *LiterActive* or at bedfordstmartins .com/meyerpoetry.

MARGARET ATWOOD (B. 1939)

you fit into me   1971

you fit into me
like a hook into an eye

a fish hook
an open eye

© Sophie Bassouls/CORBIS SYGMA.

If you blinked on a second reading, you got the point of this poem because you recognized that the simile "like a hook into an eye" gives way to a play on words in the final two lines. There the hook and eye, no longer a pleasant domestic image of fitting closely together, become a literal, sharp fishhook and a human eye. The wordplay qualifies the simile and drastically alters the tone of this poem by creating a strong and unpleasant surprise.

A *metaphor,* like a simile, makes a comparison between two unlike things, but it does so implicitly, without words such as *like* or *as:* "Mrs. Cook's coffee is a punch in the stomach." Metaphor asserts the identity of dissimilar things. Macbeth tells us that life *is* a "brief candle," life *is* "a walking shadow," life *is* "a poor player," life *is* "a tale / Told by an idiot." Metaphor transforms people, places, objects, and ideas into whatever the poet imagines them to be, and if metaphors are effective, the reader's experience, understanding, and appreciation of what is described are enhanced. Metaphors are frequently more demanding than similes because they are not signaled by particular words. They are both subtle and powerful.

Here is a poem about presentiment, a foreboding that something terrible is about to happen.

EMILY DICKINSON (1830–1886)

Presentiment — is that long Shadow — on the lawn —

ca. 1863

Presentiment — is that long Shadow — on the lawn —
Indicative that Suns go down —

The notice to the startled Grass
That Darkness — is about to pass —

The metaphors in this poem define the abstraction "Presentiment." The sense of foreboding that Dickinson expresses is identified with a particular moment — the moment when darkness is just about to envelop an otherwise tranquil, ordinary scene. The speaker projects that fear onto the "startled Grass" so that it seems any life must be frightened by the approaching "Shadow" and "Darkness" — two richly connotative words associated with death. The metaphors obliquely tell us ("tell it slant" was Dickinson's motto, remember) that presentiment is related to a fear of death, and, more important, the metaphors convey the feelings that attend that idea.

Some metaphors are more subtle than others because their comparison of terms is less explicit. Notice the difference between the following two metaphors, both of which describe a shaggy derelict refusing to leave the warmth of a hotel lobby: "He was a mule standing his ground" is a quite explicit comparison. The man is a mule; X is Y. But this metaphor is much more covert: "He brayed his refusal to leave." This second version is an ***implied metaphor*** because it does not explicitly identify the man with a mule. Instead it hints at or alludes to the mule. Braying is associated with mules and is especially appropriate in this context because of those animals' reputation for stubbornness. Implied metaphors can slip by readers, but they offer the alert reader the energy and resonance of carefully chosen, highly concentrated language.

Some poets write extended comparisons in which part or all of the poem consists of a series of related metaphors or similes. Extended metaphors are more common than extended similes. In "Catch" (p. 28),

Robert Francis creates an **extended metaphor** that compares poetry to a game of catch. The entire poem is organized around this comparison, just as all of the elements in E. E. Cummings's "she being Brand" (p. 73) are clustered around the extended comparison of a car and a woman. Because these comparisons are at work throughout the entire poem, they are called **controlling metaphors.** Extended comparisons can serve as a poem's organizing principle; they are also a reminder that in good poems metaphor and simile are not merely decorative but inseparable from what is expressed.

Notice the controlling metaphor in this poem, published posthumously by a woman whose contemporaries identified her more as a wife and mother than as a poet. Bradstreet's first volume of poetry, *The Tenth Muse,* was published by her brother-in-law in 1650 without her prior knowledge.

Anne Bradstreet (CA. 1612–1672)

The Author to Her Book   *1678*

Thou ill-formed offspring of my feeble brain,
Who after birth did'st by my side remain,
Till snatched from thence by friends, less wise than true,
Who thee abroad exposed to public view;
Made thee in rags, halting, to the press to trudge,   5
Where errors were not lessened, all may judge.
At thy return my blushing was not small,
My rambling brat (in print) should mother call;
I cast thee by as one unfit for light,
Thy visage was so irksome in my sight;   10
Yet being mine own, at length affection would
Thy blemishes amend, if so I could:
I washed thy face, but more defects I saw,
And rubbing off a spot, still made a flaw.
I stretched thy joints to make thee even feet,   15
Yet still thou run'st more hobbling than is meet;
In better dress to trim thee was my mind,
But nought save homespun cloth in the house I find.
In this array, 'mongst vulgars may'st thou roam;
In critics' hands beware thou dost not come;   20
And take thy way where yet thou are not known.
If for thy Father asked, say thou had'st none;
And for thy Mother, she alas is poor,
Which caused her thus to send thee out of door.

The extended metaphor likening her book to a child came naturally to Bradstreet and allowed her to regard her work both critically and affectionately. Her conception of the book as her child creates just the right tone of amusement, self-deprecation, and concern.

The controlling metaphor in the following poem is identified by the title. The game of chess in which these two players are engaged is simultaneously literal and metaphoric.

ROSARIO CASTELLANOS (1925–1974)

Chess   1988

TRANSLATED BY MAUREEN AHERN

Because we were friends and sometimes loved each other,
perhaps to add one more tie
to the many that already bound us,
we decided to play games of the mind.

We set up a board between us;   5
equally divided into pieces, values,
and possible moves.
We learned the rules, we swore to respect them,
and the match began.

We've been sitting here for centuries, meditating   10
ferociously
how to deal the one last blow that will finally
annihilate the other one forever.

CONSIDERATIONS FOR CRITICAL THINKING AND WRITING

1. **FIRST RESPONSE.** Why do the players decide to play chess? Are you surprised by the effect the game has on their relationship?

2. Why is chess a particularly resonant controlling metaphor? Explain why chess is more evocative than, say, cards or checkers.

3. How does the poem's diction suggest tensions between the two players that go beyond a literal game of chess? Which lines are especially suggestive to you?

4. Do you think the players are men, women, or a man and a woman? Explain your response. How does the gender of the players affect your reading of the poem?

OTHER FIGURES

Perhaps the humblest figure of speech — if not one of the most familiar — is the pun. A *pun* is a play on words that relies on a word having more than one meaning or sounding like another word. For example, "A fad is in one era and out the other" is the sort of pun that produces obligatory groans.

But most of us find pleasant and interesting surprises in puns. Here's one that has a slight edge to its humor.

EDMUND CONTI (B. 1929)

Pragmatist   1985

Apocalypse soon
Coming our way
Ground zero at noon
Halve a nice day.

Grimly practical under the circumstances, the pragmatist divides the familiar cheerful cliché by half. As simple as this poem is, its tone is mixed because it makes us laugh and wince at the same time.

Puns can be used to achieve serious effects as well as humorous ones. Although we may have learned to underrate puns as figures of speech, it is a mistake to underestimate their power and the frequency with which they appear in poetry. A close examination, for example, of Henry Reed's "Naming of Parts" (p. 176), Robert Frost's "Design" (p. 373), or almost any lengthy passage from a Shakespeare play will confirm the value of puns.

Synecdoche is a figure of speech in which part of something is used to signify the whole: a neighbor is a "wagging tongue" (a gossip); a criminal is placed "behind bars" (in prison). Less typically, synecdoche refers to the whole used to signify the part: "Germany invaded Poland"; "Princeton won the fencing match." Clearly, certain individuals participated in these activities, not all of Germany or Princeton. Another related figure of speech is **metonymy,** in which something closely associated with a subject is substituted for it: "She preferred the silver screen [motion pictures] to reading." "At precisely ten o'clock the paper shufflers [office workers] stopped for coffee."

Synecdoche and metonymy may overlap and are therefore sometimes difficult to distinguish. Consider this description of a disapproving minister entering a noisy tavern: "As those pursed lips came through the swinging door, the atmosphere was suddenly soured." The pursed lips signal the presence of the minister and are therefore a synecdoche, but they additionally suggest an inhibiting sense of sin and guilt that makes the bar patrons feel uncomfortable. Hence the pursed lips are also a metonymy, as they are in this context so closely connected with religion. Although the distinction between synecdoche and metonymy can be useful, when a figure of speech overlaps categories, it is usually labeled a metonymy.

Knowing the precise term for a figure of speech is, finally, less important than responding to its use in a poem. Consider how metonymy and synecdoche convey the tone and meaning of the following poem.

DYLAN THOMAS (1914–1953)
The Hand That Signed the Paper 1936

The hand that signed the paper felled a city;
Five sovereign fingers taxed the breath,
Doubled the globe of dead and halved a
    country;
These five kings did a king to death.

The mighty hand leads to a sloping shoulder,
The finger joints are cramped with chalk;
A goose's quill has put an end to murder
That put an end to talk.

The hand that signed the treaty bred a fever,
And famine grew, and locusts came;
Great is the hand that holds dominion over
Man by a scribbled name.

The five kings count the dead but do not soften
The crusted wound nor stroke the brow;
A hand rules pity as a hand rules heaven;
Hands have no tears to flow.

© Hulton-Deutsch Collection/CORBIS.

10

Explore contexts
for Dylan Thomas
on *LiterActive*.

15

The "hand" in this poem is a synecdoche for a powerful ruler because it is a part of someone used to signify the entire person. The "goose's quill" is a metonymy that also refers to the power associated with the ruler's hand. By using these figures of speech, Thomas depersonalizes and ultimately dehumanizes the ruler. The final synecdoche tells us that "Hands have no tears to flow." It makes us see the political power behind the hand as remote and inhuman. How is the meaning of the poem enlarged when the speaker says, "A hand rules pity as a hand rules heaven"?

One of the ways writers energize the abstractions, ideas, objects, and animals that constitute their created worlds is through **personification,** the attribution of human characteristics to nonhuman things: temptation pursues the innocent; trees scream in the raging wind; mice conspire in the cupboard. We are not explicitly told that these things are people; instead, we are invited to see that they behave like people. Perhaps it is human vanity that makes personification a frequently used figure of speech. Whatever the reason, personification, a form of metaphor that connects the nonhuman with the human, makes the world understandable in human terms. Consider this concise example from William Blake's *The Marriage of Heaven and Hell,* a long poem that takes delight in attacking conventional morality: "Prudence is a rich ugly old maid courted by Incapacity." By personifying prudence, Blake transforms what is usually considered a virtue into a comic figure hardly worth emulating.

Often related to personification is another rhetorical figure called **apostrophe,** an address either to someone who is absent and therefore cannot hear the speaker or to something nonhuman that cannot comprehend.

The following poems are rich in figurative language. As you read and study them, notice how their figures of speech vivify situations, clarify ideas, intensify emotions, and engage your imagination. Although the terms for the various figures discussed in this chapter are useful for labeling the particular devices used in poetry, they should not be allowed to get in the way of your response to a poem. Don't worry about rounding up examples of figurative language. First relax and let the figures work their effects on you. Use the terms as a means of taking you further into poetry, and they will serve your reading well.

POEMS FOR FURTHER STUDY

GARY SNYDER (B. 1930)
How Poetry Comes to Me   *1992*

It comes blundering over the
Boulders at night, it stays
Frightened outside the
Range of my campfire
I go to meet it at the
Edge of the light

CONSIDERATIONS FOR CRITICAL THINKING AND WRITING

1. **FIRST RESPONSE.** How does personification in this poem depict the creative process?
2. Why do you suppose Snyder makes each successive line shorter?
3. **CREATIVE RESPONSE.** How would eliminating the title change your understanding of the poem? Substitute another title that causes you to reinterpret it.

MARGARET ATWOOD (B. 1939)
February   *1995*

Winter. Time to eat fat
and watch hockey. In the pewter mornings, the cat,
a black fur sausage with yellow
Houdini eyes, jumps up on the bed and tries
to get onto my head. It's his   5
way of telling whether or not I'm dead.
If I'm not, he wants to be scratched; if I am
he'll think of something. He settles
on my chest, breathing his breath
of burped-up meat and musty sofas,   10

purring like a washboard. Some other tomcat,
not yet a capon, has been spraying our front door,
declaring war. It's all about sex and territory,
which are what will finish us off
in the long run. Some cat owners around here   15
should snip a few testicles. If we wise
hominids were sensible, we'd do that too,
or eat our young, like sharks.
But it's love that does us in. Over and over
again, *He shoots, he scores!* and famine   20
crouches in the bedsheets, ambushing the pulsing
eiderdown, and the windchill factor hits
thirty below, and pollution pours
out of our chimneys to keep us warm.
February, month of despair,   25
with a skewered heart in the centre.
I think dire thoughts, and lust for French fries
with a splash of vinegar.
Cat, enough of your greedy whining
and your small pink bumhole.   30
Off my face! You're the life principle,
more or less, so get going
on a little optimism around here.
Get rid of death. Celebrate increase. Make it be spring.

CONSIDERATIONS FOR CRITICAL THINKING AND WRITING

1. **FIRST RESPONSE.** How do your own associations with February compare
   with the speaker's?

2. Explain how the poem is organized around an extended metaphor that de-
   fines winter as a "Time to eat fat / and watch hockey" (lines 1-2).

3. Explain the paradox in "it's love that does us in" (line 19).

4. What theme(s) do you find in the poem? How is the cat central to them?

WILLIAM CARLOS WILLIAMS (1883-1963)

To Waken an Old Lady   1921

Old age is
a flight of small
cheeping birds
skimming
bare trees   5
above a snow glaze.
Gaining and failing
they are buffeted
by a dark wind —
But what?   10
On harsh weedstalks

and you're lost in the pounding particulars
of fly rafters, siding, hypotenuse, and load,
until nothing seems level or true
but the scorn of the tape's clucked tongue,   10

let the nub of your plainspoken pencil prevail
and it's up! Functional. Tight as a sonnet.
It will last forever (or at least for awhile)
though the critics come sit on it, and sit on it.

CONSIDERATIONS FOR CRITICAL THINKING AND WRITING

1. **FIRST RESPONSE.** Explain how the poem's diction contributes to the extended simile. Why is the language of building especially appropriate here?
2. What is the effect of the repetition and sounds in the final line? How does that affect the poem's tone?
3. Consult the Glossary of Literary Terms (p. 741) for the definition of a sonnet. To what extent does "Building an Outhouse" conform to a sonnet's structure?

ELAINE MAGARRELL (B. 1928)

The Joy of Cooking   *1988*

I have prepared my sister's tongue,
scrubbed and skinned it,
trimmed the roots, small bones, and gristle.
Carved through the hump it slices thin and neat.
Best with horseradish   5
and economical — it probably will grow back.
Next time perhaps a creole sauce
or mold of aspic?

I will have my brother's heart,
which is firm and rather dry,   10
slow cooked. It resembles muscle
more than organ meat
and needs an apple-onion stuffing
to make it interesting at all.
Although beef heart serves six   15
my brother's heart barely feeds two.
I could also have it braised
and served in sour sauce.

CONSIDERATIONS FOR CRITICAL THINKING AND WRITING

1. **FIRST RESPONSE.** Describe the poem's tone. Do you find it amusing, bitter, or something else?

2. How are the tongue and heart used to characterize the sister and brother in this poem?

3. Describe the speaker's tone. What effect does the title have on your determining the tone?

CONNECTION TO ANOTHER SELECTION

1. Write an essay that explains how cooking becomes a way of talking about something else in this poem and in Sally Croft's "Home-Baked Bread" (p. 126).

RUTH FAINLIGHT (B. 1931)

The Clarinettist

2002

Pale round arms raising her clarinet
at the exact angle, she sways, then halts,
poised for the music

like a horse that gathers itself up before the leap
with the awkward, perfect, only   5
possible movement

an alto in a quattrocento chorus, blond head
lifted from the score, open-mouthed
for hallelujah

a cherub on a ceiling cornice leaning out   10
from heaped-up clouds of opalescent pink,
translucent blue

a swimmer breasting frothy surf like ripping through
lace curtains, a dancer centred as a spinning top,
an August moon   15

alone, in front of the orchestra, the conductor's
other, and unacknowledged opposite,
she starts the tune.

CONSIDERATIONS FOR CRITICAL THINKING AND WRITING

1. **FIRST RESPONSE.** This poem is structured as one long sentence. How does this structure create a kind of suspense as the clarinettist is "poised for the music"?

2. How do the similes and metaphors capture the moment that the clarinettist "starts the tune"? What sort of description of her emerges from them?

3. **CREATIVE RESPONSE.** Create a similar three-line stanza that adds to Fainlight's description and maintains the poem's tone.

Perspective

JOHN R. SEARLE (B. 1932)
Figuring Out Metaphors   1979

If you hear somebody say, "Sally is a block of ice," or, "Sam is a pig," you are likely to assume that the speaker does not mean what he says literally, but that he is speaking metaphorically. Furthermore, you are not likely to have very much trouble figuring out what he means. If he says, "Sally is a prime number between 17 and 23," or "Bill is a barn door," you might still assume he is speaking metaphorically, but it is much harder to figure out what he means. The existence of such utterances — utterances in which the speaker means metaphorically something different from what the sentence means literally — poses a series of questions for any theory of language and communication: What is metaphor, and how does it differ from both literal and other forms of figurative utterances? Why do we use expressions metaphorically instead of saying exactly and literally what we mean? How do metaphorical utterances work, that is, how is it possible for speakers to communicate to hearers when speaking metaphorically inasmuch as they do not say what they mean? And why do some metaphors work and others do not?

From *Expression and Meaning*

CONSIDERATIONS FOR CRITICAL THINKING AND WRITING

1. Searle poses a series of important questions. Write an essay that explores one of these questions, basing your discussion on the poems in this chapter.

2. **CREATIVE RESPONSE.** Try writing a brief poem that provides a context for the line "Sally is a prime number between 17 and 23" or the line "Bill is a barn door." Your task is to create a context so that either one of these metaphoric statements is as readily understandable as "Sally is a block of ice" or "Sam is a pig." Share your poem with your classmates and explain how the line generated the poem you built around it.

Web Research the poets in this chapter at bedfordstmartins.com/ meyerpoetry.

6

Symbol, Allegory, and Irony

© Barbara Savage Cheresh.

Poetry is serious business; literature is the apparatus through which the world tries to keep intact its important ideas and feelings.
— MARY OLIVER

SYMBOL

A *symbol* is something that represents something else. An object, person, place, event, or action can suggest more than its literal meaning. A hand-shake between two world leaders might be simply a greeting, but if it is done ceremoniously before cameras, it could be a symbolic gesture signify-ing unity, issues resolved, and joint policies that will be followed. We live surrounded by symbols. When a $100,000 Mercedes-Benz comes roaring by in the fast lane, we get a quick glimpse of not only an expensive car but an entire lifestyle that suggests opulence, broad lawns, executive offices, and power. One of the reasons some buyers are willing to spend roughly the cost of five Chevrolets for a single Mercedes-Benz is that they are aware of the car's symbolic value. A symbol is a vehicle

Explore the poetic elements in this chapter on *LiterActive* or at bedfordstmartins.com/meyerpoetry.

for two things at once: it functions as itself, and it implies meanings beyond itself.

The meanings suggested by a symbol are determined by the context in which they appear. The Mercedes could symbolize very different things depending on where it was parked. Would an American political candidate be likely to appear in a Detroit blue-collar neighborhood with such a car? Probably not. Although a candidate might be able to afford the car, it would be an inappropriate symbol for someone seeking votes from all of the people. As a symbol, the German-built Mercedes would backfire if voters perceived it as representing an entity partially responsible for layoffs of automobile workers or, worse, as a sign of decadence and corruption. Similarly, a huge portrait of Mao Tse-tung conveys different meanings to residents of Beijing than it would to farmers in Prairie Center, Illinois. Because symbols depend on contexts for their meaning, literary artists provide those contexts so that the reader has enough information to determine the probable range of meanings suggested by a symbol.

In the following poem the speaker describes walking at night. How is the night used symbolically?

ROBERT FROST (1874–1963)

Acquainted with the Night   *1928*

I have been one acquainted with the night.
I have walked out in rain — and back in rain.
I have outwalked the furthest city light.

I have looked down the saddest city lane.
I have passed by the watchman on his beat   5
And dropped my eyes, unwilling to explain.

I have stood still and stopped the sound of feet
When far away an interrupted cry
Came over houses from another street,

But not to call me back or say good-by;   10
And further still at an unearthly height
One luminary clock against the sky

Proclaimed the time was neither wrong nor right.
I have been one acquainted with the night.

In approaching this or any poem, you should read for literal meanings first and then allow the elements of the poem to invite you to symbolic readings, if they are appropriate. Here the somber tone suggests that the lines have symbolic meaning, too. The flat matter-of-factness created by the repetition of "I have" (lines 1–5, 7, 14) understates the symbolic subject matter of the poem, which is, finally, more about the "night" located in the speaker's mind or soul than it is about walking away from a city and back again. The speaker is "acquainted with the night." The importance of this phrase is emphasized by Frost's title and by the fact that he begins and ends the poem with it. Poets frequently use this kind of repetition to alert readers to details that carry more than literal meanings.

The speaker in this poem has personal knowledge of the night but does not indicate specifically what the night means. To arrive at the potential meanings of the night in this context, it is necessary to look closely at its connotations, along with the images provided in the poem. The connotative meanings of night suggest, for example, darkness, death, and grief. By drawing on these connotations, Frost uses a ***conventional symbol*** — something that is recognized by many people to represent certain ideas. Roses conventionally symbolize love or beauty; laurels, fame; spring, growth; the moon, romance. Poets often use conventional symbols to convey tone and meaning.

Frost uses the night as a conventional symbol, but he also develops it into a **literary** or **contextual symbol** that goes beyond traditional, public meanings. A literary symbol cannot be summarized in a word or two. It tends to be as elusive as experience itself. The night cannot be reduced to or equated with darkness or death or grief, but it evokes those associations and more. Frost took what perhaps initially appears to be an overworked, conventional symbol and prevented it from becoming a cliché by deepening and extending its meaning.

The images in "Acquainted with the Night" lead to the poem's symbolic meaning. Unwilling, and perhaps unable, to explain explicitly to the watchman (and to the reader) what the night means, the speaker nevertheless conveys feelings about it. The brief images of darkness, rain, sad city lanes, the necessity for guards, the eerie sound of a distressing cry coming over rooftops, and the "luminary clock against the sky" proclaiming "the time was neither wrong nor right" all help to create a sense of anxiety in this tight-lipped speaker. Although we cannot know what unnamed personal experiences have acquainted the speaker with the night, the images suggest that whatever the night means, it is somehow associated with insomnia, loneliness, isolation, coldness, darkness, death, fear, and a sense of alienation from humanity and even time. Daylight — ordinary daytime thoughts and life itself — seems remote and unavailable in this poem. The night is literally the period from sunset to sunrise, but, more important, it is an internal state of being felt by the speaker and revealed through the images.

Frost used symbols rather than an expository essay that would explain the conditions that cause these feelings because most readers can provide their own list of sorrows and terrors that evoke similar emotions. Through symbol, the speaker's experience is compressed and simultaneously expanded by the personal darkness that each reader brings to the poem. The suggestive nature of symbols makes them valuable for poets and evocative for readers.

ALLEGORY

Unlike expansive, suggestive symbols, **allegory** is a narration or description usually restricted to a single meaning because its events, actions, characters, settings, and objects represent specific abstractions or ideas. Although the elements in an allegory may be interesting in themselves, the emphasis tends to be on what they ultimately mean. Characters may be given names such as Hope, Pride, Youth, and Charity; they have few, if any, personal qualities beyond their abstract meanings. These personifications are a form of extended metaphor, but their meanings are severely restricted. They are not symbols because, for instance, the meaning of a character named Charity is precisely that virtue.

There is little or no room for broad speculation and exploration in allegories. If Frost had written "Acquainted with the Night" as an allegory, he might have named his speaker Loneliness and had him leave the City of Despair to walk the Streets of Emptiness, where Crime, Poverty, Fear, and other characters would define the nature of city life. The literal elements in an allegory tend to be de-emphasized in favor of the message. Symbols, however, function both literally and symbolically, so that "Acquainted with the Night" is about both a walk and a sense that something is terribly wrong.

Allegory especially lends itself to **didactic poetry,** which is designed to teach an ethical, moral, or religious lesson. Many stories, poems, and plays are concerned with values, but didactic literature is specifically created to convey a message. "Acquainted with the Night" does not impart advice or offer guidance. If the poem argued that city life is self-destructive or sinful, it would be didactic; instead, it is a lyric poem that expresses the emotions and thoughts of a single speaker.

Although allegory is often enlisted in didactic causes because it can so readily communicate abstract ideas through physical representations, not all allegories teach a lesson. Here is a poem describing a haunted palace while also establishing a consistent pattern that reveals another meaning.

EDGAR ALLAN POE (1809–1849)
The Haunted Palace 1839

I

In the greenest of our valleys,
    By good angels tenanted,
Once a fair and stately palace —
    Radiant palace — reared its head.
In the monarch Thought's dominion — 5
    It stood there!
Never seraph spread a pinion
    Over fabric half so fair.

II

Banners yellow, glorious, golden,
    On its roof did float and flow;
(This — all this — was in the olden
    Time long ago)
And every gentle air that dallied,
    In that sweet day,
Along the ramparts plumed and pallid,
    A wingèd odor went away.

10
15

III

Wanderers in that happy valley
    Through two luminous windows saw
Spirits moving musically
    To a lute's well-tunèd law,
Round about a throne, where sitting
    (Porphyrogene!)°   *born to purple, royal*
In state his glory well befitting,
    The ruler of the realm was seen.

20

IV

And all with pearl and ruby glowing
    Was the fair palace door,
Through which came flowing, flowing, flowing
    And sparkling evermore,
A troop of Echoes whose sweet duty
    Was but to sing,
In voices of surpassing beauty,
    The wit and wisdom of their king.

25
30

V

But evil things, in robes of sorrow,
    Assailed the monarch's high estate;
(Ah, let us mourn, for never morrow
    Shall dawn upon him, desolate!)
And, round about his home, the glory
    That blushed and bloomed
Is but a dim-remembered story
    Of the old time entombed.

35
40

VI

And travelers now within that valley,
    Through the red-litten windows see
Vast forms that move fantastically
    To a discordant melody;

While, like a rapid ghastly river,   45
   Through the pale door,
A hideous throng rush out forever,
   And laugh — but smile no more.

    On one level this poem describes how a once happy palace is desolated by "evil things" (line 33). If the reader pays close attention to the diction, however, an allegorical meaning becomes apparent on a second reading. A systematic pattern develops in the choice of words used to describe the palace, so that it comes to stand for a human mind. The palace, banners, windows, door, echoes, and throng are equated with a person's head, hair, eyes, mouth, voice, and laughter. That mind, once harmoniously ordered, is overthrown by evil, haunting thoughts that lead to the mad laughter in the poem's final lines. Once the general pattern is seen, the rest of the details fall neatly into place to strengthen the parallels between the surface description of a palace and the allegorical representation of a disordered mind.

    Modern writers generally prefer symbol over allegory because they tend to be more interested in opening up the potential meanings of an experience instead of transforming it into a closed pattern of meaning. Perhaps the major difference is that while allegory may delight a reader's imagination, symbol challenges and enriches it.

IRONY

Another important resource writers use to take readers beyond literal meanings is *irony,* a technique that reveals a discrepancy between what appears to be and what is actually true. Here is a classic example in which appearances give way to the underlying reality.

EDWIN ARLINGTON ROBINSON (1869–1935)

Richard Cory   *1897*

Whenever Richard Cory went down town,
We people on the pavement looked at him:
He was a gentleman from sole to crown,
Clean favored, and imperially slim.

And he was always quietly arrayed,   5
And he was always human when he talked;
But still he fluttered pulses when he said,
"Good-morning," and he glittered when he walked.

And he was rich — yes, richer than a king —
And admirably schooled in every grace: 10
In fine, we thought that he was everything
To make us wish that we were in his place.

So on we worked, and waited for the light,
And went without the meat, and cursed the bread;
And Richard Cory, one calm summer night,   15
Went home and put a bullet through his head.

Richard Cory seems to have it all. Those less fortunate, the "people on the pavement," regard him as well-bred, handsome, tasteful, and richly endowed with both money and grace. Until the final line of the poem, the reader, like the speaker, is charmed by Cory's good fortune, so quietly expressed in his decent, easy manner. That final, shocking line, however, shatters the appearances of Cory's life and reveals him to have been a desperately unhappy man. While everyone else assumes that Cory represented "everything" to which they aspire, the reality is that he could escape his miserable life only as a suicide. This discrepancy between what appears to be true and what actually exists is known as ***situational irony:*** what happens is entirely different from what is expected. We are not told why Cory shoots himself; instead, the irony in the poem shocks us into the recognition that appearances do not always reflect realities.

Words are also sometimes intended to be taken at other than face value. ***Verbal irony*** is saying something different from what is meant. After reading "Richard Cory," to say "That rich gentleman sure was happy" is ironic. The tone of voice would indicate that just the opposite was meant; hence verbal irony is usually easy to detect in spoken language. In literature, however, a reader can sometimes take literally what a writer intends ironically. The remedy for this kind of misreading is to pay close attention to the poem's context. There is no formula that can detect verbal irony, but contradictory actions and statements as well as the use of understatement and overstatement can often be signals that verbal irony is present.

Consider how verbal irony is used in this poem.

KENNETH FEARING (1902–1961)

AD   *1938*

Wanted: Men;
Millions of men are *wanted at once* in a big new field;
New, tremendous, thrilling, great.
If you've ever been a figure in the chamber of horrors,
If you've ever escaped from a psychiatric ward,   5
If you thrill at the thought of throwing poison into wells, have heavenly
    visions of people, by the thousands, dying in flames —

Once Marines tramped
from the newsreel of his imagination;
now children plot to spray graffiti   25
in parrot-brilliant colors
across the Victorian mustache
and monocle.

CONSIDERATIONS FOR CRITICAL THINKING AND WRITING

1. **FIRST RESPONSE.** Describe the speaker's sense of the past as well as the present. In what sense do two very different cultures collide in this poem?

2. What do you think is the poem's central theme? How do the images and symbols work together to contribute to the theme?

3. **CRITICAL STRATEGIES.** Read the section on new historicist and cultural criticism (pp. 656–58) in Chapter 25, "Critical Strategies for Reading," and then do some research on Theodore Roosevelt's role in the Spanish-American War and on what was happening in the Boston public school system in the late 1980s. How does this information affect your reading of the poem?

RENNIE MCQUILKIN (B. 1936)
The Lighters   *1999*

In her eighty-ninth year, she's reducing
her inventory — china to the children, mementos
to the trash — but in her boudoir
keeps half a dozen square-shouldered Zippos,

her husband's initials on one,   5
the best man's on a second, the rest anyone's guess.
Dry-chambered, their spark wheels rusted shut,
they are lined up gravely on a jewelry chest

full of antique gap-toothed keys,
elaborate scrollwork on their hilts, fit to open   10
high-backed steamer trunks, perhaps the secret entrance
to a sunken garden

where every night the dry-bones assemble
in mothballed flannels and handknit sweaters
to roll their own, light up   15
like fireflies and, sotte voce, remember her.

CONSIDERATIONS FOR CRITICAL THINKING AND WRITING

1. **FIRST RESPONSE.** How are the lighters more than simply mementos? What meanings are associated with them?

2. Discuss McQuilkin's use of diction. How does it contribute to the poem's mood?

3. How would you describe the physical appearance of this woman?

CONNECTION TO ANOTHER SELECTION

1. Compare the treatment of this elderly woman with that of William Carlos Williams's "To Waken an Old Lady" (p. 144). How is aging depicted in each poem?

CARL SANDBURG (1878–1967)

Buttons

1905

I have been watching the war map slammed up for advertising in front
    of the newspaper office.
Buttons — red and yellow buttons — blue and black buttons — are shoved
    back and forth across the map.

A laughing young man, sunny with freckles,
Climbs a ladder, yells a joke to somebody in the crowd,
And then fixes a yellow button one inch west
And follows the yellow button with a black button one inch west.

(Ten thousand men and boys twist on their bodies in a red soak along a
    river edge,
Gasping of wounds, calling for water, some rattling death in their
    throats.)
Who would guess what it cost to move two buttons one inch on the war
    map here in front of the newspaper office where the freckle-faced
    young man is laughing to us?

CONSIDERATIONS FOR CRITICAL THINKING AND WRITING

1. **FIRST RESPONSE.** Why is the date of this poem significant?

2. Discuss the symbolic meaning of the buttons and explain why you think the symbolism is too spelled out or not.

3. What purpose does the "laughing young man, sunny with freckles" serve in the poem?

CONNECTION TO ANOTHER SELECTION

1. Discuss the symbolic treatment of war in this poem, Kenneth Fearing's "AD" (p. 162), and Henry Reed's "Naming of Parts" (p. 176).

WALLACE STEVENS (1879–1955)

Anecdote of the Jar   1923

I placed a jar in Tennessee,
And round it was, upon a hill.
It made the slovenly wilderness
Surround that hill.

The wilderness rose up to it,   5
And sprawled around, no longer wild.
The jar was round upon the ground
And tall and of a port in air.

It took dominion everywhere.
The jar was gray and bare.   10
It did not give of bird or bush,
Like nothing else in Tennessee.

CONSIDERATIONS FOR CRITICAL THINKING AND WRITING

1. **FIRST RESPONSE.** How is the jar different from its surroundings? What effect does the jar's placement have upon the "slovenly wilderness"?

2. What do you make of all the "round" sounds in lines 2, 4, 6, and 7? How do they echo the relationship between the jar and the wilderness?

3. In what sense might this poem be regarded as an anecdote about the power and limitations of art and nature?

CONNECTION TO ANOTHER SELECTION

1. Compare the thematic function of the jar in Stevens's poem with that of John Keats's "Ode on a Grecian Urn" (p. 96). What important similarities and differences do you see in the meanings of each? Discuss why you think Stevens and Keats share similar or different ideas about art.

WILLIAM STAFFORD (1914–1993)

Traveling through the Dark   1962

Traveling through the dark I found a deer
dead on the edge of the Wilson River road.
It is usually best to roll them into the canyon:
that road is narrow; to swerve might make more dead.

By glow of the tail-light I stumbled back of the car   5
and stood by the heap, a doe, a recent killing;
she had stiffened already, almost cold.
I dragged her off; she was large in the belly.

My fingers touching her side brought me the reason —
her side was warm; her fawn lay there waiting,   10
alive, still, never to be born.
Beside that mountain road I hesitated.

The car aimed ahead its lowered parking lights;
under the hood purred the steady engine.
I stood in the glare of the warm exhaust turning red;   15
around our group I could hear the wilderness listen.

I thought hard for us all — my only swerving —
then pushed her over the edge into the river.

CONSIDERATIONS FOR CRITICAL THINKING AND WRITING

1. **FIRST RESPONSE.** Notice the description of the car in this poem: the "glow of the tail-light," the "lowered parking lights," and how the engine "purred." How do these and other details suggest symbolic meanings for the car and the "recent killing"?

2. Discuss the speaker's tone. Does the speaker seem, for example, tough, callous, kind, sentimental, confused, or confident?

3. What is the effect of the last stanza's having only two lines rather than the established four lines of the previous stanzas?

4. Discuss the appropriateness of this poem's title. In what sense has the speaker "thought hard for us all"? What are those thoughts?

5. Is this a didactic poem?

ANDREW HUDGINS (B. 1951)

Seventeen   *1991*

Ahead of me, the dog reared on its rope,
and swayed. The pickup took a hard left turn,
and the dog tipped off the side. He scrambled, fell,
and scraped along the hot asphalt
before he tumbled back into the air.   5
I pounded on my horn and yelled. The rope
snapped and the brown dog hurtled into the weeds.
I braked, still pounding on my horn. The truck
stopped too.

           We met halfway, and stared   10
down at the shivering dog, which flinched
and moaned and tried to flick its tail.
Most of one haunch was scraped away
and both hind legs were twisted. *You stupid shit!*
I said. He squinted at me. "Well now, bud —   15
you best watch what you say to me."
I'd never cussed a grown-up man before.

I nodded. I figured on a beating. He grinned.
"You so damn worried about that ole dog,
he's yours." He strolled back to his truck,   20
gunned it, and slewed off, spraying gravel.
The dog whined harshly.

                              By the road,
gnats rose waist-high as I waded through
the dry weeds, looking for a rock.   25
I knelt down by the dog — tail flick —
and slammed the rock down twice. The first
blow did the job, but I had planned for two.
My hands swept up and down again. I grabbed
the hind legs, swung twice, and heaved the dog   30
into a clump of butterfly weed and vetch.
But then I didn't know that they had names,
those roadside weeds. His truck was a blue Ford,
the dog a beagle. I was seventeen.
The gnats rose, gathered to one loose cloud,   35
then scattered through coarse orange and purple weeds.

Considerations for Critical Thinking and Writing

1. **First response.** Hudgins has described "Seventeen" as a "rite of passage."
   How does the title focus this idea?

2. What kind of language does Hudgins use to describe the injured dog (lines
   1–14)? What is its effect?

3. Characterize the speaker and the driver of the pickup. What clues does the
   poem provide to the way each perceives the other?

4. Might killing the dog be understood as a symbolic action? Try to come up
   with more than one interpretation for the speaker's actions.

Connections to Other Selections

1. Write an essay that compares the speakers and themes of "Seventeen" and
   "Traveling through the Dark."

2. In an essay discuss the speakers' attitudes toward dogs in "Seventeen" and
   Ronald Wallace's "Dogs" (p. 235). What do these attitudes reveal about the
   speakers?

Alden Nowlan (1933–1983)

The Bull Moose   1962

Down from the purple mist of trees on the mountain,
lurching through forests of white spruce and cedar,
stumbling through tamarack swamps,
came the bull moose
to be stopped at last by a pole-fenced pasture.   5

Too tired to turn or, perhaps, aware
there was no place left to go, he stood with the cattle.
They, scenting the musk of death, seeing his great head
like the ritual mask of a blood god, moved to the other end
of the field, and waited.   10

The neighbors heard of it, and by afternoon
cars lined the road. The children teased him
with alder switches and he gazed at them
like an old, tolerant collie. The women asked
if he could have escaped from a Fair.   15

The oldest man in the parish remembered seeing
a gelded moose yoked with an ox for plowing.
The young men snickered and tried to pour beer
down his throat, while their girl friends took their pictures.

The bull moose let them stroke his tick-ravaged flanks,   20
let them pry open his jaws with bottles, let a giggling girl
plant a little purple cap
of thistles on his head.

When the wardens came, everyone agreed it was a shame
to shoot anything so shaggy and cuddlesome.   25
He looked like the kind of pet
women put to bed with their sons.

So they held their fire. But just as the sun dropped in the river
the bull moose gathered his strength
like a scaffolded king, straightened and lifted his horns   30
so that even the wardens backed away as they raised their rifles.
When he roared, people ran to their cars. All the young men
leaned on their automobile horns as he toppled.

CONSIDERATIONS FOR CRITICAL THINKING AND WRITING

1. **FIRST RESPONSE.** How does the speaker present the moose and the towns-people? How are the moose and townspeople contrasted? Discuss specific lines to support your response.

2. Explain how the symbols in this poem point to a conflict between human-ity and nature. What do you think the speaker's attitude toward this con-flict is?

3. **CRITICAL STRATEGIES.** Read the section on mythological criticism (pp. 660–62) in Chapter 25, "Critical Strategies for Reading," and write an essay on "The Bull Moose" that approaches the poem from a mythological perspective.

CONNECTION TO ANOTHER SELECTION

1. In an essay compare and contrast how the animals portrayed in "The Bull Moose" and in Stafford's "Traveling through the Dark" (p. 169) are used as symbols.

JULIO MARZÁN (B. 1946)

Ethnic Poetry

1994

The ethnic poet said: "The earth is maybe
a huge maraca / and the sun a trombone /
and life / is to move your ass / to slow beats."
The ethnic audience roasted a suckling pig.

The ethnic poet said: "Oh thank Goddy, Goddy /   5
I be me, my toenails curled downward /
deep, deep, deep into Mama earth."
The ethnic audience shook strands of sea shells.

The ethnic poet said: "The sun was created black /
so we should imagine light / and also dream /   10
a walrus emerging from the broken ice."
The ethnic audience beat on sealskin drums.

The ethnic poet said: "Reproductive organs /
Eagles nesting California redwoods /
Shut up and listen to my ancestors."   15
The ethnic audience ate fried bread and honey.

The ethnic poet said: "Something there is that
doesn't love a wall / That sends
the frozen-ground-swell under it."
The ethnic audience deeply understood humanity.   20

CONSIDERATIONS FOR CRITICAL THINKING AND WRITING

1. **FIRST RESPONSE.** What is the implicit definition of ethnic poetry in this
   poem?

2. The final stanza quotes lines from Robert Frost's "Mending Wall" (p. 359).
   Read the entire poem. Why do you think Marzán chooses these lines and
   this particular poem as one kind of ethnic poetry?

3. What is the poem's central irony? Pay particular attention to the final line.
   What is being satirized here?

4. **CRITICAL STRATEGIES.** Read the section on the literary canon (pp. 646–47) in
   Chapter 25, "Critical Strategies for Reading," and consider how the forma-
   tion of the literary canon is related to the theme of "Ethnic Poetry."

CONNECTION TO ANOTHER SELECTION

1. Write an essay that discusses the speaker's ideas about what poetry should
   be in "Ethnic Poetry" and in Langston Hughes's "Formula" (p. 403).

SHERMAN ALEXIE (B. 1966)

On the Amtrak from Boston to New York City   *1993*

The white woman across the aisle from me says, "Look,
look at all the history, that house
on the hill there is over two hundred years old,"
as she points out the window past me

into what she has been taught. I have learned   5
little more about American history during my few days
back East than what I expected and far less
of what we should all know of the tribal stories

whose architecture is 15,000 years older
than the corners of the house that sits   10
museumed on the hill. "Walden Pond,"
the woman on the train asks, "Did you see Walden Pond?"

and I don't have a cruel enough heart to break
her own by telling her there are five Walden Ponds
on my little reservation out West   15
and at least a hundred more surrounding Spokane,

the city I pretend to call my home. "Listen,"
I could have told her. "I don't give a shit
about Walden. I know the Indians were living stories
around that pond before Walden's grandparents were born   20

and before his grandparents' grandparents were born.
I'm tired of hearing about Don-fucking-Henley saving it, too,
because that's redundant. If Don Henley's brothers and sisters
and mothers and fathers hadn't come here in the first place

then nothing would need to be saved."   25
But I didn't say a word to the woman about Walden
Pond because she smiled so much and seemed delighted
that I thought to bring her an orange juice

back from the food car. I respect elders
of every color. All I really did was eat   30
my tasteless sandwich, drink my Diet Pepsi
and nod my head whenever the woman pointed out

another little piece of her country's history
while I, as all Indians have done
since this war began, made plans   35
for what I would do and say the next time

somebody from the enemy thought I was one of their own.

CONSIDERATIONS FOR CRITICAL THINKING AND WRITING

1. **FIRST RESPONSE.** To what extent does this poem constitute a history of
   white/Indian relations in America?

2. How does the white woman's view of history differ from the Indian's?

3. What is the symbolic function of Henry David Thoreau's *Walden* for each of the characters?

4. Why do you think the speaker expresses such frustration and anger concerning Don Henley (from the popular group The Eagles) who is well known for having raised concert benefit funds to save the woods around Walden Pond from commercial development?

CONNECTIONS TO OTHER SELECTIONS

1. Write an essay in which you discuss how you think the Indian in Alexie's poem would respond to Lydia Huntley Sigourney's "Indian Names" (p. 622). Explain why you think the speaker would be appreciative, ironic, or both.

2. Compare the themes in Alexie's poem with those in Louise Erdrich's "Dear John Wayne" (p. 475).

JAMES MERRILL (1926–1995)

Casual Wear   *1984*

Your average tourist: Fifty. 2.3
Times married. Dressed, this year, in Ferdi Plinthbower
Originals. Odds 1 to 9
Against her strolling past the Embassy

Today at noon. Your average terrorist: 5
Twenty-five. Celibate. No use for trends,
At least in clothing. Mark, though, where it ends.
People have come forth made of colored mist

Unsmiling on one hundred million screens
To tell of his prompt phone call to the station,   10
"Claiming responsibility" — devastation
Signed with a flourish, like the dead wife's jeans.

CONSIDERATIONS FOR CRITICAL THINKING AND WRITING

1. **FIRST RESPONSE.** What is the effect of the statistics in this poem?

2. Describe the speaker's tone. Is it appropriate for the subject matter? Explain why or why not.

3. Comment on the ironies that emerge from the final two lines. How are the tourist and terrorist linked by the speaker's description? Explain why you think the speaker sympathizes more with the tourist or the terrorist — or with neither.

CONNECTION TO ANOTHER SELECTION

1. Compare the satire in this poem with that in Peter Meinke's "The ABC of Aerobics" (p. 285). What is satirized in each poem? Which satire do you think is more pointed?

HENRY REED (1914–1986)

Naming of Parts

1946

Today we have naming of parts. Yesterday,
We had daily cleaning. And tomorrow morning,
We shall have what to do after firing. But today,
Today we have naming of parts. Japonica
Glistens like coral in all of the neighboring gardens,   5
          And today we have naming of parts.

This is the lower sling swivel. And this
Is the upper sling swivel, whose use you will see,
When you are given your slings. And this is the piling swivel,
Which in your case you have not got. The branches   10
Hold in the gardens their silent, eloquent gestures,
          Which in our case we have not got.

This is the safety-catch, which is always released
With an easy flick of the thumb. And please do not let me
See anyone using his finger. You can do it quite easy   15
If you have any strength in your thumb. The blossoms
Are fragile and motionless, never letting anyone see
          Any of them using their finger.

And this you can see is the bolt. The purpose of this
Is to open the breech, as you see. We can slide it   20
Rapidly backwards and forwards: we call this
Easing the spring. And rapidly backwards and forwards
The early bees are assaulting and fumbling the flowers:
          They call it easing the Spring.

They call it easing the Spring: it is perfectly easy   25
If you have any strength in your thumb: like the bolt,
And the breech, and the cocking-piece, and the point of balance,
Which in our case we have not got; and the almond-blossom
Silent in all of the gardens and the bees going backwards and forwards,
          For today we have naming of parts.   30

CONSIDERATIONS FOR CRITICAL THINKING AND WRITING

1. **FIRST RESPONSE.** Characterize the two speakers in this poem. Identify the lines spoken by each. How do their respective lines differ in tone?
2. What is the effect of the last line of each stanza?
3. How do ambiguities and puns contribute to the poem's meaning?
4. What symbolic contrast is made between the rifle instruction and the gardens? How is this contrast ironic?

RACHEL HADAS (B. 1948)

The Compact

2003

The short steep ride in the red bus uphill
from the Girls' School to the Boys' School left
time to whip our compacts out and powder
cheeks, noses. What for? For the boys? Well, yes,
we might have answered if we had been asked.   5
No one asked. Good thing. We didn't know.
Those uphill rides were forty years ago.

If every gesture halves a hidden whole,
if every moment twins a hidden half,
then my thumb clicking that pink plastic catch   10
(sweet whiff of powder; flash of a tiny mirror)
opens not only the compact but also
the first half of a parenthesis
stretching its arms out, longing to be closed.

CONSIDERATIONS FOR CRITICAL THINKING AND WRITING

1. **FIRST RESPONSE.** Discuss the denotative meanings of the "compact" as well
   as its potential symbolic meanings.
2. Why is it appropriate that the school bus is red (rather than the usual yel-
   low) and that the trip is an uphill ride?
3. How do the final lines effectively end the poem?

ROBERT BROWNING (1812–1889)

My Last Duchess

1842

Ferrara °

That's my last Duchess painted on the wall,
Looking as if she were alive. I call
That piece a wonder, now: Frà Pandolf's °
    hands
Worked busily a day, and there she stands.
Will't please you sit and look at her? I said
"Frà Pandolf" by design, for never read
Strangers like you that pictured countenance,
The depth and passion of its earnest glance,
But to myself they turned (since none puts by

Courtesy of the National Portrait Gallery, London.

Ferrara: In the sixteenth century, the duke of this Italian city arranged to marry a second time after the mysterious death of his very young first wife.   3 *Frà Pandolf:* A fictitious artist.

The curtain I have drawn for you, but I)   10
And seemed as they would ask me, if they durst,
How such a glance came there; so, not the first
Are you to turn and ask thus. Sir, 'twas not
Her husband's presence only, called that spot
Of joy into the Duchess' cheek: perhaps   15
Frà Pandolf chanced to say "Her mantle laps
Over my lady's wrist too much," or "Paint
Must never hope to reproduce the faint
Half-flush that dies along her throat": such stuff
Was courtesy, she thought, and cause enough   20
For calling up that spot of joy. She had
A heart — how shall I say? — too soon made glad,
Too easily impressed; she liked whate'er
She looked on, and her looks went everywhere.
Sir, 'twas all one! My favor at her breast,   25
The dropping of the daylight in the West,
The bough of cherries some officious fool
Broke in the orchard for her, the white mule
She rode with round the terrace — all and each
Would draw from her alike the approving speech,   30
Or blush, at least. She thanked men, — good! but thanked
Somehow — I know not how — as if she ranked
My gift of a nine-hundred-years-old name
With anybody's gift. Who'd stoop to blame
This sort of trifling? Even had you skill   35
In speech — which I have not — to make your will
Quite clear to such an one, and say, "Just this
Or that in you disgusts me; here you miss,
Or there exceed the mark" — and if she let
Herself be lessoned so, nor plainly set   40
Her wits to yours, forsooth, and made excuse,
— E'en then would be some stooping; and I choose
Never to stoop. Oh sir, she smiled, no doubt,
Whene'er I passed her; but who passed without
Much the same smile? This grew; I gave commands;   45
Then all smiles stopped together. There she stands
As if alive. Will't please you rise? We'll meet
The company below, then. I repeat,
The Count your master's known munificence
Is ample warrant that no just pretense   50
Of mine for dowry will be disallowed;
Though his fair daughter's self, as I avowed
At starting, is my object. Nay, we'll go
Together down, sir. Notice Neptune, though,
Taming a sea-horse, thought a rarity,   55
Which Claus of Innsbruck° cast in bronze for me!

Explore contexts
for Robert Browning
on *LiterActive*.

56 *Claus of Innsbruck:* Also a fictitious artist.

CONSIDERATIONS FOR CRITICAL THINKING AND WRITING

1. **FIRST RESPONSE.** What do you think happened to the duchess?

2. To whom is the duke addressing his remarks about the duchess in this poem? What is ironic about the situation?

3. Why was the duke unhappy with his first wife? What does this reveal about the duke? What does the poem's title suggest about his attitude toward women in general?

4. What seems to be the visitor's response (lines 53–54) to the duke's account of his first wife?

CONNECTION TO ANOTHER SELECTION

1. Write an essay describing the ways in which the speakers of "My Last Duchess" and Katharyn Howd Machan's "Hazel Tells LaVerne" (p. 77) inadvertently reveal themselves.

WILLIAM BLAKE (1757–1827)

The Chimney Sweeper   1789

When my mother died I was very young,
And my father sold me while yet my tongue
Could scarcely cry " 'weep! 'weep! 'weep! 'weep!"
So your chimneys I sweep, and in soot I sleep.

There's little Tom Dacre, who cried when his head,   5
That curled like a lamb's back, was shaved: so I said
"Hush, Tom! never mind it, for when your head's bare
You know that the soot cannot spoil your white hair."

And so he was quiet, and that very night,
As Tom was a-sleeping, he had such a sight!   10
That thousands of sweepers, Dick, Joe, Ned, and Jack,
Were all of them locked up in coffins of black.

And by came an Angel who had a bright key,
And he opened the coffins and set them all free;
Then down a green plain leaping, laughing, they run,   15
And wash in a river, and shine in the sun.

Then naked and white, all their bags left behind,
They rise upon clouds and sport in the wind;
And the Angel told Tom, if he'd be a good boy,
He'd have God for his father, and never want joy.   20

And so Tom awoke; and we rose in the dark,
And got with our bags and our brushes to work.
Though the morning was cold, Tom was happy and warm;
So if all do their duty they need not fear harm.

CONSIDERATIONS FOR CRITICAL THINKING AND WRITING

1. **FIRST RESPONSE.** Discuss the validity of this statement: " 'The Chimney Sweeper' is a sentimental poem about a shameful eighteenth-century social problem; such a treatment of child abuse cannot be taken seriously."
2. Characterize the speaker in this poem and describe his tone. Is his tone the same as the poet's? Consider especially lines 7, 8, and 24.
3. What is the symbolic value of the dream in lines 11 to 20?
4. Why is irony central to the meaning of this poem?

WALT WHITMAN (1819–1892)

From Song of Myself

1881

6

A child said *What is the grass?* fetching it to me with full hands;
How could I answer the child? I do not know what it is any more than he.

I guess it must be the flag of my disposition, out of hopeful green stuff
    woven.

Or I guess it is the handkerchief of the Lord,
A scented gift and remembrancer designedly dropt,   5
Bearing the owner's name someway in the corners, that we may see and
    remark, and say *Whose?*

Or I guess the grass is itself a child, the produced babe of the vegetation.

Or I guess it is a uniform hieroglyphic,
And it means, Sprouting alike in broad zones and narrow zones,
Growing among black folks as among white,   10
Kanuck, Tuckahoe, Congressman, Cuff,° I give them the same, I receive
    them the same.

And now it seems to me the beautiful uncut hair of graves.

Tenderly will I use you curling grass,
It may be you transpire from the breasts of young men,
It may be if I had known them I would have loved them,   15
It may be you are from old people, or from offspring taken soon out of
    their mothers' laps,
And here you are the mothers' laps.

This grass is very dark to be from the white heads of old mothers,
Darker than the colorless beards of old men,
Dark to come from under the faint red roofs of mouths.   20

O I perceive after all so many uttering tongues,
And I perceive they do not come from the roofs of mouths for nothing.

---

11 *Kanuck . . . Cuff:* Kanuck, a French Canadian; Tuckahoe, a Virginian; Cuff, an African American.

I wish I could translate the hints about the dead young men and women,
And the hints about old men and mothers, and the offspring taken soon
    out of their laps.

What do you think has become of the young and old men?   25
And what do you think has become of the women and children?

They are alive and well somewhere,
The smallest sprout shows there is really no death,
And if ever there was it led forward life, and does not wait at the end to
    arrest it,
And ceas'd the moment life appear'd.   30

All goes onward and outward . . . and nothing collapses,
And to die is different from what any one supposed, and luckier.

Considerations for Critical Thinking and Writing

1. **FIRST RESPONSE.** What does the grass mean to the speaker? Describe the various symbolic possibilities offered in lines 1–11. What seems to be the most important symbolic meaning?

2. Describe the tone of lines 12–26. Explain why these lines are or aren't representative of the poem's entire tone.

3. How does the final line compare with your own view of death?

Connection to Another Selection

1. Compare attitudes toward death in Whitman's poem and in Emily Dickinson's "I heard a Fly buzz — when I died —" (p. 324).

Gary Soto (B. 1952)

Behind Grandma's House   1985

At ten I wanted fame. I had a comb
And two Coke bottles, a tube of Bryl-creem.
I borrowed a dog, one with
Mismatched eyes and a happy tongue,
And wanted to prove I was tough
In the alley, kicking over trash cans,
A dull chime of tuna cans falling.
I hurled light bulbs like grenades
And men teachers held their heads,
Fingers of blood lengthening
On the ground. I flicked rocks at cats,
Their goofy faces spurred with foxtails.
I kicked fences. I shooed pigeons.
I broke a branch from a flowering peach
And frightened ants with a stream of spit.   15
I said "*Chale*," "In your face," and "No way
Daddy-O" to an imaginary priest

Courtesy of Gary Soto.

Until grandma came into the alley,
Her apron flapping in a breeze,
Her hair mussed, and said, "Let me help you,"
And punched me between the eyes.

Explore contexts
for Gary Soto
on *LiterActive*.   20

CONSIDERATIONS FOR CRITICAL THINKING AND WRITING

1. **FIRST RESPONSE.** What is the central irony of this poem?
2. How does the speaker characterize himself at ten?
3. Though the "grandma" appears only briefly, she seems, in a sense, fully characterized. How would you describe her? Why do you think she says, "Let me help you"?

CONNECTION TO ANOTHER SELECTION

1. Write an essay comparing the themes of "Behind Grandma's House" and Sharon Olds's "Rite of Passage" (p. 279).

Perspective

EZRA POUND (1885–1972)
On Symbols   *1912*

I believe that the proper and perfect symbol is the natural object, that if a man uses "symbols" he must so use them that their symbolic function does not obtrude; so that *a* sense, and the poetic quality of the passage, is not lost to those who do not understand the symbol as such, to whom, for instance, a hawk is a hawk.

From "Prolegomena," *Poetry Review,* February 1912

CONSIDERATIONS FOR CRITICAL THINKING AND WRITING

1. Discuss whether you agree with Pound that the "perfect symbol" is a "natural object" that does not insist on being read as a symbol.
2. Write an essay in which you discuss Alden Nowlan's "The Bull Moose" (p. 171) as an example of the "perfect symbol" Pound proposes.

Web Research the
poets in this chapter at
bedfordstmartins.com/
meyerpoetry.

7

Sounds

Bettmann/CORBIS.

In a poem the words should be as
pleasing to the ear as the meaning is
to the mind.
— MARIANNE MOORE

LISTENING TO POETRY

Poems yearn to be read aloud. Much of their energy, charm, and beauty
comes to life only when they are heard. Poets choose and arrange words for
their sounds as well as for their meanings. Most poetry is best read with
your lips, teeth, and tongue because they serve to artic-
ulate the effects that sound may have in a poem. When   Explore
a voice is breathed into a good poem, there is pleasure   the poetic elements
in the reading, the saying, and the hearing.   in this chapter on
                                                            LiterActive or at
     The earliest poetry — before writing and painting —   bedfordstmartins
was chanted or sung. The rhythmic quality of such oral performances   .com/meyerpoetry.
served two purposes: it helped the chanting bard remember the lines and it
entertained audiences with patterned sounds of language, which were
sometimes accompanied by musical instruments. Poetry has always been
closely related to music. Indeed, as the word suggests, lyric poetry evolved

from songs. "Western Wind" (p. 38), an anonymous Middle English lyric, survived as song long before it was written down. Had Robert Frost lived in a nonliterate society, he probably would have sung some version — a very different version to be sure — of "Acquainted with the Night" (p. 157) instead of writing it down. Even though Frost creates a speaking rather than a singing voice, the speaker's anxious tone is distinctly heard in any careful reading of the poem.

Like lyrics, early narrative poems were originally part of an anonymous oral folk tradition. A **ballad** such as "Bonny Barbara Allan" (p. 585) told a story that was sung from one generation to the next until it was finally transcribed. Since the eighteenth century, this narrative form has sometimes been imitated by poets who write **literary ballads**. John Keats's "La Belle Dame sans Merci" (p. 610) is, for example, a more complex and sophisticated nineteenth-century reflection of the original ballad traditions that developed in the fifteenth century and earlier. In considering poetry as sound, we should not forget that poetry traces its beginnings to song.

These next lines exemplify poetry's continuing relation to song. What poetic elements can you find in this ballad, which was adapted by Paul Simon and Art Garfunkel and became a popular antiwar song in the 1960s?

ANONYMOUS

Scarborough Fair

date unknown

Where are you going? To Scarborough Fair?
Parsley, sage, rosemary, and thyme,
Remember me to a bonny lass there,
For once she was a true lover of mine.

Tell her to make me a cambric shirt,   5
Parsley, sage, rosemary, and thyme,
Without any needle or thread work'd in it,
And she shall be a true lover of mine.

Tell her to wash it in yonder well,
Parsley, sage, rosemary, and thyme,   10
Where water ne'er sprung nor a drop of rain fell,
And she shall be a true lover of mine.

Tell her to plough me an acre of land,
Parsley, sage, rosemary, and thyme,
Between the sea and the salt sea strand,   15
And she shall be a true lover of mine.

Tell her to plough it with one ram's horn,
Parsley, sage, rosemary, and thyme,
And sow it all over with one peppercorn,
And she shall be a true lover of mine.   20

At just the right moments Swenson transposes letters to create amusing sound effects and wild wordplays. Although there is a story lurking in "A Nosty Fright," any serious attempt to interpret its meaning is confronted with "a EEP KOFF sign." Instead, we are invited to enjoy the delicious sounds the poet has cooked up.

Few poems revel in sound so completely. More typically, the sounds of a poem contribute to its meaning rather than become its meaning. Consider how sound is used in the next poem.

EMILY DICKINSON (1830–1886)

A Bird came down the Walk —   *c. 1862*

A Bird came down the Walk —
He did not know I saw —
He bit an Angleworm in halves
And ate the fellow, raw,

And then he drank a Dew   5
From a convenient Grass —
And then hopped sidewise to the Wall
To let a Beetle pass —

He glanced with rapid eyes
That hurried all around —   10
They looked like frightened Beads, I thought —
He stirred his Velvet Head

Like one in danger, Cautious,
I offered him a Crumb
And he unrolled his feathers   15
And rowed him softer home —

Than Oars divide the Ocean,
Too silver for a seam —
Or Butterflies, off Banks of Noon
Leap, plashless as they swim.   20

This description of a bird offers a close look at how differently a bird moves when it hops on the ground than when it flies in the air. On the ground the bird moves quickly, awkwardly, and irregularly as it plucks up a worm, washes it down with dew, and then hops aside to avoid a passing beetle. The speaker recounts the bird's rapid, abrupt actions from a somewhat superior, amused perspective. By describing the bird in human terms (as if, for example, it chose to eat the worm "raw"), the speaker is almost condescending. But when the attempt to offer a crumb fails and the frightened bird flies off, the speaker is left looking up instead of down at the bird.

With that shift in perspective the tone shifts from amusement to awe in response to the bird's graceful flight. The jerky movements of lines 1 to 13 give way to the smooth motion of lines 15 to 20. The pace of the first three stanzas is fast and discontinuous. We tend to pause at the end of each line, and this reinforces a sense of disconnected movements. In contrast, the final six lines are to be read as a single sentence in one flowing movement, lubricated by various sounds.

Read again the description of the bird flying away. Several o-sounds contribute to the image of the serene, expansive, confident flight, just as the s-sounds serve as smooth transitions from one line to the next. Notice how these sounds are grouped in the following vertical columns:

unrolled	softer	too	his	Ocean	Banks
rowed	Oars	Noon	feathers	silver	plashless
home	Or		softer	seam	as
Ocean	off		Oars	Butterflies	swim

This blending of sounds (notice how "Leap, plashless" brings together the p- and l-sounds without a ripple) helps convey the bird's smooth grace in the air. Like a feathered oar, the bird moves seamlessly in its element.

The repetition of sounds in poetry is similar to the function of the tones and melodies that are repeated, with variations, in music. Just as the patterned sounds in music unify a work, so do the words in poems, which have been carefully chosen for the combinations of sounds they create. These sounds are produced in a number of ways.

The most direct way in which the sound of a word suggests its meaning is through **onomatopoeia,** which is the use of a word that resembles the sound it denotes: *quack, buzz, rattle, bang, squeak, bowwow, burp, choo-choo, ding-a-ling, sizzle.* The sound and sense of these words are closely related, but such words represent a very small percentage of the words available to us. Poets usually employ more subtle means for echoing meanings.

Onomatopoeia can consist of more than just single words. In its broadest meaning the term refers to lines or passages in which sounds help to convey meanings, as in these lines from Updike's "Player Piano":

> My stick fingers click with a snicker
> And, chuckling, they knuckle the keys.

The sharp, crisp sounds of these two lines approximate the sounds of a piano; the syllables seem to "click" against one another. Contrast Updike's rendition with the following lines:

> My long fingers play with abandon
> And, laughing, they cover the keys.

The original version is more interesting and alive because the sounds of the words are pleasurable and reinforce the meaning through a careful blending of consonants and vowels.

Alliteration is the repetition of the same consonant sounds at the beginnings of nearby words: "*descending dewdrops*," "*luscious lemons*." Sometimes the term is also used to describe the consonant sounds within words: "*trespasser's reproach*," "*wedded lady*." Alliteration is based on sound rather than spelling. "*Keen*" and "*car*" alliterate, but "*car*" does not alliterate with "*cite*." Rarely is heavy-handed alliteration effective. Used too self-consciously, it can be distracting instead of strengthening meaning or emphasizing a relation between words. Consider the relentless *h*'s in this line: "Horrendous horrors haunted Helen's happiness." Those *h*'s certainly suggest that Helen is being pursued, but they have a more comic than serious effect because they are overdone.

Assonance is the repetition of the same vowel sound in nearby words: "*asleep under a tree*," "*time and tide*," "*haunt*" and "*awesome*," "*each evening*." Both alliteration and assonance help to establish relations among words in a line or a series of lines. Whether the effect is **euphony** (lines that are musically pleasant to the ear and smooth, like the final lines of Dickinson's "A Bird came down the Walk—") or **cacophony** (lines that are discordant and difficult to pronounce, like the claim that "never my numb plunker fumbles" in Updike's "Player Piano"), the sounds of words in poetry can be as significant as the words' denotative or connotative meanings.

This next poem provides a feast of sounds. Read the poem aloud and try to determine the effects of its sounds.

GALWAY KINNELL (B. 1927)

Blackberry Eating   *1980*

I love to go out in late September
among the fat, overripe, icy, black
    blackberries
to eat blackberries for breakfast,
the stalks very prickly, a penalty
they earn for knowing the black art
of blackberry-making; and as I stand among
    them
lifting the stalks to my mouth, the ripest
    berries
fall almost unbidden to my tongue,

Photo by Charlie Nye.

as words sometimes do, certain peculiar words
like *strengths* or *squinched*,   10
many-lettered, one-syllabled lumps,
which I squeeze, squinch open, and splurge well
in the silent, startled, icy, black language
of blackberry-eating in late September.

CONSIDERATIONS FOR CRITICAL THINKING AND WRITING

1. **FIRST RESPONSE.** What types of sounds does Kinnell use throughout this poem? What categories can you place them in? What is the effect of these sounds?

2. How do lines 4-6 fit into the poem? What does this prickly image add to the poem?

3. Explain what you think the poem's theme is.

4. Write an essay that considers the speaker's love of blackberry eating along with the speaker's appetite for words. How are the two blended in the poem?

RHYME

Like alliteration and assonance, *rhyme* is a way of creating sound patterns. Rhyme, broadly defined, consists of two or more words or phrases that repeat the same sounds: *happy* and *snappy*. Rhyme words often have similar spellings, but that is not a requirement of rhyme; what matters is that the words sound alike: *vain* rhymes with *reign* as well as *rain*. Moreover, words may look alike but not rhyme at all. In *eye rhyme* the spellings are similar, but the pronunciations are not, as with *bough* and *cough*, or *brow* and *blow*.

Not all poems use rhyme. Many great poems have no rhymes, and many weak verses use rhyme as a substitute for poetry. These are especially apparent in commercial messages and greeting-card lines. At its worst, rhyme is merely a distracting decoration that can lead to dullness and predictability. But used skillfully, rhyme creates lines that are memorable and musical.

Here is a poem using rhyme that you might remember the next time you are in a restaurant.

RICHARD ARMOUR (1906–1989)

Going to Extremes   *1954*

Shake and shake
  The catsup bottle
None'll come —
  And then a lot'll.

The experience recounted in Armour's poem is common enough, but the rhyme's humor is special. The final line clicks the poem shut — an effect that is often achieved by the use of rhyme. That click provides a sense of a satisfying and fulfilled form. Rhymes have a number of uses: they can emphasize words, direct a reader's attention to relations between words, and provide an overall structure for a poem.

Rhyme is used in the following poem to imitate the sound of cascading water.

ROBERT SOUTHEY (1774–1843)

From "The Cataract of Lodore" *1820*

"How does the water

Come down at Lodore?"

. . . .

From its sources which well
  In the tarn on the fell;
    From its fountains
    In the mountains,   5
  Its rills and its gills;
Through moss and through brake,
    It runs and it creeps
    For awhile, till it sleeps   10
    In its own little lake.
  And thence at departing,
  Awakening and starting,
  It runs through the reeds
    And away it proceeds,   15
  Through meadow and glade,
    In sun and in shade,
  And through the wood-shelter,
    Among crags in its flurry,
      Helter-skelter,   20
      Hurry-scurry.
  Here it comes sparkling,
And there it lies darkling;
Now smoking and frothing
    Its tumult and wrath in,   25
    Till in this rapid race
      On which it is bent,
      It reaches the place
      Of its steep descent.

    The cataract strong   30
    Then plunges along,
  Striking and raging
    As if a war waging
Its caverns and rocks among:
    Rising and leaping,   35
  Sinking and creeping,

> Swelling and sweeping,
> Showering and springing,
>> Flying and flinging,
>>> Writhing and ringing,   40
> Eddying and whisking,
> Spouting and frisking,
> Turning and twisting,
>> Around and around
>> With endless rebound!   45
> Smiting and fighting,
>> A sight to delight in;
> Confounding, astounding,
> Dizzying and deafening the ear with its sound.
> . . . .
> Dividing and gliding and sliding,   50
> And falling and brawling and spawling,
> And driving and riving and striving,
> And sprinkling and twinkling and wrinkling,
> And sounding and bounding and rounding,
> And bubbling and troubling and doubling,   55
> And grumbling and rumbling and tumbling,
> And clattering and battering and shattering;
> Retreating and beating and meeting and sheeting,
> Delaying and straying and playing and spraying,
> Advancing and prancing and glancing and dancing,   60
> Recoiling, turmoiling and toiling and boiling,
> And gleaming and streaming and steaming and beaming,
> And rushing and flushing and brushing and gushing,
> And flapping and rapping and clapping and slapping,
> And curling and whirling and purling and twirling,   65
> And thumping and plumping and bumping and jumping,
> And dashing and flashing and splashing and clashing;
> And so never ending, but always descending,
> Sounds and motions forever and ever are blending,
> All at once and all o'er, with a mighty uproar;   70
> And this way the water comes down at Lodore.

This deluge of rhymes consists of "Sounds and motions forever and ever . . . blending" (line 69). The pace quickens as the water creeps from its mountain source and then descends in rushing cataracts. As the speed of the water increases, so do the number of rhymes, until they run in fours: "dashing and flashing and splashing and clashing" (line 67). Most rhymes meander through poems instead of flooding them; nevertheless, Southey's use of rhyme suggests how sounds can flow with meanings. "The Cataract of Lodore" has been criticized, however, for overusing onomatopoeia. Some readers find the poem silly; others regard it as a brilliant example of sound effects. What do you think?

A variety of types of rhyme is available to poets. The most common form, *end rhyme,* comes at the ends of lines (lines 14–17).

> It runs through the reeds
>   And away it proceeds,
> Through meadow and glade,
>   In sun and in shade.

Internal rhyme places at least one of the rhymed words within the line, as in "Dividing and gliding and sliding" (line 50) or, more subtly, in the fourth and final words of "In mist or cloud, on mast or shroud."

The rhyming of single-syllable words such as *glade* and *shade* is known as *masculine rhyme,* as we see in these lines from A. E. Housman:

> Loveliest of trees, the cherry now
> Is hung with bloom along the bough.

Rhymes using words of more than one syllable are also called masculine when the same sound occurs in a final stressed syllable, as in *defend, contend; betray, away.* A *feminine rhyme* consists of a rhymed stressed syllable followed by one or more rhymed unstressed syllables, as in *butter, clutter; gratitude, attitude; quivering, shivering.* This rhyme is evident in John Millington Synge's verse:

> Lord confound this surly sister,
> Blight her brow and blotch and blister.

All of the examples so far have been *exact rhymes* because they share the same stressed vowel sounds as well as any sounds that follow the vowel. In *near rhyme* (also called *off rhyme, slant rhyme,* and *approximate rhyme*), the sounds are almost but not exactly alike. There are several kinds of near rhyme. One of the most common is *consonance,* an identical consonant sound preceded by a different vowel sound: *home, same; worth, breath; trophy, daffy.* Near rhyme can also be achieved by using different vowel sounds with identical consonant sounds: *sound, sand; kind, conned; fellow, fallow.* The dissonance of *blade* and *blood* in the following lines from Wilfred Owen helps to reinforce their grim tone:

> Let the boy try along this bayonet-blade
> How cold steel is, and keen with hunger of blood.

Near rhymes greatly broaden the possibility for musical effects in English, a language that, compared with Spanish or Italian, contains few exact rhymes. Do not assume, however, that a near rhyme represents a failed attempt at exact rhyme. Near rhymes allow a musical subtlety and variety and can avoid the sometimes overpowering jingling effects that exact rhymes may create.

These basic terms hardly exhaust the ways in which the sounds in poems can be labeled and discussed, but the terms can help you to describe how poets manipulate sounds for effect. Read "God's Grandeur" (p. 194) aloud and try to determine how the sounds of the lines contribute to their sense.

Perspective

DAVID LENSON (B. 1945)

On the Contemporary Use of Rhyme   1988

One impediment to a respectable return to rhyme is the popular survival of "functional" verse: greeting cards, pedagogical and mnemonic devices ("Thirty days hath September"), nursery rhymes, advertising jingles, and of course song lyrics. Pentameters, irregular rhymes, and free verse aren't much use in song-writing, where the meter has to be governed by the time signature of the music.

Far from universities, there has been a revival of rhymed couplets in rap music, in which, to the accompaniment of synthesizers, vocalists deliver lengthy first-person narratives in tetrameter. While most writing teachers would dismiss such lyrics as doggerel, the aim of the songs is really not so far from that of Alexander Pope: to use rhyme to sharpen social insight, in the hope that the world may be reordered.

From *The Chronicle of Higher Education*, February 24, 1988

CONSIDERATIONS FOR CRITICAL THINKING AND WRITING

1. Read some contemporary song lyrics from a wide range of groups or vocal-ists. Is Lenson correct in his assessment that irregular rhyme is not much use in songwriting?

2. Examine the rhymed couplets of some rap music. Discuss whether they are used "to sharpen social insight." What is the effect of using rhymes in rap music?

3. What is your own response to rhymed poetry? Do you like yours with or without? What do you think informs your preference?

SOUND AND MEANING

GERARD MANLEY HOPKINS (1844–1889)

God's Grandeur   1877

The world is charged with the grandeur of God
   It will flame out, like shining from shook foil;°   *shaken gold foil*
   It gathers to a greatness, like the ooze of oil
Crushed.° Why do men then now not reck his rod?°
Generations have trod, have trod, have trod;   5
   And all is seared with trade; bleared, smeared with toil;

4 *Crushed:* Olives crushed in their oil;   *reck his rod:* Obey God.

Of the bells, bells, bells, bells,
   Bells, bells, bells —
In the clamor and the clangor of the bells!

IV

  Hear the tolling of the bells —   70
     Iron bells!
What a world of solemn thought their monody compels!
   In the silence of the night,
   How we shiver with affright
At the melancholy menace of their tone!   75
   For every sound that floats
   From the rust within their throats
     Is a groan.
    And the people — ah, the people —
    They that dwell up in the steeple,   80
     All alone,
 And who tolling, tolling, tolling,
  In that muffled monotone,
 Feel a glory in so rolling
   On the human heart a stone —   85
 They are neither man nor woman —
 They are neither brute nor human —
   They are Ghouls: —
  And their king it is who tolls: —
  And he rolls, rolls, rolls,   90
   Rolls
   A pæan from the bells!
 And his merry bosom swells
   With the pæan of the bells!
 And he dances, and he yells;   95
Keeping time, time, time,
In a sort of Runic rhyme,
   To the pæan of the bells —
   Of the bells:
Keeping time, time, time,   100
In a sort of Runic rhyme,
   To the throbbing of the bells —
 Of the bells, bells, bells —
  To the sobbing of the bells;
Keeping time, time, time,   105
  As he knells, knells, knells.
In a happy Runic rhyme,
  To the rolling of the bells —
 Of the bells, bells, bells: —
  To the tolling of the bells —   110
Of the bells, bells, bells, bells,
   Bells, bells, bells —
To the moaning and the groaning of the bells.

CONSIDERATIONS FOR CRITICAL THINKING AND WRITING

1. **FIRST RESPONSE.** How does Poe create the sounds of each kind of bell in each of the poem's four sections?
2. How is onomatopoeia used in each section to echo meanings?
3. What is the effect of the many repetitions of the word *bells*?
4. How does the length of the lines in the poem create musical rhythms?
5. What kinds of rhymes are used to achieve sound effects?
6. What do you think is the theme of "The Bells"?

CONNECTION TO ANOTHER SELECTION

1. Compare Poe's sound effects with Southey's in "The Cataract of Lodore" (p. 191). Which poem do you find more effective in its use of sound? Explain why.

LEWIS CARROLL (CHARLES LUTWIDGE DODGSON/1832–1898)

Jabberwocky   *1871*

'Twas brillig, and the slithy toves
   Did gyre and gimble in the wabe:
All mimsy were the borogoves,
   And the mome raths outgrabe.

"Beware the Jabberwock, my son!   5
   The jaws that bite, the claws that catch!
Beware the Jubjub bird, and shun
   The frumious Bandersnatch!"

He took his vorpal sword in hand;
   Long time the manxome foe he sought —   10
So rested he by the Tumtum tree,
   And stood awhile in thought.

And, as in uffish thought he stood,
   The Jabberwock, with eyes of flame,
Came whiffling through the tulgey wood,   15
   And burbled as it came!

One, two! One, two! And through and through
   The vorpal blade went snicker-snack!
He left it dead, and with its head
   He went galumphing back.   20

"And hast thou slain the Jabberwock?
   Come to my arms, my beamish boy!
O frabjous day! Callooh, Callay!"
   He chortled in his joy.

'Twas brillig, and the slithy toves   25
    Did gyre and gimble in the wabe:
All mimsy were the borogoves,
    And the mome raths outgrabe.

CONSIDERATIONS FOR CRITICAL THINKING AND WRITING

1. **FIRST RESPONSE.** What happens in this poem? Does it have any meaning?
2. Not all of the words used in this poem appear in dictionaries. In *Through the Looking Glass,* Humpty Dumpty explains to Alice that " 'slithy' means 'lithe and slimy.' 'Lithe' is the same as 'active.' You see it's like a portmanteau — there are two meanings packed up into one word." Are there any other portmanteau words in the poem?
3. Which words in the poem sound especially meaningful, even if they are devoid of any denotative meanings?

CONNECTION TO ANOTHER SELECTION

1. Compare Carroll's strategies for creating sound and meaning with those used by Swenson in "A Nosty Fright" (p. 186).

WILLIAM HEYEN (B. 1940)

The Trains   *1984*

Signed by Franz Paul Stangl, Commandant,
there is in Berlin a document,
an order of transmittal from Treblinka:

248 freight cars of clothing,
400,000 gold watches,   5
25 freight cars of women's hair.

Some clothing was kept, some pulped for paper.
The finest watches were never melted down.
All the women's hair was used for mattresses, or dolls.

Would these words like to use some of that same paper?   10
One of those watches may pulse in your own wrist.
Does someone you know collect dolls, or sleep on human hair?

He is dead at last, Commandant Stangl of Treblinka,
but the camp's three syllables still sound like freight cars
straining around a curve, Treblinka,   15

Treblinka. Clothing, time in gold watches,
women's hair for mattresses and dolls' heads.
Treblinka. The trains from Treblinka.

CONSIDERATIONS FOR CRITICAL THINKING AND WRITING

1. **FIRST RESPONSE.** How does the sound of the word *Treblinka* inform your understanding of the poem?

2. Why does the place name of Treblinka continue to resonate over time? To learn more about Treblinka, search the Web, perhaps starting at ushm.org, the site of the United States Holocaust Memorial Museum.

3. Why do you suppose Heyen uses the word *in* instead of *on* in line 11?

4. Why is sound so important for establishing the tone of this poem? In what sense do the "camp's three syllables still sound like freight cars"?

5. **CRITICAL STRATEGIES.** Read the section on reader-response strategies (pp. 662–64) in Chapter 25, "Critical Strategies for Reading." How does this poem make you feel? Why?

ELIZA GRISWOLD

Occupation   *2003*

The prostitutes in Kabul tap their feet
beneath their faded burkas° in the heat.
For bread or fifteen cents, they'll take a man to bed —
their husbands dead, their seven kids unfed —
and thanks to occupation, rents have risen twentyfold,
their chickens, pots, and carpets have been sold
and women's flesh now worth its weight in tin.
Two years ago, the Talibs favored boys and left the girls alone.
A woman then was worth her weight in stone.

2 *burkas:* Traditional garments that cover the body and face of Muslim women.

CONSIDERATIONS FOR CRITICAL THINKING AND WRITING

1. **FIRST RESPONSE.** How does Griswold depict women's lives in Afghanistan both before and after the American occupation there?

2. Comment on the possible meanings of the title and their relation to one another.

3. Discuss the effect of the rhymes and how they enhance the themes.

HENRY WADSWORTH LONGFELLOW (1807–1882)

The Tide Rises, the Tide Falls   *1880*

The tide rises, the tide falls,
The twilight darkens, the curlew calls;
Along the sea-sands damp and brown
The traveller hastens toward the town.
    And the tide rises, the tide falls.   5

Darkness settles on roofs and walls,
But the sea, the sea in the darkness calls;
The little waves, with their soft, white hands,
Efface the footprints in the sands,
    And the tide rises, the tide falls.   10

The morning breaks; the steeds in their stalls
Stamp and neigh, as the hostler calls;
The day returns, but nevermore
Returns the traveller to the shore,
    And the tide rises, the tide falls.   15

CONSIDERATIONS FOR CRITICAL THINKING AND WRITING

1. **FIRST RESPONSE.** Describe the tonal effect of the repeated lines and rhymes.
2. What is the nature of the "darkness" in lines 6–7?
3. What do you think is the purpose of the horses stamping and neighing in the final stanza?

JOHN DONNE (1572–1631)

Song   *1633*

Go and catch a falling star
    Get with child a mandrake root,°
Tell me where all past years are,
    Or who cleft the Devil's foot,
Teach me to hear mermaids singing,   5
    Or to keep off envy's stinging,
          And find
          What wind
Serves to advance an honest mind.

If thou be'st borne to strange sights,   10
    Things invisible to see,
Ride ten thousand days and nights,
    Till age snow white hairs on thee,
Thou, when thou return'st, wilt tell me
    All strange wonders that befell thee,   15
          And swear
          Nowhere
Lives a woman true, and fair.

If thou findst one, let me know,
    Such a pilgrimage were sweet —   20
Yet do not, I would not go,
    Though at next door we might meet;

2 *mandrake root:* This V-shaped root resembles the lower half of the human body.

Though she were true, when you met her,
  And last, till you write your letter,
      Yet she   25
      Will be
False, ere I come, to two or three.

CONSIDERATIONS FOR CRITICAL THINKING AND WRITING

1. **FIRST RESPONSE.** What is the speaker's tone in this poem? What is his view of a woman's love? What does the speaker's use of hyperbole reveal about his emotional state?

2. Do you think Donne wants the speaker's argument to be taken seriously? Is there any humor in the poem?

3. Most of these lines end with masculine rhymes. What other kinds of rhymes are used for end rhymes?

ALEXANDER POPE (1688–1774)

From An Essay on Criticism   1711

But most by numbers° judge a poet's song;   *versification*
And smooth or rough, with them, is right or wrong;
In the bright muse though thousand charms conspire,
Her voice is all these tuneful fools admire;
Who haunt Parnassus° but to please their ear,   5
Not mend their minds; as some to church repair,
Not for the doctrine, but the music there.
These equal syllables alone require,
Though oft the ear the open vowels tire;
While expletives° their feeble aid do join;   10
And ten low words oft creep in one dull line;
While they ring round the same unvaried chimes,
With sure returns of still expected rhymes;
Where'er you find "the cooling western breeze,"
In the next line, it "whispers through the trees":   15
If crystal streams "with pleasing murmurs creep,"
The reader's threatened (not in vain) with "sleep":
Then, at the last and only couplet fraught
With some unmeaning thing they call a thought,
A needless Alexandrine° ends the song,   20
That, like a wounded snake, drags its slow length along.
Leave such to tune their own dull rhymes, and know
What's roundly smooth, or languishingly slow;
And praise the easy vigor of a line,
Where Denham's strength, and Waller's° sweetness join.   25

5 *Parnassus:* A Greek mountain sacred to the Muses.   10 *expletives:* Unnecessary words used to fill a line, as the *do* in this line.   20 *Alexandrine:* A twelve-syllable line, as line 21. 25 *Denham's . . . Waller's:* Sir John Denham (1615–1669) and Edmund Waller (1606–1687) were poets who used heroic couplets.

True ease in writing comes from art, not chance,
As those move easiest who have learned to dance.
'Tis not enough no harshness gives offense,
The sound must seem an echo to the sense:
Soft is the strain when Zephyr° gently blows,   *the west wind*   30
And the smooth stream in smoother numbers flows;
But when loud surges lash the sounding shore,
The hoarse, rough verse should like the torrent roar:
When Ajax° strives some rock's vast weight to throw,
The line too labors, and the words move slow;   35
Not so, when swift Camilla° scours the plain,
Flies o'er th' unbending corn, and skims along the main.

34 *Ajax:* A Greek warrior famous for his strength in the Trojan War.   36 *Camilla:* A goddess famous for her delicate speed.

Considerations for Critical Thinking and Writing

1. **FIRST RESPONSE.** In these lines Pope describes some faults he finds in poems and illustrates those faults within the lines that describe them. How do the sounds in lines 4, 9, 10, 11, and 21 illustrate what they describe?

2. What is the objection to the "expected rhymes" in lines 12–17? How do they differ from Pope's end rhymes?

3. Some lines discuss how to write successful poetry. How do lines 23, 24, 32–33, 35, 36, and 37 illustrate what they describe?

4. Do you agree that in a good poem "The sound must seem an echo to the sense"?

Haki R. Madhubuti (b. 1942)

The B Network   *1998*

brothers bop & pop and be-bop in cities locked up
and chained insane by crack and other acts
of desperation computerized in pentagon cellars producing
boppin brothers boastin of being better, best & beautiful.

if the boppin brothers are beautiful where are the sisters   5
who seek brotherman with a drugless head unbossed or beaten
by the bodacious West?

in a time of big wind being blown by boastful brothers,
will other brothers beat back backwardness to better & best
without braggart bosses beatin butts,   10
takin names and diggin graves?

beatin badness into bad may be urban but is it beautiful & serious?
or is it betrayal in an era of prepared easy death hangin on
corners trappin young brothers before they know the
difference between big death and big life?   15

brothers bop & pop and be-bop in cities locked up
and chained insane by crack and other acts
of desperation computerized in pentagon cellars producing
boppin brothers boastin of being better, best, beautiful
and definitely not *Black*.   20

the critical best is that
brothers better be the best if they are to avoid backwardness
brothers better be the best if they are to conquer beautiful bigness
Comprehend that bad is only *bad* if it's big, Black and better
than boastful braggarts belittling our best and brightest   25
with bosses seeking inches when miles are better.

brothers need to bop to being Black & bright & above board
the black train of beautiful wisdom that is bending this bind
toward a new & knowledgeable beginning that is
bountiful & bountiful & beautiful   30
While be-boppin to be
better than the test,
brotherman.

better yet write the exam.

Considerations for Critical Thinking and Writing

1. **FIRST RESPONSE.** Read this poem aloud. How is that a different experience from reading it silently?

2. Why has the poet included all those words beginning with *b*? How do you explain the title?

3. What is the speaker's assessment of the status of African Americans in the United States? What sort of advice, if any, is offered to them?

4. Comment on the possible interpretations of the final line.

Connection to Another Selection

1. Compare the style and themes of "The B Network" with Langston Hughes's "Dream Boogie" (p. 410).

Maxine Hong Kingston (b. 1940)
Restaurant   *1981*

for Lilah Kan

The main cook lies sick on a banquette, and
      his assistant
has cut his thumb. So the quiche cook takes
their places at the eight-burner range, and
      you and I

Courtesy of Gail K. Evenari.

get to roll out twenty-three rounds of pie
dough and break a hundred eggs, four at a crack,   5
and sift out shell with a China cap, pack
spinach in the steel sink, squish and squeeze
the water out, and grate a full moon of cheese.
Pam, the pastry chef, who is baking Choco-
late Globs (once called Mulattos) complains about the disco,   10
which Lewis, the salad man, turns up louder out of spite.
"Black so-called musician," "Broads. Whites."
The porters, who speak French, from the Ivory Coast,
sweep up droppings and wash the pans without soap.
We won't be out of here until three A.M. In this basement,   15
I lose my size. I am a bent-over
child, Gretel or Jill, and I can
lift a pot as big as a tub with both hands.
Using a pitchfork, you stoke the broccoli and bacon.
Then I find you in the freezer, taking   20
a nibble of a slab of chocolate as big as a table.
We put the quiches in the oven, then we are able
to stick our heads up out of the sidewalk into the night
and wonder at the clean diners behind glass in candlelight.

Considerations for Critical Thinking and Writing

1. **First response.** How do the sounds of this poem contribute to the descriptions of what goes on in the restaurant kitchen? How do they contribute to the diners?

2. In what sense does the speaker "lose [her] size" in the kitchen? How would you describe her?

3. Examine the poem's rhymes. What effect do they have on your reading?

4. Describe the tone of the final line. How does it differ from the rest of the poem?

Connection to Another Selection

1. Write an essay analyzing how the kitchen activities described in this poem and in Elaine Magarrell's "The Joy of Cooking" (p. 153) are used to convey the themes of these poems.

Paul Humphrey (b. 1915)

Blow   *1983*

Her skirt was lofted by the gale;
When I, with gesture deft,
Essayed to stay her frisky sail
She luffed, and laughed, and left.

CONSIDERATIONS FOR CRITICAL THINKING AND WRITING

1. **FIRST RESPONSE.** How do alliteration and assonance contribute to the euphonic effects in this poem?
2. What is the poem's controlling metaphor? Why is it especially appropriate?
3. Explain the ambiguity of the title.

ROBERT FRANCIS (1901–1987)

The Pitcher

1953

His art is eccentricity, his aim
How not to hit the mark he seems to aim at,

His passion how to avoid the obvious,
His technique how to vary the avoidance.

The others throw to be comprehended. He   5
Throws to be a moment misunderstood.

Yet not too much. Not errant, arrant, wild,
But every seeming aberration willed.

Not to, yet still, still to communicate
Making the batter understand too late.   10

CONSIDERATIONS FOR CRITICAL THINKING AND WRITING

1. **FIRST RESPONSE.** Explain how each pair of lines in this poem works together to describe the pitcher's art.
2. Consider how the poem itself works the way a good pitcher does. Which lines illustrate what they describe?
3. Comment on the effects of the poem's rhymes. How are the final two lines different in their rhyme from the previous lines? How does sound echo sense in lines 9–10?
4. Write an essay that considers "The Pitcher" as an extended metaphor for talking about poetry. How well does the poem characterize strategies for writing poetry as well as pitching?
5. Write an essay that develops an extended comparison between writing or reading poetry and playing or watching another sport.

CONNECTION TO ANOTHER SELECTION

1. Write an essay comparing "The Pitcher" with another work by Francis, "Catch" (p. 28). One poem defines poetry implicitly, the other defines it explicitly. Which poem do you prefer? Why?

Perspective

DYLAN THOMAS (1914–1953)
On the Words in Poetry   1961

You want to know why and how I just began to write poetry. . . .

To answer . . . this question, I should say I wanted to write poetry in the beginning because I had fallen in love with words. The first poems I knew were nursery rhymes, and before I could read them for myself I had come to love just the words of them, the words alone. What the words stood for, symbolized, or meant, was of very secondary importance. What mattered was the *sound* of them as I heard them for the first time on the lips of the remote and incomprehensible grown-ups who seemed, for some reason, to be living in my world. And these words were, to me, as the notes of bells, the sounds of musical instruments, the noises of wind, sea, and rain, the rattle of milkcarts, the clopping of hooves on cobbles, the fingering of branches on a window pane, might be to someone, deaf from birth, who has miraculously found his hearing. I did not care what the words said, overmuch, not what happened to Jack and Jill and the Mother Goose rest of them; I cared for the shapes of sound that their names, and the words describing their actions, made in my ears; I cared for the colors the words cast on my eyes. I realize that I may be, as I think back all that way, romanticizing my reactions to the simple and beautiful words of those pure poems; but that is all I can honestly remember, however much time might have falsified my memory. I fell in love — that is the only expression I can think of, at once, and am still at the mercy of words, though sometimes now, knowing a little of their behavior very well, I think I can influence them slightly and have even learned to beat them now and then, which they appear to enjoy. I tumbled for words at once. And, when I began to read the nursery rhymes for myself, and, later, to read other verses and ballads, I knew that I had discovered the most important things, to me, that could be ever. There they were, seemingly lifeless, made only of black and white, but out of them, out of their own being, came love and terror and pity and pain and wonder and all the other vague abstractions that make our ephemeral lives dangerous, great, and bearable. Out of them came the gusts and grunts and hiccups and heehaws of the common fun of the earth; and though what the words meant was, in its own way, often deliciously funny enough, so much funnier seemed to me, at that almost forgotten time, the shape and shade and size and noise of the words as they hummed, strummed, jugged, and galloped along. That was the time of innocence; words burst upon me, unencumbered by trivial or portentous association; words were their springlike selves, fresh with Eden's dew, as they flew out of the air. They made their own original associations as they sprang and shone. The words "Ride a cock-horse to Banbury Cross" were as haunting to me, who did not know then what a cock-horse was nor cared a damn where Banbury Cross might be, as, much later, were such lines as John Donne's "Go and catch a falling star, Get with child a mandrake root," which also I could not understand when I first read them. And as I read more and more, and it was not all verse, by any means, my love for the real life of words increased until I knew that I must live *with* them and *in* them always. I knew, in fact, that I must be a writer of words, and nothing else. The first thing was to feel and know their sound and substance; what I was going to do with those words, what use I was going to make of them, what I was going to *say* through them, would come later. I knew I had to know them most intimately in all their forms and moods, their ups and downs, their chops and changes, their needs and demands. (Here, I am afraid, I am beginning to talk too vaguely. I do not like writing *about* words, because then I often use bad and wrong and stale and wooly words. What I like to do is treat words as a craftsman does his wood or stone or what-have-you, to hew, carve, mold, coil, polish, and plane them into patterns, sequences, sculptures, fugues of sound expressing some lyrical impulse, some spiritual doubt or conviction, some dimly-realized truth I must try to reach and realize.)

From *Early Prose Writings*

CONSIDERATIONS FOR CRITICAL THINKING AND WRITING

1. Why does Thomas value nursery rhymes so highly? What nursery rhyme was your favorite as a child? Why were you enchanted by it?

2. Explain what you think Thomas would have to say about Lewis Carroll's "Jabberwocky" (p. 200) or May Swenson's "A Nosty Fright" (p. 186).

3. Consider Thomas's comparison at the end of this passage, in which he likens a poet's work to a craftsman's. In what sense is making poetry similar to sculpting, painting, or composing music? What are some of the significant differences?

Web Research the poets in this chapter at bedfordstmartins.com/meyerpoetry.

8

Patterns of Rhythm

I would define, in brief, the Poetry of words as the Rhythmical Creation of Beauty. Its sole arbiter is Taste.
—EDGAR ALLAN POE[1]

The rhythms of everyday life surround us in regularly recurring movements and sounds. As you read these words, your heart pulsates while somewhere else a clock ticks, a cradle rocks, a drum beats, a dancer sways, a foghorn blasts, a wave recedes, or a child skips. We may tend to overlook rhythm because it is so tightly woven into the fabric of our experience, but it is there nonetheless, one of the conditions of life. Rhythm is also one of the conditions of speech because the voice alternately rises and falls as words are stressed or unstressed and as the pace quickens or slackens. In poetry *rhythm* refers to the recurrence of stressed and unstressed sounds. Depending on how the sounds are arranged, this can result in a pace that is fast or slow, choppy or smooth.

Explore the poetic element in this chapter on *LiterActive* or at bedfordstmartins.com/meyerpoetry.

[1]Photograph by W. S. Hartshorn. 1848. Prints and Photographs Division, Library of Congress.

SOME PRINCIPLES OF METER

Poets use rhythm to create pleasurable sound patterns and to reinforce meanings. "Rhythm," Edith Sitwell once observed, "might be described as, to the world of sound, what light is to the world of sight. It shapes and gives new meaning." Prose can use rhythm effectively too, but prose that does so tends to be an exception. The following exceptional lines are from a speech by Winston Churchill to the House of Commons after Allied forces lost a great battle to German forces at Dunkirk during World War II:

> We shall not flag or fail. We shall go on to the end. We shall fight in France, we shall fight on the seas and oceans, we shall fight with growing confidence and growing strength in the air, we shall defend our island, whatever the cost may be, we shall fight on the beaches, we shall fight on the landing grounds, we shall fight in the fields and in the streets, we shall fight in the hills; we shall never surrender.

The stressed repetition of "we shall" bespeaks the resolute singleness of purpose that Churchill had to convey to the British people if they were to win the war. Repetition is also one of the devices used in poetry to create rhythmic effects. In the following excerpt from "Song of the Open Road," Walt Whitman urges the pleasures of limitless freedom on his reader:

> Allons!° the road is before us!   *Let's go!*
> It is safe — I have tried it — my own feet have tried it well — be not detain'd!
> Let the paper remain on the desk unwritten, and the book on the
>   shelf unopen'd!
> Let the tools remain in the workshop! Let the money remain unearn'd!
> Let the school stand! mind not the cry of the teacher!   5
> Let the preacher preach in his pulpit! Let the lawyer plead in the
>   court, and the judge expound the law.
>
> Camerado,° I give you my hand!   *friend*
> I give you my love more precious than money,
> I give you myself before preaching or law;
> Will you give me yourself? will you come travel with me?   10
> Shall we stick by each other as long as we live?

These rhythmic lines quickly move away from conventional values to the open road of shared experiences. Their recurring sounds are not created by rhyme or alliteration and assonance (see Chapter 7) but by the repetition of words and phrases.

Although the repetition of words and phrases can be an effective means of creating rhythm in poetry, the more typical method consists of patterns of accented or unaccented syllables. Words contain syllables that are either stressed or unstressed. A **stress** (or **accent**) places more emphasis on one syllable than on another. We say "*syl*lable" not "syl*lable*," "*em*phasis" not "em*pha*sis." We routinely stress syllables when we speak: "*Is* she con*tent* with the *con*tents of the *yel*low *pack*age?" To distinguish between two people we might say "Is *she* con*tent*. . . ?" In this way stress can be used to emphasize a particular word in a sentence. Poets often arrange words so that the desired meaning is suggested by the rhythm; hence emphasis is controlled by the poet rather than left entirely to the reader.

When a rhythmic pattern of stresses recurs in a poem, the result is **meter.** Taken together, all the metrical elements in a poem make up what is called the poem's **prosody. Scansion** consists of measuring the stresses in a line to determine its metrical pattern. Several methods can be used to mark lines. One widely used system uses ´ for a stressed syllable and ˘ for an unstressed syllable. In a sense, the stress mark represents the equivalent of tapping one's foot to a beat:

> Híckŏrў, díckŏrў, dóck,
> The móuse răn úp thĕ clóck.
> The clóck strŭck óne,
> Ănd dówn hĕ rún,
> Híckŏrў, díckŏrў, dóck.

In the first two lines and the final line of this familiar nursery rhyme we hear three stressed syllables. In lines 3 and 4, where the meter changes for variety, we hear just two stressed syllables. The combination of stresses provides the pleasure of the rhythm we hear.

To hear the rhythms of "Hickory, dickory, dock" does not require a formal study of meter. Nevertheless, an awareness of the basic kinds of meter that appear in English poetry can enhance your understanding of how a poem achieves its effects. Understanding the sound effects of a poem and having a vocabulary with which to discuss those effects can intensify your pleasure in poetry. Although the study of meter can be extremely technical, the terms used to describe the basic meters of English poetry are relatively easy to comprehend.

The **foot** is the metrical unit by which a line of poetry is measured. A foot usually consists of one stressed and one or two unstressed syllables. A vertical line is used to separate the feet: "The clock | struck one" consists of two feet. A foot of poetry can be arranged in a variety of patterns; here are five of the chief ones:

Foot	Pattern	Example
iamb	˘ ´	ăwáy
trochee	´ ˘	Lóvelў
anapest	˘ ˘ ´	ŭndĕrstánd
dactyl	´ ˘ ˘	déspĕrătĕ
spondee	´ ´	déad sét

The most common lines in English poetry contain meters based on iambic feet. However, even lines that are predominantly iambic will often include variations to create particular effects. Other important patterns include trochaic, anapestic, and dactylic feet. The spondee is not a sustained meter but occurs for variety or emphasis.

Iambic
What kept | his eyes | from giv | ing back | the gaze
Trochaic
He was | louder | than the | preacher
Anapestic
I am called | to the front | of the room
Dactylic
Sing it all | merrily

These meters have different rhythms and can create different effects. Iambic and anapestic are known as **rising meters** because they move from unstressed to stressed sounds, while trochaic and dactylic are known as **falling meters.** Anapests and dactyls tend to move more lightly and rapidly than iambs or trochees. Although no single kind of meter can be considered always better than another for a given subject, it is possible to determine whether the meter of a specific poem is appropriate for its subject. A serious poem about a tragic death would most likely not be well served by lilting rhythms. Keep in mind, too, that though one or another of these four basic meters might constitute the predominant rhythm of a poem, variations can occur within lines to change the pace or call attention to a particular word.

A **line** is measured by the number of feet it contains. Here, for example, is an iambic line with three feet: "If she | should write | a note." These are the names for line lengths:

monometer: one foot	pentameter: five feet
dimeter: two feet	hexameter: six feet
trimeter: three feet	heptameter: seven feet
tetrameter: four feet	octameter: eight feet

By combining the name of a line length with the name of a foot, we can describe the metrical qualities of a line concisely. Consider, for example, the pattern of feet and length of this line:

I didn't want the boy to hit the dog.

The iambic rhythm of this line falls into five feet; hence it is called **iambic pentameter.** Iambic is the most common pattern in English poetry because its rhythm appears so naturally in English speech and writing. Unrhymed iambic pentameter is called **blank verse;** Shakespeare's plays are built on such lines.

Less common than the iamb, trochee, anapest, or dactyl is the **spondee,** a two-syllable foot in which both syllables are stressed (´ ´). Note the effect of the spondaic foot at the beginning of this line:

Give me a look, give me a face
That makes simplicity a grace;
Robes loosely flowing, hair as free;
Such sweet neglect more taketh me   10
Then all th' adulteries of art.
They strike mine eyes, but not my heart.

CONSIDERATIONS FOR CRITICAL THINKING AND WRITING

1. **FIRST RESPONSE.** What are the speaker's reservations about the lady in the first stanza? What do you think "sweet" means in line 6?

2. What does the speaker want from the lady in the second stanza? How has the meaning of "sweet" shifted from line 6 to line 10? What other words in the poem are especially charged with connotative meanings?

3. How do the rhythms of Jonson's lines help to reinforce meanings? Pay particular attention to lines 6 and 12.

CONNECTION TO ANOTHER SELECTION

1. Write an essay comparing the themes of "Still to Be Neat" and Herrick's preceding poem, "Delight in Disorder." How do the speakers make similar points but from different perspectives?

2. How does the rhythm of "Still to Be Neat" compare with that of "Delight in Disorder"? Which do you find more effective? Explain why.

DIANE BURNS (B. 1950)

Sure You Can Ask Me a Personal Question   *1981*

How do you do?
    No, I am not Chinese.
No, not Spanish.
    No, I am American Indi — uh, Native American.
No, not from India.   5
    No, not Apache.
No, not Navajo.
    No, not Sioux.
No, we are not extinct.
    Yes, Indin.   10
Oh?
    So that's where you got those high cheekbones.
Your great grandmother, huh?
    An Indian Princess, huh?
Hair down to there?   15
    Let me guess. Cherokee?
Oh, so you've had an Indian friend?
    That close?

Oh, so you've had an Indian lover?
    That tight?   20
Oh, so you've had an Indian servant?
    That much?
Yeah, it was awful what you guys did to us.
    It's real decent of you to apologize.
No. I don't know where you can get peyote.   25
    No, I don't know where you can get Navajo rugs real cheap.
No, I didn't make this. I bought it at Bloomingdales.
    Thank you. I like your hair too.
I don't know if anyone knows whether or not Cher is really Indian.
    No, I didn't make it rain tonight.   30
Yeah. Uh-huh. Spirituality.
    Uh-huh. Yeah. Spirituality. Uh-huh. Mother
Earth. Yeah. Uh-huh. Uh-huh. Spirituality.
    No. I didn't major in archery.
Yeah, a lot of us drink too much.   35
    Some of us can't drink enough.
This ain't no stoic look.
    This is my face.

CONSIDERATIONS FOR CRITICAL THINKING AND WRITING

1. **FIRST RESPONSE.** What sort of person do you imagine the speaker is addressing?

2. Discuss the poem's humor. Does it also have a serious theme? Explain.

3. What is the effect of the phrases repeated throughout the poem?

WILLIAM BLAKE (1757–1827)
The Lamb   *1789*

    Little Lamb, who made thee?
    Dost thou know who made thee?
Gave thee life, and bid thee feed
By the stream and o'er the mead;
Gave thee clothing of delight,
Softest clothing, wooly, bright;
Gave thee such a tender voice,
Making all the vales rejoice?
    Little Lamb, who made thee?
    Dost thou know who made thee?

    Little Lamb, I'll tell thee,
    Little Lamb, I'll tell thee:
He is callèd by thy name,
For he calls himself a Lamb.
He is meek, and he is mild;   15

Courtesy of the National Portrait Gallery, London.

He became a little child.
I a child, and thou a lamb,
We are callèd by his name.
    Little Lamb, God bless thee!
    Little Lamb, God bless thee!   20

Explore contexts
for William Blake
on *LiterActive*.

CONSIDERATIONS FOR CRITICAL THINKING AND WRITING

1. **FIRST RESPONSE.** This poem is from Blake's *Songs of Innocence*. Describe its
   tone. How do the meter, rhyme, and repetition help to characterize the
   speaker's voice?

2. Why is it significant that the animal addressed by the speaker is a lamb?
   What symbolic value would be lost if the animal were, for example, a doe?

3. How does the second stanza answer the question raised in the first? What is
   the speaker's view of the creation?

WILLIAM BLAKE (1757–1827)

The Tyger   1794

Tyger! Tyger! burning bright
In the forests of the night,
What immortal hand or eye
Could frame thy fearful symmetry?

In what distant deeps or skies   5
Burnt the fire of thine eyes?
On what wings dare he aspire?
What the hand dare seize the fire?

And what shoulder, and what art,
Could twist the sinews of thy heart?   10
And when thy heart began to beat,
What dread hand? and what dread feet?

What the hammer? what the chain?
In what furnace was thy brain?
What the anvil? what dread grasp   15
Dare its deadly terrors clasp?

When the stars threw down their spears,
And watered heaven with their tears,
Did he smile his work to see?
Did he who made the Lamb make thee?   20

Tyger! Tyger! burning bright
In the forests of the night,
What immortal hand or eye
Dare frame thy fearful symmetry?

CONSIDERATIONS FOR CRITICAL THINKING AND WRITING

1. **FIRST RESPONSE.** This poem from Blake's *Songs of Experience* is often paired with "The Lamb." Describe the poem's tone. Is the speaker's voice the same here as in "The Lamb"? Which words are repeated, and how do they contribute to the tone?

2. What is revealed about the nature of the tiger by the words used to describe its creation? What do you think the tiger symbolizes?

3. Unlike in "The Lamb," more than one question is raised in "The Tyger." What are these questions? Are they answered?

4. Compare the rhythms in "The Lamb" and "The Tyger." Each basically uses a seven-syllable line, but the effects are very different. Why?

5. Using these two poems as the basis of your discussion, describe what distinguishes innocence from experience.

CARL SANDBURG (1878–1967)

Chicago   *1916*

Hog Butcher for the World,
Tool Maker, Stacker of Wheat,
Player with Railroads and the Nation's Freight Handler;
Stormy, husky, brawling,
City of the Big Shoulders: 5

They tell me you are wicked and I believe them, for I have seen your painted
        women under the gas lamps luring the farm boys.
And they tell me you are crooked and I answer: Yes, it is true I have seen the
        gunman kill and go free to kill again.
And they tell me you are brutal and my reply is: On the faces of women and
        children I have seen the marks of wanton hunger.
And having answered so I turn once more to those who sneer at this my city,
        and I give them back the sneer and say to them:
Come and show me another city with lifted head singing so proud to be alive
        and coarse and strong and cunning.   10
Flinging magnetic curses amid the toil of piling job on job, here is a tall bold
        slugger set vivid against the little soft cities;
Fierce as a dog with tongue lapping for action, cunning as a savage pitted
        against the wilderness,
Bareheaded,
Shoveling,
Wrecking,   15
Planning,
Building, breaking, rebuilding,
Under the smoke, dust all over his mouth, laughing with white teeth,
Under the terrible burden of destiny laughing as a young man laughs,
Laughing even as an ignorant fighter laughs who has never lost a battle,   20

Bragging and laughing that under his wrist is the pulse, and under his ribs
    the heart of the people,
  Laughing!
Laughing the stormy, husky, brawling laughter of Youth, half-naked,
    sweating, proud to be Hog Butcher, Tool Maker, Stacker of Wheat,
    Player with Railroads and Freight Handler to the Nation.

CONSIDERATIONS FOR CRITICAL THINKING AND WRITING

1. **FIRST RESPONSE.** Sandburg's personification of Chicago creates a strong identity for the city. Explain why you find the city attractive or not.
2. How do the length and rhythm of lines 1–5 compare with the final lines?
3. **CREATIVE RESPONSE.** Using "Chicago" as a model for style, try writing a tribute or condemnation about a place that you know well. Make an effort to use vivid images and stylistic techniques that capture its rhythms.

CONNECTION TO ANOTHER SELECTION

1. Compare "Chicago" with William Blake's "London" (p. 121) in style and theme.

ALFRED, LORD TENNYSON (1809–1892)
The Charge of the Light Brigade   *1855*

1

Half a league, half a league,
  Half a league onward,
All in the valley of Death
  Rode the six hundred.
"Forward, the Light Brigade!   5
Charge for the guns!" he said:
Into the valley of Death
  Rode the six hundred.

2

"Forward, the Light Brigade!"
Was there a man dismayed?   10
Not though the soldier knew
  Some one had blundered:
Their's not to make reply,
Their's not to reason why,
Their's but to do and die: 15
Into the valley of Death
  Rode the six hundred.

3

Cannon to right of them,
Cannon to left of them,
Cannon in front of them   20
   Volleyed and thundered;
Stormed at with shot and shell,
Boldly they rode and well,
Into the jaws of Death,
Into the mouth of Hell   25
   Rode the six hundred.

4

Flashed all their sabers bare,
Flashed as they turned in air
Sabring the gunners there,
Charging an army, while   30
   All the world wondered:
Plunged in the battery-smoke
Right through the line they broke;
Cossack and Russian
Reeled from the saber-stroke   35
   Shattered and sundered.
Then they rode back, but not
   Not the six hundred.

5

Cannon to right of them,
Cannon to left of them,   40
Cannon behind them
   Volleyed and thundered;
Stormed at with shot and shell,
While horse and hero fell,
They that had fought so well   45
Came through the jaws of Death,
Back from the mouth of Hell,
All that was left of them,
   Left of six hundred.

6

When can their glory fade?   50
O the wild charge they made!
   All the world wondered.
Honor the charge they made!
Honor the Light Brigade,
   Noble six hundred!   55

She pats, clicks, taps
shoes riffing the floor,   10
arms defy gravity,
legs scissor perfectly,
feet notes soar
from the glossy floor,
scatter from table to table   15
like fire licking the air.

She clicks, pats, taps
shoes shocking the floor,
arms swirl, whirl,
legs stamp, swing,   20
feet notes smokebeat
the floor, the floor
just when jazz leaps out of
the hornman's angled trumpet.

She taps, clicks, pats,   25
this sister firing the floor,
arms propel endless circles,
long legs slide, glide,
displace air, filling space,
red dress snaring the danceway,   30
black feather bobbing as she taps.

CONSIDERATIONS FOR CRITICAL THINKING AND WRITING

1. **FIRST RESPONSE.** Explain whether or not you think this vivid description of
   a dancer has a theme.
2. How does Moore's use of punctuation and repetition affect the poem's
   rhythm?
3. Why do you think Moore changes the word order in lines 1, 9, 17, and 25?

RONALD WALLACE (B. 1945)

Dogs   *1997*

When I was six years old I hit one with
a baseball bat. An accident, of course,
and broke his jaw. They put that dog to sleep,
a euphemism even then I knew
could not excuse me from the lasting wrath   5
of memory's flagellation. My remorse
could dog me as it would, it wouldn't keep
me from the life sentence that I drew:

For I've been barked at, bitten, nipped, knocked flat,
slobbered over, humped, sprayed, beshat,   10
by spaniel, terrier, retriever, bull, and Dane.

But through the years what's given me most pain
of all the dogs I've been the victim of
are those whose slow eyes gazed at me, in love.

CONSIDERATIONS FOR CRITICAL THINKING AND WRITING

1. **FIRST RESPONSE.** Discuss the relationship between the poem's first sentence and its last. What's happened to the speaker in between?
2. Comment on the rhyme scheme. Would you characterize it as obvious or subtle? Explain why.
3. How does Wallace's use of caesura and enjambment affect the poem's rhythm?

CONNECTIONS TO OTHER SELECTIONS

1. Compare this poem's theme with that of John Updike's "Dog's Death" (p. 24).
2. In an essay, discuss the strategies used in this sonnet and Shakespeare's "My mistress' eyes are nothing like the sun" (p. 243) to create emotion in the reader.

Perspective

LOUISE BOGAN (1897–1970)

On Formal Poetry

1953

What is formal poetry? It is poetry written in form. And what is *form*? The elements of form, so far as poetry is concerned, are meter and rhyme. Are these elements merely mold and ornaments that have been impressed upon poetry from without? Are they indeed restrictions which bind and fetter language and the thought and emotion behind, under, within language in a repressive way? Are they arbitrary rules which have lost all validity since they have been broken to good purpose by "experimental poets," ancient and modern? Does the breaking up of form, or its total elimination, always result in an increase of power and of effect; and is any return to form a sort of relinquishment of freedom, or retreat to old fogeyism?

From *A Poet's Alphabet*

CONSIDERATIONS FOR CRITICAL THINKING AND WRITING

1. Choose one of the questions Bogan raises and write an essay in response to it using two or three poems from this chapter to illustrate your answer.
2. Try writing a poem in meter and rhyme. Does the experience make your writing feel limited or not?

Web Research the poets in this chapter at bedfordstmartins.com/meyerpoetry.

9

Poetic Forms

© Tom Jorgensen/The University of Iowa.

A short poem need not be small.
— MARVIN BELL

Poems come in a variety of shapes. Although the best poems always have their own unique qualities, many of them also conform to traditional patterns. Frequently the *form* of a poem — its overall structure or shape — follows an already established design. A poem that can be categorized by the patterns of its lines, meter, rhymes, and stanzas is considered a *fixed form* because it follows a prescribed model such as a sonnet. However, poems written in a fixed form do not always fit models precisely; writers sometimes work variations on traditional forms to create innovative effects.

Not all poets are content with variations on traditional forms. Some prefer to create their own structures and shapes. Poems that do not conform to established patterns of meter, rhyme, and stanza are called *free verse* or *open form* poetry. (See Chapter 10 for further discussion of open forms.) This kind of poetry creates its own ordering principles through the careful arrangement of words and phrases in line lengths that embody rhythms appropriate to the meaning. Modern and contemporary poets in particular have learned to use the blank space on the page as a significant functional element (for a striking example, see Cummings's "in Just-," p. 267). Good poetry of this kind is structured in ways that can be as demanding, interesting, and satisfying as fixed forms. Open and fixed forms represent different poetic styles, but they are identical in the sense that both use language in concentrated ways to convey meanings, experiences, emotions, and effects.

SOME COMMON POETIC FORMS

A familiarity with some of the most frequently used fixed forms of poetry is useful because it allows for a better understanding of how a poem works. Classifying patterns allows us to talk about the effects of established rhythm and rhyme and recognize how significant variations from them affect the pace and meaning of the lines. An awareness of form also allows us to anticipate how a poem is likely to proceed. As we shall see, a sonnet creates a different set of expectations in a reader from those of, say, a limerick. A reader isn't likely to find in limericks the kind of serious themes that often make their way into sonnets. The discussion that follows identifies some of the important poetic forms frequently encountered in English poetry.

The shape of a fixed-form poem is often determined by the way in which the lines are organized into stanzas. A *stanza* consists of a grouping of lines, set off by a space, that usually has a set pattern of meter and rhyme. This pattern is ordinarily repeated in other stanzas throughout the poem. What is usual is not obligatory, however; some poems may use a different pattern for each stanza, somewhat like paragraphs in prose.

Traditionally, though, stanzas do share a common *rhyme scheme,* the pattern of end rhymes. We can map out rhyme schemes by noting patterns of rhyme with lowercase letters: the first rhyme sound is designated *a,* the second becomes *b,* the third *c,* and so on. Using this system, we can describe the rhyme scheme in the following poem this way: *aabb, ccdd, eeff.*

A. E. HOUSMAN (1859–1936)
Loveliest of trees, the cherry now   *1896*

Loveliest of trees, the cherry now   *a*
Is hung with bloom along the bough,   *a*
And stands about the woodland ride   *b*
Wearing white for Eastertide.   *b*

Now, of my threescore years and ten,   *c*   5
Twenty will not come again,   *c*
And take from seventy springs a score,   *d*
It only leaves me fifty more.   *d*

And since to look at things in bloom   *e*
Fifty springs are little room,   *e*   10
About the woodlands I will go   *f*
To see the cherry hung with snow.   *f*

CONSIDERATIONS FOR CRITICAL THINKING AND WRITING

1. **FIRST RESPONSE.** What is the speaker's attitude in this poem toward time and life?

2. Why is spring an appropriate season for the setting rather than, say, winter?

3. Paraphrase each stanza. How do the images in each reinforce the poem's themes?

4. Lines 1 and 12 are not intended to rhyme, but they are close. What is the effect of the near rhyme of "now" and "snow"? How does the rhyme enhance the theme?

Poets often create their own stanzaic patterns; hence there is an infinite number of kinds of stanzas. One way of talking about stanzaic forms is to describe a given stanza by how many lines it contains.

A *couplet* consists of two lines that usually rhyme and have the same meter; couplets are frequently not separated from each other by space on the page. A *heroic couplet* consists of rhymed iambic pentameter. Here is an example from Alexander Pope's "Essay on Criticism":

One science only will one genius fit;   *a*
So vast is art, so narrow human wit: *a*
Not only bounded to peculiar arts,   *b*
But oft in those confined to single parts.   *b*

A *tercet* is a three-line stanza. When all three lines rhyme they are called a *triplet*. Two triplets make up this captivating poem.

ROBERT HERRICK (1591–1674)

Upon Julia's Clothes   1648

Whenas in silks my Julia goes,   *a*
Then, then, methinks, how sweetly flows   *a*
That liquefaction of her clothes.   *a*

Next, when I cast mine eyes, and see   *b*
That brave vibration, each way free,   *b*
O, how that glittering taketh me!   *b*

CONSIDERATIONS FOR CRITICAL THINKING AND WRITING

1. **FIRST RESPONSE.** What purpose does alliteration serve in this poem?

2. Comment on the effect of the meter. How is it related to the speaker's description of Julia's clothes?

3. Look up the word *brave* in the *Oxford English Dictionary.* Which of its meanings is appropriate to describe Julia's movement? Some readers interpret lines 4–6 to mean that Julia has no clothes on. What do you think?

CONNECTION TO ANOTHER SELECTION

1. Compare the tone of this poem with that of Paul Humphrey's "Blow" (p. 207). Are the situations and speakers similar? Is there any difference in tone between these two poems?

Terza rima consists of an interlocking three-line rhyme scheme: *aba, bcb, cdc, ded,* and so on. Dante's *Divine Comedy* uses this pattern, as does Robert Frost's "Acquainted with the Night" (p. 157) and Percy Bysshe Shelley's "Ode to the West Wind" (p. 257).

A *quatrain,* or four-line stanza, is the most common stanzaic form in the English language and can have various meters and rhyme schemes (if any). The most common rhyme schemes are *aabb, abba, aaba,* and *abcb.* This last pattern is especially characteristic of the popular *ballad stanza,* which consists of alternating eight- and six-syllable lines. Samuel Taylor Coleridge adopted this pattern in "The Rime of the Ancient Mariner"; here is one representative stanza:

All in a hot and copper sky
The bloody Sun, at noon,
Right up above the mast did stand,
No bigger than the Moon.

There are a number of longer stanzaic forms, and the list of types of stanzas could be extended considerably, but knowing these three most basic patterns should prove helpful to you in talking about the form of a great many poems. In addition to stanzaic forms, there are fixed forms that characterize entire poems. Lyric poems can be, for example, sonnets, villanelles, sestinas, or epigrams.

Sonnet

The *sonnet* has been a popular literary form in English since the sixteenth century, when it was adopted from the Italian *sonnetto,* meaning "little song." A sonnet consists of fourteen lines, usually written in iambic pentameter. Because the sonnet has been such a favorite form, writers have experimented with many variations on its essential structure. Nevertheless, there are two basic types of sonnets: the Italian and the English.

The *Italian sonnet* (also known as the *Petrarchan sonnet,* from the fourteenth-century Italian poet Petrarch) divides into two parts. The first eight lines (the *octave*) typically rhyme *abbaabba.* The final six lines (the *sestet*) may vary; common patterns are *cdecde, cdcdcd,* and *cdccdc.* Very often the

Seamus Heaney (b. 1939)

The Forge   1969

All I know is a door into the dark.
Outside, old axles and iron hoops rusting;
Inside, the hammered anvil's short-pitched ring,
The unpredictable fantail of sparks
Or hiss when a new shoe toughens in water.   5
The anvil must be somewhere in the centre,
Horned as a unicorn, at one end square,
Set there immoveable: an altar
Where he expends himself in shape and music.
Sometimes, leather-aproned, hairs in his nose,   10
He leans out on the jamb, recalls a clatter
Of hoofs where traffic is flashing in rows;
Then grunts and goes in, with a slam and flick
To beat real iron out, to work the bellows.

Considerations for Critical Thinking and Writing

1. **First response.** In addition to providing a vivid description of a forge, what else does this poem offer about its portrait of a blacksmith?

2. How does the speaker's assertion that "All I know is a door into the dark" comment on the rest of the poem?

3. What kind of sonnet is "The Forge"?

Molly Peacock (b. 1947)

Desire   1984

It doesn't speak and it isn't schooled,
like a small foetal animal with wettened fur.
It is the blind instinct for life unruled,
visceral frankincense and animal myrrh.
It is what babies bring to kings,   5
an eyes-shut, ears-shut medicine of the heart
that smells and touches endings and beginnings
without the details of time's experienced *part-*
fit-into-part-fit-into-part. Like a paw,
it is blunt; like a pet who knows you   10
and nudges your knee with its snout — but more raw
and blinder and younger and more divine, too,
than the tamed wild — it's the drive for what is real,
deeper than the brain's detail: the drive to feel.

CONSIDERATIONS FOR CRITICAL THINKING AND WRITING

1. **FIRST RESPONSE.** Taken together, what do all of the metaphors that appear in this poem reveal about the speaker's conception of desire?

2. What is the "it" being described in lines 3–5? How do the allusions to the three wise men relate to the other metaphors used to define desire?

3. How is this English sonnet structured? What is the effect of its irregular meter?

CONNECTION TO ANOTHER SELECTION

1. Compare the treatment of desire in this poem with that of Sharon Olds's "Last Night" (p. 85). In an essay, identify the theme of each poem and compare their conceptions of desire. How alike are these two poems?

MARK JARMAN (B. 1952)

Unholy Sonnet

1993

After the praying, after the hymn-singing,
After the sermon's trenchant commentary
On the world's ills, which make ours secondary,
After communion, after the hand-wringing,
And after peace descends upon us, bringing   5
Our eyes up to regard the sanctuary
And how the light swords through it, and how, scary
In their sheer numbers, motes of dust ride, clinging —
There is, as doctors say about some pain,
Discomfort knowing that despite your prayers,   10
Your listening and rejoicing, your small part
In this communal stab at coming clean,
There is one stubborn remnant of your cares
Intact. There is still murder in your heart.

CONSIDERATIONS FOR CRITICAL THINKING AND WRITING

1. **FIRST RESPONSE.** Describe the rhyme scheme and structure of this sonnet. Explain why it is an English or Italian sonnet.

2. What are the effects of the use of "after" in lines 1, 2, 4, and 5 and "there" in lines 9, 13, and 14?

3. In what sense might this poem be summed up as a "communal stab" (line 12)? Discuss the accuracy of this assessment.

4. **CREATIVE RESPONSE.** Try writing a reply to the theme of Jarman's poem using the same sonnet form that he uses.

CONNECTIONS TO OTHER SELECTIONS

1. Jarman has said that his "Unholy Sonnets" (there are about twenty of them) are modeled after John Donne's *Holy Sonnets* but that he does not

share the same Christian assumptions about faith and mercy that inform Donne's sonnets. Instead, Jarman says, he "work[s] against any assumption or shared expression of faith, to write a devotional poetry against the grain." Keeping this statement in mind, write an essay comparing and contrasting the tone and theme of Jarman's sonnet with John Donne's "Batter My Heart" (p. 596) or "Death Be Not Proud" (p. 290).

Villanelle

The ***villanelle*** is a fixed form consisting of nineteen lines of any length divided into six stanzas: five tercets and a concluding quatrain. The first and third lines of the initial tercet rhyme; these rhymes are repeated in each subsequent tercet (*aba*) and in the final two lines of the quatrain (*abaa*). Moreover, line 1 appears in its entirety as lines 6, 12, and 18, while line 3 appears as lines 9, 15, and 19. This form may seem to risk monotony, but in competent hands a villanelle can create haunting echoes, as in Dylan Thomas's "Do Not Go Gentle into That Good Night."

DYLAN THOMAS (1914–1953)

Do Not Go Gentle into That Good Night   *1952*

Do not go gentle into that good night,
Old age should burn and rave at close of day;
Rage, rage against the dying of the light.

Though wise men at their end know dark is right,
Because their words had forked no lightning they   5
Do not go gentle into that good night.

Good men, the last wave by, crying how bright
Their frail deeds might have danced in a green bay,
Rage, rage against the dying of the light.

Wild men who caught and sang the sun in flight,   10
And learn, too late, they grieved it on its way,
Do not go gentle into that good night.

Grave men, near death, who see with blinding sight
Blind eyes could blaze like meteors and be gay,
Rage, rage against the dying of the light.   15

And you, my father, there on the sad height,
Curse, bless, me now with your fierce tears, I pray.
Do not go gentle into that good night.
Rage, rage against the dying of the light.

Considerations for Critical Thinking and Writing

1. **FIRST RESPONSE.** How does Thomas vary the meanings of the poem's two refrains: "Do not go gentle into that good night" and "Rage, rage against the dying of the light"?

2. Thomas's father was close to death when this poem was written. How does the tone contribute to the poem's theme?

3. How is "good" used in line 1?

4. Characterize the men who are "wise" (line 4), "Good" (7), "Wild" (10), and "Grave" (13).

5. What do figures of speech contribute to this poem?

6. Discuss this villanelle's sound effects.

Wendy Cope (b. 1945)

Lonely Hearts   1986

Can someone make my simple wish come true?
Male biker seeks female for touring fun.
Do you live in North London? Is it you?

Gay vegetarian whose friends are few,
I'm into music, Shakespeare and the sun.   5
Can someone make my simple wish come true?

Executive in search of something new —
Perhaps bisexual woman, arty, young.
Do you live in North London? Is it you?

Successful, straight and solvent? I am too —   10
Attractive Jewish lady with a son.
Can someone make my simple wish come true?

I'm Libran, inexperienced and blue—
Need slim non-smoker, under twenty-one.
Do you live in North London? Is it you?   15

Please write (with photo) to Box 152
Who knows where it may lead once we've begun?
Can someone make my simple wish come true?
Do you live in North London? Is it you?

Considerations for Critical Thinking and Writing

1. **FIRST RESPONSE.** Why does the repetitive form of the villanelle seem particularly appropriate for the subject matter of "Lonely Hearts"?

2. How closely does "Lonely Hearts" conform to the conventional form of the villanelle? Are there any significant variations that produce interesting effects?

3. How are the several speakers' voices in the poem unified by tone?

Limerick

The **limerick** is always light and humorous. Its usual form consists of five predominantly anapestic lines rhyming *aabba;* lines 1, 2, and 5 contain three feet, while lines 3 and 4 contain two. Limericks have delighted everyone from schoolchildren to sophisticated adults, and they range in subject matter from the simply innocent and silly to the satiric or obscene. The sexual humor helps to explain why so many limericks are written anonymously. Here is one that is anonymous but more concerned with physics than physiology.

ANONYMOUS

There was a young lady named Bright

There was a young lady named Bright,
Who traveled much faster than light,
   She started one day
   In a relative way,
And returned on the previous night.

This next one is a particularly clever definition of a limerick.

LAURENCE PERRINE (B. 1915)

The limerick's never averse   *1982*

The limerick's never averse
To expressing itself in a terse
   Economical style,
   And yet, all the while,
The limerick's *always* a verse.

CONSIDERATIONS FOR CRITICAL THINKING AND WRITING

1. **FIRST RESPONSE.** How does this limerick differ from others you know? How is it similar?
2. Scan Perrine's limerick. How do the lines measure up to the traditional fixed metrical pattern?
3. Try writing a limerick. Use the following basic pattern.

    ˘ ˘ ´   ˘ ˘ ´   ˘ ˘ ´
    ˘ ˘ ´   ˘ ˘ ´   ˘ ˘ ´
         ˘ ˘ ´   ˘ ˘ ´
         ˘ ˘ ´   ˘ ˘ ´
    ˘ ˘ ´   ˘ ˘ ´   ˘ ˘ ´

You might begin with a friend's name or the name of your school or town. Your instructor is, of course, fair game, too, provided your tact matches your wit.

The next selection is a real tongue twister.

KEITH CASTO
She Don't Bop 1987

A nervous young woman named Trudy
Was at odds with a horn player, Rudy.
His horn so annoyed her
The neighbors would loiter
To watch Rudy toot Trudy fruity.

Haiku

Another brief fixed poetic form, borrowed from the Japanese, is the **haiku.** A haiku is usually described as consisting of seventeen syllables organized into three unrhymed lines of five, seven, and five syllables. Owing to language difference, however, English translations of haiku are often only approximated, because a Japanese haiku exists in time (Japanese syllables have duration). The number of syllables in our sense is not as significant as the duration. These poems typically present an intense emotion or vivid image of nature, which, in the Japanese, are also designed to lead to a spiritual insight.

MATSUO BASHŌ (1644–1694)
Under cherry trees *date unknown*

Under cherry trees
Soup, the salad, fish and all . . .
Seasoned with petals.

CAROLYN KIZER (B. 1925)
After Bashō 1984

Tentatively, you
slip onstage this evening,
pallid, famous moon.

Sonia Sanchez (b. 1935)

c'mon man hold me 1998

c'mon man hold me
touch me before time love me
from behind your eyes.

> ### Considerations for Critical Thinking and Writing
>
> 1. **First response.** What different emotions do these three haiku evoke?
> 2. What differences and similarities are there between the effects of a haiku and those of an epigram?
> 3. **Creative response.** Compose a haiku. Try to make it as allusive and suggestive as possible.

Elegy

An elegy in classical Greek and Roman literature was written in alternating hexameter and pentameter lines. Since the seventeenth century, however, the term *elegy* has been used to describe a lyric poem written to commemorate someone who is dead. The word is also used to refer to a serious meditative poem produced to express the speaker's melancholy thoughts. Elegies no longer conform to a fixed pattern of lines and stanzas, but their characteristic subject is related to death and their tone is mournfully contemplative.

Theodore Roethke (1908–1963)

Elegy for Jane 1953
My Student, Thrown by a Horse

I remember the neckcurls, limp and damp as tendrils;
And her quick look, a sidelong pickerel smile;
And how, once startled into talk, the light syllables leaped for her,
And she balanced in the delight of her thought,
A wren, happy, tail into the wind,   5
Her song trembling the twigs and small branches.
The shade sang with her;
The leaves, their whispers turned to kissing;
And the mold sang in the bleached valleys under the rose.

Oh, when she was sad, she cast herself down into such a pure depth,   10
Even a father could not find her:
Scraping her cheek against straw;
Stirring the clearest water.

My sparrow, you are not here,
Waiting like a fern, making a spiny shadow.   15
The sides of wet stones cannot console me,
Nor the moss, wound with the last light.

If only I could nudge you from this sleep,
My maimed darling, my skittery pigeon.
Over this damp grave I speak the words of my love: 20
I, with no rights in this matter,
Neither father nor lover.

CONSIDERATIONS FOR CRITICAL THINKING AND WRITING

1. **FIRST RESPONSE.** Does this elegy use any kind of formal pattern for its structure? What holds it together?

2. List the images that compare Jane to nature. How is she depicted by these images?

3. Describe the shift in tone that begins in line 14. How do the speaker's feelings change in lines 14–22?

4. What is the significance of Jane having been the speaker's student? How does that affect your reading of lines 21–22?

CONNECTION TO ANOTHER SELECTION

1. Compare "Elegy for Jane" with A. E. Housman's "To an Athlete Dying Young" (p. 606). How does each poem avoid sentimentality in its description of a young person who had died?

ANDREW HUDGINS (B. 1951)

Elegy for My Father, Who Is Not Dead   *1991*

One day I'll lift the telephone
and be told my father's dead. He's ready.
In the sureness of his faith, he talks
about the world beyond this world
as though his reservations have   5
been made. I think he wants to go,
a little bit — a new desire
to travel building up, an itch
to see fresh worlds. Or older ones.
He thinks that when I follow him   10
he'll wrap me in his arms and laugh,
the way he did when I arrived
on earth. I do not think he's right.
He's ready. I am not. I can't
just say good-bye as cheerfully   15
as if he were embarking on a trip

to make my later trip go well.
I see myself on deck, convinced
his ship's gone down, while he's convinced
I'll see him standing on the dock   20
and waving, shouting, Welcome back.

Considerations for Critical Thinking and Writing

1. **FIRST RESPONSE.** Why does this speaker elegize his father if the father "is
   not dead"?
2. How does the speaker's view of immortality differ from his father's?
3. Explain why you think this is an optimistic or a pessimistic poem — or ex-
   plain why these two categories fail to describe the poem.
4. In what sense can this poem be regarded as an elegy?

Connection to Another Selection

1. Write an essay comparing attitudes toward death in this poem and in
   Dylan Thomas's "Do Not Go Gentle into That Good Night" (p. 247). Both
   speakers invoke their fathers, nearer to death than they are; what impact
   does this have?

Ode

An **ode** is characterized by a serious topic and formal tone, but no pre-
scribed formal pattern describes all odes. In some odes the pattern of each
stanza is repeated throughout, while in others each stanza introduces a
new pattern. Odes are lengthy lyrics that often include lofty emotions con-
veyed by a dignified style. Typical topics include truth, art, freedom, justice,
and the meaning of life. Frequently such lyrics tend to be more public than
private, and their speakers often use apostrophe.

Percy Bysshe Shelley (1792–1822)
Ode to the West Wind   *1820*

I

O wild West Wind, thou breath of Autumn's being,
Thou, from whose unseen presence the leaves dead
Are driven, like ghosts from an enchanter fleeing,

Yellow, and black, and pale, and hectic red,
Pestilence-stricken multitudes: O thou,   5
Who chariotest to their dark wintry bed

The wingèd seeds, where they lie cold and low,
Each like a corpse within its grave, until
Thine azure sister of the Spring shall blow

Her clarion o'er the dreaming earth, and fill   10
(Driving sweet buds like flocks to feed in air)
With living hues and odors plain and hill:

Wild Spirit, which art moving everywhere;
Destroyer and preserver; hear, oh, hear!

II

Thou on whose stream, mid the steep sky's commotion,   15
Loose clouds like earth's decaying leaves are shed,
Shook from the tangled boughs of Heaven and Ocean,

Angels° of rain and lightning: there are spread   *messengers*
On the blue surface of thine airy surge,
Like the bright hair uplifted from the head   20

Of some fierce Maenad,° even from the dim verge
Of the horizon to the zenith's height,
The locks of the approaching storm. Thou dirge

Of the dying year, to which this closing night
Will be the dome of a vast sepulcher,   25
Vaulted with all thy congregated might

Of vapors, from whose solid atmosphere
Black rain, and fire, and hail will burst: oh, hear!

III

Thou who didst waken from his summer dreams
The blue Mediterranean, where he lay,   30
Lulled by the coil of his crystálline streams,

Beside a pumice isle in Baiae's bay,°
And saw in sleep old palaces and towers
Quivering within the wave's intenser day,

All overgrown with azure moss and flowers   35
So sweet, the sense faints picturing them! Thou
For whose path the Atlantic's level powers

Cleave themselves into chasms, while far below
The sea-blooms and the oozy woods which wear
The sapless foliage of the ocean, know   40

Thy voice, and suddenly grow gray with fear,
And tremble and despoil themselves: oh, hear!

---

21 *Maenad:* In Greek mythology, a frenzied worshipper of Dionysus, god of wine and
fertility.   32 *Baiae's bay:* A bay in the Mediterranean Sea.

IV

If I were a dead leaf thou mightest bear;
If I were a swift cloud to fly with thee;
A wave to pant beneath thy power, and share   45

The impulse of thy strength, only less free
Than thou, O uncontrollable! If even
I were as in my boyhood, and could be

The comrade by thy wanderings over Heaven,
As then, when to outstrip thy skyey speed   50
Scarce seemed a vision; I would ne'er have striven

As thus with thee in prayer in my sore need.
Oh, lift me as a wave, a leaf, a cloud!
I fall upon the thorns of life! I bleed!

A heavy weight of hours has chained and bowed   55
One too like thee: tameless, and swift, and proud.

V

Make me thy lyre,° even as the forest is:
What if my leaves are falling like its own!
The tumult of thy mighty harmonies

Will take from both a deep, autumnal tone,   60
Sweet though in sadness. Be thou, Spirit fierce,
My spirit! Be thou me, impetuous one!

Drive my dead thoughts over the universe
Like withered leaves to quicken a new birth!
And, by the incantation of this verse,   65

Scatter, as from an unextinguished hearth
Ashes and sparks, my words among mankind!
Be through my lips to unawakened earth

The trumpet of a prophecy! O Wind,
If Winter comes, can Spring be far behind?   70

57 *Make me thy lyre:* Sound is produced on an Aeolian lyre, or wind harp, by wind blowing across its strings.

CONSIDERATIONS FOR CRITICAL THINKING AND WRITING

1. **FIRST RESPONSE.** Write a summary of each of this ode's five sections.
2. What is the speaker's situation? What is his "sore need" (line 52)? What does the speaker ask of the wind in lines 57–70?
3. What does the wind signify in this ode? How is it used symbolically?
4. Determine the meter and rhyme of the first five stanzas. How do these elements contribute to the ode's movement? Is this pattern continued in the other four sections?

MARY JO SALTER (B. 1954)

Home Movies: A Sort of Ode   *1999*

Because it hadn't seemed enough,
after a while, to memorialize
more Christmases, the three-layer cakes
ablaze with birthday candles, the blizzard
Billy took a shovel to,   5
Phil's lawn mower tour of the yard,
the tree forts, the shoot-'em-ups
between the boys in new string ties
and cowboy hats and holsters,
or Mother sticking a bow as big   10
as Mouseketeer ears in my hair,

my father sometimes turned the gaze
of his camera to subjects more
artistic or universal:
rapt close-ups of a rose's face;   15
a real-time sunset (nearly an hour);
what one assumes were brilliant autumn
leaves before their colors faded
to dry beige on the aging film;
a great deal of pacing, at the zoo,   20
by polar bears and leopards caged,
he seemed to say, like him.

What happened between him and her
is another story. And just as well
we have no movie of it, only   25
some unforgiving scowls she gave
through terrifying, ticking silence
when he must have asked her (no
sound track) for a smile.
Yet the scenes I keep reversing to   30
are private: not those generic cherry
blossoms at the full, or the brave
daffodil after a snowfall;

instead, it's the re-run surprise
of the unshuttered, prefab blanks   35
of windows at the back of the house,
and how the lines of aluminum
siding are scribbled on with meaning
only for us who lived there.
It's the pair of elephant bookends   40
I'd forgotten, with the upraised trunks
like handles, and the books they sought
to carry in one block to a future
that scattered all of us.

And look: it's the stoneware mixing bowl   45
figured with hand-holding dancers

handed down so many years
ago to my own kitchen, still
valueless, unbroken. Here
she's happy, teaching us to dye   50
some Easter eggs in it, a Grecian
urn of sorts near which — a foster
child of silence and slow time
myself — I smile because she does,
and patiently await my turn.   55

CONSIDERATIONS FOR CRITICAL THINKING AND WRITING

1. **FIRST RESPONSE.** To what extent does this poem conform to the definitions
   of *ode*?

2. Describe the speaker's family life based on the images provided by the
   home movies.

3. **CREATIVE RESPONSE.** Write an ode to a computer or other household appli-
   ance that expresses a particular attitude about it.

CONNECTION TO ANOTHER SELECTION

1. Lines 51–52 allude to John Keats's "Ode on a Grecian Urn" (p. 96). Read
   Keats's poem and discuss the purpose of the allusion in Salter's ode.

Parody

A *parody* is a humorous imitation of another, usually serious, work. It can
take any fixed or open form because parodists imitate the tone, language,
and shape of the original. While a parody may be teasingly close to a work's
style, it typically deflates the subject matter to make the original seem ab-
surd. Parody can be used as a kind of literary criticism to expose the defects
in a work, but it is also very often an affectionate acknowledgment that a
well-known work has become both institutionalized in our culture and fair
game for some fun. Read Andrew Marvell's "To His Coy Mistress" (p. 81)
and then study this parody.

PETER DE VRIES (1910–1993)
To His Importunate Mistress   1986

Andrew Marvell Updated

Had we but world enough, and time,
My coyness, lady, were a crime,
But at my back I always hear
Time's wingèd chariot, striking fear
The hour is nigh when creditors   5

Will prove to be my predators.
As wages of our picaresque,
Bag lunches bolted at my desk
Must stand as fealty to you
For each expensive rendezvous.   10
Obeisance at your marble feet
Deserves the best-appointed suite,
And would have, lacked I not the pelf
To pleasure also thus myself;
But aptly sumptuous amorous scenes   15
Rule out the rake of modest means.

Since mistress presupposes wife,
It means a doubly costly life;
For fools by second passion fired
A second income is required,   20
The earning which consumes the hours
They'd hoped to spend in rented bowers.
To hostelries the worst of fates
That weekly raise their daily rates!
I gather, lady, from your scoffing   25
A bloke more solvent in the offing.
So revels thus to rivals go
For want of monetary flow.
How vexing that inconstant cash
The constant suitor must abash,   30
Who with excuses vainly pled
Must rue the undisheveled bed,
And that for paltry reasons given
His conscience may remain unriven.

Considerations for Critical Thinking and Writing

1. **FIRST RESPONSE.** To what extent does this poem duplicate Marvell's style? How does it differ?

2. How is De Vries's use of "mistress" different from Marvell's? How does the speaker's complaint in this poem differ from that in "To His Coy Mistress"?

3. Explain how "picaresque" is used in line 7.

4. **CREATIVE RESPONSE.** Choose a poet whose work you know reasonably well or would like to know better and determine what is characteristic about his or her style. Then choose a poem to parody. It's probably best to attempt a short poem or a section of a long work. If you have difficulty selecting an author, you might consider Herrick, Blake, Keats, Dickinson, Whitman, or Frost, as a number of their works are included in this book.

Connection to Another Selection

1. Read Anthony Hecht's "The Dover Bitch" (p. 529), a parody of Arnold's "Dover Beach" (p. 115). Write an essay comparing the effectiveness of Hecht's parody with that of De Vries's "To His Importunate Mistress." Which parody do you prefer? Explain why.

Here's a parody for all seasons — not just Christmas — that brings together two popular icons of our culture.

X. J. KENNEDY (B. 1929)

A Visit from St. Sigmund   *1993*

Freud is just an old Santa Claus.
    — Margaret Mead°

'Twas the night before Christmas, when all through each kid
Not an Ego was stirring, not even an Id.
The hangups were hung by the chimney with care
In hopes that St. Sigmund Freud soon would be there.
The children in scream class had knocked off their screams,   5
Letting Jungian archetypes dance through their dreams,
And Mamma with her bra off and I on her lap
Had just snuggled down when a vast thunderclap
Boomed and from my unconscious arose such a chatter
As Baptist John's teeth made on Salome's platter.   10
Away from my darling I flew like a flash,
Tore straight to the bathroom and threw up, and — *smash!*
Through the windowpane hurtled and bounced on the floor
A big brick — holy smoke, it was hard to ignore.
As I heard further thunderclaps — lo and behold —   15
Came a little psychiatrist eighty years old.
He drove a wheeled couch pulled by five fat psychoses
And the gleam in his eye might induce a hypnosis.
Like subliminal meanings his coursers they came
And, consulting his notebook, he called them by name: 20
"Now Schizo, now Fetish, now Fear of Castration!
On Paranoia! on Penis-fixation!
Ach, yes, that big brick through your glass I should mention:
Just a simple device to compel your attention.
You need, boy, to be in an analyst's power: 25
You talk, I take notes — fifty schillings an hour."
A bag full of symbols he'd slung on his back;
He looked smug as a junk-peddler laden with smack
Or a shrewd politician soliciting votes
And his chinbeard was stiff as a starched billygoat's.   30
Then laying one finger aside of his nose,
He chortled, "What means this? Mein Gott, I suppose
There's a meaning in fingers, in candles und wicks,
In mouseholes und doughnut holes, steeples und sticks.
You see, it's the imminent prospect of sex   35

Margaret Mead (1901–1978): Noted American anthropologist.

That makes all us humans run round till we're wrecks,
Und each innocent infant since people began
Wants to bed with his momma und kill his old man;
So never you fear that you're sick as a swine —
Your hangups are every sane person's und mine.   40
Even Hamlet was hot for his mom — there's the rub;
Even Oedipus Clubfoot was one of the club.
Hmmm, that's humor unconscious." He gave me rib-pokes
And for almost two hours explained phallic jokes.
Then he sprang to his couch, to his crew gave a nod,   45
And away they all flew like the concept of God.
In the worst of my dreams I can hear him shout still,
"Merry Christmas to all! In the mail comes my bill."

CONSIDERATIONS FOR CRITICAL THINKING AND WRITING

1. **FIRST RESPONSE.** What makes Freud a particularly appropriate substitute for Santa Claus? How does this substitute facilitate the poem's humor?

2. What is the tone of this parody? How does the quotation from Margaret Mead help to establish the poem's tone?

3. What do you think is the poet's attitude toward Freud? Cite specific lines to support your point.

4. Is the focus of this parody the Christmas story or Freud? Explain your response.

Picture Poem

By arranging lines into particular shapes, poets can sometimes organize typography into *picture poems* of what they describe. Words have been arranged into all kinds of shapes, from apples to light bulbs. Notice how the shape of this next poem embodies its meaning.

MICHAEL McFEE (B. 1954)

In Medias Res°

1985

His waist
like the plot
thickens, wedding
pants now breathtaking,
belt no longer the cinch   5
it once was, belly's cambium
expanding to match each birthday,
his body a wad of anonymous tissue
swung in the same centrifuge of years
that separates a house from its foundation,   10
undermining sidewalks grim with joggers
and loose-filled graves and families
and stars collapsing on themselves,
no preservation society capable
of plugging entropy's dike,   15
under his zipper's sneer
a belly hibernation-
soft, ready for
the kill.

In Medias Res: A Latin term for a story that begins "in the middle of things."

CONSIDERATIONS FOR CRITICAL THINKING AND WRITING

1. **FIRST RESPONSE.** Explain how the title is related to this poem's shape. How
   is the meaning related?
2. Identify the puns. How do they work in the poem?
3. What is "cambium" (line 6)? Why is the phrase "belly's cambium" especially
   appropriate?
4. What is the tone of this poem? Is it consistent throughout?

Perspectives

ROBERT MORGAN (B. 1944)

On the Shape of a Poem

1983

In the body of the poem, lineation is part flesh and part skeleton, as form is the
towpath along which the burden of content, floating on the formless, is
pulled. All language is both mental and sacramental, is not "real" but is the
working of lip and tongue to subvert the "real." Poems empearl irritating facts
until they become opalescent spheres of moment, not so much résumés of his-
tory as of human faculties working with pain. Every poem is necessarily a frag-
ment empowered by its implicitness. We sing to charm the snake in our spines,

to make it sway with the pulse of the world, balancing the weight of conscious-
ness on the topmost vertebra.

From *Epoch*, Fall/Winter 1983

CONSIDERATIONS FOR CRITICAL THINKING AND WRITING

1. Explain Morgan's metaphors for describing lineation and form in a poem.
   Why are these metaphors useful?
2. Choose one of the poems in this chapter that makes use of a particular
   form and explain how it is "a fragment empowered by its implicitness."

ELAINE MITCHELL (B. 1924)

Form

1994

Is it a corset
or primal wave?
Don't try to force it.

Even endorse it
to shape and deceive.   5
Ouch, too tight a corset.

Take it off. No remorse. It
's an ace up your sleeve.
No need to force it.

Can you make a horse knit?   10
Who would believe?
Consider. Of course, it

might be a resource. Wit,
your grateful slave.
Form. Sometimes you force it,   15

sometimes divorce it
to make it behave.
So don't try to force it.
Respect a good corset.

CONSIDERATIONS FOR CRITICAL THINKING AND WRITING

1. **FIRST RESPONSE.** What is the speaker's attitude toward form?
2. Explain why you think the form of this poem does or does not conform to
   the speaker's advice.
3. Why is the metaphor of a corset a particularly apt image for this poem?

Research the
poets in this chapter at
bedfordstmartins.com/
meyerpoetry.

10

Open Form

> I believe every space and comma is a living part of the poem and has its function, just as every muscle and pore of the body has its function. And the way the lines are broken is a functioning part essential to the poem's life.
> —DENISE LEVERTOV

By permission of David Geier and New Directions.

Many poems, especially those written in the twentieth century, are composed of lines that cannot be scanned for a fixed or predominant meter. Moreover, very often these poems do not rhyme. Known as *free verse* (from the French, *vers libre*), such lines can derive their rhythmic qualities from the repetition of words, phrases, or grammatical structures; the arrangement of words on the printed page; or some other means. In recent years the term **open form** has been used in place of *free verse* to avoid the erroneous suggestion that this kind of poetry lacks all discipline and shape.

Although the following two poems do not use measurable meters, they do have rhythm.

E. E. CUMMINGS (1894–1962)

in Just-   *1923*

in Just-
spring   when the world is mud-
luscious the little
lame balloonman

<pre>
whistles   far   and wee   5

and eddieandbill come
running from marbles and
piracies and it's
spring

when the world is puddle-wonderful   10

the queer
old balloonman whistles
far   and   wee
and bettyandisbel come dancing

from hop-scotch and jump-rope and   15

it's
spring
and

    the

        goat-footed   20

balloonMan   whistles
far
and
wee
</pre>

Explore contexts
for E. E. Cummings
on *LiterActive*.

Considerations for Critical Thinking and Writing

1. **First Response.** What is the effect of this poem's arrangement of words and use of space on the page? How would the effect differ if the text was written out in prose?

2. What is the effect of Cummings's combining the names "eddieandbill" and "bettyandisbel"?

3. The allusion in line 20 refers to Pan, a Greek god associated with nature. How does this allusion add to the meaning of the poem?

Walt Whitman (1819–1892)

From "I Sing the Body Electric"   1855

O my body! I dare not desert the likes of you in other men and women,
    nor the likes of the parts of you,
I believe the likes of you are to stand or fall with the likes of the soul, (and
    that they are the soul,)
I believe the likes of you shall stand or fall with my poems, and that they
    are my poems.
Man's, woman's, child's, youth's, wife's, husband's, mother's, father's,
    young man's, young woman's poems.

Head, neck, hair, ears, drop and tympan of the
    ears.
Eyes, eye-fringes, iris of the eye, eyebrows, and
    the waking or sleeping of the lids,
Mouth, tongue, lips, teeth, roof of the mouth,
    jaws, and the jaw-hinges,
Nose, nostrils of the nose, and the partition,
Cheeks, temples, forehead, chin, throat, back
    of the neck, neck-slue,
Strong shoulders, manly beard, scapula, hind-
    shoulders, and the ample
    side-round of the chest,
Upper-arm, armpit, elbow-socket, lower-arm,
    arm-sinews, arm-bones,
Wrist and wrist-joints, hand, palm, knuckles,
    thumb, forefinger, finger-joints, finger-
    nails,

Courtesy of the Bayley-Whitman Collection
of Ohio Wesleyan University of Delaware,
Ohio.

Broad breast-front, curling hair of the breast,
    breast-bone, breast-side,
Ribs, belly, backbone, joints of the backbone,
Hips, hip-sockets, hip-strength, inward and outward round, man-balls,
    man-root,   15
Strong set of thighs, well carrying the trunk above,
Leg-fibers, knee, knee-pan, upper-leg, under-leg,
Ankles, instep, foot-ball, toes, toe-joints, the heel;
All attitudes, all the shapeliness, all the belongings of my or your body or
    of any one's body, male or female,
The lung-sponges, the stomach-sac, the bowels sweet and clean,   20
The brain in its folds inside the skull-frame,
Sympathies, heart-valves, palate-valves, sexuality, maternity,
Womanhood, and all that is a woman, and the man that comes from
    woman,
The womb, the teats, nipples, breast-milk, tears, laughter, weeping, love-
    looks, love-perturbations and risings,
The voice, articulation, language, whispering, shouting aloud,   25
Food, drink, pulse, digestion, sweat, sleep, walking, swimming,
Poise on the hips, leaping, reclining, embracing, arm-curving and
    tightening,
The continual changes of the flex of the mouth, and around the eyes,
The skin, the sunburnt shade, freckles, hair,
The curious sympathy one feels when feeling with the hand the naked
    meat of the body,   30
The circling rivers the breath, and breathing it in and out,
The beauty of the waist, and thence of the hips, and thence downward
    toward the knees,
The thin red jellies within you or within me, the bones and the marrow
    in the bones,
The exquisite realization of health;
O I say these are not the parts and poems of the body only, but of the soul, 35
O I say now these are the soul!

CONSIDERATIONS FOR CRITICAL THINKING AND WRITING

1. **FIRST RESPONSE.** What informs this speaker's attitude toward the human body?

2. Read the poem aloud. Is it simply a tedious enumeration of body parts, or do the lines achieve some kind of rhythmic cadence?

Perspective

WALT WHITMAN (1819–1892)
On Rhyme and Meter 1855

The poetic quality is not marshaled in rhyme or uniformity or abstract addresses to things nor in melancholy complaints or good precepts, but is the life of these and much else and is in the soul. The profit of rhyme is that it drops seeds of a sweeter and more luxuriant rhyme, and of uniformity that it conveys itself into its own roots in the ground out of sight. The rhyme and uniformity of perfect poems show the free growth of metrical laws and bud from them as unerringly and loosely as lilacs or roses on a bush, and take shapes as compact as the shapes of chestnuts and oranges and melons and pears, and shed the perfume impalpable to form. The fluency and ornaments of the finest poems or music or orations or recitations are not independent but dependent. All beauty comes from beautiful blood and a beautiful brain. If the greatnesses are in conjunction in a man or woman it is enough . . . the fact will prevail through the universe . . . but the gaggery and gilt of a million years will not prevail. Who troubles himself about his ornaments or fluency is lost.

From the preface to the 1855 edition of *Leaves of Grass*

CONSIDERATIONS FOR CRITICAL THINKING AND WRITING

1. According to Whitman, what determines the shape of a poem?
2. Why does Whitman prefer open forms over fixed forms such as the sonnet?
3. Is Whitman's poetry devoid of any structure or shape? Choose one of his poems (listed in the index) to illustrate your answer.

Open form poetry is sometimes regarded as formless because it is unlike the strict fixed forms of a sonnet, villanelle, or sestina. But even though open form poems may not employ traditional meters and rhymes, they still rely on an intense use of language to establish rhythms and relations between meaning and form. Open form poems use the arrangement of words and phrases on the printed page, pauses, line lengths, and other means to create unique forms that express their particular meaning and tone.

Cummings's "in Just-" and the excerpt from Whitman's "I Sing the Body Electric" demonstrate how the white space on a page and rhythmic cadences can be aligned with meaning, but there is one kind of open form poetry that doesn't even look like poetry on a page. A ***prose poem*** is printed as prose and represents, perhaps, the most clear opposite of fixed forms. Here is a brief example.

LOUIS JENKINS (B. 1942)

The Prose Poem 2000

The prose poem is not a real poem, of course. One of the major differences is that the prose poet is simply too lazy or too stupid to break the poem into lines. But all writing, even the prose poem, involves a certain amount of skill, just the way throwing a wad of paper, say, into a wastebasket at a distance of twenty feet, requires a certain skill, a skill that, though it may improve hand-eye coordination, does not lead necessarily to an ability to play basketball. Still, it takes practice and thus gives one a way to pass the time, chucking one paper after another at the basket, while the teacher drones on about the poetry of Tennyson.

CONSIDERATIONS FOR CRITICAL THINKING AND WRITING

1. **FIRST RESPONSE.** What is the effect of this prose poem? Does it have a theme?
2. What, if anything, is poetic in this work?
3. Arrange the lines so that they look like poetry on a page. What determines where you break the lines?

Much of the poetry published today is written in open form; however, many poets continue to take pleasure in the requirements imposed by fixed forms. Some write both fixed form and open form poetry. Each kind offers rewards to careful readers as well. Here are several more open form poems that establish their own unique patterns.

GALWAY KINNELL (B. 1927)

After Making Love We Hear Footsteps 1980

For I can snore like a bullhorn
or play loud music
or sit up talking with any reasonably sober Irishman
and Fergus will only sink deeper
into his dreamless sleep, which goes by all in one flash,   5
but let there be that heavy breathing
or a stifled come-cry anywhere in the house
and he will wrench himself awake
and make for it on the run — as now, we lie together,
after making love, quiet, touching along the length of our bodies,   10

familiar touch of the long-married,
and he appears — in his baseball pajamas, it happens,
the neck opening so small
he has to screw them on, which one day may make him wonder
about the mental capacity of baseball players —   15
and says, "Are you loving and snuggling? May I join?"
He flops down between us and hugs us and snuggles himself to sleep,
his face gleaming with satisfaction at being this very child.

In the half darkness we look at each other
and smile   20
and touch arms across his little, startlingly muscled body —
this one whom habit of memory propels to the ground of his making,
sleeper only the mortal sounds can sing awake,
this blessing love gives again into our arms.

CONSIDERATIONS FOR CRITICAL THINKING AND WRITING

1. **FIRST RESPONSE.** Explore Kinnell's line endings. Why does he break the lines where he does?
2. How does the speaker's language reveal his character?
3. Describe the shift in tone between lines 18 and 19 with the shift in focus from child to adult. How does the use of space here emphasize this shift?
4. Do you think this poem is sentimental? Explain why or why not.

CONNECTION TO ANOTHER SELECTION

1. Discuss how this poem helps to bring into focus the sense of loss Robert Frost evokes in "Home Burial" (p. 361).

KELLY CHERRY (B. 1940)

Alzheimer's   *1990*

He stands at the door, a crazy old man
Back from the hospital, his mind rattling
Like the suitcase, swinging from his hand,
That contains shaving cream, a piggy bank,
A book he sometimes pretends to read,   5
His clothes. On the brick wall beside him
Roses and columbine slug it out for space, claw the mortar.
The sun is shining, as it does late in the afternoon
In England, after rain.
Sun hardens the house, reifies it,   10
Strikes the iron grillwork like a smithy
And sparks fly off, burning in the bushes —
The rosebushes —
While the white wood trim defines solidity in space.

GARY GILDNER (B. 1938)

First Practice   1984

After the doctor checked to see
we weren't ruptured,
the man with the short cigar took us
under the grade school,
where we went in case of attack   5
or storm, and said
he was Clifford Hill, he was
a man who believed dogs
ate dogs, he had once killed
for his country, and if   10
there were any girls present
for them to leave now.
                          No one
left. OK, he said, he said I take
that to mean you are hungry   15
men who hate to lose as much
as I do. OK. Then
he made two lines of us
facing each other,
and across the way, he said,   20
is the man you hate most
in the world,
and if we are to win
that title I want to see how.
But I don't want to see   25
any marks when you're dressed,
he said. He said, *Now.*

CONSIDERATIONS FOR CRITICAL THINKING AND WRITING

1. **FIRST RESPONSE.** Do you recognize this coach? How does he compare with your own experience with sports coaches?

2. Comment on the significance of Clifford Hill's name.

3. Locate examples of irony in the poem and explain how they contribute to the theme.

4. Discuss the effect of line spacing in line 13.

CONNECTION TO ANOTHER SELECTION

1. Write an essay comparing the coach in this poem and the teacher in Judy Page Heitzman's "The Schoolroom on the Second Floor of the Knitting Mill" (p. 508).

MARILYN NELSON WANIEK (B. 1946)
Emily Dickinson's Defunct   *1978*

She used to
pack poems
in her hip pocket.
Under all the
gray old lady   5
clothes she was
dressed for action.
She had hair,
imagine,
in certain places, and   10
believe me
she smelled human
on a hot summer day.
Stalking snakes
or counting   15
the thousand motes
in sunlight
she walked just
like an Indian.
She was New England's   20
favorite daughter,
she could pray
like the devil.
She was a
two-fisted woman,   25
this babe.
All the flies
just stood around
and buzzed
when she died.   30

CONSIDERATIONS FOR CRITICAL THINKING AND WRITING

1. **FIRST RESPONSE.** How does the speaker characterize Dickinson? Explain why this characterization is different from the popular view of Dickinson.

2. How does the diction of the poem serve to characterize the speaker?

3. Discuss the function of the poem's title.

CONNECTIONS TO OTHER SELECTIONS

1. Waniek alludes to at least two other poems in "Emily Dickinson's Defunct." The title refers to E. E. Cummings's "Buffalo Bill 's" (p. 595), and the final lines (27–30) refer to Dickinson's "I heard a Fly buzz—when I died—" (p. 324). Read those poems and write an essay discussing how they affect your reading of Waniek's poem.

Jeffrey Harrison (b. 1957)

Horseshoe Contest   *1999*

East Woodstock, Connecticut
Fourth of July

After the parade
of tractors and fire trucks,
old cars and makeshift floats,
after speeches by
the minister and selectman,   5
after the cakewalk and hayrides
and children's games
are over and the cornet band
has packed up its instruments
and left the gazebo,   10
the crowd on the town
green begins to gather
around the horseshoe pit
where a tournament
has been going on all day   15
and is now down
to the four or five
best players — the same ones
every year, these old guys
who, beneath their feigned   20
insouciance, care about this
more than anything.
The stakes are high:
their names on a plaque,
their pride, their whole idea   25
of who they are,
held onto since high school
when they played football
or ran track — something
unchanging at their core,   30
small but of a certain heft.
Limber as gunslingers
preparing for a showdown,
they step up in pairs
to take their turns   35
pitching the iron shoes,
lofting these emblems
of luck with a skill
both deliberate and
offhand, landing ringer   40
after ringer, metal
clashing against metal,

while the others, those
who entered the contest
just for the hell of it   45
and who dropped out
hours ago, their throws
going wild or just
not good enough, stand
quietly at the sidelines,   50
watching with something close
to awe as their elders
stride with the casual
self-consciousness of heroes,
becoming young again   55
in the crowd's hush
and the flush of suspense,
elevated for these moments
like a horseshoe hanging
in the sunlit air   60
above them, above their lives
as dairymen and farmers,
their bodies moving
with a kind of knowledge
unknown to most of us   65
and too late for most of us
to learn — though I'd give
almost anything
to be able to do anything
that well.   70

CONSIDERATIONS FOR CRITICAL THINKING AND WRITING

1. **FIRST RESPONSE.** How does Harrison economically create a picture of a July 4th celebration in lines 1–10?

2. In what sense are the "stakes . . . high" for the horseshoe tournament players? Why is the tournament important to the speaker?

3. Type out this poem as a prose paragraph. How is the experience of reading the poem different from reading the paragraph? What do the line breaks of the poem contribute to your reading experience?

ROBERT HASS (B. 1941)

A Story about the Body   *1989*

The young composer, working that summer at an artists' colony, had watched her for a week. She was Japanese, a painter, almost sixty, and he thought he was in love with her. He loved her work, and her work was like the way she moved her body, used her hands, looked at him directly when she made amused and considered answers to his questions. One night, walking back from a concert, they came to her door and she turned to him and said, "I think you would like to have me. I would like that too, but I must tell you that I have had a double mastectomy," and when he didn't understand, "I've lost both my breasts." The radiance that he had carried around in his belly and chest cavity — like music — withered very quickly, and he made himself look at her when he said, "I'm sorry. I don't think I could." He walked back to his own cabin through the pines, and in the morning he found a small blue bowl on the porch outside his door. It looked to be full of rose petals, but he found when he picked it up that the rose petals were on top; the rest of the bowl — she must have swept them from the corners of her studio — was full of dead bees.

CONSIDERATIONS FOR CRITICAL THINKING AND WRITING

1. **FIRST RESPONSE.** Why this title? What other potential titles can you come up with that evoke your reading of the poem?

2. What impression about the "young composer" do you derive from the poem?

3. Why are bees very appropriate in the final line rather than, for example, moths?

CONNECTIONS TO OTHER SELECTIONS

1. Discuss the treatments of love in this poem and John Frederick Nims's "Love Poem" (p. 44).

2. Read T. E. Hulme's "On the Differences between Poetry and Prose" (p. 131) and write an essay on what you think Hulme would have to say about "A Story about the Body."

SHARON OLDS (B. 1942)

Rite of Passage 1983

As the guests arrive at my son's party
they gather in the living room —
short men, men in first grade
with smooth jaws and chins.
Hands in pockets, they stand around   5
jostling, jockeying for place, small fights
breaking out and calming. One says to another
How old are you? Six. I'm seven. So?
They eye each other, seeing themselves
tiny in the other's pupils. They clear their   10
throats a lot, a room of small bankers,
they fold their arms and frown. *I could beat you
up,* a seven says to a six,
the dark cake, round and heavy as a
turret, behind them on the table. My son,   15
freckles like specks of nutmeg on his cheeks,

chest narrow as the balsa keel of a
model boat, long hands
cool and thin as the day they guided him
out of me, speaks up as a host   20
for the sake of the group.
We could easily kill a two-year-old,
he says in his clear voice. The other
men agree, they clear their throats
like Generals, they relax and get down to   25
playing war, celebrating my son's life.

CONSIDERATIONS FOR CRITICAL THINKING AND WRITING

1. **FIRST RESPONSE.** In what sense is this birthday party a "Rite of Passage"?
2. How does the speaker transform these six- and seven-year-old boys into men? What is the point of doing so?
3. Comment on the appropriateness of the image of the cake in lines 14–15.
4. Why does the son's claim that "We could easily kill a two-year-old" (line 22) come as such a shock at that point in the poem?

CONNECTION TO ANOTHER SELECTION

1. Discuss the use of irony in "Rite of Passage" and Wilfred Owen's "Dulce et Decorum Est" (p. 122). Which do you think is a more effective antiwar poem? Explain why.

JULIO MARZÁN (B. 1946)

The Translator at the Reception for Latin American Writers
                                                                 1997

Air-conditioned introductions,
then breezy Spanish conversation
fan his curiosity to know
what country I come from.
"Puerto Rico and the Bronx."   5

Spectacled downward eyes
translate disappointment
like a poison mushroom
puffed in his thoughts as if,
after investing a sizable   10
intellectual budget, transporting
a huge cast and camera crew
to film on location
Mayan pyramid grandeur,
indigenes whose ancient gods   15
and comet-tail plumage
inspire a glorious epic

of revolution across a continent,
he received a lurid script
for a social documentary   20
rife with dreary streets
and pathetic human interest,
meager in the profits of high culture.

Understandably he turns,
catches up with the hostess,   25
praising the uncommon quality
of her offerings of cheese.

CONSIDERATIONS FOR CRITICAL THINKING AND WRITING

1. **FIRST RESPONSE.** What is the speaker's attitude toward the person he meets at the reception? What lines in particular lead you to that conclusion?
2. Why is that person so disappointed about "Puerto Rico and the Bronx"?
3. Explain lines 6–23. How do they reveal both the speaker and the person encountered at the reception?
4. Why is the setting of this poem significant?

CAROLINA HOSPITAL (B. 1957)

The Hyphenated Man   *2004*

Do you wake up each day
with an urge for a bagel
with café con leche?°   *with milk*
Do you flip back and forth
through *The Miami Herald* comparing every word   5
to *El Nuevo Herald*?
Do you circle around back alleys
trying to decide between McDonalds and
Pollo Tropical?
Do you feel guilty buying Cuban bread   10
at Publix,
while getting a cheesecake at Sedanos?
At Thanksgiving, do you creep into the kitchen
to put mojito° on the turkey,   *Cuban rum drink*
and then complain at Christmas because   15
there's lechón° instead of turkey?   *pork*
Do you find yourself Two-Stepping
to salsa beat and dancing güaracha
to every other jazz beat?
Does your heart skip a beat for Sonia Braga   20
while longing wistfully for the days of Doris Day?
If so my friend,
then you are the hyphenated man.
Yes, H-Y-P-H-E-N.

The hyphenated man   25
lurks beneath that confident exterior
and it's time you consider
Hyphens Anonymous,
where the confused straddlers find refuge
and solace.   30
They meet once a week,
talk Spanglish to their heart's content,
eat mariquitas° with hot dogs, and   *Cuban dish*
cuban coffee with Dunkin Donuts,
without explanations or alienations   35
Not the twelve step program,
but the three step dilemma.
Join today and
get off the see-saw,
jump off the fence,   40
slide down the hill,
cross the bridge,
get into the circle,
turn from the mirror.
Don't get off the wagon,   45
get on the hyphen.
Do not delay.
Hyphens Anonymous can help you forget
who you are
or better   50
who you wish you could be.

Considerations for Critical Thinking and Writing

1. **FIRST RESPONSE.** What is the speaker's attitude toward the hyphenated man?

2. Is the hyphenated man's life enhanced or diminished by living in two cultures?

3. How do you interpret lines 48–51? Why is the tone of these lines different from the rest of the poem?

Connection to Another Selection

1. Compare the theme of Hospital's poem with that of John Mitchum and Howard Barnes's "The Hyphen" (p. 486).

Robert Morgan (b. 1944)
Overalls   *1990*

Even the biggest man will look
babylike in overalls, bib
up to his neck holding the trousers
high on his belly, with no chafing

at the waist, no bulging over   5
the belt. But it's the pockets on
the chest that are most interesting,
buttons and snaps like medals, badges,
flaps open with careless ease, thin
sheath for the pencil, little pockets   10
and pouches and the main zipper
compartment like a wallet over
the heart and the slit where the watch
goes, an eye where the chain is caught.
Every bit of surface is taken   15
up with patches, denim mesas
and envelopes, a many-level
cloth topography. And below,
the loops for hampers and pliers
like holsters for going armed   20
and armored yet free-handed
into the field another day
for labor's playful war with time.

CONSIDERATIONS FOR CRITICAL THINKING AND WRITING

1. **FIRST RESPONSE.** How does the poem's last line announce its theme?
2. Why is it that the "pockets on / the chest . . . are most interesting" to the speaker?
3. Describe the way images of childhood and adulthood, along with work and war, are interwoven in Morgan's treatment of overalls.

ANONYMOUS

The Frog   *date unknown*

What a wonderful bird the frog are!
When he stand he sit almost;
When he hop he fly almost.
He ain't got no sense hardly;
He ain't got no tail hardly either.
When he sit, he sit on what he ain't got almost.

CONSIDERATIONS FOR CRITICAL THINKING AND WRITING

1. **FIRST RESPONSE.** How is the poem a description of the speaker as well as of a frog?
2. Though this poem is ungrammatical, it does have a patterned structure. How does the pattern of sentences create a formal structure?

TATO LAVIERA (B. 1951)

AmeRícan   *1985*

we gave birth to a new generation,
AmeRícan, broader than lost gold
never touched, hidden inside the
puerto rican mountains.

we gave birth to a new generation,   5
AmeRícan, it includes everything
imaginable you-name-it-we-got-it
society.

we gave birth to a new generation,
AmeRícan salutes all folklores,   10
european, indian, black, spanish,
and anything else compatible:

AmeRícan,   singing to composer pedro flores'° palm
              trees high up in the universal sky!

AmeRícan,   sweet soft spanish danzas gypsies   15
              moving lyrics la *española*° cascabelling   *Spanish*
              presence always singing at our side!

AmeRícan,   beating jíbaro° modern troubadours
              crying guitars romantic continental
              bolero love songs!   20

AmeRícan,   across forth and across back
              back across and forth back
              forth across and back and forth
              our trips are walking bridges!

              it all dissolved into itself, the attempt   25
              was truly made, the attempt was truly
              absorbed, digested, we spit out
              the poison, we spit out the malice,
              we stand, affirmative in action,
              to reproduce a broader answer to the   30
              marginality that gobbled us up abruptly!

AmeRícan,   walking plena-rhythms° in new york,
              strutting beautifully alert, alive,
              many turning eyes wondering,
              admiring!   35

AmeRícan,   defining myself my own way any way many
              ways Am e Rícan, with the big R and the
              accent on the í!

---

13 *pedro flores:* Puerto Rican composer of popular romantic songs.   18 *jíbaro:* A particu-
lar style of music played by Puerto Rican mountain farmers.   32 *plena-rhythms:* African–
Puerto Rican folklore, music, and dance.

AmeRícan,	like the soul gliding talk of gospel
	boogie music!

40

AmeRícan,	speaking new words in spanglish tenements,
	fast tongue moving street corner *"que*
	corta"° talk being invented at the insistence
	of a smile!

that cuts

AmeRícan,	abounding inside so many ethnic english
	people, and out of humanity, we blend
	and mix all that is good!

45

AmeRícan,	integrating in new york and defining our
	own *destino,*° our own way of life,

destiny

AmeRícan,	defining the new america, humane america,
	admired america, loved america, harmonious
	america, the world in peace, our energies
	collectively invested to find other civili-
	zations, to touch God, further and further,
	to dwell in the spirit of divinity!

50

55

AmeRícan,	yes, for now, for i love this, my second
	land, and i dream to take the accent from
	the altercation, and be proud to call
	myself american, in the u.s. sense of the
	word, AmeRícan, America!

60

CONSIDERATIONS FOR CRITICAL THINKING AND WRITING

1. **FIRST RESPONSE.** How does the arrangement of lines communicate a sense of energy and vitality?

2. How does the speaker portray Puerto Ricans living in the United States?

3. How does the poet describe the United States?

CONNECTION TO ANOTHER SELECTION

1. In an essay consider the themes, styles, and tones of "AmeRícan" and Carolina Hospital's "The Hyphenated Man" (p. 281).

PETER MEINKE (B. 1932)
The ABC of Aerobics

1983

Air seeps through alleys and our diaphragms
balloon blackly with this mix of
carbon monoxide and the thousand corrosives a city
doles out free to its constituents;
everyone's jogging through Edgemont Park,
frightened by death and fatty tissue,

5

gasping at the maximal heart rate,
hoping to outlive all the others streaming
in the lanes like lemmings lurching toward their last
jump. I join in despair   10
knowing my arteries jammed with
lint and tobacco, lard and bourbon — my
medical history a noxious marsh:
newts and moles slink through the sodden veins,
owls hoot in the lungs' dark branches;   15
probably I shall keel off the john like
queer Uncle George and lie on the bathroom floor
raging about Shirley Clark, my true love in
seventh grade, God bless her wherever she lives
tied to that turkey who hugely   20
undervalues the beauty of her tiny earlobes, one
view of which (either one: they are both perfect)
would add years to my life and I could skip these
x-rays, turn in my insurance card, and trade
yoga and treadmills and jogging and zen and   25
zucchini for drinking and dreaming of her, breathing hard.

Considerations for Critical Thinking and Writing

1. **FIRST RESPONSE.** How does the title help to establish a pattern throughout the poem? How does the pattern contribute to the poem's meaning?

2. How does the speaker feel about exercise? How do his descriptions of his physical condition serve to characterize him?

3. A primer is a book that teaches children to read or introduces them, in an elementary way, to the basics of a subject. The title "The ABC of Aerobics" indicates that this poem is meant to be a primer. What is it trying to teach us? Is its final lesson serious or ironic?

4. Discuss Meinke's use of humor. Is it effective?

Connections to Other Selections

1. Write an essay comparing the way Sharon Olds connects sex and exercise in "Sex without Love" (p. 93) with Meinke's treatment here.

2. Compare the voice in this poem with that in Galway Kinnell's "After Making Love We Hear Footsteps" (p. 271). Which do you find more appealing? Why?

Found Poem

This next selection is a ***found poem,*** unintentional verse discovered in a nonpoetic context, such as a conversation, news story, or an advertisement. Found poems are playful reminders that the words in poems are very often the language we use every day. Whether such found language should be regarded as a poem is an issue left for you to consider.

Donald Justice (1925–2004)
Order in the Streets *1969*

*(From instructions printed on a child's toy, Christmas 1968, as reported in
the* New York Times)

1. 2. 3.
Switch on.

Jeep rushes
to the scene
of riot 5

Jeep goes
in all directions
by mystery action.

Jeep stops periodically
to turn hood over 10

machine gun appears
with realistic
shooting noise.

After putting down riot,
jeep goes 15
back to the headquarters.

Considerations for Critical Thinking and Writing

1. **FIRST RESPONSE.** What is the effect of arranging these instructions in discrete lines? How are the language and meaning enhanced by this arrangement?

2. **CREATIVE RESPONSE.** Look for phrases or sentences in ads, textbooks, labels, or directions — in anything that might inadvertently contain provocative material that would be revealed by arranging the words in verse lines. You may even discover some patterns of rhyme and rhythm. After arranging the lines, explain why you organized them as you did.

Web Research the poets in this chapter at bedfordstmartins.com/meyerpoetry.

11

Combining the Elements
of Poetry: A Writing Process

In poetry you have a form looking for
a subject and a subject looking for a
form. When they come together
successfully you have a poem.
—W. H. AUDEN

© Bettmann/CORBIS.

THE ELEMENTS TOGETHER

The elements of poetry that you have studied in the first ten chapters of
this book offer a vocabulary and series of perspectives that open up avenues
of inquiry into a poem. As you have learned, there are many potential routes
that you can take. By asking questions, for example, about the speaker, dic-
tion, figurative language, sounds, rhythm, tone, or theme, you clarify your
understanding while simultaneously sensitizing yourself to elements and
issues especially relevant to the poem under consideration. This process of
careful, informed reading allows you to see how the various elements of
the poem reinforce its meanings.

A poem's elements do not exist in isolation, however. They work to-
gether to create a complete experience for the reader. Knowing how the ele-
ments combine helps you understand the poem's structure and to
appreciate it as a whole. Robert Herrick's "Delight in Disorder" (p. 226), for

example, is more easily understood (and the humor of the poem is better appreciated) when meter and rhyme are considered together with the poem's meaning. Musing about how he is more charmed by a naturally disheveled appearance than by those that seem contrived, the speaker lists several attributes of dishevelment and concludes that they

> Do more bewitch me than when art
> Is too precise in every part.

Noticing how the couplet's precise and sing-songy rhythm combines with the solid, obvious, and final rhyme of *art* / *part* helps in understanding what the speaker means by "too precise," as the lines are a little too precise themselves. Noticing this, you may even want to chart how rhythm and rhyme work together throughout the early (more disheveled) lines of the poem. Finding a pattern in the ways the elements work together throughout the poem will help you understand how the poem works.

MAPPING THE POEM

When you write about a poem, you are, in some ways, providing a guide for a place that might otherwise seem unfamiliar and remote. Put simply, writing enables you to chart a work so that you can comfortably move around in it to discuss or write about what interests you. Your paper represents a record and a map of your intellectual journey through the poem, pointing out the things worth noting and your impressions about them. Your role as writer is to offer insights into the challenges, pleasures, and discoveries that the poem harbors. These insights are a kind of sightseeing, as you navigate the various elements of the poem to make some overall point about it.

This chapter shows you how one student, Rose Bostwick, moves through the stages of writing about how a poem's elements combine for a final effect. Included here are Rose's annotated version of the poem, her first response, her informal outline, and the final draft of an explication of John Donne's "Death Be Not Proud." A detailed explanation of what is implicit in a poem, an explication requires a line-by-line examination of the poem. (For more on explication, see page 695 in Chapter 26, "Reading and Writing.") After reviewing the elements of poetry covered in the preceding chapters, Rose read the poem (which follows) several times, paying careful attention to diction, figurative language, irony, symbol, rhythm, sound, and so on. Her final paper is more concerned with the overall effect of the combination of elements than with a line-by-line breakdown, and her annotated version of the poem details her attention to that task. As you read and reread "Death Be Not Proud," keep notes on how *you* think the elements of this poem work together and to what overall effect.

John Donne (1572–1631)

John Donne, now regarded as a major poet of the early seventeenth century, wrote love poems at the beginning of his career but shifted to religious themes after converting from Catholicism to Anglicanism in the early 1590s. Although trained in law, he was also ordained a priest and became dean of St. Paul's Cathedral in London in 1621. The following poem, from "Holy Sonnets," reflects both his religious faith and his ability to create elegant arguments in verse.

Courtesy of the National Portrait Gallery, London.

Death Be Not Proud   *1611*

Death be not proud, though some have callèd thee
Mighty and dreadful, for thou art not so;
For those whom thou think'st thou dost overthrow
Die not, poor Death, nor yet canst thou kill me.
From rest and sleep, which but thy pictures° be,   *images* 5
Much pleasure; then from thee much more must flow,
And soonest our best men with thee do go,
Rest of their bones, and soul's delivery.°   *deliverance*
Thou art slave to Fate, Chance, kings, and desperate men,
And dost with Poison, War, and Sickness dwell;   10
And poppy or charms can make us sleep as well,
And better than thy stroke; why swell'st° thou then?   *swell with pride*
One short sleep past, we wake eternally
And death shall be no more; Death, thou shalt die.

Considerations for Critical Thinking and Writing

1. **First response.** Why doesn't the speaker fear death? Explain why you find the argument convincing or not.

2. How does the speaker compare death with rest and sleep in lines 5–8? What is the point of this comparison?

3. Discuss the poem's rhythm by examining the breaks and end-stopped lines. How does the poem's rhythm contribute to its meaning?

4. What are the signs that this poem is structured as a sonnet?

ASKING QUESTIONS ABOUT THE ELEMENTS

After reading a poem, use the Questions for Responsive Reading and Writing (pp. 61–62) to help you think, talk, and write about any poem. Before you do, though, be sure that you have read the poem several times without worrying actively about interpretation. With poetry, as with all literature, it's important to allow yourself the pleasure of enjoying whatever makes itself apparent to you. On subsequent readings, use the questions to understand and appreciate how the poem works; remember to keep in mind that not all questions will necessarily be relevant to a particular poem. A good starting point is to ask yourself what elements are exemplified in the parts of the poem that particularly interest you. Then ask the Questions for Responsive Reading and Writing that relate to those elements. Finally, as you begin to get a sense of what elements are important to the poem and how those elements fit together, it often helps to put your impressions on paper.

A SAMPLE CLOSE READING

An Annotated Version of "Death Be Not Proud"

As she read the poem closely several times, Rose annotated it with impressions and ideas that would lead to insights on which her analysis would be built. Her close examination of the poem's elements allowed her to understand how its parts contribute to its overall effect; her annotations provide a useful map of her thinking.

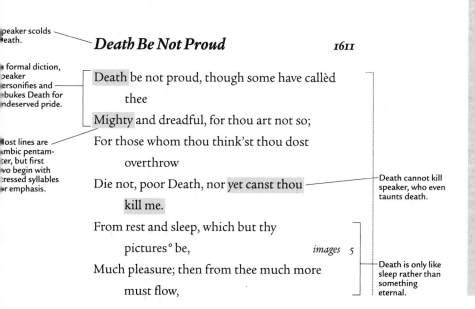

Speaker scolds Death.

A formal diction, speaker personifies and rebukes Death for undeserved pride.

Most lines are iambic pentameter, but first two begin with stressed syllables for emphasis.

Death Be Not Proud   1611

Death be not proud, though some have callèd
    thee
Mighty and dreadful, for thou art not so;
For those whom thou think'st thou dost
    overthrow
Die not, poor Death, nor yet canst thou
    kill me.
From rest and sleep, which but thy
    pictures° be,   *images* 5
Much pleasure; then from thee much more
    must flow,

Death cannot kill speaker, who even taunts death.

Death is only like sleep rather than something eternal.

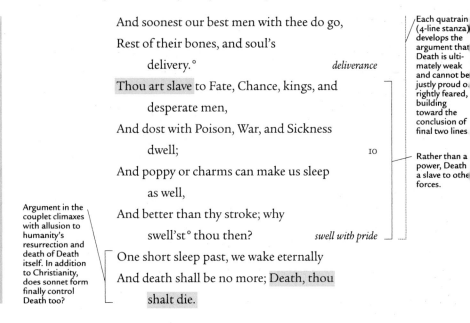

And soonest our best men with thee do go,

Rest of their bones, and soul's

delivery.°   *deliverance*

Thou art slave to Fate, Chance, kings, and

desperate men,

And dost with Poison, War, and Sickness

dwell;   10

And poppy or charms can make us sleep

as well,

And better than thy stroke; why

swell'st° thou then?   *swell with pride*

One short sleep past, we wake eternally

And death shall be no more; Death, thou

shalt die.

Margin annotations:

Each quatrain (4-line stanza) develops the argument that Death is ultimately weak and cannot be justly proud or rightly feared, building toward the conclusion of final two lines.

Rather than a power, Death a slave to other forces.

Argument in the couplet climaxes with allusion to humanity's resurrection and death of Death itself. In addition to Christianity, does sonnet form finally control Death too?

A SAMPLE FIRST RESPONSE

After Rose carefully read "Death Be Not Proud" and had a sense of how the elements work, she took the first step toward a formal explication by writing informally about the relevant elements and addressing the question *Why doesn't the speaker fear death? Explain why you find the argument convincing or not.* Note that at this point, she was not as concerned with textual evidence and detail as she would need to be in her final paper.

I've read the poem "Death Be Not Proud" by John Donne a few times now, and I have a sense of how it works. The poem is a sonnet, and each of the three quatrains presents a piece of the argument that Death should not be proud, because it is not really all-powerful, and may even be a source of pleasure. As a reader, I resist this seeming paradox at first, but I know it must be a trick, a riddle of some sort that the poem will proceed to untangle. I think one of the reasons the poem comes off as such a powerful statement is that Donne at first seems to be playful and paradoxical in his characterizations of Death. He's almost teasing Death. But beneath the teasing tone you feel the strong foundation of the real reason Death should not be proud--Donne's faith in the immortality of the soul. The poem begins to feel more solemn as it progresses, as the hints at the idea of immortality become more clearly articulated.

Donne utilizes two literary conventions to increase the effect of this poem: he uses the convention of personifying death, so that he can address it directly, and he uses the metaphor of death as a kind of sleep. These two things determine the tone and the progression from playful to solemn in the poem.

The last clause of the poem (line 14) plays with the paradoxical-seeming character of what he's been declaring. Ironically, it seems the only thing susceptible to death is death itself. Or, when death becomes powerless is when it only has power over itself.

ORGANIZING YOUR THOUGHTS

Showing in a paper how different elements of a particular poem work together is often quite challenging. While you may have a clear intuitive sense of what elements are important to the poem and how they complement one another, it is important to organize your thoughts in such a way as to make the relationships clear to your audience. The simplest way is to go line by line, but that can quickly become rote for writer and reader. Because you will want to organize your paper in the way that best serves your thesis, it may help to write an informal outline that charts how you think the argument moves. You may find, for example, that the argument is not persuasive if you start with the final lines and go back to the beginning of the poem or passage. However you decide to organize your argument, keep in mind that a single idea, or thesis, will have to run thoughout the entire paper.

A SAMPLE INFORMAL OUTLINE

In her informal outline (following), Rose discovers that her argument works best if she begins at the beginning. Note how, though her later paper concerns itself with how several elements of poetry contribute to the poem's theme and message, her informal outline concerns itself much more with what that message is and how it develops as the poem progresses. She will fill in the details later.

<u>Thesis</u>: *From the very first word, addressing "Death" directly, Donne uses the literary conventions of personifying death and comparing it to sleep to begin an argument that Death should not be proud of its might or dreadfulness. But these two elements of his argument come to be seen as the superficial points when the true reason for death's powerlessness becomes clear. The Christian belief in the immortality of the soul is the reason for death's powerlessness and likeness to sleep.*

<u>Body of essay</u>: *Show how argument proceeds by quatrains from playful address to Death, and statement that Death is much like sleep, its "picture," to statement that Death is "slave" to other forces (and so should not be*

proud of being the mightiest), to the couplet, which articulates clearly the idea of immortality and gives the final paradox, "Death, thou shalt die."

<u>Conclusion</u>: *Donne's faith in the immortality of the soul enables him to "prove" in this argument that Death is truly like its metaphorical representation, sleep. Faith allows him to derive a source for this conventional trope, and it allows him to state his truth in paradoxes. He relies on the conventional idea that death is an end, and a conqueror, and the only all-powerful force, to make the paradoxes that lend his argument the force of mystery — the mystery of faith.*

THE ELEMENTS AND THEME

As you create an informal outline, your understanding of the poem will grow, change, and finally, solidify. You will develop a much clearer sense of what the poem's elements combine to create, and you will have chosen a scheme for organizing your argument. The next step before drafting is to determine the paper's thesis, which will not only keep your paper focused but will also help you center your thoughts. For papers that discuss how the elements of poetry come together, the thesis is a single and concise statement of what the elements combine to create — the idea around which all the elements revolve. In the earlier discussion of Robert Herrick's "Delight in Disorder," for example, the two elements, rhythm and rhyme, work together to create the speaker's self-directed irony. To state this as a thesis, we might say that by making his own rhythm and rhyme "too precise," Herrick's speaker is making fun of himself while complimenting a certain type of woman. (You may ask yourself if he's doing a little flirting.)

Once you understand how all of the elements of the poem fit together and have articulated your understanding in the thesis statement, the next step is to flesh out your argument. By including quotations from the poem to illustrate the points you will be making, you will better explain exactly how each element relates to the others and, more specifically, to your thesis, and you will have created a finished paper that helps readers navigate the poem's geography.

A SAMPLE EXPLICATION

The Use of Conventional Metaphors for Death in John Donne's "Death Be Not Proud"

In Rose's final draft, she focuses on the use of metaphor in "Death Be Not Proud." Her essay provides a coherent reading that relates each line of the poem to the speaker's intense awareness of death. Although the essay discusses each stanza in order, the introductory paragraph provides a brief overview explaining how the poem's metaphor and arguments contribute to its total meaning. In addition, Rose does not hesitate to discuss a line out of sequence when it can be usefully connected to another phrase. She also works quotations into her sentences to support her points. When she adds something to a quotation to clarify it, she encloses her words in brackets so that they will not be mistaken for the poet's, and she uses a slash to indicate line divisions: "soonest . . . with thee do go, / [for] Rest of their bones, and soul's delivery." Finally, because the essay focuses on a short poem, it is not necessary to include line numbers, though they would be required in a study of a longer work. As you read through her final draft, remember that the word *explication* comes from the Latin *explicare*, "to unfold." How successful do you think Rose is at unfolding this poem to reveal how its elements — here ranging from metaphor, structure, meter, personification, paradox, and irony to theme — contribute to its meaning?

Bostwick 1

Rose Bostwick

English 101

Prof. Hart

February 24, 2006

The Use of Conventional Metaphors for Death

in John Donne's "Death Be Not Proud"

In the sonnet that begins "Death be not proud . . ." John Donne argues that death is not "mighty and dreadful," but is more like its metaphorical representation, sleep. Death, Donne puts forth, is even a source of pleasure and rest. The poet builds this argument on two foundations. One is made up of the metaphors and literary conventions for death: death is compared with sleep and is often personified so that it can be addressed directly. The poem is an address to death that at first seems paradoxical and somewhat playful, but which then rises in all the emotion of faith as it reveals the second foundation of the argument--the Christian belief in the immortality of the soul. Seen against the backdrop of this belief, death loses its powerful threat and is seen as only a metaphorical sleep, or rest.

> Thesis providing interpretation of the poem's use of metaphor and how it contributes to the poem's central argument.

Bostwick 2

Discussion of
how form and
meter
contribute to
the poem's
central
argument.

The poem is an ironic argument that proceeds according to the structure of the sonnet form. Each quatrain contains a new development or aspect of the argument, and the final couplet serves as a conclusion. The metrical scheme is mainly iambic pentameter, but in several places in the poem, the stress pattern is altered for emphasis. For example, the first foot of the poem is inverted, so that "Death," the first word, receives the stress. This announces to us right away that Death is being personified and addressed. This inversion also serves to begin the poem energetically and forcefully. The second line behaves in the same way. The first syllable of "Mighty" receives the stress, emphasizing the meaning of the word and its assumed relation to Death.

Discussion
of how
personifica-
tion con-
tributes to
the poem's
central
argument.

This first quatrain offers the first paradox and sets up the argument that death has been conventionally personified with the wrong attributes, might and dreadfulness. The poet tells death not to be proud, "though some have called thee / Mighty and dreadful," because, he says, death is not so. Donne will turn this conventional characterization of death on its head with the paradox of the third and fourth lines: he says the people overthrown by death (as if by a conqueror) "Die not, poor death, nor yet canst thou kill me." These lines establish the paradox of death not being able to cause death.

Discussion
of how
metaphor
of sleep and
idea of
immortality
support the
poem's
central
argument.

The next quatrain will not begin to answer the question of why this paradox is so, but will posit another slight paradox--the idea of death as pleasurable. In lines 5–8, Donne uses the literary convention of describing death as a metaphorical sleep, or rest, to construct the argument that death must give pleasure: "From rest and sleep, which but thy pictures be, / Much pleasure, then from thee much more must flow." At this point, the argument seems almost playful, but is carefully hinting at the solemnity of the deeper foundation of the belief in immortality. The metaphor of sleep for death includes the idea of waking; one doesn't sleep forever. The next two lines put forth the idea that death is pleasurable enough to be desired by "our best men" who "soonest . . . with thee do go, / [for] Rest of their bones, and soul's delivery." This last line comes closer to announcing the true reason for death's powerlessness and pleasure: it is the way to the "soul's delivery" from the body and life on earth, and implicitly, into another, better realm.

Bostwick 3

A new reason for death's powerlessness arises in the next four lines. The poet says to death:

> Thou art slave to Fate, Chance, kings, and desperate men,
>
> And dost with Poison, War, and Sickness dwell;
>
> And poppy or charms can make us sleep as well,
>
> And better than thy stroke; why swell'st thou then?

Donne argues here that there are forces more powerful than death that actually control it. Fate and chance determine when death occurs, and to whom it comes. Kings, with the powers of law and war, can summon death and throw it on whom they wish. And desperate men, murderers or suicides, can also summon death with the strength of their emotions. In lines 11 and 12, Donne again uses the metaphor of death as a kind of sleep, but says that drugs or "charms" give one a better sleep than death. And he asks playfully why death should be so proud, after all these illustrations of its weakness have been given: "why swell'st thou then?"

> *[side note: Discussion of how language and tone contribute to the poem's central argument.]*

Finally, with the last couplet, Donne reveals the true, deeper reason behind his argument that death should not be proud of its power. These lines also offer an explanation of the metaphor for death of sleep, or rest:

> One short sleep past, we wake eternally
>
> And death shall be no more; Death, thou shalt die.

After death, the soul lives on, according to Christian theology and belief. In the Christian heaven, where the soul is immortal, death will no longer exist, and so this last paradox, "Death, thou shalt die," becomes true. Again in this line, a significant inversion of metrical stress occurs. "Death," in the second clause, receives the stress, recalling the first line, emphasizing that it is an address and giving the clause a forceful sense of finality. His belief in the immortality of the soul enables Donne to "prove" in this argument that death is in actuality like its metaphorical representation, sleep. His faith allows him to derive a source for this conventional metaphor and to "disprove" the metaphor of death as an all-powerful conqueror. His Christian beliefs also allow him to state his truth in paradoxes, the mysteries that are justified by the mystery of faith.

> *[side note: Discussion of function of religious faith in the poem and how word order and meter create emphasis.]*

> *[side note: Conclusion supporting thesis in context of poet's beliefs.]*

Before you begin writing your own paper on poetry, review the Suggestions for Approaching Poetry (pp. 40–41) and Chapter 2, "Writing about Poetry," particularly the Questions for Responsive Reading and Writing (pp. 61–62). These suggestions and questions will help you to focus and sharpen your critical thinking and writing. You'll also find help in Chapter 26, "Reading and Writing," which offers a systematic overview of choosing a topic, developing a thesis, and organizing various types of assignments. If you use outside sources for the paper, be sure to acknowledge them adequately by using the conventional documentation procedures detailed in Chapter 27, "The Literary Research Paper."

Web Research John Donne at bedfordstmartins.com/ meyerpoetry.

Approaches
to Poetry

12

A Study of Emily Dickinson

My business is circumference.
— EMILY DICKINSON

In this chapter you'll find a variety of poems by Emily Dickinson so that you can study her work in some depth. While this collection is not wholly representative of her work, it does offer enough poems to suggest some of the techniques and concerns that characterize her writings. The poems speak not only to readers but also to one another. That's natural enough: the more familiar you are with a writer's work, the easier it is to perceive and enjoy the strategies and themes the poet uses. If you are asked to write about a number of poems by the same author, you may find useful the Questions for Writing about an Author in Depth (p. 342) and the sample paper on Dickinson's attitudes toward religious faith in four of her poems (pp. 345–47).

Explore contexts for Emily Dickinson on *LiterActive*.

Emily E, Dickinson.

This daguerreotype of Emily Dickinson, taken shortly after her sixteenth birthday, and the silhouette (*opposite page*), created when she was fourteen years old, are the only authenticated mechanically produced images of the poet.

A BRIEF BIOGRAPHY

Emily Dickinson (1830–1886) grew up in a prominent and prosperous household in Amherst, Massachusetts. Along with her younger sister, Lavinia, and older brother, Austin, she experienced a quiet and reserved family life headed by her father, Edward Dickinson. In a letter to Austin at law school, she once described the atmosphere in her father's house as

(*Below*) This recently discovered print of a mid-1850s daguerreotype, acquired by the scholar Philip F. Gura in 2000, is believed to represent the poet in her twenties.
By permission of the Collection of Philip and Leslie Gura.
(*Right*) The silhouette shows Dickinson at age fourteen.
Amherst College Archives and Special Collections. Used by permission of the Trustees of Amherst College.

Edward Dickinson.

By permission of the Houghton Library. Harvard University Dickinson Collection. © The President and Fellows of Harvard College.

Letter from Emily Dickinson to cousin William Cowper Dickinson.

Courtesy of the Todd-Bingham Picture Collection, Manuscripts and Archives, Yale University Library. © The President and Fellows of Harvard College.

Susan Gilbert Dickinson.

Courtesy of the Todd-Bingham Picture
Collection, Manuscripts and Archives,
Yale University Library.

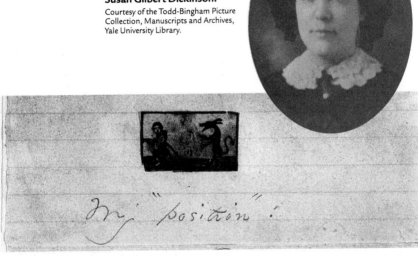

Letter from Emily Dickinson to Susan Gilbert Dickinson.

By permission of the Houghton Library, Harvard University MS Am 1118.5 (B114). © The President and Fellows of Harvard College.

(*Opposite page*) Shown here are the poet's father, Edward Dickinson, a prominent public figure in Amherst, and a page from a letter sent to her cousin William Cowper Dickinson. Emily Dickinson sometimes included in her correspondence images cut from books and magazines. This illustrated letter reads "Life is but a Strife — / T'is a bubble — / T'is a dream — / And man is but a little *boat* / Which paddles down the stream —"

(*This page*) Following a party held next door at the home of Dickinson's brother Austin and sister-in-law Susan (*top*), the poet was reprimanded by her father for staying out too late. The next day, Dickinson wrote a playful note to Susan that included a cartoon poking fun at her father. The note reads: "My 'position'" and features an image of a young person pursued by a dragonlike creature, cut from the Dickinsons' copy of the *New England Primer*, a book of moral lessons. The note concludes: "P.S. — Lest you misapprehend, the unfortunate insect upon the *left* is Myself, while the Reptile upon the *right*, is my more immediate friends, and connections [*sic*]."

"pretty much all sobriety." Her mother, Emily Norcross Dickinson, was not as powerful a presence in her life; she seems not to have been as emotionally accessible as Dickinson would have liked. Her daughter is said to have characterized her as not the sort of mother "to whom you hurry when you are troubled." Both parents raised Dickinson to be a cultured Christian woman who would one day be responsible for a family of her own. Her father attempted to protect her from reading books that might "joggle" her mind, particularly her religious faith, but Dickinson's individualistic instincts and irreverent sensibilities created conflicts that did not allow her to fall into step with the conventional piety, domesticity, and social duty prescribed by her father and the orthodox Congregationalism of Amherst.

The Dickinsons were well known in Massachusetts. Her father was a lawyer and served as the treasurer of Amherst College (a position Austin eventually took up as well), and her grandfather was one of the college's founders. Although nineteenth-century politics, economics, and social issues do not appear in the foreground of her poetry, Dickinson lived in a family environment that was steeped in them: her father was an active town official and served in the General Court of Massachusetts, the state senate, and the U.S. House of Representatives.

Dickinson, however, withdrew not only from her father's public world but also from almost all social life in Amherst. She refused to see most people, and aside from a single year at South Hadley Female Seminary (now Mount Holyoke College), one excursion to Philadelphia and Washington, and several brief trips to Boston to see a doctor about eye problems, she lived all her life in her father's house. She dressed only in white and developed a reputation as a reclusive eccentric. Dickinson selected her own society carefully and frugally. Like her poetry, her relationship to the world was intensely reticent. Indeed, during the last twenty years of her life she rarely left the house.

Though Dickinson never married, she had significant relationships with several men who were friends, confidants, and mentors. She also enjoyed an intimate relationship with her friend Susan Huntington Gilbert, who became her sister-in-law by marrying Austin. Susan and her husband lived next door and were extremely close with Dickinson. Biographers have attempted to find in a number of her relationships the source for the passion of some of her love poems and letters. Several possibilities have been put forward as the person she addressed in three letters as "Dear Master": Benjamin Newton, a clerk in her father's office who talked about books with her; Samuel Bowles, editor of the *Springfield Republican* and friend of the family; the Reverend Charles Wadsworth, a Presbyterian preacher with a reputation for powerful sermons; and an old friend and widower, Judge Otis P. Lord. Despite these speculations, no biographer has been able to identify definitively the object of Dickinson's love. What matters, of course, is not with whom she was in love — if, in fact, there was any single person — but that she wrote about such passions so intensely and convincingly in her poetry.

Choosing to live life internally within the confines of her home, Dickinson brought her life into sharp focus, for she also chose to live within the limitless expanses of her imagination—a choice she was keenly aware of and which she described in one of her poems this way: "I dwell in Possibility—" (p. 322). Her small circle of domestic life did not impinge on her creative sensibilities. Like Henry David Thoreau, she simplified her life so that doing without was a means of being within. In a sense she redefined the meaning of deprivation because being denied something—whether faith, love, literary recognition, or some other desire—provided a sharper, more intense understanding than she would have experienced had she achieved what she wanted: "'Heaven,'" she wrote, "is what I cannot reach!" This poem (p. 316), along with many others, such as "Water, is taught by thirst" (p. 313) and "Success is counted sweetest / By those who ne'er succeed" (p. 312), suggests just how persistently she saw deprivation as a way of sensitizing herself to the value of what she was missing. For Dickinson, hopeful expectation was always more satisfying than achieving a golden moment. Perhaps that's one reason she was so attracted to John Keats's poetry (see, for example, his "Ode on a Grecian Urn," p. 96).

Dickinson enjoyed reading Keats as well as Emily and Charlotte Brontë; Robert and Elizabeth Barrett Browning; Alfred, Lord Tennyson; and George Eliot. Even so, these writers had little or no effect on the style of her writing. In her own work she was original and innovative, but she did draw on her knowledge of the Bible, classical myths, and Shakespeare for allusions and references in her poetry. She also used contemporary popular church hymns, transforming their standard rhythms into free-form hymn meters. Among American writers she appreciated Ralph Waldo Emerson and Thoreau, but she apparently felt Walt Whitman was better left unread. She once mentioned to Thomas Wentworth Higginson, a leading critic with whom she corresponded about her poetry, that as for Whitman "I never read his Book—but was told that he was disgraceful" (for the kind of Whitman poetry she had been warned against, see his "I Sing the Body Electric," p. 268). Nathaniel Hawthorne, however, intrigued her with his faith in the imagination and his dark themes: "Hawthorne appals—entices," a remark that might be used to describe her own themes and techniques.

AN INTRODUCTION TO HER WORK

Today, Dickinson is regarded as one of America's greatest poets, but when she died at the age of fifty-six after devoting most of her life to writing poetry, her nearly two thousand poems—only a dozen of which were published, anonymously, during her lifetime—were unknown except to a small number of friends and relatives. Dickinson was not recognized as a major poet until the twentieth century, when modern readers ranked her as a major new voice whose literary innovations were unmatched by any other nineteenth-century poet in the United States.

Dickinson neither completed many poems nor prepared them for publication. She wrote her drafts on scraps of paper, grocery lists, and the backs of recipes and used envelopes. Early editors of her poems took the liberty of making them more accessible to nineteenth-century readers when several volumes of selected poems were published in the 1890s. The poems were made to appear like traditional nineteenth-century verse by assigning them titles, rearranging their syntax, normalizing their grammar, and regularizing their capitalizations. Instead of dashes editors used standard punctuation; instead of the highly elliptical telegraphic lines so characteristic of her poems editors added articles, conjunctions, and prepositions to make them more readable and in line with conventional expectations. In addition, the poems were made more predictable by organizing them into categories such as friendship, nature, love, and death. Not until 1955, when Thomas Johnson published Dickinson's complete works in a form that attempted to be true to her manuscript versions, did readers have the opportunity to see the full range of her style and themes.

Like that of Robert Frost, Dickinson's popular reputation has sometimes relegated her to the role of a New England regionalist who writes quaint uplifting verses that touch the heart. In 1971 that image was mailed first class all over the country by the U.S. Postal Service. In addition to issuing a commemorative stamp featuring a portrait of Dickinson, the Postal Service affixed the stamp to a first-day-of-issue envelope that included an engraved rose and one of her poems. Here's the poem chosen from among the nearly two thousand she wrote:

If I can stop one Heart from breaking   *c. 1864*

If I can stop one Heart from breaking
I shall not live in vain
If I can ease one Life the Aching
or cool one Pain

Or help one fainting Robin
Unto his Nest again
I shall not live in Vain.

This is typical not only of many nineteenth-century popular poems but also of the kind of verse that can be found in contemporary greeting cards. The speaker tells us what we imagine we should think about and makes the point simply with a sentimental image of a "fainting Robin." To point out that robins don't faint or that altruism isn't necessarily the only rule of conduct by which one should live one's life is to make trouble for this poem. Moreover, its use of language is unexceptional; the metaphors used, like that robin, are a bit weary. If this poem were characteristic of Dickinson's poetry, the U.S. Postal Service probably would not have been urged to issue a stamp in her honor, nor would you be reading her poems in this anthology or many others. Here's a poem by Dickinson that is more typical of her writing:

If I shouldn't be alive *c. 1860*

If I shouldn't be alive
When the Robins come,
Give the one in Red Cravat,
A Memorial crumb.

If I couldn't thank you,
Being fast asleep,
You will know I'm trying
With my Granite lip!

This poem is more representative of Dickinson's sensibilities and techniques. Although the first stanza sets up a rather mild concern that the speaker might not survive the winter (a not uncommon fear for those who fell prey to pneumonia, for example, during Dickinson's time), the concern can't be taken too seriously — a gentle humor lightens the poem when we realize that all robins have red cravats and are therefore the speaker's favorite. Furthermore, the euphemism that describes the speaker "Being fast asleep" in line 6 makes death seem not so threatening after all. But the sentimental expectations of the first six lines — lines that could have been written by any number of popular nineteenth-century writers — are dashed by the penultimate word of the last line. *Granite* is the perfect word here because it forces us to reread the poem and to recognize that it's not about feeding robins or offering a cosmetic treatment of death; rather, it's a bone-chilling description of a corpse's lip that evokes the cold, hard texture and grayish color of tombstones. These lips will never say "thank you" or anything else.

Instead of the predictable rhymes and sentiments of "If I can stop one Heart from breaking," this poem is unnervingly precise in its use of language and tidily points out how much emphasis Dickinson places on an individual word. Her use of near rhyme with "asleep" and "lip" brilliantly mocks a euphemistic approach to death by its jarring dissonance. This is a better poem, not because it's grim or about death, but because it demonstrates Dickinson's skillful use of language to produce a shocking irony.

Dickinson found irony, ambiguity, and paradox lurking in the simplest and commonest experiences. The materials and subject matter of her poetry are quite conventional. Her poems are filled with robins, bees, winter light, household items, and domestic duties. These materials represent the range of what she experienced in and around her father's house. She used them because they constituted so much of her life and, more important, because she found meanings latent in them. Though her world was simple, it was also complex in its beauties and its terrors. Her lyric poems capture impressions of particular moments, scenes, or moods, and she characteristically focuses on topics such as nature, love, immortality, death, faith, doubt, pain, and the self.

Though her materials were conventional, her treatment of them was innovative because she was willing to break whatever poetic conventions stood in the way of the intensity of her thought and images. Her conciseness, brevity, and wit are tightly packed. Typically she offers her observations via one or two images that reveal her thought in a powerful manner. She once characterized her literary art by writing "My business is circumference." Her method is to reveal the inadequacy of declarative statements by evoking qualifications and questions with images that complicate firm assertions and affirmations. In one of her poems she describes her strategies this way: "Tell all the Truth but tell it slant—/ Success in Circuit lies." This might well stand as a working definition of Dickinson's aesthetics and is embodied in the following poem:

The Thought beneath so slight a film —   *c. 1860*

The Thought beneath so slight a film —
Is more distinctly seen —
As laces just reveal the surge —
Or Mists — the Apennine°   *Italian mountain range*

Paradoxically, "Thought" is more clearly understood precisely because a slight "film"—in this case language—covers it. Language, like lace, enhances what it covers and reveals it all the more—just as a mountain range is more engaging to the imagination if it is covered in mists rather than starkly presenting itself. Poetry for Dickinson intensifies, clarifies, and organizes experience.

Dickinson's poetry is challenging because it is radical and original in its rejection of most traditional nineteenth-century themes and techniques. Her poems require active engagement from the reader because she seems to leave out so much with her elliptical style and remarkable contracting metaphors. But these apparent gaps are filled with meaning if we are sensitive to her use of devices such as personification, allusion, symbolism, and startling syntax and grammar. Because her use of dashes is sometimes puzzling, it helps to read her poems aloud to hear how carefully the words are arranged. What might initially seem intimidating on a silent page can surprise the reader with meaning when heard. It's also worth keeping in mind that Dickinson was not always consistent in her views and that they can change from poem to poem, depending on how she felt at a given moment. For example, her definition of religious belief in " 'Faith' is a fine invention" (p. 343) reflects an ironically detached wariness in contrast to the faith embraced in "I never saw a Moor —" (p. 344). Dickinson was less interested in absolute answers to questions than she was in examining and exploring their "circumference."

Because Dickinson's poems are all relatively brief (none is longer than fifty lines), they invite browsing and sampling, but perhaps a useful way into their highly metaphoric and witty world is this "how to" poem that reads almost like a recipe:

To make a prairie it takes a clover and one bee   *date unknown*

To make a prairie it takes a clover and one bee,
One clover, and a bee,
And revery.
The revery alone will do,
If bees are few.

This quiet but infinite claim for a writer's imagination brings together the range of ingredients in Dickinson's world of domestic and ordinary natural details. Not surprisingly, she deletes rather than adds to the recipe, because the one essential ingredient is the writer's creative imagination. *Bon appétit.*

Chronology

1830	Born December 10 in Amherst, Massachusetts.
1840	Starts her first year at Amherst Academy.
1847–48	Graduates from Amherst Academy and enters South Hadley Female Seminary (now Mount Holyoke College).
1855	Visits Philadelphia and Washington, D.C.
1857	Ralph Waldo Emerson lectures in Amherst.
1862	Starts corresponding with Thomas Wentworth Higginson, asking for advice about her poems.
1864	Visits Boston for eye treatments.
1870	Higginson visits her in Amherst.
1873	Higginson visits her for a second and final time.
1874	Her father dies in Boston.
1875	Her mother suffers from paralysis.
1882	Her mother dies.

1886	Dies on May 15 in Amherst, Massachusetts.
1890	First edition of her poetry, edited by Mabel Loomis Todd and Thomas Wentworth Higginson, is published.
1955	Thomas H. Johnson publishes *The Poems of Emily Dickinson* in three volumes, thereby making available her poetry known to that date.

Success is counted sweetest   *c. 1859*

Success is counted sweetest
By those who ne'er succeed.
To comprehend a nectar
Requires sorest need.

Not one of all the purple Host   5
Who took the Flag today
Can tell the definition
So clear of Victory

As he defeated — dying —
On whose forbidden ear   10
The distant strains of triumph
Burst agonized and clear!

CONSIDERATIONS FOR CRITICAL THINKING AND WRITING

1. **FIRST RESPONSE.** How is "success" defined in this poem? To what extent does that definition agree with your own understanding of the word?
2. What do you think is meant by the use of "comprehend" in line 3? How can a nectar be comprehended?
3. Why do the defeated understand victory better than the victorious?
4. Discuss the effect of the poem's final line.

CONNECTION TO ANOTHER SELECTION

1. In an essay compare the themes of this poem with those of John Keats's "Ode on a Grecian Urn" (p. 96).

These are the days when Birds come back —   *c. 1859*

These are the days when Birds come back —
A very few — a Bird or two —
To take a backward look.

These are the days when skies resume
The old — old sophistries   of June —   5
A blue and gold mistake.

Oh fraud that cannot cheat the Bee —
Almost thy plausibility
Induces my belief.

Till ranks of seeds their witness bear —   10
And softly thro' the altered air
Hurries a timid leaf.

Of Sacrament of summer days,
Oh Last Communion   in the Haze —
Permit a child to join.   15

The sacred emblems to partake —
Thy consecrated bread to take
And thine immortal wine!

CONSIDERATIONS FOR CRITICAL THINKING AND WRITING

1. **FIRST RESPONSE.** This poem was long known by the title "Indian Summer" (supplied by an unauthorized editor). How does an awareness of this bit of information affect your reading of the poem?

2. In what sense are "These . . . days" regarded as a "fraud" by the speaker?

3. Discuss the significance of the religious allusions in stanzas 5 and 6. What, finally, do you think is the speaker's attitude toward Indian summer?

Water, is taught by thirst   *c. 1859*

Water, is taught by thirst.
Land — by the Oceans passed.
Transport — by throe —
Peace — by its battles told —
Love, by Memorial Mold —
Birds, by the Snow.

CONSIDERATIONS FOR CRITICAL THINKING AND WRITING

1. **FIRST RESPONSE.** Which image in the poem do you find most powerful? Explain why.

2. How is the paradox of each line of the poem resolved? How is the first word of each line "taught" by the phrase that follows it?

3. **CREATIVE RESPONSE.** Try your hand at writing similar lines in which something is "taught."

CONNECTIONS TO OTHER SELECTIONS

1. What does this poem have in common with "Success is counted sweetest" (p. 312) ? Which poem do you think is more effective? Explain why.

2. How is the crucial point of this poem related to "I like a look of Agony," (p. 317)?

Safe in their Alabaster Chambers —

1859 version

Safe in their Alabaster Chambers —
Untouched by Morning
And untouched by Noon —
Sleep the meek members of the Resurrection —
Rafter of satin,   5
And Roof of stone.

Light laughs the breeze
In her Castle above them —
Babbles the Bee in a stolid Ear,
Pipe the Sweet Birds in ignorant cadence —   10
Ah, what sagacity perished here!

Safe in their Alabaster Chambers —

1861 version

Safe in their Alabaster Chambers —
Untouched by Morning —
And untouched by Noon —
Lie the meek members of the Resurrection —
Rafter of Satin — and Roof of Stone!   5

Grand go the Years — in the Crescent — above them —
Worlds scoop their arcs —
And Firmaments — row —
Diadems — drop — and Doges° — surrender —
Soundless as dots — on a Disc of Snow —   10

9 *Doges:* Chief magistrates of Venice from the twelfth to the sixteenth centuries.

CONSIDERATIONS FOR CRITICAL THINKING AND WRITING

1. **FIRST RESPONSE.** Dickinson permitted the 1859 version of this poem, entitled "The Sleeping," to be printed in the *Springfield Republican.* The second version she sent privately to Thomas Wentworth Higginson. Why do you suppose she would agree to publish the first but not the second version?

2. Are there any significant changes in the first stanzas of the two versions? If you answered yes, explain the significance of the changes.

3. Describe the different kinds of images used in the two second stanzas. How do those images affect the tones and meanings of those stanzas?

4. Discuss why you prefer one version of the poem to the other.

CONNECTIONS TO OTHER SELECTIONS

1. Compare the theme in the 1861 version with the theme of Robert Frost's "Design" (p. 373).

2. In an essay discuss the attitude toward death in the 1859 version and in "Apparently with no surprise" (p. 344).

Portraits are to daily faces

c. 1860

Portraits are to daily faces
As an Evening West,
To a fine, pedantic sunshine —
In a satin Vest!

CONSIDERATIONS FOR CRITICAL THINKING AND WRITING

1. **FIRST RESPONSE.** Dickinson once described her literary art this way: "My business is circumference." Does this poem fit her characterization of her poetry?

2. How is the basic strategy of this poem similar to the following statement: "Doorknob is to door as button is to sweater"?

3. Identify the four metonymies in the poem. Pay close attention to their connotative meanings.

4. If you don't know the meaning of "pedantic," look it up in a dictionary. How does its meaning affect your reading of "fine"?

CONNECTIONS TO OTHER SELECTIONS

1. Compare Dickinson's view of poetry in this poem with Robert Francis's perspective in "Catch" (p. 28). What important similarities and differences do you find?

2. Write an essay describing Robert Frost's strategy in "Mending Wall" (p. 359) or "Birches" (p. 365) as the business of circumference.

3. How is the theme of this poem related to the central idea in "The Thought beneath so slight a film —" (p. 310)?

4. Compare the use of the word "fine" here with its use in "'Faith' is a fine invention" (p. 343).

Some keep the Sabbath going to Church —

c. 1860

Some keep the Sabbath going to Church —
I keep it, staying at Home —
With a Bobolink for a Chorister —
And an Orchard, for a Dome —

Some keep the Sabbath in Surplice°   *holy robes*   5
I just wear my Wings —
And instead of tolling the Bell, for Church,
Our little Sexton — sings.

God preaches, a noted Clergyman —
And the sermon is never long,   10
So instead of getting to Heaven, at last —
I'm going, all along.

CONSIDERATIONS FOR CRITICAL THINKING AND WRITING

1. **FIRST RESPONSE.** What is the effect of referring to "Some" people?
2. Characterize the speaker's tone.
3. How does the speaker distinguish himself or herself from those who go to church?
4. How might "Surplice" be read as a pun?
5. According to the speaker, how should the Sabbath be observed?

CONNECTION TO ANOTHER SELECTION

1. Write an essay that discusses nature in this poem and in Walt Whitman's "When I Heard the Learn'd Astronomer" (p. 629).

"Heaven" — is what I cannot reach! c. 1861

"Heaven" — is what I cannot reach!
The Apple on the Tree —
Provided it do hopeless — hang —
That — "Heaven" is — to Me!

The Color, on the Cruising Cloud —   5
The interdicted Land —
Behind the Hill — the House behind —
There — Paradise — is found!

Her teasing Purples — Afternoons —
The credulous — decoy —   10
Enamored — of the Conjuror —
That spurned us — Yesterday!

CONSIDERATIONS FOR CRITICAL THINKING AND WRITING

1. **FIRST RESPONSE.** How does the speaker define heaven? How does that definition compare with conventional views of heaven?
2. Look up the myth of Tantalus and explain the allusion in line 3.
3. Given the speaker's definition of heaven, how do you think he or she would describe hell?

CONNECTIONS TO OTHER SELECTIONS

1. Write an essay that discusses desire in this poem and in "Water, is taught by thirst" (p. 313).
2. Discuss the speaker's attitudes toward pleasure in this poem and in Sharon Olds's "Last Night" (p. 85).

I reason, Earth is short —

c. 1862

I reason, Earth is short —
And Anguish — absolute —
And many hurt,
But, what of that?

I reason, we could die —   5
The best Vitality
Cannot excel Decay,
But, what of that?

I reason, that in Heaven —
Somehow, it will be even —   10
Some new Equation, given —
But, what of that?

CONSIDERATIONS FOR CRITICAL THINKING AND WRITING

1. **FIRST RESPONSE.** What attitudes does the speaker have toward mortality and immortality?
2. Paraphrase each of the stanzas and explain how they are thematically related to one another.
3. Discuss the effects of the poem's repeated lines.
4. **CRITICAL STRATEGIES.** Read the section on critical thinking (pp. 643–46) in Chapter 25, "Critical Strategies for Reading," and research critical commentary on this poem. Write an essay describing the range of interpretations that you find. Which interpretation do you think is the most convincing? Why?

What Soft — Cherubic Creatures —

1862

What Soft — Cherubic Creatures —
These Gentlewomen are —
One would as soon assault a Plush —
Or violate a Star —

Such Dimity° Convictions —   *sheer cotton fabric* 5
A Horror so refined
Of freckled Human Nature —
Of Deity — ashamed —

It's such a common — Glory —
A Fisherman's — Degree —   10
Redemption — Brittle Lady —
Be so — ashamed of Thee —

CONSIDERATIONS FOR CRITICAL THINKING AND WRITING

1. **FIRST RESPONSE.** Characterize the "Gentlewomen" in this poem.
2. How do the sounds produced in the first line help to reinforce their meaning?

Manuscript page for "What Soft—Cherubic Creatures—" (p. 319), taken from one of Dickinson's forty fascicles—small booklets hand-sewn with white string that contained her poetry as well as other miscellaneous writings. These fascicles are important for Dickinson scholars, as this manuscript page makes clear: her style to some extent resists translation into the conventions of print.

This was a Poet—It is That

c. 1862

This was a Poet—It is That
Distills amazing sense
From ordinary Meanings—
And Attar so immense

From the familiar species   5
That perished by the Door—
We wonder it was not Ourselves
Arrested it—before—

Of Pictures, the Discloser—
The Poet—it is He—   10
Entitles Us—by Contrast—
To ceaseless Poverty—

Of Portion—so unconscious—
The Robbing—could not harm—
Himself—to Him—a Fortune—   15
Exterior—to Time—

CONSIDERATIONS FOR CRITICAL THINKING AND WRITING

1. **FIRST RESPONSE.** According to the speaker, what powers does a poet have? Why are these powers important?
2. Explain the metaphors of "Poverty" (line 12) and "Fortune" (line 15) and how they contribute to the poem's theme.

CONNECTIONS TO OTHER SELECTIONS

1. Write an essay about a life lived in imagination as depicted in this poem and in "I dwell in Possibility—" (p. 322).
2. Discuss "A Bird came down the Walk—" (p. 187) as an example of a poem that "Distills amazing sense / From ordinary Meanings—" (lines 2–3).

After great pain, a formal feeling comes —

c. 1862

After great pain, a formal feeling comes—
The Nerves sit ceremonious, like Tombs—
The stiff Heart questions was it He, that bore,
And Yesterday, or Centuries before?

The Feet, mechanical, go round—   5
Of Ground, or Air, or Ought—
A Wooden way
Regardless grown,
A Quartz contentment, like a stone—

This is the Hour of Lead — 10
Remembered, if outlived,
As Freezing persons, recollect the Snow —
First — Chill — then Stupor — then the letting go —

CONSIDERATIONS FOR CRITICAL THINKING AND WRITING

1. **FIRST RESPONSE.** What do you think has caused the speaker's pain?

2. How does the rhythm of the lines create a slow, somber pace?

3. Discuss why "the Hour of Lead" (line 10) could serve as a useful title for this poem.

CONNECTIONS TO OTHER SELECTIONS

1. How might this poem be read as a kind of sequel to "The Bustle in a House" (p. 328)?

2. Write an essay that discusses this poem in relation to Robert Frost's "Home Burial" (p. 361).

I heard a Fly buzz — when I died — c. 1862

I heard a Fly buzz — when I died —
The Stillness in the Room
Was like the Stillness in the Air —
Between the Heaves of Storm —

The Eyes around — had wrung them dry — 5
And Breaths were gathering firm
For that last Onset — when the King
Be witnessed — in the Room —

I willed my Keepsakes — Signed away
What portion of me be 10
Assignable — and then it was
There interposed a Fly —

With Blue — uncertain stumbling Buzz —
Between the light — and me —
And then the Windows failed — and then 15
I could not see to see —

CONSIDERATIONS FOR CRITICAL THINKING AND WRITING

1. **FIRST RESPONSE.** What was expected to happen "when the King" was "witnessed"? What happened instead?

2. Why do you think Dickinson chooses a fly rather than perhaps a bee or gnat?

3. What is the effect of the last line? Why not end the poem with "I could not see" instead of the additional "to see"?

4. Discuss the sounds in the poem. Are there any instances of onomatopoeia?

CONNECTIONS TO OTHER SELECTIONS

1. Contrast the symbolic significance of the fly with the spider in Walt Whitman's "A Noiseless Patient Spider" (p. 149).

2. Consider the meaning of "light" in this poem and in "There's a certain Slant of light" (p. 696).

One need not be a Chamber — to be Haunted —   *c. 1863*

One need not be a Chamber — to be Haunted —
One need not be a House —
The Brain has Corridors — surpassing
Material Place —

Far safer, of a Midnight Meeting   5
External Ghost
Than its interior Confronting —
That Cooler Host.

Far safer, through an Abbey gallop,
The Stones a'chase —   10
Than Unarmed, one's a'self encounter —
In lonesome Place —

Ourself behind ourself, concealed —
Should startle most —
Assassin hid in our Apartment   15
Be Horror's least.

The Body — borrows a Revolver —
He bolts the Door —
O'erlooking a superior spectre —
Or More —   20

CONSIDERATIONS FOR CRITICAL THINKING AND WRITING

1. **FIRST RESPONSE.** Paraphrase the poem. Which stanza is most difficult to paraphrase? Why?

2. What is the poem's controlling metaphor? Explain why you think it is effective or not.

3. What is the "superior spectre" in line 19?

CONNECTIONS TO OTHER SELECTIONS

1. Compare and contrast this poem with Edgar Allan Poe's "The Haunted Palace" (p. 159) and Jim Stevens's "Schizophrenia" (p. 148). In an essay explain which poem you find the most frightening.

Because I could not stop for Death —   *c. 1863*

Because I could not stop for Death —
He kindly stopped for me —
The Carriage held but just Ourselves —
And Immortality.

We slowly drove — He knew no haste   5
And I had put away
My labor and my leisure too,
For His Civility —

We passed the School, where Children strove
At Recess — in the Ring —   10
We passed the Fields of Gazing Grain —
We passed the Setting Sun —

Or rather — He passed Us —
The Dews drew quivering and chill —
For only Gossamer, my Gown —   15
My Tippet° — only Tulle —   shawl

We paused before a House that seemed
A Swelling of the Ground —
The Roof was scarcely visible —
The Cornice — in the Ground —   20

Since then — 'tis Centuries — and yet
Feels shorter than the Day
I first surmised the Horses' Heads
Were toward Eternity —

CONSIDERATIONS FOR CRITICAL THINKING AND WRITING

1. **FIRST RESPONSE.** Why couldn't the speaker "stop for Death"?

2. How is death personified in this poem? How does the speaker respond to him? Why are they accompanied by Immortality?

3. What is the significance of the things they "passed" in the third stanza?

4. What is the "House" in lines 17–20?

5. Discuss the rhythm of the lines. How, for example, is the rhythm of line 14 related to its meaning?

CONNECTIONS TO OTHER SELECTIONS

1. Compare the tone of this poem with that of Dickinson's "Apparently with no surprise" (p. 344).

2. Write an essay comparing Dickinson's view of death in this poem and in "If I shouldn't be alive" (p. 309). Which poem is more powerful for you? Explain why.

I felt a Cleaving in my Mind —

c. 1864

I felt a Cleaving in my Mind —
As if my Brain had split —
I tried to match it — Seam by Seam —
But could not make them fit.

The thought behind, I strove to join
Unto the thought before —
But Sequence ravelled out of Sound
Like Balls — upon a Floor.

CONSIDERATIONS FOR CRITICAL THINKING AND WRITING

1. **FIRST RESPONSE.** What is going on in the speaker's mind?
2. What is the poem's controlling metaphor? Describe the simile in lines 7 and 8. How does it clarify further the first stanza?
3. Discuss the rhymes. How do they reinforce meaning?

CONNECTION TO ANOTHER SELECTION

1. Compare the power of the speaker's mind described here with the power of imagination described in "To make a prairie it takes a clover and one bee" (p. 311).

A Light exists in Spring

c. 1864

A Light exists in Spring
Not present on the Year
At any other period —
When March is scarcely here

A Color stands abroad   5
On Solitary Fields
That Science cannot overtake
But Human Nature feels.

It waits upon the Lawn,
It shows the furthest Tree   10
Upon the furthest Slope you know
It almost speaks to you.

Then as Horizons step
Or Noons report away
Without the Formula of sound   15
It passes and we stay —

A quality of loss
Affecting our Content
As Trade had suddenly encroached
Upon a Sacrament.   20

CONSIDERATIONS FOR CRITICAL THINKING AND WRITING

1. **FIRST RESPONSE.** Based on Dickinson's description, how would you characterize the nature of the light on a New England March day? How is that light different from that of a summer's day?
2. What kinds of feelings are evoked in the speaker by the light?
3. How are "Science" and "Trade" depicted in contrast to what "Human Nature feels"?

CONNECTION TO ANOTHER SELECTION

1. Compare Dickinson's thematic use of light in this poem and in "There's a certain Slant of light" (p. 696).

Oh Sumptuous moment   *c. 1868*

Oh Sumptuous moment
Slower go
That I may gloat on thee —
'Twill never be the same to starve
Now I abundance see —

Which was to famish, then or now —
The difference of Day
Ask him unto the Gallows led —
With morning in the sky

CONSIDERATIONS FOR CRITICAL THINKING AND WRITING

1. **FIRST RESPONSE.** How do the sounds of the first stanza contribute to its meaning?
2. What kind of moment do you imagine the speaker is describing?
3. How do the final three lines shed light on the meaning of lines 1-6?

CONNECTIONS TO OTHER SELECTIONS

1. Compare and contrast the themes of this poem, "Water, is taught by thirst" (p. 313), and "'Heaven' — is what I cannot reach!" (p. 316).

The Bustle in a House   *c. 1866*

The Bustle in a House
The Morning after Death
Is solemnest of industries
Enacted upon Earth —

The Sweeping up the Heart
And putting Love away
We shall not want to use again
Until Eternity.

CONSIDERATIONS FOR CRITICAL THINKING AND WRITING

1. **FIRST RESPONSE.** What is the relationship between love and death in this poem?
2. Why do you think mourning (notice the pun in line 2) is described as industry?
3. Discuss the tone of the poem's ending. Consider whether you think it is hopeful, sad, resigned, or some other mood.

CONNECTIONS TO OTHER SELECTIONS

1. Compare this poem with "After great pain, a formal feeling comes—" (p. 323). Which poem is, for you, a more powerful treatment of mourning?
2. How does this poem qualify "I like a look of Agony," (p. 317)? Does it contradict the latter poem? Explain why or why not.

Tell all the Truth but tell it slant—   c. 1868

Tell all the Truth but tell it slant—
Success in Circuit lies
Too bright for our infirm Delight
The Truth's superb surprise

As Lightning to the Children eased
With explanation kind
The Truth must dazzle gradually
Or every man be blind—

CONSIDERATIONS FOR CRITICAL THINKING AND WRITING

1. **FIRST RESPONSE.** What do you think the first line means? Why should truth be told "slant" and circuitously?
2. How does the second stanza explain the first?
3. How is this poem an example of its own theme?

CONNECTIONS TO OTHER SELECTIONS

1. How does the first stanza of "I know that He exists" (p. 344) suggest an idea similar to this poem's? Why do you think the last eight lines of the former aren't similar in theme to this poem?
2. Write an essay on Dickinson's attitudes about the purpose and strategies of poetry by considering this poem as well as "The Thought beneath so slight a film—" (p. 310) and "Portraits are to daily faces" (p. 315).

A Word dropped careless on a Page   *c. 1873*

A Word dropped careless on a Page
May stimulate an eye
When folded in perpetual seam
The Wrinkled Maker lie

Infection in the sentence breeds
We may inhale Despair
At distances of Centuries
From the Malaria—

CONSIDERATIONS FOR CRITICAL THINKING AND WRITING

1. **FIRST RESPONSE.** What sort of power does Dickinson attribute to the written word?
2. Who is the "Wrinkled Maker" in line 4?
3. Discuss the effects of the poem's rhymes.
4. Consult a dictionary definition of *malaria*. Why is it a particularly appropriate word choice for this poem?

There is no Frigate like a Book   *c. 1873*

There is no Frigate like a Book
To take us Lands away
Nor any Coursers like a Page
Of prancing Poetry—
This Traverse may the poorest take
Without oppress of Toll—
How frugal is the Chariot
That bears the Human soul.

CONSIDERATIONS FOR CRITICAL THINKING AND WRITING

1. **FIRST RESPONSE.** Which lines present reading as a mode of transportation? Why do you think that is an effective controlling metaphor in a poem about the value of books?
2. How does the poem's rhythm suggest a kind of "prancing Poetry"?

CONNECTION TO ANOTHER SELECTION

1. Compare the tone of this poem with that of the preceding, "A Word dropped careless on a Page."

I took one Draught of Life —

date unknown

I took one Draught of Life —
I'll tell you what I paid —
Precisely an existence —
The market price, they said.

They weighed me, Dust by Dust —
They balanced Film with Film,
Then handed me my Being's worth —
A single Dram of Heaven!

CONSIDERATIONS FOR CRITICAL THINKING AND WRITING

1. **FIRST RESPONSE.** What is the relationship between life and death in this poem?
2. What do you think "balanced Film with Film" refers to in line 6?
3. Explain whether or not you read the final two lines as an optimistic or a pessimistic view of the afterlife.

CONNECTION TO ANOTHER SELECTION

1. Discuss the meaning of heaven in this poem and in "'Heaven' — is what I cannot reach!" (p. 316).

Perspectives on Emily Dickinson

EMILY DICKINSON

A Description of Herself

1862

Mr Higginson,
Your kindness claimed earlier gratitude — but I was ill — and write today, from my pillow.
Thank you for the surgery — it was not so painful as I supposed. I bring you others° — as you ask — though they might not differ —
While my thought is undressed — I can make the distinction, but when I put them in the Gown — they look alike, and numb.
You asked how old I was? I made no verse — but one or two° — until this winter — Sir —
I had a terror — since September — I could tell to none — and so I sing, as the Boy does by the Burying Ground — because I am afraid — You inquire my Books — For Poets — I have Keats — and Mr and Mrs Browning. For Prose — Mr Ruskin — Sir Thomas Browne — and the Revelations. I went to school — but in your manner of the phrase — had no education. When a little Girl, I had a

---

others: Dickinson had sent poems to Higginson for his opinions and enclosed more with this letter.   *one or two:* Actually she had written almost 300 poems.

friend, who taught me Immortality—but venturing too near, himself—he never returned—Soon after, my Tutor, died—and for several years, my Lexicon—was my only companion—Then I found one more—but he was not contented I be his scholar—so he left the Land.

You ask of my Companions Hills—Sir—and the Sundown—and a Dog—large as myself, that my Father bought me—They are better than Beings—because they know—but do not tell—and the noise in the Pool, at Noon—excels my Piano. I have a Brother and Sister—My Mother does not care for thought—and Father, too busy with his Briefs—to notice what we do—He buys me many Books—but begs me not to read them—because he fears they joggle the Mind. They are religious—except me—and address an Eclipse, every morning—whom they call their "Father." But I fear my story fatigues you—I would like to learn—Could you tell me how to grow—or is it unconveyed—like Melody—or Witchcraft?

From a letter to Thomas Wentworth Higginson, April 25, 1862

Considerations for Critical Thinking and Writing

1. What impression does this letter give you of Dickinson?
2. What kinds of thoughts are there in the foreground of her thinking?
3. To what extent is the style of her letter writing like that of her poetry?

THOMAS WENTWORTH HIGGINSON (1823–1911)
On Meeting Dickinson for the First Time   1870

A large county lawyer's house, brown brick, with great trees & a garden—I sent up my card. A parlor dark & cool & stiffish, a few books & engravings & an open piano. . . .

A step like a pattering child's in entry & in glided a little plain woman with two smooth bands of reddish hair & a face a little like Belle Dove's; not plainer—with no good feature—in a very plain & exquisitely clean white pique & a blue net worsted shawl. She came to me with two day lilies which she put in a sort of childlike way into my hand & said "These are my introduction" in a soft frightened breathless childlike voice—& added under her breath Forgive me if I am frightened; I never see strangers & hardly know what I say—but she talked soon & thenceforward continuously—& deferentially—sometimes stopping to ask me to talk instead of her—but readily recommencing . . . thoroughly ingenuous & simple . . . & saying many things which you would have thought foolish & I wise—& some things you wd. hv. liked. I add a few over the page. . . .

"Women talk; men are silent; that is why I dread women."
"My father only reads on Sunday—he reads *lonely* & *rigorous* books."
"If I read a book [and] it makes my whole body so cold no fire ever can warm me I know *that* is poetry. If I feel physically as if the top of my head were

taken off, I know *that* is poetry. These are the only ways I know it. Is there any other way."

"How do most people live without any thoughts. There are many people in the world (you must have noticed them in the street) How do they live. How do they get strength to put on their clothes in the morning"

"When I lost the use of my Eyes it was a comfort to think there were so few real *books* that I could easily find some one to read me all of them"

"Truth is such a *rare* thing it is delightful to tell it."

"I find ecstasy in living—the mere sense of living is joy enough"

I asked if she never felt want of employment, never going off the place & never seeing any visitor "I never thought of conceiving that I could ever have the slightest approach to such a want in all future time" (& added) "I feel that I have not expressed myself strongly enough."

From a letter to his wife, August 16, 1870

CONSIDERATIONS FOR CRITICAL THINKING AND WRITING

1. How old is Dickinson when Higginson meets her? Does this description seem commensurate with her age? Explain why or why not.

2. Choose one of the quotations from Dickinson that Higginson includes and write an essay about what it reveals about her.

MABEL LOOMIS TODD (1856–1932)

The Character *of Amherst*   1881

I must tell you about the *character* of Amherst. It is a lady whom the people call the *Myth*. She is a sister of Mr. Dickinson, & seems to be the climax of all the family oddity. She has not been outside of her own house in fifteen years, except once to see a new church, when she crept out at night, & viewed it by moonlight. No one who calls upon her mother & sister ever see her, but she allows little children once in a great while, & one at a time, to come in, when she gives them cake or candy, or some nicety, for she is very fond of little ones. But more often she lets down the sweetmeat by a string, out of a window, to them. She dresses wholly in white, & her mind is said to be perfectly wonderful. She writes finely, but no one *ever* sees her. Her sister, who was at Mrs. Dickinson's party, invited me to come & sing to her mother sometime. . . . People tell me the *myth* will hear every note—she will be near, but unseen. . . . Isn't that like a book? So interesting.

From a letter to her parents, November 6, 1881

CONSIDERATIONS FOR CRITICAL THINKING AND WRITING

1. Todd, who in the 1890s would edit Dickinson's poems and letters, had known her for only two months when she wrote this letter. How does Todd characterize Dickinson?

2. Does this description seem positive or negative to you? Explain your answer.

3. A few of Dickinson's poems, such as "Much Madness is divinest Sense—" (p. 321), suggest that she was aware of this perception of her. Refer to her poems in discussing Dickinson's response to this perception.

RICHARD WILBUR (B. 1921)

On Dickinson's Sense of Privation 1960

What did Emily Dickinson do, as a poet, with her sense of privation? One thing she quite often did was to pose as the laureate and attorney of the empty-handed, and question God about the economy of His creation. Why, she asked, is a fatherly God so sparing of His presence? Why is there never a sign that prayers are heard? Why does Nature tell us no comforting news of its Maker? Why do some receive a whole loaf, while others must starve on a crumb? Where is the benevolence in shipwreck and earthquake? By asking such questions as these, she turned complaint into critique, and used her own sufferings as experiential evidence about the nature of the deity. The God who emerges from these poems is a God who does not answer, an unrevealed God whom one cannot confidently approach through Nature or through doctrine.

But there was another way in which Emily Dickinson dealt with her sentiment of lack — another emotional strategy which was both more frequent and more fruitful. I refer to her repeated assertion of the paradox that privation is more plentiful than plenty; that to renounce is to possess the more; that "The Banquet of abstemiousness / Defaces that of wine." We all know how the poet illustrated this ascetic paradox in her behavior — how in her latter years she chose to live in relative retirement, keeping the world, even in its dearest aspects, at a physical remove. She would write her friends, telling them how she missed them, then flee upstairs when they came to see her; afterward, she might send a note of apology, offering the odd explanation that "We shun because we prize." Any reader of Dickinson biographies can furnish other examples, dramatic or homely, of this prizing and shunning, this yearning and renouncing: in my own mind's eye is a picture of Emily Dickinson watching a gay circus caravan from the distance of her chamber window.

From "Sumptuous Destitution" in *Emily Dickinson: Three Views*, by Richard Wilbur, Louise Bogan, and Archibald MacLeish

CONSIDERATIONS FOR CRITICAL THINKING AND WRITING

1. Which poems by Dickinson reprinted in this anthology suggest that she was "the laureate and attorney of the empty-handed"?

2. Which poems suggest that "privation is more plentiful"?

3. Of these two types of poems, which do you prefer? Write an essay that explains your preference.

SANDRA M. GILBERT (B. 1936) AND
SUSAN GUBAR (B. 1944)

On Dickinson's White Dress   *1979*

Today a dress that the Amherst Historical Society assures us is *the* white dress Dickinson wore — or at least one of her "Uniforms of Snow" — hangs in a drycleaner's plastic bag in the closet of the Dickinson homestead. Perfectly preserved, beautifully flounced and tucked, it is larger than most readers would have expected this self-consciously small poet's dress to be, and thus reminds visiting scholars of the enduring enigma of Dickinson's central metaphor, even while it draws gasps from more practical visitors, who reflect with awe upon the difficulties of maintaining such a costume. But what exactly did the literal and figurative whiteness of this costume represent? What rewards did it offer that would cause an intelligent woman to overlook those practical difficulties? Comparing Dickinson's obsession with whiteness to [Herman] Melville's, William R. Sherwood suggests that "it reflected in her case the Christian mystery and not a Christian enigma . . . a decision to announce . . . the assumption of a worldly death that paradoxically involved regeneration." This, he adds, her gown — "a typically slant demonstration of truth" — should have revealed "to anyone with the wit to catch on."[1]

We might reasonably wonder, however, if Dickinson herself consciously intended her wardrobe to convey any one message. The range of associations her white poems imply suggests, on the contrary, that for her, as for Melville, white is the ultimate symbol of enigma, paradox, and irony, "not so much a color as the visible absence of color, and at the same time the concrete of all colors." Melville's question [in *Moby-Dick*] might, therefore, also be hers: "is it for these reasons that there is such a dumb blankness, full of meaning, in a wide landscape of snows — a colorless, all-color of atheism from which we shrink?" And his concluding speculation might be hers too, his remark "that the mystical cosmetic which produces every one of [Nature's] hues, the great principle of light, for ever remains white or colorless in itself, and if operating without medium upon matter, would touch all objects . . . with its own blank tinge." For white, in Dickinson's poetry, frequently represents both the energy (the white heat) of Romantic creativity, and the loneliness (the polar cold) of the renunciation or tribulation Romantic creativity may demand, both the white radiance of eternity — or Revelation — and the white terror of a shroud.

> From *The Madwoman in the Attic: The Woman Writer*
> *and the Nineteenth-Century Literary Imagination*

[1] *Circumference and Circumstance: Stages in the Mind and Art of Emily Dickinson* (New York: Columbia UP, 1968) 152, 231.

CONSIDERATIONS FOR CRITICAL THINKING AND WRITING

1. What meanings do Gilbert and Gubar attribute to Dickinson's white dress?
2. Discuss the meaning of the implicit whiteness in "Safe in their Alabaster Chambers —" (p. 314) and "After great pain, a formal feeling comes —" (p. 323). To what extent do these poems incorporate the meanings of whiteness that Gilbert and Gubar suggest?

3. What other possible reasons can you think of that would account for Dickinson's wearing only white?

CYNTHIA GRIFFIN WOLFF (B. 1935)

On the Many Voices in Dickinson's Poetry 1986

There were many "Voices." This fact has sometimes puzzled Dickinson's readers. One poem may be delivered in a child's Voice; another in the Voice of a young woman scrutinizing nature and the society in which she makes her place. Sometimes the Voice is that of a woman self-confidently addressing her lover in a language of passion and sexual desire. At still other times, the Voice of the verse seems so precariously balanced at the edge of hysteria that even its calmest observations grate like the shriek of dementia. There is the Voice of the housewife and the Voice that has recourse to the occasionally agonizing, occasionally regal language of the conversion experience of latter-day New England Puritanism. In some poems the Voice is distinctive principally because it speaks in the aftermath of wounding and can comprehend extremities of pain. Moreover, these Voices are not always entirely distinct from one another: the child's Voice that opens a poem may yield to the Voice of a young woman speaking the idiom of ardent love; in a different poem, the speaker may fall into a mood of almost religious contemplation in an attempt to analyze or define such abstract entities as loneliness or madness or eternity; the diction of the housewife may be conflated with the sovereign language of the New Jerusalem, and taken together, they may render some aspect of the wordsmith's labor. No manageable set of discrete categories suffices to capture the diversity of discourse, and any attempt to simplify Dickinson's methods does violence to the verse.

Yet there is a paradox here. This is, by no stretch of the imagination, a body of poetry that might be construed as a series of lyrics spoken by many different people. Disparate as these many Voices are, somehow they all appear to issue from the same "self." . . . It is the enigmatic "Emily Dickinson" readers suppose themselves to have found in this poetry, even in the extreme case when Dickinson's supposed speaker is male. One explanation for this sense of intrinsic unity in the midst of diversity is the persistence with which Dickinson addresses the same set of problems, using a remarkably durable repertoire of linguistic modes. Evocations of injury and wounding—threats to the coherence of the self—appear in the earliest poems and continue until the end; ways of rendering face-to-face encounters change, but this preoccupation with "interview" is sustained by metaphors of "confrontation" that weave throughout. The summoning of one or another Voice in a given poem, then, is not an unself-conscious emotive reflection of Emily Dickinson's mood at the moment of creation. Rather, each different Voice is a calculated tactic, an attempt to touch her readers and engage them intimately with the poetry. Each Voice had its unique advantages; each its limitations. A poet self-conscious in her craft, she calculated this element as carefully as every other.

From *Emily Dickinson*

CONSIDERATIONS FOR CRITICAL THINKING AND WRITING

1. From the poems in this anthology, try adding to the list of voices Wolff cites.

2. Despite the many voices in Dickinson's poetry, why, according to Wolff, is there still a "sense of intrinsic unity" in her poetry?

3. Choose a Dickinson poem and describe how the choice of voice is a "calculated tactic."

PAULA BENNETT (B. 1936)

On "I heard a Fly buzz—when I died —"   1990

Dickinson's rage against death, a rage that led her at times to hate both life and death, might have been alleviated, had she been able to gather hard evidence about an afterlife. But, of course, she could not. "The *Bareheaded life—under the grass—*," she wrote to Samuel Bowles in c. 1860, "worries one like a Wasp." If death was the gate to a better life in "the childhood of the kingdom of Heaven," as the sentimentalists—and Christ—claimed, then, perhaps, there was compensation and healing for life's woes. . . . But how do we know? What can we know? In "I heard a Fly buzz—when I died," Dickinson concludes that we do not know much. . . .

Like many people in her period, Dickinson was fascinated by death-bed scenes. How, she asked various correspondents, did this or that person die? In particular, she wanted to know if their deaths revealed any information about the nature of the afterlife. In this poem, however, she imagines her own death-bed scene, and the answer she provides is grim, as grim (and, at the same time, as ironically mocking) as anything she ever wrote.

In the narrowing focus of death, the fly's insignificant buzz, magnified tenfold by the stillness in the room, is all that the speaker hears. This kind of distortion in scale is common. It is one of the "illusions" of perception. But here it is horrifying because it defeats every expectation we have. Death is supposed to be an experience of awe. It is the moment when the soul, departing the body, is taken up by God. Hence the watchers at the bedside wait for the moment when the "King" (whether God or death) "be witnessed" in the room. And hence the speaker assigns away everything but that which she expects God (her soul) or death (her body) to take.

What arrives instead, however, is neither God nor death but a fly, "[w]ith Blue—uncertain—stumbling Buzz," a fly, that is, no more secure, no more sure, than we are. Dickinson had associated flies with death once before in the exquisite lament, "How many times these low feet / staggered." In this poem, they buzz "on the / chamber window," and speckle it with dirt, reminding us that the housewife, who once protected us from such intrusions, will protect us no longer. Their presence is threatening but only in a minor way, "dull" like themselves. They are a background noise we do not have to deal with yet.

In "I heard a Fly buzz," on the other hand, there is only one fly and its buzz is not only foregrounded. Before the poem is over, the buzz takes up the entire field of perception, coming between the speaker and the "light" (of day, of life, of knowledge). It is then that the "Windows" (the eyes that are the windows of the soul as well as, metonymically, the light that passes through the panes of glass) "fail" and the speaker is left in darkness—in death, in ignorance. She cannot "see" to "see" (understand).

Given that the only sure thing we know about "life after death" is that flies—in their adult form and more particularly, as maggots—devour us, the poem is at the very least a grim joke. In projecting her death-bed scene, Dickinson confronts her ignorance and gives back the only answer human knowledge can with any certainty give. While we may hope for an afterlife, no one, not even the dying, can prove it exists.

From *Emily Dickinson: Woman Poet*

CONSIDERATIONS FOR CRITICAL THINKING AND WRITING

1. According to Bennett, what is the symbolic value of the fly?

2. Does Bennett leave out any significant elements of the poem in her analysis? Explain why you think she did or did not.

3. Choose a Dickinson poem and write a detailed analysis that attempts to account for all of its major elements.

MARTHA NELL SMITH (B. 1953)

On *"Because I could not stop for Death—"*   *1993*

That this poem begins and ends with humanity's ultimate dream of self-importance—Immortality and Eternity—could well be the joke central to its meaning, for Dickinson carefully surrounds the fantasy of living ever after with the dirty facts of life—dusty carriage rides, schoolyards, and farmers' fields. Many may contend that, like the Puritans and metaphysicals before her, Dickinson pulls the sublime down to the ridiculous but unavoidable facts of existence, thus imbues life on earth with its real import. On the other hand, Dickinson may have argued otherwise. Very late in her life, she wrote, "When Jesus tells us about his Father, we distrust him. When he shows us his Home, we turn away, but when he confides to us that he is 'acquainted with Grief,' we listen, for that is also an Acquaintance of our own." Instead of sharing their faith, Dickinson may be showing the community around her, most of whom were singing "When we all get to Heaven what a day of rejoicing that will be," how selfishly selective is their belief in a system that bolsters egocentrism by assuring believers not only that their individual identities will survive death, but also that they are one of the exclusive club of the saved. Waiting for the return of Eden or Paradise, which "is always eligible" and which she "never believed . . . to be a superhuman site," those believers may simply find themselves gathering dust. Surrounded by the faithful, Dickinson struggled with trust and doubt in Christian promises herself, but whether she believed in salvation or even in immortality is endlessly debatable. Readers can select poems and letters and construct compelling arguments to prove that she did or did not. But for every declaration evincing belief, there is one like that to Elizabeth Holland:

The Fiction of "Santa Claus" always reminds me of the reply to my early question of "Who made the Bible" — "Holy Men moved by the Holy Ghost," and though I have now ceased my investigations, the Solution is insufficient —

What "Because I could not stop for Death —" will not allow is any hard and fast conclusion to be drawn about the matter. Once again . . . by mixing tropes and tones Dickinson underscores the importance of refusing any single-minded response to a subject and implicitly attests to the power in continually opening possibilities by repeatedly posing questions.

> From *Comic Power in Emily Dickinson,* by Suzanne Juhasz,
> Cristanne Miller, and Martha Nell Smith

CONSIDERATIONS FOR CRITICAL THINKING AND WRITING

1. In what sense, according to Smith, could a joke be central to the meaning of "Because I could not stop for Death —"?

2. Compare the potential joke in this poem and in "I know that He exists" (p. 344). How is your reading of each poem influenced by considering them together?

3. Read the sample paper on "Religious Faith in Four Poems by Emily Dickinson" (pp. 345-47) and write an analysis of "Because I could not stop for Death —" that supports or refutes the paper's thesis.

RONALD WALLACE (B. 1945)

Miss Goff   1994

When Zack Pulanski brought the plastic vomit
and slid it slickly to the vinyl floor
and raised his hand, and her tired eyes fell on it
with horror, the heartless classroom lost in laughter
as the custodian slyly tossed his saw dust on it   5
and pushed it, grinning, through the door,
she reached into her ancient corner closet
and found some Emily Dickinson mimeos there

which she passed out. And then, herself
passed out on the cold circumference of her desk.   10
And everybody went their merry ways
but me, who, chancing on one unexpected phrase
after another, sat transfixed until dusk.
Me and Miss Goff, the top of our heads taken off.

CONSIDERATIONS FOR CRITICAL THINKING AND WRITING

1. How does the joke played on Miss Goff in the first stanza give way to something more serious in the second stanza? Explain the shift in tone.

2. Characterize Miss Goff. How does the poem's diction reveal some of her personality?

3. Dickinson once described her own poetry by writing that "my business is circumference," and she made an attempt to define poetry with this comment: "If I read a book and it makes my whole body so cold no fire can ever warm me, I know *that* is poetry. If I feel physically as if the top of my head were taken off, I know *that* is poetry." How are these statements relevant to your understanding of Wallace's poem?

4. Discuss the use of irony in "Miss Goff."

Two Complementary Critical Readings

Charles R. Anderson (1902–1999)

Eroticism in "Wild Nights — Wild Nights!"   1960

The frank eroticism of this poem might puzzle the biographer of a spinster, but the critic can only be concerned with its effectiveness as a poem. Unless one insists on taking the "I" to mean Emily Dickinson, there is not even any reversal of the lovers' roles (which has been charged, curiously enough, as a fault in this poem). The opening declaration — "Wild Nights should be / Our luxury!" — sets the key of her song, for *luxuria* included the meaning of lust as well as lavishness of sensuous enjoyment, as she was Latinist enough to know. This is echoed at the end in "Eden," her recurring image, in letters and poems, for the paradise of earthly love. The theme here is that of sexual passion which is lawless, outside the rule of "Chart" and "Compass." But it lives by a law of its own, the law of Eden, which protects it from mundane wind and wave.

This is what gives the magic to her climactic vision, "Rowing in Eden," sheltered luxuriously in those paradisiac waters while the wild storms of this world break about them. Such love was only possible before the Fall. Since then the bower of bliss is frugal of her leases, limiting each occupant to "an instant" she says in another poem, for "Adam taught her Thrift / Bankrupt once through his excesses." In the present poem she limits her yearning to the mortal term, just "Tonight." But this echoes the surge of ecstasy that initiated her song and gives the reiterated "Wild Nights!" a double reference, to the passionate experience in Eden as well as to the tumult of the world shut out by it. So she avoids the chief pitfall of the love lyric, the tendency to exploit emotion for its own sake. Instead she generates out of the conflicting aspects of love, its ecstasy and its brevity, the symbol that contains the poem's meaning.

From Emily Dickinson's Poetry: Stairway of Surprise

Considerations for Critical Thinking and Writing

1. According to Anderson, what is the theme of "Wild Nights — Wild Nights!"?

2. How does Anderson discuss the poem's "frank eroticism"? How detailed is his discussion?

3. If there is a "reversal of the lovers' roles" in this poem, do you think it represents, as some critics have charged, "a fault in this poem"? Explain why or why not.

4. Compare Anderson's treatment of this poem with David S. Reynolds's reading that follows. Discuss which one you find more useful and explain why.

DAVID S. REYNOLDS (B. 1949)
Popular Literature and "Wild Nights — Wild Nights!"   *1988*

It is not known whether Dickinson had read any of the erotic literature of the day or if she knew of the stereotype of the sensual woman. Given her fascination with sensational journalism and with popular literature in general, it is hard to believe she would not have had at least some exposure to erotic literature. At any rate, her treatment of the daring theme of woman's sexual fantasy in this deservedly famous poem bears comparison with erotic themes as they appeared in popular sensational writings. The first stanza of the poem provides an uplifting or purification of sexual fantasy not distant from the effect of [Walt] Whitman's cleansing rhetoric, which, as we have seen, was consciously designed to counteract the prurience of the popular "love plot." Dickinson's repeated phrase "Wild Nights" is a simple but dazzling metaphor that communicates wild passion — even lust — but simultaneously lifts sexual desire out of the scabrous by fusing it with the natural image of the night. The second verse introduces a second nature image, the turbulent sea and the contrasting quiet port, which at once universalizes the passion and purifies it further by distancing it through a more abstract metaphor. Also, the second verse makes clear that this is not a poem of sexual consummation but rather of pure fantasy and sexual impossibility. Unlike popular erotic literature, the poem portrays neither a consummated seduction nor the heartless deception that it involves. There is instead a pure, fervent fantasy whose frustration is figured forth in the contrasting images of the ocean (the longed-for-but-never-achieved consummation) and the port (the reality of the poet's isolation). The third verse begins with an image, "Rowing in Eden," that further uplifts sexual passion by yoking it with a religious archetype. Here as elsewhere, Dickinson capitalizes nicely on the new religious style, which made possible such fusions of the divine and the earthly. The persona's concluding wish to "moor" in the sea expresses the sustained intense sexual longing and the simultaneous frustration of that longing. In the course of the poem, Dickinson has communicated great erotic passion, and yet, by effectively projecting this passion through unusual nature and religious images, has rid it of even the tiniest residue of sensationalism.

> From *Beneath the American Renaissance: The Subversive Imagination*
> *in the Age of Emerson and Melville*

CONSIDERATIONS FOR CRITICAL THINKING AND WRITING

1. According to Reynolds, how do Dickinson's images provide a "cleansing" effect in the poem?
2. Explain whether you agree that the poem portrays a "pure, fervent fantasy" or something else.

3. Does Reynolds's reading of the poem compete with Anderson's or complement it? Explain your answer.

4. Given the types of critical strategies described in Chapter 25, how would you characterize Anderson's and Reynolds's approaches?

Questions for Writing about an Author in Depth

As you read multiple works by the same author you're likely to be struck by the similarities and differences in those selections. You'll begin to recognize situations, events, characters, issues, perspectives, styles, and strategies — even recurring words or phrases — that provide a kind of signature, making the poems in some way identifiable with that particular writer.

The following questions can help you to respond to multiple works by the same author. They should help you to listen to how a writer's works can speak to one another and to you. Additional useful questions can be found in other chapters of this book. See Chapter 2, "Writing about Poetry," and Arguing about Literature (p. 685) in Chapter 26, "Reading and Writing."

1. What topics reappear in the writer's work? What seem to be the major concerns of the author?

2. Does the author have a definable worldview that can be discerned from work to work? Is, for example, the writer liberal, conservative, apolitical, or religious?

3. What social values come through in the author's work? Does he or she seem to identify with a particular group or social class?

4. Is there a consistent voice or point of view from work to work? Is it a persona or the author's actual self?

5. How much of the author's own life experiences and historical moment make their way into the works?

6. Does the author experiment with style from work to work, or are the works mostly consistent with one another?

7. Can the author's work be identified with a literary tradition, such as *carpe diem* poetry, that aligns his or her work with that of other writers?

8. What is distinctive about the author's writing? Is the language innovative? Are the themes challenging? Are the voices conventional? Is the tone characteristic?

9. Could you identify another work by the same author without a name being attached to it? What are the distinctive features that allow you to do so?

10. Do any of the writer's works seem *not* to be by that writer? Why?

11. What other writers are most like this author in style and content? Why?

12. Has the writer's work evolved over time? Are there significant changes or developments? Are there new ideas and styles, or do the works remain largely the same?

13. How would you characterize the author's writing habits? Is it possible to anticipate what goes on in different works, or are you surprised by their content or style?

14. Can difficult or ambiguous passages in a work be resolved by referring to a similar passage in another work?

15. What does the writer say about his or her own work? Do you trust the teller or the tale? Which do you think is more reliable?

A SAMPLE IN-DEPTH STUDY

The following paper was written for an assignment that called for an analysis (about 750 words) on any topic that could be traced in three or four poems by Dickinson. The student, Michael Weitz, chose "'Faith' is a fine invention," "I know that He exists," "I never saw a Moor —," and "Apparently with no surprise."

Previous knowledge of a writer's work can set up useful expectations in a reader. In the case of the four Dickinson poems included in this section, religion emerges as a central topic linked to a number of issues, including faith, immortality, skepticism, and the nature of God. The student selected these poems because he noticed Dickinson's intense interest in religious faith owing to the many poems that explore a variety of religious attitudes in her work. He chose these four because they were closely related, but he might have found equally useful clusters of poems about love, nature, domestic life, or writing. What especially intrigued him was some of the information he read about Dickinson's sternly religious father and the orthodox nature of the religious values of her hometown of Amherst, Massachusetts. Because this paper was not a research paper, he did not pursue these issues beyond the level of the general remarks provided in an introduction to her poetry (though he might have). He did, however, use this biographical and historical information as a means of framing his search for poems that were related to one another. In doing so he discovered consistent concerns along with contradictory themes that became the basis of his paper.

"Faith" is a fine invention   *c. 1860*

"Faith" is a fine invention
When Gentlemen can *see* —
But *Microscopes* are prudent
In an Emergency.

I know that He exists

c. 1862

I know that He exists.
Somewhere — in Silence —
He has hid his rare life
From our gross eyes.

'Tis an instant's play.   5
'Tis a fond Ambush —
Just to make Bliss
Earn her own surprise!

But — should the play
Prove piercing earnest —   10
Should the glee-glaze —
In Death's — stiff — stare —

Would not the fun
Look too expensive!
Would not the jest —   15
Have crawled too far!

I never saw a Moor —

c. 1865

I never saw a Moor —
I never saw the Sea —
Yet know I how the Heather looks
And what a Billow be.

I never spoke with God
Nor visited in Heaven —
Yet certain am I of the spot
As if the Checks were given —

Apparently with no surprise

c. 1884

Apparently with no surprise
To any happy Flower
The Frost beheads it at its play —
In accidental power —
The blond Assassin passes on —
The Sun proceeds unmoved
To measure off another Day
For an Approving God.

A SAMPLE STUDENT PAPER

Religious Faith in Four Poems by Emily Dickinson

Michael Weitz

Professor Pearl

English 270

May 5, 2006

Religious Faith in Four Poems by Emily Dickinson

Throughout much of her poetry, Emily Dickinson wrestles with complex notions of God, faith, and religious devotion. She adheres to no consistent view of religion; rather, her poetry reveals a vision of God and faith that is constantly evolving. Dickinson's gods range from the strict and powerful Old Testament father to a loving spiritual guide to an irrational and ridiculous imaginary figure. Through these varying images of God, Dickinson portrays contrasting images of the meaning and validity of religious faith. Her work reveals competing attitudes toward religious devotion as conventional religious piety struggles with a more cynical perception of God and religious worship.

> Introduction providing overview of faith in Dickinson's work

> Thesis analyzing poet's attitudes toward God and religion

Dickinson's "I never saw a Moor--" reveals a vision of traditional religious sensibilities. Although the speaker readily admits that "I never spoke with God / Nor visited in Heaven," her devout faith in a supreme being does not waver. The poem appears to be a straightforward profession of true faith stemming from the argument that the proof of God's existence is the universe's existence. Dickinson's imagery therefore evolves from the natural to the supernatural, first establishing her convictions that Moors and Seas exist, in spite of her lack of personal contact with either. This leads to the foundation of her religious faith, again based not on physical experience but on intellectual convictions. The speaker professes that she believes in the existence of Heaven even without conclusive evidence: "Yet certain am I of the spot / As if the Checks were given--" But the appearance of such idealistic views of God and faith in "I never saw a Moor--" are transformed in Dickinson's other poems into a much more skeptical vision of the validity of religious piety.

> Analysis of religious piety in "I never saw a Moor--" supported with textual evidence

> Contrast between attitudes in "Moor" and other poems

While faith is portrayed as an authentic and deeply important quality in "I never saw a Moor--," Dickinson's "'Faith' is a fine invention" portrays faith as much less essential. Faith is defined in the poem as "a fine invention" suggesting that it is created by man for man and therefore is not a crucial aspect of the natural universe. Thus the strong idealistic faith of "I never saw a Moor--" becomes discredited in the face of scientific rationalism. The speaker compares religious faith with actual microscopes, both of which are meant to enhance one's vision in some way. But "Faith" is useful only "When Gentlemen can <u>see</u>--" already; "In an Emergency," when one ostensibly cannot see, "<u>Microscopes</u> are prudent." Dickinson pits religion against science, suggesting that science, with its tangible evidence and rational attitude, is a more reliable lens through which to view the world. Faith is irreverently reduced to a mere invention and one that is ultimately less useful than microscopes or other scientific instruments.

Rational, scientific observations are not the only contributing factor to the portrayal of religious skepticism in Dickinson's poems; nature itself is seen to be incompatible in some ways with conventional religious ideology. In "Apparently with no surprise," the speaker recognizes the inexorable cycle of natural life and death as a morning frost kills a flower. But the tension in this poem stems not from the "happy Flower" struck down by the frost's "accidental power" but from the apparent indifference of the "Approving God" who condones this seemingly cruel and unnecessary death. God is seen as remote and uncompromising, and it is this perceived distance between the speaker and God that reveals the increasing absurdity of traditional religious faith. The speaker understands that praying to God or believing in religion cannot change the course of nature, and as a result feels so helplessly distanced from God that religious faith becomes virtually meaningless.

Dickinson's religious skepticism becomes even more explicit in "I know that He exists," in which the speaker attempts to understand the connection between seeing God and facing death. In this poem Dickinson characterizes God as a remote and mysterious figure; the speaker mockingly asserts, "I know that He exists," even though "He has hid his rare life / From our gross eyes." The skepticism toward religious faith revealed in this poem stems from the speaker's recog-

---

Analysis of scientific rationalism in "'Faith' is a fine invention" supported with textual evidence

Analysis of God and nature in "Apparently with no surprise" supported with textual evidence

Analysis of characterization of God in "I know that He exists" supported with textual evidence

nition of the paradoxical quest that people undertake to know and to see God. A successful attempt to see God, to win the game of hide-and-seek that He apparently is orchestrating, results inevitably in death. With this recognition the speaker comes to view religion as an absurd and reckless game in which the prize may be "Bliss" but more likely is "Death's--stiff--stare--" For to see God and to meet one's death as a result certainly suggests that the game of trying to see God (the so-called "fun") is much "too expensive" and that religion itself is a "jest" that, like the serpent in Genesis, has "crawled too far."

Ultimately, the vision of religious faith that Dickinson describes in her poems is one of suspicion and cynicism. She cannot reconcile the physical world to the spiritual existence that Christian doctrine teaches, and as a result the traditional perception of God becomes ludicrous. "I never saw a Moor--" does attempt to sustain a conventional vision of religious devotion, but Dickinson's poems overall are far more likely to suggest that God is elusive, indifferent, and often cruel, thus undermining the traditional vision of God as a loving father worthy of devout worship. Thus, not only religious faith but also those who are religiously faithful become targets for Dickinson's irreverent criticism of conventional belief.

> Conclusion providing well-supported final analysis of poet's views on God and faith.

SUGGESTED TOPICS FOR LONGER PAPERS

1. Irony is abundant in Dickinson's poetry. Choose five poems from this chapter that strike you as especially ironic and discuss her use of irony in each. Taken individually and collectively, what do these poems suggest to you about the poet's sensibilities and her ways of looking at the world?

2. Readers have often noted that Dickinson's poetry does not reflect very much of the social, political, economic, religious, and historical events of her lifetime. Using the poems in this chapter as the basis of your discussion, what can you say about the contexts in which Dickinson wrote? What kind of world do you think she inhabited, and how did she respond to it?

> Web Research Emily Dickinson at bedfordstmartins.com/meyerpoetry.

13

A Study of Robert Frost

A poem . . . begins as a lump in the throat, a sense of wrong, a home-sickness, a love-sickness. . . . It finds the thought and the thought finds the words.

— ROBERT FROST

Every poem is doubtlessly affected by the personal history of its composer, but Robert Frost's poems are especially known for their reflection of New England life. Although the poems included in this chapter evoke the landscapes of Frost's life and work, the depth and range of those landscapes are far more complicated than his popular reputation typically acknowledges. He was an enormously private man and a much more subtle poet than many of his readers have expected him to be. His poems warrant careful, close readings. As you explore his poetry, you may find useful the Questions for Writing about an

Explore contexts for Robert Frost on *LiterActive*.

Robert Frost

Author in Depth (p. 342) as a means of stimulating your thinking about his life and work.

A BRIEF BIOGRAPHY

Few poets have enjoyed the popular success that Robert Frost (1874–1963) achieved during his lifetime, and no twentieth-century American poet has had his or her work as widely read and honored. Frost is as much associated with New England as the stone walls that help define its landscape; his reputation, however, transcends regional boundaries. Although he was named poet laureate of Vermont only two years before his death, he was for many years the nation's unofficial poet laureate. Frost collected honors the way some people pick up burrs on country walks. Among his awards were four Pulitzer Prizes, the Bollingen Prize, a Congressional Medal, and dozens of honorary degrees. Perhaps his most moving appearance was his

Robert Frost at age eighteen (1892), the year he graduated from high school. "Education," Frost once said, "is the ability to listen to almost anything without losing your temper or your self-confidence."
Courtesy of Rauner Special Collections Library, Dartmouth College.

Robert Frost at age forty-seven (1921) at Stone Cottage in Shaftsbury, Vermont. Frost wrote, "I would have written of me on my stone: / I had a lover's quarrel with the world." Courtesy of Rauner Special Collections Library, Dartmouth College.

Robert Frost at his writing desk in Franconia, New Hampshire, 1915. "I have never started a poem whose end I knew," Frost said, "writing a poem is discovering."

recitation of "The Gift Outright" for millions of Americans at the inauguration of John F. Kennedy in 1961.

Frost's recognition as a poet is especially remarkable because his career as a writer did not attract any significant attention until he was nearly forty years old. He taught himself to write while he labored at odd jobs, taught school, or farmed.

Frost's early identity seems very remote from the New England soil. Although his parents were descended from generations of New Englanders, he was born in San Francisco and was named Robert Lee Frost after the Confederate general. After his father died in 1885, his mother moved the family back to Massachusetts to live with relatives. Frost graduated from high school sharing valedictorian honors with the classmate who would become his wife three years later. Between high school and marriage, he attended Dartmouth College for a few months and then taught. His teaching prompted him to enroll in Harvard in 1897, but after less than two years he withdrew without a degree (though Harvard would eventually award him an honorary doctorate in 1937, four years after Dartmouth conferred its honorary degree on him). For the next decade, Frost read and wrote poems when he was not chicken farming or teaching. In 1912, he sold his farm and moved his family to England, where he hoped to find the audience that his poetry did not have in America.

Three years in England made it possible for Frost to return home as a poet. His first two volumes of poetry, *A Boy's Will* (1913) and *North of Boston* (1914), were published in England. During the next twenty years, honors and awards were conferred on collections such as *Mountain Interval* (1916), *New Hampshire* (1923), *West-Running Brook* (1928), and *A Further Range* (1936). These are the volumes on which most of Frost's popular and critical reputation rests. Later collections include *A Witness Tree* (1942), *A Masque of Reason* (1945), *Steeple Bush* (1947), *A Masque of Mercy* (1947), *Complete Poems* (1949), and *In the Clearing* (1962). In addition to publishing his works, Frost endeared himself to audiences throughout the country by presenting his poetry almost as conversations. He also taught at a number of schools, including Amherst College, the University of Michigan, Harvard University, Dartmouth College, and Middlebury College.

Frost's countless poetry readings generated wide audiences eager to claim him as their poet. The image he cultivated resembled closely what the public likes to think a poet should be. Frost was seen as a lovable, wise old man; his simple wisdom and cracker-barrel sayings appeared comforting and homey. From this Yankee rustic, audiences learned that "There's a lot yet that isn't understood" or "We love the things we love for what they are" or "Good fences make good neighbors."

In a sense, Frost packaged himself for public consumption. "I am . . . my own salesman," he said. When asked direct questions about the meanings of his poems, he often winked or scratched his head to give the impression that the customer was always right. To be sure, there is a simplicity in Frost's language, but that simplicity does not fully reflect the depth of the man, the complexity of his themes, or the richness of his art.

The folksy optimist behind the public lectern did not reveal his private troubles to his audiences, although he did address those problems at his writing desk. Frost suffered from professional jealousies, anger, and depression. His family life was especially painful. Three of his four children died: a son at the age of four, a daughter in her late twenties from tuberculosis, and another son by suicide. His marriage was filled with tension. Although Frost's work is landscaped with sunlight, snow, birches, birds, blueberries, and squirrels, it is important to recognize that he was also intimately "acquainted with the night," a phrase that serves as the haunting title of one of his poems (see p. 157).

As a corrective to Frost's popular reputation, one critic, Lionel Trilling, described the world Frost creates in his poems as a "terrifying universe," characterized by loneliness, anguish, frustration, doubts, disappointment, and despair. To point this out is not to annihilate the pleasantness and even good-natured cheerfulness that can be enjoyed in Frost's poetry, but it is to say that Frost is not so one-dimensional as he is sometimes assumed to be. Frost's poetry requires readers who are alert and willing to penetrate the simplicity of its language to see the elusive and ambiguous meanings that lie below the surface.

AN INTRODUCTION TO HIS WORK

Frost's treatment of nature helps to explain the various levels of meaning in his poetry. The familiar natural world his poems evoke is sharply detailed. We hear icy branches clicking against themselves, we see the snow-white trunks of birches, we feel the smarting pain of a twig lashing across a face. The aspects of the natural world Frost describes are designated to give pleasure, but they are also frequently calculated to provoke thought. His use of nature tends to be symbolic. Complex meanings are derived from simple facts, such as a spider killing a moth or the difference between fire and ice (see "Design," p. 373, and "Fire and Ice," p. 369). Although Frost's strategy is to talk about particular events and individual experiences, his poems evoke universal issues.

Frost's poetry has strong regional roots and is "versed in country things," but it flourishes in any receptive imagination because, in the final analysis, it is concerned with human beings. Frost's New England landscapes are the occasion rather than the ultimate focus of his poems. Like the rural voices he creates in his poems, Frost typically approaches his themes indirectly. He explained the reason for this in a talk titled "Education by Poetry":

> Poetry provides the one permissible way of saying one thing and meaning another. People say, "Why don't you say what you mean?" We never do that, do we, being all of us too much poets. We like to talk in parables and in hints and in indirections — whether from diffidence or some other instinct.

The result is that the settings, characters, and situations that make up the subject matter of Frost's poems are vehicles for his perceptions about life.

In "Stopping by Woods on a Snowy Evening" (p. 370), for example, Frost uses the kind of familiar New England details that constitute his poetry for more than descriptive purposes. He shapes them into a meditation on the tension we sometimes feel between life's responsibilities and the "lovely, dark, and deep" attraction that death offers. When the speaker's horse "gives his harness bells a shake," we are reminded that we are confronting a universal theme as well as a quiet moment of natural beauty.

Among the major concerns that appear in Frost's poetry are the fragility of life, the consequences of rejecting or accepting the conditions of one's life, the passion of inconsolable grief, the difficulty of sustaining intimacy, the fear of loneliness and isolation, the inevitability of change, the tensions between the individual and society, and the place of tradition and custom.

Whatever theme is encountered in a poem by Frost, a reader is likely to agree with him that "the initial delight is in the surprise of remembering something I didn't know." To achieve that fresh sense of discovery, Frost allowed himself to follow his instincts; his poetry

> inclines to the impulse, it assumes direction with the first line laid down, it runs a course of lucky events, and ends in a clarification of life — not necessarily a

great clarification, such as sects and cults are founded on, but in a momentary stay against confusion.

This description from "On The Figure a Poem Makes" (see p. 377 for the complete essay), Frost's brief introduction to *Complete Poems,* may sound as if his poetry is formless and merely "lucky," but his poems tend to be more conventional than experimental: "The artist in me," as he put the matter in one of his poems, "cries out for design."

From Frost's perspective, "free verse is like playing tennis with the net down." He exercised his own freedom in meeting the challenges of rhyme and meter. His use of fixed forms such as couplets, tercets, quatrains, blank verse, and sonnets was not slavish because he enjoyed working them into the natural English speech patterns — especially the rhythms, idioms, and tones of speakers living north of Boston — that give voice to his themes. Frost often liked to use "Stopping by Woods on a Snowy Evening" as an example of his graceful way of making conventions appear natural and inevitable. He explored "the old ways to be new."

Frost's eye for strong, telling details was matched by his ear for natural speech rhythms. His flexible use of what he called "iambic and loose iambic" enabled him to create moving lyric poems that reveal the personal thoughts of a speaker and dramatic poems that convincingly characterize people caught in intense emotional situations. The language in his poems appears to be little more than a transcription of casual and even rambling speech, but it is in actuality Frost's poetic creation, carefully crafted to reveal the joys and sorrows that are woven into people's daily lives. What is missing from Frost's poems is artificiality, not art. Consider this poem.

The Road Not Taken   *1916*

Two roads diverged in a yellow wood,
And sorry I could not travel both
And be one traveler, long I stood
And looked down one as far as I could
To where it bent in the undergrowth;   5

Then took the other, as just as fair,
And having perhaps the better claim,
Because it was grassy and wanted wear;
Though as for that the passing there
Had worn them really about the same,   10

And both that morning equally lay
In leaves no step had trodden black.
Oh, I kept the first for another day!
Yet knowing how way leads on to way,
I doubted if I should ever come back.   15

I shall be telling this with a sigh
Somewhere ages and ages hence:
Two roads diverged in a wood, and I—
I took the one less traveled by,
And that has made all the difference.   20

This poem intrigues readers because it is at once so simple and so deeply resonant. Recalling a walk in the woods, the speaker describes how he came to a fork in the road, which forced him to choose one path over another. Though "sorry" that he "could not travel both," he made a choice after carefully weighing his two options. This, essentially, is what happens in the poem; there is no other action. However, the incident is charged with symbolic significance by the speaker's reflections on the necessity and consequences of his decision.

The final stanza indicates that the choice concerns more than simply walking down a road, for the speaker says that choosing the "less traveled" path has affected his entire life—that "that has made all the difference." Frost draws on a familiar enough metaphor when he compares life to a journey, but he is also calling attention to a less commonly noted problem: despite our expectations, aspirations, appetites, hopes, and desires, we can't have it all. Making one choice precludes another. It is impossible to determine what particular decision the speaker refers to: perhaps he had to choose a college, a career, a spouse; perhaps he was confronted with mutually exclusive ideas, beliefs, or values. There is no way to know because Frost wisely creates a symbolic choice and implicitly invites us to supply our own circumstances.

The speaker's reflections about his choice are as central to an understanding of the poem as the choice itself; indeed, they may be more central. He describes the road taken as "having perhaps the better claim, / Because it was grassy and wanted wear"; he prefers the "less traveled" path. This seems to be an expression of individualism, which would account for "the difference" his choice made in his life. But Frost complicates matters by having the speaker also acknowledge that there was no significant difference between the two roads; one was "just as fair" as the other; each was "worn . . . really about the same"; and "both that morning equally lay / In leaves no step had trodden black."

The speaker imagines that in the future, "ages and ages hence," he will recount his choice with "a sigh" that will satisfactorily explain the course of his life, but Frost seems to be having a little fun here by showing us how the speaker will embellish his past decision to make it appear more dramatic. What we hear is someone trying to convince himself that the choice he made significantly changed his life. When he recalls what happened in the "yellow wood," a color that gives a glow to that irretrievable moment when his life seemed to be on verge of a momentous change, he appears more concerned with the path he did not choose than with the one he took. Frost shrewdly titles the poem to suggest the speaker's sense of loss at not being able to "travel both" roads. When the speaker's reflections about his choice are examined, the poem reveals his nostalgia instead of affirming his decision to travel a self-reliant path in life.

The rhymed stanzas of "The Road Not Taken" follow a pattern established in the first five lines (*abaab*). This rhyme scheme reflects, perhaps, the speaker's efforts to shape his life into a pleasing and coherent form. The natural speech rhythms Frost uses allow him to integrate the rhymes unobtrusively, but there is a slight shift in lines 19 and 20, when the speaker asserts self-consciously that the "less traveled" road—which we already know to be basically the same as the other road—"made all the difference." Unlike all of the other rhymes in the poem, "difference" does not rhyme precisely with "hence." The emphasis that must be placed on "differ*ence*" to make it rhyme perfectly with "hence" may suggest that the speaker is trying just a little too hard to pattern his life on his earlier choice in the woods.

Perhaps the best way to begin reading Frost's poetry is to accept the invitation he placed at the beginning of many volumes of his poems. "The Pasture" means what it says of course; it is about taking care of some farm chores, but it is also a means of "saying one thing in terms of another."

The Pasture   *1913*

I'm going out to clean the pasture spring;
I'll only stop to rake the leaves away
(And wait to watch the water clear, I may):
I shan't be gone long.—You come too.

I'm going out to fetch the little calf
That's standing by the mother. It's so young
It totters when she licks it with her tongue.
I shan't be gone long.—You come too.

"The Pasture" is a simple but irresistible songlike invitation to the pleasure of looking at the world through the eyes of a poet.

Chronology

1874	Born on March 26 in San Francisco.
1885	Father dies and family moves to Lawrence, Massachusetts.
1892	Graduates from Lawrence High School.
1893–94	Studies at Dartmouth College.
1895	Marries his high school sweetheart, Elinor White.
1897–99	Studies at Harvard College.

1900	Moves to a farm in West Derry, New Hampshire.
1912	Moves to England, where he farms and writes.
1913	*A Boy's Will* is published in London.
1914	*North of Boston* is published in London.
1915	Moves to a farm near Franconia, New Hampshire.
1916	Elected to National Institute of Letters.
1917–20	Teaches at Amherst College.
1919	Moves to South Shaftsbury, Vermont.
1921–23	Teaches at the University of Michigan.
1923	*Selected Poems* and *New Hampshire* are published; the latter is awarded a Pulitzer Prize.
1928	*West-Running Brook* is published.
1930	*Collected Poems* is published.
1936	*A Further Range* is published; teaches at Harvard.
1938	Wife dies.
1939–42	Teaches at Harvard.
1942	*A Witness Tree,* which is awarded a Pulitzer Prize, is published.
1943–49	Teaches at Dartmouth.
1945	*A Masque of Reason* is published.
1947	*Steeple Bush* and *A Masque of Mercy* are published.
1949	*Complete Poems* (enlarged) is published.
1961	Reads "The Gift Outright" at President John F. Kennedy's inauguration.
1963	Dies on January 29 in Boston.

Mowing   *1913*

There was never a sound beside the wood but one,
And that was my long scythe whispering to the ground.
What was it it whispered? I knew not well myself;
Perhaps it was something about the heat of the sun,
Something, perhaps, about the lack of sound —   5
And that was why it whispered and did not speak.
It was no dream of the gift of idle hours,
Or easy gold at the hand of fay or elf:
Anything more than the truth would have seemed too weak
To the earnest love that laid the swale in rows,   10
Not without feeble-pointed spikes of flowers
(Pale orchises), and scared a bright green snake.

The fact is the sweetest dream that labour knows.
My long scythe whispered and left the hay to make.

CONSIDERATIONS FOR CRITICAL THINKING AND WRITING

1. **FIRST RESPONSE.** Describe the tone of "Mowing." How does reading the poem aloud affect your understanding of it?

2. Discuss the image of the scythe. Do you think it has any symbolic value? Explain why or why not.

3. Paraphrase the poem. What do you think its thematic significance is?

4. Describe the type of sonnet Frost uses in "Mowing."

My November Guest   1913

My Sorrow, when she's here with me,
   Thinks these dark days of autumn rain
Are beautiful as days can be;
She loves the bare, the withered tree;
   She walks the sodden pasture lane.   5

Her pleasure will not let me stay.
   She talks and I am fain to list:
She's glad the birds are gone away,
She's glad her simple worsted grey
   Is silver now with clinging mist.   10

The desolate, deserted trees,
   The faded earth, the heavy sky,
The beauties she so truly sees,
She thinks I have no eye for these,
   And vexes me for reason why.   15

Not yesterday I learned to know
   The love of bare November days
Before the coming of the snow,
But it were vain to tell her so,
   And they are better for her praise.   20

CONSIDERATIONS FOR CRITICAL THINKING AND WRITING

1. **FIRST RESPONSE.** How is "Sorrow" personified? What sort of relationship does the speaker have with her?

2. What kind of tone do the poem's images create?

3. What do you think is this poem's theme?

CONNECTION TO ANOTHER SELECTION

1. Compare Frost's treatment of November with Margaret Atwood's evocation of "February" (p. 143). Explain why you prefer one poem over the other.

5. This poem was first published in 1914; Frost read it to an audience when he visited Russia in 1962. What do these facts suggest about the symbolic value of "Mending Wall"?

CONNECTIONS TO OTHER SELECTIONS

1. How do you think the neighbor in this poem would respond to Dickinson's idea of imagination in "To make a prairie it takes a clover and one bee" (p. 311)?
2. What similarities and differences does the neighbor have with the people Frost describes in "Neither Out Far nor In Deep" (p. 373)?

Home Burial   *1914*

He saw her from the bottom of the stairs
Before she saw him. She was starting down,
Looking back over her shoulder at some fear.
She took a doubtful step and then undid it
To raise herself and look again. He spoke   5
Advancing toward her: "What is it you see
From up there always — for I want to know."
She turned and sank upon her skirts at that,
And her face changed from terrified to dull.
He said to gain time: "What is it you see,"   10
Mounting until she cowered under him.
"I will find out now — you must tell me, dear."
She, in her place, refused him any help
With the least stiffening of her neck and silence.
She let him look, sure that he wouldn't see,   15
Blind creature; and awhile he didn't see.
But at last he murmured, "Oh," and again, "Oh."

"What is it — what?" she said.

                    "Just that I see."

"You don't," she challenged. "Tell me what it is."   20

"The wonder is I didn't see at once.
I never noticed it from here before.
I must be wonted° to it — that's the reason.   *accustomed*
The little graveyard where my people are!
So small the window frames the whole of it.   25
Not so much larger than a bedroom, is it?
There are three stones of slate and one of marble,
Broad-shouldered little slabs there in the sunlight
On the sidehill. We haven't to mind *those*.
But I understand: it is not the stones,   30
But the child's mound —"

                                "Don't, don't, don't, don't," she cried.

She withdrew, shrinking from beneath his arm
That rested on the banister, and slid downstairs;
And turned on him with such a daunting look,   35
He said twice over before he knew himself:
"Can't a man speak of his own child he's lost?"

"Not you! — Oh, where's my hat? Oh, I don't need it!
I must get out of here. I must get air.
I don't know rightly whether any man can."   40

"Amy! Don't go to someone else this time.
Listen to me. I won't come down the stairs."
He sat and fixed his chin between his fists.
"There's something I should like to ask you, dear."

"You don't know how to ask it."   45

                        "Help me, then."
Her fingers moved the latch for all reply.

"My words are nearly always an offense.
I don't know how to speak of anything
So as to please you. But I might be taught,   50
I should suppose. I can't say I see how.
A man must partly give up being a man
With women-folk. We could have some arrangement
By which I'd bind myself to keep hands off
Anything special you're a-mind to name.   55
Though I don't like such things 'twixt those that love.
Two that don't love can't live together without them.
But two that do can't live together with them."
She moved the latch a little. "Don't — don't go.
Don't carry it to someone else this time.   60
Tell me about it if it's something human.
Let me into your grief. I'm not so much
Unlike other folks as your standing there
Apart would make me out. Give me my chance.
I do think, though, you overdo it a little.   65
What was it brought you up to think it the thing
To take your mother-loss of a first child
So inconsolably — in the face of love.
You'd think his memory might be satisfied —"

"There you go sneering now!"   70

                        "I'm not, I'm not!

You make me angry. I'll come down to you.
God, what a woman! And it's come to this,
A man can't speak of his own child that's dead."

"You can't because you don't know how to speak.   75
If you had any feelings, you that dug
With your own hand — how could you? — his little grave;

I saw you from that very window there,
Making the gravel leap and leap in air,
Leap up, like that, like that, and land so lightly   80
And roll back down the mound beside the hole.
I thought, Who is that man? I didn't know you.
And I crept down the stairs and up the stairs
To look again, and still your spade kept lifting.
Then you came in. I heard your rumbling voice   85
Out in the kitchen, and I don't know why,
But I went near to see with my own eyes.
You could sit there with the stains on your shoes
Of the fresh earth from your own baby's grave
And talk about your everyday concerns.   90
You had stood the spade up against the wall
Outside there in the entry, for I saw it."

"I shall laugh the worst laugh I ever laughed.
I'm cursed. God, if I don't believe I'm cursed."

"I can repeat the very words you were saying.   95
'Three foggy mornings and one rainy day
Will rot the best birch fence a man can build.'
Think of it, talk like that at such a time!
What had how long it takes a birch to rot
To do with what was in the darkened parlor   100
You *couldn't* care! The nearest friends can go
With anyone to death, comes so far short
They might as well not try to go at all.
No, from the time when one is sick to death,
One is alone, and he dies more alone.   105
Friends make pretense of following to the grave.
But before one is in it, their minds are turned
And making the best of their way back to life
And living people, and things they understand.
But the world's evil. I won't have grief so   110
If I can change it. Oh, I won't, I won't!"

"There, you have said it all and you feel better.
You won't go now. You're crying. Close the door.
The heart's gone out of it: why keep it up.
Amy! There's someone coming down the road!"   115

"*You* — oh, you think the talk is all. I must go —
Somewhere out of this house. How can I make you —"

"If — you — do!" She was opening the door wider.
"Where do you mean to go? First tell me that.
I'll follow and bring you back by force. I *will!* —"   120

Considerations for Critical Thinking and Writing

1. **FIRST RESPONSE.** This poem tells a story of a relationship. Is the husband insensitive and indifferent to his wife's grief? Characterize the wife. Has Frost invited us to sympathize with one character more than with the other?

2. How has the burial of the child within sight of the stairway window affected the relationship of the couple in this poem? Is the child's grave a symptom or a cause of the conflict between them?

3. What is the effect of splitting the iambic pentameter pattern in lines 18 and 19, 31 and 32, 45 and 46, and 70 and 71?

4. Is the conflict resolved at the conclusion of the poem? Do you think the husband and wife will overcome their differences?

After Apple-Picking   *1914*

My long two-pointed ladder's sticking through a tree
Toward heaven still,
And there's a barrel that I didn't fill
Beside it, and there may be two or three
Apples I didn't pick upon some bough.   5
But I am done with apple-picking now.
Essence of winter sleep is on the night,
The scent of apples: I am drowsing off.
I cannot rub the strangeness from my sight
I got from looking through a pane of glass   10
I skimmed this morning from the drinking trough
And held against the world of hoary grass.
It melted, and I let it fall and break.
But I was well
Upon my way to sleep before it fell,   15
And I could tell
What form my dreaming was about to take.
Magnified apples appear and disappear,
Stem end and blossom end,
And every fleck of russet showing clear.   20
My instep arch not only keeps the ache,
It keeps the pressure of a ladder-round.
I feel the ladder sway as the boughs bend.
And I keep hearing from the cellar bin
The rumbling sound   25
Of load on load of apples coming in.
For I have had too much
Of apple-picking: I am overtired
Of the great harvest I myself desired.
There were ten thousand thousand fruit to touch,   30
Cherish in hand, lift down, and not let fall.
For all
That struck the earth,
No matter if not bruised or spiked with stubble,
Went surely to the cider-apple heap   35
As of no worth.
One can see what will trouble

This sleep of mine, whatever sleep it is.
Were he not gone,
The woodchuck could say whether it's like his   40
Long sleep, as I describe its coming on,
Or just some human sleep.

CONSIDERATIONS FOR CRITICAL THINKING AND WRITING

1. **FIRST RESPONSE.** How does this poem illustrate Frost's view that "Poetry provides the one permissible way of saying one thing and meaning another"? When do you first sense that the detailed description of apple picking is being used that way?

2. What comes after apple picking? What does the speaker worry about in the dream beginning in line 18?

3. Why do you suppose Frost uses apples rather than, say, pears or squash?

Birches   *1916*

When I see birches bend to left and right
Across the lines of straighter darker trees,
I like to think some boy's been swinging them.
But swinging doesn't bend them down to stay
As ice-storms do. Often you must have seen them   5
Loaded with ice a sunny winter morning
After a rain. They click upon themselves
As the breeze rises, and turn many-colored
As the stir cracks and crazes their enamel.
Soon the sun's warmth makes them shed crystal shells   10
Shattering and avalanching on the snow-crust—
Such heaps of broken glass to sweep away
You'd think the inner dome of heaven had fallen.
They are dragged to the withered bracken by the load,
And they seem not to break; though once they are bowed   15
So low for long, they never right themselves:
You may see their trunks arching in the woods
Years afterwards, trailing their leaves on the ground
Like girls on hands and knees that throw their hair
Before them over their heads to dry in the sun.   20
But I was going to say when Truth broke in
With all her matter-of-fact about the ice-storm,
I should prefer to have some boy bend them
As he went out and in to fetch the cows—
Some boy too far from town to learn baseball,   25
Whose only play was what he found himself,
Summer or winter, and could play alone.
One by one he subdued his father's trees
By riding them down over and over again

Until he took the stiffness out of them,   30
And not one but hung limp, not one was left
For him to conquer. He learned all there was
To learn about not launching out too soon
And so not carrying the tree away
Clear to the ground. He always kept his poise   35
To the top branches, climbing carefully
With the same pains you use to fill a cup
Up to the brim, and even above the brim.
Then he flung outward, feet first, with a swish,
Kicking his way down through the air to the ground.   40
So was I once myself a swinger of birches.
And so I dream of going back to be.
It's when I'm weary of considerations,
And life is too much like a pathless wood
Where your face burns and tickles with the cobwebs   45
Broken across it, and one eye is weeping
From a twig's having lashed across it open.
I'd like to get away from earth awhile
And then come back to it and begin over.
May no fate willfully misunderstand me   50
And half grant what I wish and snatch me away
Not to return. Earth's the right place for love:
I don't know where it's likely to go better.
I'd like to go by climbing a birch tree,
And climb black branches up a snow-white trunk,   55
Toward heaven, till the tree could bear no more,
But dipped its top and set me down again.
That would be good both going and coming back.
One could do worse than be a swinger of birches.

Considerations for Critical Thinking and Writing

1. **FIRST RESPONSE.** What do you think the swinging of birches symbolizes?

2. Why does the speaker in this poem prefer the birches to have been bent by boys instead of ice storms?

3. How is "earth" (line 52) described in the poem? Why does the speaker choose it over "heaven" (line 56)?

4. How might the effect of this poem be changed if it were written in heroic couplets instead of blank verse?

5. **CRITICAL STRATEGIES.** Read the section on reader-response strategies (pp. 662–64) in Chapter 25, "Critical Strategies for Reading." Trace your response to this poem over three successive careful readings. How does your understanding of the poem change or develop?

A Girl's Garden

1916

A neighbor of mine in the village
    Likes to tell how one spring
When she was a girl on the farm, she did
    A childlike thing.

One day she asked her father   5
    To give her a garden plot
To plant and tend and reap herself,
    And he said, "Why not?"

In casting about for a corner
    He thought of an idle bit   10
Of walled-off ground where a shop had stood,
    And he said, "Just it."

And he said, "That ought to make you
    An ideal one-girl farm,
And give you a chance to put some strength   15
    On your slim-jim arm."

It was not enough of a garden,
    Her father said, to plow;
So she had to work it all by hand,
    But she don't mind now.   20

She wheeled the dung in the wheelbarrow
    Along a stretch of road;
But she always ran away and left
    Her not-nice load,

And hid from anyone passing.   25
    And then she begged the seed.
She says she thinks she planted one
    Of all things but weed.

A hill each of potatoes,
    Radishes, lettuce, peas,   30
Tomatoes, beets, beans, pumpkins, corn
    And even fruit trees.

And yes, she has long mistrusted
    That a cider apple tree
In bearing there today is hers,   35
    Or at least may be.

Her crop was a miscellany
    When all was said and done,
A little bit of everything,
    A great deal of none.   40

Now when she sees in the village
    How village things go,
Just when it seems to come in right,
    She says, "*I* know!"

"It's as when I was a farmer —"   45
  Oh, never by way of advice!
And she never sins by telling the tale
  To the same person twice.

CONSIDERATIONS FOR CRITICAL THINKING AND WRITING

1. **FIRST RESPONSE.** Write a paraphrase of the poem. What do you think it is about?

2. Why do you suppose Frost uses a narrator to tell the story about the girl instead of having her tell the story herself?

3. What purpose does the father's character serve in the poem?

4. Discuss the distinction that is made between the "ideal one-girl farm" (line 14) and "How village things go" (42).

CONNECTIONS TO OTHER SELECTIONS

1. Compare the narrator in this poem to the narrator in "Stopping by Woods on a Snowy Evening" (p. 370). How, in each poem, do simple activities reveal something about the narrator?

2. Discuss the narrator's treatment of the neighbor in this poem and in "Mending Wall" (p. 359).

"Out, Out —" °   *1916*

The buzz-saw snarled and rattled in the yard
And made dust and dropped stove-length sticks of wood,
Sweet-scented stuff when the breeze drew across it.
And from there those that lifted eyes could count
Five mountain ranges one behind the other   5
Under the sunset far into Vermont.
And the saw snarled and rattled, snarled and rattled,
As it ran light, or had to bear a load.
And nothing happened: day was all but done.
Call it a day, I wish they might have said   10
To please the boy by giving him the half hour
That a boy counts so much when saved from work.
His sister stood beside them in her apron
To tell them "Supper." At the word, the saw,
As if to prove saws knew what supper meant,   15
Leaped out at the boy's hand, or seemed to leap —
He must have given the hand. However it was,
Neither refused the meeting. But the hand!
The boy's first outcry was a rueful laugh,
As he swung toward them holding up the hand   20

"Out, Out —": From Act V, Scene v, of Shakespeare's *Macbeth*.

Half in appeal, but half as if to keep
The life from spilling. Then the boy saw all —
Since he was old enough to know, big boy
Doing a man's work, though a child at heart —
He saw all spoiled. "Don't let him cut my hand off —   25
The doctor, when he comes. Don't let him, sister!"
So. But the hand was gone already.
The doctor put him in the dark of ether.
He lay and puffed his lips out with his breath.
And then — the watcher at his pulse took fright.   30
No one believed. They listened at his heart.
Little — less — nothing! — and that ended it.
No more to build on there. And they, since they
Were not the one dead, turned to their affairs.

CONSIDERATIONS FOR CRITICAL THINKING AND WRITING

1. **FIRST RESPONSE.** This narrative poem is about the accidental death of a Vermont boy. What is the purpose of the story? Some readers have argued that the final lines reveal the speaker's callousness and indifference. What do you think?

2. How does Frost's allusion to *Macbeth* contribute to the meaning of this poem? Does the speaker seem to agree with the view of life expressed in Macbeth's lines?

3. **CRITICAL STRATEGIES.** Read the section on Marxist criticism (pp. 665–66) in Chapter 25, "Critical Strategies for Reading." How do you think a Marxist critic would interpret the family and events described in this poem?

CONNECTIONS TO OTHER SELECTIONS

1. What are the similarities and differences in theme between this poem and Frost's "Nothing Gold Can Stay" (p. 371)?

2. Write an essay comparing how grief is handled by the boy's family in this poem and the couple in "Home Burial" (p. 361).

3. Compare the tone and theme of "'Out, Out—'" with those of Stephen Crane's "A Man Said to the Universe" (p. 164).

Fire and Ice   *1923*

Some say the world will end in fire,
Some say in ice.
From what I've tasted of desire
I hold with those who favor fire.
But if it had to perish twice,
I think I know enough of hate
To say that for destruction ice
Is also great
And would suffice.

CONSIDERATIONS FOR CRITICAL THINKING AND WRITING

1. **FIRST RESPONSE.** What characteristics of human behavior does the speaker associate with fire and ice?
2. What theories about the end of the world are alluded to in lines 1 and 2?
3. How does the speaker's use of understatement and rhyme affect the tone of this poem?

Stopping by Woods on a Snowy Evening

1923

Whose woods these are I think I know.
His house is in the village, though;
He will not see me stopping here
To watch his woods fill up with snow.

My little horse must think it queer   5
To stop without a farmhouse near
Between the woods and frozen lake
The darkest evening of the year.

He gives his harness bells a shake
To ask if there is some mistake.   10
The only other sound's the sweep
Of easy wind and downy flake.

The woods are lovely, dark and deep,
But I have promises to keep,
And miles to go before I sleep,   15
And miles to go before I sleep.

CONSIDERATIONS FOR CRITICAL THINKING AND WRITING

1. **FIRST RESPONSE.** What is the significance of the setting in this poem? How is tone conveyed by the images?
2. What does the speaker find appealing about the woods? What is the purpose of the horse in the poem?
3. Although the last two lines are identical, they are not read at the same speed. Why the difference? What is achieved by the repetition?
4. What is the poem's rhyme scheme? What is the effect of the rhyme in the final stanza?

CONNECTION TO ANOTHER SELECTION

1. What do you think Frost might have to say about Thylias Moss's version of this poem, "Interpretation of a Poem by Frost" (p. 151)?

Neither Out Far nor In Deep

1936

The people along the sand
All turn and look one way.
They turn their back on the land.
They look at the sea all day.

As long as it takes to pass   5
A ship keeps raising its hull;
The wetter ground like glass
Reflects a standing gull.

The land may vary more;
But wherever the truth may be —   10
The water comes ashore,
And the people look at the sea.

They cannot look out far.
They cannot look in deep.
But when was that ever a bar   15
To any watch they keep?

CONSIDERATIONS FOR CRITICAL THINKING AND WRITING

1. **FIRST RESPONSE.** Frost built this poem around a simple observation that raises some questions. Why do people at the beach almost always face the ocean? What feelings and thoughts are evoked by looking at the ocean?

2. Notice how the verb *look* takes on added meaning as the poem progresses. What are the people looking for?

3. How does the final stanza extend the poem's significance?

4. Does the speaker identify with the people described, or does he ironically distance himself from them?

Design   — white on white

1936

begins w/ "I"

I found a dimpled spider, fat and white,   a
On a white heal-all,° holding up a moth   b
Like a white piece of rigid satin cloth —   b
Assorted characters of death and blight   a
Mixed ready to begin the morning right,   a   5
Like the ingredients of a witches' broth —   b
A snow-drop spider, a flower like a froth,   b
And dead wings carried like a paper kite.   a

What had the flower to do with being white,   a   *what brought them together?*
The wayside blue and innocent heal-all?   c   *Gd? fate? design?*
What brought the kindred spider to that height,   a   10
Then steered the white moth thither in the night? a

2 *heal-all:* A common flower, usually blue, once used for medicinal purposes.

but not

What of the existence of evil ?
malevolent mover

What but design of darkness to appall? — C
If design govern in a thing so small. C

CONSIDERATIONS FOR CRITICAL THINKING AND WRITING

1. **FIRST RESPONSE.** What kinds of speculations are raised in the poem's final two lines? Consider the meaning of the title. Is there more than one way to read it?

2. How does the division of the octave and sestet in this sonnet serve to organize the speaker's thoughts and feelings? What is the predominant rhyme? How does that rhyme relate to the poem's meaning?

3. Which words seem especially rich in connotative meanings? Explain how they function in the sonnet.

4. **CRITICAL STRATEGIES.** Read the section on formalist strategies (pp. 648–50) in Chapter 25, "Critical Strategies for Reading." Which words seem especially rich in connotative meanings? Explain how they function in the sonnet.

CONNECTIONS TO OTHER SELECTIONS

1. Compare the ironic tone of "Design" with the tone of William Hathaway's "Oh, Oh" (p. 26). What would you have to change in Hathaway's poem to make it more like Frost's?

2. In an essay discuss Frost's view of God in this poem and Dickinson's perspective in "I know that He exists" (p. 344).

3. Compare "Design" with "In White," Frost's early version of it (p. 376).

The Silken Tent

1942

She is as in a field a silken tent
At midday when a sunny summer breeze
Has dried the dew and all its ropes relent,
So that in guys° it gently sways at ease,   *ropes that steady a tent*
And its supporting central cedar pole,   5
That is its pinnacle to heavenward
And signifies the sureness of the soul,
Seems to owe naught to any single cord,
But strictly held by none, is loosely bound
By countless silken ties of love and thought   10
To everything on earth the compass round,
And only by one's going slightly taut
In the capriciousness of summer air
Is of the slightest bondage made aware.

CONSIDERATIONS FOR CRITICAL THINKING AND WRITING

1. **FIRST RESPONSE.** What is being compared in this sonnet? How does the detail accurately describe both elements of the comparison?

2. How does the form of this one-sentence sonnet help to express its theme? Pay particular attention to the final three lines.

3. How do the sonnet's sounds contribute to its meaning?

The Most of It   1942

He thought he kept the universe alone;
For all the voice in answer he could wake
Was but the mocking echo of his own
From some tree-hidden cliff across the lake.
Some morning from the boulder-broken beach   5
He would cry out on life, that what it wants
Is not its own love back in copy speech,
But counter-love, original response.
And nothing ever came of what he cried
Unless it was the embodiment that crashed   10
In the cliff's talus on the other side,
And then in the far-distant water splashed,
But after a time allowed for it to swim,
Instead of proving human when it neared
And someone else additional to him,   15
As a great buck it powerfully appeared,
Pushing the crumpled water up ahead,
And landed pouring like a waterfall,
And stumbled through the rocks with horny tread,
And forced the underbrush — and that was all.   20

CONSIDERATIONS FOR CRITICAL THINKING AND WRITING

1. **FIRST RESPONSE.** Discuss the significance of the title. To what does "It" refer?

2. Why do you suppose Frost uses a third-person speaker instead of a first-person narrator?

3. The presence of the "great buck" seems to warrant a symbolic reading. What do you make of it?

4. Explain what you think is the poem's theme(s).

CONNECTION TO ANOTHER SELECTION

1. Compare the tone of this poem with "Neither Out Far nor In Deep" (p. 373) as third-person narratives.

Perspectives on Robert Frost

ROBERT FROST

"In White": An Early Version of "Design"   *1912*

A dented spider like a snow drop white
On a white Heal-all, holding up a moth
Like a white piece of lifeless satin cloth —
Saw ever curious eye so strange a sight? —
Portent in little, assorted death and blight   5
Like the ingredients of a witches' broth? —
The beady spider, the flower like a froth,
And the moth carried like a paper kite.

What had that flower to do with being white,
The blue prunella every child's delight.   10
What brought the kindred spider to that height?
(Make we no thesis of the miller's° plight.)   *miller moth*
What but design of darkness and of night?
Design, design! Do I use the word aright?

ends w/ "I"

CONSIDERATIONS FOR CRITICAL THINKING AND WRITING

1. Read "In White" and "Design" (p. 373) aloud. Which version sounds better to you? Why?

2. Compare these versions line for line, paying particular attention to word choice. List the differences and try to explain why you think Frost revised the lines.

3. How does the change in titles reflect a shift in emphasis in the poem?

ROBERT FROST

On the Living Part of a Poem   *1914*

The living part of a poem is the intonation entangled somehow in the syntax, idiom, and meaning of a sentence. It is only there for those who have heard it previously in conversation. . . . It is the most volatile and at the same time important part of poetry. It goes and the language becomes dead language, the poetry dead poetry. With it go the accents, the stresses, the delays that are not the property of vowels and syllables but that are shifted at will with the sense. Vowels have length there is no denying. But the accent of sense supersedes all other accent, overrides it and sweeps it away. I will find you the word *come* variously used in various passages, a whole, half, third, fourth, fifth, and sixth note. It is as long as the sense makes it. When men no longer know the intonations on which we string our words they will fall back on what I may call the absolute length of our syllables, which is the length we would give them in passages that meant nothing. . . . I say you can't read a single good sentence with the salt in it unless you have previously heard it spoken. Neither can you with the help of all the characters and diacritical marks pronounce a single word unless you have previously heard it actually pronounced. Words exist in the mouth not books.

From a letter to Sidney Cox in *A Swinger of Birches: A Portrait of Robert Frost*

CONSIDERATIONS FOR CRITICAL THINKING AND WRITING

1. Why does Frost place so much emphasis on hearing poetry spoken?
2. Choose a passage from "Home Burial" (p. 361) or "After Apple-Picking" (p. 364) and read it aloud. How does Frost's description of his emphasis on intonation help explain the effects he achieves in the passage you have selected?
3. Do you think it is true that all poetry must be heard? Do "words exist in the mouth not books"?

AMY LOWELL (1874–1925)
On Frost's Realistic Technique 1915

I have said that Mr. Frost's work is almost photographic. The qualification was unnecessary, it is photographic. The pictures, the characters, are reproduced directly from life, they are burnt into his mind as though it were a sensitive plate. He gives out what has been put in unchanged by any personal mental process. His imagination is bounded by what he has seen, he is confined within the limits of his experience (or at least what might have been his experience) and bent all one way like the windblown trees of New England hillsides.

From a review of *North of Boston*, *The New Republic*, February 20, 1915

CONSIDERATIONS FOR CRITICAL THINKING AND WRITING

1. Consider the "photographic" qualities of Frost's poetry by discussing particular passages that strike you as having been "reproduced directly from life."
2. Write an essay that supports or refutes Lowell's assertion that "he gives out what has been put in unchanged by any personal mental process."

ROBERT FROST
On the Figure a Poem Makes 1939

Abstraction is an old story with the philosophers, but it has been like a new toy in the hands of the artists of our day. Why can't we have any one quality of poetry we choose by itself? We can have in thought. Then it will go hard if we can't in practice. Our lives for it.

Granted no one but a humanist much cares how sound a poem is if it is only *a* sound. The sound is the gold in the ore. Then we will have the sound out alone and dispense with the inessential. We do till we make the discovery that the object in writing poetry is to make all poems sound as different as possible from each other, and the resources for that of vowels, consonants, punctuation, syntax, words, sentences, meter are not enough. We need the help of context — meaning — subject matter. That is the greatest help towards variety. All that can be done with words is soon told. So also with meters — particularly in our language where there are virtually but two, strict iambic and loose iambic. The ancients with many were still poor if they depended on meters for all tune. It is painful to watch our sprung-rhythmists straining at the point of omitting one short from a foot for relief from monotony. The possibilities for tune from the dramatic tones of meaning struck across the rigidity of a limited meter are endless. And we are back in poetry as merely one more art of having something to say, sound or unsound. Probably better if sound, because deeper and from wider experience.

Then there is this wildness whereof it is spoken. Granted again that it has an equal claim with sound to being a poem's better half. If it is a wild tune, it is a poem. Our problem then is, as modern abstractionists, to have the wildness pure; to be wild with nothing to be wild about. We bring up as aberrationists, giving way to undirected associations and kicking ourselves from one chance suggestion to another in all directions as of a hot afternoon in the life of a grasshopper. Theme alone can steady us down. Just as the first mystery was how a poem could have a tune in such a straightness as meter, so the second mystery is how a poem can have wildness and at the same time a subject that shall be fulfilled.

It should be of the pleasure of a poem itself to tell how it can. The figure a poem makes. It begins in delight and ends in wisdom. The figure is the same as for love. No one can really hold that the ecstasy should be static and stand still in one place. It begins in delight, it inclines to the impulse, it assumes direction with the first line laid down, it runs a course of lucky events, and ends in a clarification of life — not necessarily a great clarification, such as sects and cults are founded on, but in a momentary stay against confusion. It has denouement. It has an outcome that though unforeseen was predestined from the first image of the original mood — and indeed from the very mood. It is but a trick poem and no poem at all if the best of it was thought of first and saved for the last. It finds its own name as it goes and discovers the best waiting for it in some final phrase at once wise and sad — the happy-sad blend of the drinking song.

No tears in the writer, no tears in the reader. No surprise for the writer, no surprise for the reader. For me the initial delight is in the surprise of remembering something I didn't know I knew. I am in a place, in a situation, as if I had materialized from cloud or risen out of the ground. There is a glad recognition of the long lost and the rest follows. Step by step the wonder of unexpected supply keeps going. The impressions most useful to my purpose seem always those I was unaware of and so made no note of at the time when taken, and the conclusion is come to that like giants we are always hurling experience ahead of us to pave the future with against the day when we may want to strike a line of purpose across it for somewhere. The line will have the more charm for not being mechanically straight. We enjoy the straight crookedness of a good walking stick. Modern instruments of precision are being used to make things crooked as if by eye and hand in the old days.

I tell how there may be a better wildness of logic than of inconsequence. But the logic is backward, in retrospect, after the act. It must be more felt than seen ahead like prophecy. It must be a revelation, or a series of revelations, as much for the poet as for the reader. For it to be that there must have been the greatest freedom of the material to move about in it and to establish relations in it regardless of time and space, previous relation, and everything but affinity. We prate of freedom. We call our schools free because we are not free to stay away from them till we are sixteen years of age. I have given up my democratic prejudices and now willingly set the lower classes free to be completely taken care of by the upper classes. Political freedom is nothing to me. I bestow it right and left. All I would keep for myself is the freedom of my material — the condition of body and mind now and then to summons aptly from the vast chaos of all I have lived through.

Scholars and artists thrown together are often annoyed at the puzzle of where they differ. Both work for knowledge; but I suspect they differ most importantly in the way their knowledge is come by. Scholars get theirs with conscientious thoroughness along projected lines of logic; poets theirs cavalierly and as it happens in and out of books. They stick to nothing deliberately, but let what will stick to them like burrs where they walk in the fields. No acquirement is on assignment, or even self-assignment. Knowledge of the second kind is much more available in the wild free ways of wit and art. A school boy may be defined as one who can tell you what he knows in the order in which he learned it. The artist must value himself as he snatches a thing from some previous order in time and space into a new order with not so much as a ligature clinging to it of the old place where it was organic.

More than once I should have lost my soul to radicalism if it had been the originality it was mistaken for by its young converts. Originality and initiative are what I ask for my country. For myself the originality need be no more than the freshness of a poem run in the way I have described: from delight to wisdom. The figure is the same as for love. Like a piece of ice on a hot stove the poem must ride on its own melting. A poem may be worked over once it is in being, but may not be worried into being. Its most precious quality will remain its having run itself and carried away the poet with it. Read it a hundred times: it will forever keep its freshness as a metal keeps its fragrance. It can never lose its sense of a meaning that once unfolded by surprise as it went.

From *Complete Poems of Robert Frost*

CONSIDERATIONS FOR CRITICAL THINKING AND WRITING

1. Frost places a high premium on sound in his poetry because it "is the gold in the ore." Choose one of Frost's poems in this book and explain the effects of its sounds and how they contribute to its meaning.

2. Discuss Frost's explanation of how his poems are written. In what sense is the process both spontaneous and "predestined"?

3. What do you think Frost means when he says he's given up his "democratic prejudices"? Why is "political freedom" nothing to him?

4. Write an essay that examines in more detail the ways scholars and artists "come by" knowledge.

5. Explain what you think Frost means when he writes that "like a piece of ice on a hot stove the poem must ride on its own melting."

ROBERT FROST

On the Way to Read a Poem   *1951*

The way to read a poem in prose or verse is in the light of all the other poems ever written. We may begin anywhere. We *duff* into our first. We read that imperfectly (thoroughness with it would be fatal), but the better to read the second. We read the second the better to read the third, the third the better to read the fourth, the fourth better to read the fifth, the fifth the better to read the first again, or the second if it so happens. For poems are not meant to be read in course any more than they are to be made a study of. I once made a resolve never to put any book to any use it wasn't intended for by its author. Improvement will not be a progression but a widening circulation. Our instinct is to settle down like a revolving dog and make ourselves at home among the poems, completely at our ease as to how they should be taken. The same people will be apt to take poems right as know how to take a hint when there is one and not to take a hint when none is intended. Theirs is the ultimate refinement.

From "Poetry and School," *Atlantic Monthly*, June 1951

CONSIDERATIONS FOR CRITICAL THINKING AND WRITING

1. Given your own experience, how good is Frost's advice about reading in general and his poems in particular?

2. In what sense is a good reader like a "revolving dog" and a person who knows "how to take a hint"?

3. Frost elsewhere in this piece writes, "One of the dangers of college to anyone who wants to stay a human reader (that is to say a humanist) is that he will become a specialist and lose his sensitive fear of landing on the lovely too hard. (With beak and talon.)" Write an essay in response to this concern. Do you agree with Frost's distinction between a "human reader" and a "specialist"?

HERBERT R. COURSEN JR.   (B. 1932)

A Parodic Interpretation of "Stopping by Woods on a Snowy Evening"   *1962*

Much ink has spilled on many pages in exegesis of this little poem. Actually, critical jottings have only obscured what has lain beneath critical noses all these years. To say that the poem means merely that a man stops one night to observe a snowfall, or that the poem contrasts the mundane desire for creature comfort with the sweep of aesthetic appreciation, or that it renders worldly responsibilities paramount, or that it reveals the speaker's latent death-wish is to miss the point rather badly. Lacking has been that mind simple enough to see what is *really* there. . . .

The "darkest evening of the year" in New England is December 21st, a date near that on which the western world celebrates Christmas. It may be that December 21st *is* the date of the poem, or (and with poets this seems more likely) that this is the closest the poet can come to Christmas without giving it all away. Who has "promises to keep" at or near this date, and who must traverse much territory to fulfill these promises? Yes, and who but St. Nick would know the location of *each* home? Only he would know who had "just settled down for a long winter's nap" (the poem's third line — "He will not see me stopping here" — is clearly a veiled allusion) and would not be out inspecting his acreage this night. The unusual phrase "fill up with snow," in the poem's fourth line, is a transfer of Santa's occupational preoccupation to the countryside; he is mulling the filling of countless stockings hung above countless fireplaces by countless careful children. "Harness bells," of course, allude to "Sleighing Song," a popular Christmas tune of the time the poem was written in which the refrain "Jingle Bells! Jingle Bells!" appears; thus again are we put on the Christmas track. The "little horse," like the date, is another attempt at poetic obfuscation. Although the "rein-reindeer" ambiguity has been eliminated from the poem's final version,[1] probably because too obvious, we may speculate that the animal is really a reindeer disguised as a horse by the poet's desire for obscurity, a desire which we must concede has been fulfilled up to now.

The animal is clearly concerned, like the faithful Rudolph — another possible allusion (post facto, hence unconscious) — lest his master fail to complete his mission. Seeing no farmhouse in the second quatrain, but pulling a load of presents, no wonder the little beast wonders! It takes him a full two quatrains to rouse his driver to remember all the empty stockings which hang ahead. And Santa does so reluctantly at that, poor soul, as he ponders the myriad farmhouses and villages which spread between him and his own "winter's nap." The modern St. Nick, lonely and overworked, tosses no "Happy Christmas to all and to all a good night!" into the precipitation. He merely shrugs his shoulders and resignedly plods away.

From "The Ghost of Christmas Past: 'Stopping by Woods
on a Snowy Evening,' " *College English,* December 1962

---

[1] The original draft contained the following line: "That bid me give the reins a shake" (Stageberg-Anderson, *Poetry as Experience* [New York, 1952], p. 457). [Coursen's note.]

CONSIDERATIONS FOR CRITICAL THINKING AND WRITING

1. Is this critical spoof at all credible? Does the interpretation hold any water? Is the evidence reasonable? Why or why not? Which of the poem's details are accounted for and which are ignored?

2. Choose a Frost poem and try writing a parodic interpretation of it.

3. What criteria do you use to distinguish between a sensible interpretation of a poem and an absurd one? In an essay compare and contrast your criteria with the criteria suggested by Peter Rabinowitz in his perspective "On Close Readings" (p. 670).

BLANCHE FARLEY (B. 1937)

The Lover Not Taken 1984

Committed to one, she wanted both
And, mulling it over, long she stood,
Alone on the road, loath
To leave, wanting to hide in the undergrowth.
This new guy, smooth as a yellow wood 5

Really turned her on. She liked his hair,
His smile. But the other, Jack, had a claim
On her already and she had to admit, he did wear
Well. In fact, to be perfectly fair,
He understood her. His long, lithe frame 10

Beside hers in the evening tenderly lay.
Still, if this blond guy dropped by someday,
Couldn't way just lead on to way?
No. For if way led on and Jack
Found out, she doubted if he would ever come back. 15

Oh, she turned with a sigh.
Somewhere ages and ages hence,
She might be telling this. "And I —"
She would say, "stood faithfully by."
But by then who would know the difference? 20

With that in mind, she took the fast way home,
The road by the pond, and phoned the blond.

CONSIDERATIONS FOR CRITICAL THINKING AND WRITING

1. Which Frost poem is the object of this parody?
2. Describe how the stylistic elements mirror Frost's poem.
3. Does this parody seem successful to you? Explain what makes a successful parody.
4. **CREATIVE RESPONSE.** Choose a Frost poem — or a portion of one if it is long — and try writing a parody of it.

PETER D. POLAND

On "Neither Out Far nor In Deep" 1994

Robert Frost's cryptic little lyric "Neither Out Far nor In Deep" remains as elusive as "the truth" that is so relentlessly pursued in the poem itself. The poem is very much "about" this search for truth, and scholars, for the most part, persistently maintain that such effort is both necessary and noble, adding slowly but inexorably to the storehouse of human knowledge. Suggestive though such an interpretation might be, it distorts Frost's intentions — as a close examination of the curious image of "a standing gull," located strategically at the very heart of this enigmatic work (lines 7-8, its literal and thematic center), will reveal.

As "the people" stare vacantly seaward in search of "the truth," mesmerized by the mysterious, limitless sea, they closely resemble standing (as opposed to flying) gulls. Never directly stated, this comparison, so crucial to the poem's meaning, is clearly implied, and it works very much to the people's disadvantage. For the gull is doing what comes naturally, staring into the teeming sea that is its source of life (that is, of food), and it is merely resting from its life-sustaining labors. "The people," implies Frost, in literally and symbolically turning their backs on their domain, the land, to stare incessantly seaward, are unnatural. Their efforts are life-denying in the extreme.

Frost underscores the life-denying nature of their mindless staring by introducing not a flock of standing gulls, but a single gull only—surprising in that standing gulls (or, more accurately, terns, which typically station themselves en masse by the water's edge) are rarely found alone. The solitary gull points up just what "the people" are doing and how isolating and dehumanizing such activity is. So absorbed are they in their quest for "truth" that they have become oblivious of all else but their own solipsistic pursuit. They have cut themselves off from the land world and all that it represents (struggles and suffering, commitments, obligations, responsibilities) and from one another as well. They have become isolates, like the solitary gull that they resemble. Furthermore, Frost emphasizes not the bird itself but only its reflected image in the glassy surface of the shore; it is the reflected image that is the object of our concern, for it bears significantly on "the people" themselves. In an ironic version of Plato's Parable of the Cave, these relentless pursuers of truth have willfully turned their backs on the only "reality" they can ever know—the land world and all that it represents—and in so doing have been reduced to insubstantial images, shadowy reflections of true human beings engaged in genuinely fruitful human endeavor. Nameless, faceless, mindless, they have become pale copies of the real thing.

All of this adds up to one inescapable conclusion: "The people" are indeed "gulls"—that is, "dupes." In their search for ultimate reality they have been tricked, cheated, conned. It is all a fraud, insists Frost (for all that they do see is the occasional passing ship mentioned in lines 5 and 6), and he clearly holds their vain efforts in contempt. As the final stanzas make dramatically clear, they are wasting away their lives in a meaningless quest, for whatever it is and wherever it might be, "the truth" is surely not here. In short, they can look "Neither Out Far nor In Deep." So why bother?

The poem cries out for comparison with Frost's most famous work, his personal favorite, "Stopping by Woods on a Snowy Evening," wherein the seductive woods—"lovely, dark and deep"—recall the mysterious sea of "Neither Out Far nor In Deep." But the narrator of "Stopping by Woods" realizes how dangerously alluring the woods are. He realizes that he has "promises to keep," that he cannot "sleep" in the face of his societal obligations, and so he shortly turns homeward. "The people" of the present poem, however, continue to "look at the sea all day," seduced by its deep, dark, mysterious depths. Turning their backs on the land world, their world, they have violated their promises; they are asleep to their human responsibilities, as their comparison to the reflected image of a solitary gull suggests. For "gulls" they surely are.

From *The Explicator* 52.2 (Winter 1994)

CONSIDERATIONS FOR CRITICAL THINKING AND WRITING

1. Do you agree with Poland's interpretation of this poem or do you agree with the other readers he mentions who argue that the people on the shore are engaged in a "necessary and noble" pursuit of the truth?

2. How does Poland use "Stopping by Woods on a Snowy Evening" (p. 370) to further his argument?

3. Explain whether or not you think Poland's reading of "Neither Out Far nor In Deep" is consistent with your understanding of Frost's attitudes toward human aspiration in "Birches" (p. 365).

DEREK WALCOTT (B. 1930)

The Road Taken   1996

Robert Frost: the icon of Yankee values, the smell of wood smoke, the sparkle of dew, the reality of farmhouse dung, the jocular honesty of an uncle.

Why is the favorite figure of American patriotism not paternal but avuncular? Because uncles are wiser than fathers. They have humor, they keep their distance, they are bachelors, they can't be fooled by rhetoric. Frost loved playing the uncle, relishing the dry enchantment of his own voice, the homely gravel in the throat, the keep-your-distance pseudo-rusticity that suspected every stranger, meaning every reader. The voice is like its weather. It tells you to stay away until you are invited. Its first lines, in the epigraph to Frost's 1949 *Complete Poems,* are not so much invitations as warnings.

> I'm going out to clean the pasture spring;
> I'll only stop to rake the leaves away
> (And wait to watch the water clear, I may):
> I sha'n't be gone long. — You come too.

From the very epigraph, then, the surly ambiguities slide in. Why "I may"? Not for the rhyme, the desperation of doggerel, but because of this truth: that it would take too long to watch the agitated clouded water settle, that is, for as long as patience allows the poet to proceed to the next line. (Note that the parentheses function as a kind of container, or bank, or vessel, of the churned spring.) The refrain, "You come too." An invitation? An order? And how sincere is either? That is the point of Frost's tone, the authoritative but ambiguous distance of a master ironist.

Frost is an autocratic poet rather than a democratic poet. His invitations are close-lipped, wry, quiet; neither the voice nor the metrical line has the open-armed municipal mural expansion of the other democratic poet, Whitman. The people in Frost's dramas occupy a tight and taciturn locale. They are not part of Whitman's parade of blacksmiths, wheelwrights made communal by work. Besieged and threatened, their virtues are as cautious and measured as the scansion by which they are portrayed.

From Joseph Brodsky, Seamus Heaney, and Derek Walcott,
Homage to Robert Frost

Considerations for Critical Thinking and Writing

1. Why does Walcott characterize Frost as more of an uncle than a father? Explain why you agree or disagree.

2. Choose one of Frost's poems in this anthology and use it to demonstrate that he is a "master ironist."

3. Write an essay that fleshes out Walcott's observation that the people in Frost's poems are "Besieged and threatened, their virtues . . . as cautious and measured as the scansion by which they are portrayed."

Two Complementary Critical Readings

Richard Poirier (b. 1925)

On Emotional Suffocation in "Home Burial"   1977

Frost's poetry recurrently dramatizes the discovery that the sharing of a "home" can produce imaginations of uncontrollable threat inside or outside. "Home" can become the source of those fears from which it is supposed to protect us; it can become the habitation of that death whose anguish it is supposed to ameliorate. And this brings us to one of Frost's greatest poetic dramatizations of the theme, "Home Burial." [T]he pressure is shared by a husband and wife, but . . . the role of the husband is ambiguous. Though he does his best to comprehend the wife's difficulties, he is only partly able to do so. The very title of the poem means something about the couple as well as about the dead child buried in back of the house. It is as if "home" were a burial plot for all of them.

The opening lines of Frost's dramatic narratives are usually wonderfully deft in suggesting the metaphoric nature of "home," the human opportunities or imperatives which certain details represent for a husband or a wife. . . . [I]n "Home Burial," the couple are trapped inside the house, which is described as a kind of prison, or perhaps more aptly, a mental hospital. Even the wife's glance out the window can suggest to the husband the desperation she feels within the confines of what has always been his family's "home"; it looks directly on the family graveyard which now holds the body of their recently dead child: [lines 1–30 of "Home Burial" are quoted here].

The remarkable achievement here is that the husband and wife have become so nearly inarticulate in their animosities that the feelings have been transferred to a vision of household arrangements and to their own bodily movements. They and the house conspire together to create an aura of suffocation. . . . Frost's special genius is in the placement of words. The first line poses the husband as a kind of spy; the opening of the second line suggests a habituated wariness on her part, but from that point to line 5 we are shifted back to his glimpse of her as she moves obsessively again, as yet unaware of being watched, to the window. Suggestions of alienation, secretiveness, male intimidation ("advancing toward her") within a situation of mutual distrust, a miasmic fear inside as well as outside the house—we are made to sense this before anyone speaks. Initially the fault seems to lie mostly with the husband. But as soon as she catches him watching her, and as soon as he begins to talk, it is the grim mutuality of their dilemma and the shared responsibilities for it that sustain the dramatic intelligence and power of the poem.

From *Robert Frost: The Work of Knowing*

CONSIDERATIONS FOR CRITICAL THINKING AND WRITING

1. According to Poirier, how can the couple's home be regarded as a kind of "mental hospital"? Compare Poirier's view with Kearns's description in the following perspective on the house as a "marital asylum."

2. Explain why you agree or disagree that the husband's behavior is a form of "male intimidation."

3. Write an essay that discusses the "grim mutuality" of the couple's "dilemma."

KATHERINE KEARNS (B. 1949)
On the Symbolic Setting of "Home Burial"   1987

"Home Burial" may be used to clarify Frost's intimate relationships between sex, death, and madness. The physical iconography is familiar — a stairwell, a window, a doorway, and a grave — elements which Frost reiterates throughout his poetry. The marriage in "Home Burial" has been destroyed by the death of a first and only son. The wife is in the process of leaving the house, crossing the threshold from marital asylum into freedom. The house is suffocating her. Her window view of the graveyard is not enough and is, in fact, a maddening reminder that she could not enter the earth with her son. With its transparent barrier, the window is a mockery of a widened vision throughout Frost's poetry and seems to incite escape rather than quelling it; in "Home Burial" the woman can "see" through the window and into the grave in a way her husband cannot, and the fear is driving her down the steps toward the door — "She was starting down — / Looking back over her shoulder at some fear" — even before she sees her husband. He threatens to follow his wife and bring her back by force, as if he is the cause of her leaving, but his gesture will be futile because it is based on the mistaken assumption that she is escaping him. Pathetically, he is merely an obstacle toward which she reacts at first dully and then with angry impatience. He is an inanimate part of the embattled household, her real impetus for movement comes from the grave.

The house itself, reduced symbolically and literally to a womblike passageway between the bedroom and the threshold, is a correlative for the sexual tension generated by the man's insistence on his marital rights. He offers to "give up being a man" by binding himself "to keep hands off," but their marriage is already sexually damaged and empty. The man and woman move in an intricate dance, she coming downward and then retracing a step, he "Mounting until she cower[s] under him," she "shrinking from beneath his arm" to slide downstairs. Randall Jarrell examines the image of the woman sinking into "a modest, compact, feminine bundle" upon her skirts;[1] it might be further observed that this childlike posture is also very much a gesture of sexual denial, body bent, knees drawn up protectively against the breasts, all encompassed by voluminous skirts. The two are in profound imbalance, and Frost makes the wife's speech and movements the poetic equivalent of stumbling and resistance; her lines are frequently eleven syllables, and often are punctuated by spondees whose forceful but awkward slowness embodies the woman's vacillations "from terrified to dull," and from frozen and silent immobility to anger. Her egress from the house will be symbolic verification of her husband's impotence, and if she leaves it and does not come back, the house will rot as the best birch fence will rot. Unfilled, without a woman with child, it will fall into itself, an image that recurs throughout Frost's poetry. Thus the child's grave predicts the dissolution of household, . . . almost a literal "home burial."

From "'The Place Is the Asylum': Women and Nature in Robert Frost's Poetry," *American Literature*, May 1987

[1] "Robert Frost's 'Home Burial,'" in *The Moment of Poetry*, ed. Don Cameron Allen (Baltimore: Johns Hopkins UP, 1962), p. 104.

Considerations for Critical Thinking and Writing

1. How does Kearns's discussion of the stairwell, window, doorway, and grave shed light on your reading of "Home Burial"?

2. Discuss whether Kearns sympathizes more with the wife or the husband. Which character do you feel more sympathetic toward? Do you think Frost sides with one or the other? Explain your response.

3. Write an essay in which you agree or disagree with Kearns's assessment that "the wife is in the process of crossing the threshold from marital asylum into freedom."

Suggested Topics for Longer Papers

1. Research Frost's popular reputation and compare that with recent biographical accounts of his personal life. How does knowledge of his personal life affect your reading of his poetry?

2. Frost has been described as a cheerful poet of New England who creates pleasant images of the region as well as a poet who creates a troubling, frightening world bordered by anxiety, anguish, doubts, and darkness. How do the poems in this chapter support both of these readings of Frost's poetry?

(Web) Research Robert Frost at bedfordstmartins.com/ meyerpoetry.

14

A Study of Langston Hughes

I believe that poetry should be
direct, comprehensible, and the
epitome of simplicity.

— LANGSTON HUGHES

The poetry of Langston Hughes represents a significant chapter in twentieth-century American literature. The poetry included here both chronicles and evokes African American life during the middle decades of the last century. Moreover, it celebrates the culture and heritage of what is called the "Harlem Renaissance" of the 1920s, which has continued to be a vital tradition and presence in American life. As you introduce yourself to Hughes's innovative techniques and the cultural life embedded in his poetry, keep in mind the Questions for Writing about an Author in Depth (p. 342), which can serve as a guide in your explorations.

Explore contexts for Langston Hughes on *LiterActive*.

Langston Hughes

(*Left*) From the publication of *The Weary Blues* in 1926 on, Hughes was an established figure in the Harlem Renaissance, a cultural movement characterized by an explosion of black literature, theater, music, painting, and political and racial consciousness that began after the First World War. A stamp commemorating the centennial of Hughes's birth (2002) is but one illustration of his lasting impact on American poetry and culture.

© 2002 United States Postal Service. All Rights Reserved. Used with Permission. Hughes stamp image by permission of Harold Ober Associates, Incorporated.

(*Below*) Langston Hughes claimed that Walt Whitman, Carl Sandburg, and Paul Laurence Dunbar were his greatest influences as a poet. However, the experience of black America from the 1920s through the 1960s, the life and language of Harlem, and a love of jazz and the blues clearly shaped the narrative and lyrical experimentation of his poetry. Both the cover and contents of *The Weary Blues*, his first collection of poetry, reflect the influence of music on his work.

Used with permission of Maria Elena Rico Covarrubias.

In this 1932 image taken by African American photographer James VanDerZee, a Harlem couple in raccoon coats pose with a Cadillac on West 127th Street. VanDerZee once commented, "I tried to pose each person in such a way as to tell a story." His work offered America a dazzling view of black middle-class life in the 1920s and 1930s.
© Donna M. VanDerZee.

A BRIEF BIOGRAPHY

Even as a child, Langston Hughes (1902–1967) was wrapped in an important African American legacy. He was raised by his maternal grandmother, who was the widow of Lewis Sheridan Leary, one of the band of men who participated in John Brown's raid on the federal arsenal at Harpers Ferry in 1859. The raid was a desperate attempt to ignite an insurrection that would ultimately liberate slaves in the South. It was a failure. Leary was killed, but the shawl he wore, which was returned to his wife bloodstained and riddled with bullet holes, was proudly worn by Hughes's grandmother fifty years after the raid, and she used it to cover her grandson at night when he was a young boy.

Throughout his long career as a professional writer, Hughes remained true to the African American heritage he celebrated in his writings, which were frankly "racial in theme and treatment, derived from the life I know." In an influential essay published in *The Nation,* "The Negro Artist and the

The famous Lafayette Theatre, located near 132nd street on 7th Avenue, known during the Harlem Renaissance as the "Boulevard of Dreams," was one of New York's first theaters to desegregate (c. 1912). The theater (now a church) seated 2,000 people and, beginning in 1916, employed its own Lafayette Players, who performed popular and classical plays for almost exclusively black audiences. Known as the "House Beautiful" to many of its patrons, the Lafayette also showcased the blues singer Bessie Smith, the jazz composer Duke Ellington, and other prominent African American performers. Shown here is the vibrant opening night of Shakespeare's *Macbeth*, staged by Orson Welles, featuring leading actors Canada Lee and Rose McLendon, with a musical score by James P. Johnson (1936).
The Granger Collection, New York.

Racial Mountain" (1926), he insisted on the need for black artists to draw on their heritage rather than "to run away spiritually from . . . race":

> We younger Negro artists who create now intend to express our individual dark-skinned selves without fear or shame. If white people are pleased, we are glad. If they are not, it doesn't matter. We know we are beautiful. And ugly too. The tom-tom cries and the tom-tom laughs. If colored people are pleased we are glad. If they are not, their displeasure doesn't matter either. We build our temples for tomorrow, strong as we know how, and we stand on top of the mountain, free within ourselves.

That freedom was hard won for Hughes. His father, James Nathaniel Hughes, could not accommodate the racial prejudice and economic frustration that were the result of James's black and white racial ancestry. James abandoned his wife, Carrie Langston Hughes, only one year after their son was born in Joplin, Missouri, and went to find work in Mexico,

Langston Hughes testifying before the Senate Investigations Subcommittee — Senator Joseph McCarthy's subcommittee on subversive activities — on March 27, 1953. Hughes testified: "From my point [of view] it doesn't matter what the form of government is if the rights of the minorities and the poor people are respected, and if they have a chance to advance equally." (See "Un-American Investigators," p. 412.)
© Bettmann/CORBIS.

where he hoped the color of his skin would be less of an issue than in the United States. During the periods when Hughes's mother shuttled from city to city in the Midwest looking for work, she sent her son to live with his grandmother.

Hughes's spotty relationship with his father — a connection he developed in his late teens and maintained only sporadically thereafter — consisted mostly of arguments about his becoming a writer rather than an engineer and businessman as his father wished. Hughes's father could not appreciate or even tolerate his son's ambition to write about the black experience, and Hughes (whose given name was also James but who refused to be identified by it) could not abide his father's contempt for blacks. Consequently, his determination, as he put it in "The Negro Artist," "to express our individual dark-skinned selves without fear or shame" was not only a profound response to African American culture but also an intensely personal commitment that made a relationship with his own father impossible. Though Hughes had been abandoned by his father, he nevertheless felt an early and deep connection to his ancestors, as he reveals in the following poem, written while crossing the Mississippi River by train as he traveled to visit his father in Mexico, just a month after his high school graduation.

The Negro Speaks of Rivers   1921

I've known rivers:
I've known rivers ancient as the world and older than the
    flow of human blood in human veins.

My soul has grown deep like the rivers.

I bathed in Euphrates when dawns were young.   5
I built my hut near the Congo and it lulled me to sleep.
I looked upon the Nile and raised the pyramids above it.
I heard the singing of the Mississippi when Abe Lincoln
    went down to New Orleans, and I've seen its muddy
    bosom turn all golden in the sunset.   10

I've known rivers:
Ancient, dusky rivers.

My soul has grown deep like the rivers.

This poem appeared in *The Crisis,* the official publication of the National Association for the Advancement of Colored People, which eventually published more of Hughes's poems than any other magazine or journal. This famous poem's simple and direct free verse makes clear that Africa's "dusky rivers" run concurrently with the poet's soul as he draws spiritual strength as well as individual identity from the collective experience of his ancestors. The themes of racial pride and personal dignity work their way through some forty books that Hughes wrote, edited, or compiled during his forty-five years of writing.

AN INTRODUCTION TO HIS WORK

Hughes's works include volumes of poetry, novels, short stories, essays, plays, opera librettos, histories, documentaries, autobiographies, biographies, anthologies, children's books, and translations, as well as radio and television scripts. This impressive body of work makes him an important literary artist and a leading African American voice of the twentieth century. First and foremost, he considered himself a poet. He set out to be a poet who could address himself to the concerns of his people in poems that could be read with no formal training or extensive literary background. He wanted his poetry to be "direct, comprehensible, and the epitome of simplicity."

Hughes's poetry echoes the voices of ordinary African Americans and the rhythms of their music. He drew on an oral tradition of working-class folk poetry that embraced black vernacular language at a time when some middle-class blacks of the 1920s felt that the use of the vernacular was an embarrassing handicap and an impediment to social progress. Hughes's response to such concerns was unequivocal; at his readings, some of which were accompanied by jazz musicians or singers, his innovative voice found an appreciative audience. As Hughes very well knew, much of the pleasure associated with his poetry comes from reading it aloud; his many recorded readings give testimony to that pleasure.

The blues can be heard moving through Hughes's poetry as well as in the works of many of his contemporaries associated with the Harlem Renaissance, a movement of African American writers, painters, sculptors, actors, and musicians who were active in New York City's Harlem of the 1920s. Hughes's introduction to the "laughter and pain, hunger and heartache" of blues music began the year he spent at Columbia University. He dropped out after only two semesters because he preferred the night life and culture of Harlem to academic life. The sweet, sad blues songs captured for Hughes the intense pain and yearning that he saw around him and that he incorporated into poems such as "The Weary Blues" (p. 401). He also reveled in the jazz music of Harlem and discovered in its open forms and improvisations an energy and freedom that significantly influenced the style of his poetry.

Hughes's life, like the jazz music that influenced his work, was characterized by improvisation and openness. After leaving Columbia, he worked a series of odd jobs and then traveled as a merchant seaman to Africa and Europe from 1923 to 1924. He jumped ship to work for several months in the kitchen of a Paris nightclub. As he broadened his experience through travel, he continued to write poetry. After his return to the United States in 1925 he published poems in two black magazines, *The Crisis* and *Opportunity,* and met the critic Carl Van Vechten, who sent his poems to the publisher Alfred A. Knopf. He also—as a busboy in a Washington, D.C., hotel—met the poet Vachel Lindsay, who was instrumental in advancing Hughes's reputation as a poet. In 1926 Hughes published his first volume of poems, *The Weary Blues,* and enrolled in Lincoln University in Pennsylvania, his education funded by a generous patron. His second volume of verse, *Fine Clothes to the Jew,* appeared in 1927, and by the time he graduated from Lincoln in 1929 he was reading his poems publicly on a book tour of the South. Hughes ended the decade as more than a promising poet; as Countee Cullen pronounced in a mixed review of *The Weary Blues* (mixed because Cullen believed that African American poets should embrace universal themes rather than racial themes), Hughes had "arrived."

Hughes wrote more prose than poetry during the 1930s, publishing his first novel, *Not without Laughter* (1930), and a collection of stories, *The Ways of White Folks* (1934). In addition to writing a variety of magazine articles, he also worked on a number of plays and screenplays. Many of his poems from this period reflect proletarian issues. During this decade Hughes's travels took him to all points of the compass—Cuba, Haiti, the Soviet Union, China, Japan, Mexico, France, and Spain—but his general intellectual movement was decidedly toward the left. Hughes was attracted to the American Communist Party, owing to its insistence on equality for all working-class people regardless of race. Like many other Americans of the thirties, he turned his attention away from the exotic twenties and focused on the economic and political issues attending the Great Depression that challenged the freedom and dignity of common humanity.

During World War II, Hughes helped the war effort by writing jingles and catchy verses to sell war bonds and to bolster morale. His protest poems of the thirties were largely replaced by poems that returned to earlier themes centered on the everyday lives of African Americans. In 1942 Hughes described his new collection of poems, *Shakespeare in Harlem,* as "light verse. Afro-American in the blues mood . . . to be read aloud, crooned, shouted, recited, and sung. Some with gestures, some not—as you like." Soon after this collection appeared, the character of Jesse B. Simple emerged from Hughes's 1943 newspaper column for the Chicago *Defender.* Hughes developed this popular urban African American character in five humorous books published over a fifteen-year period: *Simple Speaks His Mind* (1950), *Simple Takes a Wife* (1953), *Simple Stakes a Claim* (1957), *The Best of Simple* (1961), and *Simple's Uncle Sam* (1965). Two more poetry collections appeared in the forties: *Fields of Wonder* (1947) and *One-Way Ticket* (1949).

In the 1950s and 1960s Hughes's poetry again revealed the strong influence of black music, especially in the rhythms of *Montage of a Dream Deferred* (1951) and *Ask Your Mama: 12 Moods for Jazz* (1961). From the poem "Harlem" (p. 411) in *Montage of a Dream Deferred,* Lorraine Hansberry derived the title of her 1959 play *A Raisin in the Sun.* This is only a small measure of Hughes's influence on his fellow African American writers, but it is suggestive nonetheless. For some in the 1950s, however, Hughes and his influence occasioned suspicion. He was watched closely by the FBI and the Special Committee on Un-American Activities of the House of Representatives because of his alleged communist activities in the 1930s. Hughes denied that he was ever a member of the Communist party, but he and others, including Albert Einstein and Paul Robeson, were characterized as "dupes and fellow travelers" by *Life* magazine in 1949. Hughes was subpoenaed to appear before Senator Joseph McCarthy's subcommittee on subversive activities in 1953 and listed by the FBI as a security risk until 1959. His anger and indignation over these attacks from the right can be seen in his poem "Un-American Investigators" (p. 412), published posthumously in *The Panther and the Lash* (1967).

Despite the tremendous amount that Hughes published, including two autobiographies, *The Big Sea* (1940) and *I Wonder as I Wander* (1956), he remains somewhat elusive. He never married or had friends who can lay claim to truly knowing him beyond what he wanted them to know (even though several biographies have been published). And yet Hughes is well known — not for his personal life but for his treatment of the possibilities of African American experiences and identities. Like Walt Whitman, one of his favorite writers, Hughes created a persona that spoke for more than himself. Consider Hughes's voice in the following poem.

I, Too   1925

I, too, sing America.

I am the darker brother.
They send me to eat in the kitchen
When company comes,
But I laugh,   5
And eat well,
And grow strong.

Tomorrow,
I'll be at the table
When company comes.   10
Nobody'll dare
Say to me,
"Eat in the kitchen,"
Then.

Besides,   15
They'll see how beautiful I am
And be ashamed —

I, too, am America.

The "darker brother" who celebrates America is certain of a better future when he will no longer be shunted aside by "company." The poem is characteristic of Hughes's faith in the racial consciousness of African Americans, a consciousness that reflects their integrity and beauty while simultaneously demanding respect and acceptance from others: "Nobody'll dare / Say to me, / 'Eat in the kitchen,' / Then."

Hughes's poetry reveals his hearty appetite for all humanity, his insistence on justice for all, and his faith in the transcendent possibilities of joy and hope that make room for everyone at America's table.

Chronology

1902	Born on February 1, in Joplin, Missouri.
1903–14	Lives primarily with his grandmother in Lawrence, Kansas.
1920	Graduates from high school in Cleveland.
1921–22	Attends Columbia University for one year but then drops out to work odd jobs and discover Harlem.
1923–24	Travels to Africa and Europe while working on a merchant ship.
1926	Publishes his first collection of poems, *The Weary Blues,* and enters Lincoln University in Pennsylvania.
1929	Graduates from Lincoln University.
1930	Publishes his first novel, *Not without Laughter.*
1932	Travels to the Soviet Union.
1934	Publishes his first collection of short stories, *The Ways of White Folks.*
1935	His play *Mulatto* is produced on Broadway.
1937	Covers the Spanish Civil War for the Baltimore *Afro-American.*
1938–39	Founds African American theaters in Harlem and Los Angeles.
1940	Publishes his first autobiography, *The Big Sea.*
1943	Creates the character of Simple in columns for the Chicago *Defender.*
1947	Is poet-in-residence at Atlanta University.
1949	Teaches at University of Chicago's Laboratory School.
1950	Publishes his first volume of Simple sketches, *Simple Speaks His Mind.*
1951	Publishes a translation of Federico García Lorca's *Gypsy Ballads.*
1953	Is subpoenaed to appear before Senator Joseph McCarthy's subcommittee on subversive activities in Washington, D.C.
1954–55	Publishes a number of books for young readers, including *The First Book of Jazz* and *Famous American Negroes.*
1956	Publishes his second autobiography, *I Wonder as I Wander.*
1958	Publishes *The Langston Hughes Reader.*
1960	Publishes *An African Treasury: Articles, Essays, Stories, Poems by Black Africans.*
1961	Is inducted into the National Institute of Arts and Letters.
1962	Publishes *Fight for Freedom: The Story of the NAACP.*

1963	Publishes *Five Plays by Langston Hughes.*
1964	Publishes *New Negro Poets: U.S.A.*
1965	Defends Martin Luther King Jr. from attacks by militant blacks.
1966	Is appointed by President Lyndon B. Johnson to lead the American delegation to the First World Festival of Negro Arts in Dakar.
1967	Dies on May 22 in New York City; his last volume of poems, *The Panther and the Lash,* is published posthumously.
1994	*The Collected Poems of Langston Hughes,* edited by Arnold Rampersad and David Roessel, is published.

Negro   *1922*

I am a Negro:
  Black as the night is black,
  Black like the depths of my Africa.

I've been a slave:
  Caesar told me to keep his door-steps clean.   5
  I brushed the boots of Washington.

I've been a worker:
  Under my hand the pyramids arose.
  I made mortar for the Woolworth Building.

I've been a singer: 10
  All the way from Africa to Georgia
  I carried my sorrow songs.
  I made ragtime.

I've been a victim:
  The Belgians cut off my hands in the Congo.   15
  They lynch me still in Mississippi.

I am a Negro:
  Black as the night is black,
  Black like the depths of my Africa.

CONSIDERATIONS FOR CRITICAL THINKING AND WRITING

1. **FIRST RESPONSE.** What sort of identity does the speaker claim for the "Negro"? What is the effect of the litany of roles?

2. What is the effect of the repetition of the first and last stanzas?

3. What kind of history of black people does the speaker describe?

CONNECTIONS TO OTHER SELECTIONS

1. How does Hughes's use of night and blackness in "Negro" help to explain their meaning in the poem "Dream Variations" (p. 401)?

2. Write an essay comparing the treatment of oppression in "Negro" with that in William Blake's "The Chimney Sweeper" (p. 179).

Danse Africaine   1922

The low beating of the tom-toms,
The slow beating of the tom-toms,
    Low . . . slow
    Slow . . . low —
    Stirs your blood.   5
        Dance!
A night-veiled girl
    Whirls softly into a
    Circle of light.
    Whirls softly . . . slowly,   10
Like a wisp of smoke around the fire —
    And the tom-toms beat,
    And the tom-toms beat,
And the low beating of the tom-toms
    Stirs your blood.   15

CONSIDERATIONS FOR CRITICAL THINKING AND WRITING

1. **FIRST RESPONSE.** How do the sounds of this poem build its meaning? (What *is* its meaning?)

2. What effect do the repeated rhythms have? You may need to read the poem aloud to answer.

CONNECTION TO ANOTHER SELECTION

1. **CREATIVE RESPONSE.** Try rewriting this poem based on the prescription for poetry in Hughes's "Formula" (p. 403).

Mother to Son   1922

Well, son, I'll tell you:
Life for me ain't been no crystal stair.
It's had tacks in it,
And splinters,
And boards torn up,   5
And places with no carpet on the floor —
Bare.
But all the time
I'se been a-climbin' on,
And reachin' landin's,   10

And turnin' corners,
And sometimes goin' in the dark
Where there ain't been no light.
So boy, don't you turn back.
Don't you set down on the steps   15
'Cause you finds it's kinder hard.
Don't you fall now—
For I'se still goin', honey,
I'se still climbin',
And life for me ain't been no crystal stair.   20

CONSIDERATIONS FOR CRITICAL THINKING AND WRITING

1. **FIRST RESPONSE.** How is the central metaphor of climbing stairs a particularly appropriate idea for conveying this poem's theme?

2. Try rewriting the dialect of this poem in formal diction. How does this change your response to the poem?

3. What does it imply that the stairs are crystal rather than, say, carpeted?

Jazzonia   1923

Oh, silver tree!
Oh, shining rivers of the soul!

In a Harlem cabaret
Six long-headed jazzers play.
A dancing girl whose eyes are bold   5
Lifts high a dress of silken gold.

Oh, singing tree!
Oh, shining rivers of the soul!

Were Eve's eyes
In the first garden   10
Just a bit too bold?
Was Cleopatra gorgeous
In a gown of gold?

Oh, shining tree!
Oh, silver rivers of the soul!   15

In a whirling cabaret
Six long-headed jazzers play.

CONSIDERATIONS FOR CRITICAL THINKING AND WRITING

1. **FIRST RESPONSE.** Does "Jazzonia" capture what you imagine a Harlem cabaret to have been like? Discuss the importance of the setting.

2. What is the effect of the variations in lines 1–2, 7–8, and 14–15?

3. What do the allusions to Eve and Cleopatra add to the poem's meaning? Are the questions raised about them answered?

CONNECTION TO ANOTHER SELECTION

1. Compare in an essay the rhythms of "Jazzonia" and "Danse Africaine" (p. 399).

Dream Variations   *1924*

To fling my arms wide
In some place of the sun,
To whirl and to dance
Till the white day is done.
Then rest at cool evening   5
Beneath a tall tree
While night comes on gently,
   Dark like me —
That is my dream!

To fling my arms wide   10
In the face of the sun,
Dance! Whirl! Whirl!
Till the quick day is done.
Rest at pale evening . . .
A tall, slim tree . . .   15
Night coming tenderly
   Black like me.

CONSIDERATIONS FOR CRITICAL THINKING AND WRITING

1. **FIRST RESPONSE.** What distinctions are made in the poem between night and day? Which is the dream?
2. Describe the speaker's "Dream." How might the dream be understood metaphorically?
3. How do the rhythms of the lines contribute to the poem's effects?

CONNECTIONS TO OTHER SELECTIONS

1. In an essay compare and contrast the meanings of darkness and the night in this poem and in William Stafford's "Traveling through the Dark" (p. 169).
2. Discuss the significance of the dream in this poem and in "Dream Boogie" (p. 410).

The Weary Blues   *1925*

Droning a drowsy syncopated tune,
Rocking back and forth to a mellow croon,
   I heard a Negro play.
Down on Lenox Avenue° the other night   *street in Harlem*

By the pale dull pallor of an old gas light   5
    He did a lazy sway. . . .
    He did a lazy sway. . . .
To the tune o' those Weary Blues.
With his ebony hands on each ivory key
He made that poor piano moan with melody.   10
    O Blues!
Swaying to and fro on his rickety stool
He played that sad raggy tune like a musical fool.
    Sweet Blues!
Coming from a black man's soul.   15
    O Blues!
In a deep song voice with a melancholy tone
I heard that Negro sing, that old piano moan —
    "Ain't got nobody in all this world,
        Ain't got nobody but ma self.   20
        I's gwine to quit ma frownin'
        And put ma troubles on the shelf."

Thump, thump, thump, went his foot on the floor.
He played a few chords then he sang some more —
    "I got the Weary Blues   25
        And I can't be satisfied.
        Got the Weary Blues
        And can't be satisfied —
        I ain't happy no mo'
        And I wish that I had died."
And far into the night he crooned that tune.   30
The stars went out and so did the moon.
The singer stopped playing and went to bed
While the Weary Blues echoed through his head.
He slept like a rock or a man that's dead.   35

CONSIDERATIONS FOR CRITICAL THINKING AND WRITING

1. **FIRST RESPONSE.** Write a one-paragraph description of the blues based on how the poem presents this kind of music.

2. How does the speaker's voice compare with the singer's?

3. Comment on the effects of the rhymes.

4. **CRITICAL STRATEGIES.** Read the section on formalist strategies (pp. 648–50) in Chapter 25, "Critical Strategies for Reading," and explain how the rhythm of the lines reflects their meaning.

CONNECTION TO ANOTHER SELECTION

1. Discuss "The Weary Blues" and "Lenox Avenue: Midnight" (p. 404) as vignettes of urban life in America. Do you think that these poems, though written more than seventy years ago, are still credible descriptions of city life? Explain why or why not.

Cross   *1925*

My old man's a white old man
And my old mother's black.
If ever I cursed my white old man
I take my curses back.

If ever I cursed my black old mother   5
And wished she were in hell,
I'm sorry for that evil wish
And now I wish her well.

My old man died in a fine big house.
My ma died in a shack.   10
I wonder where I'm gonna die,
Being neither white nor black?

CONSIDERATIONS FOR CRITICAL THINKING AND WRITING

1. **FIRST RESPONSE.** What do you think has caused the speaker to retract his or her hard feelings about his or her parents?

2. Discuss the possible meaning of the title.

3. Why do you think the speaker regrets having "cursed" his or her father and mother? Is it possible to determine if the speaker is male or female? Why or why not?

4. What informs the speaker's attitude toward life?

CONNECTION TO ANOTHER SELECTION

1. Read the perspective by Robert Francis, "On 'Hard' Poetry" (p. 48), and write an essay explaining why you would characterize "Cross" as "hard" or "soft" poetry.

Formula   *1926*

Poetry should treat
    Of lofty things
Soaring thoughts
    And birds with wings.

The Muse of Poetry   5
    Should not know
That roses
    In manure grow.

The Muse of Poetry
    Should not care   10
That earthly pain
    Is everywhere.

Poetry!
Treats of lofty things:
Soaring thoughts   15
And birds with wings.

CONSIDERATIONS FOR CRITICAL THINKING AND WRITING

1. **FIRST RESPONSE.** What makes this poem a parody? What assumptions about poetry are being made fun of?
2. How does "Formula" fit the prescriptions offered in the advice to greeting-card freelancers (p. 43)?

CONNECTIONS TO OTHER SELECTIONS

1. Choose any two poems by Hughes in this collection and explain why they do not fit the "Formula."
2. Write an essay that explains how Helen Farries's "Magic of Love" (p. 44) conforms to the ideas about poetry presented in "Formula."

Esthete in Harlem   *1926*

Strange,
That in this nigger place
I should meet life face to face;
When, for years, I had been seeking
Life in places gentler-speaking,
Until I came to this vile street
And found Life stepping on my feet!

CONSIDERATIONS FOR CRITICAL THINKING AND WRITING

1. **FIRST RESPONSE.** Why might an esthete find Harlem strange? What changes the speaker's mind?
2. Discuss the effect of the enjambment in lines 6–7.

Lenox Avenue: Midnight   *1926*

The rhythm of life
Is a jazz rhythm,
Honey.
The gods are laughing at us.

The broken heart of love,   5
The weary, weary heart of pain, —
Overtones,

Undertones,
To the rumble of street cars,
To the swish of rain.   10

Lenox Avenue,
Honey.
Midnight,
And the gods are laughing at us.

CONSIDERATIONS FOR CRITICAL THINKING AND WRITING

1. **FIRST RESPONSE.** What, in your own experience, is the equivalent of Lenox Avenue for the speaker?
2. For so brief a poem there are many sounds in these fourteen lines. What are they? How do they reinforce the poem's meanings?
3. What do you think is the poem's theme?

CONNECTIONS TO OTHER SELECTIONS

1. In an essay compare the theme of this poem with that of Emily Dickinson's "I know that He exists" (p. 344).
2. Compare and contrast the speaker's tone in this poem with that of the speaker in Thomas Hardy's "Hap" (p. 599).

Song for a Dark Girl   *1927*

Way Down South in Dixie
   (Break the heart of me)
They hung my black young lover
   To a cross roads tree.

Way Down South in Dixie   5
   (Bruised body high in air)
I asked the white Lord Jesus
   What was the use of prayer.

Way down South in Dixie
   (Break the heart of me)   10
Love is a naked shadow
   On a gnarled and naked tree.

CONSIDERATIONS FOR CRITICAL THINKING AND WRITING

1. **FIRST RESPONSE.** What allusion is made in the first line of each stanza? How is that allusion ironic?
2. What *is* "the use of prayer" in this poem? Is the question answered? What, in particular, leads you to your conclusion?
3. Discuss the relationship between love and hatred in the poem.

1. Compare the speaker's sensibilities in this poem and in Emily Dickinson's "If I can stop one Heart from breaking" (p. 308). What kinds of cultural assumptions are implicit in each speaker's voice?

Red Silk Stockings   *1927*

Put on yo' red silk stockings,
Black gal.
Go out an' let de white boys
Look at yo' legs.

Ain't nothin' to do for you, nohow,   5
Round this town, —
You's too pretty.

Put on yo' red silk stockings, gal,
An' tomorrow's chile'll
Be a high yaller.   10

Go out an' let de white boys
Look at yo' legs.

CONSIDERATIONS FOR CRITICAL THINKING AND WRITING

1. **FIRST RESPONSE.** Whom do you think is speaking? Describe his or her tone.
2. Discuss the racial dimensions of this poem.
3. Write a response from the girl — does she put on the red silk stockings? Explain why you imagine her reacting in a certain way.

CONNECTION TO ANOTHER SELECTION

1. Write an essay that compares relations between whites and blacks in this poem and in "Dinner Guest: Me" (p. 415).

Rent-Party° Shout: For a Lady Dancer   *1930*

Whip it to a jelly!
Too bad Jim!
Mamie's got ma man —
An' I can't find him.

Rent-Party: In Harlem during the 1920s, parties were given that charged admission to raise money for rent.

Shake that thing! O!   5
Shake it slow!
That man I love is
Mean an' low.
Pistol an' razor!
Razor an' gun!   10
If I sees ma man he'd
Better run—
For I'll shoot him in de shoulder,
Else I'll cut him down,
Cause I knows I can find him   15
When he's in de ground—
Then can't no other women
Have him layin' round.
So play it, Mr. Nappy!
Yo' music's fine!   20
I'm gonna kill that
Man o' mine!

Considerations for Critical Thinking and Writing

1. **FIRST RESPONSE.** Describe the type of music you think might be played at this party today.
2. In what sense is this poem a kind of "Shout"?
3. How is the speaker's personality characterized by her use of language?
4. How does Hughes's use of short lines affect your reading of the poem?

Drum   *1931*

Bear in mind
That death is a drum
Beating for ever
Till the last worms come
To answer its call,   5
Till the last stars fall,
Until the last atom
Is no atom at all,
Until time is lost
And there is no air   10
And space itself
Is nothing nowhere.
Death is a drum,
A signal drum,
Calling all life   15
To Come! Come!
Come!

Park Bench

1934

I live on a park bench.
You, Park Avenue.
Hell of a distance
Between us two.

I beg a dime for dinner —   5
You got a butler and a maid.
But I'm wakin' up!
Say, ain't you afraid

That I might, just maybe,
In a year or two,   10
Move on over
To Park Avenue?

Ballad of the Landlord

1940

Landlord, landlord,
My roof has sprung a leak.
Don't you 'member I told you about it
Way last week?

Landlord, landlord,   5
These steps is broken down.
When you come up yourself
It's a wonder you don't fall down.

Ten Bucks you say I owe you?
Ten Bucks you say is due?   10

Well, that's Ten Bucks more'n I'll pay you
Till you fix this house up new.

What? You gonna get eviction orders?
You gonna cut off my heat?
You gonna take my furniture and   15
Throw it in the street?

Um-huh! You talking high and mighty.
Talk on — till you get through.
You ain't gonna be able to say a word
If I land my fist on you.   20

Police! Police!
Come and get this man!
He's trying to ruin the government
And overturn the land!

Copper's whistle!   25
Patrol bell!
Arrest.

Precinct Station.
Iron cell.
Headlines in press: 30

MAN THREATENS LANDLORD
TENANT HELD NO BAIL
JUDGE GIVES NEGRO 90 DAYS IN COUNTY JAIL

CONSIDERATIONS FOR CRITICAL THINKING AND WRITING

1. **FIRST RESPONSE.** The poem incorporates both humor and serious social commentary. Which do you think is dominant? Explain.
2. Why is the literary ballad an especially appropriate form for the content of this poem?
3. How does the speaker's language simultaneously characterize him and the landlord?

CONNECTION TO ANOTHER SELECTION

1. Write an essay on landlords based on this poem and Wole Soyinka's "Telephone Conversation" (p. 538).

Morning After   *1942*

I was so sick last night I
Didn't hardly know my mind.
So sick last night I
Didn't know my mind.
I drunk some bad licker that   5
Almost made me blind.

Had a dream last night I
Thought I was in hell.
I drempt last night I
Thought I was in hell.   10
Woke up and looked around me —
Babe, your mouth was open like a well.

I said, Baby! Baby!
Please don't snore so loud.
Baby! Please!   15
Please don't snore so loud.
You jest a little bit o' woman but you
Sound like a great big crowd.

CONSIDERATIONS FOR CRITICAL THINKING AND WRITING

1. **FIRST RESPONSE.** How does the final stanza of this poem take its mood and dominant idea in a different direction from what a reader might expect based on the first two stanzas?

2. **CREATIVE RESPONSE.** Write a fourth stanza that brings the poem back to the tone of the first two stanzas.

Dream Boogie   *1951*

Good morning, daddy!
Ain't you heard
The boogie-woogie rumble
Of a dream deferred?
Listen closely: 5
You'll hear their feet
Beating out and beating out a —

  You think
  It's a happy beat?

Listen to it closely: 10
Ain't you heard
something underneath
like a —

  What did I say?

Sure,   15
I'm happy!
Take it away!

  Hey, pop!
  Re-bop!
  Mop!   20

  Y-e-a-h!

CONSIDERATIONS FOR CRITICAL THINKING AND WRITING

1. **FIRST RESPONSE.** Answer the question *"You think / It's a happy beat?"*
2. Discuss the poem's musical qualities. Which lines are most musical?
3. Describe the competing tones in the poem. Which do you think is predominant?

CONNECTIONS TO OTHER SELECTIONS

1. In an essay compare and contrast the thematic tensions in this poem and in "Harlem," the poem at the bottom of the page.
2. How are the "dreams" different in "Dream Boogie" and "Dream Variations" (p. 401)?

125th Street°   1950

Face like a chocolate bar
full of nuts and sweet.

Face like a jack-o'-lantern,
candle inside.

Face like slice of melon,
grin that wide.

125th Street: The main street in Harlem.

CONSIDERATIONS FOR CRITICAL THINKING AND WRITING

1. **FIRST RESPONSE.** How do these three similes create a vivid picture of 125th Street?
2. How does this poem confirm the poet Marvin Bell's observation that "a short poem need not be small"?

Harlem   1951

What happens to a dream deferred?

    Does it dry up
    like a raisin in the sun?
    Or fester like a sore —
    And then run?   5
    Does it stink like rotten meat?
    Or crust and sugar over —
    like a syrupy sweet?

    Maybe it just sags
    like a heavy load.   10

    Or does it explode?

CONSIDERATIONS FOR CRITICAL THINKING AND WRITING

1. **FIRST RESPONSE.** How might the question asked in this poem be raised by any individual or group whose dreams and aspirations are thwarted?

2. In some editions of Hughes's poetry the title of this poem is "Dream Deferred." What would the effect of this change be on your reading of the poem's symbolic significance?

3. How might the final line be completed as a simile? What is the effect of the speaker not completing the simile? Why is this an especially useful strategy?

CONNECTION TO ANOTHER SELECTION

1. Write an essay on the themes of "Harlem" and James Merrill's "Casual Wear" (p. 175).

Un-American Investigators 1953

The committee's fat,
Smug, almost secure
Co-religionists
Shiver with delight
In warm manure   5
As those investigated —
Too brave to name a name —
Have pseudonyms revealed
In Gentile game
    Of who,   10
    Born Jew,
    Is who?
Is not your name Lipshitz?
    Yes.
Did you not change it   15
For subversive purposes?
    No.
For nefarious gain?
    Not so.
Are you sure?   20
The committee shivers
With delight in
Its manure.

CONSIDERATIONS FOR CRITICAL THINKING AND WRITING

1. **FIRST RESPONSE.** What do you think is the political bent of the speaker? What in the poem suggests this?

2. Research in the library and online the hearings and investigations of the House of Representatives' Special Committee on Un-American Activities. How is this background information relevant to an understanding of this poem?

3. How does the speaker characterize the investigators?

4. Given the images in the poem, what might serve as a substitute for its ironic title?

CONNECTION TO ANOTHER SELECTION

1. Write an essay that connects the committee described in this poem with the speaker in E. E. Cummings's "next to of course god america i" (p. 163). What do they have in common?

Old Walt   *1954*

Old Walt Whitman
Went finding and seeking,
Finding less than sought
Seeking more than found,
Every detail minding   5
Of the seeking or the finding.

Pleasured equally
In seeking as in finding,
Each detail minding,
Old Walt went seeking   10
And finding.

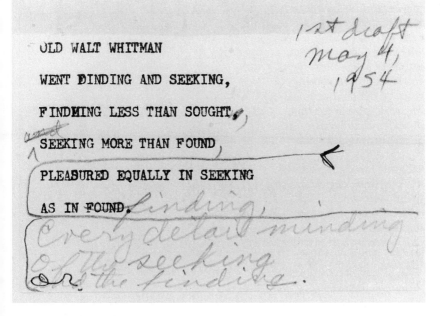

Manuscript page for "Old Walt" (1954) showing an earlier stage of the poem with Hughes's revisions.

Reprinted by permission of Harold Ober Associates, Incorporated.

Considerations for Critical Thinking and Writing

1. **FIRST RESPONSE.** Read any poem by Whitman in this book. Do you agree with the speaker's take on Whitman's poetry?

2. Write an explication of "Old Walt." (For a discussion of how to explicate a poem, see the sample explication on p. 294.)

3. What is the effect of the poem's repeated sounds?

4. To what extent do you think lines 3 and 4 could be used to describe Hughes's poetry as well as Whitman's?

Connection to Another Selection

1. How does Hughes's tribute to Whitman compare with his tribute to Frederick Douglass (p. 416)?

doorknobs 1961

The simple silly terror
of a doorknob on a door
that turns to let in life
on two feet standing,
walking, talking,   5
wearing dress or trousers,
maybe drunk or maybe sober,
maybe smiling, laughing, happy,
maybe tangled in the terror
of a yesterday past grandpa   10
when the door from out there opened
into here where I, antenna,
recipient of your coming,
received the talking image
of the simple silly terror   15
of a door that opens
at the turning of a knob
to let in life
walking, talking, standing
wearing dress or trousers,   20
drunk or maybe sober,
smiling, laughing, happy,
or tangled in the terror
of a yesterday past grandpa
not of our own doing.   25

Considerations for Critical Thinking and Writing

1. **FIRST RESPONSE.** Why is the doorknob associated with "terror"? Does it have any symbolic value, or should it be read literally?

2. How do the style and content of this poem differ from those of the other poems by Hughes in this anthology?
3. The final eight lines repeat much of the first part of the poem. What is repeated and what is changed? What is the effect of this repetition?

CONNECTION TO ANOTHER SELECTION

1. Write an essay comparing the theme of this poem with that of Jim Stevens's "Schizophrenia" (p. 148).

Dinner Guest: Me   1965

I know I am
The Negro Problem
Being wined and dined,
Answering the usual questions
That come to white mind   5
Which seeks demurely
To probe in polite way
The why and wherewithal
Of darkness U.S.A.—
Wondering how things got this way   10
In current democratic night,
Murmuring gently
Over *fraises du bois,*
"I'm so ashamed of being white."

The lobster is delicious,   15
The wine divine,
And center of attention
At the damask table, mine.
To be a Problem on
Park Avenue at eight   20
Is not so bad.
Solutions to the Problem,
Of course, wait.

CONSIDERATIONS FOR CRITICAL THINKING AND WRITING

1. **FIRST RESPONSE.** What does the speaker satirize in this description of a dinner party? Do you think this "Problem" exists today?
2. Why is line 9, "Of darkness U.S.A.—," especially resonant?
3. What effects are created by the speaker's diction?
4. Discuss the effects of the rhymes in lines 15–23.

CONNECTION TO ANOTHER SELECTION

1. Write an essay on the speaker's treatment of the diners in this poem and in Maxine Hong Kingston's "Restaurant" (p. 206).

Frederick Douglass: 1817–1895°   *1966*

Douglass was someone who,
Had he walked with wary foot
And frightened tread,
From very indecision
Might be dead,   5
Might have lost his soul,
But instead decided to be bold
And capture every street
On which he set his feet,
To route each path   10
Toward freedom's goal,
To make each highway
Choose *his* compass' choice,
To all the world cried,
Hear my voice! . . .   15
Oh, to be a beast, a bird,
Anything but a slave! he said.

Who would be free
Themselves must strike
The first blow, he said.   20

   He died in 1895.

   He is not dead.

1817–1895: Douglass was actually born in 1818; as a slave, he did not know his true birth date.

CONSIDERATIONS FOR CRITICAL THINKING AND WRITING

1. **FIRST RESPONSE.** This poem was published when the civil rights movement was very active in America. Does that information affect your reading of it?

2. What does Hughes celebrate about the life of Douglass, author of *Narrative of the Life of Frederick Douglass, an American Slave, Written by Himself* (1845)?

CONNECTION TO ANOTHER SELECTION

1. How is the speaker's attitude toward violence in this poem similar to that of the speaker in "Harlem" (p. 411)?

Perspectives on Langston Hughes

LANGSTON HUGHES

On Harlem Rent Parties 1940

Then [in the late twenties and early thirties] it was that house-rent parties began to flourish — and not always to raise the rent either. But, as often as not, to have a get-together of one's own, where you could do the black-bottom with no stranger behind you trying to do it, too. Non-theatrical, non-intellectual Harlem was an unwilling victim of its own vogue. It didn't like to be stared at by white folks. But perhaps the downtowners never knew this — for the cabaret owners, the entertainers, and the speakeasy proprietors treated them fine — as long as they paid.

The Saturday night rent parties that I attended were often more amusing than any night club, in small apartments where God knows who lived — because the guests seldom did — but where the piano would often be augmented by a guitar, or an odd cornet, or somebody with a pair of drums walking in off the street. And where awful bootleg whiskey and good fried fish or steaming chitterling were sold at very low prices. And the dancing and singing and impromptu entertaining went on until dawn came in at the windows.

These parties, often termed whist parties or dances, were usually announced by brightly colored cards stuck in the grille of apartment house elevators. Some of the cards were highly entertaining in themselves:

We got yellow girls, we've got black and tan
Will you have a good time? - YEAH MAN !

A Social Whist Party
—GIVEN BY—
MARY WINSTON
147 West 145th Street   Apt. 5

SATURDAY EVE., MARCH 19th, 1932

GOOD MUSIC   REFRESHMENTS

Almost every Saturday night when I was in Harlem I went to a house-rent party. I wrote lots of poems about house-rent parties, and ate there at many a fried fish and pig's foot — with liquid refreshments on the side. I met ladies' maids and truck drivers, laundry workers and shoe shine boys, seamstresses and porters. I can still hear their laughter in my ears, hear the soft slow music, and feel the floor shaking as the dancers danced.

From "When the Negro Was in Vogue," in *The Big Sea*

CONSIDERATIONS FOR CRITICAL THINKING AND WRITING

1. What, according to Hughes, was the appeal of the rent parties in contrast to the nightclubs?

2. Describe the tone in which Hughes recounts his memory of these parties.

DONALD B. GIBSON (B. 1933)

The Essential Optimism of Hughes and Whitman   1971

As optimists generally do, Langston Hughes and Walt Whitman lacked a sense of evil. This (and all it implies) puts Hughes in a tradition with other American writers. He stands with Whitman, Emerson, Thoreau, and later Sandburg, Lindsay, and Steinbeck, as opposed to Hawthorne, Poe, Melville, James, Faulkner, and Eliot. This is not to say that he did not recognize the existence of evil, but, as Yeats says of Emerson and Whitman, he lacked the "Vision of Evil." He did not see evil as inherent in the character of nature and man, hence he felt that the evil (small *e*) about which he wrote so frequently in his poems (lynchings, segregation, discrimination of all kinds) would be eradicated with the passage of time. Of course the Hughes of *The Panther and the Lash* (1967) is not as easily optimistic as the poet was twenty or twenty-five years before. Hughes could not have written "I, Too," or even "The Negro Speaks of Rivers" in the sixties. But the evidence as I see it has it that though he does not speak so readily about the fulfillment of the American ideal for black people, and though something of the spirit of having waited too long prevails, still the optimism remains. . . .

    Montage of a Dream Deferred (1951), included in *Selected Poems,* describes the dream as deferred, not dead nor incapable of fulfillment. There is a certain grimness in the poem, for example in its most famous section, "Harlem," which begins, "What happens to a dream deferred? / Does it dry up / like a raisin in the sun?" but the grimness is by no means unrelieved. There is, as a matter of fact, a lightness of tone throughout the poem which could not exist did the poet see the ravages of racial discrimination as manifestations of Evil. . . . The whole tone of *Montage of a Dream Deferred* is characterized by the well-known "Ballad of the Landlord." There the bitter-sweet quality of Hughes's attitude toward his subject is clear.

From "The Good Black Poet and the Good Grey Poet: The Poetry of
Hughes and Whitman," in *Langston Hughes: Black Genius, A Critical
Evaluation,* edited by Therman B. O'Daniel

CONSIDERATIONS FOR CRITICAL THINKING AND WRITING

1. What distinction does Gibson make between "Evil" and "evil"?

2. Discuss whether you agree or disagree that Hughes lacked a "Vision of Evil."

3. Why do you think Gibson writes that Hughes couldn't have written "The Negro Speaks of Rivers" (p. 393) or "I, Too" (p. 396) in the 1960s?

4. What aspects of Whitman does Hughes seem to admire in "Old Walt" (p. 413)?

James A. Emanuel (b. 1921)
Hughes's Attitudes toward Religion   1973

Religion, because of its historical importance during and after slavery, is an undeniably useful theme in the work of any major black writer. In a writer whose special province for almost forty-five years was more recent black experience, the theme is doubly vital. Hughes's personal religious orientation is pertinent. Asked about it by the Reverend Dana F. Kennedy of the "Viewpoint" radio and television show (on December 10, 1960), the poet responded:

> I grew up in a not very religious family, but I had a foster aunt who saw that I went to church and Sunday school . . . and I was very much moved, always, by the, shall I say, the rhythms of the Negro church . . . of the spirituals, . . . of those wonderful old-time sermons. . . . There's great beauty in the mysticism of much religious writing, and great help there — but I also think that we live in a world . . . of solid earth and vegetables and a need for jobs and a need for housing. . . .

Two years earlier, the poet had told John Kirkwood of British Columbia's *Vancouver Sun* (December 3, 1958): "I'm not anti-Christian. I'm not against anyone's religion. Religion is one of the innate needs of mankind. What I am against is the misuse of religion. But I won't ridicule it. . . . Whatever part of God is in anybody is not to be played with, and everybody has got a part of God in them."

These typical public protestations by Hughes boil down to his insistence that religion is naturally sacred and beautiful, and that its needed sustenance must not be exploited.

From "Christ in Alabama: Religion in the Poetry of Langston Hughes," in *Modern Black Poets,* edited by Donald B. Gibson

Considerations for Critical Thinking and Writing

1. Why do you think Emanuel asserts that, owing to slavery, religion "is an undeniably useful theme in the work of any major Black writer"?
2. How does Hughes's concern for the "solid earth and vegetables and a need for jobs and a need for housing" qualify his attitudes toward religion?

Richard K. Barksdale (b. 1915)
On Censoring "Ballad of the Landlord"   1977

In 1940, ["Ballad of the Landlord"] was a rather innocuous rendering of an imaginary dialogue between a disgruntled tenant and a tight-fisted landlord. In creating a poem about two such social archetypes, the poet was by no means taking any new steps in dramatic poetry. The literature of most capitalist and noncapitalist societies often pits the haves against the have-nots, and not infrequently the haves are wealthy men of property who "lord" it over improvident men who own nothing. So the confrontation between tenant and landlord was in 1940 just another instance of the social malevolence of a system that punished the powerless and excused the powerful. In fact, Hughes's tone of dry irony throughout the poem leads one to suspect that the poet deliberately overstated a situation and that some sardonic humor was supposed to be squeezed out of the incident. . . .

Ironically, this poem, which in 1940 depicted a highly probable incident in American urban life and was certainly not written to incite an economic revolt or promote social unrest, became, by the mid-1960s, a verboten assignment in a literature class in a Boston high school. In his Langston Hughes headnote in *Black Voices* (1967), Abraham Chapman reported that a Boston high school English teacher named Jonathan Kozol was fired for assigning it to his students. By the mid-sixties, Boston and many other American cities had become riot-torn, racial tinderboxes, and their ghettos seethed with tenant anger and discontent. So the poem gathered new meanings reflecting the times, and the word of its tenant persona bespoke the collective anger of thousands of black have-nots.

From *Langston Hughes: The Poet and His Critics*

CONSIDERATIONS FOR CRITICAL THINKING AND WRITING

1. Why do you think the Boston School Committee believed that the "Ballad of the Landlord" (p. 408) should be censored?

2. Do you agree with Barksdale that the poem is a "rather innocuous rendering" of economic and social issues? Explain your answer.

3. How did the poem acquire "new meanings reflecting the times" between the 1940s and 1960s? What new meanings might it have for readers today?

KAREN JACKSON FORD

Hughes's Aesthetics of Simplicity   *1992*

The repression of the great bulk of Hughes's poems is the result of chronic critical scorn for their simplicity. Throughout his long career, but especially after his first two volumes of poetry (readers were at first willing to assume that a youthful poet might grow to be more complex), his books received their harshest reviews for a variety of "flaws" that all originate in an aesthetics of simplicity. From his first book, *The Weary Blues* (1926), to his last one, *The Panther and the Lash* (1967), the reviews invoke a litany of faults: the poems are superficial, infantile, silly, small, unpoetic, common, jejune, iterative, and, of course, simple.[1] Even his admirers reluctantly conclude that Hughes's poetics failed. Saunders Redding flatly opposes simplicity and artfulness. "While Hughes's rejection of his own growth shows an admirable loyalty to his self-commitment as the poet of the 'simple, Negro commonfolk' . . . it does a disservice to his art."[2] James Baldwin, who recognizes the potential of simplicity

---

[1] Reviews in which these epithets appear are collected in Edward J. Mullen, *Critical Essays on Langston Hughes* (Boston: G. K. Hall) 1986. [Ford's note.]
[2] Redding's comments appear in Mullen 74. [Ford's note.]

as an artistic principle, faults the poems for "tak[ing] refuge . . . in a fake simplicity in order to avoid the very difficult simplicity of the experience."[3]

Despite a lifetime of critical disappointments, then, Hughes remained loyal to the aesthetic program he had outlined in 1926 in his decisive poetic treatise, "The Negro Artist and the Racial Mountain." There he had predicted that the common people would "give to this world its truly great Negro artist, the one who is not afraid to be himself," a poet who would explore the "great field of unused [folk] material ready for his art" and recognize that this source would provide "sufficient matter to furnish a black artist with a lifetime of creative work."[4] This is clearly a portrait of the poet Hughes would become, and he maintained his fidelity to this ideal at great cost to his literary reputation.

From "Do Right to Write Right: Langston Hughes's Aesthetics of Simplicity," *Twentieth Century Literature* 38.4 (1992)

[3] Baldwin's comments appear in Mullen 85. [Ford's note.]
[4] *The Nation* 122 (1926): 692. [Ford's note.]

CONSIDERATIONS FOR CRITICAL THINKING AND WRITING

1. What was Hughes's rationale for the value of simplicity in his poetry?

2. Explain whether or not you think there are any justifications for regarding Hughes's poetry as "superficial" and too "simple."

DAVID CHINITZ (B. 1962)

The Romanticization of Africa in the 1920s   1997

In Europe black culture was an exotic import; in America it was domestic and increasingly mass-produced. If postwar [World War I] disillusionment judged the majority culture mannered, neurotic, and repressive, Americans had an easily accessible alternative. The need for such an Other produced a discourse in which black Americans figured as barely civilized exiles from the jungle, with — so the clichés ran — tom-toms beating in their blood and dark laughter in their souls. The African American became a model of "natural" human behavior to contrast with the falsified, constrained and impotent modes of the "civilized."

Far from being immune to the lure of this discourse, for the better part of the 1920s Hughes asserted an open pride in the supposed primitive qualities of his race, the atavistic legacy of the African motherland. Unlike most of those who romanticized Africa, Hughes had at least some firsthand experience of the continent; yet he processed what he saw there in images conditioned by European primitivism, rendering "[the land] wild and lovely, the people dark and beautiful, the palm trees tall, the sun bright, and the rivers deep."[1] His short story "Luani of the Jungle," in attempting to glorify aboriginal African vigor as against European anemia, shows how predictable and unextraordinary even Hughes's primitivism could be. To discover in the descendents of

[1] *The Big Sea.* 1940. N.Y.: Thunder's Mouth, 1986, 11. [Chinitz's note.]

idealized Africans the same qualities of innate health, spontaneity, and natu-
ralness requires no great leap; one has only to identify the African American as
a displaced primitive, as Hughes does repeatedly in his first book, *The Weary
Blues*:

> They drove me out of the forest.
> They took me away from the jungles.
> I lost my trees.   ,
> I lost my silver moons.
>
> Now they've caged me
> In the circus of civilization.[2]

Hughes depicts black atavism vividly and often gracefully, yet in a way that is
entirely consistent with the popular iconography of the time. His African
Americans retain "among the skyscrapers" the primal fears and instincts of
their ancestors "among the palms in Africa."[3] The scion of Africa is still more
than half primitive: "All the tom-toms of the jungles beat in my blood, / And
all the wild hot moons of the jungles shine in my soul."[4]

From "Rejuvenation through Joy: Langston Hughes, Primitivism and Jazz,"
in American Literary History, Spring 1997

[2] *The Weary Blues*. N.Y.: Knopf, 1926, 100. [Chinitz's note.]
[3] *Ibid*. 101.
[4] *Ibid*. 102.

CONSIDERATIONS FOR CRITICAL THINKING AND WRITING

1. According to Chinitz, why did Europeans and Americans romanticize
   African culture?

2. Consider the poems published by Hughes in the 1920s reprinted in this an-
   thology. Explain whether you find any "primitivism" in these poems.

3. Later in this essay, Chinitz points out that Hughes eventually rejected the
   "reductive mischaracterizations of black culture, the commercialism, the
   sham sociology, and the downright silliness of the primitivist fad." Choose
   and discuss a poem from this anthology that you think reflects Hughes's
   later views of primitivism.

Two Complementary Critical Readings

ARNOLD RAMPERSAD (B. 1941)

On the Persona in "The Negro Speaks of Rivers"   *1985*

Here, the persona moves steadily from dimly starred personal memory ("I've
known rivers") toward a rendezvous with modern history (Lincoln going down
the Mississippi and seeing the horror of slavery that, according to legend,
would make him one day free the slaves). The death wish, benign but suffus-
ing, of its images of rivers older than human blood, of souls grown as deep
as these rivers, gives way steadily to an altering, ennobling vision whose final

effect gleams in the evocation of the Mississippi's "muddy bosom" turning at last "all golden in the sunset." Personal anguish has been alchemized by the poet into a gracious meditation on his race, whose despised ("muddy") culture and history, irradiated by the poet's vision, changes within the poem from mud into gold. This is a classic example of the essential process of creativity in Hughes.

The poem came to him, according to Hughes (accurately, it seems clear) about ten months after his Mexican illness, when he was riding a train from Cleveland to Mexico to rejoin his father. The time was sundown, the place the Mississippi outside St. Louis. "All day on the train I had been thinking of my father," he would write in *The Big Sea.* "Now it was just sunset and we crossed the Mississippi, slowly, over a long bridge. I looked out of the window of the Pullman at the great muddy river flowing down toward the heart of the South, and I began to think what that river, the old Mississippi, had meant to Negroes in the past — how to be sold down the river was the worst fate that could overtake a slave in bondage. Then I remembered reading how Abraham Lincoln had made a trip down the Mississippi on a raft, and how he had seen slavery at its worst, and had decided within himself that it should be removed from American life. Then I began to think of other rivers in our past — the Congo, and the Niger, and the Nile in Africa — and the thought came to me: 'I've known rivers,' and I put it down on the back of an envelope I had in my pocket, and within the space of ten or fifteen minutes, as the train gathered speed in the dusk, I had written this poem."

From "The Origins of Poetry in Langston Hughes,"
Southern Review 21.3 (1985)

Considerations for Critical Thinking and Writing

1. How does the biographical information that Rampersad provides affect your reading of "The Negro Speaks of Rivers" (p. 393)?

2. Describe how the poem's images support Rampersad's assertion that Hughes's personal experience is "alchemized" into a reflection on the history of his race.

ADRIAN OKTENBERG (B. 1947)

Memory in "The Negro Speaks of Rivers"   1987

"The Negro Speaks of Rivers" . . . is only the beginning of a long chain of poems by Hughes which confront, distill, extend, and transform the historical experience of black people into an art both limpid and programmatic. . . . The "I" of the poem is not that of "a" Negro but "the" Negro, suggesting the whole of the people and their history. Most of the consonants — *d*'s, *n*'s, *l*'s, *s*'s — are soft, and of the vowels, long *o*'s reoccur, contributing by sound the effect of an ancient voice. The tone of the repeated declarative sentences is muted, lulling. Every element of the poem combines to suggest that when the Negro speaks of rivers it is with the accumulated wisdom of a sage. The function of a sage is to impart the sometimes secret but long accumulated history of a people to its younger members so that they might make the lessons of the past active in the future. This impartation occurs in the central stanza of the poem:

> I bathed in the Euphrates when dawns were young.
> I built my hut near the Congo and it lulled me to sleep.
> I looked upon the Nile and raised the pyramids above it.
> I heard the singing of the Mississippi when Abe Lincoln
>   went down to New Orleans, and I've seen its muddy
>   bosom turn all golden in the sunset.

Moving by suggestion, by naming particular rivers and particular activities performed nearby, the poem implicates the whole history of African and American slavery without ever articulating the word. "I bathed in the Euphrates" and "I built my hut near the Congo" are the normal activities of natural man performed in his natural habitat. That may be an unnecessarily anthropological way of putting it, but the lines are the equivalent of the speaker having said, "I made my life undisturbed in the place where I lived." The shift — and the lesson — occurs in the next two lines. Raising the pyramids above the Nile was the act of slaves, and if ever "Abe Lincoln went down to New Orleans," it would have been in the context of American slavery and the Civil War. Implicit in the history of a people who had first been free and then enslaved is the vision of freedom regained, and therein lies the program. The final line of the poem, "My soul has grown deep like the rivers," suggests wisdom in the word *deep*. The wisdom imparted by the poem, beyond the memory of the suffering of slavery, includes a more deeply embedded memory of freedom. This is perhaps the more powerful memory, or the more sustaining one, and even if deferred, will reemerge in one form or another.

> From "From the Bottom Up: Three Radicals of the Thirties" in
> *A Gift of Tongues: Critical Challenges in Contemporary American Poetry,*
> edited by Marie Harris and Kathleen Aguero

CONSIDERATIONS FOR CRITICAL THINKING AND WRITING

1. Oktenberg characterizes the speaker of the poem as having "the accumulated wisdom of a sage." Does the knowledge that Hughes was only nineteen years old when he wrote this poem affect your response to Oktenberg's characterization? Explain why or why not.

2. Discuss whether or not you think Oktenberg's reading competes with or complements Rampersad's interpretation.

SUGGESTED TOPICS FOR LONGER PAPERS

1. Discuss Hughes's use of rhyme, meter, and sounds in five poems of your choice. How do these elements contribute to the poems' meanings?

2. Taken together, how do Hughes's poems provide a critique of relations between blacks and whites in America?

15

A Study of Julia Alvarez: Five Poems

© Daniel Cima.

> When I'm asked what made me into a writer, I point to the watershed experience of coming to this country. Not understanding the language, I had to pay close attention to each word — great training for a writer.
> — JULIA ALVAREZ

This chapter offers five poems, chosen by Julia Alvarez for this anthology, with commentaries written by the poet herself. Alvarez's insights on each work, in addition to accompanying images and documents, provide a variety of contexts — personal, cultural, and historical — for understanding and appreciating her poems.

In her introductions to each of the poems, Alvarez shares her reasons for writing, what was on her mind when she wrote each work, what she thinks now looking back at them, as well as a bird's-eye view into her writing process (see especially the drafts of the poem in progress on pp. 444–46). She also evokes the voices of those who have inspired her—muses that range from women talking and cooking in a kitchen to a character in *The Arabian Nights* to the poets Walt Whitman, Langston Hughes, and others. Alvarez writes, "A poem can be a resting place for the soul . . . a world teeming with discoveries of luminous little *ah-ha!* moments, a 'place for the genuine,' as Marianne Moore calls it." Read on and find out, for example, who her real "First Muse" was, and what, according to Alvarez, a famous American poet and the Chiquita Banana have in common.

In addition to Alvarez's inviting and richly detailed introductions, the chapter also presents a number of visual contexts, such as a photo of a 1963 civil rights demonstration in Queens, New York; the poet's passport photo taken at age ten, just before she moved back to the United States; a collection of draft manuscript pages; and an image of one of Alvarez's poems set in a bronze plaque in a sidewalk—part of "Library Way" in New York City. Further, a critical essay—which complements Alvarez's own perspectives throughout the chapter—by Kelli Lyon Johnson (p. 451) allows readers to consider Alvarez's work in a critical framework. (For a discussion of how cultural criticism that focuses on a broad range of historical as well as social, political, and economic perspectives can be used to shed light on literary works, see the opening paragraphs of Chapter 17, "A Cultural Case Study: Louise Erdrich's 'Dear John Wayne'" [p. 472]. For a discussion on reading a work alongside critical theory, see Chapter 25, "Critical Strategies for Reading" [p. 643].)

A BRIEF BIOGRAPHY

Although Julia Alvarez was born (1950) in New York City, she lived in the Dominican Republic until she was ten years old. She returned to New York after her father, a physician, was connected to a plot to overthrow the dictatorship of Rafael Trujillo, and the family had to flee. Growing up in Queens was radically different from the Latino Caribbean world she experienced during her early childhood. A new culture and new language sensitized Alvarez to her surroundings and her use of language so that emigration from the Dominican Republic to Queens was the beginning of her movement toward becoming a writer. Alvarez quotes the Polish poet Czeslaw Milosz's assertion that "Language is the only homeland" to explain her own sense that what she really settled into was not so much the United States as the English language.

Her fascination with English continued into high school and took shape in college as she became a serious writer—first at Connecticut College from 1967 to 1969 and then at Middlebury College, where she earned her B.A. in 1971. At Syracuse University she was awarded the American Academy of Poetry Prize and, in 1975, earned an M.A. in creative writing.

Since then Alvarez has served as a writer-in-residence for the Kentucky

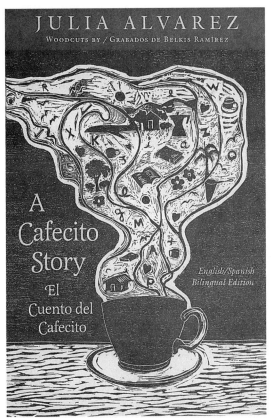

(*Left*) *A Cafecito Story* (2001), which Alvarez describes as a modern "eco-parable" or "green fable" and love story, was inspired by the author's work with local coffee growers in the Dominican Republic.

Cover image by Belkis Ramírez. Reprinted by permission.

(*Below*) Julia Alvarez with students from Middlebury College at her coffee farm, Alta Gracia, in the Dominican Republic.

Photograph courtesy of Fundacion Finca Alta Gracia.

Arts Commission, the Delaware Arts Council, and the Arts Council of Fayetteville, North Carolina. She has taught at California State College (Fresno), College of Sequoias, Phillips Andover Academy, the University of Vermont, George Washington University, the University of Illinois, and, since 1988, at Middlebury College, where she has been a professor of literature and creative writing and is currently a part-time writer-in-residence. Alvarez divides her time between Vermont and the Dominican Republic where she and her husband have set up an organic coffee farm, Alta Gracia, that supports a literacy school for children and adults. *A Cafecito Story* (2001), which Alvarez considers a "green fable" or "eco-parable," grew out of their experiences promoting fair trade and sustainability for coffee farmers in the Dominican Republic.

AN INTRODUCTION TO HER WORK

Alvarez's poetry has been widely published in journals and magazines ranging from the *New Yorker* to *Mirabella* to the *Kenyon Review*. Her book of poems, *Homecoming* (1984; a new expanded verison, *Homecoming: New and Collected Poems*, was published in 1996 by Plume/Penguin), uses simple — yet incisive — language to explore issues related to love, domestic life, and work. Her second book of poetry, *The Other Side/El Otro Lado* (1995), is a collection of meditations on her childhood memories of immigrant life that shaped her adult identity and sensibilities. Some of these concerns are also manifested in her book of essays, titled *Something to Declare* (1998), a collection that describes her abiding concerns about how to respond to competing cultures. In her third poetry collection, *The Woman I Kept to Myself* (2004), Alvarez reflects on her personal life and development as a writer from the vantage point of her mid-fifties in seventy-five poems, each consisting of three ten-line stanzas.

   In addition to writing a number of books for children and young adults, Alvarez has also published six novels. The first, *How the García Girls Lost Their Accents* (1991), is a collection of fifteen separate but interrelated stories that cover thirty years of the lives of the García sisters from the late 1950s to the late 1980s. Drawing on her own experiences, Alvarez describes the sisters fleeing the Dominican Republic and growing up Latina in the United States. *In the Time of the Butterflies* (1994) is a fictional account of a true story concerning four sisters who opposed Trujillo's dictatorship. Three of the sisters were murdered in 1960 by the government, and the surviving fourth sister recounts the events of their personal and political lives that led to her sisters' deaths. Shaped by the history of Dominican freedom and tyranny, the novel also explores the sisters' relationships to each other and their country.

   In *¡Yo!* (1997), Alvarez focuses on Yolanda, one of the García sisters from her first novel, who is now a writer. Written in the different voices of Yo's friends and family members, this fractured narrative constructs a complete picture of a woman who uses her relationships as fodder for fiction, a woman who is self-centered, aggravating, and finally lovable — who is deeply embedded in American culture while remaining aware of her Dominican roots. *¡Yo!*, which means "I" in English, is a meditation on points of view and narrative.

In the Name of Salomé (2000) is a fictional account of Salomé Ureña, who was born in the 1850s and considered to be "the Emily Dickinson of the Dominican Republic," and her daughter's efforts late in life to reconcile her relationship to her mother's reputation and her own response to Castro's revolution in Cuba. Alvarez published her sixth and most recent novel, *Saving the World*, in 2006, a story that also links two women's lives, one from the past and one from the present, around personal and political issues concerning humanitarian efforts to end smallpox in the nineteenth century and the global AIDS epidemic in the twenty-first century.

Chronology

1950	Born on March 27 in New York City.
1950–60	Raised in the Dominican Republic.
1960	Alvarez family flees the Dominican Republic for New York City after her father joins efforts to overthrow the dictatorship of Rafael Trujillo.
1961	Rafael Trujillo is assassinated.
1967–69	Attends Connecticut College.
1971	Graduates from Middlebury College with a B.A.
1975	Graduates from Syracuse University with an M.A.
1979–80	Attends Bread Loaf School of English.
1979–81	Instructor at Phillips Andover Academy.
1981–83	Visiting assistant professor at University of Vermont.
1984	Publishes *Homecoming*, a volume of poems, and *The Housekeeping Book*, a handmade book of a series of "housekeeping poems," illustrated by Carol MacDonald and Rene Schall.
1984–85	Visiting writer-in-residence at George Washington University.
1985–88	Assistant professor of English at University of Illinois.
1987–88	Awarded a National Endowment for the Arts Fellowship.
1988–98	Professor of English at Middlebury College.
1988–Present	Writer-in-residence at Middlebury College.
1991	Publishes *How the García Girls Lost Their Accents*, a novel.
1994	Publishes *In the Time of the Butterflies*, a novel.
1995	Publishes *The Other Side/El Otro Lado*, a volume of poems.
1996	Publishes *Homecoming: New and Collected Poems*, a reissue of *Homecoming* (1984) with new work included.
1997	Publishes *¡Yo!*, a novel.

1998	Publishes *Something to Declare*, a collection of essays, and *Seven Trees*, a handmade volume of poems.
2000	Publishes *In the Name of Salomé*, a novel, and *The Secret Footprints*, a picture book for children.
2001	Publishes *A Cafecito Story*, a novel or "eco-parable," and *How Tía Lola Came to ~~Visit~~ Stay*, a novel for young adults.
2002	Publishes *The Woman I Kept to Myself*, a volume of poems, and *Before We Were Free*, a novel for young adults.
2004	Publishes *A Gift of Gracias: The Legend of Altagracia*, a picture book for children, and *Finding Miracles*, a novel for young adults.
2006	Publishes *Saving the World*, a novel.

In "Queens, 1963" Alvarez remembers the neighborhood she lived in when she was a thirteen-year-old and how "Everyone seemed more American / than we, newly arrived." The tensions that arose when new immigrants and ethnic groups moved onto the block were mirrored in many American neighborhoods in 1963. Indeed, the entire nation was made keenly aware of such issues as antisegregation when demonstrations were organized across the South and a massive march on Washington in support of civil rights for African Americans drew hundreds of thousands of demonstrators who listened to Martin Luther King Jr. deliver his electrifying "I have a dream" speech. But the issues were hardly resolved, as evidenced by 1963's two best-selling books: *Happiness Is a Warm Puppy* and *Security Is a Thumb and a Blanket*, by Charles M. Schulz of *Peanuts* cartoon fame. The popularity of these books is, perhaps, understandable given the tensions that moved across the country and which seemed to culminate on November 22, 1963, when President Kennedy was assassinated in Dallas, Texas. These events are not mentioned in "Queens, 1963," but they are certainly part of the context that helps us to understand Alvarez's particular neighborhood. In the following introductory essay, Alvarez reflects on the cultural moment of 1963 and her reasons for writing the poem.

JULIA ALVAREZ

On Writing "Queens, 1963"   2006

I remember when we finally bought our very own house after three years of living in rentals. Back then, Queens, New York, was not the multicultural, multilingual place it is today. But the process was beginning. Our neighborhood was sprinkled with ethnicities, some who had been here longer than others. The Germans down the block — now we would call them German Americans — had been Americans for a couple of generations as had our Jewish neighbors, and most definitely, the Midwesterners across the street. Meanwhile, the Greek

Julia Alvarez, age ten, in her 1960 passport photo.
Courtesy of Julia Alvarez.

family next door were newcomers as were we, our accents still heavy, our cooking smells commingling across our backyard fences during mealtimes: their Greek lamb with rosemary, our Dominican habichuelas with sofrito.°

It seemed a peaceable enough kingdom until a black family moved in across the street. What a ruckus got started! Of course, it was the early 1960s: the civil rights movement was just getting under way in this country. Suddenly, our neighborhood was faced with discrimination, but coming from the very same people who themselves had felt discrimination from other, more mainstream Americans. It was my first lesson in hypocrisy and in realizing that America was still an experiment in process. The words on the Statue of Liberty

habichuelas with sofrito: Kidney beans prepared with a sautéed mixture of spices, herbs, garlic, onion, pepper, and tomato.

(see "Sometimes the Words Are So Close," p. 443) were only a promise, not yet a practice in the deep South or in Queens, New York.

In writing this poem I wanted to suggest the many ethnic families in the neighborhood. Of course, I couldn't use their real names and risk being sued. (Though, come to think of it, I've never heard of a poem being sued, have you?) Plus, there is the matter of failing memory. (This was forty-two years ago!) So I chose names that suggested other languages, other places, and also — always the poet's ear at work — names that fit in with the rhythm and cadence of the lines.

JULIA ALVAREZ

Queens, 1963   *1992*

Everyone seemed more American
than we, newly arrived,
foreign dirt still on our soles.
By year's end, a sprinkler waving
like a flag on our mowed lawn,   5
we were blended into the block,
owned our own mock Tudor house.
Then the house across the street
sold to a black family.
Cop cars patrolled our block   10
from the Castellucci's at one end
to the Balakian's on the other.
We heard rumors of bomb threats,
a burning cross on their lawn.
(It turned out to be a sprinkler.)   15
Still the neighborhood buzzed.
The barber's family, Haralambides,
our left-side neighbors, didn't want trouble.
They'd come a long way to be free!
Mr. Scott, the retired plumber,   20
and his plump midwestern wife,
considered moving back home
where white and black got along
by staying where they belonged.
They had cultivated our street   25
like the garden she'd given up
on account of her ailing back,
bad knees, poor eyes, arthritic hands.
She went through her litany daily.
Politely, my mother listened —   30
¡Ay, Mrs. Scott, qué pena!°
— her Dominican good manners
still running on automatic.
The Jewish counselor next door,

31 *qué pena:* What a shame!

had a practice in her house; 35
clients hurried up her walk
ashamed to be seen needing.
(I watched from my upstairs window,
gloomy with adolescence,
and guessed how they too must have 40
hypocritical old-world parents.)
Mrs. Bernstein said it was time
the neighborhood opened up.
As the first Jew on the block,
she remembered the snubbing she got 45
a few years back from Mrs. Scott.
But real estate worried her,
our houses' plummeting value.
She shook her head as she might
at a client's grim disclosures. 50
Too bad the world works this way.
The German girl playing the piano
down the street abruptly stopped
in the middle of a note.
I completed the tune in my head 55
as I watched *their* front door open.
A dark man in a suit
with a girl about my age
walked quickly into a car.
My hand lifted but fell 60
before I made a welcoming gesture.
On her face I had seen a look
from the days before we had melted
into the United States of America.
It was hardness mixed with hurt. 65
It was knowing she never could be
the right kind of American.
A police car followed their car.
Down the street, curtains fell back.
Mrs. Scott swept her walk 70
as if it had just been dirtied.
Then the German piano commenced
downward scales as if tracking
the plummeting real estate.
One by one I imagined the houses 75
sinking into their lawns,
the grass grown wild and tall
in the past tense of this continent
before the first foreigners owned
any of this free country. 80

CONSIDERATIONS FOR CRITICAL THINKING AND WRITING

1. **FIRST RESPONSE.** What nationalities live in this neighborhood in the New York City borough of Queens? Are they neighborly to each other?

2. In line 3, why do you suppose Alvarez writes "foreign dirt still on our soles" rather than "foreign soil still on our shoes"? What does Alvarez's particular word choice suggest about her feelings for her native country?

3. Characterize the speaker. How old is she? How does she feel about having come from the Dominican Republic? About living in the United States?

4. Do you think this poem is optimistic or pessimistic about racial relations in the United States? Explain your answer by referring to specific details in the poem.

CONSIDERATIONS FOR CRITICAL THINKING AND WRITING

1. Compare the use of irony in "Queens, 1963" with that in John Ciardi's "Suburban" (p. 518). How does irony contribute to each poem?

2. Discuss the problems immigrants encounter in this poem and in Chitra Banerjee Divakaruni's "Indian Movie, New Jersey" (p. 544).

3. Write an essay comparing and contrasting the tone and theme in "Queens, 1963" and in Tato Laviera's "AmeRícan" (p. 284).

Queens Civil Rights Demonstration 1963

In this photograph police remove a Congress of Racial Equality (CORE) demonstrator from a Queens construction site. Demonstrators blocked the delivery entrance to the site because they wanted more African Americans and Puerto Ricans hired in the building-trade industry.
Reprinted by permission of AP/Wide World Photos.

CONSIDERATIONS FOR CRITICAL THINKING AND WRITING

1. Discuss the role played by the police in this photograph and in "Queens, 1963." What attitudes toward the police do the photograph and the poem display?

2. How do you think the Scotts and Mrs. Bernstein would have responded to this photograph in 1963?

3. Compare the tensions in "Queens, 1963" to those depicted in this photo. How do the speaker's private reflections relate to this public protest?

Perspective

MARNY REQUA (B. 1971)

From an Interview with Julia Alvarez   *1997*

M.R. What was it like when you came to the United States?

J.A. When we got to Queens, it was really a shock to go from a totally Latino, *familia* Caribbean world into this very cold and kind of forbidding one in which we didn't speak the language. I didn't grow up with a tradition of writing or reading books at all. People were always telling stories but it wasn't a tradition of literary . . . reading a book or doing something solitary like that. Coming to this country I discovered books, I discovered that it was a way to enter into a portable homeland that you could carry around in your head. You didn't have to suffer what was going on around you. I found in books a place to go. I became interested in language because I was learning a language intentionally at the age of ten. I was wondering, "Why is it that word and not another?" which any writer has to do with their language. I always say I came to English late but to the profession early. By high school I was pretty set: that's what I want to do, be a writer.

M.R. Did you have culture shock returning to the Dominican Republic as you were growing up?

J.A. The culture here had an effect on me — at the time this country was coming undone with protests and flower children and drugs. Here I was back in the Dominican Republic and I wouldn't keep my mouth shut. I had my own ideas and I had my own politics, and it, I just didn't gel anymore with the family. I didn't quite feel I ever belonged in this North American culture and I always had this nostalgia that when I went back I'd belong, and then I found out I didn't belong there either.

M.R. Was it a source of inspiration to have a foot in both cultures?

J.A. I only came to that later. [Then], it was a burden because I felt torn. I wanted to be part of one culture and then part of the other. It was a time when the model for the immigrant was that you came and you became an American and you cut off your ties and that was that. My parents had that frame of mind, because they were so afraid, and they were "Learn your English" and "Become one of them," and that left out so much. Now I see the richness. Part of what I want to do with my work is that complexity, that richness. I don't want it to be simplistic and either/or.

From "The Politics of Fiction," *Frontera* magazine 5 (1997)

CONSIDERATIONS FOR CRITICAL THINKING AND WRITING

1. What do you think Alvarez means when she describes books as "a portable homeland that you could carry around in your head"?

2. Why is it difficult for Alvarez to feel that she belongs in either the Dominican or the North American culture?

3. Alvarez says that in the 1960s "the model for the immigrant was that you came and you became an American and you cut off your ties and that was that." Do you think this model has changed in the United States since then? Explain your response.

4. How might this interview alter your understanding of "Queens, 1963"? What light is shed, for example, on the speaker's feeling that her family "blended into the block" in line 6?

JULIA ALVAREZ

On Writing "Housekeeping Cages" and Her Housekeeping Poems 1998

I can still remember the first time I heard my own voice on paper. It happened a few years after I graduated from a creative writing master's program. I had earned a short-term residency at Yaddo, the writer's colony, where I was assigned a studio in the big mansion — the tower room at the top of the stairs. The rules were clear: we artists and writers were to stick to our studios during the day and come out at night for supper and socializing. Nothing was to come between us and our work.

I sat up in my tower room, waiting for inspiration. All around me I could hear the typewriters going. Before me lay a blank sheet of paper, ready for the important work I had come there to write. That was the problem, you see. I was trying to do IMPORTANT work and so I couldn't hear myself think. I was trying to pitch my voice to "Turning and turning in the widening gyre," or, "Of man's first disobedience, and the fruit of that forbidden tree, " or, "Sing in me, Muse, and through me tell the story." I was tuning my voice to these men's voices because I thought that was the way I had to sound if I wanted to be a writer. After all, the writers I read and admired sounded like that.

But the voice I heard when I listened to myself think was the voice of a woman, sitting in her kitchen, gossiping with a friend over a cup of coffee. It was the voice of Gladys singing her sad boleros, Belkis putting color on my face with tales of her escapades, Tití naming the orchids, Ada telling me love stories as we made the beds. I had, however, never seen voices like these in print. So, I didn't know poems could be written in those voices, *my* voice.

So there I was at Yaddo, trying to write something important and coming up with nothing. And then, hallelujah — I heard the vacuum going up and down the hall. I opened the door and introduced myself to the friendly, sweating woman, wielding her vacuum cleaner. She invited me down to the kitchen so we wouldn't disturb the other guests. There I met the cook, and as we all sat, drinking coffee, I paged through her old cookbook, *knead, poach, stew, whip, score, julienne, whisk, sauté, sift.* Hmm. I began hearing a music in these words. I jotted down the names of implements:

Cup, spoon, ladle, pot, kettle,
grater and peeler,
colander, corer,
waffle iron, small funnel.

"You working on a poem there?" the cook asked me.
I shook my head.

A little later, I went upstairs and wrote down in my journal this beautiful vocabulary of my girlhood. As I wrote, I tapped my foot on the floor to the rhythm of the words. I could see Mami and the aunts with the cook in the kitchen bending their heads over a pot of habichuelas, arguing about what flavor was missing—what could it be they had missed putting in it? And then, the thought of Mami recalled Gladys, the maid who loved to sing, and that thought led me through the house, the mahogany furniture that needed dusting, the beds that needed making, the big bin of laundry that needed washing.

That day, I began working on a poem about dusting. Then another followed on sewing; then came a sweeping poem, an ironing poem. Later, I would collect these into a series I called "the housekeeping poems," poems using the metaphors, details, language of my first apprenticeship as a young girl. Even later, having found my woman's voice, I would gain confidence to explore my voice as a Latina and to write stories and poems using the metaphors, details, rhythms of that first world I had left behind in Spanish.

But it began, first, by discovering my woman's voice at Yaddo where I had found it as a child. Twenty years after learning to sing with Gladys, I was reminded of the lessons I had learned in childhood: that my voice would not be found up in a tower, in those upper reaches or important places, but down in the kitchen among the women who first taught me about service, about passion, about singing as if my life depended on it.

From *Something to Declare*

Julia Alvarez
Housekeeping Cages

1994

Sometimes people ask me why I wrote a series of poems about housekeeping if I'm a feminist. Don't I want women to be liberated from the oppressive roles they were condemned to live? I don't see housekeeping that way. They were the crafts we women had, sewing, embroidering, cooking, spinning, sweeping, even the lowly dusting. And like Dylan Thomas said, we sang in our chains like the sea. Isn't it already thinking from the point of view of the oppressor to say to ourselves, what we did was nothing?

You use what you have, you learn to work the structure to create what you need. I don't feel that writing in traditional forms is giving up power, going over to the enemy. The word belongs to no one, the houses built of words belong to no one. We have to take them back from those who think they own them.

Sometimes I get in a mood. I tell myself I am taken over. I am writing under somebody else's thumb and tongue. See, English was not my first language. It was, in fact, a colonizing language to my Spanish Caribbean. But then Spanish was also a colonizer's language; after all, Spain colonized Quisqueya. There's no getting free. We are always writing in a form imposed on us. But then, I'm Scheherazade in the Sultan's room. I use structures to survive and triumph! To say what's important to me as a woman and as a Latina.

I think of form as territory that has been colonized, but that you can free. See, I feel subversive in formal verse. A voice is going to inhabit that form that was barred from entering it before! That's what I tried in the "33" poems, to use my woman's voice in a sonnet as I would use it sitting in the kitchen with a close friend, talking womanstuff. In school, I was always trying to inhabit those forms as the male writers had. To pitch my voice to "Of man's first disobedience, and the fruit. . . ." If it didn't hit the key of "Sing in me, Muse, and through me tell the story," how could it be important poetry? The only kind.

While I was in graduate school some of the women in the program started a Women's Writing Collective in Syracuse. We were musing each other into unknown writing territory. One woman advised me to listen to my own voice, deep inside, and put that down on paper. But what I heard when I listened were voices that said things like "Don't put so much salt on the lettuce, you'll wilt the salad!" I'd never heard that in a poem. So how could it be poetry? Then, with the "33" sonnet sequence, I said, I'm going to go in there and I'm going to sound like myself. I took on the whole kaboodle. I was going into form, sonnets no less. Wow.

What I wanted from the sonnet was the tradition that it offered as well as the structure. The sonnet tradition was one in which women were caged in golden cages of beloved, in perfumed gas chambers of stereotype. I wanted to go in that heavily mined and male labyrinth with the string of my own voice. I wanted to explore it and explode it too. I call my sonnets free verse sonnets. They have ten syllables per line, and the lines are in a loose iambic pentameter. But they are heavily enjambed and the rhymes are often slant-rhymes, and the rhyme scheme is peculiar to each sonnet. One friend read them and said, "I didn't know they were sonnets. They sounded like you talking!"

By learning to work the sonnet structure and yet remaining true to my own voice, I made myself at home in that form. When I was done with it, it was a totally different form from the one I learned in school. I have used other traditional forms. In my poem about sweeping, since you sweep with the broom and you dance — it's a coupling — I used rhyming couplets. I wrote a poem of advice mothers give to their daughters in a villanelle, because it's such a nagging form. But mostly the sonnet is the form I've worked with. It's the classic form in which we women were trapped, love objects, and I was trapped inside that voice and paradigm, and I wanted to work my way out of it.

My idea of traditional forms is that as women much of our heritage is trapped in them. But the cage can turn into a house if you housekeep it the right way. You housekeep it by working the words just so.

From *A Formal Feeling Comes: Poems in Form by Contemporary Women,*
edited by Annie Finch

could burn the clothes. I was not allowed to iron clothes until I was older and could be trusted to iron all different kinds of fabrics ("gabardine, organdy, wool, madras") just right.

Again, think of how ironing someone's clothes can be a metaphor for all kinds of things. You have this power to take out the wrinkles and worries from someone's outer skin! You can touch and caress and love someone and not be told that you are making a nuisance of yourself!

In writing this poem I wanted the language to mirror the process. I wanted the lines to suggest all the fussy complications of trying to get your iron into hard corners and places ("I stroked the yoke, / the breast pocket, collar and cuffs, / until the rumpled heap relaxed . . .") and then the smooth sailing of a line that sails over the line break into the next line ("into the shape / of my father's broad chest . . ."). I wanted to get the hiss of the iron in those last four lines. I revised and revised this poem, especially the verbs, most especially the verbs that have to do the actual work of the iron. When I finally got that last line with its double rhymes ("express / excess"; "love / cloth"), I felt as if I'd done a whole laundry basket worth of ironing just right.

JULIA ALVAREZ

Ironing Their Clothes   1981

With a hot glide up, then down, his shirts,
I ironed out my father's back, cramped
and worried with work. I stroked the yoke,
the breast pocket, collar and cuffs,
until the rumpled heap relaxed into the shape   5
of my father's broad chest, the shoulders shrugged off
the world, the collapsed arms spread for a hug.
And if there'd been a face above the buttondown neck,
I would have pressed the forehead out, I would
have made a boy again out of that tired man!   10

If I clung to her skirt as she sorted the wash
or put out a line, my mother frowned,
a crease down each side of her mouth.
This is no time for love! But here
I could linger over her wrinkled bedjacket,   15
kiss at the damp puckers of her wrists
with the hot tip. Here I caressed
collars, scallops, ties, pleats which made
her outfits test of the patience of my passion.
Here I could lay my dreaming iron on her lap.   20

The smell of baked cotton rose from the board
and blew with a breeze out the window
to the family wardrobe drying on the clothesline,
all needing a touch of my iron. Here I could tickle

the underarms of my big sister's petticoat   25
or secretly pat the backside of her pajamas.
For she too would have warned me not to muss
her fresh blouses, starched jumpers, and smocks,
all that my careful hand had ironed out,
forced to express my excess love on cloth.   30

CONSIDERATIONS FOR CRITICAL THINKING AND WRITING

1. **FIRST RESPONSE.** Explain how the speaker expresses her love for her family in the extended metaphor of ironing.

2. How are ironing and the poem itself expressions of the speaker's "excess love" (line 30). In what sense is her love excessive?

3. Explain how the speaker's relationship to her father differs from how she relates to her mother.

CONNECTIONS TO OTHER SELECTIONS

1. **CREATIVE RESPONSE.** Compare the descriptions of the mother in this poem and in Alvarez's "Dusting" (p. 440). Write a one-paragraph character sketch that uses vivid details and metaphoric language to describe her.

2. Discuss the perspective provided on housework in "Ironing Their Clothes" and in Natasha Trethewey's "Domestic Work, 1937" (p. 274).

JULIA ALVAREZ

On Writing "Sometimes the Words Are So Close"   2006
From the "33" Sonnet Sequence

I really believe that being a reader turns you into a writer. You connect with the voice in a poem at a deeper and more intimate level than you do with practically anyone in your everyday life. Seems like the years fall away, differences fall away, and when George Herbert asks in his poem, "The Flower,"

Who would have thought my shrivel'd heart
Could have recover'd greennesse?

You want to stroke the page and answer him, "I did, George." Instead you write a poem that responds to the feelings in his poem; you recover greenness for him and for yourself.

With the "33" sonnet sequence, I wanted the voice of the speaker to sound like a real woman speaking. A voice at once intimate and also somehow universal, essential. This sonnet #42 ["Sometimes the Words Are So Close"] is the last one in the sequence, a kind of final "testimony" about what writing is all about.

I mentioned that when you love something you read, you want to respond to it. You want to say it again, in fresh new language. Robert Frost speaks to this impulse in the poet when he says, "Don't borrow, steal!" Well, I borrowed /

stole two favorite passages. One of them is from the poem on the Statue of Liberty, which was written by Emma Lazarus (1849–1887), titled "The New Colossus" [p. 613]. These lines will sound familiar to you, I'm sure:

> Give me your tired, your poor,
> Your huddled masses yearning to breathe free,
> The wretched refuse of your teeming shore.
> Send these, the homeless, tempest-tost to me,
> I lift my lamp beside the golden door!

I think of these lines, not just as an invitation to the land of the brave and home of the free, but an invitation to poetry! A poem can be a resting place for the soul yearning to breathe free, a form that won't tolerate the misuses and abuses of language, a world teeming with discoveries and luminous little *ah-ha!* moments, a "place for the genuine," as Marianne Moore calls it in her poem, "On Poetry." William Carlos Williams said that we can't get the news from poems, practical information, hard facts, but "men die daily for lack of what is found there."

I not only agreed with this idea, but I wanted to say so in my own words, and so I echoed those lines from the Statue of Liberty in my sonnet:

> Those of you lost and yearning to be free,
> who hear these words, take heart from me.

Another favorite line comes from Walt Whitman's book-length "Leaves of Grass": "Who touches this [book] touches a man." As a young, lonely immigrant girl reading Whitman, those words made me feel so accompanied, so connected. And so I borrowed/stole that line and made it my own at the end of this poem.

JULIA ALVAREZ

Sometimes the Words Are So Close   *1982*
From the "33" Sonnet Sequence

Sometimes the words are so close I am
more who I am when I'm down on paper
than anywhere else as if my life were
practising for the real me I become
unbuttoned from the anecdotal and   5
unnecessary and undressed down
to the figure of the poem, line by line,
the real text a child could understand.
Why do I get confused living it through?
Those of you lost and yearning to be free,   10
who hear these words, take heart from me.
I once was in as many drafts as you.
But briefly, essentially, here I am.
Who touches this poem touches a woman.

Drafts of "Sometimes the Words Are So Close": A Poet's Writing Process

Sometimes the words are so close that I am
than who I am
expressed, all that I am, down on paper,
feet, legs, thigh, hips, belly, breasts, arms, finger
by finger as if the words were a hand
unbuttoning the anecdotal and
unnecessary to undress me down
to the figure of the poem, line by line,
the real text so easy to understand
I wonder I missed it in living it?
You, not if theres any left.
you, tomorrow I also felt
love and loss and longing
the lines pile up

too little for me life was my 1st draft,
I made a mess of love
but I saved some of
a brainstorm self expression
too personal, bit by bit
I salvaged some of who I was / am

myself as I couldn't live
I want you to know
why was I confused every
I wonder I missed it living it
wouldn't have known me
You of the future theres any left
too I'm here for me, my life was a
too personal, but
salvaged to mean
briefly, essentially, her life
but briefly, essentially, her life
reduced to

who touches this poem touches a woman

Sometimes the words are so close I am
more who I am when I'm down on paper
than anywhere else as if my life were
practising for the real me I become
unbuttoned from the anecdotal and
unnecessary and undressed down
to the figure of the poem, line by line
the real text a child could understand —
Why do I get confused living it through
(crossed-out lines) what I, your curious
me anymore than
but briefly, essentially, here I am
Who touches this poem touches a woman —

goes...
you...

Concone now if its touched you...

Sometimes the words are so close I am
more who I am when I'm down on paper
than anywhere else as if my life were
practising for the real me I become
unbuttoned form the anecdotal and
unnecessary and undressed down
to the figure of the poem, line by line,
the real text a child could understand.
Why do I get confused living it through?
Those of you, lost and yearning to be free,
who hear these words, take heart from me.
I ~~was~~ once was in as many drafts as you.
But briefly, essentially, here I am...
Who touches this poem touches a woman.

Concone, now it's
touched you
as I sought
to do, you'll find yourself
embraced by
mought

you'll find yourself
drawn in
brought to love

```
Sometimes the words are so close I am
more who I am when I'm down on paper
than anywhere else as if my life were
practising for the real me I become
unbuttoned from the anecdotal and
unnecessary and undressed down
to the figure of the poem, line by line,
the real text a child could understand.
Why do I get confused living it through?
Those of you, lost and yearning to be free,
who hear these words, take heart from me.
I once was in as many drafts as you.
But briefly, essentially, here I am...
Who touches this poem touches a woman.
```

pretentious

Considerations for Critical Thinking and Writing

1. **FIRST RESPONSE.** Paraphrase lines 1–9. What produces the speaker's sense of frustration?

2. How do lines 10–14 resolve the question raised in line 9?

3. Explain how Alvarez's use of punctuation serves to reinforce the poem's meanings.

4. Discuss the elements of this poem that make it a sonnet.

5. Read carefully Alvarez's early drafts and discuss how they offer insights into your understanding and interpretation of the final version.

Connections to Other Selections

1. Compare the transformative power of poetry in this poem and in Emily Dickinson's "This was a Poet—It is That" (p. 323).

2. The poem's final line echoes Walt Whitman's poem "So Long" in which he addresses the reader: "Camerado, this is no book,/Who touches this touches a man." Alvarez has said that Whitman is one of her favorite poets. Read the selections by Whitman in this anthology (check the index for titles) along with "So Long" (readily available online) and propose an explanation about why you think she admires his poetry.

JULIA ALVAREZ

On Writing "First Muse"   2006

I have to come clean about calling this poem, "First Muse."

I had another first muse in Spanish. Her name was Scheherazade and I read about her in a book my aunt gave me called *The Arabian Nights*. Scheherazade saves her life by telling the murderous sultan incredible tales night after

Perspective

KELLI LYON JOHNSON (B. 1969)

Mapping an Identity   2005

Alvarez poses the problem of how we are to understand and represent identity within the multiple migrations that characterize an increasingly global society. By "mapping a country that's not on the map," Alvarez, a Dominican immigrant forced into exile in the United States, is undertaking a journey that places her at the forefront of contemporary American letters.

The question of identity and agency is particularly acute for women, postcolonial peoples, and others upon whom an identity has traditionally been imposed. Given Alvarez's success, both commercial and artistic, a variety of groups have claimed her as a member of their communities: as woman, ethnic, exile, diaspora, Caribbean, Dominican, Latina, and American. In the keynote address at a conference for Caribbean Studies, Doña Aída Cartagena Portalatín, "the grand woman of letters in the Dominican Republic" (*Something*[1] 171) gently chides Alvarez for writing in English. "Come back to your country, to your language," she tells Alvarez. "You are a Dominican" (171). By conflating linguistic, national, and cultural identity, Portalatín underscores the importance of these factors for constructing a literary tradition that includes displaced writers like Alvarez, who quite consciously has not adopted for writing the language of her country of origin.

In response to such comments, Alvarez has asserted her own self-definition as both (and neither) Dominican and American by writing "a new place on the map" (*Something* 173). Placing herself among a multiethnic group of postcolonial authors who write in English — "Michael Ondaatje in Toronto, Maxine Hong Kingston in San Francisco, Seamus Heaney in Boston, Bharati Mukherjee in Berkeley, Marjorie Agosín in Wellesley, Edwidge Danticat in Brooklyn" (173) — Alvarez, like these authors, has altered contemporary American literature by stretching the literary cartography of the Americas. These authors have brought, through their writings, their own countries of origin into a body of work in which the word *American* expands across continents and seas and begins to recapture its original connotation.

Alvarez has also claimed membership among a *comunidad* of U.S. Latina writers — Sandra Cisneros, Ana Castillo, Judith Ortiz Cofer, Lorna Dee Cervantes, Cherríe Moraga, Helena María Viramontes, and Denise Chávez — despite her fears that "the cage of definition" will enclose her writing "with its 'Latino subject matter,' 'Latino style,' 'Latino concerns'" (169). Like these authors, Alvarez seeks to write women into a postcolonial tradition of literature that has historically excluded women, particularly in writings of exile. To counter imposed definitions and historical silences, Alvarez has found that "the best way to define myself is through stories and poems" (169). The space that Alvarez maps is thus a narrative space: the site of her emerging cartography of identity and exile.

From *Julia Alvarez: Writing a New Place on the Map*

[1] *Something to Declare*, Alvarez's collection of essays published in 1998.

CONSIDERATIONS FOR CRITICAL THINKING AND WRITING

1. Based on your reading of the poems in this chapter, which community identity — "ethnic, exile, diaspora, Caribbean, Dominican, Latina, and American" — best describes Alvarez for you?

2. In what sense does Alvarez's poetry expand "the literary cartography of the Americas"?

3. Consider "First Muse" as Alvarez's response to Portalatín's suggestion that she should write in Spanish rather than English and "[c]ome back to your country, to your language."

16

A CRITICAL CASE STUDY
T. S. Eliot's "The Love Song of J. Alfred Prufrock"

Genuine poetry can communicate
before it is understood.
—T. S. ELIOT

This chapter provides several critical approaches to a challenging but highly rewarding poem by T. S. Eliot. After studying this poem, you're likely to find yourself quoting bits of its striking imagery. At the very least, you'll recognize the lines when you hear other people fold them into their own conversations. This poem has elicited numerous critical approaches because it raises so many issues relating to history, biography, imagery, symbolism, irony, myth, and other matters. The following critical excerpts offer a small

Explore contexts for T. S. Eliot on *LiterActive*.

T.S. Eliot

T. S. Eliot began writing poetry as a student. He is shown here in 1906 at age eighteen, during his first year at Harvard. In 1910, Eliot continued his studies abroad at the Sorbonne in Paris, and at age twenty-three completed his first draft of "The Love Song of J. Alfred Prufrock" during the summer of 1911. Later in his life Eliot said, "Immature poets imitate; mature poets steal."

Reprinted by permission of the Houghton Library, Harvard University.

and partial sample of the possible formalist, biographical, historical, mythological, psychological, sociological, and other perspectives that have attempted to shed light on the poem (see Chapter 25, "Critical Strategies for Reading," for a discussion of a variety of critical methods). They should help you to enjoy the poem more by raising questions, providing insights, and inviting you further into the text.

A BRIEF BIOGRAPHY

Born into a prominent New England family that had moved to St. Louis, Missouri, Thomas Stearns Eliot (1888–1965) was a major figure in English literature between the two world wars. He studied literature and philosophy at Harvard and on the Continent, subsequently choosing to live in England for most of his life and becoming a citizen of that country in 1927. Many writers have been powerfully influenced by his allusive and challenging poetry, particularly his treatment of postwar life in *The Waste Land* (1922)

This portrait of T. S. Eliot is by the Modernist painter and writer Wyndham Lewis. The Modernist movement of art and literature, dating from the late nineteenth to the mid-twentieth century, represented a rejection of tradition, a radical departure from Victorian sentimentality, and a move toward more experimental forms of expression. Modernist writers included T. S. Eliot, James Joyce, and Virginia Woolf. One of the themes explored by Modernist authors like Eliot is alienation. He once said, "[Poetry] may make us from time to time a little more aware of the deeper unnamed feelings which form the substratum of our being, to which we rarely penetrate; for our lives are mostly a constant evasion of ourselves."

Courtesy of the Friends of the Durban Art Gallery, South Africa.

T. S. Eliot (November 10, 1959), in a pose that suggests the Prufrock persona, holding a book containing some of his earlier work during a press conference at the University of Chicago.
© Bettmann/CORBIS.

and his exploration of religious questions in *The Four Quartets* (1943). In addition, he wrote plays, including *Murder in the Cathedral* (1935) and *The Cocktail Party* (1950). He was awarded the Nobel Prize for Literature in 1948. In "The Love Song of J. Alfred Prufrock" Eliot presents a comic but serious figure who expresses through a series of fragmented images the futility, boredom, and meaninglessness associated with much of modern life.

T. S. ELIOT (1888–1965)
The Love Song of J. Alfred Prufrock   *1917*

S'io credesse che mia risposta fosse
A persona che mai tornasse al mondo,
Questa fiamma staria senza più scosse.
Ma perciocchè giammai di questo fondo

Non tornò vivo alcun, s'i'odo il vero,
Senza tema d'infamia ti rispondo.°

    Let us go then, you and I,
When the evening is spread out against the sky
Like a patient etherized upon a table;
Let us go, through certain half-deserted streets,
The muttering retreats   5
Of restless nights in one-night cheap hotels
And sawdust restaurants with oyster-shells:
Streets that follow like a tedious argument
Of insidious intent
To lead you to an overwhelming question . . .   10

Oh, do not ask, "What is it?"
Let us go and make our visit.

In the room the women come and go
Talking of Michelangelo.

    The yellow fog that rubs its back upon the window panes,   15
The yellow smoke that rubs its muzzle on the window panes
Licked its tongue into the corners of the evening,
Lingered upon the pools that stand in drains,
Let fall upon its back the soot that falls from chimneys,
Slipped by the terrace, made a sudden leap,   20
And seeing that it was a soft October night,
Curled once about the house, and fell asleep.

    And indeed there will be time°
For the yellow smoke that slides along the street,
Rubbing its back upon the window panes;   25
There will be time, there will be time
To prepare a face to meet the faces that you meet;
There will be time to murder and create,
And time for all the works and days° of hands
That lift and drop a question on your plate: 30
Time for you and time for me,
And time yet for a hundred indecisions,
And for a hundred visions and revisions,
Before the taking of a toast and tea.

Epigraph: *S'io credesse . . . rispondo:* Dante's *Inferno,* 27:58–63. In the Eighth Chasm of the Inferno, Dante and Virgil meet Guido da Montefeltro, one of the False Counselors, who is punished by being enveloped in an eternal flame. When Dante asks Guido to tell his life story, the spirit replies: "If I thought that my answer were to one who might ever return to the world, this flame would shake no more; but since from this depth none ever returned alive, if what I hear is true, I answer you without fear of infamy."

23 *there will be time:* An allusion to Ecclesiastes 3:1–8: "To everything there is a season, and a time to every purpose under heaven. . . ."

29 *works and days:* Hesiod's eighth-century B.C. poem *Works and Days* gives practical advice on how to conduct one's life in accordance with the seasons.

In the room the women come and go   35
Talking of Michelangelo.

 And indeed there will be time
To wonder, "Do I dare?" and, "Do I dare?" —
Time to turn back and descend the stair,
With a bald spot in the middle of my hair —   40
(They will say: "How his hair is growing thin!")
My morning coat, my collar mounting firmly to the chin,
My necktie rich and modest, but asserted by a simple pin —
(They will say: "But how his arms and legs are thin!")
Do I dare   45
Disturb the universe?
In a minute there is time
For decisions and revisions which a minute will reverse.

 For I have known them all already, known them all:
Have known the evenings, mornings, afternoons,   50
I have measured out my life with coffee spoons;
I know the voices dying with a dying fall
Beneath the music from a farther room.
 So how should I presume?

 And I have known the eyes already, known them all —   55
The eyes that fix you in a formulated phrase.
And when I am formulated, sprawling on a pin,
When I am pinned and wriggling on the wall,
Then how should I begin
To spit out all the butt-ends of my days and ways?   60
 And how should I presume?

 And I have known the arms already, known them all —
Arms that are braceleted and white and bare
(But in the lamplight, downed with light brown hair!)
 Is it perfume from a dress   65
 That makes me so digress?
Arms that lie along a table, or wrap about a shawl.
 And should I then presume?
 And how should I begin?

 Shall I say, I have gone at dusk through narrow streets,   70
And watched the smoke that rises from the pipes
Of lonely men in shirtsleeves, leaning out of windows? . . .

I should have been a pair of ragged claws
Scuttling across the floors of silent seas.

 And the afternoon, the evening, sleeps so peacefully!   75
Smoothed by long fingers,
Asleep . . . tired . . . or it malingers,
Stretched on the floor, here beside you and me.
Should I, after tea and cakes and ices,
Have the strength to force the moment to its crisis?   80
But though I have wept and fasted, wept and prayed,

Though I have seen my head (grown slightly bald) brought in upon a platter,°
I am no prophet — and here's no great matter;
I have seen the moment of my greatness flicker,
And I have seen the eternal Footman hold my coat, and snicker,   85
    And in short, I was afraid.

    And would it have been worth it, after all,
After the cups, the marmalade, the tea,
Among the porcelain, among some talk of you and me,
Would it have been worth while   90
To have bitten off the matter with a smile,
To have squeezed the universe into a ball°
To roll it toward some overwhelming question,
To say: "I am Lazarus,° come from the dead,
Come back to tell you all, I shall tell you all" —   95
If one, settling a pillow by her head,
    Should say: "That is not what I meant at all;
        That is not it, at all."

    And would it have been worth it, after all,
Would it have been worth while,   100
After the sunsets and the dooryards and the sprinkled streets,
After the novels, after the teacups, after the skirts that trail along the floor —
And this, and so much more? —
It is impossible to say just what I mean!
But as if a magic lantern threw the nerves in patterns on a screen: 105
Would it have been worth while
If one, settling a pillow or throwing off a shawl,
And turning toward the window, should say:
    "That is not it at all,
    That is not what I meant, at all."   110

No! I am not Prince Hamlet, nor was meant to be;
Am an attendant lord,° one that will do
To swell a progress,° start a scene or two   *state procession*
Advise the prince: withal, an easy tool,
Deferential, glad to be of use,   115
Politic, cautious, and meticulous;
Full of high sentence, but a bit obtuse;
At times, indeed, almost ridiculous —
Almost, at times, the Fool.

I grow old . . . I grow old . . .   120
I shall wear the bottoms of my trowsers rolled.

---

82 *head . . . upon a platter:* At Salome's request, Herod had John the Baptist decapitated and had the severed head delivered to her on a platter (see Matt. 14:1-12 and Mark 6:17-29).

92 *squeezed the universe into a ball:* See Andrew Marvell's "To His Coy Mistress" (p. 81), lines 41-42: "Let us roll all our strength and all / Our sweetness up into one ball."

94 *Lazarus:* The brother of Mary and Martha who was raised from the dead by Jesus (John 11:1-44). In Luke 16:19-31, a rich man asks that another Lazarus return from the dead to warn the living about their treatment of the poor.

112 *attendant lord:* Like Polonius in Shakespeare's *Hamlet.*

Shall I part my hair behind? Do I dare to eat a peach?
I shall wear white flannel trowsers, and walk upon the beach.
I have heard the mermaids singing, each to each.

I do not think that they will sing to me.   125

I have seen them riding seaward on the waves,
Combing the white hair of the waves blown back
When the wind blows the water white and black.

We have lingered in the chambers of the sea
By seagirls wreathed with seaweed red and brown,   130
Till human voices wake us, and we drown.

CONSIDERATIONS FOR CRITICAL THINKING AND WRITING

1. **FIRST RESPONSE.** What does J. Alfred Prufrock's name connote? How would you characterize him?

2. What do you think is the purpose of the epigraph from Dante's *Inferno*?

3. What is it that Prufrock wants to do? How does he behave? What does he think of himself? Which parts of the poem answer these questions?

4. Who is the "you" of line 1 and the "we" in the final lines?

5. Discuss the poem's imagery. How does the imagery reveal Prufrock's character? Which images seem especially striking to you?

CONNECTIONS TO OTHER SELECTIONS

1. Write an essay comparing Prufrock's sense of himself as an individual with that of Walt Whitman's speaker in "One's-Self I Sing" (p. 629).

2. Discuss in an essay the tone of "The Love Song of J. Alfred Prufrock" and Robert Frost's "Acquainted with the Night" (p. 157).

Perspectives on T. S. Eliot

ELISABETH SCHNEIDER (1897–1984)

Schneider uses a biographical approach to the poem to suggest that part of what went into the characterization of Prufrock were some of Eliot's own sensibilities.

Hints of Eliot in Prufrock   *1952*

Perhaps never again did Eliot find an epigraph quite so happily suited to his use as the passage from the *Inferno* which sets the underlying serious tone for *Prufrock* and conveys more than one level of its meaning: "S'io credesse che mia risposta . . . ," lines in which Guido da Montefeltro consents to tell his story to Dante only because he believes that none ever returns to the world of the living from his depth. One in Hell can bear to expose his shame only to another of the damned; Prufrock speaks to, will be understood only by, other Prufrocks (the "you and I" of the opening, perhaps), and, I imagine the epigraph also hints, Eliot himself is speaking to those who know this kind of hell. The poem, I need hardly say, is not in a literal sense autobiographical: for one thing, though it is clear that Prufrock will never marry, the poem was published in the year of Eliot's own first marriage. Nevertheless, friends who knew the young Eliot almost all describe him, retrospectively but convincingly, in Prufrockian terms; and Eliot himself once said of dramatic monologue in general that what we normally hear in it "is the voice of the poet, who has put on the costume and make-up either of some historical character, or of one out of fiction." . . . I suppose it to be one of the many indirect clues to his own poetry planted with evident deliberation throughout his prose. "What every poet starts from," he also once said, "is his own emotions," and, writing of Dante, he asserted that the *Vita nuova* "could only have been written around a personal experience," a statement that, under the circumstances, must be equally applicable to Prufrock; Prufrock was Eliot, though Eliot was much more than Prufrock. We miss the whole tone of the poem, however, if we read it as social satire only. Eliot was not either the dedicated apostle in theory, or the great exemplar in practice, of complete "depersonalization" in poetry that one influential early essay of his for a time led readers to suppose.

From "Prufrock and After: The Theme of Change," *PMLA,* October 1952

CONSIDERATIONS FOR CRITICAL THINKING AND WRITING

1. Though Schneider concedes that the poem is not literally autobiographical, she does assert that "Prufrock was Eliot." How does she argue this point? Explain why you find her argument convincing or unconvincing.

2. Find information in the library about Eliot's early career when he was writing this poem. To what extent does the poem reveal his circumstances and concerns at that point in his life?

BARBARA EVERETT

Everett's discussion of tone is used to make a distinction between Eliot and his characterization of Prufrock.

The Problem of Tone in Prufrock   *1974*

Eliot's poetry presents a peculiar problem as far as tone is concerned. *Tone* really means the way the attitude of a speaker is manifested by the inflections of his speaking voice. Many critics have already recognized that for a mixture of reasons it is difficult, sometimes almost impossible, to ascertain Eliot's tone in this way. It is not that the poetry lacks "voice," for in fact Eliot has an extraordinarily recognizable poetic voice, often imitated and justifying his own comment in the . . . *Paris Review* that "in a poem you're writing for your own voice, which is very important. You're thinking in terms of your own voice." It is this authoritative, idiosyncratic, and exact voice that holds our complete attention in poem after poem, however uninterested we are in what opinions it may seem or happen to be expressing. But Eliot too seems uninterested in what opinions it may happen to be expressing, for he invariably dissociates himself from his poems before they are even finished — before they are hardly begun — by balancing a derisory name or title against an "I," by reminding us that there is always going to be a moment at which detachment will take place or has taken place, a retrospective angle from which, far in the future, critical judgment alters the scene, and the speaking voice of the past has fallen silent. "I have known them all already, known them all." Thus whatever started to take place in the beginning of a poem by Eliot cannot truly be said to be Eliot's opinion because at some extremely early stage he began that process of dissociation to be loosely called "dramatization," a process reflected in the peculiar distances of the tone, as though everything spoken was in inverted commas.

From "In Search of Prufrock," *Critical Quarterly*, Summer 1974

CONSIDERATIONS FOR CRITICAL THINKING AND WRITING

1. According to Everett, why is it difficult to describe Eliot's tone in his poetry?

2. How does Eliot's tone make it difficult to make an autobiographical connection between Prufrock and Eliot?

3. How does Everett's reading of the relationship between Prufrock and Eliot differ from Schneider's in the preceding perspective?

MICHAEL L. BAUMANN (B. 1926)

Baumann takes a close look at the poem's images in his formalist efforts to make a point about Prufrock's character.

The "Overwhelming Question" for Prufrock   *1981*

Most critics . . . have seen the overwhelming question related to sex. . . . They have implicitly assumed — and given their readers to understand — that Prufrock's is the male's basic question: Can I?

The poet and critic Delmore Schwartz once said that "J. Alfred Prufrock is unable to make love to women of his own class and kind because of shyness, self-consciousness, and fear of rejection."[1] This is undoubtedly true, but

---

[1] "T. S. Eliot as the International Hero," *Partisan Review*, 12 (1945), 202; rpt in *T. S. Eliot: A Selected Critique*, ed. Leonard Unger (New York: Rinehart & Company, Inc., 1948), 46.

Prufrock's inability to *feel* love has something to do with his inability to *make* love, too. . . . A simple desire, lust, is more than honest Prufrock can cope with as he mounts the stairs.

But Prufrock is coping with another, less simple desire as well. . . . If birth, copulation, and death is all there is, then, once we are born, once we have copulated, only death remains (for the male of the species, at least). Prufrock, having "known them all already, known them all," having "known the evenings, mornings, afternoons," having "measured out" his life "with coffee spoons," desires death. The "overwhelming question" that assails him would no longer be the romantic rhetorical "Is life worth living?" (to which the answer is obviously No), but the more immediate shocker: "Should one commit suicide?" which is to say: "Should I?" . . .

. . . The poem makes clear that Prufrock wants more than the "entire destruction of consciousness as we understand it," a notion Prufrock expresses by wishing he were "a pair of ragged claws, / Scuttling across the floors of silent seas." Prufrock wants death itself, physical death, and the poem, I believe, is explicit about this desire.

Not only does Prufrock seem to be tired of time — "time yet for a hundred indecisions" — a tiredness that goes far beyond the acedia Prufrock is generally credited with feeling, if only because "there will be time to murder and create," time, in other words (in one sense at least) to copulate, but Prufrock is also tired of his own endless vanities, from feeling he must "prepare a face to meet the faces that you meet," to having to summon up those ironies with which to contemplate his own thin arms and legs, and, indeed, to asking if, in the rather tedious enterprise of preparing for copulation, the moment is worth "forcing to its crisis." No wonder Prufrock compares himself to John the Baptist and, in conjuring up this first concrete image of his own death, sees his head brought in upon a platter. That would be the easy way out. He had, after all, "wept and fasted, wept and prayed," but he realizes he is no prophet — and no Salome will burst into passion, will ignite for him. When the eternal Footman, Death, who holds his coat, snickers, he does so because Prufrock has let "the moment" of his "greatness" flicker, because Prufrock was unable to comply with the one imperative greatness would have thrust upon him: to kill himself. Prufrock explains: "I was afraid." Yet the achievement of his vision at the end of the poem, his being able to linger "in the chambers of the sea / By seagirls wreathed with seaweed red and brown," is an act of the imagination that only physical death can complete, unless Prufrock wants human voices to wake him, and drown him. His romantic vision demands the voluntary act: suicide. It is to be expected that he will fail in this too, as he has failed in everything else.

From "Let Us Ask 'What Is It,'" *Arizona Quarterly,* Spring 1981

CONSIDERATIONS FOR CRITICAL THINKING AND WRITING

1. Describe the evidence used by Baumann to argue that Prufrock contemplates suicide.

2. Explain in an essay why you do or do not find Baumann's argument convincing.

3. Later in his essay Baumann connects Prufrock's insistence that "No, I am not Prince Hamlet" with Hamlet's "To be or not to be" speech. How do you think this reference might be used to support Baumann's argument?

FREDERIK L. RUSCH (B. 1938)

Rusch makes use of the insights developed by Erich Fromm, a social psychologist who believed "psychic forces [are] a process of constant interaction between man's needs and the social and historical reality in which he participates."

Society and Character in "The Love Song of J. Alfred Prufrock"   *1984*

In looking at fiction, drama, and poetry from the Frommian point of view, the critic understands literature to be social portrayal as well as character portrayal or personal statement. Society and character are inextricably joined. The Frommian approach opens up the study of literary work, giving a social context to its characters, which suggests why those characters behave as they do. The Frommian approach recognizes human beings for what they are — basically gregarious individuals who are interdependent upon each other, in need of each other, and thus, to a certain degree, products of their social environments, although those environments may be inimical to their mental well-being. That is, as stated earlier, the individual's needs and drives have a social component and are not purely biological. The Frommian approach to literature assumes that a writer is — at least by implication — analyzing society and its setting as well as character. . . .

In T. S. Eliot's "The Love Song of J. Alfred Prufrock," Prufrock is talking to himself, expressing a fantasy or daydream. In his monologue, Prufrock, as noted by Grover Smith, "is addressing, as if looking into a mirror, his whole public personality."[1] Throughout the poem, Prufrock is extremely self-conscious, believing that the people in his imaginary drawing room will examine him as a specimen insect, "sprawling on a pin, / . . . pinned and wriggling on the wall. . . ." Of course, self-consciousness — being conscious of one's self — is not necessarily neurotic. Indeed, it is part of being a human being. It is only when self-consciousness, which has always led man to feel a separation from nature, becomes obsessive that we have a problem. Prufrock is certainly obsessed with his self-consciousness, convinced that everyone notices his balding head, his clothes (his prudent frocks), his thin arms and legs.

---

[1] Grover Smith, *T. S. Eliot's Poetry and Plays: A Study in Sources and Meaning* (Chicago: U of Chicago P, 1962), 16.

On one level, however, Prufrock is merely expressing the pain that all human beings must feel. Although his problem is extreme, he is quite representative of the human race:

> Self-awareness, reason, and imagination have disrupted the "harmony" that characterizes animal existence. Their emergence has made man into an anomaly, the freak of the universe. He is part of nature, subject to her physical laws and unable to change them, yet he transcends nature. He is set apart while being a part; he is homeless, yet chained to the home he shares with all creatures. . . . Being aware of himself, he realizes his powerlessness and the limitations of his existence. He is never free from the dichotomy of his existence: he cannot rid himself of his mind, even if he would want to; he cannot rid himself of his body as long as he is alive — and his body makes him want to be alive.[2]

This is the predicament of the human being. His self-awareness has made him feel separate from nature. This causes pain and sorrow. What, then, is the solution to the predicament? Fromm believed that mankind filled the void of alienation from nature with the creation of a culture, a society: "Man's existential, and hence unavoidable disequilibrium can be relatively stable when he has found, with the support of his culture, a more or less adequate way of coping with his existential problems" (*Destructiveness* 225). But, unfortunately for Prufrock, his culture and society do not allow him to overcome his existential predicament. The fact is, he is bored by his modern, urban society.

In image after image, Prufrock's mind projects boredom:

> For I have known them all already, known them all:
> Have known the evenings, mornings, afternoons,
> I have measured out my life with coffee spoons. . . .
> . . . .
>
> And I have known the eyes already, known them all —
> . . . .
>
> Then how should I begin
> To spit out all the butt-ends of my days and ways?
> . . . .
>
> And I have known the arms already, known them all —. . . .

Prufrock is completely unstimulated by his social environment, to the point of near death. The evening in which he proposes to himself to make a social visit is "etherized upon a table." The fog, as a cat, falls asleep; it is "tired . . . or it malingers, / Stretched on the floor. . . ."

Prufrock, living in a city of "half-deserted streets, / . . . one-night cheap hotels / And sawdust restaurants with oyster-shells," gets no comfort, no nurturing from his environment. He is, in the words of Erich Fromm, a "modern mass man . . . isolated and lonely" (*Destructiveness* 107). He lives in a destructive environment. Instead of providing communion with fellow human beings, it alienates him through boredom. Such boredom leads to "a state of chronic depression" that can cause the pathology of "insufficient inner productivity" in

---

[2] Erich Fromm, *The Anatomy of Human Destructiveness* (New York: Holt, Rinehart & Winston, 1973), 225.

the individual (*Destructiveness* 243). Such a lack of productivity is voiced by Prufrock when he confesses that he is neither Hamlet nor John the Baptist.

An interesting tension in "The Love Song of J. Alfred Prufrock" is caused by the reader's knowledge that Prufrock understands his own predicament quite well. Although he calls himself a fool, he has wisdom about himself and his predicament. This, however, only reinforces his depression and frustration. In his daydream, he is able to reveal truths about himself that, while they lead to self-understanding, apparently cannot alleviate his problems in his waking life. The poem suggests no positive movement out of the predicament. Prufrock is like a patient cited by Fromm, who under hypnosis envisioned "a black barren place with many masks," and when asked what the vision meant said "that everything was dull, dull, dull; that the masks represent the different roles he takes to fool people into thinking he is feeling well" (*Destructiveness* 246). Likewise, Prufrock understands that "There will be time, there will be time / To prepare a face to meet the faces that you meet. . . ." But despite his understanding of the nature of his existence, he cannot attain a more productive life.

It was Fromm's belief that with boredom "the decisive conditions are to be found in the overall environmental situation. . . . It is highly probable that even cases of severe depression-boredom would be less frequent and less intense . . . in a society where a mood of hope and love of life predominated. But in recent decades the opposite is increasingly the case, and thus a fertile soil for the development of individual depressive states is provided" (*Destructiveness* 251). There is no "mood of hope and love of life" in Prufrock's society. Prufrock is a lonely man, as lonely as "the lonely men in shirt-sleeves, leaning out of windows" of his fantasy. His only solution is to return to the animal state that his race was in before evolving into human beings.

Animals are one with nature, not alienated from their environments. They *are* nature, unselfconscious. Prufrock would return to a preconscious existence in the extreme: "I should have been a pair of ragged claws / Scuttling across the floors of silent seas." Claws *without a head* surely would not be alienated, bored, or depressed. They would seek and would need no psychological nurturing from their environment. And in the end Prufrock's fantasy of becoming claws is definitely more positive for him than his life as a human being. He completes his monologue with depressing irony, to say the least: it is with human voices waking us, bringing us back to human society, that we drown.

> From "Approaching Literature through the Social Psychology of
> Erich Fromm" in *Psychological Perspectives on Literature:
> Freudian Dissidents and Non-Freudians,* edited by Joseph Natoli

CONSIDERATIONS FOR CRITICAL THINKING AND WRITING

1. According to Rusch, why is Fromm's approach useful for understanding Prufrock's character as well as his social context?

2. In what ways is Prufrock "representative of the human race" (para. 3)? Is he like any other characters you have read about in this anthology? Explain your response.

3. In an essay consider how Rusch's analysis of Prufrock might be used to support Baumann's argument that Prufrock's "overwhelming question" is whether or not he should kill himself (p. 462).

ROBERT SWARD (B. 1933)

Sward, a poet, provides a detailed explication, framed by his own personal experiences during the Korean War.

A Personal Analysis of "The Love Song of J. Alfred Prufrock"   1996

In 1952, sailing to Korea as a U.S. Navy librarian for Landing Ship Tank 914, I read T. S. Eliot's "The Love Song of J. Alfred Prufrock." Ill-educated, a product of Chicago's public-school system, I was nineteen-years-old and, awakened by Whitman, Eliot, and Williams, had just begun writing poetry. I was also reading all the books I could get my hands on.

Eliot had won the Nobel Prize in 1948 and, curious, I was trying to make sense of poems like "Prufrock" and "The Waste Land."

"What do you know about T. S. Eliot?" I asked a young officer who'd been to college and studied English literature. I knew from earlier conversations that we shared an interest in what he called "modern poetry." A yeoman third class, two weeks at sea and bored, I longed for someone to talk to. "T. S. Eliot was born in St. Louis, Missouri, but he lives now in England and is studying to become an Englishman," the officer said, tapping tobacco into his pipe. "The 'T. S.' stands for 'tough shit.' You read Eliot's 'Love Song of J. Alfred Prufrock,' what one English prof called 'the first poem of the modern movement,' and if you don't understand it, 'tough shit.' All I can say is that's some love song."

An anthology of poetry open before us, we were sitting in the ship's all-metal, eight by eight-foot library eating bologna sandwiches and drinking coffee. Fortunately, the captain kept out of sight and life on the slow-moving (eight to ten knots), flat-bottomed amphibious ship was unhurried and anything but formal.

"Then why does Eliot bother calling it a love song?" I asked, as the ship rolled and the coffee sloshed onto a steel table. The tight metal room smelled like a cross between a diesel engine and a New York deli.

"Eliot's being ironic, sailor. 'Prufrock' is the love song of a sexually repressed and horny man who has no one but himself to sing to." Drawing on his pipe, the officer scratched his head. "Like you and I, Mr. Prufrock is a lonely man on his way to a war zone. We're sailing to Korea and we know the truth, don't we? We may never make it back. Prufrock marches like a brave soldier to a British drawing room that, he tells us, may be the death of him. He's a mock heroic figure who sings of mermaids and peaches and drowning."

Pointing to lines 129–31, the officer read aloud:

> We have lingered in the chambers of the sea
> By seagirls wreathed with seaweed red and brown
> Till human voices wake us and we drown.

"Prufrock is also singing because he's a poet. Prufrock *is* T. S. Eliot and, the truth is, Eliot is so much like Prufrock that he has to distance himself from his creation. That's why he gives the man that pompous name. Did you know

'Tough Shit,' as a young man, sometimes signed himself 'T. Stearns Eliot'? You have to see the humor — the irony — in 'Prufrock' to understand the poem."

"I read it, I hear it in my head, but I still don't get it," I confessed. "What is 'Prufrock' about?"

"'Birth, death and copulation, that's all there is.' That's what Eliot himself says. Of course the poem also touches on aging, social status, and fashion."

"Aging and fashion?" I asked.

The officer threw back his head and recited:

(They will say: "How his hair is growing thin!")
My morning coat, my collar mounting firmly to the chin,
My necktie rich and modest, but asserted by a simple pin.

He paused, then went on:

I grow old . . . I grow old . . .
I shall wear the bottoms of my trousers rolled.

"At the time the poem was written it was fashionable for young men to roll their trousers. In lines 120–21, Thomas Stearns Prufrock is laughing at himself for being middle-aged and vain.

"Anyway, 'The Love Song of J. Alfred Prufrock' is an interior monologue," said the officer, finishing his bologna sandwich and washing it down with dark rum. Wiping mustard from his mouth, he continued. "The whole thing takes place in J. Alfred Prufrock's head. That's clear, isn't it?"

I had read [Robert] Browning's "My Last Duchess" and understood about interior monologues.

"Listen, sailor: Prufrock thinks about drawing rooms, but he never actually sets foot in one. Am I right?"

"Yeah," I said after rereading the first ten lines. "I think so."

"The poem is about what goes through Prufrock's mind on his way to some upper-class drawing room. It's a foggy evening in October, and what Mr. Prufrock really needs is a drink. He's a tightass Victorian, a lonely teetotaling intellectual. Anyone else would forget the toast and marmalade and step into a pub and ask for a pint of beer."

Setting down his pipe, the naval officer opened the flask and refilled our coffee mugs.

"Every time I think I know what 'Prufrock' means it turns out to mean something else," I said. "Eliot uses too many symbols. Why doesn't he just say what he means?"

"The city — 'the lonely men in shirt-sleeves' and the 'one-night cheap hotels' — are masculine," said the officer. "That's what cities are like, aren't they: ugly and oppressive. What's symbolic — or should I say, what's obscure — about that?"

"Nothing," I said. "That's the easy part — Prufrock walking along like that."

"Okay," said the officer. "And in contrast to city streets, you've got the oppressive drawing room that, in Prufrock's mind, is feminine — 'Arms that are braceleted and white and bare' and 'the marmalade, the tea, / Among the porcelain, among some talk of you and me.'" Using a pencil, the officer underlined those images in the paperback anthology.

"You ever been to a tea party, Sward?"

"No, sir, I haven't. Not like Prufrock's."

"Well," said the officer, "I have and I have a theory about that 'overwhelming question' Prufrock wants to ask in line 10 — and again in line 93. Twice in the poem we hear about an 'overwhelming question.' What do you think he's getting at with that 'overwhelming question,' sailor?"

"Prufrock wants to ask the women what they're doing with their lives, but he's afraid they'll laugh at him," I said.

"Guess again, Sward," he said leaning back in his chair, stretching his arms.

"What's your theory, sir?"

"Sex," said the officer. "On the one hand, it's true, he wants to fit in and play the game because, after all, he's privileged. He belongs in the drawing room with the clever Englishwomen. At the same time he fantasizes. If he could, I think he'd like to shock them. Prufrock longs to put down his dainty porcelain teacup and shout, 'I am Lazarus, come from the dead, / Come back to tell you all, I shall tell you all.'"

"Why doesn't he do it?" I asked.

"Because Prufrock is convinced no matter what he says he won't reach them. He feels the English gentlewomen he's dealing with are unreachable. He believes his situation is as hopeless as theirs. He's dead and they're dead, too. That's why the poem begins with an image of sickness, 'a patient etherized upon a table,' and ends with people drowning. Prufrock is tough shit, man."

"You said you think there's a connection between Eliot the poet and J. Alfred Prufrock," I said.

"Of course there's a connection. Tommy Eliot from St. Louis, Missouri," said the officer. "Try as he will, he doesn't fit in. His English friends call him 'The American' and laugh. Tom Eliot the outsider with his rolled umbrella. T. S. Eliot is a self-conscious, make-believe Englishman and you have to understand that to understand 'Prufrock.'

"The poem is dark and funny at the same time. It's filled with humor and Prufrock is capable of laughing at himself. Just read those lines, 'Is it perfume from a dress / That makes me so digress?'"

"You were talking about Prufrock being sexually attracted to the women. How could that be if he is, as you say, 'dead.'" I asked.

"By 'dead' I mean desolate, inwardly barren, godforsaken. Inwardly, spiritually, Prufrock is a desolate creature. He's a moral man, he's a civilized man, but he's also hollow. But there's hope for him. In spite of himself, Prufrock is drawn to women.

"Look at line 64. He's attracted and repelled. Prufrock attends these teas, notices the women's arms 'downed with light brown hair!' and it scares the hell out of him because what he longs to do is to get them onto a drawing-room floor or a beach somewhere and bury his face in that same wonderfully tantalizing 'light brown hair.' What do you think of that, sailor?"

"I think you're right, sir."

"Then tell me this, Mr. Sward: Why doesn't he ask the overwhelming question? Hell, man, maybe it's not sexual. Maybe I'm wrong. Maybe what he wants to do is to ask some question like what you yourself suggested: 'What's the point in going on living when, in some sense, we're all already dead?'"

"I think he doesn't ask the question because he's so repressed, sir. He longs for physical contact, like you say, but he also wants another kind of intimacy, and he's afraid to ask for it and it's making him crazy."

"That's right, sailor. He's afraid. Eliot wrote the poem in 1911 when women were beginning to break free."

"Break free of what?" I asked.

"Of the prim and proper Victorian ideal. Suffragettes, feminists they called themselves. At the time Eliot wrote 'Prufrock,' women in England and America were catching on to the fact that they were disfranchised and had begun fighting for the right to vote, among other things, and for liberation, equality with men.

"Of course Prufrock is more prim and proper than the bored, overcivilized women in the poem. And it's ironic, isn't it, that he doesn't understand that the women are one step ahead of him. What you have in Prufrock is a man who tries to reconcile the image of real women with 'light brown hair' on their arms with some ideal, women who are a cross between the goddess Juno and a sweet Victorian maiden."

"Prufrock seems to know pretty well what he's feeling," I said. "He's not a liar and he's not a coward. To be honest, sir, I identify with Prufrock. He may try on one mask or another, but he ends up removing the mask and exposing himself."

"Now, about interior monologues: to understand 'Prufrock' you have to understand that most poems have one or more speakers and an audience, implied or otherwise. Let's go back to line 1. Who is this 'you and I' Eliot writes about?"

"Prufrock is talking to both his inner self and the reader," I said.

"How do you interpret the first ten lines?" the officer asked, pointing with his pencil.

"'Let us go then, you and I,' he's saying, let us stroll, somnolent and numb as a sedated patient, through these seedy 'half-deserted streets, / The muttering retreats / Of restless nights in one-night cheap hotels.'"

"That's it, sailor. And while one might argue that Prufrock 'wakes' at the end of the poem, he is for the most part a ghostly inhabitant of a world that is, for him, a sort of hell. He is like the speaker in the Italian epigraph from Dante's *Inferno*, who says, essentially, 'Like you, reader, I'm in purgatory and there is no way out. Nobody ever escapes from this pit and, for that reason, I can speak the truth without fear of ill fame.'

"Despairing and sick of heart, Prufrock is a prisoner. Trapped in himself and trapped in society, he attends another and another in an endless series of effete, decorous teas.

> In the room the women come and go
> Talking of Michelangelo.

"Do you get it now? Do you see what I mean when I say 'tough shit'?" said the officer.

"Yeah, I'm beginning to," I said.

"T. S. Eliot's 'Prufrock' has become so much a part of the English language that people who have never read the poem are familiar with phrases like 'I have measured out my life with coffee spoons' and 'I grow old . . . I grow old . . . / I shall wear the bottoms of my trousers rolled' and 'Do I dare to eat a peach?' and 'In the room the women come and go.'

"Do you get it now? Eliot's irregularly rhymed, 131-line interior monologue has become part of the monologue all of us carry on in our heads. We are all of us, whether we know it or not, love-hungry, sex-crazed soldiers and sailors, brave, bored and lonely. At some level in our hearts, we are all J. Alfred Prufrock, every one of us, and we are all sailing into a war zone from which, as the last line of the poem implies, we may never return."

From "T. S. Eliot's 'Love Song of J. Alfred Prufrock'" in *Touchstones: American Poets on a Favorite Poem,* edited by Robert Pack and Jay Parini

CONSIDERATIONS FOR CRITICAL THINKING AND WRITING

1. How satisfactory is this reading of the poem? Are any significant portions of the poem left out of this reading?
2. Compare the tone of this critical approach to any other in this chapter. Explain why you prefer one over another.
3. Using Sward's personal approach, write an analysis of a poem of your choice in this anthology.

SUGGESTED TOPICS FOR LONGER PAPERS

1. "The Love Song of J. Alfred Prufrock" has proved to be popular among generations of college students who are fond of quoting bits of the poem. What do you think accounts for that popularity among your own generation? Alternatively, why doesn't this poem speak to your concerns or those of your generation?
2. Of the five critical perspectives on the poem provided in this chapter, which did you find to be the most satisfying reading? Explain your response by describing how your choice opened up the poem more than the other four perspectives.

17

A CULTURAL CASE STUDY
Louise Erdrich's "Dear John Wayne"

My background is such a rich mixed bag
I'd be crazy to want to be anything else.
— LOUISE ERDRICH

Close readings allow us to appreciate and understand the literary art of
a text. These formalist approaches to literature study the intrinsic ele-
ments of a work to determine how it is constructed, emphasizing how vari-
ous elements such as diction, image, figures of speech, tone, symbol, irony,
sound, rhythm, and other literary techniques provide patterns related to
the work's meaning. Instead of examining extrinsic matters such as social,
political, and economic contexts related to a poem, formalist critics focus
on the intrinsic qualities of the text itself. A formalist might, for example,
approach Thomas Hardy's 1912 poem "The Convergence of the Twain"
(p. 89) by placing significant emphasis on the form of this poem—its
rhyming three-line stanzas—rather than the historical
contexts around the sinking of the *Titanic*. A formalist
would be more concerned with the effects produced by
these triplets rather than the identities of some of the enormously wealthy
people who went down with the ship. In more recent literary criticism,

Explore contexts
for Louise Erdrich
on *LiterActive*.

however, there has been a renewed interest in the historical and cultural contexts of works that go beyond close readings of the text.

Cultural critics pay close attention to the historical contexts of a work, but unlike literary historians, they do not limit themselves to major historical events or famous people. A cultural critic might, for example, approach "The Convergence of the Twain" not only as an opportunity to examine the "vaingloriousness" of the rich who put their faith in the technology that produced the *Titanic* but also as an occasion to investigate how poor people made jokes about the sinking to deflate the pretensions of the rich. The ironies that go unsuspected by "human vanity" can be seen to go even deeper in the nervous jokes that infiltrate popular culture when such a catastrophe occurs. Hardy's dignified, if pessimistic, poetic response can be illuminated in radically different ways such as by advertising before the voyage or the jokes and sentimental poetic eulogies published after the disaster. Cultural critics study material drawn from a broad spectrum that includes "high" culture and popular culture. A cultural critic's approach to Hardy's treatment of the *Titanic*'s fate — captained by what Hardy calls the "Spinner of the Years" — might include discussions of everything from the ship's actual construction plans to passenger cabin accommodations to manuals for lifeboat drills, as well as connections to Hardy's contemporaries, who also wrote about the *Titanic*.

The documents that follow Louise Erdrich's "Dear John Wayne" are provided to suggest how cultural criticism can be used to contextualize a literary work historically. The documents include an excerpt from an interview with Erdrich on writing as a Native American; an early American painting depicting westward migration; a book excerpt on Hollywood Indians; an interview with John Wayne; a photograph of Wayne from a western film; and an Indian perspective on the Great Plains by Chief Luther Standing Bear. These documents offer some possible approaches to understanding the culture contemporary to "Dear John Wayne." A variety of such approaches can create a wider and more informed reading of the poem while deepening one's appreciation of Erdrich's achievement in writing it.

A BRIEF BIOGRAPHY

Louise Erdrich is of Chippewa (Ojibwe), French, and German American heritage. Born in Little Falls, Minnesota, she grew up as part of the Turtle Mountain Band of Chippewa in Wahpeton, North Dakota. Her parents, who taught in a school sponsored by the Bureau of Indian Affairs, made sure that she and her six siblings were connected to their large extended Indian family and heritage. They also encouraged her to tell stories and to write: "My father used to give me a nickel for every story I wrote, and my mother wove strips of construction paper together and stapled them into

When asked in an interview when she decided to become a writer, Louise Erdrich replied: "By the time I was twenty it was clear to me that I was good for—and good at—nothing else. I hated every job I had. . . . picking cucumbers, hoeing beets, selling popcorn, lifeguarding, waitressing, selling Kentucky Fried Chicken. . . . I knew if I were to have any chance at all for happiness in work, I had better throw myself at the writing life."
© Nancy Crampton.

book covers. So at an early age I felt myself to be a published author earning substantial royalties." Those nickels were well spent, given that Erdrich has become a significant voice in American literature.

In 1972, Erdrich entered Dartmouth College in a class that was among the first group of women admitted to the school. That same year Michael Dorris arrived to direct the new Native American studies program. He and Erdrich later married and collaborated on a number of books. While studying literature, creative writing, and Native American history and culture, Erdrich won several awards for her poetry and fiction. She worked a variety of jobs in North Dakota after graduating from Dartmouth, and then enrolled in the creative writing program at Johns Hopkins University, where she earned a master's degree in 1979.

Erdrich has published two books of poetry: *Jacklight* (1984) and *Baptism of Fire* (1989). Her poems strongly evoke small-town midwestern life and her Native American roots. She now prefers writing fiction over poetry, because, she says, fiction is more suitable for the narratives she wants to tell: "I began to tell stories in the poems and then realized that there was not enough room."

Although she is an accomplished poet, Erdrich's reputation is founded primarily on her fiction. Her first novel, *Love Medicine* (1984), which won the National Book Critics Circle Award, consists of a collection of interrelated stories about a group of Native American families living on or near a North Dakota reservation populated by strong-willed, passionate characters. *Love Medicine* (1984) is part of a related series of novels, the others of which are *The Beet Queen* (1986), *Tracks* (1988), *The Bingo Palace* (1994), and *Tales of Burning Love* (1996). The series spans the period just before World War I through the 1980s.

Before her husband's death in 1997, Erdrich enjoyed a very close professional relationship with him. The two worked together on Dorris's nonfiction *The Broken Cord: A Family's Ongoing Struggle with Fetal Alcohol Syndrome* (1989) and on a romantic mystery novel titled *The Crown of Columbus* (1991), which concerns a Native American woman who, ironically, discovers Christopher Columbus. Erdrich's novel, *The Antelope Wife* (1998), though not directly related to the earlier five interlocking novels, explores the connections characters experience over generations and across bloodlines as they fiercely struggle to survive the difficulties they encounter in their complex lives. Her most recent novels are *The Last Report on the Miracles at Little No Horse* (2002), a story of the Ojibwe people of North Dakota and a priest who arrives to convert them; *The Master Butcher's Singing Club* (2003), the story of Fidelis Waldovgel, a World War I sniper and local butcher known for his singing, also set in North Dakota; and *The Painted Indian* (2005), about a mysterious Indian drum whose sounds bridge time and space for the people who encounter it.

In "Dear John Wayne" (from *Jacklight*) Erdrich creates a revealing moment in which Indians view a classic John Wayne western at a drive-in movie. The poem explores the inevitable tensions the Indians feel as the rest of the audience cheers the great western hero coming to avenge the slaughter of white settlers who displace the Indians. Writing at a time when Native Americans are increasingly asserting their rights as a people and as American citizens, Erdrich implicitly connects contemporary American attitudes toward Indians with earlier Hollywood western myths and even earlier national policies that are reflected, for example, in a telling sentence from President Andrew Johnson's message to Congress in 1867: "If the savage resists, civilization, with the ten commandments in one hand and the sword in the other, demands his immediate extermination." History and myth combine to produce an intense personal reaction to such demands, as Erdrich addresses her poem to "Dear John Wayne."

Dear John Wayne   *1984*

August and the drive-in picture is packed.
We lounge on the hood of the Pontiac
surrounded by the slow-burning spirals they sell
at the window, to vanquish the hordes of mosquitoes.
Nothing works. They break through the smoke screen for blood.   5

Always the lookout spots the Indians first,
spread north to south, barring progress.
The Sioux or some other Plains bunch
in spectacular columns, ICBM missiles,
feathers bristling in the meaningful sunset.   10

The drum breaks. There will be no parlance.
Only the arrows whining, a death-cloud of nerves
swarming down on the settlers
who die beautifully, tumbling like dust weeds
into the history that brought us all here   15
together: this wide screen beneath the sign of the bear.

The sky fills, acres of blue squint and eye
that the crowd cheers. His face moves over us,
a thick cloud of vengeance, pitted
like the land that was once flesh. Each rut,   20
each scar makes a promise: *It is
not over, this fight, not as long as you resist.*

Everything we see belongs to us.

A few laughing Indians fall over the hood
slipping in the hot spilled butter.   25
The eye sees a lot, John, but the heart is so blind.
Death makes us owners of nothing.
He smiles, a horizon of teeth
the credits reel over, and then the white fields
again blowing in the true-to-life dark.   30
The dark films over everything.
We get into the car
scratching our mosquito bites, speechless and small
as people are when the movie is done.
We are back in our skins.   35

How can we help but keep hearing his voice,
the flip side of the sound track, still playing:
*Come on, boys, we got them
where we want them, drunk, running.*
They'll give us what we want, what we need.   40
Even his disease was the idea of taking everything.
Those cells, burning, doubling, splitting out of their skins.

CONSIDERATIONS FOR CRITICAL THINKING AND WRITING

1. **FIRST RESPONSE.** How does your attitude about John Wayne as a western hero compare with the speaker's assessment in the poem?

2. What formulaic elements typical of western movies do you find in the poem? How does the speaker's use of language subtly comment on these stereotypical scenes?

3. How does the speaker describe the audience watching the film? What is the relationship between the Indians on the screen and the Indians "slipping in the hot spilled butter" (line 25)?

4. Why is the drive-in setting especially appropriate for this poem? How is the setting related to the theme?

CONNECTIONS TO OTHER SELECTIONS

1. Compare the use of irony in "Dear John Wayne" with that in Florence Cassen Mayers's "All-American Sestina" (p. 250).

2. Write an essay comparing and contrasting the tone and theme in "Dear John Wayne" and in Tato Laviera's "AmeRícan" (p. 284).

Perspectives

KATIE BACON (B. 1971)

From an Interview with Louise Erdrich   2001

K.B.   The novelist Stewart O'Nan has written that you have accomplished for Native Americans what "Richard Wright and James Baldwin achieved for African-Americans . . . Philip Roth for Jews and David Leavitt for homosexuals"—you have brought them into the mainstream of attention. Do you feel any pressure to write about certain themes because people think of you as a Native American writer? As more Native Americans have begun publishing books, do you feel freed in any way?

L.E.   First of all, I only wish what O'Nan says were true. There seems to be very little mainstream awareness of Native Americans as contemporary people. Most people still think in stereotypes—the latest being the casino-rich Indian. I have not yet become acquainted with a casino-rich Indian. The Native people I know whose tribes run casinos work extremely hard and live modestly. As for pressure to write about certain themes, no. Anything I write about comes from inside and not outside pressure. Nothing works on paper unless I feel absolutely compelled to write it, and some of what I write as a consequence may work politically and emotionally, or it simply may not.

    I do feel pleased that many other Native people are writing books, extending the view of what a Native person is, and introducing the idea of tribal literature. Not "Native" literature, but literature based in one tribal vision. For instance, Ojibwe literature is very different from Lakota, or Zuni, or Santa Clara Pueblo, or Ho-Chunk, or Mesquakie literature. Each is based in an extremely specific tradition, history, religion, worldview. . . .

K.B.   Chinua Achebe wrote in his recent book of essays, *Home and Exile*, "The twentieth century for all its many faults did witness a significant beginning, in Africa and elsewhere in the so-called Third World, of the process of 're-storying' peoples who had been knocked silent by the trauma of all sorts of dispossession." Do you see yourself as a "re-storier" for the Ojibwe—a reclaimer of narratives that were never written down or were drowned out by what was taught in school about Native Americans?

L.E.   The Ojibwe have been telling stories through and in spite of immense hardship, dispossession, and anguish. In fact, Ojibwe narrative has grown rich and subtle on the ironies of conflict. But these are the narratives Ojibwe people tell among themselves, and in Ojibwemowin. I wouldn't even begin to think of myself as a "re-storier" in that sense. I write in English, and so I suppose I function as an emissary of the between-world, that increasingly common margin where cultures mix and collide. That is in fact where many of my stories occur.

Primarily, though, I am just a storyteller, and I take them where I find them. I love stories whether they function to reclaim old narratives or occur spontaneously. Often, to my surprise, they do both. I'll follow an inner thread of a plot and find that I am actually retelling a very old story, often in a contemporary setting. I usually can't recall whether it is something I remember hearing, or something I dreamed, or read, or imagined on the spot. It all becomes confused and then the characters take over, anyway, and make the piece their own.

From "An Emissary of the Between World"
The Atlantic Unbound, January 17, 2001

CONSIDERATIONS FOR CRITICAL THINKING AND WRITING

1. Explain whether or not you agree with Erdrich's observation that "most people still think in stereotypes" about Native Americans. What examples can you think of in contemporary American culture that support or refute that claim?

2. To what extent do you think Achebe's description of people "knocked silent by the trauma of all sorts of dispossession" serves to encapsulate the theme of "Dear John Wayne"?

3. In what sense might "Dear John Wayne" make Erdrich an "emissary of the between-world" where "cultures mix and collide"?

CONSIDERATIONS FOR CRITICAL THINKING AND WRITING

1. Describe the tone of the painting *American Progress*. How do the visual details constitute an attitude toward westward expansion?

2. How does the presence of Indians in the painting (see the lower left side of the image) affect your interpretation?

3. Research the concept of American manifest destiny. Why was this a popular and compelling idea in the nineteenth century? How is this ideology worked into the painting and into "Dear John Wayne"?

John Gast, *American Progress.* This 1872 painting conveys a positive attitude about westward expansion. A woman in a white robe, symbolizing the idea of manifest destiny, moves westward across the Great Plains holding a book (education) and a telegraph wire (communication and business). Fleeing from her in the foreground, and portrayed in darkness, are the casualties of progress — bison and Native Americans. Marching forward below and behind her are images portrayed in lightness — farmers, a stagecoach, and a locomotive — symbolizing progress.

Museum of the American West Collection, Autry National Center, Los Angeles.

TERRY WILSON (B. 1941)
On Hollywood Indians

1996

*They from the beginning announced that they wanted to maintain their way of life....
And we set up those reservations so they could, and have a Bureau of Indian Affairs to
help take care of them.... Maybe we should not have humored them in wanting to stay
in that kind of primitive life-style. Maybe we should have said, "No, come join us. Be
citizens along with the rest of us...." You'd be surprised. Some of them became very
wealthy, because some of these reservations were overlaying great pools of oil. And you
can get rich pumping oil. And so I don't know what their complaint might be.*

—Ronald Reagan

Responses by Native Americans to President Ronald Reagan's answer to re-
peated requests for a policy statement addressing Indian concerns in 1988 were
surprisingly temperate, given the rage they must have felt. Their chief executive
could not imagine that Indians had a problem? The nation's most disadvan-
taged people by virtually any measure — health, education, economics, political
power — had witnessed his administration's halving of federal appropriations
for Indian programs and Reagan was bewildered at their protest? Only native
peoples, long accustomed to governmental hyperextensions of illogic and mis-
information, could eschew invective in favor of weary sighs and renewed at-
tempts at further dialogue with the Great Communicator.[1]

Perhaps Indian America should have anticipated Reagan's presidential
stance. While campaigning along the political trail to the White House, he was
asked during an interview to name those persons whose lives he would have
enjoyed living. Among those he listed were Vasco Nunez de Balboa, Hernando
Cortez, Father Junipero Serra, Meriwether Lewis, and William Clark. Cortez
and Balboa explored and invaded parts of native America and Father Serra
oversaw the establishment of California Indian missions that exploited native
labor and coerced religious conversion. The selection of Lewis and Clark, Pres-
ident Thomas Jefferson's explorers of the Louisiana Purchase, was explained in
Reagan's final listing: "And any number of those men who first crossed the
Plains in the opening of the West. In other words," he added, "I'm fascinated
by those who saw this new world when it was virtually untouched by man."[2]

Apparently Reagan regarded the native presence in America as scant or of
relative insignificance, and had no qualms about subsequent Euro-American
colonization. Where did the president get his notions about Indians and In-
dian/white relations? He was a college student in the 1930s, and any history
textbook of that period would have utilized the paradigm of the frontier to
characterize United States history. Historians invariably described the course
of nation-building in terms of the inexorable march of frontiersmen across the

---

[1] *Great Communicator:* A popular phrase used to describe President Reagan's speaking abilities.

[2] *San Francisco Chronicle,* June 22, 1988. This information appeared in the feature "The Col-
umn of Lists," compiled by Irving Wallace, David Wallechinsky, and Amy Wallace.

continent, bringing civilization to previously savage lands. Native Americans were posited as an obstacle, not unlike deserts and mountains, to be overcome and tamed. Then again, recalling the presidential penchant for fond remembrance of his Hollywood years, maybe Reagan simply acquired his understanding of history and the role of Indians in the national past through an osmotic celluloid process.

Generations of Americans, native and non-native alike, have been vastly influenced by the movie-made Indian. Not a few citizens have received their basic understanding of Native Americans almost exclusively from images cast by Hollywood. Without the threat of Indian attack, the frontier drama would not resonate. Indians were occasionally noble, always savage, and inevitably defeated by the last reel. Variations on this theme occurred, notably during the last forty years, but the lasting impressions on moviegoers have changed less than the makers of films such as *Dances with Wolves* (1990) and *Thunderheart* (1992) hoped. People act toward one another according to their perceptions, not realities. If, as I believe, the majority of the non-Indian population's attitudes, and consequently policies, toward Native Americans are based to a significant degree on notions gained from the movies, a clearer understanding of the Hollywood Indian is crucial for all those interested in the cultural survivals of the nation's smallest racial minority.

From the days of the nickelodeon through the decades of the 1960s, Native American images were prominent on movie screens. Immigrant viewers with little or no English appreciated action sequences during the silent film era that provided easily discernible heroes and villains: Feather-bedecked, bow and arrow-wielding Indians attacking wagon trains and forts, settlers and cavalrymen, filled the bad guy roles admirably. Occasionally a director would fashion a film that peered behind the war-painted faces of the savages to reveal indigenous people protecting their homelands, but until the 1950s few moviemakers questioned the validity of the Indian as a constant threat to pillage, rape, burn, and kill.

That for decades Hollywood's Indians generally represented a menace to the majority white culture is scarcely surprising. The nature of relations between Native Americans and Euro-Americans virtually demands such an interpretation of the past by non-Indians. Every nation-state was created at the expense of some to promote the welfare of others. This truism rarely figures prominently in the historical and cultural memories that make up the collective national consciousness. Moviemakers have both reflected U.S. society's mythology about Indians and reinforced and refined its images of native peoples.

Regardless of how historians have presented the frontier process, there is an inescapable unpleasantness associated with the formation of the United States: nation building necessitated the dispossession of indigenous Americans. The New World offered those who made the Atlantic crossing something that was in short supply in Europe — available land. Native peoples occupying the land constituted an obstacle to colonial America's primary goal of asserting control over territory that would yield a living and, ultimately, a way of life.

From "Celluloid Sovereignty: Hollywood's 'History' of Native Americans"
in *Legal Reelism: Movies as Legal Texts,* edited by John Denvir

CONSIDERATIONS FOR CRITICAL THINKING AND WRITING

1. Discuss the relevancy of Ronald Reagan's ideas about Indians in the 1980s to "Dear John Wayne." How does Wilson's tone in the first two paragraphs serve as a commentary on Reagan's attitudes toward Indians?

2. Comment on Wilson's assertion that "the majority of the non-Indian population's attitudes, and consequently policies, toward Native Americans are based to a significant degree on notions gained from the movies." Discuss whether or not you think this is still true today.

3. Why does Wilson find it "scarcely surprising" that "Hollywood's Indians generally represented a menace to the majority white culture"? How is this kind of fear manifested in the treatment of other minorities in contemporary life?

4. Wilson says that "nation building necessitated the dispossession of indigenous Americans" (para 7). How is this idea an important feature in the thematic landscape of Erdrich's poem?

RICHARD WARREN LEWIS (B. 1932)

From an Interview with John Wayne   *1971*

For more than 41 years, the barrel-chested physique and laconic derring-do of John Wayne have been prototypical of gung-ho virility, Hollywood style. In more than 200 films Wayne has charged the beaches of Iwo Jima, beaten back the Indians at Fort Apache and bloodied his fists in the name of frontier justice so often—and with nary a defeat—that he has come to occupy a unique niche in American folklore. . . .

His milieu is still the action Western, in which Wayne's simplistic plotlines and easily discernible good and bad guys attest to a romantic way of life long gone from the American scene—if indeed it ever really existed. Even his screen name—changed from Marion Michael Morrison—conveys the man's plain, rugged cinematic personality. Fittingly, he was the first of the Western movie heroes to poke a villain in the jaw. Wearing the symbolic white Stetson—which never seemed to fall off, even in the wildest combat—he made scores of three-and-a-half-day formula oaters such as *Pals of the Saddle* in the Thirties before being tapped by director John Ford to star in *Stagecoach*—the 1939 classic that paved the way for his subsequent success in such milestone Westerns as *Red River,* the ultimate epic of the cattle drive, and *The Alamo,* a patriotic paean financed by Wayne with $1,500,000 of his own money.

By 1969, having made the list of Top Ten box-office attractions for 19 consecutive years, Wayne had grossed more than $400,000,000 for his studios—more than any other star in motion-picture history. But because of his uncompromising squareness—and his archconservative politics—he was still largely a profit without honor in Hollywood. That oversight was belatedly reflected when his peers voted the tearful star a 1970 Oscar for his portrayal of Rooster Cogburn, the tobacco-chewing, hard-drinking, straight-shooting, patch-eyed marshal in *True Grit*—a possibly unwitting exercise in self-parody that good-naturedly spoofed dozens of his past characterizations.

Long active in Republican politics, Wayne has vigorously campaigned and helped raise funds for Nixon, Ronald Reagan, George Murphy, Barry Goldwater, and Los Angeles' maverick Democratic mayor Sam Yorty. Before the 1968 campaign, a right-wing Texas billionaire had urged Wayne to serve as Vice-Presidential running mate to George Wallace, an overture he rejected. Not least among the Texan's reasons for wanting to draft Wayne was the actor's obdurately hawkish support of the Indochina war — as glorified in his production of *The Green Berets,* which had the dubious distinction of being probably the only pro-war movie made in Hollywood during the Sixties.

.   .   .

PLAYBOY: Do you think *True Grit* is the best film you've ever made?
WAYNE: No, I don't. Two classic Westerns were better — *Stagecoach* and *Red River* — and a third, *The Searchers,* which I thought deserved more praise than it got, and *The Quiet Man* was certainly one of the best. Also the one that all the college cinematography students all the time — *The Long Voyage Home.*
PLAYBOY: Which was the worst?
WAYNE: Well, there's about 50 of them that are tied. I can't even remember the names of some of the leading ladies in those first ones, let alone the names of the pictures.
PLAYBOY: At what point in your career were you nicknamed Duke?
WAYNE: That goes back to my childhood. I was called Duke after a dog — a very good Airedale out of the Baldwin Kennels. Republic Pictures gave me a screen credit on one of the early pictures and called me Michael Burn. On another one, they called me Duke Morrison. Then they decided Duke Morrison didn't have enough prestige. My real name, Marion Michael Morrison, didn't sound American enough for them. So they came up with John Wayne. I didn't have any say in it, but I think it's a great name. It's short and strong and to the point. It took me a long time to get used to it, though. I still don't recognize it when somebody calls me John.
PLAYBOY: After giving you a new name, did the studio decide on any particular screen image for you?
WAYNE: They made me a singing cowboy. The fact that I couldn't sing — or play the guitar — became terribly embarrassing to me, especially on personal appearances. Every time I made a public appearance, the kids insisted that I sing *The Desert Song* or something. But I couldn't take along the fella who played the guitar out on one side of the camera and the fella who sang on the other side of the camera. So finally I went to the head of the studio and said, "Screw this, I can't handle it." And I quit doing those kind of pictures. They went out and brought the best hillbilly recording artist in the country to Hollywood to take my place. For the first couple of pictures, they had a hard time selling him, but he finally caught on. His name was Gene Autry. It was 1939 before I made *Stagecoach* — the picture that really made me a star.
PLAYBOY: Like *Stagecoach,* most of the 204 pictures you've made — including your latest, *Rio Lobo* — have been Westerns. Don't the plots all start to seem the same?
WAYNE: *Rio Lobo* certainly wasn't any different from most of my Westerns. Nor was *Chisum,* the one before that. But there still seems to be a very hearty public appetite for this kind of film — what some writers call a typical John Wayne Western. That's a label they use disparagingly.

PLAYBOY: Does that bother you?

WAYNE: Nope. If I depended on the critics' judgment and recognition, I'd never have gone into the motion-picture business. . . .

PLAYBOY: For years American Indians have played an important — if subordinate — role in your Westerns. Do you feel any empathy with them?

WAYNE: I don't feel we did wrong in taking this great country away from them, if that's what you're asking. Our so-called stealing of this country from them was just a matter of survival. There were great numbers of people who needed new land, and the Indians were selfishly trying to keep it for themselves.

PLAYBOY: Weren't the Indians — by virtue of prior possession — the rightful owners of the land?

WAYNE: Look, I'm sure there have been inequalities. If those inequalities are presently affecting any of the Indians now alive, they have a right to a court hearing. But what happened 100 years ago in our country can't be blamed on us today.

PLAYBOY: Indians today are still being dehumanized on reservations.

WAYNE: I'm quite sure that the concept of a Government-run reservation would have an ill effect on anyone. But that seems to be what the socialists are working for now — to have *everyone* cared for from cradle to grave.

PLAYBOY: Indians on reservations are more neglected than cared for. Even if you accept the principle of expropriation, don't you think a more humane solution to the Indian problem could have been devised?

WAYNE: This may come as a surprise to you, but I wasn't alive when reservations were created — even if I *do* look that old. I have no idea what the best method of dealing with the Indians in the 1800s would have been. Our forefathers evidently thought they were doing the right thing.

From *Playboy*, May 1971

CONSIDERATIONS FOR CRITICAL THINKING AND WRITING

1. Given Lewis's description of Wayne's reputation, how do you account for his popularity? How do you think your generation regards him?

2. Describe how Erdrich draws on Wayne's popular reputation and image to set up the conflict between white and Indian culture.

3. Discuss the significance of Wayne's personal politics and his attitudes toward Indians in relation to the poem. Explain why this enhances your understanding of Erdrich's choice for Wayne over another popular western actor.

4. Wayne died in 1979 after a battle with cancer — what he called "the Big C." Explain how this information affects your reading of the poem's final lines.

John Wayne as Cavalry Officer   1949

In the 1949 film *She Wore a Yellow Ribbon* (directed by John Ford), John Wayne stars as an aging cavalry officer fighting Indian wars. In the story of the film, set in 1876, General Custer has just been killed and Indian tribes are united and on the offensive. Wayne's character puts off retirement to lead a troop escorting two white women to safety.
Reprinted by permission of Ethan Wayne/Wayne Enterprises.

CONSIDERATIONS FOR CRITICAL THINKING AND WRITING

1. What do the sword and the fence suggest to you about the absence of Indians in this photograph?

2. Compare the image of John Wayne in this picture with the figures in Gast's *American Progress* (p. 479). What do you make of the figures' stance in each picture and their relationship to the landscape?

3. Choose one of the italicized lines in "Dear John Wayne" as a caption for this photograph and discuss its meaning to you.

John Wayne and Hyphenated Americans

John Wayne recorded the album *America, Why I Love Her* in 1973, in the midst of Watergate and the final days of the Vietnam War. Wayne presented the lyrics, many composed by close friend (Big) John Mitchum, spoken-word style, over standard patriotic tunes. His personal connection to the message and sentiment of the album is made clear in a book of the same title, published in

1977, which collects the record's lyrics and presents Wayne's own comments about each song. The album was re-released by the Estate of John Wayne in December 2001, in response to the 9/11 attacks on the Pentagon and World Trade Center. Following are the lyrics to one of the songs Wayne recorded, titled "The Hyphen." The song conveys strong opinions on American identity that are very different from those represented in Louise Erdrich's poem "Dear John Wayne" (p. 475).

JOHN MITCHUM (1919–2001) AND HOWARD BARNES

The Hyphen

1977

The Hyphen, Webster's Dictionary defines,
Is a symbol used to divide a compound word or a single word.
So it seems to me that when a man calls himself
An "Afro-American," a "Mexican-American," an "Italian-American,"
An "Irish-American," a "Jewish-American,"   5
What he's sayin' is, I'm a divided American.

Well, we all come from different places,
Different creeds and different races,
To form a nation . . . to become as one.
Yet look at the harm a line has done —   10
A simple little line and yet
As divisive as a line can get.
A crooked cross the Nazis flew,
And the Russian hammer and sickle too —
Time bombs in the lives of Man;   15
But none of these could ever fan
The flames of hatred faster than
The Hyphen.

The Russian hammer built a wall
That locks men's hearts from freedom's call.   20
A crooked cross flew overhead
Above twenty million tragic dead —
Among them men from this great nation,
Who died for freedom's preservation.
A hyphen is a line that's small;   25
It can be a bridge or be a wall.
A bridge can save you lots of time,
A wall you always have to climb.
The road to liberty lies true.
The Hyphen's use is up to you.   30

Used as a bridge, it can span
All the differences of Man.
Being free in mind and soul

Should be our most important goal.
If you use The Hyphen as a wall,   35
You'll make your life mean . . . and small.
An American is a special breed,
Whose people came to her in need.
They came to her that they might find
A world where they'd have peace of mind,   40
Where men are equal . . . and something more —
Stand taller than they stood before.

So you be wise in your decision,
And that little line won't cause division.
Let's join hands with one another . . .   45
For in this land, each man's your brother.
United we stand . . . divided we fall.
We're ʌᴍᴇʀɪᴄᴀɴs . . . and that says it all.

Considerations for Critical Thinking and Writing

1. In what sense are hyphenated Americans "divided" according to these lyrics? How might "The Hyphen" be considered Wayne's version of "Dear Louise Erdrich"?

2. What do you think about the idea that "An American is a special breed" (line 37)? Explain why you agree or disagree.

Chief Luther Standing Bear (1868–1939)

An Indian Perspective on the Great Plains   *1933*

We did not think of the great open plains, the beautiful rolling hills, and winding streams with tangled growth, as "wild." Only to the white man was nature a "wilderness" and only to him was the land "infested" with "wild" animals and "savage" people. To us it was tame. Earth was bountiful and we were surrounded with the blessings of the Great Mystery. Not until the hairy man from the east came and with brutal frenzy heaped injustices upon us and the families we loved was it "wild" for us. When the very animals of the forest began fleeing from his approach, then it was that for us the "Wild West" began.

From *Land of the Spotted Eagle*

Considerations for Critical Thinking and Writing

1. Discuss the central irony of this passage. How does it turn upside-down the assumptions associated with the western hero?

2. How might this passage be regarded as a prose poem embodying a theme similar to that of "Dear John Wayne"?

SUGGESTED TOPICS FOR LONGER PAPERS

1. Describe how various elements of Erdrich's "Dear John Wayne"—diction, image, tone, metaphor, irony, theme, symbol—constitute a meditation on immigration, assimilation into a culture, and racism.

2. Use the library or the Internet to supplement the documents provided in this chapter that help to characterize western films and their treatment of Indians. Search for and comment on additional material that provides relevant contexts for the poem.

My love is such that rivers cannot quench,
Nor ought but love from thee, give recompense.
Thy love is such I can no way repay,
The heavens reward thee manifold, I pray.   10
Then while we live, in love let's so persevere
That when we live no more, we may live ever.

CONSIDERATIONS FOR CRITICAL THINKING AND WRITING

1. **FIRST RESPONSE.** Describe the poem's tone. Is it what you'd expect from a seventeenth-century Puritan? Why or why not?

2. Consider whether Bradstreet's devotion is directed more toward her husband here on earth or toward the eternal rewards of heaven.

3. What is the paradox of the final line? How is it resolved?

CONNECTION TO ANOTHER SELECTION

1. How does the theme of this poem compare with that of Bradstreet's "Before the Birth of One of Her Children" (p. 588)? Explain why you find the poems consistent or contradictory.

The remaining poems in this case study are modern and contemporary pieces that both maintain and revise the perspectives on love provided by Marlowe, Shakespeare, and Bradstreet. As you read them, consider what each adds to your understanding of the others and of love in general.

ELIZABETH BARRETT BROWNING (1806–1861)

How Do I Love Thee?
Let Me Count the Ways   *1850*

How do I love thee? Let me count the ways.
I love thee to the depth and breadth and height
My soul can reach, when feeling out of sight
For the ends of being and ideal grace.
I love thee to the level of every day's   5
Most quiet need, by sun and candle-light.
I love thee freely, as men strive for right.
I love thee purely, as they turn from praise.
I love thee with the passion put to use
In my old griefs, and with my childhood's faith.   10
I love thee with a love I seemed to lose
With my lost saints. I love thee with the breath,
Smiles, tears, of all my life; and, if God choose,
I shall but love thee better after death.

CONSIDERATIONS FOR CRITICAL THINKING AND WRITING

1. **FIRST RESPONSE.** This poem has remained extraordinarily popular for more than 150 years. Why do you think it has been so often included in collections of love poems? What is its appeal? Does it speak to a contemporary reader? To you?

2. Comment on the effect of the diction. What kind of tone does it create?

3. Would you characterize this poem as having a religious theme — or is it a substitute for religion?

CONNECTION TO ANOTHER SELECTION

1. Compare and contrast the images, tone, and theme of this poem with those of Christina Rossetti's "Promises Like Pie-Crust" (p. 619). Explain why you find one poem more promising than the other.

EDNA ST. VINCENT MILLAY (1892–1950)

Recuerdo°   *1922*

We were very tired, we were very merry —
We had gone back and forth all night on the
    ferry.
It was bare and bright, and smelled like a
    stable —
But we looked into a fire, we leaned across a
    table,
We lay on a hill-top underneath the moon;
And the whistles kept blowing, and the dawn
    came soon.

© CORBIS.

We were very tired, we were very merry —
We had gone back and forth all night on the ferry;
And you ate an apple, and I ate a pear,
From a dozen of each we had bought somewhere;   10
And the sky went wan, and the wind came cold,
And the sun rose dripping, a bucketful of gold.

We were very tired, we were very merry,
We had gone back and forth all night on the ferry.
We hailed, "Good morrow, mother!" to a shawl-covered head,   15
And bought a morning paper, which neither of us read;
And she wept, "God bless you!" for the apples and pears,
And we gave her all our money but our subway fares.

Recuerdo: I remember (Spanish).

CONSIDERATIONS FOR CRITICAL THINKING AND WRITING

1. **FIRST RESPONSE.** This poem was a very popular representation of New York City bohemian life in Greenwich Village during the 1920s. What do you think made "Recuerdo" so appealing then?

CONSIDERATIONS FOR CRITICAL THINKING AND WRITING

1. **FIRST RESPONSE.** Explain how the images and metaphors create a sense of loss.

2. Discuss the effects of the line spacing. How do they serve as a substitute for conventional punctuation?

3. How does the allusion to Dido enrich your reading of "When You Go Away"?

CONNECTION TO ANOTHER SELECTION

1. Compare the treatment of time in this poem and in Shakespeare's "Not marble, nor the gilded monuments" (p. 491).

MARK DOTY (B. 1953)

The Embrace 1998

You weren't well or really ill yet either;
just a little tired, your handsomeness
tinged by grief or anticipation, which brought
to your face a thoughtful, deepening grace.

I didn't for a moment doubt you were dead. 5
I knew that to be true still, even in the dream.
You'd been out — at work maybe? —
having a good day, almost energetic.

We seemed to be moving from some old house
where we'd lived, boxes everywhere, things 10
in disarray: that was the *story* of my dream,
but even asleep I was shocked out of narrative

by your face, the physical fact of your face:
inches from mine, smooth-shaven, loving, alert.
Why so difficult, remembering the actual look 15
of you? Without a photograph, without strain?

So when I saw your unguarded, reliable face,
your unmistakable gaze opening all the warmth
and clarity of you — warm brown tea — we held
each other for the time the dream allowed. 20

Bless you. You came back, so I could see you
once more, plainly, so I could rest against you
without thinking this happiness lessened anything,
without thinking you were alive again.

CONSIDERATIONS FOR CRITICAL THINKING AND WRITING

1. **FIRST RESPONSE.** In what sense can "The Embrace" be read as a love poem? Explain why it does or doesn't fit your definition of a love poem.

2. Describe the tone of each of the stanzas and trace your emotional response to them as you move through the poem. What is your emotional reaction to the entire poem?

3. Describe the relation between death and love in the poem. How is that relation central to the theme?

JOAN MURRAY (B. 1945)
Play-by-Play   *1997*

Yaddo°

Would it surprise the young men
playing softball on the hill to hear the women
on the terrace admiring their bodies:
the slim waist of the pitcher, the strength
of the runner's legs, the torso of the catcher   5
rising off his knees to toss the ball back to the mound?
Would it embarrass them
to hear two women, sitting together after dinner,
praising even their futile motions:
the flex of a batter's hips   10
before his missed swing, the wide-spread stride
of a man picked off his base, the intensity
on the new man's face
as he waits on deck and fans the air?

Would it annoy them, the way some women   15
take offense when men caress them with their eyes?
And why should it surprise me that these women,
well past sixty, haven't put aside desire
but sit at ease and in pleasure,
watching the young men move above the rose garden   20
where the marble Naiads
pose and yawn in their fountain?
Who better than these women, with their sweaters
draped across their shoulders, their perspectives
honed from years of lovers, to recognize   25
the beauty that would otherwise
go unnoticed on this hill?
And will it compromise their pleasure
if I sit down at their table to listen
to the play-by-play and see it through their eyes?   30

Would it distract the young men if they realized
that three women laughing softly on the terrace

Yaddo: An artist's colony in Saratoga Springs, New York.

above closed books and half-filled wineglasses
are moving beside them on the field?
Would they want to know how they've been 35
held to the light till some motion or expression
showed the unsuspected loveliness
in a common shape or face?
Wouldn't they have liked to see how they looked
down there, as they stood for a moment at the plate, 40
bathed in the light of perfect expectation,
before their shadows lengthened, before they
walked together up the darkened hill,
so beautiful they would not have
recognized themselves? 45

CONSIDERATIONS FOR CRITICAL THINKING AND WRITING

1. **FIRST RESPONSE.** How would you answer the series of nine questions posed by the speaker?
2. What do you think the young men would have to say to the older women gazing at them?
3. Explain how the "marble Naiads" (line 21) help to set the tone.
4. Discuss the significance of the title.

CONNECTION TO ANOTHER SELECTION

1. Write an essay on the nature of desire in this poem and in Molly Peacock's "Desire" (p. 245).

BILLIE BOLTON (B. 1950)

Memorandum 2004

Courtesy of Billie Bolton.

TO: My Boyfriend from Hell
FR: Me
RE: Shit I Never Want to Hear Another Word
About as Long as I Live

1. **Your Addled Thoughts.** Anything about your ongoing interest in Lucy Liu's legs, Shania Twain's bellybutton, or Reese Witherspoon's whatever; your must-see TV dramas, your fantasy baseball addiction, or your addictions period. Anything about going anywhere with you at any time including, but not limited to: Sam's Club, Big Lots, Waffle House, church fish fries, local snake round-ups or Amvet turkey shoots, unless you promise to be the turkey.

2. Your Wireless Connection. Anything about your stage-four cell phone habit; the dames who have your cell phone number and why; who's on your speed-dial list or who left a voice mail message; anything about cell phone rebates, late fees, roaming charges, contracts or dropping your cell phone in the john by accident, even if you flush it and walk away.

3. Your Adolescent Only Child. Anything about his bed-wetting or fire-setting habits; his gang affiliation, court dates or swastika tattoo; anything about his tantrums, seizures or deep psychological need for video games and fruit roll-ups; anything about his pathological grudge against mankind or his particular beef against me.

4. Your Significant Others (female). Anything about the redneck redhead you banged in high school, the long-haired potheads you balled in your hippie days, the white trash airhead you married or the blue-haired battle-ax who pats you on the rump and pays for your dinner. Anything about your devotion to your long-suffering mother, your loopy sisters, or even the Blessed Virgin.

CONSIDERATIONS FOR CRITICAL THINKING AND WRITING

1. **FIRST RESPONSE.** What makes this a poem rather than simply a memo?
2. How does the speaker's diction and choice of details reveal her own personality?
3. **CREATIVE RESPONSE.** Using Bolton's style, tone, and form as inspiration, write a reply from the boyfriend's point of view.

CONNECTION TO ANOTHER SELECTION

1. Compare the use of descriptive detail to create tone in "Memorandum" and in Michelle Boisseau's "Self-Pity's Closet" (p. 555).

SUGGESTED TOPICS FOR LONGER PAPERS

1. Choose one of the love poems in this chapter and compare its themes with the lyrics of a contemporary love song in terms of poetic elements such as diction, tone, images, figures of speech, sounds, and rhythms.
2. Select any two poems from this chapter that were published before 1900 and compare them in style and theme with two poems published after 1900. Which set of poems, the early or the later, comes closest to representing your own sensibilities concerning love? Explain why.

19

A THEMATIC CASE STUDY
Teaching and Learning

O this learning, what a thing it is!
— WILLIAM SHAKESPEARE

National Portrait Gallery,
London.

The thematic center of this case study focuses on teaching and learning. The various literary elements that contribute to the idea or point around which the entire poem revolves are there to enhance, in this case, poems about the writers' experiences with education. Taken together, the poems represent a variety of poetic responses ranging from fond appreciation and raucous humor to bitter anger and deep grievance. These poems are likely to make you recall your own complicated and contradictory moments in school. Reading them might not make you feel better about some of your experiences, but you will, perhaps, think more deeply about what they mean to you.

Web Research the poets in this chapter at bedfordstmartins.com/meyerpoetry.

You've spent a significant portion of your life in school learning and being taught, and as you well know, the lessons come in many forms and sometimes at unexpected moments. The poems included in this section all depict a lesson of sorts—even if what has been taught and what has been learned are not always clear (and they are not always the same thing). All of the poetry included here was written within the past fifty years or so, and most of it is quite recent. The contemporary nature of these poems should allow you to make some vivid and striking connections to your own experience — and it may make you grind your teeth a bit, too. As you read, think about who is learning what, how you might link each reading with another, and how you personally respond to the work in question. The lessons discovered in this poetry will undoubtedly add to your understanding that learning is a complicated matter that goes well beyond anyone's lesson plans.

The writing assignment in Langston Hughes's "Theme for English B" is more problematic than it seems — especially for the African American student who must complete it for a white teacher. There are themes within themes in this poem.

Langston Hughes (1902–1967)
Theme for English B

1949

The instructor said,

> *Go home and write*
> *a page tonight*
> *And let that page come out of you —*
> *Then, it will be true.*
>
> 5

I wonder if it's that simple?
I am twenty-two, colored, born in Winston-Salem.
I went to school there, then Durham, then here
to this college on the hill above Harlem.
I am the only colored student in my class.   10
The steps from the hill lead down into Harlem,
through a park, then I cross St. Nicholas,
Eighth Avenue, Seventh, and I come to the Y,
the Harlem Branch Y, where I take the elevator
up to my room, sit down, and write this page: 15

It's not easy to know what is true for you or me
at twenty-two, my age. But I guess I'm what
I feel and see and hear, Harlem, I hear you:
hear you, hear me — we two — you, me, talk on this page.
(I hear New York, too.) Me — who?   20
Well, I like to eat, sleep, drink, and be in love.
I like to work, read, learn, and understand life.
I like a pipe for a Christmas present,
or records — Bessie,° bop, or Bach.
I guess being colored doesn't make me *not* like   25
the same things other folks like who are other races.

24 *Bessie:* Bessie Smith (1898?–1937), a famous blues singer.

Nothing. None of the content of this course
has value or meaning   10
Take as many days off as you like:
any activities we undertake as a class
I assure you will not matter either to you or me
and are without purpose

    Everything. A few minutes after we began last time   15
    a shaft of light suddenly descended and an angel
    or other heavenly being appeared
    and revealed to us what each woman or man must do
    to attain divine wisdom in this life and
    the hereafter   20
    This is the last time the class will meet
    before we disperse to bring the good news to all people on earth

Nothing. When you are not present
how could something significant occur?

    Everything. Contained in this classroom   25
    is a microcosm of human experience
    assembled for you to query and examine and ponder
    This is not the only place such as opportunity has been gathered

    but it was one place

And you weren't here   30

CONSIDERATIONS FOR CRITICAL THINKING AND WRITING

1. **FIRST RESPONSE.** Trace through each stanza the teacher's response to the student's question about missing class. Explain why you consider the response justified or unjustified.

2. Discuss the reasons why you think the teacher's tone is primarily sarcastic or ironic (see the Glossary of Literary Terms for clarification on the difference between the two).

3. What distinction is made between "Nothing" and "Everything"?

CONNECTION TO ANOTHER SELECTION

1. Compare the portrait of this teacher with that of any other teacher that appears in a poem of your choice from this chapter. Explain why you prefer one to the other.

MAGGIE ANDERSON (B. 1948)

The Thing You Must Remember   *1986*

The thing you must remember is how, as a child,
you worked hours in the art room, the teacher's
hands over yours, molding the little clay dog.
You must remember how nothing mattered

but the imagined dog's fur, the shape of his ears 5
and his paws. The gray clay felt dangerous, — *more danger*
What does this mean? your small hands were pressing what you couldn't
say with your limited words. When the dog's back
stiffened, then cracked to white shards
in the kiln, you learned how the beautiful 10
suffers from too much attention, how clumsy
a single vision can grow, and fragile
with trying too hard. The thing you must
remember is the art teacher's capable
hands: large, rough and grainy,
over yours, holding on. 15

CONSIDERATIONS FOR CRITICAL THINKING AND WRITING

1. **FIRST RESPONSE.** Describe how Anderson molds ideas about discipline, creativity, and art into the theme through her use of images.

2. What is the nature of the memory that the speaker insists the reader retain? Why is that memory important?

3. Why was it that the "gray clay felt dangerous"? Do you think this poem evokes a pleasant memory of something else?

CONNECTIONS TO OTHER SELECTIONS

Both poems = childhood school memories

1. Discuss the sense of direction provided by the teacher in Anderson's poem and in Judy Page Heitzman's "The Schoolroom on the Second Floor of the Knitting Mill" (p. 508).

2. What do you think is learned by the "you" of "The Thing You Must Remember" and the "we" of "Gratitude to Old Teachers" by Robert Bly (p. 503)? To what extent does the shift in pronouns indicate a shift or difference in attitudes about the learning that is described?

JEFFREY HARRISON (B. 1957)

Fork

2003

Because on the first day of class you said,
"In ten years most of you won't be writing,"
barely hiding that you hoped it would be true;
because you told me over and over, in front of the class,
that I was "hopeless," that I was wasting my time 5
but more importantly yours, that I *just didn't get it*;
because you violently scratched out every other word,
scrawled "Awk" and "Eek" in the margins
as if you were some exotic bird,
then highlighted your own remarks in pink; 10
because you made us proofread the galleys

of your how-I-became-a-famous-writer memoir;
because you wanted disciples, and got them,
and hated me for not becoming one;
because you were beautiful and knew it, and used it,   15
making wide come-fuck-me eyes
at your readers from the jackets of your books;
because when, at the end of the semester,
you grudgingly had the class over for dinner
at your over-decorated pseudo-Colonial   20
full of photographs with you at the center,
you served us take-out pizza on plastic plates
but had us eat it with your good silver;
and because a perverse inspiration rippled through me,

I stole a fork, slipping it into the pocket of my jeans,   25
then hummed with inward glee the rest of the evening
to feel its sharp tines pressing against my thigh
as we sat around you in your dark paneled study
listening to you blather on about your latest prize.
The fork was my prize. I practically sprinted   30
back to my dorm room, where I examined it:
a ridiculously ornate pattern, with vegetal swirls
and the curvaceous initials of one of your ancestors,
its flamboyance perfectly suited to your
red-lipsticked and silk-scarved ostentation.   35

That summer, after graduation, I flew to Europe,
stuffing the fork into one of the outer pouches
of my backpack. On a Eurail pass I covered ground
as only the young can, sleeping in youth hostels,
train stations, even once in the Luxembourg Gardens.   40
I'm sure you remember the snapshots you received
anonymously, each featuring your fork
at some celebrated European location: your fork
held at arm's length with the Eiffel Tower
listing in the background; your fork   45
in the meaty hand of a smiling Beefeater;
your fork balanced on Keats's grave in Rome
or sprouting like an antenna from Brunelleschi's dome;
your fork dwarfing the Matterhorn.
I mailed the photos one by one — if possible   50
with the authenticating postmark of the city
where I took them. It was my mission that summer.

That was half my life ago. But all these years
I've kept the fork, through dozens of moves
and changes — always in the same desk drawer   55
among my pens and pencils, its sharp points
spurring me on. It became a talisman
whose tarnished aura had as much to do
with me as you. You might even say your fork
made me a writer. Not you, your fork.   60

You are still the worst teacher I ever had.
You should have been fired but instead got tenure.
As for the fork, just yesterday my daughter
asked me why I keep a fork in my desk drawer,
and I realized I don't need it any more.   65
It has served its purpose. Therefore
I am returning it to you with this letter.

CONSIDERATIONS FOR CRITICAL THINKING AND WRITING

1. **FIRST RESPONSE.** How has the teacher made the speaker a writer? How has
   the fork "served its purpose"? (line 66).

2. Comment on the style of lines 1–24. How do these lines characterize both
   the speaker and teacher?

3. Describe the tone of each stanza. How does the tone change as the narra-
   tive progresses?

CONNECTIONS TO OTHER SELECTIONS

1. Consider the treatment of the writing teacher in this poem, in Halli-
   day's "Graded Paper" (p. 507), and in Wakefield's "In a Poetry Workshop"
   (p. 509). What do these portraits of teachers have in common? What signif-
   icant differences do you find?

Perspective

JEFFREY HARRISON (B. 1957)

On "Fork" as a Work of Fiction   2003

"Fork" is a persona poem and thus, essentially, a work of fiction. This fact has
disappointed the kind of reader whose first question is always, "Who is the
teacher?" There really isn't an answer to that question, since the poem is based
on a combination of disparate snippets and anecdotes — some of questionable
authority — and pure fictionalizing. Students have always told stories about
their teachers, perhaps relishing most the recounting of their bad experiences,
which lend themselves to embellishment. This poem tries to tap into — and
maybe even to parody slightly — that rich vein of complaint.

   If the poem seems autobiographical, I'd like to think it's because I was
able to take on the narrator's persona and to make the material my own. But it
does raise questions about poetic license and how much one is willing to make
up in a poem. Each poet has to find his or her own answer to that question, but
the answer can change from poem to poem, and also over time. I find myself,
in certain poems (like this one), willing to take more license than I used to. To
object to these kinds of liberties, it seems to me, is to impose unnecessary and
literal-minded restrictions on the imagination and on the possibilities of po-
etry — and to ignore the fact that there are many ways to make a poem.

CONSIDERATIONS FOR CRITICAL THINKING AND WRITING

1. Are you the "kind of reader" who is disappointed to learn that this poem — or any other work — is "pure fictionalizing"? How does this work's fictional nature affect your reading of it?

2. Harrison points out that one of his purposes in the poem may be "to parody slightly" the speaker's objections to his teacher. Explain why or why you don't find the speaker somewhat parodied.

3. Try tapping into your own "rich vein of complaint" and write a poem about a teacher that is "a combination of disparate snippets and anecdotes . . . and pure fictionalizing."

SUGGESTED TOPICS FOR LONGER PAPERS

1. Which one of the poems about teaching and learning most speaks to your own experiences as a student? As you discuss the poem's thematics, fold in your own personal response and experience using Robert Sward's essay "A Personal Analysis of 'The Love Song of J. Alfred Prufrock'" (p. 467) as a model.

2. Put together a portfolio of popular songs about school (ask around — nearly everyone can recall at least one example — or use the Internet) and analyze them in terms of their style, themes, historical context, or whatever interests you most about them.

20

A THEMATIC CASE STUDY
Humor and Satire

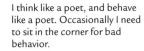

I think like a poet, and behave like a poet. Occasionally I need to sit in the corner for bad behavior.
— GARY SOTO

There is nothing wrong with a poetry that is entertaining and easy to understand.
— CHARLES BUKOWSKI

Poetry can be a hoot. There are plenty of poets that leave you smiling, grinning, chuckling, and laughing out loud because they use language that is witty, surprising, teasing, or satirical. Occasionally, their subject matter is simply wacky. There's a poem in this chapter, for example, titled "Commercial Leech Farming Today" (p. 528) that deftly squeezes humor out of bloodsucking leeches grown for treating contemporary surgical patients. Although the material might not sound promising, Thomas Lux's treatment shapes this unlikely topic into a memorable satiric theme.

Sadly, however, poetry is too often burdened with a reputation for only being formal and serious, and readers sometimes show their deference by feeling intimidated and humbled in its earnest, weighty presence. After all, poetry frequently concerns itself with matters of great consequence: its themes contemplate subjects such as God and immortality, love and death, war and peace, injustice and outrage, racism and societal ills, deprivation

516

and disease, alienation and angst, totalitarianism and terrorism, as well as a host of other tragic grievances and agonies that humanity might suffer. For readers of *The Onion*, a widely distributed satirical newspaper also available online, this prevailing grim reputation is humorously framed in a bogus story about National Poetry Month, celebrated each April to increase an awareness of the value of poetry in American life. The brief article (April 27, 2005) quotes a speaker at a fund-raising meeting of the "American Poetry Prevention Society" who cautions that "we must stop this scourge before more lives are exposed to poetry." He warns that "young people, particularly morose high-school and college students, are very susceptible to this terrible affliction." *The Onion*'s satire peels away the erroneous assumption that sorrow and tears are the only appropriate responses to a poetry "infection."

Poetry — at least in its clichéd popular form — is nearly always morosely dressed in black and rarely smiles. This severe image of somber profundity unfortunately tailors our expectations so that we assume that serious poetry cannot be playful and even downright funny or, putting the issue another way, that humorous poetry cannot be thoughtful and significant. The poems in this chapter demonstrate that serious poems can be funny and that comic poems can be thoughtful. Their humor, sometimes subtle, occasionally even savage, will serve to remind you that laughter engenders thought as well as pleasure.

FLEUR ADCOCK (B. 1934)

The Video

When Laura was born, Ceri watched.
They all gathered around Mum's bed —
Dad and the midwife and Mum's sister
and Ceri. "Move over a bit," Dad said —
he was trying to focus the camcorder   5
on Mum's legs and the baby's head.

After she had a little sister,
and Mum had gone back to being thin,
and was twice as busy, Ceri played
the video again and again.   10
She watched Laura come out, and then,
in reverse, she made her go back in.

CONSIDERATIONS FOR CRITICAL THINKING AND WRITING

1. **FIRST RESPONSE.** How does the humor in the final line produce the theme?
2. Discuss the appropriateness of Adcock's choice of "watched" in lines 1 and 10. What does the word suggest about Ceri?
3. How does the rhyme scheme affect your reading of the poem?

CONNECTION TO ANOTHER SELECTION

1. Compare the treatment of family life and the purpose of home videos in "The Video" and in Mary Jo Salter's "Home Movies: A Sort of Ode" (p. 260).

JOHN CIARDI (1916–1986)
Suburban   *1978*

Yesterday Mrs. Friar phoned. "Mr. Ciardi,
  how do you do?" she said. "I am sorry to say
this isn't exactly a social call. The fact is
  your dog has just deposited — forgive me —
a large repulsive object in my petunias."   5

I thought to ask, "Have you checked the rectal grooving
  for a positive I.D.?" My dog, as it happened,
was in Vermont with my son, who had gone fishing —
  if that's what one does with a girl, two cases of beer,
and a borrowed camper. I guessed I'd get no trout.   10

But why lose out on organic gold for a wise crack?
  "Yes, Mrs. Friar," I said, "I understand."
"Most kind of you," she said. "Not at all," I said.
  I went with a spade. She pointed, looking away.
"I always have loved dogs," she said, "but really!"   15

I scooped it up and bowed. "The animal of it.
  I hope this hasn't upset you, Mrs. Friar."
"Not really," she said, "but really!" I bore the turd
  across the line to my own petunias
and buried it till the glorious resurrection   20

when even these suburbs shall give up their dead.

CONSIDERATIONS FOR CRITICAL THINKING AND WRITING

1. **FIRST RESPONSE.** How does the speaker transform Mrs. Friar into a symbolic figure of the suburbs?

2. Why do you suppose Ciardi focuses on this particular incident to make a comment on the suburbs? What is the speaker's attitude toward suburban life?

3. **CREATIVE RESPONSE.** Write a one-paragraph physical description of Mrs. Friar that captures her character.

CONNECTION TO ANOTHER SELECTION

1. Compare the speakers' voices in "Suburban" and in John Updike's "Dog's Death" (p. 24).

Daisy Fried (b. 1967)

Wit's End

2000

My father says, "Face it, you live
   in a civilization of mirrors and sinks,"
      invading my real room, the bathroom.

I pull down an eyelid till I see the pained
   pink meniscus underneath. I "O"   5
      my mouth, poke the mascara wand

at my eyelashes, not missing
   by much. It's makeup's premonition
      of sex in the house he can't stand.

The bathroom's littered with eyeliners,   10
   tweezers, kisslipped tissues. I shed snarls
      of hair in the shower like saffron threads,

red kelp. In the mirror I paint myself a clownface
   copied from *Sassy, Seventeen, Glamour.* He
      stands in the doorway, loving   15

the used-to-be lovable 12-year-old
   formerly his. We look in the mirror:
      blush welts, orange, riding low

on my cheeks, pink lipstick leaking
   from my lip corners. Glitter-white   20
      chevrons for eyelids; Cover Girl fails

again to cover my nose-zits. Reflected, behind me,
   tangles of the unwashed bras I don't need
      trail from shower rod, shampoo rack,

hot-cold dial, soapdish, stopcock.   25
   He hates it: me mooning, me sighing,
      me incessantly hairbrushing, singing stupid

love songs. "I'll buy back the gunk!" he says.
   He'll pay twice what I spent if only I'll stop.
      I stand by the tub in the bathroom,   30

my real room. I prop up a leg, I pull up
   my skirt, start shaving thigh-stubble. I shove
      the door shut between us with my ass.

Considerations for Critical Thinking and Writing

1. **First Response.** What images and figures of speech make Fried's description of this father-daughter relationship convincing?
2. In what sense is the bathroom for the speaker "my real room" (lines 3 and 31)?

3. How does the title sum up the poem's familial conflict?
4. Explain why you think Fried treats the speaker mostly satirically or sympathetically.

CONNECTIONS TO OTHER SELECTIONS

1. Compare the tone and theme of "Wit's End" with that of Li Ho's "A Beautiful Girl Combs Her Hair" (p. 56).
2. How might the daughter in "Wit's End" be considered a youthful version of the speaker in Sylvia Plath's "Mirror" (p. 145)?

RONALD WALLACE (B. 1945)

In a Rut   *2002*

She dogs me while
I try to take a catnap.
Of course, I'm playing possum but
I can feel her watching me,
eagle-eyed, like a hawk.   5
She snakes over to my side
of the bed, and continues to
badger me. I may be a rat, but
I won't let her get my goat.
I refuse to make an   10
ass of myself, no matter
how mulish I feel.
I'm trying to make a
bee-line for sleep, but
You're a turkey! she says, and   15
I'm thinking she's no
spring chicken. She *is* a busy beaver,
though, always trying to ferret
things out. She's a bit batty,
in fact, a bit cuckoo, but   20
What's your beef, now? I say.
*Get your head out
of the sand,* she replies. *What
are you—a man, or a mouse?*
That's a lot of bull, I think;   25
she can be a real bear.
Don't horse around, now, she says.
You know you can't weasel out of it!
She's having a whale of a time,
thinking she's got me skunked, thinking   30
that she's out-foxed me.
But I know she's just crying wolf,
and I won't be cowed. Feeling

1. Compare the style and theme of Pastan's poem with that of E. E. Cummings's "she being Brand" (p. 73).

PETER SCHMITT (B. 1958)

Friends with Numbers

1995

If you make friends with numbers,
you don't need any other friends.
  —Shakuntala Devi, math genius

They are not hard to get to know:
6 and 9 keep changing their minds,
8 cuts the most graceful figure
but sleeps for an eternity,
and 7, lucky 7, takes   5
an arrow to his heart always.
5, halfway to somewhere, only
wants to patch his unicycle
tire, and 4, who'd like to stand for
something solid, has never had   10
two feet on the ground, yet flutters
gamely in the breeze like a flag.
3, for all his literary
accomplishments and pretensions
to immortality, is still   15
(I can tell you) not half the man
8 is asleep or awake. 1,
little 1. I know him better
than all the others, these numbers
who are all my friends. Only 2,   20
that strange smallest prime, can I count
as just a passing acquaintance.
Divisible by only 1
and herself, she seems on the verge,
yet, of always coming apart.   25
And though she eludes me, swanlike,
though I'd love to know her better,
still I am fine, there are others,
many, I have friends in numbers.

CONSIDERATIONS FOR CRITICAL THINKING AND WRITING

1. **FIRST RESPONSE.** How does the personification of numbers create characters in the poem?
2. Explain how the speaker's use of language helps to characterize him.

3. Discuss the various ways in which the single digits are transformed into individual visual images.

CONNECTION TO ANOTHER SELECTION

1. Discuss the originality — the fresh and unusual approach to their respective subject matter — in Schmitt's poem and in Kate Clanchy's "Spell" (p. 128). What makes these poems so interesting?

MARTÍN ESPADA (B. 1957)
The Community College Revises Its Curriculum in Response to Changing Demographics

2000

SPA 100 Conversational Spanish
2 credits

The course
is especially concerned
with giving police
the ability
to express themselves
tersely
in matters of interest
to them

CONSIDERATIONS FOR CRITICAL THINKING AND WRITING

1. **FIRST RESPONSE.** What sort of political comment do you think Espada makes in this poem?
2. Would this be a poem without the title?
3. **CREATIVE RESPONSE.** Choose a course description from your school's catalog and organize the catalog copy into poetic lines. Provide your poem with a title that offers a provocative commentary about it.

CONNECTION TO ANOTHER SELECTION

1. Compare the themes in Espada's poem and in Donald Justice's "Order in the Streets" (p. 287).

M. CARL HOLMAN (1919–1988)
Mr. Z

1967

Taught early that his mother's skin was the sign of error,
He dressed and spoke the perfect part of honor;
Won scholarships, attended the best schools,
Disclaimed kinship with jazz and spirituals;

Chose prudent, raceless views for each situation,　　　　　　5
Or when he could not cleanly skirt dissension,
Faced up to the dilemma, firmly seized
Whatever ground was Anglo-Saxonized.

In diet, too, his practice was exemplary:
Of pork in its profane forms he was wary;　　　　　　　10
Expert in vintage wines, sauces and salads,
His palate shrank from cornbread, yams and collards.

He was as careful whom he chose to kiss:
His bride had somewhere lost her Jewishness,
But kept her blue eyes; an Episcopalian　　　　　　　15
Prelate proclaimed them matched chameleon.
Choosing the right addresses, here, abroad,
They shunned those places where they might be barred;
Even less anxious to be asked to dine
Where hosts catered to kosher accent or exotic skin.　　　20

And so he climbed, unclogged by ethnic weights,
An airborne plant, flourishing without roots.
Not one false note was struck — until he died:
His subtly grieving widow could have flayed
The obit writers, ringing crude changes on a clumsy phrase:　25
"One of the most distinguished members of his race."

CONSIDERATIONS FOR CRITICAL THINKING AND WRITING

1. **FIRST RESPONSE.** What is the central irony of Mr. Z's life? What do you think of him?

2. Explain whether or not you find Holman's satiric portrait to be fair.

3. Discuss the poem's rhythms and rhymes. How do they contribute to the tone?

4. What does Mr. Z's name suggest about his identity?

CONNECTIONS TO OTHER SELECTIONS

1. Compare the satirical treatment of race in "Mr. Z" and in Langston Hughes's "Dinner Guest: Me" (p. 415).

2. Discuss the preference for "Anglo-Saxonized" (line 8) appearances in "Mr. Z" and in Janice Mirikitani's "Recipe" (p. 547).

GARY SOTO (B. 1952)

Mexicans Begin Jogging　　　　　　　　　*1995*

At the factory I worked
In the fleck of rubber, under the press
Of an oven yellow with flame,
Until the border patrol opened

Their vans and my boss waved for us to run.   5
"Over the fence, Soto," he shouted,
And I shouted that I was American.
"No time for lies," he said, and pressed
A dollar in my palm, hurrying me
Through the back door.   10

Since I was on his time, I ran
And became the wag to a short tail of Mexicans —
Ran past the amazed crowds that lined
The street and blurred like photographs, in rain.
I ran from that industrial road to the soft   15
Houses where people paled at the turn of an autumn sky.
What could I do but yell *vivas*
To baseball, milkshakes, and those sociologists
Who would clock me
As I jog into the next century   20
On the power of a great, silly grin.

Explore contexts
for Gary Soto
on *LiterActive*.

CONSIDERATIONS FOR CRITICAL THINKING AND WRITING

1. **FIRST RESPONSE.** What ironies are present in this poem?

2. Soto was born and raised in Fresno, California. How does this fact affect your reading of the first stanza?

3. In what different ways does the speaker become "the wag" (line 12) in this poem? (You may want to look up the word to consider all possible meanings.)

4. Explain lines 17–21. What serious point is being made in these humorous lines?

CONNECTION TO ANOTHER SELECTION

1. Compare the speakers' ironic attitudes toward exercise in this poem and in Peter Meinke's "The ABC of Aerobics" (p. 285).

BOB HICOK (B. 1960)

Spam leaves an aftertaste   *2002*

What does the Internet know that it sends me
unbidden the offer of a larger penis?
I'm flattered by the energy devoted
to the architecture of my body.
Brain waves noodling on girth, length, curvature   5
possibly, pictures drawn on napkins
of the device, teeth for holding, cylinder —
pneumatic, hydraulic — for stretching
who I am into who I shall be. But of all

messages to drop from the digital ether,   10
hope lives in the communiqué that I can find
out anything about anyone. So I've asked:
who am I, why am I here, if a train
leaving Chicago is subsidized
by the feds, is the romance of travel   15
dead? I'd like the skinny on where I'll be
when I die, to have a map, a seismic map
of past and future emotions, to be told
how to keep the violence I do to myself
from becoming the grenades I pitch   20
at others. The likes of Snoop.com
never get back to me, though I need
to know most of all if any of this helps.
How we can scatter our prayers so wide,
if we've become more human or less   25
in being able to share the specific
in a random way, or was it better
to ask the stars for peace or rain,
to trust the litany of our need
to the air's imperceptible embrace? Just   30
this morning I got a message
asking is anyone out there. I replied
no, I am not, are you not there too,
needing me, and if not, come over, I have
a small penis but aspirations   35
for bigger things, faith among them,
and by that I mean you and I
face to face, mouths
making the sounds once known
as conversation.   40

CONSIDERATIONS FOR CRITICAL THINKING AND WRITING

1. **FIRST RESPONSE.** Comment on the humor Hicok uses to satirize how our lives have been affected by the Internet.

2. What is the serious theme that the speaker's humor leads the reader to contemplate? How does this complicate the poem's tone?

3. How do your own experiences with spam compare with the speaker's?

CONNECTIONS TO OTHER SELECTIONS

1. How might Hicok's poem be considered a latter-day version of T. S. Eliot's "The Love Song of J. Alfred Prufrock" (p. 456)?

2. Discuss the perspective on American contemporary life implicit in "Spam leaves an aftertaste" with respect to the view offered in Tony Hoagland's "America" (p. 561).

THOMAS LUX (B. 1946)

Commercial Leech Farming Today

1997

—for Robert Sacherman

Although it never rivaled wheat, soybean,
cattle and so on farming
there was a living
in leeches
and after a period of decline   5
there is again
a living to be made
from this endeavor: they're used to reduce
the blood in tissues
after plastic surgery—eyelifts, tucks,   10
wrinkle erad, or in certain
microsurgeries—reattaching a finger, penis.
I love the capitalist
spirit. As in most businesses
the technology has improved: instead   15
of driving an elderly horse
into a leech pond, letting him die
by exsanguination,
and hauling him out
to pick the bloated blossoms   20
from his hide, it's now done at Biopharm
(the showcase operation in Swansea,
Wales)—temp control, tanks, aerator
pumps, several species,
each for a specific job. Once, 19th century,   25
they were applied to the temple
as a treatment for mental
illness. Today we know
their exact chemistry: hirudin,
a blood thinner in their saliva,   30
also an anesthesia
and dilators for the wound area.
Don't you love
the image: the Dr. lays a leech along
the tiny stitches of an eyelift.   35
Where they go after their work is done
I don't know
but I've heard no complaints
from Animal Rights
so perhaps they're retired   40
to a lake or adopted
as pets, maybe the best looking
kept to breed. I don't know. I like the story,
I like the going backwards
to ignorance   45

But the serpent (more subtle), unheard
From until now, unlocked and unappled
Eve, and Adam unabled.

Then the unthorned got thorns
And the unthistled thistles, the earth   20
Untoiled until then.

Adam unparadized — a song not
Unsung, of life's uneasying,
And Adam undone.

CONSIDERATIONS FOR CRITICAL THINKING AND WRITING

1. **FIRST RESPONSE.** The epigraph from Kevin Jackson cites a literary curiosity that inspires Wing to summarize the plot of Adam and Eve's Fall in *Paradise Lost*. How successful is she in relating the story?

2. Discuss the repetition of the poem's sounds and their effects.

3. Choose a stanza that you regard as the most effective in its images and humor and explain why.

CONNECTION TO ANOTHER SELECTION

1. Consider the ways in which "Paradise-Un" and "A Nosty Fright" by May Swenson (p. 186) demonstrate a kind of wild delight in language and its sounds.

ANN LAUINGER

Marvell Noir   2005

Sweetheart, if we had the time,
A week in bed would be no crime.
I'd light your Camels, pour your Jack;
You'd do shiatsu on my back.
When you got up to scramble eggs,   5
I'd write a sonnet to your legs,
And you could watch my stubble grow.
Yes, gorgeous, we'd take it slow.
I'd hear the whole sad tale again:
A roadhouse band; you can't trust men;   10
He set you up; you had to eat,
And bitter with the bittersweet
Was what they dished you; Ginger lied;
You weren't there when Sanchez died;
You didn't know the pearls were fake . . .   15
Aw, can it, sport! Make no mistake,
You're in it, doll, up to your eyeballs!
Tears? Please! You'll dilute our highballs,
And make that angel face a mess
For the nice Lieutenant. I confess   20
I'm nuts for you — but take the rap?

You must think I'm some other sap!
And, precious, I kind of wish I was.
Well, when they spring you, give a buzz;
Guess I'll get back to Archie's wife,   25
And you'll get twenty-five to life.
You'll have time then, more than enough,
To reminisce about the stuff
That dreams are made of, and the men
You suckered. Sadly, in the pen   30
Your kind of talent goes to waste.
But Irish bars are more my taste
Than iron ones: stripes ain't my style.
You're going down; I promise I'll
Come visit every other year.   35
Now kiss me, sweet — the squad car's here.

CONSIDERATIONS FOR CRITICAL THINKING AND WRITING

1. **FIRST RESPONSE.** The Marvell of the title refers to Andrew Marvell's "To His Coy Mistress" (p. 81). How does Lauinger's poem evoke Marvell's *carpe diem* poem (see the Glossary of Literary Terms) and the tough-guy tone of a "noir" narrative, a crime story or thriller that is especially dark?

2. Discuss the ways in which time is a central presence in the poem.

CONNECTION TO ANOTHER SELECTION

1. Compare the speaker's voice in this poem with the respective speakers in Marvell's "To His Coy Mistress" (p. 81) and Peter De Vries's "To His Importunate Mistress" (p. 261). Explain which parody you prefer — Lauinger's or De Vries's.

CHARLES BUKOWSKI (1920–1994)
poety readings   1997

poetry readings have to be some of the saddest
damned things ever,
the gathering of the clansmen and clanladies,
week after week, month after month, year
after year,
getting old together,
reading on to tiny gatherings,
still hoping their genius will be
discovered,
making tapes together, discs together,
sweating for applause
they read basically to and for
each other,
they can't find a New York publisher
or one   15

The Yale Collection of American Literature, Beinecke Rare Book and Manuscript Library, Yale University.

within miles,
but they read on and on
in the poetry holes of America,
never daunted,
never considering the possibility that   20
their talent might be
thin, almost invisible,
they read on and on
before their mothers, their sisters, their husbands,
their wives, their friends, the other poets   25
and the handful of idiots who have wandered
in
from nowhere.

I am ashamed for them,
I am ashamed that they have to bolster each other,   30
I am ashamed for their lisping egos,
their lack of guts.

if these are our creators,
please, please give me something else:

a drunken plumber at a bowling alley,   35
a prelim boy in a four rounder,
a jock guiding his horse through along the
rail,
a bartender on last call,
a waitress pouring me a coffee,   40
a drunk sleeping in a deserted doorway,
a dog munching a dry bone,
an elephant's fart in a circus tent,
a 6 p.m. freeway crush,
the mailman telling a dirty joke   45

anything
anything
but
these.

CONSIDERATIONS FOR CRITICAL THINKING AND WRITING

1. **FIRST RESPONSE.** Some readers find this poem's humor right on target while others recoil from its savage, despairing tone. What do you think?

2. What distinction is made between the poetry readers and the others described in lines 35–45? Why does the speaker prefer the latter?

3. Imagine this poem being read at a poetry reading. What kind of response do you think it would elicit?

CONNECTION TO ANOTHER SELECTION

1. Describe how poets and poems are represented in "poetry readings" and in Richard Wakefield's "In a Poetry Workshop" (p. 509). What do the two poems have in common in terms of their perspectives on the contemporary poetry scene?

21

A THEMATIC CASE STUDY
Border Crossings

As immigrants we have this enormous raw material. . . . We draw from a dual culture, with two sets of worldviews and paradigms juxtaposing each other.

— CHITRA BANERJEE DIVAKARUNI

Courtesy of the author.

© The Nobel Foundation.

I can define . . . can simplify the history of human society, the evolution of human society, as a contest between power and freedom.

— WOLE SOYINKA

This chapter brings together seven poems and a variety of images that center upon the theme of crossing borders. The borders referred to in these poems are not only those that mark geographic or political divisions but also the uncertain and indeterminate borders associated with culture, class, race, ethnicity, and gender. Even if we have never left our home state or country, we have all moved back and forth across such defining lines as we negotiate the margins and edges of our personal identities within the particular worlds we inhabit. Any first-year college student, for example, knows that college life and demanding course work represent a significant border crossing: increased academic challenges, responsibility, and autonomy likely reflect an entirely new culture for the student. By Thanksgiving vacation, students know (as do their parents and friends) that they've crossed an invisible border that causes a slight shift in their identity because they've done some growing and maturing.

The poems and visuals in this chapter explore a wide range of border crossings. Phillis Wheatley was kidnapped and forced across borders in 1761 when she was brought to America as a slave. Her poem "On Being Brought from Africa to America" offers a fascinating argument against racism. Wheatley's perspective is deepened by a diagram of a ship and an advertisement for an auction that vividly illustrate how slaves were transported and marketed. Wole Soyinka's "Telephone Conversation," paired with a poster advertising the film *Guess Who's Coming to Dinner?*, reflects the racial tensions associated with integration. These tensions are internalized in Pat Mora's "Legal Alien" and Jacalyn López García's "I Just Wanted to Be Me," which describe the dilemma of being raised as a Mexican American. Sandra M. Gilbert examines the pain caused by ethnic stereotyping in "Mafioso," which is complemented by a revealing photograph of Italian immigrant children as they are processed at Ellis Island. The anxieties felt by new immigrants and their yearnings for the life they left behind are the subject of Chitra Banerjee Divakaruni's "Indian Movie, New Jersey," which is paired with an optimistic cover of a Bollywood film soundtrack. The prejudice that causes some of the anxiety in that poem is also evident in Janice Mirikitani's "Recipe," a satire commenting on the impact of Western beauty ideals on Japanese girls and women. The relevancy of that problem is brought home in the accompanying photograph of a child holding one of Japan's most popular dolls, by Chiaki Tsukumo. Finally, Thomas Lynch's "Liberty" provides an amusing but pointed look at an Irish American who finds suburban life to be a lamentable state compared to the life of his ancestors in Ireland. The photograph of a crowded, working-class Boston suburb that follows the poem tidily captures Lynch's themes.

A list of additional thematically related poems is located at the end of this chapter.

TRANSCENDENCE AND BORDERS

Born in West Africa, Phillis Wheatley was kidnapped and brought to America in 1761 and sold to John and Susannah Wheatley of Boston. She was taught to read and write and was then freed at about the age of thirteen. Her remarkable intelligence and talents led Susannah to help her publish *Poems on Various Subjects, Religious and Moral* in 1773. The influence of religion on her poetry is clearly evident in "On Being Brought from Africa to America." Her response to having been a slave in America is complicated by her acceptance of the religion, language, and even the literary style of the white culture that she found there. The true nature of slavery is apparent, however, in the diagram of a slave ship and a slave auction advertisement. Do these documents qualify Wheatley's description of her origins and the new world into which she was brought as a slave?

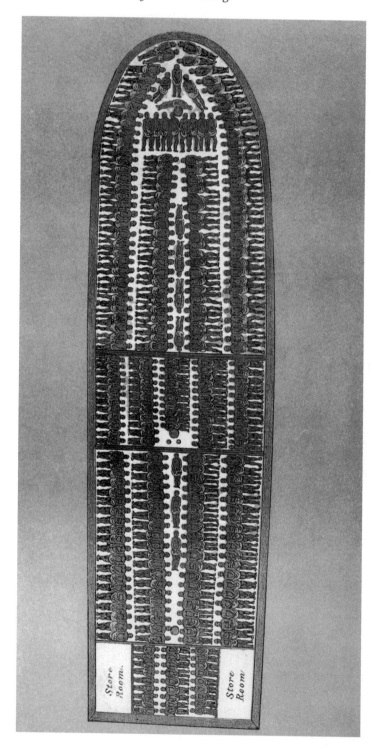

Diagram of an Eighteenth-Century Slave Ship. Often tightly packed and confined in spaces smaller than graves, slaves were subjected to inadequate ventilation and extremely unsanitary conditions. Many died of suffocation or disease during the 3,700-mile voyage from Africa to America.
Reprinted by permission of the Burstein Collection/CORBIS ©.

PHILLIS WHEATLEY (1753?–1784)

On Being Brought from Africa to America   1773

'Twas mercy brought me from my pagan land,
Taught my benighted soul to understand
That there's a God — that there's a Saviour too;
Once I redemption neither sought nor knew.
Some view our sable race with scornful eye —
"Their color is a diabolic dye."
Remember, Christians, Negroes black as Cain°
May be refined, and join the angelic train.

7 *Cain:* In the Bible, Cain murdered Abel and was therefore "marked" by God. That mark has been interpreted by some readers as the origin of dark-skinned people (see Genesis 4:1–15).

CONSIDERATIONS FOR CRITICAL THINKING AND WRITING

1. How does the speaker argue against the pervasive racist views concerning Africans in the eighteenth century?

2. Do you find the argument convincing? Explain whether your own refutation of racism would be argued on similar or other grounds.

3. What arguments are put forth on the slave-auction poster? What attitudes are revealed by its author's choice of words?

Negroes for Sale.

A Cargo of very fine stout Men and Women, in good order and fit for immediate service, just imported from the Windward Coast of Africa, in the Ship Two Brothers.— Conditions are one half Cash or Produce, the other half payable the first of January next, giving Bond and Security if required.

The Sale to be opened at 10 o'Clock each Day, in Mr. Bourdeaux's Yard, at No, 48, on the Bay.

May 19, 1784.   JOHN MITCHELL.

Thirty Seasoned Negroes

To be Sold for Credit, at Private Sale.

AMONGST which is a Carpenter, none of whom are known to be dishonest.

Also, to be sold for Cash, a regular bred young Negroe Man-Cook, born in this Country, who served several Years under an exceeding good French Cook abroad, and his Wife a middle aged Washer-Woman, (both very honest) and their two Children. Likewise, a young Man a Carpenter.

For Terms apply to the Printer.

1784 Slave-Auction Advertisement. In preparation for sale at auction, slaves were fed and washed by the ship's crew. Tar or palm oil was used to disguise sores or wounds caused by poor conditions on board.
© CORBIS.

4. Consider Wheatley's poem alongside the slave-ship diagram and the advertisement for a slave auction. How do you account for the speaker's attitude toward slavery and redemption in relation to the historical realities of slavery?

CONNECTION TO ANOTHER SELECTION

1. Compare the tone and theme of Wheatley's poem with that of Langston Hughes's "I, Too" (p. 396).

RACE AND BORDERS

The conversation Wole Soyinka allows us to overhear in a traditional English red phone booth evokes serious racial tensions as well as a humorous treatment of them. The benighted reaction of the landlady seems to be no match for the speaker's satiric wit. Race is also the issue in *Guess Who's Coming to Dinner?*, a 1967 film about an interracial couple who complicate the lives of a young white woman's parents. The mother and father regard themselves as progressive until their daughter introduces a black man as her future husband. Both the poem and the film are set in the 1960s. Do you think their themes are dated, or do they remain issues in the twenty-first century?

WOLE SOYINKA (B. 1934)

Telephone Conversation   *1960*

The price seemed reasonable, location
Indifferent. The landlady swore she lived
Off premises. Nothing remained
But self-confession. "Madam," I warned,
"I hate a wasted journey — I am African."   5
Silence. Silenced transmission of
Pressurized good-breeding. Voice, when it came,
Lipstick coated, long gold-rolled
Cigarette-holder pipped. Caught I was, foully.
"HOW DARK?" . . . I had not misheard . . . "ARE YOU LIGHT   10
OR VERY DARK?" Button B. Button A. Stench
Of rancid breath of public hide-and-speak.
Red booth. Red pillar-box. Red double-tiered
Omnibus squelching tar. It *was* real! Shamed
By ill-mannered silence, surrender   15
Pushed dumbfoundment to beg simplification.
Considerate she was, varying the emphasis —
"ARE YOU DARK? OR VERY LIGHT?" Revelation came.
"You mean — like plain or milk chocolate?"
Her assent was clinical, crushing in its light   20

Impersonality. Rapidly, wave-length adjusted,
I chose. "West African sepia" — and as afterthought,
"Down in my passport." Silence for spectroscopic
Flight of fancy, till truthfulness clanged her accent
Hard on the mouthpiece. "WHAT'S THAT?" conceding   25
"DON'T KNOW WHAT THAT IS." "Like brunette."
"THAT'S DARK, ISN'T IT?" "Not altogether.
Facially, I am brunette, but madam, you should see
The rest of me. Palm of my hand, soles of my feet
Are a peroxide blonde. Friction, caused —   30
Foolishly madam — by sitting down, has turned
My bottom raven black — One moment madam!" — sensing
Her receiver rearing on the thunderclap
About my ears — "Madam," I pleaded, "wouldn't you rather
See for yourself?"   35

Guess Who's Coming to Dinner? This 1967 film featured Hollywood's first on-screen interracial kiss, between Sidney Poitier and Katharine Houghton. Poitier was the first African American actor to play a leading role in a Hollywood film.
Reprinted by permission of Columbia Pictures and the Kobal Collection.

Considerations for Critical Thinking and Writing

1. **FIRST RESPONSE.** Characterize the landlady. What details deftly reveal her personality? Do you think the speaker's treatment of her is fair or biased? Why?

2. Describe the poem's humor. Do you think the humor undercuts or enhances the racial issues presented?

3. Describe the audience that you think *Guess Who's Coming to Dinner?* is intended for. From what perspective was this film written? Compare this to Soyinka's perspective in "Telephone Conversation."

Connection to Another Selection

1. How does Langston Hughes's "Dinner Guest: Me" (p. 415) serve as a commentary on the racial tensions explored in "Telephone Conversation" and *Guess Who's Coming to Dinner?*

IDENTITY AND BORDERS

In "Legal Alien" Pat Mora explores the difficulties of living in two different cultures simultaneously. The poem's speaker, both Mexican and American, worries that each cultural identity displaces the other, leaving the speaker standing alone between both worlds. Similarly, Jacalyn López García, a multimedia artist who combines computer art, video, and music CD-ROMs to create complex images, explores the dilemmas that she encountered while being raised as a Mexican American. How do the poem and the image evoke the tensions produced by trying to assimilate into a new culture while trying to hold onto the cultural values brought from one's native country?

Pat Mora (b. 1942)

Legal Alien   1985

Bi-lingual, Bi-cultural,
able to slip from "How's life?"
to *"Me'stan volviendo loca,"*°
able to sit in a paneled office
drafting memos in smooth English,   5
able to order in fluent Spanish
at a Mexican restaurant,
American but hyphenated,
viewed by Anglos as perhaps exotic,
perhaps inferior, definitely different,   10
viewed by Mexicans as alien,

---

3 *Me'stan . . . loca:* They are driving me crazy.

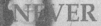

MY MOTHER'S STORY
"I raised my children speaking English only
because I did not want them to have an accent."

"I thought it would be easier for them."

"After all, I spoke English, having attended an
American school in Casas Grandes, Mexico."

"But I never had the privileges of being "white"."

"I Just Wanted to Be Me" (1997), by Jacalyn López García. In her multimedia exhibit *Glass Houses*, Garcia explores family history and issues of identity. "As we crossed the Mexican border, the border patrol would ask me my citizenship. I would reply, 'American' because my parents taught me to say that. But in California, people would ask me 'What are you?' . . . I would proudly reply 'Mexican.' It wasn't until I became a teenager that I claimed I was 'Mexican-American.'" Once, a white neighbor reported to authorities that García's mother was undocumented. "I was only seven years old when my mother was deported, my brother was six. The Christmas tree stayed up until Mom returned home in April of the following year." Reprinted by permission of the artist.

(their eyes say, "You may speak
Spanish but you're not like me")
an American to Mexicans
a Mexican to Americans   15
a handy token
sliding back and forth
between the fringes of both worlds
by smiling
by masking the discomfort   20
of being pre-judged
Bi-laterally.

CONSIDERATIONS FOR CRITICAL THINKING AND WRITING

I. **FIRST RESPONSE.** What is the nature of the discomfort the speaker experiences as an "American but hyphenated"? Explain whether you think the advantages outweigh the disadvantages.

2. What qualities do you think make someone an American? How does your description compare with your classmates' views? How do you account for the differences or similarities?

3. Discuss the appropriateness of the poem's title. How does it encapsulate the speaker's emotional as well as official status?

4. How do poet Pat Mora and artist Jacalyn López García incorporate multiple voices into their work? Why do you think they do so?

CONNECTION TO ANOTHER SELECTION

1. Compare and contrast the speaker's responses to "sliding back and forth / between the fringes of both worlds" in Mora's "Legal Alien" and in Louise Erdrich's "Dear John Wayne" (p. 475).

IMMIGRATION AND BORDERS

Ethnic stereotypes are the legacy Sandra M. Gilbert examines in "Mafioso." Her poem raises important questions about the way in which popular culture shapes our assumptions about and perceptions of ethnic groups. How much of what we regard as quintessentially Italian American is generated by films like *The Godfather* or television programs like *The Sopranos*? How did most immigrants actually work to become Americans once they arrived on the country's shores? A glimpse of the nature of that struggle is suggested by the 1911 photograph of three boys undergoing an examination at Ellis Island. Do you think the photograph supports or qualifies Gilbert's assessment of the difficulties immigrants faced upon their arrival in America?

SANDRA M. GILBERT (B. 1936)

Mafioso   1979

Frank Costello eating spaghetti in a cell at San Quentin,
Lucky Luciano mixing up a mess of bullets and
calling for parmesan cheese,
Al Capone baking a sawed-off shotgun into a
huge lasagna —   5
          are you my uncles, my
only uncles?

      O Mafiosi,
bad uncles of the barren
cliffs of Sicily — was it only you   10
that they transported in barrels
like pure olive oil
across the Atlantic?

         Was it only you
who got out at Ellis Island with   15

black scarves on your heads and cheap cigars
and no English and a dozen children?

No carts were waiting, gallant with paint,
no little donkeys plumed like the dreams of peacocks.
Only the evil eyes of a thousand buildings   20
stared across at the echoing debarcation center,
making it seem so much smaller than a piazza,

only a half dozen Puritan millionaires stood on the wharf,
in the wind colder than the impossible snows of the Abruzzi,
ready with country clubs and dynamos   25

to grind the organs out of you.

"Baggage Examined Here" (1911). Between 1880 and 1920, nearly four million Italian immigrants came to the United States, most arriving in New York City and settling in cities along the East Coast. While first- and second-class steamship passengers were quickly inspected onboard and allowed to disembark in Manhattan, third-class passengers, such as the boys in this photo, were taken to Ellis Island, where they were subjected to a series of medical examinations and interviews. Inspectors marked the immigrants' clothing with chalk, indicating the need for further examination: *Sc* for scalp disease, *G* for goiter, *H* for hernia, *L* for lameness, or *S* for senility.
© Bettmann/CORBIS.

CONSIDERATIONS FOR CRITICAL THINKING AND WRITING

1. **FIRST RESPONSE.** In what sense are the gangsters Frank Costello, Lucky Luciano, and Al Capone to be understood as "bad uncles"? How does the speaker, in particular, feel about the "uncles"?

2. Explain how nearly all of the images in the poem are associated with Italian life. Does the poem reinforce stereotypes about Italians or invoke images about them for some other purpose? If so, what other purpose?

3. What sort of people are the "Puritan millionaires" (line 23)? What is their relationship to the "bad uncles"?

4. Consider the photograph. Why was it taken? What does this image convey about attitudes toward working-class immigrants processed at Ellis Island? How do the words "Baggage Examined Here" function in the image? How do these words connect with the last line of Gilbert's poem ("to grind the organs out of you")? What comments are the photograph and poem making about the experience?

CONNECTIONS TO OTHER SELECTIONS

1. Discuss the ways in which ethnicity is used to create meaning in "Mafioso" and in Jimmy Santiago Baca's "Green Chile" (p. 117).

2. How do the attitudes conveyed in "Mafioso" and the photograph "Baggage Examined Here" compare to the sentiments expressed in Emma Lazarus's "The New Colossus" (p. 613), the poem inscribed at the base of the Statue of Liberty?

EXPECTATIONS AND BORDERS

The immigrants' dream of America is deeply present in Chitra Banerjee Divakaruni's "Indian Movie, New Jersey." The hopeful expectation that immigrants bring with them takes on a nostalgic and melancholy tone as the speaker contrasts America as imagined to the country that is experienced. The Indian movie offers yet another dream that suggests a powerful yearning for a different kind of life than the one found in New Jersey. Is the movie version of India any more or less real than the speaker's picture of America? Is this poem more about disillusionment or delusion?

CHITRA BANERJEE DIVAKARUNI (B. 1956)

Indian Movie, New Jersey   *1990*

Not like the white filmstars, all rib
and gaunt cheekbone, the Indian sex-goddess
smiles plumply from behind a flowery
branch. Below her brief red skirt, her thighs

are satisfying-solid, redeeming   5
as tree trunks. She swings her hips
and the men-viewers whistle. The lover-hero
dances in to a song, his lip-sync
a little off, but no matter, we
know the words already and sing along.   10
It is safe here, the day
golden and cool so no one sweats,
roses on every bush and the Dal Lake
clean again.
        The sex-goddess switches   15
to thickened English to emphasize
a joke. We laugh and clap. Here
we need not be embarrassed by words
dropping like lead pellets into foreign ears.
The flickering movie-light   20
wipes from our faces years of America, sons
who want mohawks and refuse to run
the family store, daughters who date
on the sly.
        When at the end the hero   25
dies for his friend who also
loves the sex-goddess and now can marry her,
we weep, understanding. Even the men
clear their throats to say, "What *qurbani!*°   *sacrifice*
What *dosti!*"° After, we mill around   *friendship*   30
unwilling to leave, exchange greetings
and good news: a new gold chain, a trip
to India. We do not speak
of motel raids, canceled permits, stones
thrown through glass windows, daughters and sons   35
raped by Dotbusters.°
        In this dim foyer
we can pull around us the faint, comforting smell
of incense and *pakoras,*° can arrange   *fried appetizers*
our children's marriages with hometown boys and girls,   40
open a franchise, win a million
in the mail. We can retire
in India, a yellow two-storied house
with wrought-iron gates, our own
Ambassador car. Or at least   45
move to a rich white suburb, Summerfield
or Fort Lee, with neighbors that will
talk to us. Here while the film-songs still echo
in the corridors and restrooms, we can trust
in movie truths: sacrifice, success, love and luck,   50
the America that was supposed to be.

---

36 *Dotbusters:* New Jersey gangs that attack Indians.

Rawal Films, *Ladki Pasand Hai (I Like This Girl)* (1971). India's massive Hindi-language film industry, known as Bollywood (a play on the word Hollywood, with the B representing Bombay), produces twice as many films as Hollywood each year, with a huge international audience. Bollywood films are churned out so quickly that sometimes scripts are handwritten and actors on set shoot scenes for multiple films. Traditionally, these colorful extravaganzas, chock full of singing, dancing, and multiple costume changes, stick to a "boy meets girl" formula — a hero and heroine fall in love and then struggle for family approval. This image is from the soundtrack to a 1971 film with a typical Bollywood plot.
Reprinted by permission of HMV Odeon. Courtesy of Niall Richardson.

CONSIDERATIONS FOR CRITICAL THINKING AND WRITING

1. **FIRST RESPONSE.** Why does the speaker feel comfortable at the movies? How is the world inside the theater different from life outside in New Jersey?

2. Explain the differences portrayed by the speaker between life in India and life in New Jersey. What connotative values are associated with each location in the poem? Discuss the irony in the final two lines.

3. How do the ideas and values of the Bollywood poster contrast with the realities conveyed in the last part of the poem?

1. Explain how the speaker's idea of "the America that was supposed to be" (line 51) compares with the nation described in Florence Cassen Mayers's "All-American Sestina" (p. 250).

BEAUTY AND BORDERS

Janice Mirikitani, a third-generation Japanese American, reflects upon dominant cultural standards of beauty in "Recipe." Women who do not meet such standards — especially women of color — can be faced with complicated decisions about how they want to appear, decisions that go far more than skin deep. Chiaki Tsukumo's 2003 photograph of a young Tokyo girl holding a popular Western-style doll demonstrates how powerful Western concepts of beauty are, even among non-Western people. Why are "Round Eyes" so desirable? What kind of price is paid for such a desire?

JANICE MIRIKITANI (B. 1942)

Recipe   *1987*

Round Eyes

Ingredients: scissors, Scotch magic transparent tape,
                eyeliner — water based, black.
                Optional: false eyelashes.

Cleanse face thoroughly.   5

For best results, powder entire face, including eyelids.
    (lighter shades suited to total effect desired)

With scissors, cut magic tape $^{1}/_{16}$" wide, $^{3}/_{4}$" – $^{1}/_{2}$" long —
depending on length of eyelid.

Stick firmly onto mid–upper eyelid area   10
    (looking down into handmirror facilitates finding
    adequate surface)

If using false eyelashes, affix first on lid, folding any
excess lid over the base of eyelash with glue.

Paint black eyeliner on tape and entire lid.   15

Do not cry.

CONSIDERATIONS FOR CRITICAL THINKING AND WRITING

1. **FIRST RESPONSE.** Discuss your response to the poem's final line.

2. Why does Mirikitani write the poem in recipe form? What is the effect of the very specific details of this recipe?

"Girl with Licca Doll," by Chiaki Tsukumo (2003). According to the Japanese toymaker Takara, "Licca-chan was developed to make girls' dreams and wishes come true" and "to nurture kindness, gentleness, and love in children." A fan's personal Web site notes that Licca-chan "hates arithmetic, but she's good at language, music, and art." Her favorite books are *Anne of Green Gables* and *A Little Princess*, and she loves eating ice cream and window-shopping. First introduced in 1967, the doll has since sold nearly fifty million units and become, according to the toymaker, a national character that has inspired a Licca-chan generation of women consumers.
Reprinted by permission of the Associated Press.

3. Why is "false eyelashes" a particularly resonant phrase in the context of this poem?

4. Consider and note the Licca doll's hair, eyes, and costume in the photograph by Chiaki Tsukumo. How do you account for the success of the Licca doll? What do you make of the toymaker's claim that the doll makes "girls' dreams and wishes come true"? What dreams and wishes do you think the toymaker is selling? How do the ideals that the toymaker (Takara) associates with the Licca doll compare with those associated with Barbie?

5. How does the paragraph connect with Mirikitani's satirical poem?

CONNECTION TO ANOTHER SELECTION

1. How might the voice in Michelle Boisseau's "Self-Pity's Closet" (p. 555) be read as a version of the speaker in "Recipe"?

FREEDOM AND BORDERS

Thomas Lynch's "Liberty" is an amusing protest against conformity, the kind of middling placidity often associated with suburban life in America. The blustery Irish speaker in this poem laments the lost world his ancestors inhabited in Ireland and longs for the "form[s] of freedom" that they once enjoyed. Though the speaker may cause us to smile, his complaint is serious nonetheless. The potential validity of his assessment of suburban life is presented visually in the accompanying photograph of Somerville, Massachusetts, a suburb of Boston. How might Lynch's speaker be considered a resident of one of those houses? Does the arrangement of the streets and houses help to explain the attitudes expressed in the poem? What are your own views about the suburbs?

THOMAS LYNCH (B. 1948)

Liberty   1998

Some nights I go out and piss on the front lawn
as a form of freedom — liberty from
porcelain and plumbing and the Great Beyond
beyond the toilet and the sewage works.
Here is the statement I am trying to make: 5
to say I am from a fierce bloodline of men
who made their water in the old way, under stars
that overarched the North Atlantic where
the River Shannon empties into sea.
The ex-wife used to say, "Why can't you pee   10
in concert with the most of humankind
who do their business tidily indoors?"
It was gentility or envy, I suppose,
because I could do it anywhere, and do
whenever I begin to feel encumbered.   15
Still, there is nothing, here in the suburbs,
as dense as the darkness in West Clare
nor any equivalent to the nightlong wind
that rattles in the hedgerow of whitethorn there
on the east side of the cottage yard in Moveen.   20
It was market day in Kilrush, years ago:
my great-great-grandfather bargained with tinkers
who claimed it was whitethorn that Christ's crown was made from.
So he gave them two and six and brought them home —
mere saplings then — as a gift for the missus,   25
who planted them between the house and garden.
For years now, men have slipped out the back door

"Somerville, Massachusetts," by Alex MacLean (1993). Between 1870 and 1915, new streetcar lines in the Boston suburb of Somerville spurred major population growth in the area. Many of the newcomers were immigrants, including Irish workers attracted by plentiful jobs at the brickyards and in the slaughtering and meatpacking industry. The two-family houses in this photograph were built around 1910 to house the new population. By World War II, these neighborhoods swelled to a population density said to be greater than that of Calcutta.
Reprinted by permission of Alex S. MacLean/Landslides.

during wakes or wedding feasts or nights of song
to pay their homage to the holy trees
and, looking up into that vast firmament,   30
consider liberty in that last townland where
they have no crowns, no crappers and no ex-wives.

CONSIDERATIONS FOR CRITICAL THINKING AND WRITING

1. **FIRST RESPONSE.** Does "gentility or envy" (line 13) get in the way of your enjoyment and appreciation of this poem? Explain why or why not.
2. Characterize the speaker and explain why you find him engaging or not. What sort of liberty does he insist upon?
3. Consider Alex MacLean's aerial photograph of Somerville, Massachusetts. What strikes you about this landscape? What is the thinking behind this

example of city planning? How does such a plan affect personal freedoms, and how might it inspire rebellion such as that of the speaker in Lynch's poem?

CONNECTION TO ANOTHER SELECTION

1. Discuss Lynch's treatment of suburban life and compare it with that of John Ciardi in "Suburban" (p. 518). What similarities are there in the themes and metaphoric strategies of these two poems?

SUGGESTED TOPICS FOR LONGER PAPERS

1. Write an essay that develops a common theme or thread that you find in all seven poems presented in this chapter. You may explore similarities or differences concerning any aspect of the border crossings they examine.
2. Choose one of the poems listed below and research at least three images that complement, extend, or qualify the poem. Select rich images that allow you to write an essay explaining how they are thematically connected to the idea of crossing borders in the poem.

Selections related to this chapter

Sherman Alexie, *On the Amtrak from Boston to New York City* (p. 174)

Jimmy Santiago Baca, *Green Chile* (p. 117)

Regina Barreca, *Nighttime Fires* (p. 39)

Michelle Boisseau, *Self-Pity's Closet* (p. 555)

Diane Burns, *Sure You Can Ask Me a Personal Question* (p. 227)

John Ciardi, *Suburban* (p. 518)

Louise Erdrich, *Dear John Wayne* (p. 475)

Martín Espada, *Bully* (p. 166)

Robert Frost, *The Road Not Taken* (p. 354)

Robert Frost, *Mending Wall* (p. 359)

Tony Hoagland, *America* (p. 561)

M. Carl Holman, *Mr. Z* (p. 524)

Carolina Hospital, *The Hyphenated Man* (p. 281)

Langston Hughes, *The Negro Speaks of Rivers* (p. 393)

Langston Hughes, *I, Too* (p. 396)

Langston Hughes, *Theme for English B* (p. 502)

Langston Hughes, *Negro* (p. 398)

Langston Hughes, *Dinner Guest: Me* (p. 415)

Tato Laviera, *AmeRícan* (p. 284)

Emma Lazarus, *The New Colossus* (p. 613)

An Anthology
of Poems

22

An Album of
Contemporary Poems

Now the role of poetry is not simply to
hold understanding in place but to help
create and hold a realm of experience.
Poetry has become a kind of tool for
knowing the world in a particular way.
—JANE HIRSHFIELD

© Jerry Bauer.

MICHELLE BOISSEAU (B. 1955)

Born in Cincinnati, Michelle Boisseau earned a B.A. and M.A. from Ohio
University and a Ph.D. from the University of Houston. She has taught lit-
erature and writing courses at Moorhead State Univer-
sity and the University of Missouri at Kansas City. She
received a National Endowment for the Arts poetry fel-
lowship as well as a number of other grants and awards;
her poetry collections include *No Private Life* (1990) and *Understory* (1996).

Web Research the
poets in this chapter
at bedfordstmartins
.com/meyerpoetry.

Self-Pity's Closet   *2003*

Depression, loneliness, anger, shame, envy,
appetite without hunger, unquenchable
thirst, secret open wounds, long parades
of punishments, resentment honed and glinting
in the sun, the wind driving a few leaves,   5
an empty bird call, the grass bent down, far off

a dog barking and barking, the skin sticky,
the crotch itchy, the tongue stinking, the eyes,
words thrust from the mouth like bottles off a bridge,
tangy molasses of disgust, dank memory   10
of backs, of eyebrows raised and cool expressions
after your vast and painful declarations,
subtle humiliations creeping up
like the smell of wet upholstery, dial tone
in the brain, the conviction that your friends   15
never really loved you, the certitude
you deserved no better, never have, stains
in the carpet, the faucet drilling the sink,
the nights raining spears of stars, the days bland
and blank as newspapers eaten slowly   20
in the bathtub, the clock, the piano,
heavy impatient books, slippery pens,
the radio, a bug bouncing against
the window: go away, make it all go away.

CONNECTIONS TO OTHER SELECTIONS

1. Compare the pain experienced by the speaker in this poem with the speaker's pain in Stephen Dobyns's "Do They Have a Reason?" (p. 559). How do the images in each poem reveal the speaker's state of mind?

2. Discuss the themes you find in this poem and in Edgar Allan Poe's "The Haunted Palace" (p. 159). Explain whether or not you think the differences between these two poems are greater than their similarities.

BILLY COLLINS (B. 1941)

Since the publication of his first book, *The Apple That Astonished Paris* (1988), Billy Collins (born in New York City in 1941) has established himself as a prominent voice in contemporary American poetry. His books include *Picnic, Lightning* (1998); *The Art of Drowning* (1995), a finalist for the Lenore Marshall Prize; *Questions about Angels* (1991), selected for the National Poetry Series and reissued in 1999; *Sailing Alone Around the Room: New and Selected Poems* (2001), and *Nine Horses* (2002). Collins was selected in 2001 as the poet laureate of the United States.

Marginalia   *1998*

Sometimes the notes are ferocious,
skirmishes against the author
raging along the borders of every page
in tiny black script.

If I could just get my hands on you,   5
Kierkegaard,° or Conor Cruise O'Brien,°
they seem to say,
I would bolt the door and beat some logic into your head.

Other comments are more offhand, dismissive —
"Nonsense." "Please!" "HA!!" —   10
that kind of thing.
I remember once looking up from my reading,
my thumb as a bookmark,
trying to imagine what the person must look like
who wrote "Don't be a ninny"   15
alongside a paragraph in *The Life of Emily Dickinson.*

Students are more modest
needing to leave only their splayed footprints
along the shore of the page.
One scrawls "Metaphor" next to a stanza of Eliot's.°   20
Another notes the presence of "Irony"
fifty times outside the paragraphs of *A Modest Proposal.*°

Or they are fans who cheer from the empty bleachers,
hands cupped around their mouths.
"Absolutely," they shout   25
to Duns Scotus° and James Baldwin.°
"Yes." "Bull's-eye." "My man!"
Check marks, asterisks, and exclamation points
rain down along the sidelines.

And if you have managed to graduate from college   30
without ever having written "Man vs. Nature"
in a margin, perhaps now
is the time to take one step forward.

We have all seized the white perimeter as our own
and reached for a pen if only to show   35
we did not just laze in an armchair turning pages;
we pressed a thought into the wayside,
planted an impression along the verge.

Even Irish monks in their cold scriptoria°
jotted along the borders of the Gospels   40
brief asides about the pains of copying,

---

6 *Kierkegaard:* Søren Aaby Kierkegaard (1813-1855), Danish philosopher and theologian.
Conor Cruise O'Brien (B. 1917): Irish historian, critic, and statesman.

20 *Eliot's:* Thomas Stearns Eliot (1888-1965), American-born English poet and critic (see
p. 453).

22 *A Modest Proposal:* An essay by English satirist Jonathan Swift (1667-1745).

26 *Duns Scotus* (1265?-1308): Scottish theologian.   *James Baldwin* (1924-1987): African American
essayist and novelist.

39 *scriptoria:* Rooms in a monastery used for writing and copying.

a bird singing near their window,
or the sunlight that illuminated their page —
anonymous men catching a ride into the future
on a vessel more lasting than themselves.   45

And you have not read Joshua Reynolds,°
they say, until you have read him
enwreathed with Blake's° furious scribbling.

Yet the one I think of most often,
the one that dangles from me like a locket,   50
was written in the copy of *Catcher in the Rye*°
I borrowed from the local library
one slow, hot summer.
I was just beginning high school then,
reading books on a davenport in my parents' living room,   55
and I cannot tell you
how vastly my loneliness was deepened,
how poignant and amplified the world before me seemed,
when I found on one page

a few greasy looking smears   60
and next to them, written in soft pencil —
by a beautiful girl, I could tell,
whom I would never meet —
"Pardon the egg salad stains, but I'm in love."

46 *Joshua Reynolds* (1723-1792): English portrait artist who entertained many of the important writers of his time.

48 *Blake's:* William Blake (1757-1827), English mystic and poet.

51 *Catcher in the Rye:* A novel (1951) about adolescence by American author J. D. Salinger (B. 1919).

CONNECTIONS TO OTHER SELECTIONS

1. Discuss the speaker's response to reading in this poem and in Philip Larkin's "A Study of Reading Habits" (p. 34). How is reading used as a measure of each speaker's character?

2. Describe the speaker's attitude toward books in this poem and in Anne Bradstreet's "The Author to Her Book" (p. 137).

STEPHEN DOBYNS (B. 1941)

Born in Orange, New Jersey, Stephen Dobyns has published more than thirty books, among them ten books of poetry and twenty novels. After graduating from Wayne State University, he earned an M.F.A. from the University of Iowa. His many awards include the Lamont Poetry Selection, the Poetry Society of America's Melville Crane Award, and Guggenheim and National

Endowment for the Humanities fellowships. His poetry collections include *Concurring Beasts* (1972), *Black Dog, Red Dog* (1984), *Cemetery Nights* (1987), *Velocities: New and Selected Poems, 1966–1992* (1994), *Common Carnage* (1996), and *Pallbearers Envying the Dead Who Ride* (1999). He has taught at a variety of schools, including the University of Iowa and Boston University.

Do They Have a Reason?   2000

Life begins, you make some friends,
what futures you plan for one another.
No failures here, no one sent to prison.
When you first start out, you can't imagine
you won't succeed, even if the road's unclear   5
and your parents call you dumb, your brother
pulls your ears, somehow you'll make it work,
even if what you want is to rob a bank,
to be a first-rate crook, but mostly we start out
idealistic — doctors, astrophysicists — or maybe   10
we have a taste for fame and money — actors,
stockbrokers — but always something at the top
and always several: Maybe I'll be this or that,
we say. And mostly our friends encourage us
just so we'll encourage them. Sure you'll be   15
a surgeon, they say, you got the hands. So we
loll about the riverbank with our first cigars
and watch the ducks float by. It's summer
and third grade is dead forever. We lean back
on our elbows and blow some smoke. I'll be   20
an astronaut, you say, and own a fleet of trucks.
You bet, says your cousin, and I'll play ball.
And he's the guy who dies a drunk at thirty-five.
Think of the moment when you at last catch on.
Some kids get it right away, others not so quick.   25
One day you experience a click in your head
as the world turns from one place to another.
Does the sky change color, the river get colder?
Like when you stroll into the local diner after school
for a Coke and a hot pretzel, a place you visit   30
every day to meet your pals, but today your pals
are having fun someplace else, and there instead
are half a dozen kids you've never seen before:
sixth graders for certain. They snatch your pack,
toss your stuff around, one tears your shirt,   35
another rips your books. What's their reason?
They don't need a reason. When the world
you love is changed for another, it's like that.

CONNECTIONS TO OTHER SELECTIONS

1. Discuss the speaker's sense of undergoing a shift in sensibility in this poem with the speaker in Andrew Hudgins's "Seventeen" (p. 170).

2. How might Sharon Olds's "Rite of Passage" (p. 279) be read as a means of providing the "reason" for what happens in Dobyns's poem?

JANE HIRSHFIELD (B. 1953)

Born in New York City, Jane Hirshfield is the author of five books of poetry, most recently *Given Sugar, Given Salt* (2001), and a collection of essays, *Nine Gates: Entering the Mind of Poetry* (1997). She has also edited and co-translated two collections of poetry by women from the past, *Women in Praise of the Sacred: Forty-three Centuries of Spiritual Poetry by Women* (1995) and *The Ink Dark Moon: Poems by Ono no Komachi and Izumi Shikibu, Women of the Ancient Court of Japan* (1990). Hirshfield's awards include the Poetry Center Book Award, the Bay Area Book Reviewers Award, Columbia University's Translation Center Award, and fellowships from the Guggenheim and Rockefeller Foundations. She has taught at the University of California at Berkeley, the University of San Francisco, and Bennington College.

August Day   *2001*

You work with what you are given —
today I am blessed, today I am given luck.
It takes the shape of a dozen ripening fruit trees,
a curtain of pole beans, a thicket of berries.
It takes the shape of a dozen empty hours.   5

In them is neither love nor love's muster of losses,
in them is no chance for harm or for good.
Does even my humanness matter?
A bear would be equally happy, this August day,
fat on the simple sweetness plucked between thorns.   10

There are some who may think, "How pitiful, how lonely."
Others must murmur, "How lazy."

I agree with them all: pitiful, lonely, lazy.
Lost to the earth and to heaven,
thoroughly drunk on its whiskeys, I wander my kingdom.   15

CONNECTIONS TO OTHER SELECTIONS

1. Discuss the moods created in "August Day" and in Margaret Atwood's "February" (p. 143). To what extent do you think each poem is successful in capturing the essence of the title's subject?

Locked Ward: Newtown, Connecticut

2005

Your tight-lipped jailer beckons
and I trail her like a moon.

The padding of her strange white shoes,
the doors she unlocks one by one —

then you are there on the edge of a cot   5
like a whipped child, with your eyes down.

There are no sharp objects in here,
only the malignant shapes

that dance out
when the strappings are undone.   10

I have brought you what you wanted
from home. A robe, a sweater —

an irony, as though what you wanted
could be mine to give so

easily. Oh I   15
would wrap you up and carry you away

to some all-powerful physician
or at least some place

they'd let you rave in peace.
Silence of the years, the sins against   20

the white page. Carried always out to sea
by the foul winds off the laundry,

the stains that cannot be removed
by any washing of the hands.

The years are mute. And yet   25
there is no end to the lament

of daughters, no end
to the sharp objects in the heart.

CONNECTIONS TO OTHER SELECTIONS

1. Discuss the parent-daughter relationship as it is revealed by the images in
   Loden's poem and in Cathy Song's "The Youngest Daughter" (p. 94).
2. Compare the themes in Loden's poem and in Emily Dickinson's "One need
   not be a Chamber — to be Haunted —" (p. 325).

Susan Minot (b. 1956)

Born and raised in Massachusetts, Susan Minot earned a B.A. at Brown University and an M.F.A. at Columbia University. Before devoting herself full-time to writing, Minot worked as an assistant editor at *Grand Street* magazine. Her stories have appeared in the *Atlantic Monthly, Harper's,* the *New Yorker, Mademoiselle,* and *Paris Review.* Her short stories have been collected in *Lust and Other Stories* (1989), and she has published four novels — *Monkeys* (1986), *Folly* (1992), *Evening* (1998), and *Rapture* (2002), as well as one volume of poetry: *Poems 4 A.M.* (2002).

Courtesy of Dinah Minot Hubley.

My Husband's Back

2005

Sunday evening.
Breakdown hour. Weeping into
a pot of burnt rice. Sun dimmed
like a light bulb gone out
behind a gray lawn of snow.   5
The baby flushed with the flu
asleep on a pillow.
The fire won't catch.
The wet wood's caked
with ice. Sitting   10
on the couch my spine
collides with all its bones
and I watch my husband
peer past the glass grate
and blow.   15
His back in a snug plaid shirt
gray and white
leaning into the woodstove
is firm and compact
like a young man's back.   20

And the giant world which swirls
in my head
stopping most thought
suddenly ceases
to spin. It sits   25
right there, the back I love,
animal and gamine, leaning
on one arm.

I could crawl on it forever
the one point in the world   30
turns out
I have travelled everywhere
to get to.

CONNECTIONS TO OTHER SELECTIONS

1. Compare Minot's "My Husband's Back" and Anne Bradstreet's "To My
   Dear and Loving Husband" (p. 492) as love poems.
2. Discuss the speakers' tones in Minot's poem and in Jane Kenyon's "The
   Shirt" (p. 496).

ROBERT MORGAN (B. 1944)

Robert Morgan is a poet and novelist who has been widely praised as the
poet laureate of Appalachia. Morgan was born and raised in North Carolina
in a small, isolated valley in the Blue Ridge Mountains. He earned his B.A.
from the University of North Carolina at Chapel Hill and his M.A. from
the University of North Carolina at Greensboro. He has published four
books of fiction since 1969, including *The Hinterlands* (1994) and *The Truest
Pleasure* (1995). He has been widely published in such magazines as *Atlantic
Monthly, New Republic, Poetry, Southern Review, Yale Review, Carolina Quar-
terly,* and *New England Review.* He has also published nine volumes of po-
etry, his latest titled *Topsoil Road* (2000). In 1971 he began teaching at
Cornell University, where, since 1992, he has been Kappa Alpha Professor
of English. He has won several awards, including four National Endow-
ment for the Arts fellowships and a Guggenheim Fellowship, and has been
included in *New Stories from the South* and *Prize Stories: The O. Henry Awards.*
His recent novel, *Gap Creek* (1999), was selected for Oprah's Book Club.

Fever Wit   2000

If a child or young adult lay
near crisis with a temperature,
bedclothes hot as from an iron,
face swollen bright as a blown coal,
neighbors and kin would gather round,   5
sitting near the bedside, leaning
close, awaiting words uttered from
delirium, the scattered phrase
and mutter from hot throat and brain.
Every mumble seemed a message   10
to interpret, each groan and wince,

jerk and whisper, a report in
testimony from other tongues,
as though the sick child glowing with
infection could see beyond in   15
fever intoxication, become
a filament for lighting their
ordinary lives with lightning glimpse
burned through the secret boundary,
the ill one privileged to say   20
across and not distort or resist
the wisdom of sickness, the vision
from pain-fire's further peaks, before
the dreaded sweat, the chill descent.

CONNECTIONS TO OTHER SELECTIONS

1. Compare the theme of this poem with that of Emily Dickinson's "Tell all the Truth but tell it slant —" (p. 329).

2. Discuss the "neighbors and kin" of this poem and "The people along the sand" in Robert Frost's "Neither Out Far nor In Deep" (p. 373).

ALBERTO RÍOS (B. 1952)

Born in Nogales, Arizona, Alberto Ríos grew up on the border between Mexico and Arizona, which is the subject of his memoir *Capriotoda* (1999). He earned a bachelor's degree and an M.F.A. from the University of Arizona. He has published several short story collections and a number of poetry collections, including *Whispering to Fool the Wind* (1982), *The Lime Orchard Woman* (1988), *Teodoro Luna's Two Kisses* (1990), and *The Smallest Muscle in the Human Body* (2002). His many awards include the Arizona Governor's Arts Award and fellowships from the Guggenheim Foundation and the National Endowment for the Arts. He teaches at Arizona State University.

The Gathering Evening   *2002*

Shadows are the patient apprentices of everything.
They follow what might be followed,

Sit with what will not move.
They take notes all day long —

We don't pay attention, we don't see   5
The dark writing of the pencil, the black notebook.

Sometimes, if you are watching carefully,
A shadow will move. You will turn to see

What has made it move, but nothing.
The shadows transcribe all night.   10

Transcription is their sleep.
We mistake night as a setting of the sun:

Night is all of them comparing notes,
So many gathering that their crowd

Makes the darkness everything.   15
Patient, patient, quiet and still.

One day they will have learned it all.
One day they will step out, in front,

And we will follow them, be their shadows,
And work for our turn —   20

The centuries it takes
To learn what waiting has to teach.

CONNECTIONS TO OTHER SELECTIONS

1. Compare the treatment of shadows in this poem and in Emily Dickinson's "Presentiment — is that long Shadow — on the lawn —" (p. 136).

2. Discuss the significance of the night in this poem and in Robert Frost's "Acquainted with the Night" (p. 157).

CATHY SONG (B. 1955)

Of Chinese and Korean descent, Cathy Song was born in Honolulu, Hawaii. After receiving her B.A. from Wellesley College, she pursued an M.A. in creative writing at Boston University. The recipient of a number of grants and awards, including the Shelley Memorial Award from the Poetry Society of America and the Hawaii Award for Literature, she has taught creative writing at various universities. Her work frequently focuses on the world of family and ancestry. Among her collections of poetry are *Picture Bride* (1983), *Frameless Windows, Squares of Light* (1988), *School Figures* (1994), and *The Land of Bliss* (2001).

A Poet in the House   *2001*

Emily's job was to think.
She was the only one of us
who had that to do.
  —Lavinia Dickinson

Seemingly small her work,
minute to the point of invisibility —
she vanished daily into paper, famished,
hungry for her next encounter —

© John Eddy.

but she opened with a string of humble   5
words necessity,
necessary as the humble work
of bringing well to water, roast to knife, cake to frost,
the coarse, loud, grunting labor of the rest of us
who complained not at all   10
for the noises she heard
we deemed divine, if
claustrophobic and esoteric —
and contented ourselves to the apparent,
the menial, set our heads   15
to the task of daily maintenance,
the simple order at the kitchen table,
while she struggled with a different thing —
the pressure seized upon her mind —
we could ourselves not bear such strain   20
and, in gratitude, heaved the bucket,
squeezed the rag, breathed the sweet,
homely odor of soap.
Lifting dirt from the floor
I swear   25
we could hear her thinking.

Connections to Other Selections

1. Compare Song's assessment of the life of a poet with the view expressed in Howard Nemerov's "Walking the Dog" (p. 521) or William Trowbridge's "Poets' Corner" (below).

2. Discuss the perspective on Dickinson in this poem and in Ron Wallace's "Miss Goff" (p. 339).

William Trowbridge

A native of Omaha, Nebraska, William Trowbridge teaches at Northwest Missouri State University. His collections of poems include *Book of Kong* (1989), *Flickers* (2000), and the forthcoming *Four Seasons*. He has been awarded the American Poet's Prize and fellowships at Ragdale, Yaddo, and the MacDowell Colony.

Poets' Corner   *1999*

They put me in right field
because I didn't pitch that well
or throw or catch or hit,
because I tried to steer the ball

like a paper plane, watched   5
Christmas gifts with big
red ribbons floating through
the strike zone, and swung
at dirt balls. So they played the odds,
sent me out there in the tall grass   10
by the Skoal sign, where I wandered
distant as the nosebleed seats
my father got us in Comiskey Park,°
my teammates looking
remote and miniature,   15
their small cries and gesticulations
like things remembered
from a dream. I went dreamy,
sun on my face, the scent
of sod and bluegrass, the lilt   20
of birdcall and early cricket
bending afternoon away
from fastballs and hook slides
to June's lazy looping
single: baseball at its best,   25
my only fear the deep fly
with my name on it,
meteoric as Jehovah
or Coach Bob Zambisi
closing in to deliver once   30
again the meaning of the game:
what it takes to play, why I had to
crouch vigilant as a soldier
in combat, which he never
had the privilege of being,   35
and stop that lolling around
with my head up my ass,
watching the birdies and picking
dandelions like some kind of
little priss, some kind   40
of Percy Bitch Shelby.

13 *Comiskey Park:* Home of the Chicago White Sox baseball team and renamed as U.S. Cellular Field.

CONNECTIONS TO OTHER SELECTIONS

1. Explain the coach's allusion to "Percy Bitch Shelby."
2. Compare the treatment of the coaches in this poem and in Gary Gildner's "First Practice" (p. 275).

23

An Album of
World Literature

My poetry has passed through the same
stages of my life; from a solitary child-
hood and an adolescence cornered in
distant, isolated countries, I set out to
make myself a part of the great human
multitude.
— PABLO NERUDA

ANNA AKHMATOVA (RUSSIA / 1889–1966)

Born in Russia, Anna Akhmatova was a poet and translator who was re-
garded as a major modern poet in Russia. Although she was expelled from
the Union of Soviet Writers during Stalin's rule, she was reclaimed by her
country in the 1960s. Her poetry is characterized by its
clarity, precision, and simplicity. Her work is translated
in *Complete Poems of Anna Akhmatova* (1990).

Web Research the
poets in this chapter
at bedfordstmartins
.com/meyerpoetry.

Lot's Wife   1922

TRANSLATED BY RICHARD WILBUR

The just man followed then his angel guide
Where he strode on the black highway, hulking and bright;
But a wild grief in his wife's bosom cried,
Look back, it is not too late for a last sight

Of the red towers of your native Sodom, the square   5
Where once you sang, the gardens you shall mourn,
And the tall house with empty windows where
You loved your husband and your babes were born.

She turned, and looking on the bitter view
Her eyes were welded shut by mortal pain;   10
Into transparent salt her body grew,
And her quick feet were rooted in the plain.

Who would waste tears upon her? Is she not
The least of our losses, this unhappy wife?
Yet in my heart she will not be forgot   15
Who, for a single glance, gave up her life.

CONNECTIONS TO OTHER SELECTIONS

1. Discuss the use of biblical allusions in "Lot's Wife" and in William Butler Yeats's "The Second Coming" (p. 636). How is an understanding of the allusions crucial to interpreting each poem?
2. Consider the "unhappy wife" in this poem and in Linda Pastan's "Marks" (p. 151). Discuss how you regard the wife in each poem.

CLARIBEL ALEGRÍA (EL SALVADOR / B. 1924)

Born in Estelí, Nicaragua, Claribel Alegría moved with her family to El Salvador within a year of her birth. A 1948 graduate of George Washington University, she considers herself a Salvadoran, and much of her writing reflects the political upheaval of recent Latin American history. In 1978 she was awarded the Casa de las Americas Prize for her book *I Survive*. A bilingual edition of her major works, *Flowers from the Volcano*, was published in 1982.

I Am Mirror   *1978*

TRANSLATED BY ELECTA ARENAL AND MARSHA GABRIELA DREYER

Water sparkles
on my skin
and I don't feel it
water streams
down my back   5
I don't feel it
I rub myself with a towel
I pinch myself in the arm

I don't feel
frightened I look at myself in the mirror
she also pricks herself
I begin to get dressed
stumbling
from the corners
shouts like lightning bolts
tortured eyes
scurrying rats
and teeth shoot forth
although I feel nothing
I wander through the streets:
children with dirty faces
ask me for charity
child prostitutes
who are not yet fifteen
the streets are paved with pain
tanks that approach
raised bayonets
bodies that fall
weeping
finally I feel my arm
I am no longer a phantom
I hurt
therefore I exist
I return to watch the scene:
children who run
bleeding
women with panic
in their faces
this time it hurts me less
I pinch myself again
and already I feel nothing
I simply reflect
what happens at my side
the tanks
are not tanks
nor are the shouts
shouts
I am a blank mirror
that nothing penetrates
my surface
is hard
is brilliant
is polished
I became a mirror
and I am fleshless
scarcely preserving
a vague memory
of pain.

10

15

20

25

30

35

40

45

50

55

CONNECTIONS TO OTHER SELECTIONS

1. Compare the ways in which Alegría uses mirror images to reflect life in El Salvador with Sylvia Plath's concerns in "Mirror" (p. 145).

2. Write an essay comparing the speaker's voice in this poem with that in William Blake's "London" (p. 121). How do the speakers evoke emotional responses to what they describe?

YEHUDA AMICHAI (ISRAEL / 1924–2000)

Considered a leading Hebrew poet, Yehuda Amichai was born in Germany in 1924 and later moved with his family to Jerusalem. Amichai fought with the Jewish Brigade of the British Army during World War II and in the War of Independence. After the war, he attended Hebrew University. His first volume of poetry, *Achshav Uve-Yamin HaAharim* (*Now and in Other Days*), appeared in 1955 and immediately attracted the interest of the poetry-reading public. Widely read and admired outside his country, his works have been translated into thirty-three languages. His *Collected Poems* appeared in 1963; he is also the author of two novels and a book of short stories. *The Selected Poems of Yehuda Amichai* was published in 1996.

Jerusalem, 1985   *1985*

TRANSLATED BY CHANA BLOCH

Scribbled wishes stuck between the stones
of the Wailing Wall:
bits of crumpled, wadded paper.

And across the way, stuck in an old iron gate
half-hidden by jasmine:
"Couldn't make it,
I hope you'll understand."

CONNECTION TO ANOTHER SELECTION

1. Consider the use of irony in this poem and in Emily Dickinson's "I know that He exists" (p. 344).

MAHMOUD DARWISH (PALESTINE / B. 1942)

Born in Al Birweh, a village near Galilee in what is now Israel, Mahmoud Darwish has devoted his life and writing to his Palestinian homeland from which he has been exiled. His commitment to independence for Palestine is evident in his work for the Palestine Liberation Organization and in his publication of more than twenty books of poetry that include *Sand and Other Poems* (1986), *Adam of Two Edens* (2000), and *The Raven's Ink* (2001). In 2001 he was awarded the Lannan Prize for Cultural Freedom. Darwish remains a major literary voice for the Palestinians.

Identity Card   1980

TRANSLATED FROM THE ARABIC BY DENYS JOHNSON-DAVIES

Put it on record.
   I am an Arab
And the number of my card is fifty thousand
I have eight children
And the ninth is due after summer.   5
What's there to be angry about?

Put it on record.
   I am an Arab
Working with comrades of toil in a quarry.
I have eight children   10
For them I wrest the loaf of bread,
The clothes and exercise books
From the rocks
And beg for no alms at your door,
   Lower not myself at your doorstep.   15
   What's there to be angry about?

Put it on record.
   I am an Arab.
I am a name without a title,
Patient in a country where everything   20
Lives in a whirlpool of anger.
   My roots
   Took hold before the birth of time
   Before the burgeoning of the ages,
   Before cypress and olive trees,   25
   Before the proliferation of weeds.

My father is from the family of the plough
   Not from highborn nobles.
And my grandfather was a peasant
   Without line or genealogy.   30
My house is a watchman's hut
   Made of sticks and reeds.
Does my status satisfy you?
   I am a name without a surname.

Put it on record.   35
   I am an Arab.
Color of hair: jet black.

Color of eyes: brown.
My distinguishing features:
    On my head the *'iqal* cords over a *keffiyeh*   40
    Scratching him who touches it.
My address:
    I'm from a village, remote, forgotten,
    Its streets without name
    And all its men in the fields and quarry.   45

    What's there to be angry about?

Put it on record.
    I am an Arab.
You stole my forefathers' vineyards
    And land I used to till,   50
    I and all my children,
    And you left us and all my grandchildren
    Nothing but these rocks.
    Will your government be taking them too
    As is being said?   55

So!
    Put it on record at the top of page one:
    I don't hate people,
    I trespass on no one's property.
And yet, if I were to become hungry   60
    I shall eat the flesh of my usurper.
    Beware, beware of my hunger
    And of my anger!

CONNECTIONS TO OTHER SELECTIONS

1. Discuss the relation between anger and political history in "Identity Card" and in Langston Hughes's "Harlem" (p. 411).
2. Consider "Identity Card" and Norman Stock's "What I Said" (p. 234) as two halves of a dialogue that voice personal responses to public, political events. In what sense do the two poems speak to each other?

TASLIMA NASRIN (BANGLADESH / B. 1962)

Born in Mymensingh, East Pakistan (now Bangladesh), Taslima Nasrin earned her medical degree in 1984. In addition to working as a physician in Dacca hospitals, she made a career as a prolific writer of fiction, poetry, and nonfiction, focusing particularly on women's oppression. Her widely translated writing has been condemned by conservative mullahs and religious fundamentalists, who have demanded that her books be banned and that she be executed. Since the early 1990s she has lived in the United States, Calcutta, and Europe, where the European Parliament awarded her the Sakharov Prize in Freedom of Thought in 1994. Her collections of poetry include *The Game in Reverse* (1995).

At the Back of Progress...

1995

TRANSLATED FROM THE BENGALI BY CAROLYNE WRIGHT AND MOHAMMAD NURUL HUDA

The fellow who sits in the air-conditioned office
is the one who in his youth raped
          a dozen or so young girls
and at the cocktail party, he's secretly stricken with lust
fastening his eyes on the belly button of some lovely.   5
In the five-star hotels, this fellow frequently
        tries out his different tastes
        in sex acts with a variety of women.
This fellow goes home and beats his wife
        over a handkerchief   10
        or a shirt collar.
This fellow sits in his office and talks with people
        puffing on a cigarette
        and shuffling through his files.

        Ringing the bell he calls his employee   15
            shouts at him
        orders the bearer to bring tea
            and drinks.
    This fellow gives out character references for people.

The employee who's speaking in such a low voice   20
that no one knows or would ever suspect
how much he could raise his voice at home,
        how foul his language could be
        how vile his behavior.
Gathering with his buddies, he buys some movie tickets   25
and kicking back on the porch outside, indulges
        in loud harangues on politics, art and literature.
Someone is committing suicide   his mother
            or his grandmother
            or his great-grandmother.   30
Returning home he beats his wife
        over a bar of soap or
        the baby's pneumonia.

The bearer who brings the tea
who keeps the lighter in his pocket   35
and who gets a couple of *tākā* as a tip:
he's divorced his first wife for her sterility,
his second wife for giving birth to a daughter,

he's divorced his third wife for not bringing dowry.
Returning home, this fellow beats his fourth wife   40
over a couple of green chiles or a handful of cooked rice.

CONNECTIONS TO OTHER SELECTIONS

1. Discuss the status of women in Nasrin's poem and in Eliza Griswold's "Occupation" (p. 202). Which poem, in your opinion, presents women in a more desperate situation? Explain your response.
2. Compare the treatment of men in Nasrin's poem and in Daisy Fried's "Wit's End" (p. 519). How do the cultural differences depicted in the poems result in divergent tones?

PABLO NERUDA (CHILE / 1904–1973)

Born in Chile, Pablo Neruda insisted all of his life on the connection between poetry and politics. He was an activist and a Chilean diplomat in a number of countries during the 1920s and 1930s and remained politically active until his death. Neruda was regarded as a great and influential poet (he was awarded the Nobel Prize in 1971) whose poetry ranged from specific political issues to the yearnings of romantic love. Among his many works are *Twenty Love Poems and a Song of Despair* (1924), *Residence on Earth* (three series, 1925–45), *Spain in the Heart* (1937), *The Captain's Verses* (1952), and *Memorial of Isla Negra* (1964).

The United Fruit Co. 1950

TRANSLATED BY ROBERT BLY

When the trumpet sounded, it was
all prepared on the earth,
and Jehovah parceled out the earth
to Coca-Cola, Inc., Anaconda,
Ford Motors, and other entities: 5
The Fruit Company, Inc.
reserved for itself the most succulent,
the central coast of my own land,
the delicate waist of America.
It rechristened its territories   10
as the "Banana Republics"
and over the sleeping dead,
over the restless heroes
who brought about the greatness,
the liberty and the flags,   15

it established the comic opera:
abolished the independencies,
presented crowns of Caesar,
unsheathed envy, attracted
the dictatorship of the flies,   20
Trujillo flies, Tacho flies,
Carias flies, Martinez flies,
Ubico flies, damp flies
of modest blood and marmalade,
drunken flies who zoom   25
over the ordinary graves,
circus flies, wise flies
well trained in tyranny.

Among the bloodthirsty flies
the Fruit Company lands its ships,   30
taking off the coffee and the fruit;
the treasure of our submerged
territories flows as though
on plates into the ships.

Meanwhile Indians are falling   35
into the sugared chasms
of the harbors, wrapped
for burial in the mist of the dawn:
a body rolls, a thing
that has no name, a fallen cipher,   40
a cluster of dead fruit
thrown down on the dump.

Connections to Other Selections

1. Discuss the political perspective in this poem and in Julio Marzán's "The Translator at the Reception for Latin American Writers" (p. 280). What significant similarities are there between the two poems?

2. Contrast the treatment of fruit in this poem and in Galway Kinnell's "Blackberry Eating" (p. 189).

Octavio Paz (Mexico / 1914–1998)

Born in Mexico City, Octavio Paz studied at the National Autonomous University and in 1943 helped found one of Mexico's most important literary reviews, the *Prodigal Son*. He served in the Mexican diplomatic corps in Paris, New Delhi, and New York. Much of Paz's poetry reflects Hispanic traditions and European modernism as well as Buddhism. In 1990 he received the Nobel Prize for Literature. Paz's major works include *Sun Stone* (1958), *The Violent Season* (1958), *Salamander* (1962), *Blanco* (1966), *Eastern Rampart* (1968), *Renga* (1971), and *Collected Poems, 1957–1987* (1987).

The Street   1963

A long silent street.
I walk in blackness and I stumble and fall
and rise, and I walk blind, my feet
stepping on silent stones and dry leaves.
Someone behind me also stepping on stones, leaves: 5
if I slow down, he slows;
if I run, he runs. I turn: nobody.
Everything dark and doorless.
Turning and turning among these corners
which lead forever to the street   10
where nobody waits for, nobody follows me,
where I pursue a man who stumbles
and rises and says when he sees me: nobody.

Connections to Other Selections

1. How does the speaker's anxiety in this poem compare with that in Robert Frost's "Acquainted with the Night" (p. 157)?
2. Write an essay comparing the tone of this poem and that of Langston Hughes's "Lenox Avenue: Midnight" (p. 404).

Yousif al-Saʿigh   (Iraq / b. 1932)

Born in Mousil, Yousif al-Saʿigh was educated at the University of Baghdad and is a teacher and writer of poetry, fiction, and nonfiction. His work has appeared in more than fourteen books. *Poems*, his collected poetry translated into English, was published in 1992. "An Iraqi Evening" offers a poignant glimpse of his country's home front during a war.

An Iraqi Evening   1992

TRANSLATED BY SAADI A SIMAWE, RALPH SAVARESE, AND CHUCK MILLER

Clips from the battlefield
in an Iraqi evening:
a peaceable home
two boys
preparing their homework   5
a little girl
absentmindedly drawing on scrap paper
funny pictures.
— breaking news coming shortly.

The entire house becomes ears   10
ten Iraqi eyes glued to the screen in frightened silence.
Smells mingle:
the smell of war
and the smell of just baked bread.
The mother raises her eyes to a photo on the wall   15
whispering
— May God protect you
and she begins preparing supper
quietly
and in her mind   20
clips float past of the battlefield
carefully selected for hope.

    [18 Feburary 1986]°

[18 February 1986]: The Iran-Iraq war was fought from 1980 to 1988 and claimed an estimated 150,000 Iraqis.

CONNECTIONS TO OTHER SELECTIONS

1. Compare the attitudes expressed toward war in "An Iraqi Evening" and in Alfred, Lord Tennyson's "The Charge of the Light Brigade" (p. 231).

2. Discuss how the images in "An Iraqi Evening" and in Dylan Thomas's "The Hand That Signed the Paper" (p. 140) create the respective tone for each poem.

LÉOPOLD SÉDAR SENGHOR (SENEGAL / 1906–2001)

Born in Senegal, Léopold Sédar Senghor was educated in Dakar and Paris. He was a founder of a movement that sought to restore pride in African cultures — a philosophy that was termed *negritude,* meaning the customs and traditions that were long suppressed by colonial rule. In addition to his successful career as a poet, Senghor was also president of Senegal for twenty years.

Totem   *1945*

TRANSLATED BY MELVIN DIXON

I must hide him down in my deepest veins
The Ancestor whose stormy skin
Streaks with lightning and thunder
He is the guardian animal I must hide
Lest I burst the dam of scandal.
He is my loyal blood demanding loyalty,

Protecting my naked pride against myself
And the arrogance of fortunate races . . .

CONNECTIONS TO OTHER SELECTIONS

1. Discuss the significance of the symbols in "Totem" and in Alden Nowlan's "The Bull Moose" (p. 171). Despite their differing subject matter, how can the poems' themes be related to one another?
2. Consider what race means to the speakers in "Totem" and in M. Carl Holman's "Mr. Z" (p. 524).

SHU TING (CHINA / B. 1952)

Born in the Fujian Province of China, Shu Ting (whose real name is Gong Peiyu) was forced in 1969 to live in the countryside for three years, because her father was accused of being hostile to the Cultural Revolution. There she began to read Western literature and write. On her return to the city of Xiamen in 1972, she worked in factories and continued writing poetry that made her one of China's most popular poets and a member of the Chinese Writers' Association. She has been a correspondent for the *Beijing Review* and continues to write poetry that has been translated into ten languages. Two of her poetry collections have been translated into English: *Selected Poems* (1994) and *The Mist of My Heart* (1995).

O Motherland, Dear Motherland   1979

TRANSLATED BY FANG DAI, DENNIS DING, AND EDWARD MORIN

I am the old broken waterwheel beside your river
That has composed a centuries-old song of weariness;
I'm the smoke-smudged miner's lamp on your forehead
That lights your snail-like crawl through the cave of history.
I'm the withered rice-ear, the washed-out roadbed,   5
The barge mired in a silt shoal
As the tow rope cuts
Deeply into your shoulder
— O Motherland.

I am poverty,   10
I'm sorrow,
I'm the bitterly painful hope
Of your generations.
I am the flowers strewn from Apsara's° flowing sleeves

---

14 *Apsara's:* Flying Apsaras, or spirits, played music for the Buddhas.

That after thousands of years still have not reached earth   15
— O Motherland.

I am your untarnished ideal
Just broken away from the cobweb of myths;
I'm a bud of the ancient lotus blanketed under your snow,
I'm your smiling dimple wet with tears;   20
Your newly drawn lime-white starting line.
I'm the scarlet dawn emerging with long shimmering rays
— O Motherland.

I am numbered among your billions,
The sum of your nine million square kilometers.   25
You with the scar-blemished breast
Have nurtured me,
Me the confused, the ponderer, the seething,
So that from my body of flesh and blood
You might eke out   30
Your prosperity, your glory, and your freedom
— O Motherland,
My dear Motherland.

CONNECTIONS TO OTHER SELECTIONS

1. Compare the speaker's tone in this poem and in Mahmoud Darwish's "Identity Card" (p. 574).
2. Discuss the view of China in this poem and the perspective on the United States in Florence Cassen Mayers's "All-American Sestina" (p. 250).

WISŁAWA SZYMBORSKA (POLAND / B. 1923)

Born in Poland, Wisława Szymborska has lived in Cracow since the age of eight. She steadfastly refuses to reveal autobiographical details, insisting that her poems should speak for themselves. With the exception of *Sounds, Feelings, Thoughts: Seventy Poems by Wisława Szymborska* (1981), translated and introduced by Magnus J. Krynski and Robert A. Maguire, and *View with a Grain of Sand: Selected Poems* (1995), translated by Stanislaw Barańczak and Clare Cavanagh, only some of Szymborska's poems have been translated into English. Three of her later poetry collections — as yet untranslated — are *There But for the Grace* (1972), *A Great Number* (1976), and *The People of the Bridge* (1986). She was awarded the Nobel Prize for Literature in 1996.

Nothing's a Gift

1993

TRANSLATED BY STANISLAW BARAŃCZAK AND CLARE CAVANAGH

Nothing's a gift, it's all on loan.
I'm drowning in debts up to my ears.
I'll have to pay for myself
with my self,
give up my life for my life.   5

Here's how it's arranged:
The heart can be repossessed,
the liver, too,
and each single finger and toe.

Too late to tear up the terms,   10
my debts will be repaid,
and I'll be fleeced,
or, more precisely, flayed.

I move about the planet
in a crush of other debtors.   15
Some are saddled with the burden
of paying off their wings.
Others must, willy-nilly,
account for every leaf.

Every tissue in us lies   20
on the debit side.
Not a tentacle or tendril
is for keeps.

The inventory, infinitely detailed,
implies we'll be left   25
not just empty-handed
but handless, too.

I can't remember
where, when, and why
I let someone open   30
this account in my name.

We call the protest against this
the soul.
And it's the only item
not included on the list.   35

CONNECTIONS TO OTHER SELECTIONS

1. Compare attitudes toward the body in this poem and Walt Whitman's "I Sing the Body Electric" (p. 268).

2. Discuss the themes in this poem and in William Wordsworth's "The World Is Too Much with Us" (p. 242).

TOMAS TRANSTRÖMER (SWEDEN / B. 1931)

Born in Stockholm, Tomas Tranströmer has had his work translated more than any other contemporary Scandinavian poet. He has worked as a psychologist with juvenile offenders and people with disabilities. His poetry collections include *Night Vision* (1971), *Windows and Stones: Selected Poems* (1972), *Truth Barriers* (1978), *Selected Poems* (1981), and *New Selected Poems* (1997). Among his awards are the Petrarch Prize (1981) and a lifetime subsidy from the government of Sweden.

April and Silence   *1991*

TRANSLATED BY ROBIN FULTON

Spring lies desolate.
The velvet-dark ditch
crawls by my side
without reflections.

The only thing that shines   5
is yellow flowers.

I am carried in my shadow
like a violin
in its black box.

The only thing I want to say   10
glitters out of reach
like the silver
in a pawnbroker's.

CONNECTIONS TO OTHER SELECTIONS

1. Discuss the description of spring in this poem and in William Carlos Williams's "Spring and All" (p. 631).

2. In an essay explain how the dictions used in this poem and Martín Espada's "Latin Night at the Pawnshop" (p. 78) contribute to the poems' meanings and tone.

24

A Collection
of Poems

© Imogen Cunningham Trust

If there were no poetry on any day in the
world, poetry would be invented that
day. For there would be an intolerable
hunger.
— MURIEL RUKEYSER

ANONYMOUS (TRADITIONAL SCOTTISH BALLAD)
Bonny Barbara Allan

date unknown

It was in and about the Martinmas° time,
    When the green leaves were afalling,
That Sir John Graeme, in the West Country,
    Fell in love with Barbara Allan.

He sent his men down through the town,   5
    To the place where she was dwelling:
"Oh haste and come to my master dear,
    Gin° ye be Barbara Allan."   *if*

1 *Martinmas:* St. Martin's Day, November 11.

Web Research the
poets in this chapter at
bedfordstmartins.com/
meyerpoetry.

O hooly,° hooly rose she up,   *slowly*
    To the place where he was lying,   10
And when she drew the curtain by:
    "Young man, I think you're dying."

"O it's I'm sick, and very, very sick,
    And 'tis a' for Barbara Allan." —
"O the better for me ye's never be,   15
    Tho your heart's blood were aspilling."

"O dinna ye mind,° young man," she said,   *don't you remember*
    "When ye was in the tavern adrinking,
That ye made the health° gae round and round,   *toasts*
    And slighted Barbara Allan?"   20

He turned his face unto the wall,
    And death was with him dealing:
"Adieu, adieu, my dear friends all,
    And be kind to Barbara Allan."

And slowly, slowly raise her up,   25
    And slowly, slowly left him,
And sighing said she could not stay,
    Since death of life had reft him.

She had not gane a mile but twa,
    When she heard the dead-bell ringing,
And every jow° that the dead-bell geid,   30 *stroke*
    It cried, "Woe to Barbara Allan!"

"O mother, mother, make my bed!
    O make it saft and narrow!
Since my love died for me today,   35
    I'll die for him tomorrow."

WILLIAM BLAKE (1757–1827)

The Garden of Love   *1794*

I went to the Garden of Love,
And saw what I never had seen:
A Chapel was built in the midst,
Where I used to play on the green.

And the gates of this Chapel were shut,   5
And "Thou shalt not" writ over the door;
So I turned to the Garden of Love
That so many sweet flowers bore;

And I saw it was filled with graves,
And tomb-stones where flowers should be;   10

Explore contexts
for William Blake on
LiterActive.

And Priests in black gowns were walking their rounds,
And binding with briars my joys and desires.

WILLIAM BLAKE (1757–1827)
Infant Sorrow   1992

My mother groand! my father wept.
Into the dangerous world I leapt:
Helpless naked piping loud:
Like a fiend hid in a cloud.

Struggling in my fathers hands:
Striving against my swadling bands
Bound and weary I thought best
To sulk upon my mothers breast.

ROBERT BLY (B. 1926)
Snowfall in the Afternoon   1962

1

The grass is half-covered with snow.
It was the sort of snowfall that starts in late afternoon.
And now the little houses of the grass are growing dark.

2

If I reached my hands down, near the earth,
I could take handfuls of darkness!   5
A darkness was always there, which we never noticed.

3

As the snow grows heavier, the cornstalks fade farther away,
And the barn moves nearer to the house.
The barn moves all alone in the growing storm.

4

The barn is full of corn, and moving toward us now,   10
Like a hulk blown toward us in a storm at sea;
All the sailors on deck have been blind for many years.

ANNE BRADSTREET (CA. 1612–1672)

Before the Birth of One of Her Children

1678

All things within this fading world hath end,
Adversity doth still our joys attend;
No ties so strong, no friends so dear and sweet,
But with death's parting blow is sure to meet.
The sentence past is most irrevocable,   5
A common thing, yet oh, inevitable.
How soon, my Dear, death may my steps attend,
How soon't may be thy lot to lose thy friend,
We both are ignorant, yet love bids me
These farewell lines to recommend to thee,   10
That when that knot's untied that made us one,
I may seem thine, who in effect am none.
And if I see not half my days that's due,
What nature would, God grant to yours and you;
The many faults that well you know I have   15
Let be interred in my oblivious grave;
If any worth or virtue were in me,
Let that live freshly in thy memory
And when thou feel'st no grief, as I no harms,
Yet love thy dead, who long lay in thine arms,   20
And when thy loss shall be repaid with gains
Look to my little babes, my dear remains.
And if thou love thyself, or loved'st me,
These O protect from stepdame's° injury.   *stepmother's*
And if chance to thine eyes shall bring this verse,   25
With some sad sighs honor my absent hearse;
And kiss this paper for thy love's dear sake,
Who with salt tears this last farewell did take.

ELIZABETH BARRETT BROWNING (1806–1861)

My letters! all dead paper, mute and white!

1850

My letters! all dead paper, mute and white!
And yet they seem alive and quivering
Against my tremulous hands which loose the string
And let them drop down on my knee to-night.
This said, — he wished to have me in his sight   5
Once, as a friend: this fixed a day in spring
To come and touch my hand . . . a simple thing,
Yet I wept for it! — this, . . . the paper's light . . .
Said, *Dear, I love thee*; and I sank and quailed
As if God's future thundered on my past.
This said, *I am thine* — and so its ink has paled   10

GEORGE GORDON, LORD BYRON   (1788–1824)

She Walks in Beauty

1814

From Hebrew Melodies

I

She walks in Beauty, like the night
        Of cloudless climes and starry skies;
And all that's best of dark and bright
        Meet in her aspect and her eyes:
Thus mellowed to that tender light   5
        Which Heaven to gaudy day denies.

II

One shade the more, one ray the less,
        Had half impaired the nameless grace
Which waves in every raven tress,
        Or softly lightens o'er her face;   10
Where thoughts serenely sweet express,
        How pure, how dear their dwelling-place.

III

And on that cheek, and o'er that brow,
        So soft, so calm, yet eloquent,
The smiles that win, the tints that glow,   15
        But tell of days in goodness spent,
A mind at peace with all below,
        A heart whose love is innocent!

LUCILLE CLIFTON   (B. 1936)

this morning (for the girls of eastern high school)

1987

this morning
this morning
              i met myself

coming in

a bright
jungle girl
shining
quick as a snake
a tall

© Christopher Felver.

tree girl a   10
me girl

       i met myself
this morning
coming in

and all day   15
i have been
a black bell
ringing
i survive

       survive   20

survive

JUDITH ORTIZ COFER (B. 1952)

The Game   *1993*

The little humpbacked girl
did not go to school,
but was kept home to help her mother,
an unsmiling woman with other children
whose spines were not twisted   5
into the symbol of a family's shame.

At birth,
on first seeing the child
curled into a question mark,
the eternal *why*   10
she would have to carry home,
she gave her the name of Cruz,
for the cross Christ bore
to Calvary.

In my house,   15
we did not speak of her affliction,
but acted as if Cruz,
whose lovely head
sat incongruously upon a body
made of stuck-together parts —   20
like a child's first attempt
at cutting and pasting a paper doll —
was the same
as any of my other friends.

But when she stood at our door,   25
waiting for me to go out and play,
Mother fell silent, awed, perhaps,
by the sight
of one of her God's small mysteries.

Running to her backyard,   30
Cruz and I would enter a playhouse
she had built of palm fronds
where we'd play her favorite game: "family."
I was always cast in the role
of husband or child — perfect   35
in my parts — I'd praise her lavishly
for the imaginary dishes
she placed before me,
while she laughed, delighted
at my inventions, lost in the game,   40
until it started getting too late
to play pretend.

SAMUEL TAYLOR COLERIDGE (1772–1834)

Kubla Khan: or, a Vision in a Dream°   *1798*

In Xanadu did Kubla Khan°
    A stately pleasure-dome decree:
Where Alph, the sacred river, ran
Through caverns measureless to man
    Down to a sunless sea.   5

So twice five miles of fertile ground
With walls and towers were girdled round:
And here were gardens bright with sinuous rills
Where blossomed many an incense-bearing tree;
And there were forests ancient as the hills,   10
Enfolding sunny spots of greenery.

But oh! that deep romantic chasm which slanted
Down the green hill athwart a cedarn cover!°
A savage place! as holy and enchanted
As e'er beneath a waning moon was haunted   15
By woman wailing for her demon-lover!
And from this chasm, with ceaseless turmoil seething,
As if this earth in fast thick pants were breathing,
A mighty fountain momently was forced,
Amid whose swift half-intermitted burst   20
Huge fragments vaulted like rebounding hail,
Of chaffy grain beneath the thresher's flail:
And 'mid these dancing rocks at once and ever

Vision in a Dream: This poem came to Coleridge in an opium-induced dream, but he was interrupted by a visitor while writing it down. He was later unable to remember the rest of the poem.

1 *Kubla Khan:* The historical Kublai Khan (1216–1294, grandson of Genghis Khan) was the founder of the Mongol dynasty in China.

13 *athwart . . . cover:* Spanning a grove of cedar trees.

It flung up momently the sacred river.
Five miles meandering with a mazy motion   25
Through wood and dale the sacred river ran,
Then reached the caverns measureless to man,
And sank in tumult to a lifeless ocean:
And 'mid this tumult Kubla heard from far
Ancestral voices prophesying war!   30
   The shadow of the dome of pleasure
   Floated midway on the waves;
   Where was heard the mingled measure
   From the fountain and the caves.
It was a miracle of rare device,   35
A sunny pleasure-dome with caves of ice!

   A damsel with a dulcimer
   In a vision once I saw:
   It was an Abyssinian maid,
   And on her dulcimer she played,   40
   Singing of Mount Abora.
   Could I revive within me
   Her symphony and song,
   To such a deep delight 'twould win me,
That with music loud and long,   45
I would build that dome in air,
That sunny dome! those caves of ice!
And all who heard should see them there,
And all should cry, Beware! Beware!
His flashing eyes, his floating hair!   50
Weave a circle round him thrice,
And close your eyes with holy dread,
For he on honey-dew hath fed,
And drunk the milk of Paradise.

RICHARD CRASHAW (1613–1649)

An Epitaph upon a Young Married Couple, Dead and Buried Together   1646

To these, whom death again did wed,
This grave's their second marriage-bed.
For though the hand of fate could force
'Twixt soul and body a divorce,
It could not sunder man and wife   5
'Cause they both livéd but one life.
Peace, good reader. Do not weep.
Peace, the lovers are asleep.
They, sweet turtles, folded lie
In the last knot love could tie.   10
And though they lie as they were dead,

Their pillow stone, their sheets of lead,
(Pillow hard, and sheets not warm)
Love made the bed; they'll take no harm;
Let them sleep, let them sleep on.   15
Till this stormy night be gone,
Till th' eternal morrow dawn;
Then the curtains will be drawn
And they wake into a light,
Whose day shall never die in night.   20

E. E. Cummings (1894–1962)

Buffalo Bill 's°   *1923*

Buffalo Bill 's
defunct
    who used to
      ride a watersmooth-silver
                  stallion   5
and break onetwothreefourfive pigeonsjustlikethat
                    Jesus

he was a handsome man
              and what i want to know is
how do you like your blueeyed boy   10
Mister Death

Buffalo Bill: William Frederick Cody (1846–1917) was an American frontier scout and Indian killer turned international circus showman with his Wild West show, which employed Sitting Bull and Annie Oakley.

Gregory Djanikian (b. 1949)

When I First Saw Snow   *1989*

Tarrytown, N.Y.

Bing Crosby was singing "White Christmas"
    on the radio, we were staying at my aunt's house
    waiting for papers, my father was looking for a job.
We had trimmed the tree the night before,
    sap had run on my fingers and for the first time   5
    I was smelling pine wherever I went.
Anais, my cousin, was upstairs in her room
    listening to Danny and the Juniors.
Haigo was playing Monopoly with Lucy, his sister,
    Buzzy, the boy next door, had eyes for her   10
    and there was a rattle of dice, a shuffling

of Boardwalk, Park Place, Marvin Gardens.
There were red bows on the Christmas tree.
It had snowed all night.
My boot buckles were clinking like small bells   15
    as I thumped to the door and out
    onto the gray planks of the porch dusted with snow.
The world was immaculate, new,
    even the trees had changed color,
    and when I touched the snow on the railing   20
    I didn't know what I had touched, ice or fire.
I heard, "I'm dreaming . . ."
I heard, "At the hop, hop, hop . . . oh, baby."
I heard "B & O" and the train in my imagination
    was whistling through the great plains.   25
And I was stepping off,
I was falling deeply into America.

John Donne (1572–1631)

The Apparition
c. 1600

When by thy scorn, O murderess, I am dead,
    And that thou thinkst thee free
From all solicitation from me,
Then shall my ghost come to thy bed,
And thee, feigned vestal, in worse arms shall see;   5
Then thy sick taper° will begin to wink,   *candle*
And he, whose thou art then, being tired before,
Will, if thou stir, or pinch to wake him, think
    Thou call'st for more,
And in false sleep will from thee shrink.   10
And then, poor aspen wretch, neglected, thou,
Bathed in a cold quicksilver sweat, wilt lie
    A verier° ghost than I.   *truer*
What I will say, I will not tell thee now,
Lest that preserve thee; and since my love is spent,   15
I had rather thou shouldst painfully repent,
Than by my threatenings rest still innocent.

John Donne (1572–1631)

Batter My Heart
1610

Batter my heart, three-personed God; for You
As yet but knock, breathe, shine, and seek to mend;
That I may rise and stand, o'erthrow me, and bend
Your force, to break, blow, burn, and make me new.

I, like an usurped town, to another due,   5
Labor to admit You, but Oh, to no end!
Reason, Your viceroy in me, me should defend,
But is captived, and proves weak or untrue.
Yet dearly I love You, and would be loved fain.
But am betrothed unto Your enemy: 10
Divorce me, untie, or break that knot again,
Take me to You, imprison me, for I,
Except You enthrall me, never shall be free,
Nor ever chaste, except You ravish me.

JOHN DONNE (1572–1631)

The Flea   *1633*

Mark but this flea, and mark in this°
How little that which thou deny'st me is;
It sucked me first, and now sucks thee,
And in this flea our two bloods mingled be;
Thou know'st that this cannot be said   5
A sin, nor shame, nor loss of maidenhead,
      Yet this enjoys before it woo,
        And pampered swells with one blood made of two,
          And this, alas, is more than we would do.°

Oh stay, three lives in one flea spare,   10
Where we almost, yea more than, married are.
This flea is you and I, and this
Our marriage bed, and marriage temple is;
Though parents grudge, and you, we're met
And cloistered in these living walls of jet.   15
      Though use° make you apt to kill me,   *habit*
      Let not to that, self-murder added be,
        And sacrilege, three sins in killing three.

Cruel and sudden, hast thou since
Purpled thy nail in blood of innocence?   20
Wherein could this flea guilty be,
Except in that drop which it sucked from thee?
Yet thou triumph'st, and say'st that thou
Find'st not thyself, nor me, the weaker now;
      'Tis true; then learn how false, fears be;   25
      Just so much honor, when thou yield'st to me,
        Will waste, as this flea's death took life from thee.

---

1 *mark in this:* Take note of the moral lesson in this object.   9 *more than we would do:* That
is, if we do not join our blood in conceiving a child.

GEORGE ELIOT (MARY ANN EVANS / 1819–1880)

In a London Drawingroom

1865

The sky is cloudy, yellowed by the smoke.
For view there are the houses opposite,
Cutting the sky with one long line of wall
Like solid fog: far as the eye can stretch
Monotony of surface and of form   5
Without a break to hang a guess upon.
No bird can make a shadow as it flies,
For all its shadow, as in ways o'erhung
By thickest canvas, where the golden rays
Are clothed in hemp. No figure lingering   10
Pauses to feed the hunger of the eye
Or rest a little on the lap of life.
All hurry on and look upon the ground
Or glance unmarking at the passersby.
The wheels are hurrying, too, cabs, carriages   15
All closed, in multiplied identity.
The world seems one huge prison-house and court
Where men are punished at the slightest cost,
With lowest rate of color, warmth, and joy.

CHARLOTTE PERKINS GILMAN (1860–1935)

Anonymous – No clear speaker

Whatever Is

1903

What about our minds keeps us from the truth?

Whatever is we only know   a
As in our minds we find it so;   a
    No staring fact is half so clear   b
    As one dim, preconceived idea —   b
No matter how the fact may glow.   a   5

Vainly may Truth her trumpet blow   a
To stir our minds; like heavy dough   a
    They stick to what they think — won't hear   b
        Whatever is.

Our ancient myths in solid row   a   10
Stand up — we simply have to go   a
    And choke each fiction old and dear   b
    Before the modest facts appear;   b
Then we may grasp, reluctant, slow,   a
        Whatever is.   15

SAM HAMILL (B. 1942)

Sheepherder Coffee 2003

I used to like sheepherder coffee,
a cup of grounds in my old enameled pot,
then three cups of water and a fire,

and when it's hot, boiling into froth,
a half cup of cold water 5
to bring the grounds to the bottom.

It was strong and bitter and good
as I squatted on the riverbank,
under the great redwoods, all those years ago.

Some days, it was nearly all I got. 10
I was happy with my dog,
and cases of books in my funky truck.

But when I think of that posture now,
I can't help but think
of Palestinians huddled in their ruins, 15

the Afghani shepherd with his bleating goats,
the widow weeping, sending off her sons,
the Tibetan monk who can't go home.

There are fewer names for coffee
than for love. Squatting, they drink, 20
thinking, waiting for whatever comes.

THOMAS HARDY (1840–1928)

Hap 1866

If but some vengeful god would call to me
From up the sky, and laugh: "Thou suffering thing,
Know that thy sorrow is my ecstasy,
That thy love's loss is my hate's profiting!"

Then would I bear it, clench myself, and die, 5
Steeled by the sense of ire unmerited;
Half-eased in that a Powerfuller than I
Had willed and meted me the tears I shed.

But not so. How arrives it joy lies slain,
And why unblooms the best hope ever sown? 10
— Crass Casualty obstructs the sun and rain,
And dicing Time for gladness casts a moan. . . .
These purblind Doomsters had as readily strown
Blisses about my pilgrimage as pain.

THOMAS HARDY (1840–1928)
In Time of "The Breaking of Nations"°

1915

1

Only a man harrowing clods
    In a slow silent walk
With an old horse that stumbles and nods
    Half asleep as they stalk.

2

Only thin smoke without flame   5
    From the heaps of couch-grass;
Yet this will go onward the same
    Though Dynasties pass.

3

Yonder a maid and her wight°   *man*
    Come whispering by: 10
War's annals will cloud into night
    Ere their story die.

The Breaking of Nations: See Jeremiah 51:20: "Thou art my battle axe and weapons of war: for with thee will I break in pieces the nations, and with thee will I destroy kingdoms."

JOY HARJO (B. 1951)
The Path to the Milky Way Leads through Los Angeles

2000

There are strangers above me, below me and all around me and we are all
strange in this place of recent invention.
This city named for angels appears naked and stripped of anything
    resembling
the shaking of turtle shells, the songs of human voices on a summer night
outside Okmulgee.°   5
Yet, it's perpetually summer here, and beautiful. The shimmer of gods is easier
to perceive at sunrise or dusk,
when those who remember us here in the illusion of the marketplace
turn toward the changing of the sun and say our names.
We matter to somebody,   10
We must matter to the strange god who imagines us as we revolve together in
the dark sky on the path to the Milky Way.

5 *Okmulgee:* The name of a city in Oklahoma and the Creek word for bubbling water.

We can't easily see that starry road from the perspective of the crossing of
boulevards, can't hear it in the whine of civilization or taste the minerals of
planets in hamburgers.   15
But we can buy a map here of the stars' homes, dial a tone for dangerous love,
choose from several brands of water or a hiss of oxygen for gentle
    rejuvenation.
Everyone knows you can't buy love but you can still sell your soul for less
    than a song to a stranger who will sell it to someone else for a profit
until you're owned by a company of strangers
in the city of the strange and getting stranger.   20
I'd rather understand how to sing from a crow
who was never good at singing or much of anything
but finding gold in the trash of humans.
So what are we doing here I ask the crow parading on the ledge of falling that
hangs over this precarious city?   25
Crow° just laughs and says *wait, wait and see* and I am waiting and not seeing
anything, not just yet.
But like crow I collect the shine of anything beautiful I can find.

26 *Crow:* A mythic Native American trickster character.

Frances E. W. Harper (1825–1911)

Learning to Read   1872

Very soon the Yankee teachers
    Came down and set up school;
But oh! how the Rebs did hate it, —
    It was agin' their rule

Our masters always tried to hide   5
    Book learning from our eyes;
Knowledge did'nt agree with slavery —
    'Twould make us all too wise.

But some of us would try to steal
    A little from the book,   10
And put the words together,
    And learn by hook or crook.

I remember Uncle Caldwell,
    Who took pot-liquor fat
And greased the pages of his book,   15
    And hid it in his hat.

And had his master ever seen
    The leaves upon his head,
He'd have thought them greasy papers,
    But nothing to be read.   20

And there was Mr. Turner's Ben
    Who heard the children spell,
And picked the words right up by heart,
    And learned to read 'em well.

Well the Northern folks kept sending   25
    The Yankee teachers down
And they stood right up and helped us,
    Though Rebs did sneer and frown,

And, I longed to read my Bible,
    For precious words it said;   30
But when I begun to learn it,
    Folks just shook their heads,

And said there is no use trying,
    Oh! Chloe, you're too late;
But as I was rising sixty,   35
    I had no time to wait.

So I got a pair of glasses,
    And straight to work I went,
And never stopped till I could read
    The hymns and Testament.   40

Then I got a little cabin —
    A place to call my own —
And I felt as independent
    As the queen upon her throne.

GEORGE HERBERT (1593–1633)

The Collar

1633

I struck the board° and cried, "No more;   *table*
          I will abroad!
What? shall I ever sigh and pine?
My lines and life are free, free as the road,
    Loose as the wind, as large as store.°   5
        Shall I be still in suit?°   *serving another*
    Have I no harvest but a thorn
    To let me blood, and not restore
What I have lost with cordial° fruit?   *restorative*
        Sure there was wine   10
    Before my sighs did dry it; there was corn
        Before my tears did drown it.
    Is the year only lost to me?

5 *store:* A storehouse or warehouse.

Have I no bays° to crown it,   *triumphal wreaths*
No flowers, no garlands gay? All blasted?   15
    All wasted?
Not so, my heart; but there is fruit,
    And thou hast hands.
Recover all thy sigh-blown age
On double pleasures: leave thy cold dispute   20
Of what is fit, and not. Forsake thy cage,
    Thy rope of sands,
Which petty thoughts have made, and made to thee
    Good cable, to enforce and draw,
      And be thy law,   25
While thou didst wink and wouldst not see.
      Away! take heed;
      I will abroad.
Call in thy death's-head° there; tie up thy fears.
    He that forbears   30
    To suit and serve his need,
      Deserves his load."
But as I raved and grew more fierce and wild
    At every word,
Methought I heard one calling, *Child!*   35
    And I replied, *My Lord.*

29 *death's-head:* A skull, reminder of mortality.

CONRAD HILBERRY (B. 1928)

The Calvinist   *1999*

I like to think words go
their own way—like *waterspout*
or *sleep* or *Aztec soup*—but
in the chamber just behind

my tongue a Calvinist   5
sits at a thin-legged desk,
interjecting, editing. He
adds his touch, wrapping

a small message around the leg
of each pigeon as it comes   10
from the dovecote. The words
fly out, clattering white

against the sky, circling,
flashing in the sun like bits
of torn paper. But then   15
they feel the compass-pull,

feel the slight weight
of the message on their legs
and in a ragged line
head for home.   20

GERARD MANLEY HOPKINS (1844–1889)

Hurrahing in Harvest   *1877*

Summer ends now; now, barbarous in beauty, the stooks° arise   *sheaves*
    Around; up above, what wind-walks! what lovely behaviour
    Of silk-sack clouds! has wilder, wilful-wavier
Meal-drift moulded ever and melted across skies?

I walk, I lift up, I lift up heart, eyes,   5
    Down all that glory in the heavens to glean our Saviour;
    And, éyes, heárt, what looks, what lips yet gave you a
Rapturous love's greeting of realer, of rounder replies?

And the azurous hung hills are his world-wielding shoulder
    Majestic — as a stallion stalwart, very-violet-sweet! —   10
These things, these things were here and but the beholder
    Wanting; which two when they once meet,
The heart rears wings bold and bolder
    And hurls for him, O half hurls earth for him off under his feet.

GERARD MANLEY HOPKINS (1844–1889)

Pied Beauty   *1877*

Glory be to God for dappled things —
        For skies of couple-color as a brinded cow;
                For rose-moles all in stipple upon trout that swim;
Fresh-firecoal chestnut-falls;° finches' wings;   *fallen chestnut*
        Landscape plotted and pieced — fold, fallow, and plow;   5
                And all trades, their gear and tackle and trim.

All things counter, original, spare, strange;
        Whatever is fickle, freckled (who knows how?)
                With swift, slow; sweet, sour; adazzle, dim;
He fathers-forth whose beauty is past change: 10
                Praise him.

GERARD MANLEY HOPKINS (1844–1889)
The Windhover°
1877

To Christ Our Lord

I caught this morning morning's minion,° king-   *favorite*
  dom of daylight's dauphin, dapple-dawn-drawn Falcon, in his riding
  Of the rolling level underneath him steady air, and striding
High there, how he rung upon the rein of a wimpling wing
In his ecstasy! then off, off forth on swing,   5
  As a skate's heel sweeps smooth on a bow-bend: the hurl and gliding
  Rebuffed the big wind. My heart in hiding
Stirred for a bird, — the achieve of, the mastery of the thing!

Brute beauty and valour and act, oh, air, pride, plume, here
  Buckle!° AND the fire that breaks from thee then, a billion 10
Times told lovelier, more dangerous, O my chevalier!

  No wonder of it: shéer plód makes plough down sillion° *furrow*
Shine, and blue-bleak embers, ah my dear,
  Fall, gall themselves, and gash gold-vermilion.

The Windhover: "A name for the kestrel [a kind of small hawk], from its habit of hovering or
hanging with its head to the wind" [*OED*]. 10 *Buckle:* To join, to equip for battle, to
crumple.

A. E. HOUSMAN (1859–1936)
Is my team ploughing
1896

"Is my team ploughing,
  That I was used to drive
And hear the harness jingle
  When I was man alive?"

Ay, the horses trample,   5
  The harness jingles now;
No change though you lie under
  The land you used to plough.

"Is football playing
  Along the river shore,   10
With lads to chase the leather,
  Now I stand up no more?"

Ay, the ball is flying,
  The lads play heart and soul;
The goal stands up, the keeper   15
  Stands up to keep the goal.

"Is my girl happy,
    That I thought hard to leave,
And has she tired of weeping
    As she lies down at eve?"   20

Ay, she lies down lightly,
    She lies not down to weep:
Your girl is well contented.
    Be still, my lad, and sleep.

"Is my friend hearty,   25
    Now I am thin and pine,
And has he found to sleep in
    A better bed than mine?"

Yes, lad, I lie easy,
    I lie as lads would choose;   30
I cheer a dead man's sweetheart,
    Never ask me whose.

A. E. HOUSMAN (1859–1936)

To an Athlete Dying Young   *1896*

The time you won your town the race
We chaired° you through the marketplace;
Man and boy stood cheering by,
And home we brought you shoulder-high.

Today, the road all runners come,   5
Shoulder-high we bring you home,
And set you at your threshold down,
Townsman of a stiller town.

Smart lad, to slip betimes away
From fields where glory does not stay,   10
And early though the laurel° grows
It withers quicker than the rose.

Eyes the shady night has shut
Cannot see the record cut,
And silence sounds no worse than cheers   15
After earth has stopped the ears:

Now you will not swell the rout
Of lads that wore their honors out,
Runners whom renown outran
And the name died before the man.   20

---

2 *chaired:* Carried on the shoulders in triumphal parade.   11 *laurel:* Flowering shrub traditionally used to fashion wreaths of honor.

To set, before its echoes fade,
The fleet foot on the sill of shade,
And hold to the low lintel up
The still-defended challenge-cup.

And round that early-laureled head   25
Will flock to gaze the strengthless dead,
And find unwithered on its curls
The garland briefer than a girl's.

JULIA WARD HOWE (1819–1910)
Battle-Hymn of the Republic   1862

Mine eyes have seen the glory of the coming of the Lord:
He is trampling out the vintage where the grapes of wrath are stored;
He hath loosed the fateful lightning of his terrible swift sword:
        His truth is marching on.

I have seen Him in the watch-fires of a hundred circling camps;   5
They have builded Him an altar in the evening dews and damps;
I can read His righteous sentence by the dim and flaring lamps.
        His day is marching on.

I have read a fiery gospel, writ in burnished rows of steel:
"As ye deal with my contemners, so with you my grace shall deal;   10
Let the Hero, born of woman, crush the serpent with his heel,
        Since God is marching on."

He has sounded forth the trumpet that shall never call retreat;
He is sifting out the hearts of men before his judgment-seat:
Oh! be swift, my soul, to answer Him! be jubilant, my feet!   15
        Our God is marching on.

In the beauty of the lilies Christ was born across the sea,
With a glory in his bosom that transfigures you and me:
As he died to make men holy, let us die to make men free,
    While God is marching on.   20

BEN JONSON (1573–1637)
On My First Son   1603

Farewell, thou child of my right hand,° and joy.
My sin was too much hope of thee, loved boy;
Seven years thou wert lent to me, and I thee pay,
Exacted by thy fate, on the just day.°   *his birthday*

---

1 *child of my right hand:* This phrase translates the Hebrew name "Benjamin," Jonson's son.

Oh, could I lose all father° now. For why   *fatherhood* 5
Will man lament the state he should envỳ? —
To have so soon 'scaped world's and flesh's rage,
And, if no other misery, yet age.
Rest in soft peace, and asked, say, "Here doth lie
Ben Jonson his best piece of poetry,"   10
For whose sake henceforth all his vows be such
As what he loves may never like too much.

BEN JONSON (1573–1637)

To Celia   *1616*

Drink to me only with thine eyes,
    And I will pledge with mine;
Or leave a kiss but in the cup,
    And I'll not ask for wine.
The thirst that from the soul doth rise   5
    Doth ask a drink divine;
But might I of Jove's nectar sup,
    I would not change for thine.

I sent thee late a rosy wreath,
    Not so much honoring thee   10
As giving it a hope that there
    It could not withered be.
But thou thereon didst only breathe,
    And sent'st it back to me;
Since when it grows, and smells, I swear,   15
    Not of itself but thee.

JUNE JORDAN (1936–2002)

The Reception   *1994*

Doretha wore the short blue lace last night
and William watched her drinking so she fight
with him in flying collar slim-jim orange
tie and alligator belt below the navel pants uptight

'I flirt. You hear me? Yes I flirt.   5
Been on my pretty knees all week
to clean the rich white downtown dirt
the greedy garbage money reek.

I flirt. Damned right. You look at me.'
But William watched her carefully   10
his mustache shaky she could see
him jealous, 'which is how he always be

at parties.' Clementine and Wilhelmina
looked at trouble in the light blue lace
and held to George while Roosevelt Senior   15
circled by the yella high and bitterly light blue face

He liked because she worked
the crowded room like clay like molding men
from dust to muscle jerked
the arms and shoulders moving when   20
she moved.

The Lord Almighty Seagrams
bless
Doretha in her short blue dress
and Roosevelt waiting for his chance: 25
a true gut-funky blues to make her really dance.

JOHN KEATS (1795–1821)

To one who has been long in city pent   *1816*

To one who has been long in city pent,
 'Tis very sweet to look into the fair
  And open face of heaven, — to breathe a prayer
Full in the smile of the blue firmament.
Who is more happy, when, with heart's content,   5
 Fatigued he sinks into some pleasant lair
  Of wavy grass, and reads a debonair
And gentle tale of love and languishment?

Returning home at evening, with an ear
 Catching the notes of Philomel,° — an eye   *A nightingale* 10
Watching the sailing cloudlet's bright career,
 He mourns that day so soon has glided by:
E'en like the passage of an angel's tear
  That falls through the clear ether silently.

JOHN KEATS (1795–1821)

The Human Seasons   *1818*

Four seasons fill the measure of the year;
 Four seasons are there in the mind of man.
He hath his lusty spring, when fancy clear
 Takes in all beauty with an easy span:
He hath his summer, when luxuriously   5
 He chews the honied cud of fair spring thoughts,
Till, in his soul dissolv'd, they come to be
 Part of himself. He hath his autumn ports

And havens of repose, when his tired wings
    Are folded up, and he content to look   10
On mists in idleness: to let fair things
    Pass by unheeded as a threshold brook.
He hath his winter too of pale misfeature,
Or else he would forget his mortal nature.

John Keats (1795–1821)
When I have fears that I may cease to be   *1818*

When I have fears that I may cease to be
    Before my pen has gleaned my teeming brain,
Before high-piled books, in charactery,°   *print*
    Hold like rich garners the full ripened grain;
When I behold, upon the night's starred face,   5
    Huge cloudy symbols of a high romance,
And think that I may never live to trace
    Their shadows, with the magic hand of chance;
And when I feel, fair creature of an hour,
    That I shall never look upon thee more,   10
Never have relish in the faery° power   *magic*
    Of unreflecting love; — then on the shore
Of the wide world I stand alone, and think
Till love and fame to nothingness do sink.

John Keats (1795–1821)
La Belle Dame sans Merci°   *1819*

O what can ail thee, knight-at-arms,
    Alone and palely loitering?
The sedge has withered from the lake,
    And no birds sing.

O what can ail thee, knight-at-arms,   5
    So haggard and so woe-begone?
The squirrel's granary is full,
    And the harvest's done.

I see a lily on thy brow,
    With anguish moist and fever dew,
And on thy cheeks a fading rose   10
    Fast withereth too.

La Belle Dame sans Merci: This title is borrowed from a medieval poem and means "The Beautiful Lady without Mercy."

I met a lady in the meads,
  Full beautiful — a faery's child,
Her hair was long, her foot was light,   15
  And her eyes were wild.

I made a garland for her head,
  And bracelets too, and fragrant zone;°   *belt*
She looked at me as she did love,
  And made sweet moan.   20

I set her on my pacing steed,
  And nothing else saw all day long,
For sidelong would she bend, and sing
  A faery's song.

She found me roots of relish sweet,   25
  And honey wild, and manna dew,
And sure in language strange she said,
  "I love thee true."

She took me to her elfin grot,
  And there she wept, and sighed full sore,   30
And there I shut her wild wild eyes
  With kisses four.

And there she lullèd me asleep,
  And there I dreamed — Ah! woe betide!
The latest° dream I ever dreamed   *last* 35
  On the cold hill side.

I saw pale kings and princes too,
  Pale warriors, death-pale were they all;
They cried — "La Belle Dame sans Merci
  Hath thee in thrall!"   40

I saw their starved lips in the gloam,
  With horrid warning gapèd wide,
And I awoke and found me here,
  On the cold hill's side.

And this is why I sojourn here,   45
  Alone and palely loitering,
Though the sedge has withered from the lake,
  And no birds sing.

Yusef Komunyakaa (b. 1947)

Slam, Dunk, & Hook   *1992*

Fast breaks. Lay ups. With Mercury's
Insignia on our sneakers,
We outmaneuvered the footwork
Of bad angels. Nothing but a hot

Swish of strings like silk   5
Ten feet out. In the roundhouse
Labyrinth our bodies
Created, we could almost
Last forever, poised in midair
Like storybook sea monsters.   10
A high note hung there
A long second. Off
The rim. We'd corkscrew
Up & dunk balls that exploded
The skullcap of hope & good   15
Intention. Bug-eyed, lanky,
All hands & feet . . . sprung rhythm.
We were metaphysical when girls
Cheered on the sidelines.
Tangled up in a falling,   20
Muscles were a bright motor
Double-flashing to the metal hoop
Nailed to our oak.
When Sonny Boy's mama died
He played nonstop all day, so hard   25
Our backboard splintered.
Glistening with sweat, we jibed
& rolled the ball off our
Fingertips. Trouble
Was there slapping a blackjack   30
Against an open palm.
Dribble, drive to the inside, feint,
& glide like a sparrow hawk.
Layups. Fast breaks.
We had moves we didn't know   35
We had. Our bodies spun

On swivels of bone & faith,
Through a lyric slipknot
Of joy, & we knew we were
Beautiful & dangerous.   40

TED KOOSER (B. 1939)

A Death at the Office   *1980*

The news goes desk to desk
like a memo: *Initial
and pass on.* Each of us marks
Surprised or *Sorry.*

The management came early   5
and buried her nameplate

Mother with infant down the rocks.° Their moans
The vales redoubled to the hills, and they
     To heaven. Their martyred blood and ashes sow   10
O'er all the Italian fields, where still doth sway
     The triple Tyrant;° that from these may grow
     A hundredfold, who, having learnt thy way,
     Early may fly the Babylonian woe.°

5–8 *in thy book . . . rocks:* On Easter Day, 1655, 1,700 members of the Waldensian sect were massacred in Piedmont by the duke of Savoy's forces.

12 *triple Tyrant:* The Pope, with his three-crowned tiara, has authority on earth and in Heaven and Hell.

14 *Babylonian woe:* The destruction of Babylon, symbol of vice and corruption, at the end of the world (see Rev. 17–18). Protestants interpreted the "Whore of Babylon" as the Roman Catholic Church.

John Milton (1608–1674)

When I consider how my light is spent   *c. 1655*

When I consider how my light is spent,°
     Ere half my days in this dark world and wide,
     And that one talent° which is death to hide
Lodged with me useless, though my soul more bent
To serve therewith my Maker, and present   5
     My true account, lest He returning chide;
     "Doth God exact day-labor, light denied?"
I fondly° ask. But Patience, to prevent   *foolishly*
That murmur, soon replies, "God doth not need
     Either man's work or His own gifts. Who best   10
     Bear His mild yoke, they serve Him best. His state
Is kingly: thousands at His bidding speed,
     And post o'er land and ocean without rest;
     They also serve who only stand and wait."

1 *how my light is spent:* Milton had been totally blind since 1651.   3 *that one talent:* Refers to Jesus' parable of the talents (units of money), in which a servant entrusted with a talent buries it rather than invests it and is punished on his master's return (Matt. 25:14–30).

N. Scott Momaday (b. 1934)

Crows in a Winter Composition   *1976*

This morning the snow,
The soft distances
Beyond the trees
In which nothing appeared —

Nothing appeared.   5
The several silences,
Imposed one upon another,
Were unintelligible.

I was therefore ill at ease
When the crows came down,   10
Whirling down and calling,
Into the yard below
And stood in a mindless manner
On the gray, luminous crust,
Altogether definite, composed,   15
In the bright enmity of my regard,
In the hard nature of crows.

SARAH MORGAN BRYAN PIATT (1836–1919)

A New Thanksgiving   *1910*

For war, plague, pestilence, flood, famine, fire,
   For Christ discrowned, for false gods set on high;
For fools, whose hands must have their hearts' desire,
   We thank Thee — in the darkness — and so die.

For shipwreck: Oh, the sob of strangling seas! —   5
   No matter. For the snake that charms the dove;
And (is it not the bitterest of all these?)
   We thank Thee — in our blind faith — even for Love.

For breaking hearts; for all that breaks the heart;
   For Death, the one thing after all the rest,   10
We thank Thee, O our Father! Thou who art,
   And wast, and shalt be — knowing these are best.

MARGE PIERCY (B. 1936)

For the Young Who Want To   *1982*

Talent is what they say
you have after the novel
is published and favorably
reviewed. Beforehand what
you have is a tedious   5
delusion, a hobby like knitting.

Work is what you have done
after the play is produced
and the audience claps.

Before that friends keep asking   10
when you are planning to go
out and get a job.

Genius is what they know you
had after the third volume
of remarkable poems. Earlier   15
they accuse you of withdrawing,
ask why you don't have a baby,
call you a bum.

The reason people want M.F.A.'s,
take workshops with fancy names   20
when all you can really
learn is a few techniques,
typing instructions and some-
body else's mannerisms

is that every artist lacks   25
a license to hang on the wall
like your optician, your vet
proving you may be a clumsy sadist
whose fillings fall into the stew
but you're certified a dentist.   30

The real writer is one
who really writes. Talent
is an invention like phlogiston°
after the fact of fire.
Work is its own cure. You have to   35
like it better than being loved.

33 *phlogiston:* A pre-nineteenth century term used to explain (erroneously) why things
burned.

SIR WALTER RALEIGH (1554–1618)

The Nymph's Reply to the Shepherd   *1600*

If all the world and love were young,
And truth in every shepherd's tongue,
These pretty pleasures might me move
To live with thee and be thy love.

Time drives the flocks from field to fold,   5
When rivers rage and rocks grow cold,
And Philomel° becometh dumb;   *nightingale*
The rest complains of cares to come.

The flowers do fade, and wanton fields
To wayward winter reckoning yields;   10
A honey tongue, a heart of gall,
Is fancy's spring, but sorrow's fall.

Thy gowns, thy shoes, thy beds of roses,
Thy cap, thy kirtle, and thy posies
Soon break, soon wither, soon forgotten —   15
In folly ripe, in reason rotten.

Thy belt of straw and ivy buds,
Thy coral clasps and amber studs,
All these in me no means can move
To come to thee and be thy love.   20

But could youth last and love still breed,
Had joys no date° nor age no need,   *end*
Then these delights my mind might move
To live with thee and be thy love.

Christina Georgina Rossetti
(1830–1894)

Some Ladies Dress in Muslin Full and White   *c. 1848*

© Bettmann/CORBIS.

      Some ladies dress in muslin full and
          white,
Some gentlemen in cloth succinct and black;
Some patronise a dog-cart, some a hack,
      Some think a painted clarence only
          right.
      Youth is not always such a pleasing
          sight:
Witness a man with tassels on his back;
Or woman in a great-coat like a sack,
      Towering above her sex with horrid height.
If all the world were water fit to drown,
      There are some whom you would not teach to swim,   10
    Rather enjoying if you saw them sink:
    Certain old ladies dressed in girlish pink,
With roses and geraniums on their gown.
      Go to the basin, poke them o'er the rim —

Christina Georgina Rossetti (1830–1894)

In Progress   *1862*

Ten years ago it seemed impossible
    That she should ever grow so calm as this,
    With self-remembrance in her warmest kiss
And dim dried eyes like an exhausted well.

Slow-speaking when she has some fact to tell,   5
    Silent with long-unbroken silences,
    Centred in self yet not unpleased to please,
Gravely monotonous like a passing bell.

Mindful of drudging daily common things,
    Patient at pastime, patient at her work,   10
Wearied perhaps but strenuous certainly.
Sometimes I fancy we may one day see
    Her head shoot forth seven stars from where they lurk
And her eyes lightnings and her shoulders wings.

CHRISTINA GEORGINA ROSSETTI (1830–1894)

The World   *1862*

    By day she wooes me, soft, exceeding fair:
    But all night as the moon so changeth she;
    Loathsome and foul with hideous leprosy
        And subtle serpents gliding in her hair.
        By day she wooes me to the outer air,   5
    Ripe fruits, sweet flowers, and full satiety:
    But thro' the night, a beast she grins at me,
        A very monster void of love and prayer.
    By day she stands a lie: by night she stands
        In all the naked horror of the truth   10
With pushing horns and clawed and clutching hands.
        Is this a friend indeed; that I should sell
    My soul to her, give her my life and youth,
    Till my feet, cloven too, take hold on hell?

CHRISTINA GEORGINA ROSSETTI (1830–1894)

Promises Like Pie-Crust°   *1896*

Promise me no promises,
    So will I not promise you;
Keep we both our liberties,
    Never false and never true:
Let us hold the die uncast,   5
    Free to come as free to go;
For I cannot know your past,
    And of mine what can you know?

You, so warm, may once have been
    Warmer towards another one;   10

Pie-Crust: An old English proverb: "Promises are like pie-crust, made to be broken."

I, so cold, may once have seen
    Sunlight, once have felt the sun:
Who shall show us if it was
    Thus indeed in time of old?
Fades the image from the glass   15
    And the fortune is not told.

If you promised, you might grieve
    For lost liberty again;
If I promised, I believe
    I should fret to break the chain: 20
Let us be the friends we were,
    Nothing more but nothing less;
Many thrive on frugal fare
    Who would perish of excess.

WILLIAM SHAKESPEARE (1564–1616)

That time of year thou mayst in me behold   *1609*

That time of year thou mayst in me behold
When yellow leaves, or none, or few, do hang
Upon those boughs which shake against the cold,
Bare ruined choirs, where late the sweet birds sang.
In me thou see'st the twilight of such day   5
As after sunset fadeth in the west;
Which by and by black night doth take away,
Death's second self,° that seals up all in rest.   *sleep*
In me thou see'st the glowing of such fire,
That on the ashes of his youth doth lie,   10
As the deathbed whereon it must expire,
Consumed with that which it was nourished by.
    This thou perceiv'st, which makes thy love more strong,
    To love that well which thou must leave ere long.

Explore contexts
for William Shakespeare
on *LiterActive*.

WILLIAM SHAKESPEARE (1564–1616)

When forty winters shall besiege thy brow   *1609*

When forty winters shall besiege thy brow
And dig deep trenches in thy beauty's field,
Thy youth's proud livery, so gazed on now,
Will be a tattered weed,° of small worth held.   *garment*
Then being asked where all thy beauty lies,   5
Where all the treasure of thy lusty days,
To say within thine own deep-sunken eyes

Were an all-eating shame and thriftless praise.
How much more praise deserved thy beauty's use
If thou couldst answer, "This fair child of mine   10
Shall sum my count and make my old excuse,"
Proving his beauty by succession thine.
    This were to be new made when thou art old,
    And see thy blood warm when thou feel'st it cold.

WILLIAM SHAKESPEARE (1564–1616)

When, in disgrace with Fortune and men's eyes   *1609*

When, in disgrace with Fortune and men's eyes,
I all alone beweep my outcast state,
And trouble deaf heaven with my bootless cries,
And look upon myself and curse my fate,
Wishing me like to one more rich in hope,   5
Featured like him, like him with friends possessed,
Desiring this man's art, and that man's scope,
With what I most enjoy contented least,
Yet in these thoughts myself almost despising,
Haply I think on thee, and then my state,   10
Like to the lark at break of day arising
From sullen earth, sings hymns at heaven's gate;
    For thy sweet love remembered such wealth brings
    That then I scorn to change my state with kings.

PERCY BYSSHE SHELLEY (1792–1822)

Ozymandias°   *1818*

I met a traveler from an antique land
Who said: Two vast and trunkless legs of stone
Stand in the desert. . . . Near them, on the sand,
Half sunk, a shattered visage lies, whose frown,
And wrinkled lip, and sneer of cold command,   5
Tell that its sculptor well those passions read
Which yet survive, stamped on these lifeless things,
The hand that mocked them, and the heart that fed:

Ozymandias: Greek name for Ramses II, pharaoh of Egypt for sixty-seven years during the thirteenth century B.C. His colossal statue lies prostrate in the sands of Luxor. Napoleon's soldiers measured it (56 feet long, ear 3½ feet long, weight 1,000 tons). Its inscription, according to the Greek historian Diodorus Siculus, was "I am Ozymandias, King of Kings; if anyone wishes to know what I am and where I lie, let him surpass me in some of my exploits."

And on the pedestal these words appear:
"My name is Ozymandias, King of Kings: 10
Look on my works, ye Mighty, and despair!"
Nothing beside remains. Round the decay
Of that colossal wreck, boundless and bare
The lone and level sands stretch far away.

SIR PHILIP SIDNEY (1554–1586)

Loving in Truth, and Fain in Verse My Love to Show   *1591*

Loving in truth, and fain in verse my love to show,
That she, dear she, might take some pleasure of my pain,
Pleasure might cause her read, reading might make her know,
Knowledge might pity win, and pity grace obtain,
I sought fit words to paint the blackest face of woe,   5
Studying inventions fine, her wits to entertain,
Oft turning others' leaves, to see if thence would flow
Some fresh and fruitful showers upon my sunburnt brain.
But words came halting forth, wanting Invention's stay;
Invention, Nature's child, fled step-dame° Study's blows;   *stepmother*   10
And others' feet still seemed but strangers in my way.
Thus great with child to speak, and helpless in my throes,
Biting my truant pen, beating myself for spite:
"Fool," said my Muse to me, "look in thy heart and write."

LYDIA HUNTLEY SIGOURNEY (1791–1865)

Indian Names   *1834*

*"How can the red men be forgotten, while so many of
our states and territories, bays, lakes and rivers, are
indelibly stamped by names of their giving?"*

Ye say they all have passed away,
    That noble race and brave,
That their light canoes have vanished
    From off the crested wave;
That 'mid the forests where they roamed   5
    There rings no hunter shout,
But their name is on your waters,
    Ye may not wash it out.

'Tis where Ontario's billow
    Like Ocean's surge is curled,   10
Where strong Niagara's thunders wake
    The echo of the world.
Where red Missouri bringeth
    Rich tribute from the west,
And Rappahannock sweetly sleeps   15
    On green Virginia's breast.

Ye say their cone-like cabins,
    That clustered o'er the vale,
Have fled away like withered leaves
    Before the autumn gale,   20
But their memory liveth on your hills,
    Their baptism on your shore,
Your everlasting rivers speak
    Their dialect of yore.

Old Massachusetts wears it,   25
    Within her lordly crown,
And broad Ohio bears it,
    Amid his young renown;
Connecticut hath wreathed it
    Where her quiet foliage waves,   30
And bold Kentucky breathed it hoarse
    Through all her ancient caves.

Wachuset hides its lingering voice
    Within his rocky heart,
And Alleghany graves its tone   35
    Throughout his lofty chart;
Monadnock on his forehead hoar
    Doth seal the sacred trust,
Your mountains build their monument,
    Though ye destroy their dust.   40

Ye call these red-browed brethren
    The insects of an hour,
Crushed like the noteless worm amid
    The regions of their power;
Ye drive them from their father's lands,   45
    Ye break of faith the seal,
But can ye from the court of Heaven
    Exclude their last appeal?

Ye see their unresisting tribes,
    With toilsome step and slow,   50
On through the trackless desert pass,
    A caravan of woe;
Think ye the Eternal's ear is deaf?
    His sleepless vision dim?
Think ye the *soul's blood* may not cry   55
    From that far land to him?

DAVID R. SLAVITT (B. 1935)

Height 2001

*The question that he frames in all but words
is what to make of a diminished thing.*
　　　　　　　— Robert Frost

My doctor, for some obscure reason, is checking
not only my weight but (he's kidding, right?) my height. . . .
This is for pediatricians, and parents who mark
the growth of their little darlings on door frames. But now
he adjusts the metal rod to the top of my head　　　　　　　　　5
and discovers a diminution. I am not, he tells me,
six feet anymore, but five feet ten and a half. . . .
And what (aside from the obvious wise-ass answer)
is the difference?
　　　　　　　　I'm not — as I was, as I thought of myself —　　10
tall. I was proud of that height I'd done nothing to earn.
If it simply happened, whatever talent I have
also just happened, as grace does, or love. And now
it's gone. As grace can go, or love. And we do
what we can to accept and adjust. (What choice do we have?)　　15
I'm average. Of middling stature. I stand up as straight
as I can, the way I was taught to do as a boy,
but it doesn't help, won't change me, can't bring back
that not altogether insignificant edge
I used to have. With this slight shift in perspective,　　　　　20
no longer *de haut en bas,*° there may be new lessons
I apparently need to learn in humility, faith,
or simply that resignation that age should provide.
A tall order, it may yet come in time.

21 *de haut en bas:* From top to bottom (French).

WALLACE STEVENS (1879–1955)

The Emperor of Ice-Cream 1923

Call the roller of big cigars,
The muscular one, and bid him whip
In kitchen cups concupiscent curds.°
Let the wenches dawdle in such dress

3 *concupiscent curds:* "The words 'concupiscent curds' have no genealogy; they are merely expressive: at least, I hope they are expressive. They express the concupiscence of life, but, by contrast with the things in relation in the poem, they express or accentuate life's destitution, and it is this that gives them something more than a cheap lustre" (Wallace Stevens, *Letters* [New York: Knopf, 1960], p. 500).

As they are used to wear, and let the boys   5
Bring flowers in last month's newspapers.
Let be be finale of seem.°
The only emperor is the emperor of ice-cream.

Take from the dresser of deal,
Lacking the three glass knobs, that sheet   10
On which she embroidered fantails once
And spread it so as to cover her face.
If her horny feet protrude, they come
To show how cold she is, and dumb.
Let the lamp affix its beam.   15
The only emperor is the emperor of ice-cream.

7 *Let . . . seem:* "The true sense of 'Let be be finale of seem' is let being become the conclusion
or denouement of appearing to be: in short, ice cream is an absolute good. The poem is
obviously not about ice cream, but about being as distinguished from seeming to be" (*Letters,*
p. 341).

ALFRED, LORD TENNYSON (1809–1892)

Ulysses°   *1833*

   It little profits that an idle king,
By this still hearth, among these barren crags,
Matched with an agèd wife,° I mete and dole   *Penelope*
Unequal laws unto a savage race,
That hoard, and sleep, and feed, and know not me.   5
   I cannot rest from travel; I will drink
Life to the lees. All times I have enjoyed
Greatly, have suffered greatly, both with those
That loved me, and alone; on shore, and when
Through scudding drifts the rainy Hyades°   10
Vexed the dim sea. I am become a name;
For always roaming with a hungry heart
Much have I seen and known — cities of men
And manners, climates, councils, governments,
Myself not least, but honored of them all —   15
And drunk delight of battle with my peers,
Far on the ringing plains of windy Troy.
I am a part of all that I have met;
Yet all experience is an arch wherethrough
Gleams that untraveled world, whose margin fades   20
For ever and for ever when I move.

Ulysses: Ulysses, the hero of Homer's epic poem the *Odyssey,* is presented by Dante in *The
Inferno,* XXVI, as restless after his return to Ithaca and eager for new adventures.

10 *Hyades:* Five stars in the constellation Taurus, supposed by the ancients to predict rain
when they rose with the sun.

How dull it is to pause, to make an end,
To rust unburnished, not to shine in use!
As though to breathe were life. Life piled on life
Were all too little, and of one to me   25
Little remains; but every hour is saved
From that eternal silence, something more,
A bringer of new things; and vile it were
For some three suns to store and hoard myself,
And this gray spirit yearning in desire   30
To follow knowledge like a sinking star,
Beyond the utmost bound of human thought.

    This is my son, mine own Telemachus,
To whom I leave the scepter and the isle —
Well-loved of me, discerning to fulfill   35
This labor, by slow prudence to make mild
A rugged people, and through soft degrees
Subdue them to the useful and the good.
Most blameless is he, centered in the sphere
Of common duties, decent not to fail   40
In offices of tenderness, and pay
Meet adoration to my household gods,
When I am gone. He works his work, I mine.

    There lies the port; the vessel puffs her sail:
There gloom the dark, broad seas. My mariners,   45
Souls that have toiled, and wrought, and thought with me —
That ever with a frolic welcome took
The thunder and the sunshine, and opposed
Free hearts, free foreheads — you and I are old;
Old age hath yet his honor and his toil.   50
Death closes all; but something ere the end,
Some work of noble note, may yet be done,
Not unbecoming men that strove with Gods.
The lights begin to twinkle from the rocks;
The long day wanes; the slow moon climbs; the deep   55
Moans round with many voices. Come, my friends.
'Tis not too late to seek a newer world.
Push off, and sitting well in order smite
The sounding furrows; for my purpose holds
To sail beyond the sunset, and the baths   60
Of all the western stars, until I die.
It may be that the gulfs will wash us down;
It may be we shall touch the Happy Isles,°
And see the great Achilles,° whom we knew.
Though much is taken, much abides; and though   65

---

63 *Happy Isles:* Elysium, the home after death of heroes and others favored by the gods. It was thought by the ancients to lie beyond the sunset in the uncharted Atlantic.   64 *Achilles:* The hero of Homer's *Iliad.*

We are not now that strength which in old days
Moved earth and heaven, that which we are, we are:
One equal temper of heroic hearts,
Made weak by time and fate, but strong in will
To strive, to seek, to find, and not to yield. 70

ALFRED, LORD TENNYSON (1809–1892)

Tears, Idle Tears 1847

    Tears, idle tears, I know not what they mean,
Tears from the depth of some divine despair
Rise in the heart, and gather to the eyes,
In looking on the happy Autumn-fields,
And thinking of the days that are no more. 5

    Fresh as the first beam glittering on a sail,
That brings our friends up from the underworld,
Sad as the last which reddens over one
That sinks with all we love below the verge;
So sad, so fresh, the days that are no more. 10

    Ah, sad and strange as in dark summer dawns
The earliest pipe of half-awaken'd birds
To dying ears, when unto dying eyes
The casement° slowly grows a glimmering square; *window*
So sad, so strange, the days that are no more. 15

    Dear as remember'd kisses after death,
And sweet as those by hopeless fancy feign'd
On lips that are for others; deep as love,
Deep as first love, and wild with all regret;
O Death in Life, the days that are no more. 20

DYLAN THOMAS (1914–1953)

Fern Hill 1946

Now as I was young and easy under the apple boughs
About the lilting house and happy as the grass was green,
    The night above the dingle starry,
      Time let me hail and climb
     Golden in the heydays of his eyes, 5
And honored among wagons I was prince of the apple towns
And once below a time I lordly had the trees and leaves

    Trail with daisies and barley
    Down the rivers of the windfall light.

And as I was green and carefree, famous among the barns   10
About the happy yard and singing as the farm was home,
    In the sun that is young once only,
        Time let me play and be
    Golden in the mercy of his means,
And green and golden I was huntsman and herdsman, the calves   15
Sang to my horn, the foxes on the hills barked clear and cold,
    And the sabbath rang slowly
    In the pebbles of the holy streams.

All the sun long it was running, it was lovely, the hay
Fields high as the house, the tunes from the chimneys, it was air   20
    And playing, lovely and watery
        And fire green as grass.
    And nightly under the simple stars
As I rode to sleep the owls were bearing the farm away,
All the moon long I heard, blessed among stables, the nightjars   25
    Flying with the ricks, and the horses
        Flashing into the dark.

And then to awake, and the farm, like a wanderer white
With the dew, come back, the cock on his shoulder; it was all
    Shining, it was Adam and maiden,   30
        The sky gathered again
    And the sun grew round that very day.
So it must have been after the birth of the simple light
In the first, spinning place, the spellbound horses walking warm
    Out of the whinnying green stable   35
        On to the fields of praise.

And honored among foxes and pheasants by the gay house
Under the new made clouds and happy as the heart was long,
    In the sun born over and over,
        I ran my heedless ways,   40
    My wishes raced through the house-high hay
And nothing I cared, at my sky-blue trades, that time allows
In all his tuneful turning so few and such morning songs
    Before the children green and golden
        Follow him out of grace,   45
Nothing I cared, in the lamb white days, that time would take me
Up to the swallow-thronged loft by the shadow of my hand,
    In the moon that is always rising,
        Nor that riding to sleep
    I should hear him fly with the high fields   50
And wake to the farm forever fled from the childless land.
Oh as I was young and easy in the mercy of his means,
    Time held me green and dying
    Though I sang in my chains like the sea.

WALT WHITMAN (1819–1892)

I Heard You Solemn-Sweet Pipes of the Organ   *1861*

I heard you solemn-sweet pipes of the organ as last Sunday
    morn I pass'd the church,
Winds of autumn, as I walk'd the woods at dusk I heard your
    long-stretch'd sighs up above so mournful,
I heard the perfect Italian tenor singing at the opera, I heard
    the soprano in the midst of the quartet singing;
Heart of my love! you too I heard murmuring low through
    one of the wrists around my head,
Heard the pulse of you when all was still ringing little bells
    last night under my ear.

WALT WHITMAN (1819–1892)

When I Heard the Learn'd Astronomer   *1865*

When I heard the learn'd astronomer,
When the proofs, the figures, were ranged in columns before me,
When I was shown the charts and diagrams, to add, divide, and measure them,
When I sitting heard the astronomer where he lectured with much applause
    in the lecture-room,
How soon unaccountable I became tired and sick,
Till rising and gliding out I wandered off by myself,
In the mystical moist night-air, and from time to time,
Looked up in perfect silence at the stars.

WALT WHITMAN (1819–1892)

One's-Self I Sing   *1867*

One's-Self I sing, a simple separate person,
Yet utter the word Democratic, the word En-Masse.

Of physiology from top to toe I sing,
Not physiognomy alone nor brain alone is worthy for the Muse, I say the
    Form complete is worthier far,
The Female equally with the Male I sing.

Of Life immense in passion, pulse, and power,
Cheerful, for freest action formed under the laws divine,
The Modern Man I sing.

RICHARD WILBUR (B. 1921)

Love Calls Us to the Things of This World °   *1956*

The eyes open to a cry of pulleys,°
And spirited from sleep, the astounded soul
Hangs for a moment bodiless and simple
As false dawn.
         Outside the open window   5
The morning air is all awash with angels.
Some are in bed-sheets, some are in blouses,
Some are in smocks: but truly there they are.
Now they are rising together in calm swells
Of halcyon feeling, filling whatever they wear   10
With the deep joy of their impersonal breathing;
Now they are flying in place, conveying
The terrible speed of their omnipresence, moving
And staying like white water; and now of a sudden
They swoon down into so rapt a quiet   15
That nobody seems to be there.
                The soul shrinks

         From all that it is about to remember,
From the punctual rape of every blessèd day,
And cries,
      "Oh, let there be nothing on earth but laundry,   20
Nothing but rosy hands in the rising steam
And clear dances done in the sight of heaven."

Yet, as the sun acknowledges
With a warm look the world's hunks and colors,   25
The soul descends once more in bitter love
To accept the waking body, saying now
In a changed voice as the man yawns and rises,

"Bring them down from their ruddy gallows;
Let there be clean linen for the backs of thieves;   30
Let lovers go fresh and sweet to be undone,
And the heaviest nuns walk in a pure floating
Of dark habits,
         keeping their difficult balance."

Loves Calls Us . . . : From St. Augustine's *Commentary on the Psalms.* 1 *pulleys:* Grooved
wheels at each end of a laundry line; clothes are hung on the line and advance as the line is
moved.

WILLIAM WORDSWORTH (1770–1850)

Mutability

1822

From low to high doth dissolution climb,
And sink from high to low, along a scale
Of awful° notes, whose concord shall not fail;   *awe-filled*
A muscial but melancholy chime,
Which they can hear who meddle not with crime,   5
Nor avarice, nor over-anxious care.
Truth fails not; but her outward forms that bear
The longest date do melt like frosty rime,
That in the morning whitened hill and plain
And is no more; drop like the tower sublime   10
Of yesterday, which royally did wear
His crown of weeds, but could not even sustain
Some casual shout that broke the silent air,
Or the unimaginable touch of Time.

MITSUYE YAMADA (B. 1923)

A Bedtime Story

1976

Once upon a time,
an old Japanese legend
goes as told
by Papa,
an old woman traveled through   5
many small villages
seeking refuge
for the night.

Each door opened
a sliver   10
in answer to her knock
then closed.
Unable to walk
any further
she wearily climbed a hill   15
found a clearing
and there lay down to rest
a few moments to catch
her breath.

The village town below   20
lay asleep except
for a few starlike lights.
Suddenly the clouds opened
and a full moon came into view
over the town.   25

The old woman sat up
turned toward
the village town
and in supplication
called out   30
Thank you people
of the village,
If it had not been for your
kindness
in refusing me a bed   35
for the night
these humble eyes would never
have seen this
memorable sight.

Papa paused, I waited.   40
In the comfort of our
hilltop home in Seattle
overlooking the valley,
I shouted
"That's the *end*?"   45

WILLIAM BUTLER YEATS (1865–1939)

The Second Coming°   *1921*

Turning and turning in the widening gyre°
The falcon cannot hear the falconer;
Things fall apart; the center cannot hold;
Mere anarchy is loosed upon the world,
The blood-dimmed tide is loosed, and
        everywhere
The ceremony of innocence is drowned;
The best lack all conviction, while the worst
Are full of passionate intensity.

Surely some revelation is at hand;
Surely the Second Coming is at hand.   10
The Second Coming! Hardly are those words out

© Hulton-Deutsch Collection/CORBIS.

When a vast image out of *Spiritus Mundi*°   *Soul of the world*
Troubles my sight: somewhere in sands of the desert
A shape with lion body and the head of a man,
A gaze blank and pitiless as the sun,   15
Is moving its slow thighs, while all about it
Reel shadows of the indignant desert birds.

Explore contexts
for William Butler Yeats
on *LiterActive*.

The Second Coming: According to Matthew 24:29–44, Christ will return to earth after a time of tribulation to reward the righteous and establish the millennium of heaven on earth. Yeats saw his troubled time as the end of the Christian era and feared the portents of the new cycle.

1 *gyre:* Widening spiral of a falcon's flight, used by Yeats to describe the cycling of history.

The darkness drops again; but now I know
That twenty centuries of stony sleep
Were vexed to nightmare by a rocking cradle,   20
And what rough beast, its hour come round at last,
Slouches towards Bethlehem to be born?

WILLIAM BUTLER YEATS (1865–1939)

Leda and the Swan°   *1924*

A sudden blow: the great wings beating still
Above the staggering girl, her thighs caressed
By the dark webs, her nape caught in his bill,
He holds her helpless breast upon his breast.

How can those terrified vague fingers push   5
The feathered glory from her loosening thighs?
And how can body, laid in that white rush,
But feel the strange heart beating where it lies?

A shudder in the loins engenders there
The broken wall, the burning roof and tower   10
And Agamemnon dead.
                              Being so caught up,
So mastered by the brute blood of the air,
Did she put on his knowledge with his power
Before the indifferent beak could let her drop?   15

Leda and the Swan: In Greek myth, Zeus in the form of a swan seduced Leda and fathered
Helen of Troy (whose abduction started the Trojan War) and Clytemnestra, Agamemnon's
wife and murderer. Yeats thought of Zeus's appearance to Leda as a type of annunciation,
like the angel appearing to Mary.

WILLIAM BUTLER YEATS (1865–1939)

Sailing to Byzantium°   *1927*

I

That is no country for old men.° The young
In one another's arms, birds in the trees
— Those dying generations — at their song,
The salmon-falls, the mackerel-crowded seas

Byzantium: Old name for the modern city of Istanbul, capital of the Eastern Roman Empire,
ancient artistic and intellectual center. Yeats uses Byzantium as a symbol for "artificial" (and
therefore, deathless) art and beauty, as opposed to the beauty of the natural world, which is
bound to time and death.

1 *That . . . men:* Ireland, part of the time-bound world.

Fish, flesh, or fowl, commend all summer long   5
Whatever is begotten, born and dies.
Caught in that sensual music all neglect
Monuments of unaging intellect.

II

An aged man is but a paltry thing,
A tattered coat upon a stick, unless   10
Soul clap its hands and sing, and louder sing
For every tatter in its mortal dress,
Nor is there singing school but studying
Monuments of its own magnificence;
And therefore I have sailed the seas and come   15
To the holy city of Byzantium.

III

O sages standing in God's holy fire
As in the gold mosaic of a wall,
Come from the holy fire, perne in a gyre,°
And be the singing-masters of my soul.   20
Consume my heart away; sick with desire
And fastened to a dying animal
It knows not what it is; and gather me
Into the artifice of eternity.

IV

Once out of nature I shall never take   25
My bodily form from any natural thing,
But such a form as Grecian goldsmiths make
Of hammered gold and gold enameling
To keep a drowsy Emperor awake;°
Or set upon a golden bough° to sing   30
To lords and ladies of Byzantium
Of what is past, or passing, or to come.

---

19 *perne in a gyre:* Bobbin making a spiral pattern.   27–29 *such . . . awake:* "I have read somewhere that in the Emperor's palace at Byzantium was a tree made of gold and silver, and artificial birds that sang." [Yeats's note.]   30 *golden bough:* In Greek legend, Aeneas had to pluck a golden bough from a tree in order to descend into Hades. As soon as the bough was plucked, another grew in its place.

WILLIAM BUTLER YEATS (1865–1939)

Crazy Jane Talks with the Bishop   *1933*

I met the Bishop on the road
And much said he and I.
"Those breasts are flat and fallen now,
Those veins must soon be dry;
Live in a heavenly mansion,   5
Not in some foul sty."

"Fair and foul are near of kin,
And fair needs foul," I cried.
"My friends are gone, but that's a truth
Nor grave nor bed denied,   10
Learned in bodily lowliness
And in the heart's pride.

"A woman can be proud and stiff
When on love intent;
But Love has pitched his mansion in   15
The place of excrement;
For nothing can be sole or whole
That has not been rent."

Critical Thinking and Writing about Poetry

25

Critical Strategies
for Reading

Great literature is simply language
charged with meaning to the utmost
possible degree.
— EZRA POUND

National Portrait
Gallery, London.

The answers you get from literature
depend upon the questions you pose.
— MARGARET ATWOOD

CRITICAL THINKING

Maybe this has happened to you: the assignment is to consider a work, let's
say Nathaniel Hawthorne's *The Scarlet Letter*, and write an analysis of some
aspect of it that interests you, taking into account critical sources that
comment on and interpret the work. You cheerfully
begin research in the library but quickly find yourself
bewildered by several seemingly unrelated articles. The
first traces the thematic significance of images of light
and darkness in the novel; the second makes a case for
Hester Prynne as a liberated woman; the third argues that Arthur Dimmes-
dale's guilt is a projection of Hawthorne's own emotions; and the fourth
analyzes the introduction, "The Custom House," as an attack on bourgeois

Web Explore
the critical approaches
in this chapter on
LiterActive or at
bedfordstmartins.com/
meyerpoetry.

values. These disparate treatments may seem random and capricious—a confirmation of your worst suspicions that interpretations of literature are hit-or-miss excursions into areas that you know little about or didn't know even existed. But if you understand that the articles are written from different perspectives—formalist, feminist, psychological, and Marxist—and that the purpose of each is to enhance your understanding of the work by discussing a particular element of it, then you can see that their varying strategies represent potentially interesting ways of opening up the text that might otherwise never have occurred to you. There are many ways to approach a text, and a useful first step is to develop a sense of direction, an understanding of how a perspective—your own or a critic's—shapes a discussion of a text.

This chapter offers an introduction to critical approaches to literature by outlining a variety of strategies for reading poetry, fiction, or drama. The emphasis is of course on poetry, and to that end the approaches focus on Robert Frost's "Mending Wall" (p. 359); a rereading of that well-known poem will equip you for the discussions that follow. In addition to the emphasis on this poem to illustrate critical approaches, some fiction and drama examples are also included along the way to demonstrate how these critical approaches can be applied to any genre. These strategies include approaches that have long been practiced by readers who have used, for example, the insights gleaned from biography and history to illuminate literary works as well as more recent approaches, such as those used by feminist, reader-response, and deconstructionist critics. Each of these perspectives is sensitive to image, symbol, tone, irony, and other literary elements that you have been studying, but each also casts those elements in a special light. The formalist approach emphasizes how the elements within a work achieve their effects, whereas biographical and psychological approaches lead outward from the work to consider the author's life and other writings. Even broader approaches, such as historical and sociological perspectives, connect the work to historic, social, and economic forces. Mythological readings represent the broadest approach, because they discuss the cultural and universal responses readers have to a work.

Any given strategy raises its own types of questions and issues while seeking particular kinds of evidence to support itself. An awareness of the assumptions and methods that inform an approach can help you to understand better the validity and value of a given critic's strategy for making sense of a work. More important, such an understanding can widen and deepen the responses of your own reading.

The critical thinking that goes into understanding a professional critic's approach to a work should not be foreign to you because you have already used essentially the same kind of thinking to understand the work itself. The skills you have developed to produce a literary *analysis* that, for example, describes how a character, symbol, or rhyme scheme supports a theme are also useful for reading literary criticism, because such skills allow you to keep track of how the parts of a critical approach create a particular reading of a literary work. When you analyze a poem, story, or play by closely examining how its various elements relate to the whole, your *interpretation* — your articulation of what the work means to you as supported by an analysis of its elements — necessarily involves choosing what you focus on in the work. The same is true of professional critics.

Critical readings presuppose choices in the kinds of material that are discussed. An analysis of the setting of Robert Frost's "Home Burial" (p. 361) would probably bring into focus the oppressive environment of the couple's domestic life rather than, say, the economic history of New England farming. The economic history of New England farming might be useful to a Marxist critic concerned with how class is revealed in "Home Burial," but for a formalist critic interested in identifying the unifying structures of the poem such information would be irrelevant.

The Perspectives, Complementary Readings, and Critical Case Studies in this anthology offer opportunities to read critics who are using a wide variety of approaches to analyze and interpret texts. In the critical case study on T. S. Eliot's "The Love Song of J. Alfred Prufrock" (Chapter 16), for instance, Elisabeth Schneider offers a biographical interpretation of Prufrock by suggesting that Eliot shared some of his character's sensibilities. In contrast, Michael L. Baumann argues that Prufrock's character can be understood through a close examination of the poem's images. Each of these critics raises different questions, examines different evidence, and makes different assumptions to interpret Prufrock's character. Being aware of those differences — teasing them out so that you can see how they lead to competing conclusions — is a useful way to analyze the analysis itself. What is left out of an interpretation is sometimes as significant as what is included. As you read the critics, it's worth reminding yourself that your own critical thinking skills can help you to determine the usefulness of a particular approach.

The following overview is neither exhaustive in the types of critical approaches covered nor complete in its presentation of the complexities inherent in them, but it should help you to develop an appreciation of the intriguing possibilities that attend literary interpretation. The emphasis in this chapter is on ways of thinking about literature rather than on daunting lists of terms, names, and movements. Although a working knowledge of critical schools may be valuable and necessary for a fully informed use of a given critical approach, the aim here is more modest and practical. This chapter is no substitute for the shelves of literary criticism that can be found in your library, but it does suggest how readers using different perspectives organize their responses to texts.

The summaries of critical approaches that follow are descriptive, not evaluative. Each approach has its advantages and limitations, but those matters are best left to further study. Like literary artists, critics have their personal values, tastes, and styles. The appropriateness of a specific critical approach will depend, at least in part, on the nature of the literary work under discussion as well as on your own sensibilities and experience. However, any approach, if it is to enhance understanding, requires sensitivity, tact, and an awareness of the various literary elements of the text, including, of course, its use of language.

Successful critical approaches avoid eccentric decodings that reveal so-called hidden meanings; if there is no apparent evidence of a given meaning, this is because it is nonexistent in the text, not because the author has attempted to hide it in some way. For a parody of this sort of critical excess, see "A Parodic Interpretation of 'Stopping by Woods on a Snowy Evening'" (p. 380), in which Herbert R. Coursen Jr. has some fun with a Robert Frost poem and Santa Claus while making a serious point about the dangers of overly ingenious readings. Literary criticism attempts, like any valid hypothesis, to account for phenomena — the text — without distorting or misrepresenting what it describes.

THE LITERARY CANON: DIVERSITY AND CONTROVERSY

Before looking at the various critical approaches discussed in this chapter, it makes sense to consider first which literature has been traditionally considered worthy of such analysis. The discussion in the Introduction called The Changing Literary Canon (p. 6) may have already alerted you to the fact that in recent years many more works by women, minorities, and writers from around the world have been considered by scholars, critics, and teachers to merit serious study and inclusion in what is known as the literary canon. This increasing diversity has been celebrated by those who believe that multiculturalism taps new sources for the discovery of great literature while raising significant questions about language, culture, and society. At the same time, others have perceived this diversity as a threat to the established, traditional canon of Western culture.

The debates concerning whose work should be read, taught, and written about have sometimes been acrimonious as well as lively and challenging. Bitter arguments have been waged recently on campuses and in the media over what has come to be called "political correctness." Two camps — roughly — have formed around these debates: liberals and conservatives (the appropriateness of these terms is debatable but the oppositional positioning is unmistakable). The liberals are said to insist on politically correct views from colleagues and students opening-up the curriculum to multicultural texts from Asia, Africa, Latin America, and elsewhere, and to encourage more tolerant attitudes about race, class, gender, and sexual orientation. These revisionists, seeking a change in traditional attitudes, are sometimes accused of intimidating the opposition into silence and substituting ideological dogma for reason and truth. The conservatives are also portrayed as ideologues; in their efforts to preserve what they regard as the best from the past, they refuse to admit that Western classics, mostly written by white male Europeans, represent only a portion of human experience. These traditionalists are seen as advocating values that are neither universal nor eternal but merely privileged and entrenched. Conservatives are charged with refusing to acknowledge that their values also represent a political agenda, which is implicit in their preference for the works of canonical authors such as Homer, Virgil, Shakespeare, Milton, Tolstoy, and Faulkner. The reductive and contradictory nature of this national debate between liberals and conservatives has been neatly summed up by Katha Pollitt: "Read the conservatives' list and produce a nation of sexists and racists — or a nation of philosopher kings. Read the liberals' list and produce a nation of spiritual relativists — or a nation of open-minded world citizens" ("Canon to the Right of Me . . . ," *The Nation,* Sept. 23, 1991, p. 330).

These troubling and extreme alternatives can be avoided, of course, if the issues are not approached from such absolutist positions. Solutions to these issues cannot be suggested in this limited space, and, no doubt, solutions will evolve over time, but we can at least provide a perspective. Books — regardless of what list they are about — are not likely to unite a fragmented nation or to disunite a unified one. It is perhaps more useful and accurate to see issues of canonicity as reflecting political changes rather than being the primary causes of them. This is not to say that books don't have an impact on readers — that *Uncle Tom's Cabin,* for instance, did not galvanize antislavery sentiments in nineteenth-century America — but that book lists do not by themselves preserve or destroy the status quo.

It's worth noting that the curricula of American universities have always undergone significant and, some would say, wrenching changes. Only a little more than one hundred years ago there was strong opposition to teaching English, as well as other modern languages, alongside programs dominated by Greek and Latin. Only since the 1920s has American literature been made a part of the curriculum, and just five decades ago writers such as Emily Dickinson, Robert Frost, W. H. Auden, and Marianne Moore were regarded with the same raised eyebrows that today might be raised about contemporary writers such as Sharon Olds, Martín Espada, Rita Dove, or Billy Collins. New voices do not drown out the past; they build on and eventually become part of it as newer writers take their place alongside them. Neither resistance to change nor a denial of the past will have its way with the canon. Though both impulses are widespread, neither is likely to dominate the other, because there are too many reasonable, practical readers and teachers who instead of replacing Shakespeare, Frost, and other canonical writers have supplemented them with writers who have been neglected because they were from non-Western cultures or because they represented disenfranchised segments of the Western canon. These readers experience the current debates about the canon not as a binary opposition but as an opportunity to explore important questions about continuity and change in our literature, culture, and society.

FORMALIST STRATEGIES

Formalist critics focus on the formal elements of a work — its language, structure, and tone. A formalist reads literature as an independent work of art rather than as a reflection of the author's state of mind or as a representation of a moment in history. Historic influences on a work, an author's intentions, or anything else outside the work are generally not treated by formalists (this is particularly true of the most famous modern formalists, known as the **New Critics,** who dominated American criticism from the 1940s through the 1960s). Instead, formalists offer intense examinations of the relationship between form and meaning within a work, emphasizing the subtle complexity of how a work is arranged. This kind of close reading pays special attention to what are often described as *intrinsic* matters in a literary work — diction, irony, paradox, metaphor, and symbol, for instance — as well as larger elements, such as plot, characterization, and narrative technique. Formalists examine how these elements work together to give a coherent shape to a work while contributing to its meaning. The answers to the questions formalists raise about how the shape and effect of a work are related come from the work itself. Other kinds of information that go beyond the text — biography, history, politics, economics, and so on — are typically regarded by formalists as *extrinsic* matters, which are considerably less important than what goes on within the autonomous text.

Poetry especially lends itself to close readings, because a poem's relative brevity allows for detailed analyses of nearly all of its words and how they achieve their effects. For a sample formalist reading of how a pervasive sense of death is worked into a poem, see "A Reading of Dickinson's 'There's a certain Slant of light'" (p. 696).

Formalist strategies are also useful for analyzing drama and fiction. In his well-known essay "The World of *Hamlet*," Maynard Mack explores Hamlet's character and predicament by paying close attention to the words and images that Shakespeare uses to build a world in which appearances mask reality and mystery is embedded in scene after scene. Mack points to recurring terms, such as *apparition, seems, assume,* and *put on,* as well as repeated images of acting, clothing, disease, and painting, to indicate the treacherous surface world Hamlet must penetrate to get to the truth. This pattern of deception provides an organizing principle around which Mack offers a reading of the entire play:

> Hamlet's problem, in its crudest form, is simply the problem of the avenger: he must carry out the injunction of the ghost and kill the king. But this problem . . . is presented in terms of a certain kind of world. The ghost's injunction to act becomes so inextricably bound up for Hamlet with the character of the world in which the action must be taken — its mysteriousness, its baffling appearances, its deep consciousness of infection, frailty, and loss — that he cannot come to terms with either without coming to terms with both.

Although Mack places *Hamlet* in the tradition of revenge tragedy, his reading of the play emphasizes Shakespeare's arrangement of language rather than literary history as a means of providing an interpretation that accounts for various elements of the play. Mack's formalist strategy explores how diction reveals meaning and how repeated words and images evoke and reinforce important thematic significances.

A formalist reading of Robert Frost's "Mending Wall" leads to an examination of the tensions produced by the poem's diction, repetitions, and images that take us beyond a merely literal reading. The speaker describes how every spring he and his neighbor walk beside the stone wall bordering their respective farms to replace the stones that have fallen during winter. As they repair the wall, the speaker wonders what purpose the wall serves, given that "My apple trees will never get across / And eat the cones under his pines"; his neighbor, however, "only says, 'Good fences make good neighbors.'" The moment described in the poem is characteristic of the rural New England life that constitutes so much of Frost's poetry, but it is also typical of how he uses poetry as a means of "saying one thing in terms of another," as he once put it in an essay titled "Education by Poetry."

Just as the speaker teases his neighbor with the idea that the apple trees won't disturb the pines, so, too, does Frost tease the reader into looking at what it is "that doesn't love a wall." Frost's use of language in the poem does not simply consist of homespun casual phrases enlisted to characterize rural neighbors. From the opening lines, the "Something . . . that doesn't love a wall" and "That sends the frozen-ground swell under it" is, on the literal level, a frost heave that causes the stones to tumble from the wall. But after several close readings of the poem, we can see the implicit pun in these lines suggesting that it is *Frost* who objects to the wall, thus aligning the poet's perspective with the speaker's. A careful examination of some of the other formal elements in the poem supports this reading.

In contrast to the imaginative wit of the speaker who raises fundamental questions about the purpose of any wall, the images associated with his neighbor indicate that he is a traditionalist who "will not go behind his father's saying." Moreover, the neighbor moves "like an old-stone savage" in "darkness" that is attributed to his rigid, tradition-bound, walled-in sensibilities rather than to "the shade of trees." Whereas the speaker's wit and intelligence are manifested by his willingness to question the necessity or desirability of "walling in or walling out" anything, his benighted neighbor can only repeat again that "good fences make good neighbors." The stone-heavy darkness of the neighbor's mind is emphasized by the contrasting light wit and agility of the speaker, who speculates: "Before I built a wall I'd ask to know . . . to whom I was like to give offense." The pun on the final word of this line makes a subtle but important connection between giving "offense" and creating "a fence." Frost's careful use of diction, repetition, and images deftly reveals and reinforces thematic significances suggesting that the stone wall serves as a symbol of isolation, confinement, fear, and even savagery. The neighbor's conservative, tradition-bound, mindless support of the wall is a foil to the speaker's — read Frost's — poetic, liberal response, which imagines and encourages the possibilities of greater freedom and brotherhood.

Although this brief discussion of some of the formal elements of Frost's poem does not describe all there is to say about how they produce an effect and create meaning, it does suggest the kinds of questions, issues, and evidence that a formalist strategy might raise in providing a close reading of the text itself.

BIOGRAPHICAL STRATEGIES

A knowledge of an author's life can help readers understand his or her work more fully. Events in a work might follow actual events in a writer's life just as characters might be based on people known by the author. Ernest Hemingway's "Soldier's Home" is a story about the difficulties of a World War I veteran named Krebs returning to his small hometown in Oklahoma, where he cannot adjust to the pious assumptions of his family and neighbors. He refuses to accept their innocent blindness to the horrors he has witnessed during the war. They have no sense of the brutality of modern life; instead they insist he resume his life as if nothing has happened. There is plenty of biographical evidence to indicate that Krebs's unwillingness to lie about his war experiences reflects Hemingway's own responses on his return to Oak Park, Illinois, in 1919. Krebs, like Hemingway, finds he has to leave the sentimentality, repressiveness, and smug complacency that threaten to render his experiences unreal: "the world they were in was not the world he was in."

An awareness of Hemingway's own war experiences and subsequent disillusionment with his hometown can be readily developed through available biographies, letters, and other of his written works. Consider, for example, this passage from *By Force of Will: The Life and Art of Ernest Hemingway*, in which Scott Donaldson describes Hemingway's response to World War I:

> In poems, as in [*A Farewell to Arms*], Hemingway expressed his distaste for the first war. The men who had to fight the war did not die well:
>
> > Soldiers pitch and cough and twitch —
> >   All the world roars red and black;
> > Soldiers smother in a ditch,
> >   Choking through the whole attack.
>
> And what did they die for? They were "sucked in" by empty words and phrases —
>
> > King and country,
> > Christ Almighty,

And the rest,
Patriotism,
Democracy,
Honor —

which spelled death. The bitterness of these outbursts derived from the distinction Hemingway drew between the men on the line and those who started the wars that others had to fight.

This kind of information can help to deepen our understanding of just how empathetically Krebs is presented in the story. Relevant facts about Hemingway's life will not make "Soldier's Home" a better written story than it is, but such information can make clearer the source of Hemingway's convictions and how his own experiences inform his major concerns as a storyteller.

Some formalist critics — some New Critics, for example — argue that interpretation should be based exclusively on internal evidence rather than on any biographical information outside the work. They argue that it is not possible to determine an author's intention and that the work must stand by itself. Although this is a useful caveat for keeping the work in focus, a reader who finds biography relevant would argue that biography can at the very least serve as a control on interpretation. A reader who, for example, finds Krebs at fault for not subscribing to the values of his hometown would be misreading the story, given both its tone and the biographical information available about the author. Although the narrator never *tells* the reader that Krebs is right or wrong for leaving town, the story's tone sides with his view of things. If, however, someone were to argue otherwise, insisting that the tone is not decisive and that Krebs's position is problematic, a reader familiar with Hemingway's own reactions could refute that argument with a powerful confirmation of Krebs's instincts to withdraw. Hence, many readers find biography useful for interpretation.

However, it is also worth noting that biographical information can complicate a work. For example, readers who interpret "Mending Wall" as a celebration of an iconoclastic sensibility that seeks to break down the psychological barriers and physical walls that separate human beings may be surprised to learn that very few of Frost's other writings support this view. His life was filled with emotional turmoil; it has been described by a number of biographers as egocentric and vindictive rather than generous and open to others. He once commented that "I always hold that we get forward as much by hating as by loving." Indeed, many facts about Frost's life — as well as many of the speakers in his poems — are typified by depression, alienation, tension, suspicion, jealous competitiveness, and suicidal tendencies. Instead of challenging wall-builders, Frost more characteristically built walls of distrust around himself among his family, friends, and colleagues. In this biographical context, it is especially noteworthy that it is the speaker of "Mending Wall" who alone repairs the damage done to the walls by hunters, and it is he who initiates each spring the rebuilding of the wall. However much he may question its value, the speaker does, after all, rebuild the wall between himself and his neighbor. This biographical approach raises provocative questions about the text. Does the poem suggest that boundaries and walls are, in fact, necessary? Are walls a desirable foundation for relationships between people? Although these and other questions raised by a biographical approach cannot be answered here, this kind of biographical perspective certainly adds to the possibilities of interpretation.

Sometimes biographical information does not change our understanding so much as it enriches our appreciation of a work. It matters, for instance, that much of John Milton's poetry, so rich in visual imagery, was written after he became blind; and it is just as significant — to shift to a musical example — that a number of Ludwig van Beethoven's greatest works, including the *Ninth Symphony,* were composed after he succumbed to total deafness.

PSYCHOLOGICAL STRATEGIES

Given the enormous influence that Sigmund Freud's psychoanalytic theories had on twentieth-century interpretations of human behavior, it is nearly inevitable that most people have some familiarity with his ideas about dreams, unconscious desires, and sexual repression, as well as his terms for different aspects of the psyche — the id, ego, and superego. Psychological approaches to literature draw on Freud's theories and other psychoanalytic theories to understand more fully the text, the writer, and the reader. Critics use such approaches to explore the motivations of characters and the symbolic meanings of events, while biographers speculate about a writer's own motivations — conscious or unconscious — in a literary work. Psychological approaches are also used to describe and analyze the reader's personal responses to a text.

Although it is not feasible to explain psychoanalytic terms and concepts in so brief a space as this, it is possible to suggest the nature of a psychological approach. It is a strategy based heavily on the idea of the existence of a human unconscious — those impulses, desires, and feelings about which a person is unaware but that influence emotions and behavior.

Central to a number of psychoanalytic critical readings is Freud's concept of what he called the **Oedipus complex,** a term derived from Sophocles' tragedy *Oedipus the King.* This complex is predicated on a boy's unconscious rivalry with his father for his mother's love and his desire to eliminate his father in order to take his father's place with his mother. The female version of the psychological conflict is known as the **Electra complex,** a term used to describe a daughter's unconscious rivalry for her father. The name comes from a Greek legend about Electra, who avenged the death of her father, Agamemnon, by killing her mother. In *The Interpretation of Dreams,*

Freud explains why *Oedipus the King* "moves a modern audience no less than it did the contemporary Greek one." What unites their powerful attraction to the play is an unconscious response:

> There must be something which makes a voice within us ready to recognize the compelling force of destiny in the *Oedipus*. . . . His destiny moves us only because it might have been ours — because the oracle laid the same curse upon us before our birth as upon him. It is the fate of all of us, perhaps, to direct our first sexual impulse towards our mother and our first hatred and our first murderous wish against our father. Our dreams convince us that this is so. King Oedipus, who slew his father Laius and married his mother Jocasta, merely shows us the fulfillment of our own childhood wishes . . . and we shrink back from him with the whole force of the repression by which those wishes have since that time been held down within us.

In this passage Freud interprets the unconscious motives of Sophocles in writing the play, Oedipus in acting within it, and the audience in responding to it.

A further application of the Oedipus complex can be observed in a classic interpretation of *Hamlet* by Ernest Jones, who used this concept to explain why Hamlet delays in avenging his father's death. This reading has been tightly summarized by Norman Holland, a recent psychoanalytic critic, in *The Shakespearean Imagination*. Holland shapes the issues into four major components:

> One, people over the centuries have been unable to say why Hamlet delays in killing the man who murdered his father and married his mother. Two, psychoanalytic experience shows that every child wants to do just exactly that. Three, Hamlet delays because he cannot punish Claudius for doing what he himself wished to do as a child and, unconsciously, still wishes to do: he would be punishing himself. Four, the fact that this wish is unconscious explains why people could not explain Hamlet's delay.

Although the Oedipus complex is, of course, not relevant to all psychological interpretations of literature, interpretations involving this complex do offer a useful example of how psychoanalytic critics tend to approach a text.

The situation in Frost's "Mending Wall" is not directly related to an Oedipus complex, but the poem has been read as a conflict in which the "father's saying" represents the repressiveness of a patriarchal order that challenges the speaker's individual poetic consciousness. "Mending Wall" has also been read as another kind of struggle with repression. In "Up against the 'Mending Wall': The Psychoanalysis of a Poem by Frost" Edward Jayne offers a detailed reading of the poem as "the overriding struggle to suppress latent homosexual attraction between two men separated by a wall" (*College English* 1973). Jayne reads the poem as the working out of "unconscious homosexual inclinations largely repugnant to Frost and his need to divert and sublimate them." Regardless of whether or not a reader finds these arguments convincing, it is clear that the poem does have something to do with powerful forms of repression. And what about the reader's response? How might a psychological approach account for different responses from readers who argue that the poem calls for either a world that includes walls or one that dismantles them? One needn't be versed in psychoanalytic terms to entertain this question.

HISTORICAL STRATEGIES

Historians sometimes use literature as a window onto the past, because literature frequently provides the nuances of a historic period that cannot be readily perceived through other sources. The characters in Harriet Beecher Stowe's novel *Uncle Tom's Cabin* (1852) display, for example, a complex set of white attitudes toward blacks in mid-nineteenth-century America that is absent from more traditional historic documents such as census statistics or state laws. Another way of approaching the relationship between literature and history, however, is to use history as a means of understanding a literary work more clearly. The plot pattern of pursuit, escape, and capture in nineteenth-century slave narratives had a significant influence on Stowe's plotting of action in *Uncle Tom's Cabin*. This relationship demonstrates that the writing contemporary to an author is an important element of the history that helps to shape a work. There are many ways to talk about a work's historical and cultural dimensions. Such readings treat a literary text as a document reflecting, producing, or being produced by the social conditions of its time, giving equal focus to the social milieu and the work itself. Four historical strategies that have been especially influential are literary history criticism, Marxist criticism, new historicist criticism, and cultural criticism.

Literary History Criticism

Literary historians shift the emphasis from the period to the work. Hence a literary historian might also examine mid-nineteenth-century abolitionist attitudes toward blacks to determine whether Stowe's novel is representative of those views or significantly to the right or left of them. Such a study might even indicate how closely the book reflects racial attitudes of twentieth-century readers. A work of literature may transcend time to the extent that it addresses the concerns of readers over a span of decades or centuries, but it remains for the literary historian a part of the past in which it was composed, a past that can reveal more fully a work's language, ideas, and purposes.

Literary historians move beyond both the facts of an author's personal life and the text itself to the social and intellectual currents in which the author composed the work. They place the work in the context of its time (as do many critical biographers who write "life and times" studies), and sometimes they make connections with other literary works that may have influenced the author. The basic strategy of literary historians is to illuminate the historic background in order to shed light on some aspect of the work itself.

In Hemingway's "Soldier's Home" we learn that Krebs had been at Belleau Wood, Soissons, the Champagne, St. Mihiel, and the Argonne. Although nothing is said of these battles in the story, they were among the most bloody battles of the war; the wholesale butchery and staggering casualties incurred by both sides make credible the way Krebs's unstated but lingering memories have turned him into a psychological prisoner of war. Knowing something about the ferocity of those battles helps us account for Krebs's response in the story. Moreover, we can more fully appreciate Hemingway's refusal to have Krebs lie about the realities of war for the folks back home if we are aware of the numerous poems, stories, and plays published during World War I that presented war as a glorious, manly, transcendent sacrifice for God and country. Juxtaposing those works with "Soldier's Home" brings the differences into sharp focus.

Similarly, a reading of William Blake's poem "London" (p. 121) is less complete if we do not know of the horrific social conditions — the poverty, disease, exploitation, and hypocrisy — that characterized the city Blake laments in the late eighteenth century.

One last example: the potential historical meaning of the wall that is the subject of Frost's "Mending Wall" might be more distinctly seen if it is placed in the context of its publication date, 1914, when the world was on the verge of collapsing into the violent political landscape of World War I. The insistence that "Good fences make good neighbors" suggests a grim, ironic tone in the context of European nationalist hostilities that seemed to be moving inexorably toward war. The larger historical context for the poem would have been more apparent to its readers contemporary with World War I, but a historical reconstruction of the horrific tensions produced by shifting national borders and shattered walls during the war can shed some light on the larger issues that may be at stake in the poem. Moreover, an examination of Frost's attitudes toward the war and America's potential involvement in it could help to produce a reading of the meaning and value of a world with or without walls.

Marxist Criticism

Marxist readings developed from the heightened interest in radical reform during the 1930s, when many critics looked to literature as a means of furthering proletarian social and economic goals, based largely on the writings of Karl Marx. **Marxist critics** focus on the ideological content of a work — its explicit and implicit assumptions and values about matters such as culture, race, class, and power. Marxist studies typically aim at not only revealing and clarifying ideological issues but also correcting social injustices. Some Marxist critics have used literature to describe the competing socioeconomic interests that too often advance capitalist money and power rather than socialist morality and justice. They argue that criticism, like literature, is essentially political because it either challenges or supports economic oppression. Even if criticism attempts to ignore class conflicts, it is politicized, according to Marxists, because it supports the status quo.

It is not surprising that Marxist critics pay more attention to the content and themes of literature than to its form. A Marxist critic would more likely be concerned with the exploitive economic forces that cause Willy Loman to feel trapped in Arthur Miller's *Death of a Salesman* than with the playwright's use of nonrealistic dramatic techniques to reveal Loman's inner thoughts. Similarly, a Marxist reading of Frost's "Mending Wall" might draw on the poet's well-known conservative criticisms of President Franklin Delano Roosevelt's New Deal during the 1930s as a means of reading conservative ideology into the poem. Frost's deep suspicions of collective enterprise might suggest to a Marxist that the wall represents the status quo, that is, a capitalist construction that unnaturally divides individuals (in this case, the poem's speaker from his neighbor) and artificially defies nature. Complicit in their own oppression, both farmers, to a lesser and greater degree, accept the idea that "good fences make good neighbors," thereby maintaining and perpetuating an unnatural divisive order that oppresses and is mistakenly perceived as necessary and beneficial. A Marxist reading would see the speaker's and neighbor's conflicts as not only an individual issue but also part of a larger class struggle.

New Historicist Criticism

Since the 1960s a development in historical approaches to literature known as *new historicism* has emphasized the interaction between the historic context of a work and a modern reader's understanding and interpretation of the work. In contrast to many traditional literary historians, however, new historicists attempt to describe the culture of a period by reading many different kinds of texts that traditional historians might have previously left for sociologists and anthropologists. New historicists attempt to read a period in all of its dimensions, including political, economic, social, and esthetic concerns. These considerations could be used to explain something about the nature of rural New England life early in the twentieth century. The process of mending the stone wall authentically suggests how this tedious job simultaneously draws the two men together and keeps them apart. Pamphlets and other contemporary writings about farming and maintaining property lines could offer insight into either the necessity or the uselessness of the spring wall-mending rituals. A new historicist might find useful how advice offered in texts about running a farm reflect or refute the speaker's or neighbor's competing points of view in the poem.

New historicist criticism acknowledges more fully than traditional historical approaches the competing nature of readings of the past and thereby tends to offer new emphases and perspectives. New historicism reminds us that there is not only one historic context for "Mending Wall." The year before Frost died, he visited Moscow as a cultural ambassador from the United States. During this 1962 visit — only one year after the Soviet Union's construction of the Berlin Wall — he read "Mending Wall" to his Russian audience. Like the speaker in that poem, Frost clearly enjoyed the "mischief" of that moment, and a new historicist would clearly find intriguing the way the poem was both intended and received in so volatile a context. By emphasizing that historical perceptions are governed, at least in part, by our own concerns and preoccupations, new historicists sensitize us to the fact that the history on which we choose to focus is colored by being reconstructed from our own present moment. This reconstructed history affects our reading of texts.

Cultural Criticism

Cultural critics, like new historicists, focus on the historical contexts of a literary work, but they pay particular attention to popular manifestations of social, political, and economic contexts. Popular culture — mass-produced and consumed cultural artifacts, today ranging from advertising to popular fiction to television to rock music — and "high" culture are given equal emphasis. A cultural critic might be interested in looking at how Baz Luhrmann's movie version of *Romeo and Juliet* (1996) was influenced by the fragmentary nature of MTV videos. Adding the "low" art of everyday life to "high" art opens up previously unexpected and unexplored areas of criticism. Cultural critics use widely eclectic strategies drawn from new historicism, psychology, gender studies, and deconstructionism (to name only a handful of approaches) to analyze not only literary texts but also radio talk shows, comic strips, calendar art, commercials, travel guides, and baseball cards. Because all human activity falls within the ken of cultural criticism, nothing is too minor or major, obscure or pervasive, to escape the range of its analytic vision.

Cultural criticism also includes *postcolonial criticism,* the study of cultural behavior and expression in relationship to the formerly colonized world. Postcolonial criticism refers to the analysis of literary works by writers from countries and cultures that at one time were controlled by colonizing powers — such as Indian writers during or after British colonial rule. The term also refers to the analysis of literary works written about colonial cultures by writers from the colonizing country. Many of these kinds of analyses point out how writers from colonial powers sometimes misrepresent colonized cultures by reflecting more of their own values: Joseph Conrad's *Heart of Darkness* (published in 1899) represents African culture differently from the way Chinua Achebe's *Things Fall Apart* does, for example. Cultural criticism and postcolonial criticism represent a broad range of approaches to examining race, gender, and class in historical contexts in a variety of cultures.

A cultural critic's approach to Frost's "Mending Wall" might emphasize how the poem reflects New England farmers' attitudes toward hunters, or it might examine how popular poems about stone walls contemporary to "Mending Wall" endorse such wall building instead of making problematic the building of walls between neighbors as Frost does. Each of these perspectives can serve to create a wider and more informed understanding of the poem. For a deeper sense of the range of documents used by cultural critics to shed light on literary works and the historical contexts in which they are written and read, see Chapter 17, "A Cultural Case Study: Louise Erdrich's 'Dear John Wayne.'"

GENDER STRATEGIES

Gender critics explore how ideas about men and women — what is masculine and feminine — can be regarded as socially constructed by particular cultures. According to some critics, sex is determined by simple biological and anatomical categories of male or female, and gender is determined by a culture's values. Thus ideas about gender and what constitutes masculine and feminine behavior are created by cultural institutions and conditioning. A gender critic might, for example, focus on Frost's characterization of the narrator's neighbor as an emotionally frozen son of a father who overshadowed his psychological and social development. The narrator's rigid masculinity would then be seen as a manifestation of socially constructed gender identity in the 1910s. Gender criticism expands categories and definitions of what is masculine or feminine and tends to regard sexuality as more complex than merely masculine or feminine, heterosexual or homosexual. Gender criticism, therefore, has come to include gay and lesbian criticism as well as feminist criticism. Although there are complex and sometimes problematic relationships among these approaches because some critics argue that heterosexuals and homosexuals are profoundly biologically different, gay and lesbian criticism, like feminist criticism, can be usefully regarded as a subset of gender criticism.

Feminist Criticism

Like Marxist critics, *feminist critics* would also be interested in examining the status quo in "Mending Wall," because they seek to correct or supplement what they regard as a predominantly male-dominated critical perspective with a feminist consciousness. Like other forms of sociological criticism, feminist criticism places literature in a social context, and, like those of Marxist criticism, its analyses often have sociopolitical purposes—purposes that might explain, for example, how images of women in literature reflect the patriarchal social forces that have impeded women's efforts to achieve full equality with men.

Feminists have analyzed literature by both men and women in an effort to understand literary representations of women as well as the writers and cultures that create them. Related to concerns about how gender affects the way men and women write about each other is an interest in whether women use language differently from the way men do. Consequently, feminist critics' approach to literature is characterized by the use of a broad range of disciplines—among them history, sociology, psychology, and linguistics—to provide a perspective sensitive to feminist issues.

A feminist approach to Frost's "Mending Wall" might initially appear to offer few possibilities given that no women appear in the poem and that no mention or allusion is made about women. And that is precisely the point: the landscape presented in the poem is devoid of women. Traditional gender roles are evident in the poem because it is men, not women, who work outdoors building walls and who discuss the significance of their work. For a feminist critic, the wall might be read as a symbol of patriarchal boundaries that are defined exclusively by men. If the wall can be seen as a manifestation of the status quo built upon the "father's saying[s]," then mending the wall each year and keeping everything essentially the same—with women securely out of the picture—essentially benefits the established patriarchy. The boundaries are reconstructed and rationalized in the absence of any woman's potential efforts to offer an alternative to the boundaries imposed by the men's rebuilding of the wall. Perhaps one way of considering the value of a feminist perspective on this work can be discerned if a reader imagines the speaker or the neighbor as a woman and how that change might extend the parameters of their conversation about the value of the wall.

Gay and Lesbian Criticism

Gay and lesbian critics focus on a variety of issues, including how homosexuals are represented in literature, how they read literature, and whether sexuality and gender are culturally constructed or innate. Gay critics have produced new readings and discovered homosexual concerns in writers such as Herman Melville and Henry James, while lesbian critics have done the same with writers such as Emily Dickinson and Sylvia Plath. Some readers have found in "Mending Wall," for example, homosexual tensions between the narrator and his neighbor that are suppressed by both men as they build their wall to fence in forbidden and unbidden desires. Although gay and lesbian readings often raise significant interpretative controversies among critics, they have opened up provocative discussions of seemingly familiar texts.

MYTHOLOGICAL STRATEGIES

Mythological approaches to literature attempt to identify what in a work creates deep, universal responses in readers. Whereas psychological critics interpret the symbolic meanings of characters and actions in order to understand more fully the unconscious dimensions of an author's mind, a character's motivation, or a reader's response, mythological critics (also frequently referred to as archetypal critics) interpret the hopes, fears, and expectations of entire cultures.

In this context myth is not to be understood simply as referring to stories about imaginary gods who perform astonishing feats in the causes of love, jealousy, or hatred. Nor are myths to be judged as merely erroneous, primitive accounts of how nature runs its course and humanity its affairs. Instead, literary critics use myths as a strategy for understanding how human beings try to account for their lives symbolically. Myths can be a window onto a culture's deepest perceptions about itself, because myths attempt to explain what otherwise seems unexplainable: a people's origin, purpose, and destiny.

All human beings have a need to make sense of their lives, whether they are concerned about their natural surroundings, the seasons, sexuality, birth, death, or the very meaning of existence. Myths help people organize their experiences; these systems of belief (less formally held than religious or political tenets but no less important) embody a culture's assumptions and values. What is important to the mythological critic is not the validity or truth of those assumptions and values; what matters is that they reveal common human concerns.

It is not surprising that although the details of mythic stories vary enormously, the essential patterns are often similar, because these myths attempt to explain universal experiences. There are, for example, numerous myths that redeem humanity from permanent death through a hero's resurrection and rebirth. For Christians the resurrection of Jesus symbolizes the ultimate defeat of death and coincides with the rebirth of nature's fertility in spring. Features of this rebirth parallel the Greek myths of Adonis and Hyacinth, who die but are subsequently transformed into living flowers; there are also similarities that connect these stories to the reincarnation of the Indian Buddha or the rebirth of the Egyptian Osiris. To be sure, important differences exist among these stories, but each reflects a basic human need to limit the power of death and to hope for eternal life.

Mythological critics look for underlying, recurrent patterns in literature that reveal universal meanings and basic human experiences for readers regardless of when or where they live. The characters, images, and themes that symbolically embody these meanings and experiences are called *archetypes.* This term designates universal symbols, which evoke deep and perhaps unconscious responses in a reader because archetypes bring with them the heft of our hopes and fears since the beginning of human time. Surely one of the most powerfully compelling archetypes is the death/

rebirth theme that relates the human life cycle to the cycle of the seasons. Many others could be cited and would be exhausted only after all human concerns were cataloged, but a few examples can suggest some of the range of plots, images, and characters addressed.

Among the most common literary archetypes are stories of quests, initiations, scapegoats, meditative withdrawals, descents to the underworld, and heavenly ascents. These stories are often filled with archetypal images: bodies of water that may symbolize the unconscious or eternity or baptismal rebirth; rising suns, suggesting reawakening and enlightenment; setting suns, pointing toward death; colors such as green, evocative of growth and fertility, or black, indicating chaos, evil, and death. Along the way are earth mothers, fatal women, wise old men, desert places, and paradisal gardens. No doubt your own reading has introduced you to any number of archetypal plots, images, and characters.

Mythological critics attempt to explain how archetypes are embodied in literary works. Employing various disciplines, these critics articulate the power a literary work has over us. Some critics are deeply grounded in classical literature, whereas others are more conversant with philology, anthropology, psychology, or cultural history. Whatever their emphases, however, mythological critics examine the elements of a work in order to make larger connections that explain the work's lasting appeal.

A mythological reading of Sophocles' *Oedipus the King*, for example, might focus on the relationship between Oedipus's role as a scapegoat and the plague and drought that threaten to destroy Thebes. The city is saved and the fertility of its fields restored only after the corruption is located in Oedipus. His subsequent atonement symbolically provides a kind of rebirth for the city. Thus the plot recapitulates ancient rites in which the well-being of a king was directly linked to the welfare of his people. If a leader were sick or corrupt, he had to be replaced in order to guarantee the health of the community.

A similar pattern can be seen in the rottenness that Shakespeare exposes in Hamlet's Denmark. *Hamlet* reveals an archetypal pattern similar to that of *Oedipus the King*: not until the hero sorts out the corruption in his world and in himself can vitality and health be restored in his world. Hamlet avenges his father's death and becomes a scapegoat in the process. When he fully accepts his responsibility to set things right, he is swept away along with the tide of intrigue and corruption that has polluted life in Denmark. The new order — established by Fortinbras at the play's end — is achieved precisely because Hamlet is willing and finally able to sacrifice himself in a necessary purgation of the diseased state.

These kinds of archetypal patterns exist potentially in any literary period. Frost's "Mending Wall," for example, is set in spring, an evocative season that marks the end of winter and earth's renewal. The action in the poem, however, does not lead to a celebration of new life and human community; instead there is for the poem's speaker and his neighbor an annual ritual to "set the wall between us as we go" — a ritual that separates and divides human experience rather than unifying it. We can see that the rebuilding of the wall runs counter to nature itself because the stones are so round that "We have to use a spell to make them balance." The speaker also resists the wall and sets out to subvert it by toying with the idea of challenging his neighbor's assumption that "good fences make good neighbors," a seemingly ancient belief passed down through one "father's saying" to the next. The speaker, however, does not heroically overcome the neighbor's ritual; he merely points out that the wall is not needed where it is. The speaker's acquiescence results in the continuation of a ritual that confirms the old order rather than overthrowing the "old-stone savage," who demands the dark isolation and separateness associated with the "gaps" produced by winter's frost. The neighbor's old order prevails despite nature's and the speaker's protestations. From a mythological critic's perspective, the wall might itself be seen as a "gap," an unnatural disruption of nature and the human community.

READER-RESPONSE STRATEGIES

Reader-response criticism, as its name implies, focuses on the reader rather than the work itself. This approach to literature describes what goes on in the reader's mind during the process of reading a text. In a sense, all critical approaches (especially psychological and mythological criticism) concern themselves with a reader's response to literature, but there is a stronger emphasis in reader-response criticism on the reader's active construction of the text. Although many critical theories inform reader-response criticism, all ***reader-response critics*** aim to describe the reader's experience of a work: in effect we get a reading of the reader, who comes to the work with certain expectations and assumptions, which are either met or not met. Hence the consciousness of the reader — produced by reading the work — is the subject matter of reader-response critics. Just as writing is a creative act, so is reading, as it also produces a text.

Reader-response critics do not assume that a literary work is a finished product with fixed formal properties, as, for example, formalist critics do. Instead, the literary work is seen as an evolving creation of the reader's as he or she processes characters, plots, images, and other elements while reading. Some reader-response critics argue that this act of creative reading is, to a degree, controlled by the text, but it can produce many interpretations of the same text by different readers. There is no single definitive reading of a work, because the crucial assumption is that readers create rather than discover meanings in texts. Readers who have gone back to works they had read earlier in their lives often find that a later reading draws very different responses from them. What earlier seemed unimportant is now crucial; what at first seemed central is now barely worth noting. The reason, put simply, is that two different people have read the same text. Reader-response critics are not after the "correct" reading of the text or what the author presumably intended; instead they are interested in the reader's experience with the text.

These experiences change with readers; although the text remains the same, the readers do not. Social and cultural values influence readings, so that, for example, an avowed Marxist would be likely to come away from Miller's *Death of a Salesman* with a very different view of American capitalism than that of, say, a successful sales representative, who might attribute Willy Loman's fall more to his character than to the American economic system. Moreover, readers from different time periods respond differently to texts. An Elizabethan — concerned perhaps with the stability of monarchical rule — might respond differently to Hamlet's problems than would a twentieth-century reader well versed in psychology and concepts of what Freud called the Oedipus complex. This is not to say that anything goes, that Miller's play can be read as an amoral defense of cheating and rapacious business practices or that *Hamlet* is about the dangers of living away from home. The text does, after all, establish some limits that allow us to reject certain readings as erroneous. But reader-response critics do reject formalist approaches that describe a literary work as a self-contained object, the meaning of which can be determined without reference to any extrinsic matters, such as the social and cultural values assumed by either the author or the reader.

Reader-response criticism calls attention to how we read and what influences our readings. It does not attempt to define what a literary work means on the page but rather what it does to an informed reader — a reader who understands the language and conventions used in a given work. Reader-response criticism is not a rationale for mistaken or bizarre readings of works but an exploration of the possibilities for a plurality of readings shaped by the readers' experience with the text. This kind of strategy can help us understand how our responses are shaped by both the text and ourselves.

Frost's "Mending Wall" illustrates how reader-response critical strategies read the reader. Among the first readers of the poem in 1914, those who were eager to see the United States enter World War I might have been inclined to see the speaker as an imaginative thinker standing up for freedom rather than antiquated boundaries and sensibilities that don't know what they are "walling in or walling out." But for someone whose son could be sent to the trenches of France to fight the Germans, the phrase "Good fences make good neighbors" might sound less like an unthinking tradition and more like solid, prudent common sense. In each instance the reader's circumstances could have an effect on his or her assessment of the value of walls and fences. Certainly the Russians who listened to Frost's reading of "Mending Wall" in 1962, only one year after the construction of the Berlin Wall, had a very different response from the Americans who heard about Frost's reading and who relished the discomfort they thought the reading had caused the Russians.

By imagining different readers we can imagine a variety of responses to the poem that are influenced by the readers' own impressions, memories, or experiences. Such imagining suggests the ways in which reader-response criticism opens up texts to a number of interpretations. As one final example, consider how readers' responses to "Mending Wall" would be affected if the poem were printed in two different magazines, read in the context of either the *Farmer's Almanac* or the *New Yorker.* What assumptions and beliefs would each magazine's readership be likely to bring to the poem? How do you think the respective experiences and values of each magazine's readers would influence their readings?

DECONSTRUCTIONIST STRATEGIES

Deconstructionist critics insist that literary works do not yield fixed, single meanings. They argue that there can be no absolute knowledge about anything because language can never say what we intend it to mean. Anything we write conveys meanings we did not intend, so the deconstructionist argument goes. Language is not a precise instrument but a power whose meanings are caught in an endless web of possibilities that cannot be untangled. Accordingly, any idea or statement that insists on being understood separately can ultimately be "deconstructed" to reveal its relations and connections to contradictory and opposite meanings.

Unlike other forms of criticism, deconstructionism seeks to destabilize meanings instead of establishing them. In contrast to formalists such as the New Critics, who closely examine a work in order to call attention to how its various components interact to establish a unified whole, deconstructionists try to show how a close examination of a text's language inevitably reveals conflicting, contradictory impulses that "deconstruct" or break down its apparent unity.

Although deconstructionists and New Critics both examine the language of a text closely, deconstructionists focus on the gaps and ambiguities that reveal a text's instability and indeterminacy, whereas New Critics look for patterns that explain how the text's fixed meaning is structured. Deconstructionists painstakingly examine the competing meanings within the text rather than attempt to resolve them into a unified whole.

The questions deconstructionists ask are aimed at discovering and describing how a variety of possible readings are generated by the elements of a text. In contrast to a New Critic's concerns about the ultimate meaning of a work, a deconstructionist's primary interest is in how the use of language—diction, tone, metaphor, symbol, and so on—yields only provisional, not definitive, meanings. Consider, for example, the following excerpt from an American Puritan poet, Anne Bradstreet. The excerpt is from "The Flesh and the Spirit" (1678), which consists of an allegorical debate between two sisters, the body and the soul. During the course of the debate, Flesh, a consummate materialist, insists that Spirit values ideas that do not exist and that her faith in idealism is both unwarranted and insubstantial in the face of the material values that earth has to offer—riches, fame, and physical pleasure. Spirit, however, rejects the materialistic worldly argument that the only ultimate reality is physical reality and pledges her faith in God:

> Mine eye doth pierce the heavens and see
> What is invisible to thee.
> My garments are not silk nor gold,
> Nor such like trash which earth doth hold,
> But royal robes I shall have on,
> More glorious than the glist'ring sun;
> My crown not diamonds, pearls, and gold,
> But such as angels' heads enfold
> The city where I hope to dwell,
> There's none on earth can parallel;
> The stately walls both high and strong,
> Are made of precious jasper stone;
> The gates of pearl, both rich and clear,
> And angels are for porters there;
> The streets thereof transparent gold,
> Such as no eye did e'er behold;
> A crystal river there doth run,
> Which doth proceed from the Lamb's throne.

A deconstructionist would point out that Spirit's language—her use of material images such as jasper stone, pearl, gold, and crystal—cancels the explicit meaning of the passage by offering a supermaterialistic reward to the spiritually faithful. Her language, in short, deconstructs her intended meaning by using the same images that Flesh would use to describe the rewards of the physical world. A deconstructionist reading, then, reveals the impossibility of talking about the invisible and spiritual worlds without using materialistic (that is, metaphoric) language. Thus Spirit's very language demonstrates a contradiction and conflict in her conviction that the world of here and now must be rejected for the hereafter. Her language deconstructs her meaning.

Deconstructionists look for ways to question and extend the meanings of a text. In Frost's "Mending Wall," for example, the speaker presents himself as being on the side of the imaginative rather than hidebound, rigid responses to life. He seems to value freedom and openness rather than restrictions and narrowly defined limits. Yet his treatment of his Yankee farmer neighbor can be read as condescending and even smug in its superior attitude toward his neighbor's repeating his "father's saying," as if he were "an old-stone savage armed." The condescending attitude hardly suggests a robust sense of community and shared humanity. Moreover, for all the talk about unnecessary conventions and traditions, a deconstructionist would likely be quick to point out that Frost writes the poem in blank verse—unrhymed iambic pentameter—rather than free verse; hence the very regular rhythms of the narrator's speech may be seen to deconstruct its liberationist meaning.

As difficult as it is controversial, deconstructionism is not easily summarized or paraphrased. For an example of deconstructionism in practice and how it differs from New Criticism, see Andrew P. Debicki's "New Criticism and Deconstructionism: Two Attitudes in Teaching Poetry" in *Perspectives* (p. 667).

Perspectives on Critical Reading

SUSAN SONTAG (B. 1933)

Against Interpretation   *1964*

Like the fumes of the automobile and of heavy industry which befoul the urban atmosphere, the effusion of interpretations of art today poisons our sensibilities. In a culture whose already classical dilemma is the hypertrophy of the intellect at the expense of energy and sensual capability, interpretation is the revenge of the intellect upon art.

Even more. It is the revenge of the intellect upon the world. To interpret is to impoverish, to deplete the world—in order to set up a shadow world of "meanings." It is to turn *the* world into *this* world. ("This world"! As if there were any other.)

The world, our world, is depleted, impoverished enough. Away with all duplicates of it, until we again experience more immediately what we have. . . .

In most modern instances, interpretation amounts to the philistine refusal to leave the work of art alone. Real art has the capacity to make us nervous. By reducing the work of art to its content and then interpreting *that,* one tames the work of art. Interpretation makes art manageable, conformable.

This philistinism of interpretation is more rife in literature than in any other art. For decades now, literary critics have understood it to be their task to translate the elements of the poem or play or novel or story into something else.

From *Against Interpretation*

CONSIDERATIONS FOR CRITICAL THINKING AND WRITING

1. What are Sontag's objections to interpretation? Explain whether you agree or disagree with them.

2. In what sense does interpretation make art "manageable" and "conformable"?

3. In an essay explore what you take to be both the dangers of interpretation and its contributions to your understanding of literature.

Annette Kolodny (b. 1941)

On the Commitments of Feminist Criticism

1980

If feminist criticism calls anything into question, it must be that dog-eared myth of intellectual neutrality. For what I take to be the underlying spirit or message of any consciously ideologically premised criticism — that is, that ideas are important *because* they determine the ways we live, or want to live, in the world — is vitiated by confining those ideas to the study, the classroom, or the pages of our books. To write chapters decrying the sexual stereotyping of women in our literature, while closing our eyes to the sexual harassment of our women students and colleagues; to display Katharine Hepburn and Rosalind Russell in our courses on "The Image of the Independent Career Women in Film," while managing not to notice the paucity of female administrators on our own campus; to study the women who helped make universal enfranchisement a political reality, while keeping silent about our activist colleagues who are denied promotion or tenure; to include segments on "Women in the Labor Movement" in our American studies or women's studies courses, while remaining willfully ignorant of the department secretary fired for efforts to organize a clerical workers' union; to glory in the delusions of "merit," "privilege," and "status" which accompany campus life in order to insulate ourselves from the millions of women who labor in poverty — all this is not merely hypocritical; it destroys both the spirit and the meaning of what we are about.

> From "Dancing through the Minefield: Some Observations on the Theory, Practice, and Politics of a Feminist Literary Criticism," *Feminist Studies* 6, 1980

Considerations for Critical Thinking and Writing

1. Why does Kolodny reject "intellectual neutrality" as a "myth"? Explain whether you agree or disagree with her point of view.

2. Kolodny argues that feminist criticism can be used as an instrument for social reform. Discuss the possibility and desirability of her position. Do you think other kinds of criticism can and should be used to create social change?

Andrew P. Debicki (b. 1934)

New Criticism and Deconstructionism: Two Attitudes in Teaching Poetry

1985

[Let's] look at the ways in which a New Critic and a deconstructivist might handle a poem. My first example, untitled, is a work by Pedro Salinas, which I first analyzed many years ago and which I have recently taught to a group of students influenced by deconstruction:

> Sand: sleeping on the beach today
> and tomorrow caressed
> in the bosom of the sea:

the sun's today, water's prize tomorrow.
Softly you yield
to the hand that presses you
and go away with the first
courting wind that appears.
Pure and fickle sand,
changing and clear beloved,
I wanted you for my own,
and held you against my chest and soul.
But you escaped with the waves, the wind, the sun,
and I remained without a beloved,
my face turned to the wind which robbed her,
and my eyes to the far-off sea in which she had
green loves in a green shelter.

My original study of this poem, written very much in the New Critical tradition, focused on the unusual personification of sand as beloved and on the metaphorical pattern that it engendered. In the first part of the work, the physical elusiveness of sand (which slips through one's hand, flies with the wind, moves from shore to sea) evokes a coquettish woman, yielding to her lover and then escaping, running off with a personified wind, moving from one being to another. Watching these images, the reader gradually forgets that the poem is metaphorically describing sand and becomes taken up by the unusual correspondences with the figure of a flirting woman. When in the last part of the poem the speaker laments his loss, the reader is drawn into his lament for a fickle lover who has abandoned him.

Continuing a traditional analysis of this poem, we would conclude that its unusual personification/metaphor takes us beyond a literal level and leads us to a wider vision. The true subject of this poem is not sand, nor is it a flirt who tricks a man. The comparison between sand and woman, however, has made us feel the elusiveness of both, as well as the effect that this elusiveness has had on the speaker, who is left sadly contemplating it at the end of the poem. The poem has used its main image to embody a general vision of fleetingness and its effects.

My analysis, as developed thus far, is representative of a New Critical study. It focuses on the text and its central image, it describes a tension produced within the text, and it suggests a way in which this tension is resolved so as to move the poem beyond its literal level. In keeping with the tenets of traditional analytic criticism, it shows how the poem conveys a meaning that is far richer than its plot or any possible conceptual message. But while it is careful not to reduce the poem to a simple idea or to an equivalent of its prose summary, it does attempt to work all of its elements into a single interpretation which would satisfy every reader . . . : it makes all of the poem's meanings reside in its verbal structures, and it suggests that those meanings can be discovered and combined into a single cohesive vision as we systematically analyze those structures.

By attempting to find a pattern that will incorporate and resolve the poem's tensions, however, this reading leaves some loose ends, which I noticed even in my New Critical perspective — and which I found difficult to explain. To see the poem as the discovery of the theme of fleetingness by an insightful speaker, we have to ignore the fanciful nature of the comparison, the whimsical attitude to reality that it suggests, and the excessively serious lament of the speaker, which is difficult to take at face value — he laments the loss of *sand* with the excessive emotion of a romantic lover! The last lines, with their evocation of the beloved/sand in an archetypal kingdom of the sea, ring a bit hollow. Once we notice all of this, we see the speaker as being somehow unreliable in his strong response to the situation. He tries too hard to equate the loss of sand with the loss of love, he paints himself as too much of a romantic, and he loses our assent when we realize that his rather cliché declarations are not very fitting. Once we become aware of the speaker's limitations, our perspective about the poem changes: we come to see its "meaning" as centered, not on the theme of fleetingness as such, but on a portrayal of the speaker's exaggerated efforts to embody this theme in the image of sand.

For the traditional New Critic, this would pose a dilemma. The reading of the poem as a serious embodiment of the theme of evanescence is undercut by an awareness of the speaker's unreliability. One can account for the conflict between readings, to some extent, by speaking of the poem's use of irony and by seeing a tension between the theme of evanescence and the speaker's excessive concern with an imaginary beloved (which blinds him to the larger issues presented by the poem). That still leaves unresolved, however, the poem's final meaning and effect. In class discussions, in fact, a debate between those students who asserted that the importance of the poem lay in its engendering the theme of fleetingness and those who noted the absurdity of the speaker often ended in an agreement that this was a "problem poem" which never resolved or integrated its "stresses" and its double vision. . . .

The deconstructive critic, however, would not be disturbed by a lack of resolution in the meanings of the poem and would use the conflict between interpretations as the starting point for further study. Noting that the view of evanescence produced by the poem's central metaphor is undercut by the speaker's unreliability, the deconstructive critic would explore the play of signification that the undercutting engenders. Calling into question the attempt to neatly define evanescence, on the one hand, and the speaker's excessive romanticism on the other, the poem would represent, for this critic, a creative confrontation of irresoluble visions. The image of the sand as woman, as well as the portrayal of the speaker, would represent a sort of "seam" in the text, an area of indeterminacy that would open the way to further readings. This image lets us see the speaker as a sentimental poet, attempting unsuccessfully to define evanescence by means of a novel metaphor but getting trapped in the theme of lost love, which he himself has engendered; it makes us think of the inadequacy of language, of the ways in which metaphorical expression and the clichés of a love lament can undercut each other.

Once we adopt such a deconstructivist perspective, we will find in the text details that will carry forward our reading. The speaker's statement that he held "her" against his "chest and his soul" underlines the conflict in his perspective: it juggles a literal perspective (he rubs sand against himself) and a metaphorical one (he reaches for his beloved), but it cannot fully combine them — "soul" is ludicrously inappropriate in reference to the former. The reader, noting the inappropriateness, has to pay attention to the inadequacy of language as used here. All in all, by engendering a conflict between various levels and perspectives, the poem makes us feel the incompleteness of any one reading, the way in which each one is a "misreading" (not because it is wrong, but because it is incomplete), and the creative lack of closure in the poem. By not being subject to closure, in fact, this text becomes all the more exciting: its view of the possibilities and limitations of metaphor, language, and perspective seems more valuable than any static portrayal of "evanescence."

The analyses I have offered of this poem exemplify the different classroom approaches that would be taken by a stereotypical New Critic, on the one hand, and a deconstructive critic on the other. Imbued with the desire to come to an overview of the literary work, the former will attempt to resolve its tensions (and probably remain unsatisfied with the poem). Skeptical of such a possibility and of the very existence of a definable "work," the latter will focus on the tensions that can be found in the text as vehicles for multiple readings. Given his or her attitude to the text, the deconstructive critic will not worry about going beyond its "limits" (which really do not exist). This will allow, of course, for more speculative readings; it will also lead to a discussion of ways in which the text can be extended and "cured" in successive readings, to the fact that it reflects on the process of its own creation, and to ways in which it will relate to other texts.

> From *Writing and Reading DIFFERENTLY: Deconstruction*
> *and the Teaching of Composition and Literature,*
> edited by G. Douglas Atkins and Michael L. Johnson

Considerations for Critical Thinking and Writing

1. Explain how the New Critical and deconstructionist approaches to the Salinas poem differ. What kinds of questions are raised by each? What elements of the poem are focused on in each approach?

2. Write an essay explaining which reading of the poem you find more interesting. In your opening paragraph define what you mean by "interesting."

3. Choose one of the critical strategies for reading discussed in this chapter and discuss Salinas's poem from that perspective.

PETER RABINOWITZ (B. 1944)

On Close Readings   *1988*

Belief in close reading may be the nearest thing literary scholars have to a shared critical principle. Academics who teach literature tend to accept as a matter of course that good reading is slow, attentive to linguistic nuance (especially figurative language), and suspicious of surface meanings.

Close reading is a fundamental link between the New Critics and the Yale deconstructionists. Indeed, deconstructionist J. Hillis Miller has gone so far as to characterize what he saw as an attack on close reading by Gerald Graff as "a major treason against our profession." Similarly, what Naomi Schor calls "clitoral" feminist criticism, and its "hermeneutics focused on the detail," is a variant of close reading. So is much reader-response criticism.

Despite its broad acceptance by scholars, however, close reading is not the natural, the only, or always the best way to approach a text. I'm not suggesting that it should never be taught or used. But I do want to argue that close reading rests on faulty assumptions about how literature is read, which can lead, especially in the classroom, to faulty prescriptions about how it *ought* to be read.

The fact is that there are a variety of ways to read, all of which engage the reader in substantially different kinds of activity. Which kind depends in part on the reader and his or her immediate purpose. Teasing out the implicit homo-erotic tendencies in [Ivan] Turgenev's *Asya,* for instance, is a different activity from trying to determine its contribution to the development of first-person narrative techniques. In part, the way one reads also varies from text to text. Different authors, different genres, different periods, different cultures expect readers to approach texts in different ways.

The bias in academe toward close reading reduces that multiplicity. While all close readers obviously don't read in exactly the same way, the variations have a strong family resemblance. Their dominance in the aristocracy of critical activity — virtually undiminished by the critical revolutions of the last twenty years — can skew evaluation, distort interpretation, discourage breadth of vision, and separate scholars from students and other ordinary readers.

David Daiches was not being eccentric when he argued that literary value depends on the "degree to which the work lends itself" to the kind of reading demanded by New Critical theory. The schools in vogue may change, but we still assign value to what fits our prior conceptions of reading, and the academically sanctioned canon consequently consists largely of texts that respond well to close reading.

Once you give priority to close reading, you implicitly favor figurative writing over realistic writing, indirect expression over direct expression, deep meaning over surface meaning, form over content, and the elite over the popular. In the realm of poetry, that means giving preference to lyric over narrative poems, and in the realm of fiction, to symbolism and psychology over plot. Such preferences, in turn, devalue certain voices. A writer directly confronting brute oppression, for instance, is apt to be ranked below another who has the luxury minutely to explore the details of subtle middle-class crises. Thus, for a close reader, the unresonant prose of Harriet Wilson's *Our Nig* will automatically make the novel seem less "good" than Henry James's more intricate *What Maisie Knew,* although the racist brutality endured by Ms. Wilson's heroine is arguably more important for our culture — and thus more deserving of our consideration — than the affluent sexual merry-go-round that dizzies Maisie.

It would be bad enough if the preference for close reading simply meant that texts that didn't measure up were chucked onto a noncanonical pile — then, at least, the rebellious could rummage through the rejects. But close reading also has an insidious effect on interpretation. Not only do we reject many works that don't fit; more damaging, we also twist many others until they *do* fit.

Yet we fail to recognize the magnitude of this distortion. One of the major problems with much current critical practice is the tendency to underestimate the extent to which texts can serve as mirrors — not of the external world but of the reader, who is apt to find in a text not what is really there but what he expects or wants to find. . . .

When reading for class, many students read closely, but few continue the practice once they've left college. In fact, most people — including teachers —

who really enjoy literature recognize that close reading is a special kind of interpretive practice. Literary scholars are apt to make a distinction between "real reading" and "reading for fun"; most nonacademic readers are likely to divide "real reading" from "reading for class." In either case, an artificial split is created between academe and "real life," which leads to theories that devalue the kinds of reading (and therefore the kinds of books) that engage most readers most of the time.

If I'm against close reading, then what am I for? The obvious alternative is pluralism.

We can legitimately show our students that different writers in different social, historical, and economic contexts write for different purposes and with different expectations. Likewise, we can teach our students that different readers (or the same reader under different circumstances) read for different reasons.

We must also give our students actual practice in various kinds of reading. For example, an introductory literature course should include many different sorts of texts: long novels as well as lyric poems; realistic (even didactic) works as well as symbolic ones; writing aimed at a broad audience as well as at a literate elite. The course should also include different kinds of tasks. Students should learn to approach a given text in several different ways, at least some of which arise out of their personal and cultural situations. Most important, we must help our students to be self-conscious about what they are doing, and to realize that every decision about how to read opens certain doors only by closing others.

It is not simply that learning new, less rigid ways of reading increases the number of works we can enjoy and learn from. More important, learning to read in different ways allows us to enjoy a wider range of texts and gain new perspectives on our cultural assumptions. Only such flexible reading leads to intellectual growth, for it is only that kind of reading that can enable us to be conscious of — and therefore able to deal effectively with — the narrowness of "standard" interpretive techniques.

From "Our Evaluation of Literature Has Been Distorted
by Academe's Bias toward Close Readings of Texts,"
Chronicle of Higher Education, April 6, 1988

Considerations for Critical Thinking and Writing

1. Why does Rabinowitz object to the bias toward close reading as the primary way to approach a literary work? Explain why you agree or disagree.

2. According to Rabinowitz, how does a critical emphasis on close reading affect the formation of the canon?

3. In an essay discuss Rabinowitz's observation that an emphasis on close reading "devalue[s] the kinds of reading (and therefore the kinds of books) that engage most readers most of the time."

HARRIET HAWKINS (B. 1939)

Should We Study King Kong *or* King Lear? *1988*

There is nothing either good or bad, but thinking makes it so.
            —Hamlet

Troilus: *What's aught but as 'tis valued?*
Hector: *But value dwells not in particular will:*
   It holds its estimate and dignity
   As well wherein 'tis precious of itself
   As in the prizer.
                    —Troilus and Cressida

To what degree is great literature—or bad literature—an artificial category? Are there any good—or bad—reasons why most societies have given high status to certain works of art and not to others? Could Hamlet be right in concluding that there is *nothing* either good or bad but thinking—or critical or ideological discourse—makes it so? Or are certain works of art so precious, so magnificent—or so trashy—that they obviously ought to be included in the canon or expelled from the classroom? So far as I know, there is not now any sign of a critical consensus on the correct answer to these questions either in England or in the United States.

In England there are, on the one hand, eloquent cases for the defense of the value of traditional literary studies, like Dame Helen Gardner's last book, *In Defence of the Imagination.* On the other hand, there are critical arguments insisting that what really counts is not what you read, but the way that you read it. You might as well study *King Kong* as *King Lear,* because what matters is not the script involved, but the critical or ideological virtues manifested in your own "reading" of whatever it is that you are reading. Reviewing a controversial book entitled *Re-Reading English,* the poet Tom Paulin gives the following account of the issues involved in the debate:

> The contributors are collectively of the opinion that English literature is a dying subject and they argue that it can be revived by adopting a "socialist pedagogy" and introducing into the syllabus "other forms of writing and cultural production than the canon of literature" . . . it is now time to challenge "hierarchical" and "elitist" conceptions of literature and to demolish the bourgeois ideology which has been "naturalised" as literary value. . . . They wish to develop "a politics of reading" and to redefine the term "text" in order to admit newspaper reports, songs, and even mass demonstrations as subjects for tutorial discussion. Texts no longer have to be books: indeed, "it may be more democratic to study *Coronation Street* [England's most popular soap opera] than *Middlemarch.*"

However one looks at these arguments, it seems indisputably true that the issues involved are of paramount critical, pedagogical, and social importance. There are, however, any number of different ways to look at the various arguments. So far as I am, professionally, concerned, they raise the central question, "Why should any of us still study, or teach, Shakespeare's plays (or *Paradise Lost* or *The Canterbury Tales*)?" After all, there are quite enough films, plays, novels, and poems being produced today (to say nothing of all those "other forms of writing," including literary criticism, that are clamoring for our attention) to satisfy anyone interested in high literature, or popular genres, or any form of "cultural production" whatsoever. They also raise the obviously reflexive question: "Assuming that all traditionally 'canonized' works were eliminated, overnight, from the syllabus of every English department in the world, would not comparable problems of priority, value, elitism, ideological pressure, authoritarianism, and arbitrariness almost(?) immediately arise with reference to *whatever* works — of whatsoever kind and nature — were substituted for them?"

If, say, the place on the syllabus currently assigned to *King Lear* were reassigned to *King Kong,* those of us currently debating the relative merits of the Quarto, the Folio, or a conflated version of *King Lear* would, *mutatis mutandis,*° have to decide whether to concentrate classroom attention on the "classic" version of *King Kong,* originally produced in 1933, or to focus on the 1974 remake (which by now has many ardent admirers of its own). Although classroom time might not allow the inclusion of both, a decision to exclude either version might well seem arbitrary or authoritarian and so give rise to grumbles about the "canon." Moreover, comparable questions of "canonization" might well arise with reference to other films excluded from a syllabus that included either version (or both versions) of *King Kong.* For example: why assign class time to *King Kong* and not to (say) *Slave Girls of the White Rhinoceros*? Who, if any, of us has the right to decide whether *King Lear* or *King Kong* or the *Slave Girls* should, or should not, be included on, or excluded from, the syllabus? And can the decision to include, or exclude, any one of them be made, by any one of us, on any grounds whatsoever that do *not* have to do with comparative merit, or comparative value judgments, or with special interests — that is, with the aesthetic or ideological priorities, preferences, and prejudices of the assigners of positions on whatever syllabus there is? And insofar as most, if not all, of our judgments and preferences are comparative, are they not, inevitably, hierarchical?

Is there, in fact, any form of endeavor or accomplishment known to the human race — from sport to ballet to jazz to cooking — wherein comparative standards of excellence comparable to certain "hierarchical" and "elitist" conceptions of literature are nonexistent? Even bad-film buffs find certain bad films more gloriously bad than others. And, perhaps significantly given its comparatively short lifetime, the avant-garde cinema has, by now, produced snobs to rival the most elitist literary critic who ever lived, such as the one who thus puts down a friend who likes ordinary Hollywood films:

> Ah that's all right for you, I know the sort you are, but give me a private job that's shot on faded sepia sixteen millimetre stock with non-professional actors . . . no story and dialogue in French *any day of the week.*

What is striking about this snob's assumption is how characteristic it is of a long tradition of critical elitism that has consistently sneered at popular genres (e.g., romance fiction, soap operas, horror films, westerns, etc.) that are tainted by the profit motive and so tend to "give the public what it wants" in the way of sentimentality, sensationalism, sex, violence, romanticism, and the like.

From "*King Lear* to *King Kong* and Back: Shakespeare and Popular Modern Genres" in "*Bad*" *Shakespeare: Revaluations of the Shakespeare Canon,* edited by Maurice Charney

mutatis mutandis: Substituting different terms (Latin).

CONSIDERATIONS FOR CRITICAL THINKING AND WRITING

1. Do you agree or disagree that "great literature – or bad literature – [is] an artificial category"? Explain why.

2. Why would problems of "priority, value, elitism, ideological pressure, authoritarianism, and arbitrariness" probably become issues for evaluating any new works that replaced canonized works?

3. Write an essay in which you argue for (or against) studying popular arts (for example, popular song lyrics) alongside the works of classic writers such as Shakespeare.

MORRIS DICKSTEIN (B. 1940)

On the Social Responsibility of the Critic   1993

Many critics today, as if in violent reaction to the reading habits of the ordinary citizen, are haunted by the fear of becoming the passive consumer of ideological subtexts or messages. As the country grew more conservative in the eighties, many academic critics turned more radical, and this led to an onslaught by national magazines and media pundits on political correctness, the supposed left-wing and multicultural orthodoxy in American universities.

Here we encounter a number of puzzling paradoxes about "reading" in America today. As reading diminishes – not in absolute terms but in relation to other ways of receiving information – as reading loses its hold on people, the metaphor of reading constantly expands. Molecular biologists like Robert Pollack talk about "reading DNA," the structure of genetic transmission in each living cell. Students of urban life discuss "the city as text" and how to read it, as they did at a conference I attended in 1989. Film scholars publish books about "how to read a film" reflecting on our constantly expanding (and increasingly undifferentiated) notion of what constitutes a text. And literary critics over the past sixty years have developed ever more subtle and complex ways of reading those texts, often using obscure, specialized language that itself resists being read.

As educators worry about the role of video and electronic media in displacing the written word, as the skills of ordinary readers seem to languish, the sophistication and territorial ambition of academic readers continue to grow, widening a split that has been one of the hallmarks of the modern period. The common reader still exists, but many professional readers dissociate themselves on principle from the habits of the tribe: they deliberately read against the grain of the text, against common sense, against most people's way of reading – indeed, against their own way of reading in their ordinary lives. If the reader of *Scarlett* or *Gone with the Wind* reads passively, wanting to be possessed and carried away by a book, as by an old-fashioned movie or piece of music, the critical reader, influenced by theory and by the new historicism, has developed an active, aggressive, even adversarial approach to writing. What Paul Ricoeur in his book on Freud calls the "hermeneutics of suspicion" has become a primary feature of academic criticism, which aims above all to disclose the institutional pressures and ideological formations that speak through texts and influence us as we read.° . . .

Our advanced criticism is especially marked by the suspicion and the hostility with which it performs such operations: its failure to distinguish art from propaganda, literature from advertising; its fierce resistance to the mental framework of the works it examines. "All right, what's wrong with this book?" asks one programmatically suspicious instructor of the students in her humanities class, to make sure they don't get taken in by those "great" books. Some of our recent ideological criticism turns the social understanding of literature, which can be intrinsically valuable, into an all too predictable exercise in debunking and demystification. . . .

The role of the critic is not to read notionally and cleverly, and certainly not to castigate writers for their politics, but to raise ordinary reading to its highest power—to make it more insightful, more acute, without losing touch with our deepest personal responses. It is ironic to speak for the social responsibility of the writer while betraying the public sphere of reading. Criticism, even academic criticism, is neither a sect nor a priesthood but ultimately a public trust, mediating between artists or writers and their often puzzled audience. . . .

A naive reading, anchored in wonder, must remain an indispensable moment of a more self-conscious reading, not just a piece of scaffolding to be kicked away as our suspicion and professionalism take over. We need a better balance between the naive and suspicious readers in ourselves: between the willing suspension of disbelief and our ability to withhold ourselves and read skeptically; between our appreciation of art and our wary knowledge of its persuasive power; between a sympathy for the author as an individual like ourselves—working out creative problems, making contingent choices—and our critical sense of a literary work as the discursive formation of a cultural moment.

From "Damaged Literacy: The Decay of Reading," *Profession 93*

What . . . read: Paul Ricoeur (1913–2005), a French philosopher and critic, author of *Freud and Philosophy: An Essay on Interpretation* (1970). Hermeneutics refers to the theory and method of perceiving and interpreting texts.

CONSIDERATIONS FOR CRITICAL THINKING AND WRITING

1. Do you think video and electronic media are "displacing the written word"? What evidence can you point to in your own experience that refutes or supports this claim?

2. What do you think Dickstein means when he refers to academic criticism as "a public trust"? What should the function of criticism be, according to Dickstein? In what sense is the role of the critic "to raise ordinary reading to its highest power"?

3. What criticism does Dickstein level against contemporary literary criticism? Explain why you agree or disagree with his perspective.

26

Reading and Writing

I can't write five words but that I change seven.

— DOROTHY PARKER

© Bettmann/CORBIS.

THE PURPOSE AND VALUE OF WRITING ABOUT LITERATURE

Introductory literature courses typically include three components: reading, discussion, and writing. Students usually find the readings a pleasure, the class discussions a revelation, and the writing assignments — at least initially — a little intimidating. Writing an analysis of the symbolic use of a wall in Robert Frost's "Mending Wall" (p. 359) or in Herman Melville's story "Bartleby, the Scrivener," for example, may seem considerably more daunting than making a case for animal rights or analyzing a campus newspaper editorial that calls for grade reforms. Like Bartleby, you might want to respond with "I would prefer not to." Literary topics are not, however, all that different from the kinds of papers assigned in English composition courses; many of the same skills are required for both. Regardless of the type of paper, you must develop a thesis and support it with evidence in language that is clear and persuasive.

Whether the subject matter is a marketing survey, a political issue, or a literary work, writing is a method of communicating information and perceptions. Writing teaches. But before writing becomes an instrument for informing the reader, it serves as a means of learning for the writer. An essay is a process of discovery as well as a record of what has been discovered. One of the chief benefits of writing is that we frequently realize what we want to say only after trying out ideas on a page and seeing our thoughts take shape in language.

More specifically, writing about a literary work encourages us to be better readers because it requires a close examination of the elements of a short story, poem, or play. To determine how plot, character, setting, point of view, style, tone, irony, or any number of other literary elements function in a work, we must study them in relation to one another as well as separately. Speed-reading won't do. To read a text accurately and validly — neither ignoring nor distorting significant details — we must return to the work repeatedly to test our responses and interpretations. By paying attention to details and being sensitive to the author's use of language, we develop a clearer understanding of how the work conveys its effects and meanings.

Nevertheless, students sometimes ask why it is necessary or desirable to write about a literary work. Why not allow stories, poems, and plays to speak for themselves? Isn't it presumptuous to interpret Hemingway, Dickinson, or Shakespeare? These writers do, of course, speak for themselves, but they do so indirectly. Literary criticism does not seek to replace the text by explaining it but to enhance our readings of works by calling attention to elements that we might have overlooked or only vaguely sensed.

Another misunderstanding about the purpose of literary criticism is that it crankily restricts itself to finding faults in a work. Critical essays are sometimes mistakenly equated with newspaper and magazine reviews of recently published works. Reviews typically include summaries and evaluations to inform readers about a work's nature and quality, but critical essays assume that readers are already familiar with a work. Although a critical essay may point out limitations and flaws, most criticism — and certainly the kind of essay usually written in an introductory literature course — is designed to explain, analyze, and reveal the complexities of a work. Such sensitive consideration increases our appreciation of the writer's achievement and significantly adds to our enjoyment of a short story, poem, or play. In short, the purpose and value of writing about literature are that doing so leads to greater understanding and pleasure.

READING THE WORK CLOSELY

Know the piece of literature you are writing about before you begin your essay. Think about how the work makes you feel and how it is put together. The more familiar you are with how the various elements of the text convey effects and meanings, the more confident you will be explaining whatever perspective on it you ultimately choose. Do not insist that everything make sense on a first reading. Relax and enjoy yourself; you can be attentive and still allow the author's words to work their magic on you. With subsequent readings, however, go more slowly and analytically as you try to establish relations between characters, actions, images, or whatever else seems important. Ask yourself why you respond as you do. Think as you read, and notice how the parts of a work contribute to its overall nature. Whether the work is a short story, poem, or play, you will read relevant portions of it over and over, and will very likely find more to discuss in each review if the work is rich.

It's best to avoid reading other critical discussions of a work before you are thoroughly familiar with it. There are several good reasons for following this advice. By reading interpretations before you know a work, you deny yourself the pleasure of discovery. That is a bit like starting with the last chapter in a mystery novel. But perhaps even more important than protecting the surprise and delight that a work might offer is that a premature reading of a critical discussion will probably short-circuit your own responses. You will see the work through the critic's eyes and have to struggle with someone else's perceptions and ideas before you can develop your own.

Reading criticism can be useful, but not until you have thought through your own impressions of the text. A guide should not be permitted to become a tyrant. This does not mean, however, that you should avoid background information about a work — for example, that the title of Peter De Vries's "To His Importunate Mistress" (p. 262) alludes to Andrew Marvell's earlier *carpe diem* poem, "To His Coy Mistress" (p. 81). Knowing something about the author as well as historic and literary contexts can help to create expectations that enhance your reading.

ANNOTATING THE TEXT
AND JOURNAL NOTE-TAKING

As you read, get in the habit of annotating your texts. Whether you write marginal notes, highlight, underline, or draw boxes and circles around important words and phrases, you'll eventually develop a system that allows you to retrieve significant ideas and elements from the text. Another way to record your impressions of a work — as with any other experience — is to keep a journal. By writing down your reactions to characters, images, language, actions, and other matters in a reading journal, you can often determine why you like or dislike a work or feel sympathetic or antagonistic to an author or discover paths into a work that might have eluded you if you hadn't preserved your impressions. Your journal notes and annotations may take whatever form you find useful; full sentences and grammatical correctness are not essential (unless they are to be handed in and your instructor requires that), though they might allow you to make better sense of your own reflections days later. The point is simply to put in writing thoughts that you can retrieve when you need them for class discussion or a writing assignment. Consider the following student annotation of the first twenty-four lines of Andrew Marvell's "To His Coy Mistress" and the journal entry that follows it:

Annotated Text

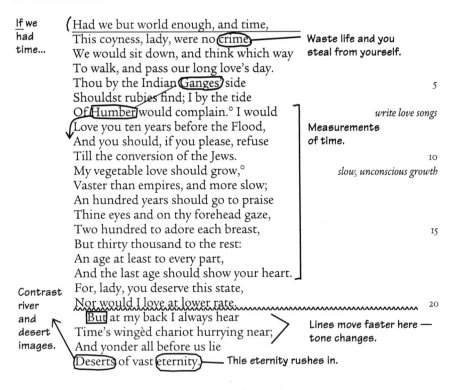

If we had time...

(Had we but world enough, and time,
This coyness, lady, were no crime   — Waste life and you steal from yourself.
We would sit down, and think which way
To walk, and pass our long love's day.
Thou by the Indian Ganges' side   5
Shouldst rubies find; I by the tide
Of Humber would complain.° I would   *write love songs*
Love you ten years before the Flood,   Measurements
And you should, if you please, refuse   of time.
Till the conversion of the Jews.   10
My vegetable love should grow,°   *slow, unconscious growth*
Vaster than empires, and more slow;
An hundred years should go to praise
Thine eyes and on thy forehead gaze,
Two hundred to adore each breast,   15
But thirty thousand to the rest:
An age at least to every part,
And the last age should show your heart.
For, lady, you deserve this state,
Nor would I love at lower rate.   20

Contrast river and desert images.

But at my back I always hear
Time's wingèd chariot hurrying near;   Lines move faster here — tone changes.
And yonder all before us lie
Deserts of vast eternity.   — This eternity rushes in.

Journal Note

He'd be patient and wait for his "mistress" if they had the time--sing songs, praise her, adore her, etc. But they don't have that much time according to him. He seems to be patient but he actually begins by calling patience--her coyness--a "crime." Looks to me like he's got his mind made up from the beginning of the poem. Where's her response? I'm not sure about him.

This journal note responds to some of the effects noted in the annotations of the poem; it's an excellent beginning for making sense of the speaker's argument in the poem.

Taking notes will preserve your initial reactions to the work. Many times first impressions are the best. Your response to a peculiar character, a striking phrase, or a subtle pun might lead to larger perceptions. The student paper on "The Love Song of J. Alfred Prufrock" (p. 700), for example, began with the student making notes in the margins of the text about the disembodied images of eyes and arms that appear in the poem. This, along with the fragmentary thoughts and style of the speaker, eventually led her to examine the significance of the images and how they served to characterize Prufrock.

You should take detailed notes only after you've read through the work. If you write too many notes during the first reading, you're likely to disrupt your response. Moreover, until you have a sense of the entire work, it will be difficult to determine how connections can be made among its various elements. In addition to recording your first impressions and noting significant passages, images, diction, and so on, you should consult the Questions for Responsive Reading and Writing on page 61. These questions can assist you in getting inside a work as well as organizing your notes.

Inevitably, you will take more notes than you finally use in the paper. Note-taking is a form of thinking aloud, but because your ideas are on paper you don't have to worry about forgetting them. As you develop a better sense of a potential topic, your notes will become more focused and detailed.

CHOOSING A TOPIC

If your instructor assigns a topic or offers a choice from among an approved list of topics, some of your work is already completed. Instead of being asked to come up with a topic about Emily Dickinson's poems in this anthology, you may be assigned a three-page essay that specifically discusses "Dickinson's Treatment of Grief in 'The Bustle in a House.'" You also have the assurance that a specified topic will be manageable within the suggested number of pages. Unless you ask your instructor for permission to write on a different or related topic, be certain to address yourself to the assignment. An essay that does not discuss grief but instead describes Dickinson's relationship with her father would be missing the point. Notice, too, that there is room even in an assigned topic to develop your own approach. One question that immediately comes to mind is whether grief defeats or helps the speaker in the poem. Assigned topics do not relieve you of thinking about an aspect of a work, but they do focus your thinking.

At some point during the course, you may have to begin an essay from scratch. You might, for example, be asked to write about a poem that somehow impressed you or that seemed particularly well written or filled with insights. Before you start considering a topic, you should have a sense of how long the paper will be, because the assigned length can help to determine the extent to which you should develop your topic. Ideally, the paper's length should be based on how much space you deem necessary to present your discussion clearly and convincingly, but if you have any doubts and no specific guidelines have been indicated, ask. The question is important; a topic that might be appropriate for a three-page paper could be too narrow for ten pages. Three pages would probably be adequate for a discussion of the speaker's view of death in John Keats's "To Autumn." Conversely, it would be futile to try to summarize Keats's use of sensuality in his poetry in even ten pages; the topic would have to be narrowed to something like "Images of Sensuality in 'La Belle Dame sans Merci.'" Be sure that the topic you choose can be adequately covered in the assigned number of pages.

Once you have a firm sense of how much you are expected to write, you can begin to decide on your topic. If you are to choose what work to write about, select one that genuinely interests you. Too often students pick a poem, because it is mercifully short or seems simple. Such works can certainly be the subjects of fine essays, but simplicity should not be the major reason for selecting them. Choose a work that has moved you so that you have something to say about it. The student who wrote about "The Love Song of J. Alfred Prufrock" was initially attracted to the poem's imagery because she had heard a friend (no doubt an English major) jokingly quote Prufrock's famous lament that "I should have been a pair of ragged claws / Scuttling across the floors of silent seas." Her paper then grew out of her curiosity about the meaning of the images. When a writer is engaged in a topic, the paper has a better chance of being interesting to a reader.

After you have settled on a particular work, your notes and annotations of the text should prove useful for generating a topic. The student paper on Prufrock developed naturally from the notes (p. 700) that the student jotted down about the images. If you think with a pen in your hand, you are likely to find when you review your notes that your thoughts have clustered into one or more topics. Perhaps there are patterns of imagery that seem to make a point about life. There may be symbols that are ironically paired or levels of diction that reveal certain qualities about the speaker. Your notes and annotations on such aspects can lead you to a particular effect or impression. Having chuckled your way through Peter Meinke's "The ABC of Aerobics" (p. 285), you may discover that your notations about the poem's humor point to a serious satire of society's values.

DEVELOPING A THESIS

When you are satisfied that you have something interesting to say about a work and that your notes have led you to a focused topic, you can formulate a *thesis*, the central idea of the paper. Whereas the topic indicates what the paper focuses on (the disembodied images in "Prufrock," for example), the thesis explains what you have to say about the topic (the frightening images of eyes, arms, and claws reflect Prufrock's disjointed, fragmentary response to life). The thesis should be a complete sentence (though sometimes it may require more than one sentence) that establishes your topic in clear, unambiguous language. The thesis may be revised as you get further into the topic and discover what you want to say about it, but once the thesis is firmly established it will serve as a guide for you and your reader, because all of the information and observations in your essay should be related to the thesis.

One student on an initial reading of Andrew Marvell's "To His Coy Mistress" (p. 81) saw that the male speaker of the poem urges a woman to love now before time runs out for them. This reading gave him the impression that the poem is a simple celebration of the pleasures of the flesh, but on subsequent readings he underlined or noted these images: "Time's wingèd chariot hurrying near"; "Deserts of vast eternity"; "marble vault"; "worms"; "dust"; "ashes"; and these two lines: "The grave's a fine and private place, / But none, I think, do there embrace."

By listing these images associated with time and death, he established an inventory that could be separated from the rest of his notes on point of view, character, sounds, and other subjects. Inventorying notes allows patterns to emerge that you might have only vaguely perceived otherwise. Once these images are grouped, they call attention to something darker and more complex in Marvell's poem than a first impression might suggest.

These images may create a different feeling about the poem, but they still don't explain very much. One simple way to generate a thesis about a literary work is to ask the question "why?" Why do these images appear in the poem? Why does the speaker in William Stafford's "Traveling through the Dark" (p. 169) push the dead deer into the river? Why does disorder appeal so much to the speaker in Robert Herrick's "Delight in Disorder" (p. 226)? Your responses to these kinds of questions can lead to a thesis.

Writers sometimes use freewriting to help themselves explore possible answers to such questions. It can be an effective way of generating ideas. Freewriting is exactly that: the technique calls for nonstop writing without concern for mechanics or editing of any kind. Freewriting for ten minutes or so on a question will result in fragments and repetitions, but it can also produce some ideas. Here's an example of a student's response to the question about the images in "To His Coy Mistress":

He wants her to make love. Love poem. There's little time. Her crime. He exaggerates. Sincere? Sly? What's he want? She says nothing — he says it all. What about deserts, ashes, graves, and worms? Some love poem. Sounds like an old Vincent Price movie. Full of sweetness but death creeps in. Death — hurry hurry! Tear pleasures. What passion! Where's death in this? How can a love poem be so ghoulish?

She does nothing. Maybe frightened? Convinced? Why death? Love and death — time — death.

This freewriting contains several ideas; it begins by alluding to the poem's plot and speaker, but the central idea seems to be death. This emphasis led the student to five potential thesis statements for his essay about the poem:

1. "To His Coy Mistress" is a difficult poem.
2. Death in "To His Coy Mistress."
3. There are many images of death in "To His Coy Mistress."
4. "To His Coy Mistress" celebrates the pleasures of the flesh but it also recognizes the power of death to end that pleasure.
5. On the surface, "To His Coy Mistress" is a celebration of the pleasures of the flesh, but this witty seduction is tempered by a chilling recognition of the reality of death.

The first statement is too vague to be useful. In what sense is the poem difficult? A more precise phrasing, indicating the nature of the difficulty, is needed. The second statement is a topic rather than a thesis. Because it is not a sentence, it does not express a complete idea about how the poem treats death. Although this could be an appropriate title, it is inadequate as a thesis statement. The third statement, like the first one, identifies the topic, but even though it is a sentence, it is not a complete idea that tells us anything significant beyond the fact it states. After these preliminary attempts to develop a thesis, the student remembered his first impression of the poem and incorporated it into his thesis statement. The fourth thesis is a useful approach to the poem because it limits the topic and indicates how it will be treated in the paper: the writer will begin with an initial impression of the poem and then go on to qualify it. However, the fifth thesis is better than the fourth because it indicates a shift in tone produced by the ironic relationship between death and flesh. An effective thesis, like this one, makes a clear statement about a manageable topic and provides a firm sense of direction for the paper.

Most writing assignments in a literature course require you to persuade readers that your thesis is reasonable and supported with evidence. Papers that report information without comment or evaluation are simply summaries. Similarly, a paper that merely pointed out the death images in "To His Coy Mistress" would not contain a thesis, but a paper that attempted to make a case for the death imagery as a grim reminder of how vulnerable flesh is would involve persuasion. In developing a thesis, remember that you are expected not merely to present information but to argue a point.

ARGUING ABOUT LITERATURE

An argumentative essay is designed to make persuasive your interpretation of a work. Arguing about literature doesn't mean that you're engaged in an angry, antagonistic dispute (though controversial topics do sometimes engender heated debates). Instead, argumentation requires that you present your interpretation of a work (or a portion of it) by supporting your discussion with clearly defined terms, ample evidence, and a detailed analysis of relevant portions of the text.

If you have a choice, it's generally best to write about a topic that you feel strongly about. Even if you don't like cats you might find Jane Kenyon's "The Blue Bowl" (p. 125) just the sort of treatment that helps explain why you don't want one. On the other hand, if you're a cat fan, the poem may suggest something essential about cats that you've experienced but have never quite put your finger on. If your essay is to be interesting and convincing, what is important is that it be written from a strong point of view that persuasively argues your evaluation, analysis, and interpretation of a work. It is not enough to say that you like or dislike a work; instead you must give your reader some ideas and evidence that can be accepted or rejected based on the quality of the answers to the questions you raise.

One way to come up with persuasive answers is to generate good questions that will lead you further into the text and to critical issues related to it. Notice how the Perspectives, Complementary Readings, and Critical Case Studies in this anthology raise significant questions and issues about texts from a variety of points of view. Moreover, the critical strategies for reading summarized in Chapter 25 can be a resource for raising questions that can be shaped into an argument. The following lists of questions for the critical approaches covered in Chapter 25 should be useful for discovering arguments you might make about a short story, poem, or play. The page number that follows each heading refers to the discussion in the anthology for that particular approach.

Formalist Questions (p. 648)

1. How do various elements of the work — plot, character, point of view, setting, tone, diction, images, symbol, and so on — reinforce its meanings?
2. How are the elements related to the whole?
3. What is the work's major organizing principle? How is its structure unified?
4. What issues does the work raise? How does the work's structure resolve those issues?

Biographical Questions (p. 650)

1. Are facts about the writer's life relevant to your understanding of the work?

2. Are characters and incidents in the work versions of the writer's own experiences? Are they treated factually or imaginatively?
3. How do you think the writer's values are reflected in the work?

Psychological Questions (p. 652)

1. How does the work reflect the author's personal psychology?
2. What do the characters' emotions and behavior reveal about their psychological states? What types of personalities are they?
3. Are psychological matters such as repression, dreams, and desire presented consciously or unconsciously by the author?

Historical Questions (p. 654)

1. How does the work reflect the period in which it was written?
2. What literary or historical influences helped to shape the work's form and content?
3. How important is the historical context to interpreting the work?

Marxist Questions (p. 655)

1. How are class differences presented in the work? Are characters aware or unaware of the economic and social forces that affect their lives?
2. How do economic conditions determine the characters' lives?
3. What ideological values are explicit or implicit?
4. Does the work challenge or affirm the social order it describes?

New Historicist Questions (p. 656)

1. What kinds of documents outside the work seem especially relevant for shedding light on the work?
2. How are social values contemporary to the work reflected or refuted in the work?
3. How does your own historical moment affect your reading of the work and its historical reconstruction?

Cultural Studies Questions (p. 657)

1. What does the work reveal about the cultural behavior contemporary to it?
2. How does popular culture contemporary to the work reflect or challenge the values implicit or explicit in the work?
3. What kinds of cultural documents contemporary to the work add to your reading of it?
4. How do your own cultural assumptions affect your reading of the work and the culture contemporary to it?

Gender Studies Questions (p. 658)

1. How are the lives of men and women portrayed in the work? Do the men and women in the work accept or reject these roles?
2. Is the work's form and content influenced by the author's gender?
3. What attitudes are explicit or implicit concerning heterosexual, homosexual, or lesbian relationships? Are these relationships sources of conflict? Do they provide resolutions to conflicts?
4. Does the work challenge or affirm traditional ideas about men and women and same-sex relationships?

Mythological Questions (p. 660)

1. How does the story resemble other stories in plot, character, setting, or use of symbols?
2. Does the work present archetypes such as quests, initiations, scapegoats, or withdrawals and returns?
3. Does the protagonist undergo any kind of transformation such as a movement from innocence to experience that seems archetypal?
4. Do any specific allusions to myths shed light on the text?

Reader-Response Questions (p. 662)

1. How do you respond to the work?
2. How do your own experiences and expectations affect your reading and interpretation?
3. What is the work's original or intended audience? To what extent are you similar to or different from that audience?
4. Do you respond in the same way to the work after more than one reading?

Deconstructionist Questions (p. 664)

1. How are contradictory and opposing meanings expressed in the work?
2. How does meaning break down or deconstruct itself in the language of the text?
3. Would you say that ultimate definitive meanings are impossible to determine and establish in the text? Why? How does that affect your interpretation?
4. How are implicit ideological values revealed in the work?

These questions will not apply to all texts, and they are not mutually exclusive. They can be combined to explore a text from several critical perspectives simultaneously. A feminist approach to Anne Bradstreet's "The Author to Her Book" (p. 137) could also use Marxist concerns about class to make observations about the oppression of women's lives in the historical context of the seventeenth century. Your use of these questions should allow you to discover significant issues from which you can develop an argumentative essay that is organized around clearly defined terms, relevant evidence, and a persuasive analysis.

ORGANIZING A PAPER

After you have chosen a manageable topic and developed a thesis — a central idea about it — you can begin to organize your paper. Your thesis, even if it is still somewhat tentative, should help you decide what information will need to be included and provide you with a sense of direction.

Consider again the sample thesis in the section on developing a thesis:

> On the surface, "To His Coy Mistress" is a celebration of the pleasures of the flesh,
> but this witty seduction is tempered by a chilling recognition of the reality of
> death.

This thesis indicates that the paper can be divided into two parts: the pleasures of the flesh and the reality of death. It also indicates an order: because the central point is to show that the poem is more than a simple celebration, the pleasures of the flesh should be discussed first so that another, more complex reading of the poem can follow. If the paper began with the reality of death, its point would be anticlimactic.

Having established such a broad and informal outline, you can draw on your underlinings, margin notations, and notecards for the subheadings and evidence required to explain the major sections of your paper. This next level of detail would look like the following:

1. Pleasures of the flesh

    Part of the traditional tone of love poetry

2. Recognition of death

    Ironic treatment of love

    Diction

    Images

    Figures of speech

    Symbols

    Tone

This list was initially a jumble of terms, but the student arranged the items so that each of the two major sections leads to a discussion of tone. (The student also found it necessary to drop some biographical information from his notes because it was irrelevant to the thesis.) The list indicates that the first part of the paper will establish the traditional tone of love poetry that celebrates the pleasures of the flesh, while the second part will present a more detailed discussion about the ironic recognition of death. The emphasis is on the latter because that is the point to be argued in the paper. Hence the thesis has helped to organize the parts of the paper, establish an order, and indicate the paper's proper proportions.

The next step is to fill in the subheadings with information from your notes. Many experienced writers find that making lists of information to be included under each subheading is an efficient way to develop paragraphs. For a longer paper (perhaps a research paper), you should be able to develop a paragraph or more on each subheading. On the other hand, a shorter paper may require that you combine several subheadings in a paragraph. You may also discover that while an informal list is adequate for a brief paper, a ten-page assignment could require a more detailed outline. Use the method that is most productive for you. Whatever the length of the essay, your presentation must be in a coherent and logical order that allows your reader to follow the argument and evaluate the evidence. The quality of your reading can be demonstrated only by the quality of your writing.

WRITING A DRAFT

The time for sharpening pencils, arranging your desk, and doing almost anything else instead of writing has ended. The first draft will appear on the page only if you stop avoiding the inevitable and sit, stand up, or lie down to write. It makes no difference how you write, just so you do. Now that you have developed a topic into a tentative thesis, you can assemble your notes and begin to flesh out whatever outline you have made.

Be flexible. Your outline should smoothly conduct you from one point to the next, but do not permit it to railroad you. If a relevant and important idea occurs to you now, work it into the draft. By using the first draft as a means of thinking about what you want to say, you will very likely discover more than your notes originally suggested. Plenty of good writers don't use outlines at all but discover ordering principles as they write. Do not attempt to compose a perfectly correct draft the first time around. Grammar, punctuation, and spelling can wait until you revise. Concentrate on what you are saying. Good writing most often occurs when you are in hot pursuit of an idea rather than in a nervous search for errors.

To make revising easier, leave wide margins and extra space between lines so that you can easily add words, sentences, and corrections. Write on only one side of the paper. Your pages will be easier to keep track of that way, and, if you have to clip a paragraph to place it elsewhere, you will not lose any writing on the other side.

If you are working on a word processor, you can take advantage of its capacity to make additions and deletions as well as move entire paragraphs by making just a few simple keyboard commands. Some software programs can also check spelling and certain grammatical elements in your writing. It's worth remembering, however, that though a clean copy fresh off a printer may look terrific, it will read only as well as the thinking and writing that have gone into it. Many writers prudently store their data on disks and print their pages each time they finish a draft to avoid losing any material because of power failures or other problems. These printouts are also easier to read than the screen when you work on revisions.

Once you have a first draft on paper, you can delete material that is unrelated to your thesis and add material necessary to illustrate your points and make your paper convincing. The student who wrote "Disembodied Images in 'The Love Song of J. Alfred Prufrock'" (p. 700) wisely dropped a paragraph that questioned whether Prufrock displays chauvinistic attitudes toward women. Although this could be an interesting issue, it has nothing to do with the thesis, which explains how the images reflect Prufrock's inability to make a meaningful connection to his world.

Remember that your initial draft is only that. You should go through the paper many times — and then again — working to substantiate and clarify your ideas. You may even end up with several entire versions of the paper. Rewrite. The sentences within each paragraph should be related to a single topic. Transitions should connect one paragraph to the next so that there are no abrupt or confusing shifts. Awkward or wordy phrasing or unclear sentences and paragraphs should be mercilessly poked and prodded into shape.

Writing the Introduction and Conclusion

After you have clearly and adequately developed the body of your paper, pay particular attention to the introductory and concluding paragraphs. It's probably best to write the introduction — at least the final version of it — last, after you know precisely what you are introducing. Because this paragraph is crucial for generating interest in the topic, it should engage the reader and provide a sense of what the paper is about. There is no formula for writing effective introductory paragraphs, because each writing situation is different — depending on the audience, topic, and approach — but if you pay attention to the introductions of the essays you read, you will notice a variety of possibilities. The introductory paragraph to the Prufrock paper, for example, is a straightforward explanation of why the disembodied images are important for understanding Prufrock's character. The rest of the paper then offers evidence to support this point.

Concluding paragraphs demand equal attention because they leave the reader with a final impression. The conclusion should provide a sense of closure instead of starting a new topic or ending abruptly. In the final paragraph about the disembodied images in "Prufrock" the student explains their significance in characterizing Prufrock's inability to think of himself or others as complete and whole human beings. We now see that the images of eyes, arms, and claws are reflections of the fragmentary nature of Prufrock and his world. Of course, the body of your paper is the most important part of your presentation, but do remember that first and last impressions have a powerful impact on readers.

Using Quotations

Quotations can be a valuable means of marshaling evidence to illustrate and support your ideas. A judicious use of quoted material will make your points clearer and more convincing. Here are some guidelines that should help you use quotations effectively.

1. Brief quotations (four lines or fewer of prose or three lines or fewer of poetry) should be carefully introduced and integrated into the text of your paper with quotation marks around them.

> According to the narrator, Bertha "had a reputation for strictness." He tells us that she always "wore dark clothes, dressed her hair simply, and expected contrition and obedience from her pupils."

For brief poetry quotations, use a slash to indicate a division between lines.

> The concluding lines of Blake's "The Tyger" pose a disturbing question: "What immortal hand or eye / Dare frame thy fearful symmetry?"

Lengthy quotations should be separated from the text of your paper. More than three lines of poetry should be double-spaced and centered on the page. More than four lines of prose should be double-spaced and indented ten spaces from the left margin, with the right margin the same as for the text. Do *not* use quotation marks for the passage; the indentation indicates that the passage is a quotation. Lengthy quotations should not be used in place of your own writing. Use them only if they are absolutely necessary.

2. If any words are added to a quotation, use brackets to distinguish your addition from the original source.

> "He [Young Goodman Brown] is portrayed as self-righteous and disillusioned."

Any words inside quotation marks and not in brackets must be precisely those of the author. Brackets can also be used to change the grammatical structure of a quotation so that it fits into your sentence.

> Smith argues that Chekhov "present[s] the narrator in an ambivalent light."

If you drop any words from the source, use an ellipsis (three spaced periods) to indicate that the omission is yours.

> "Early to bed . . . makes a man healthy, wealthy, and wise."

Use an ellipsis preceding a period to indicate an omission at the end of a sentence.

"Early to bed and early to rise makes a man healthy . . . ."

Use a single line of spaced periods to indicate the omission of a line or more of poetry or more than one paragraph of prose.

Nothing would sleep in that cellar, dank as a ditch,

Bulbs broke out of boxes hunting for chinks in the dark,

. . . .

Nothing would give up life:

Even the dirt kept breathing a small breath.

3. You will be able to punctuate quoted material accurately and confidently if you observe these conventions.
Place commas and periods inside quotation marks.

"Even the dirt," Roethke insists, "kept breathing a small breath."

Even though a comma does not appear after "dirt" in the original quotation, it is placed inside the quotation mark. The exception to this rule occurs when a parenthetical reference to a source follows the quotation.

"Even the dirt," Roethke insists, "kept breathing a small breath" (11).

Punctuation marks other than commas or periods go outside the quotation marks unless they are part of the material quoted.

What does Roethke mean when he writes that "the dirt kept breathing a small breath"?

Yeats asked, "How can we know the dancer from the dance?"

REVISING AND EDITING

Put some distance — a day or so if you can — between yourself and each draft of your paper. The phrase that seemed just right on Wednesday may be revealed as all wrong on Friday. You'll have a better chance of detecting lumbering sentences and thin paragraphs if you plan ahead and give yourself the time to read your paper from a fresh perspective. Through the process of revision, you can transform a competent paper into an excellent one.

Begin by asking yourself if your approach to the topic requires any rethinking. Is the argument carefully thought out and logically presented? Are there any gaps in the presentation? How well is the paper organized? Do the paragraphs lead into one another? Does the body of the paper deliver what the thesis promises? Is the interpretation sound? Are any relevant and important elements of the work ignored or distorted to advance the thesis? Are the points supported with evidence? These large questions should be addressed before you focus on more detailed matters. If you uncover serious problems as a result of considering these questions, you'll probably have quite a lot of rewriting to do, but at least you will have the opportunity to correct the problems — even if doing so takes several drafts.

A useful technique for spotting awkward or unclear moments in the paper is to read it aloud. You might also try having a friend read it aloud to you. If your handwriting is legible, your friend's reading — perhaps accompanied by hesitations and puzzled expressions — could alert you to passages that need reworking. Having identified problems, you can readily correct them on a word processor or on the draft provided you've skipped lines and used wide margins. The final draft you hand in should be neat and carefully proofread for any inadvertent errors.

The following checklist offers questions to ask about your paper as you revise and edit it. Most of these questions will be familiar to you; however, if you need help with any of them, ask your instructor or review the appropriate section in a composition handbook.

Questions for Revising and Editing

1. Is the topic manageable? Is it too narrow or too broad?
2. Is the thesis clear? Is it based on a careful reading of the work?
3. Is the paper logically organized? Does it have a firm sense of direction?
4. Is your argument persuasive? Do you use evidence from the text to support your main points?
5. Should any material be deleted? Do any important points require further illustration or evidence?
6. Does the opening paragraph introduce the topic in an interesting manner?
7. Are the paragraphs developed, unified, and coherent? Are any too short or long?
8. Are there transitions linking the paragraphs?
9. Does the concluding paragraph provide a sense of closure?
10. Is the tone appropriate? Is it unduly flippant or pretentious?
11. Is the title engaging and suggestive?
12. Are the sentences clear, concise, and complete?

(continued)

13. Are simple, complex, and compound sentences used for variety?

14. Have technical terms been used correctly? Are you certain of the meanings of all of the words in the paper? Are they spelled correctly?

15. Have you documented any information borrowed from books, articles, or other sources? Have you quoted too much instead of summarizing or paraphrasing secondary material?

16. Have you used a standard format for citing sources (see p. 720)?

17. Have you followed your instructor's guidelines for the manuscript format of the final draft?

18. Have you carefully proofread the final draft?

When you proofread your final draft, you may find a few typographical errors that must be corrected but do not warrant printing an entire page again. Provided there are not more than a handful of such errors throughout the page, they can be corrected as shown in the following passage. This example condenses a short paper's worth of errors; no single passage should be this shabby in your essay.

To add a letter or word, use a caret on the line where the addition ^is^ needed. To delete a word draw a single line through ~~through~~ it. Run-on words are separated by a vertical|line, and inadvertent spaces are closed like t⌣his. Transposed letters are indicated this w⌣ay. New paragraphs are noted with the sign ¶ in front of where the next paragraph is to begin. ¶ Unless you . . .

These sorts of errors can be minimized by proofreading on the screen and simply entering corrections as you go along.

MANUSCRIPT FORM

The novelist and poet Peter De Vries once observed in his characteristically humorous way that he very much enjoyed writing but that he couldn't bear the "paper work." Behind this playful pun is a half-serious impatience with the mechanics of it all. You may feel some of that too, but this is not the time to allow a thoughtful, carefully revised paper to trip over minor details that can be easily accommodated. The final draft you hand in to your instructor should not only read well but look neat. If your instructor does not provide specific instructions concerning the paper's format, follow these guidelines.

1. Papers (particularly long ones) should be typed, double-spaced, on 8½ × 11-inch paper. Avoid transparent paper such as onionskin; it is diffi-

cult to read and write comments on. If you compose on a word processor be certain that the print is legible. If your instructor accepts handwritten papers, write legibly in ink on only one side of a wide-lined page.

2. Use a one-inch margin at the top, bottom, and sides of each page. Unless you are instructed to include a separate title page, type your name, instructor's name, course number and section, and date on separate lines one inch below the upper-left corner of the first page. Double-space between these lines and then center the title below the date. Do not underline or put quotation marks around your paper's title, but do use quotation marks around the titles of poems, short stories, or other brief works, and underline the titles of books and plays (a sample paper title: "Mending Wall" and Other Boundaries in Frost's <u>North of Boston</u>). Begin the text of your paper two spaces below the title. If you have used secondary sources, center the heading "Notes" or "Works Cited" one inch from the top of a separate page and then double-space between it and the entries.

3. Number each page consecutively, beginning with page 1, a half inch from the top of the page in the upper-right corner.

4. Gather the pages with a paper clip rather than staples, folders, or some other device. That will make it easier for your instructor to handle the paper.

TYPES OF WRITING ASSIGNMENTS

The types of papers most frequently assigned in literature classes are explication, analysis, and comparison and contrast. Most writing about literature involves some combination of these skills. This section includes a sample explication, an analysis, and a comparison and contrast paper. For a sample research paper that demonstrates a variety of strategies for documenting outside sources, see page 729. For other examples of student papers, see pages 698, 700, and 707.

Explication

The purpose of this approach to a literary work is to make the implicit explicit. ***Explication*** is a detailed explanation of a passage of poetry or prose. Because explication is an intensive examination of a text line by line, it is mostly used to interpret a short poem in its entirety or a brief passage from a long poem, short story, or play. Explication can be used in any kind of paper when you want to be specific about how a writer achieves a certain effect. An explication pays careful attention to language: the connotations of words, allusions, figurative language, irony, symbol, rhythm, sound, and so on. These elements are examined in relation to one another and to the work's overall effect and meaning.

The simplest way to organize an explication is to move through the passage line by line, explaining whatever seems significant. It is wise to avoid, however, an assembly-line approach that begins each sentence with "In line one. . . ." Instead, organize your paper in whatever way best serves your thesis. You might find that the right place to start is with the final lines, working your way back to the beginning of the poem or passage. The following sample explication on Emily Dickinson's "There's a certain Slant of light" does just that. The student's opening paragraph refers to the final line of the poem in order to present her thesis. She explains that though the poem begins with an image of light, it is not a bright or cheery poem but one concerned with "the look of Death." Because the last line prompted her thesis, that is where she begins the explication.

You might also find it useful to structure a paper by discussing various elements of literature, so that you have a paragraph on connotative words followed by one on figurative language and so on. However your paper is organized, keep in mind that the aim of an explication is not simply to summarize the passage but to comment on the effects and meanings produced by the author's use of language in it. An effective explication (the Latin word *explicare* means "to unfold") displays a text to reveal how it works and what it signifies. Although writing an explication requires some patience and sensitivity, it is an excellent method for coming to understand and appreciate the elements and qualities that constitute literary art.

A SAMPLE EXPLICATION

A Reading of Dickinson's "There's a certain Slant of light"

The sample paper by Bonnie Katz is the result of an assignment calling for an explication of about 750 words on any poem by Emily Dickinson. Katz selected "There's a certain Slant of light."

EMILY DICKINSON (1830–1886)

There's a certain Slant of light   *c. 1861*

There's a certain Slant of light,
Winter Afternoons —
That oppresses, like the Heft
Of Cathedral Tunes —

Heavenly Hurt, it gives us —   5
We can find no scar,
But internal difference,
Where the Meanings, are —

None may teach it — Any —
'Tis the Seal Despair —   10
An imperial affliction
Sent us of the Air —

When it comes, the Landscape listens —
Shadows — hold their breath —
When it goes, 'tis like the Distance   15
On the look of Death —

    This essay comments on every line of the poem and provides a coherent reading that relates each line to the speaker's intense awareness of death. Although the essay discusses each stanza in the order that it appears, the introductory paragraph provides a brief overview explaining how the poem's images contribute to its total meaning. In addition, the student does not hesitate to discuss a line out of sequence when it can be usefully connected to another phrase. This is especially apparent in the third paragraph, in her discussion of stanzas 2 and 3. The final paragraph describes some of the poem's formal elements. It might be argued that this discussion could have been integrated into the previous paragraphs rather than placed at the end, but the student does make a connection in her concluding sentence between the pattern of language and its meaning.

    Several other matters are worth noticing. The student works quotations into her own sentences to support her points. She quotes exactly as the words appear in the poem, even Dickinson's irregular use of capital letters. When something is added to a quotation to clarify it, it is enclosed in brackets so that the essayist's words will not be mistaken for the poet's: "Seal [of] Despair." A slash is used to separate line divisions as in "imperial affliction / Sent us of the Air." And, finally, because the essay focuses on a short poem, it is not necessary to include line numbers, though they would be required in a study of a longer work.

Bonnie Katz

Professor Quiello

English 109–2

October 26, 2006

A Reading of Dickinson's

"There's a certain Slant of light"

Because Emily Dickinson did not provide titles for her poetry, editors follow the customary practice of using the first line of a poem as its title. However, a more appropriate title for "There's a certain Slant of light," one that suggests what the speaker in the poem is most concerned about, can be drawn from the poem's last line, which ends with "the look of Death." Although the first line begins with an image of light, nothing bright, carefree, or cheerful appears in the poem. Instead, the predominant mood and images are darkened by a sense of despair resulting from the speaker's awareness of death.

In the first stanza, the "certain Slant of light" is associated with "Winter Afternoons," a phrase that connotes the end of a day, a season, and even life itself. Such light is hardly warm or comforting. Not a ray or beam, this slanting light suggests something unusual or distorted and creates in the speaker a certain slant on life that is consistent with the cold, dark mood that winter afternoons can produce. Like the speaker, most of us have seen and felt this sort of light: it "oppresses" and pervades our sense of things when we encounter it. Dickinson uses the senses of hearing and touch as well as sight to describe the overwhelming oppressiveness that the speaker experiences. The light is transformed into sound by a simile that tells us it is "like the Heft / Of Cathedral Tunes." Moreover, the "Heft" of that sound--the slow, solemn measures of tolling church bells and organ music--weighs heavily on our spirits. Through the use of shifting imagery, Dickinson evokes a kind of spiritual numbness that we keenly feel and perceive through our senses.

By associating the winter light with "Cathedral Tunes," Dickinson lets us know that the speaker is concerned about more than the weather. Whatever it is that "oppresses" is related by connotation to faith, mortality, and God. The second and third stanzas offer several suggestions about this connection. The pain caused by the light is a "Heavenly Hurt." This "imperial affliction / Sent us

Thesis providing overview of explication

Line-by-line explication of first stanza, focusing on connotations of words and imagery, in relation to mood and meaning of poem as a whole; supported with references to the text

of the Air" apparently comes from God above, and yet it seems to be part of the very nature of life. The oppressiveness we feel is in the air, and it can neither be specifically identified at this point in the poem nor be eliminated, for "None may teach it--Any." All we know is that existence itself seems depressing under the weight of this "Seal [of] Despair." The impression left by this "Seal" is stamped within the mind or soul rather than externally. "We can find no scar," but once experienced this oppressiveness challenges our faith in life and its "Meanings."

> Explication of second, third, and fourth stanzas, focusing on connotations of words and imagery in relation to mood and meaning of poem as a whole; supported with references to the text

The final stanza does not explain what those "Meanings" are, but it does make clear that the speaker is acutely aware of death. As the winter daylight fades, Dickinson projects the speaker's anxiety onto the surrounding landscape and shadows, which will soon be engulfed by the darkness that follows this light: "the Landscape listens-- / Shadows--hold their breath." This image firmly aligns the winter light in the first stanza with darkness. Paradoxically, the light in this poem illuminates the nature of darkness. Tension is released when the light is completely gone, but what remains is the despair that the "imperial affliction" has imprinted on the speaker's sensibilities, for it is "like the Distance / On the look of Death." There can be no relief from what that "certain Slant of light" has revealed because what has been experienced is permanent--like the fixed stare in the eyes of someone who is dead.

The speaker's awareness of death is conveyed in a thoughtful, hushed tone. The lines are filled with fluid l and s sounds that are appropriate for the quiet, meditative voice in the poem. The voice sounds tentative and uncertain-- perhaps a little frightened. This seems to be reflected in the slightly irregular meter of the lines. The stanzas are trochaic with the second and fourth lines of each stanza having five syllables, but no stanza is identical because each works a slight variation on the first stanza's seven syllables in the first and third lines. The rhymes also combine exact patterns with variations. The first and third lines of each stanza are not exact rhymes, but the second and fourth lines are exact so that the paired words are more closely related: Afternoons, Tunes; scar, are; Despair, Air; and breath, Death. There is a pattern to the poem, but it is unobtrusively woven into the speaker's voice in much the same way that "the look of Death" is subtly present in the images and language of the poem.

> Explication of the elements of rhythm and sound throughout poem

> Conclusion tying explication of rhythm and sound with explication of words and imagery in previous paragraphs

Analysis

The preceding sample essay shows how an explication examines in detail the important elements in a work and relates them to the whole. An *analysis,* however, usually examines only a single element — such as diction, character, point of view, symbol, tone, or irony — and relates it to the entire work. An analytic topic separates the work into parts and focuses on a specific one; you might consider "Point of View in 'The Love Song of J. Alfred Prufrock,'" "Patterns of Rhythm in Robert Browning's 'My Last Duchess,'" or "Irony in 'The Road Not Taken.'" The specific element must be related to the work as a whole or it will appear irrelevant. It is not enough to point out that there are many death images in Andrew Marvell's "To His Coy Mistress"; the images must somehow be connected to the poem's overall effect.

Whether an analytic paper is just a few pages or many, it cannot attempt to discuss everything about the work it is considering. Only those elements that are relevant to the topic can be treated. This kind of focusing makes the topic manageable; this is why most papers that you write will probably be some form of analysis. Explications are useful for a short passage, but a line-by-line commentary on a story, play, or long poem simply isn't practical. Because analysis allows you to consider the central effect or meaning of an entire work by studying a single important element, it is a useful and common approach to longer works.

A SAMPLE ANALYSIS

Disembodied Images in "The Love Song of J. Alfred Prufrock"

Beth Hart's paper analyzes some of the images in T. S. Eliot's "The Love Song of J. Alfred Prufrock" (the poem appears on p. 456). The assignment simply called for an essay of approximately 750 words on a poem written in the twentieth century. The approach was left to the student.

The idea for this essay began with Hart asking herself why there are so many fragmentary, disjointed images in the poem. The initial answer to this question was that "The disjointed images are important for understanding Prufrock's character." This answer was the rough beginning of a tentative thesis. What still had to be explained, though, was how the images are important. To determine the significance of the disjointed images, Hart jotted down some notes based on her underlinings and marginal notations.

Prufrock	Images
odd name--nervous, timid?	fog
"indecisions," "revisions"	lost, wandering

confessional tone, self-conscious	watching eyes
	ladies' arms
"bald spot"	polite talk, meaningless talk
"afraid"	"ragged claws" that scuttle
questioning, tentative	oppressive
"I am not Prince Hamlet"	distorted
"I grow old"	weary longing
wake--to drown	entrapped--staircase

From these notes Hart saw that the images—mostly fragmented and disjointed—suggested something about Prufrock's way of describing himself and his world. This insight led eventually to the final version of her thesis statement: "Eliot's use of frightening disembodied images such as eyes, arms, and claws reflects Prufrock's terror at having to face a world to which he feels no meaningful connection." Her introductory paragraph concludes with this sentence so that her reader can fully comprehend why she then discusses the images of eyes, arms, and claws that follow.

The remaining paragraphs present details that explain the significance of the images of eyes in the second paragraph, the arms in the third, the claws in the fourth, and in the final paragraph all three images are the basis for concluding that Prufrock's vision of the world is disconnected and disjointed.

Hart's notes certainly do not constitute a formal outline, but they were useful to her in establishing a thesis and recognizing what elements of the poem she needed to cover in her discussion. Her essay is sharply focused, well organized, and generally well written (though some readers might wish for a more engaging introductory paragraph that captures a glint of Prufrock's "bald spot" or some other small detail in order to generate some immediate interest in his character).

Beth Hart

Professor Lucas

English 110–3

March 30, 2006

Disembodied Images in

"The Love Song of J. Alfred Prufrock"

T. S. Eliot's poem "The Love Song of J. Alfred Prufrock" addresses the

dilemma of a man who finds himself trapped on the margins of the social world,

unable to make any meaningful interpersonal contact because of his deep-

seated fear of rejection and misunderstanding. Prufrock feels acutely discon-

nected from society, which makes him so self-conscious that he is frightened

into a state of social paralysis. His overwhelming self-consciousness, disillusion-

ment with social circles, and lack of connection with those around him are re-

vealed through Eliot's use of fragmented imagery. Many of the predominant

images are disembodied pieces of a whole, revealing that Prufrock sees the world

not as fully whole or complete, but as disjointed, fragmented parts of the whole.

Eliot's use of frightening disembodied images such as eyes, arms, and claws

reflects Prufrock's terror at having to face a world to which he feels no meaning-

ful connection.

Eliot suggests Prufrock's acute self-consciousness through the fragmentary

image of "eyes." Literally, these eyes merely represent the people who surround

Prufrock, but this disembodied image reveals his obsessive fear of being watched

and judged by others. His confession that "I have known the eyes already, known

them all-- / The eyes that fix you in a formulated phrase" (lines 55-56) suggests

how deeply he resists being watched, and how uncomfortable he is with himself,

both externally--referring in part to his sensitivity to the "bald spot in the

middle of my hair" (40)--and internally--his relentless self-questioning "'Do I

dare?' and, 'Do I dare?'" (38). The disembodied eyes force the reader to recog-

nize the oppression of being closely watched, and so to share in Prufrock's

painful self-awareness. Prufrock's belief that the eyes have the terrifying and

violent power to trap him like a specimen insect "pinned and wriggling on the

Margin annotations:

Thesis providing overview of writer's analysis

Analysis of the meaning of fragmented imagery in the poem

Close analysis of "eyes" supported with references to the text

wall" (58), to be scrutinized in its agony, further reveals the terror of the floating, accusatory image of the eyes.

The disembodied image of "arms" also reflects Prufrock's distorted vision of both himself and others around him. His acknowledgment that he has "known the arms already, known them all-- / Arms that are braceleted and white and bare" (62-63) relates to the image of the eyes, yet focuses on a very different aspect of the people surrounding Prufrock. Clearly, the braceleted arms belong to women, and that these arms are attached to a perfumed dress (65) suggests that these arms belong to upper-class, privileged women. This is partially what makes the disembodied image of the arms so frightening for Prufrock: he is incapable of connecting with a woman the way he, as a man, is expected to. The image of the arms, close enough to Prufrock to reveal their down of "light brown hair" (64), suggests the potential for reaching out and possibly touching Prufrock. The terrified self-consciousness that the image elicits in him leads Prufrock to wish that he could leave his own body and take on the characteristics of yet another disembodied image.

> Close analysis of "arms" supported with references to the text

Prufrock's despairing declaration, "I should have been a pair of ragged claws / Scuttling across the floors of silent seas" (73-74), offers yet another example of his vision of the world as fragmented and incomplete. The "pair of claws" that he longs to be not only connotes a complete separation from the earthly life that he finds so threatening, so painful, and so meaningless, but also suggests an isolation from others that would allow Prufrock some freedom and relief from social pressures. However, this image of the claws as a form of salvation for Prufrock in fact offers little suggestion of actual progress from his present circumstances; crabs can only "scuttle" from side to side and are incapable of moving directly forward or backward. Similarly, Prufrock is trapped in a situation in which he feels incapable of moving either up or down the staircase (39). Thus, this disembodied image of the claws serves to remind the reader that Prufrock is genuinely trapped in a life that offers him virtually no hope of real connection or wholeness.

> Close analysis of "claws" supported with references to the text

The fragmented imagery that pervades "The Love Song of J. Alfred Prufrock" emphasizes and clarifies Prufrock's vision of the world as disconnected and disjointed. The fact that Prufrock thinks of people in terms of their individual component parts (specifically, eyes and arms) suggests his lack of understanding of people as whole and complete beings. This reflects his vision of himself as a fragmentary self, culminating in his wish to be not a whole crab, but merely a pair of disembodied claws. By use of these troubling images Eliot infuses the poem with the pain of Prufrock's self-awareness and his confusion at the lack of wholeness he feels in his world.

Conclusion of analysis echoes the thesis and draws in points made in previous paragraphs

Hart's essay suggests a number of useful guidelines for analytic papers:

1. Only those points related to the thesis are included. In another type of paper the significance of Eliot's epigraph from Dante, for example, might have been more important than the imagery.

2. The analysis keeps the images in focus while at the same time indicating how they are significant in revealing Prufrock's character.

3. The title is a useful lead into the paper; it provides a sense of what the topic is.

4. The introductory paragraph is direct and clearly indicates that the paper will argue that the images serve to reveal Prufrock's character.

5. Brief quotations are deftly incorporated into the text of the paper to illustrate points. We are told what we need to know about the poem as evidence is provided to support ideas. There is no unnecessary summary.

6. The paragraphs are well developed, unified, and coherent. They flow naturally from one to another. Notice, for example, the smooth transition worked into the final sentence of the third paragraph and the first sentence of the fourth paragraph.

7. Hart makes excellent use of her careful reading and notes by finding revealing connections among the details she has observed.

8. As events in the poem are described, the present tense is used. This avoids awkward tense shifts and lends an immediacy to the discussion.

9. The concluding paragraph establishes the significance of why the images should be seen as a reflection of Prufrock's character and provides a sense of closure by relating the images of Prufrock's disjointed world with the images of his fragmentary self.

10. In short, Hart has demonstrated that she has read the work closely, has understood the function of the images in the revelation of Prufrock's sensibilities, and has argued her thesis convincingly by using evidence from the poem.

Comparison and Contrast

Another essay assignment in literature courses often combined with analytic topics is the type that requires you to write about similarities and differences between or within works. You might be asked to discuss "How Sounds Express Meanings in May Swenson's 'A Nosty Fright' and Lewis Carroll's 'Jabberwocky'" or "Love and Hate in Robert Frost's 'Fire and Ice.'" A ***comparison*** of either topic would emphasize their similarities, while a ***contrast*** would stress their differences. It is possible, of course, to include both perspectives in a paper if you find significant likenesses and differences. A comparison of Andrew Marvell's "To His Coy Mistress" (p. 81) and Richard Wilbur's "A Late Aubade" (p. 84) would, for example, yield similarities, because each poem describes a man urging his lover to make the most of their precious time together; however, important differences also exist in the tone and theme of each poem that would constitute a contrast. (You should, incidentally, be aware that the term *comparison* is sometimes used inclusively to refer to both similarities and differences. If you are assigned a comparison of two works, be sure that you understand what your instructor's expectations are; you may be required to include both approaches in the essay.)

When you choose your own topic, the paper will be more successful—more manageable—if you write on works that can be meaningfully related to each other. Although Robert Herrick's "To the Virgins, to Make Much of Time" (p. 79) and T. S. Eliot's "The Love Song of J. Alfred Prufrock" (p. 456) both have something to do with hesitation, the likelihood of anyone making a connection between the two that reveals something interesting and important is remote—though perhaps not impossible if the topic were conceived imaginatively and tactfully. Choose a topic that encourages you to ask significant questions about each work; the purpose of a comparison or contrast is to understand the works more clearly for having examined them together.

Choose works to compare or contrast that intersect with each other in some significant way. They may, for example, be written by the same author or about the same subject. Perhaps you can compare their use of some technique, such as irony or point of view. Regardless of the specific topic, be sure to have a thesis that allows you to organize your paper around a central idea that argues a point about the two works. If you merely draw up a list of similarities or differences without a thesis in mind, your paper will be little more than a series of observations with no apparent purpose. Keep in the foreground of your thinking what the comparison or contrast reveals about the works.

There is no single way to organize comparative papers as each topic is likely to have its own particular issues to resolve, but it is useful to be aware of two basic patterns that can be helpful with a comparison, a contrast, or a combination of both. One method that can be effective for relatively short papers consists of dividing the paper in half, first discussing one work and then the other. Here, for example, is a partial informal outline for a discussion of Langston Hughes's "Un-American Investigators" (p. 412) and Tato Laviera's "AmeRícan" (p. 284); the topic is a comparison and contrast:

"Two Views of America by Hughes and Laviera"

1. "Un-American Investigators"

    a. Diction

    b. Images

    c. Allusions

    d. Themes

2. "AmeRícan"

    a. Diction

    b. Images

    c. Allusions

    d. Themes

This organizational strategy can be effective provided that the second part of the paper combines the discussion of "AmeRícan" with references to "Un-American Investigators" so that the thesis is made clear and the paper is unified without being repetitive. If the two poems were treated entirely separately, then the discussion would be merely parallel rather than integrated. In a lengthy paper, this organization probably would not work well because a reader would have difficulty remembering the points made in the first half as he or she reads on.

Thus for a longer paper it is usually better to create a more integrated structure that discusses both works as you take up each item in your outline. Shown here in partial outline is the second basic pattern using the elements just cited.

1. Diction
   a. "Un-American Investigators"
   b. "AmeRícan"
2. Images
   a. "Un-American Investigators"
   b. "AmeRícan"
3. Allusions
   a. "Un-American Investigators"
   b. "AmeRícan"
4. Themes
   a. "Un-American Investigators"
   b. "AmeRícan"

This pattern allows you to discuss any number of topics without requiring that your reader recall what you first said about the diction of "Un-American Investigators" before you discuss the diction of "AmeRícan" many pages later. However you structure your comparison or contrast paper, make certain that a reader can follow its elements and keep track of its thesis.

A SAMPLE COMPARISON

Andrew Marvell and Sharon Olds Seize the Day

The following paper responds to an assignment that required a comparison and contrast — about 1,000 words — of two assigned poems. The student chose to write an analysis of two very different *carpe diem* poems.

In the following comparison essay, Christina Smith focuses on the male and female *carpe diem* voices of Andrew Marvell's "To His Coy Mistress" (p. 81) and Sharon Olds's "Last Night" (p. 85). After introducing the topic in the first paragraph, she takes up the two poems in a pattern similar to the first outline suggested for "Two Views of America by Hughes and Laviera." Notice how Smith works in subsequent references to Marvell's poem as she discusses Olds's so that her treatment is integrated and we are reminded why she is comparing the two works. Her final paragraph sums up her points without being repetitive and reiterates the thesis with which she began.

Christina Smith
English 109-10
Professor Monroe
April 2, 2006

Andrew Marvell and Sharon Olds Seize the Day

In her 1996 poem "Last Night," Sharon Olds never mentions Andrew Mar-
vell's 1681 poem "To His Coy Mistress." Through a contemporary lens, however,
she firmly qualifies Marvell's seventeenth-century masculine perspective. Mar-
vell's speaker attempts to woo a young woman and convince her to have sexual
relations with him. His seize-the-day rhetoric argues that "his mistress" should
let down her conventional purity and enjoy the moment, his logic being that we
are grave-bound anyway, so why not? Although his poetic pleading is effective,
both stylistically and argumentatively, Marvell's speaker obviously assumes that
the coy mistress will succumb to his grasps at her sexuality. Further, and most
important, the speaker takes for granted that the female must be persuaded to
love. His smooth talk leaves no room for a feminine perspective, be it a slap in
the face or a sharing of his carpe diem attitudes. Olds accommodates Marvell's
masculine speaker but also deftly takes poetic license in the cause of female
freedom and sensuously lays out her own scenario. Through describing a per-
sonal sexual encounter both erotically and with jarring rawness, Olds's female
speaker demonstrates that women have just as many lustful urges as the men
who would seduce them; she presents sex as neither solely a male quest nor a
female sacrifice. "Last Night" takes a female perspective on sex and fully ex-
plores it at its most raw and basic level.

"To His Coy Mistress" is in a regular rhyme scheme, as each line rhymes with
the next--almost like a compilation of couplets. And this, accompanied by tradi-
tional iambic pentameter, lays the foundation for a forcefully flowing speech, a
command for the couple to just do it. By the end of the poem the speaker seems
to expect his mistress to capitulate. Marvell's speaker declares at the start that
if eternity were upon them, he would not mind putting sex aside and paying her
unending homage. "Had we but world enough, and time, / This coyness, lady,

were no crime. / We would sit down, and think which way / To walk, and pass our long love's day" (lines 1-4). He proclaims that he would love her "ten years before the Flood" (8) and concedes that she "should, if you please, refuse / Till the conversion of the Jews" (9-10). This eternal love-land expands as Marvell asserts that his "vegetable love should grow / Vaster than empires, and more slow" (11-12). Every part of her body would be admired for an entire "age" because "lady, you deserve this state, / Nor would I love at lower rate" (19-20). He would willingly wait but, alas, circumstances won't let him. She'll have to settle for the here and now, and he must show her that life is not an eternity but rather an alarm clock.

The speaker laments that "at my back I always hear / Time's wingèd chariot hurrying near" (21-22). He then cleverly draws a picture of what exactly eternity does have in store for them, namely barren "Deserts" where her "beauty shall no more be found" (25) while "worms shall try / That long preserved virginity" (27-28) and her "quaint honor turn to dust" (29). This death imagery is meant to frighten her for not having lived enough. He astutely concedes that "The grave's a fine and private place, / But none, I think, do there embrace" (31-32), thereby making even more vivid the nightmare he has just laid before her. Although he must make his grim argument, he does not want to dampen the mood, so he quickly returns to her fair features.

"Now," the speaker proclaims, "while the youthful hue / Sits on thy skin like morning dew, / And while thy willing soul transpires / At every pore with instant fires, / Now let us sport us while we may" (33-37). The speaker has already made the decision for her. Through sex, their energies will become one--they will "roll" their "strength" and "sweetness up into one ball" (41) as they "tear" their "pleasures with rough strife" (43). If the two of them cannot have eternity and make the "sun / Stand still" (45-46), then they will seize the day, combine and celebrate their humanity, and "make [the sun] run" (46). The speaker makes a vivid case in favor of living for the moment. His elaborate images of the devotion of his mistress deserves, the inevitability of death, and the vivaciousness of human life are compelling. Three hundred years later, however, Sharon Olds demonstrates that women no longer need--or may never have needed--this lesson, because they share the same desires.

Olds's poem may be read as a contemporary response, though likely unintentional, to "To His Coy Mistress." This poet's fine and private place is not the grave, as it was in Marvell's poetic persuasion, but rather her own sexual encounter. The hard language of the poem, describing this act of sex as a "death-grip / holding to life" (13-14), suggests a familiarity with Marvell's own implications of death. More importantly, her speaker needs no rationale to live fully; she just does. She has sex on her own, willingly, knowingly, and thoroughly.

Unlike "To His Coy Mistress," the poem has no rhyme scheme and has little meter or conventional form. The free verse tells the sexual story in an unconfined, open way. The poem flows together with urgent, sexual images drawn from a place in which nothing exists but biological instinct. It is organic at its most raw, basic level. The speaker and her lover unite "like dragonflies / in the sun, 100 degrees at noon, / the ends of their abdomens stuck together" (2-4). Whereas Marvell's lovers race against time, Olds's seem unaware of it altogether. The only sense of time in the poem is in reference to the morning after sex; the act itself is suspended in an unmeasured space in the speaker's memory. Any descriptive details are reserved for the encounter itself, and the setting is undefined. So it is the language of biology-- "something twisting and / twisting out of a chrysalis, / enormous, without language, all / head, all shut eyes" (6-9)-- that evokes erotic images. There is no foreplay, "No kiss, / no tenderness" (12-13), but the poem does not hint at a power struggle either. The speaker suggests mutuality, describing the lovers as "like violent hands clasped tight" (15). The two are "barely moving" (16), and when they "[start] to die" (19), they do so together.

Afterwards, they return to themselves, away from the sensual, all-consuming world in which they reveled. However, the speaker has not literally or figuratively exhausted the natural world yet. She describes their hairlines as "wet as the arc of a gateway after / a cloudburst" (25-26). The cloudburst is itself a sudden, almost violent phenomenon, not unlike this sexual moment, and though she emerges from the encounter, it stays with her as a vivid memory.

Revisiting memories of the experience the next day allows the speaker to examine the moment, and she reflects in line 26 that it ended in peaceful sleep. The last lines stand in contrast to Marvell's speaker, whose desperate, pleading tone is filled with tension rather than the relief of consummation. As the poem draws to a close (26-29), we see that this sexual encounter is an experience that, however raw, is rooted in tenderness. The erotic language of biology is in her own voice as she describes the two waking in the morning "clasped, fragrant, buoyant" (28). Olds's subject does not have to be persuaded by an excited man to be a sexual being; her sexuality seeps into her normal life, she wakes the next morning "almost afraid" (1) by it, and we marvel at its depth. Unlike Marvell's speaker, who remains eternally poised to "tear our pleasures," Olds's speaker is steeped in those pleasures.

27

The Literary
Research Paper

Does anyone know a good poet who's a
vegetarian?
— DONALD HALL

© Nancy Crampton.

WRITING A LITERARY RESEARCH PAPER

A close reading of a primary source such as a short story, poem, or play can
give insights into a work's themes and effects, but sometimes you will want
to know more. A published commentary by a critic who knows the work
well and is familiar with the author's life and times can provide insights
that otherwise may not be available. Such comments and interpretations —
known as *secondary sources* — are, of course, not a substitute for the work it-
self, but they often can take you into a work further than if you made the
journey by yourself.

After imagination, good sense, and energy, perhaps the next most im-
portant quality for writing a research paper is the ability to organize mate-
rial. A research paper on a literary topic requires a writer to take account
of quite a lot at once: the text, ideas, sources, and documentation tech-
niques all make demands on one's efforts to present a topic clearly and
convincingly.

713

The following list should give you a sense of what goes into creating a research paper. Although some steps on the list can be folded into one another, they offer an overview of the work that will involve you.

1. Choosing a topic
2. Finding sources
3. Evaluating sources
4. Taking notes
5. Developing a thesis
6. Organizing an outline
7. Writing drafts
8. Revising
9. Documenting sources
10. Preparing the final draft and proofreading

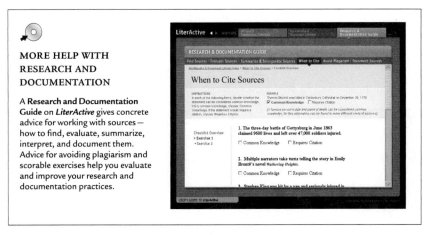

MORE HELP WITH RESEARCH AND DOCUMENTATION

A **Research and Documentation Guide** on *LiterActive* gives concrete advice for working with sources — how to find, evaluate, summarize, interpret, and document them. Advice for avoiding plagiarism and scorable exercises help you evaluate and improve your research and documentation practices.

Even if you have never written a research paper, you most likely have already had experience choosing a topic, developing a thesis, organizing an outline, and writing a draft that you then revised, proofread, and handed in. Those skills represent six of the ten items on the list. This chapter briefly reviews some of these steps and focuses on the remaining tasks, unique to research paper assignments.

CHOOSING A TOPIC

Chapter 26 discusses the importance of reading a work closely and taking careful notes as a means of generating topics for writing about literature. If you know a work well and record your understanding of it in notes, you'll have impressions and ideas to choose from for potential topics. You may find it useful to review the information on pages 679–81 before reading the advice about putting together a research paper in this chapter.

The student author of the sample research paper "Individuality and Community in Frost's 'Mowing' and 'Mending Wall'" (p. 729) was asked to write a five-page paper that demonstrated some familiarity with published critical perspectives on two Robert Frost poems of her choice. Before looking into critical discussions of the poems, she read them several times, taking notes and making comments in the margin of her textbook on each reading.

What prompted her choice of "Mending Wall," for example, was a class discussion that focused on the poem's speaker's questioning the value and necessity of the wall in contrast to his neighbor's insistence on it. At one point, however, the boundaries of the discussion opened up to the possibility that the wall is important to both characters in the poem rather than only the neighbor. It is, after all, the speaker, not the neighbor, who repairs the damage to the wall caused by hunters and who initiates the rebuilding of the wall. Why would he do that if he wanted the wall down? Only after having thoroughly examined the poem did the student go to the library to see what professional critics had to say about this question.

FINDING SOURCES

Whether your college library is large or small, its reference librarians can usually help you locate secondary sources about a particular work or author. Unless you choose a very recently published poem, play, or essay about which little or nothing has been written, you should be able to find out more about a literary work efficiently and quickly. Even if a work has been published recently, you can probably find relevant information on the Internet (see Electronic Sources, p. 717). Here are some useful reference sources that can help you to establish both an overview of a potential topic and a list of relevant books and articles.

Annotated List of References

> *American Writers.* 4 vols. New York: Scribner's, 1979. Chronological essays offer biography and criticism of major American writers.
> Baker, Nancy L., and Nancy Huling. *A Research Guide for Undergraduate Students: English and American Literature.* 6th ed. New York: MLA, 2006. Especially designed for students; a useful guide to reference sources.
> Bryer, Jackson, ed. *Sixteen Modern American Authors: A Survey of Research and Criticism.* New York: Norton, 1990. Extensive bibliographic essays on Sherwood Anderson, Willa Cather, Hart Crane, Theodore Dreiser, T. S. Eliot, William Faulkner, F. Scott Fitzgerald, Robert Frost, Ernest Hemingway, Eugene O'Neill, Ezra Pound, Edwin Arlington Robinson, John Steinbeck, Wallace Stevens, William Carlos Williams, and Thomas Wolfe.

Contemporary Literary Criticism. A multivolume series. Detroit: Gale, 1973-. Brief biographies of contemporary authors along with excerpts from reviews and criticism of their work.

Corse, Larry B., and Sandra B. Corse. *Articles on American and British Literature: An Index to Selected Periodicals, 1950–1977.* Athens, Ohio: Swallow, 1981. Specifically designed for students using small college libraries.

Dictionary of Literary Biography. Detroit: Gale, 1978-. A multivolume series in progress of American, British, and world writers that provides useful biographical and critical overviews.

Elliot, Emory, et al. *Columbia Literary History of the United States.* New York: Columbia UP, 1998. This updates the discussions in Spiller (p. 717) and reflects recent changes in the canon.

Harner, James L. *Literary Research Guide: A Guide to Reference Sources for the Study of Literature in English and Related Topics.* 4th ed. New York: MLA, 2002. A selective but extensive annotated guide to important bibliographies, abstracts, databases, histories, surveys, dictionaries, encyclopedias, and handbooks; an invaluable research tool with extensive, useful indexes.

Holman, C. Hugh, and William Harmon. *A Handbook to Literature.* 8th ed. New York: Macmillan, 1999. A thorough dictionary of literary terms that also provides brief, clear overviews of literary movements such as Romanticism.

Kuntz, Joseph M., and Nancy C. Martinez. *Poetry Explication: A Checklist of Interpretation since 1925 of British and American Poems Past and Present.* Boston: Hall, 1980.

Merriam-Webster's Encyclopedia of Literature. Springfield, MA: Merriam-Webster, 1995. A guide to authors, works, terms, periods, and topics for world literature.

MLA International Bibliography of Books and Articles on Modern Language and Literature. New York: MLA, 1921-. Compiled annually; a major source for articles and books. Also available online and on CD-ROM.

The New Cambridge Bibliography of English Literature. 5 vols. Cambridge, England: Cambridge UP, 1967-77. An important source on the literature from 600 to 1950.

Ousby, Ian, ed. *The Cambridge Guide to English Literature.* 2d ed. Cambridge, England: Cambridge UP, 1994. A valuable overview.

The Oxford History of English Literature. 13 vols. Oxford, England: Oxford UP, 1945-. The most comprehensive literary history.

The Penguin Companion to World Literature. 4 vols. New York: McGraw-Hill, 1969-71. Covers classical, Asian, African, European, English, and American literature.

Preminger, Alex, and T. V. F. Brogan, eds. *The New Princeton Encyclopedia of Poetry and Poetics.* Princeton, NJ: Princeton UP, 1993. Includes entries on technical terms and poetic movements.

Rees, Robert, and Earl N. Harbert. *Fifteen American Authors before 1900: Bibliographic Essays on Research and Criticism.* Madison: U of Wiscon-

sin P, 1984. Among the writers covered are Stephen Crane and Emily
Dickinson.

Spiller, Robert E., et al. *Literary History of the United States.* 4th ed. 2 vols.
New York: Macmillan, 1974. Coverage of literary movements and indi-
vidual writers from colonial times to the 1960s.

These sources are available in the reference sections of most college li-
braries; ask a reference librarian to help you locate them.

Electronic Sources

You can locate materials in a variety of sources, including card catalogs, spe-
cialized encyclopedias, bibliographies, and indexes to periodicals. Library
Web sites also provide online databases that you can access from home.
This can be an efficient way to establish a bibliography on a specific topic.
Consult a reference librarian about how to use your library's online re-
sources and to determine whether online research is feasible for your topic.

In addition to the many electronic databases ranging from your li-
brary's computerized holdings to the many specialized CD-ROMs avail-
able, such as *MLA International Bibliography* (a major source for articles and
books on literary topics), the Internet also connects millions of sites with
primary sources (the full texts of stories, poems, plays, and essays) and sec-
ondary sources (biography or criticism). If you have not had practice with
research on the Web, it is a good idea to get guidance from your instructor
or a librarian, and by using your library's home page as a starting point.
Browsing on the Internet can be absorbing as well as informative, but un-
less you have plenty of time to spare, don't wait until the last minute to lo-
cate your electronic sources. You might find yourself trying to find reliable,
professional sources among thousands of sites if you enter an unqualified
entry such as "Charles Dickens." Once you are familiar with the Web, how-
ever, you'll find its research potential both fascinating and rewarding.

Do remember that your own college library offers a broad range of
electronic sources. If you're feeling uncertain, intimidated, and profoundly
unplugged, your reference librarians are there to help you to get started.
Once you take advantage of their advice and tutorials, you'll soon find that
negotiating the World Wide Web can be an efficient means of research for
almost any subject.

EVALUATING SOURCES AND TAKING NOTES

Evaluate your sources for their reliability and the quality of their evidence.
Check to see if an article or book has been superseded by later studies; try
to use up-to-date sources. A popular magazine article will probably not
be as authoritative as an article in a scholarly journal. Sources that are well
documented with primary and secondary materials usually indicate that the

author has done his or her homework. Books printed by university presses and established trade presses are preferable to books privately printed. But there are always exceptions. If you are uncertain about how to assess a book, try to find out something about the author. Are there any other books listed in the catalog that indicate the author's expertise? What do book reviews say about the work? Three valuable indexes to book reviews of literary studies are *Book Review Digest, Book Review Index,* and *Index to Book Reviews in the Humanities.* Your reference librarian can show you how to use these important tools for evaluating books. Reviews can be a quick means to get a broad perspective on writers and their works because reviewers often survey previous approaches to the topic under discussion.

A cautionary note: assessing online sources can be more problematic than evaluating print sources because anyone with a computer and online access can publish on the Internet. Be sure to determine the nature of your sources and their authority. Is the site the work of a professional or an amateur? Is the information likely to be reliable? Is it biased? Is it documented? Before placing your trust in an Internet source, make sure that it warrants your confidence.

As you prepare a list of reliable sources relevant to your topic, record the necessary bibliographic information so that it will be available when you make up the list of works cited for your paper. For a book include the author, complete title, place of publication, publisher, and date. For an article include author, complete title, name of periodical, volume number, date of issue, and page numbers. For an Internet source, include the author, complete title, database title, periodical or site name, date of posting of the site (or last update), name of institution or organization, date when you accessed the source, and the network address (URL).

Once you have assembled a tentative bibliography, you will need to take notes on your readings. Be sure to keep track of where the information comes from by recording the author's name and page number. If you use more than one work by the same author include a brief title as well as the author's name.

DEVELOPING A THESIS AND ORGANIZING THE PAPER

As the notes on "Mowing" and "Mending Wall" accumulated, the student sorted them into topics including

1. Publication history of the poems
2. Frost's experiences as a farmer
3. Critics' readings of the poems
4. The speaker's attitude toward the wall

5. The neighbor's attitude toward the wall

6. Mythic elements in the poems

7. Does the wall have any positive value?

8. How do the speaker and neighbor characterize themselves?

9. Humor and tone in the poems

10. Frost as a regional poet

The student quickly saw that items 1, 2, 6, and 10 were not directly related to her topic concerning why the speaker initiates the rebuilding of the wall. The remaining numbers (3-5, 7-9) are the topics taken up in the paper. The student had begun her reading of secondary sources with a tentative thesis that stemmed from her question about why the poem's speaker helps his neighbor to rebuild the wall. That "why" shaped itself into the expectation that she would have a thesis something like this: "The speaker helps to rebuild the wall because. . . ."

She assumed she would find information that indicated some specific reason. But the more she read the more she discovered that there was no single explanation provided by the poem or by critics' readings of the poem. Instead, through the insights provided by her sources, she began to see that the wall had several important functions in the poem. The perspective she developed into her thesis — that the wall "provided a foundation upon which the men build a personal sense of identity" — allowed her to incorporate a number of the critics' insights into her paper in order to shed light on why the speaker helps to rebuild the wall.

Because the assignment was relatively brief, the student did not write up a formal outline but instead organized her stacks of usable notecards and proceeded to write the first draft from them.

REVISING

After writing your first draft, you should review the advice and the Questions for Revising and Editing on pages 692–94 so that you can read your paper with an objective eye. Two days after writing her next-to-last draft, the writer of "Individuality and Community in Frost's 'Mowing' and 'Mending Wall'" realized that she had allotted too much space for critical discussions of the humor in the poem that were not directly related to her approach. She realized that it was not essential to point out and discuss the puns in the poem; hence she corrected this by simply deleting most references to the poem's humor. The point is that she saw this herself after she took some time to approach the paper from a fresh perspective.

DOCUMENTING SOURCES
AND AVOIDING PLAGIARISM

You must acknowledge the use of a source when you (1) quote someone's exact words, (2) summarize or borrow someone's opinions or ideas, or (3) use information and facts that are not considered to be common knowledge. The purpose of this documentation is to acknowledge your sources, to demonstrate that you are familiar with what others have thought about the topic, and to provide your reader access to the same sources. If your paper is not adequately documented, it will be vulnerable to a charge of *plagiarism* — the presentation of someone else's work as your own. Conscious plagiarism is easy to avoid; honesty takes care of that for most people. However, there is a more problematic form of plagiarism that is often inadvertent. Whether inadequate documentation is conscious or not, plagiarism is a serious matter and must be avoided. Papers can be evaluated only by what is on the page, not by their writers' intentions.

Let's look more closely at what constitutes plagiarism. Consider the following passage quoted from A. R. Coulthard, "Frost's 'Mending Wall,'" *Explicator* 45 (Winter 1987): 40:

> "Mending Wall" has many of the features of an "easy" poem aimed at high-minded readers. Its central symbol is the accessible stone wall to represent separation, and it appears to oppose isolating barriers and favor love and trust, the stuff of Golden Treasury of Inspirational Verse.

Now read this plagiarized version:

> "Mending Wall" is an easy poem that appeals to high-minded readers who take inspiration from its symbolism of the stone wall, which seems to oppose isolating barriers and support trusting love.

Though the writer has shortened the passage and made some changes in the wording, this paragraph is basically the same as Coulthard's. Indeed, several of his phrases are lifted almost intact. (Notice, however, that the plagiarized version seems to have missed Coulthard's irony and, therefore, misinterpreted and misrepresented the passage.) Even if a parenthetical reference had been included at the end of the passage and the source included in "Works Cited," the language of this passage would still be plagiarism because it is presented as the writer's own. Both language and ideas must be acknowledged.

Here is an adequately documented version of the passage:

> A. R. Coulthard points out that "high-minded readers" mistakenly assume that "Mending Wall" is a simple inspirational poem that uses the symbolic wall to reject isolationism and to support, instead, a sense of human community (40).

This passage makes absolutely clear that the observation is Coulthard's, and it is written in the student's own language with the exception of one quoted phrase. Had Coulthard not been named in the passage, the parenthetical reference would have included his name: (Coulthard 40).

Some mention should be made of the notion of common knowledge before we turn to the standard format for documenting sources. Observations and facts that are widely known and routinely included in many of your sources do not require documentation. It is not necessary to cite a source for the fact that Alfred, Lord Tennyson, was born in 1809 or that Frost writes about New England. Sometimes it will be difficult for you to determine what common knowledge is for a topic that you know little about. If you are in doubt, the best strategy is to supply a reference.

There are two basic ways to document sources. Traditionally, sources have been cited in footnotes at the bottom of each page or in endnotes grouped together at the end of the paper. Here is how a portion of the sample paper on "Mending Wall" would look if footnotes were used instead of parenthetical documentation:

> It remains one of Frost's more popular poems, and, as Douglas Wilson notes, "one of the most famous in all of American poetry."[1]
>
> [1]Douglas L. Wilson, "The Other Side of the Wall," Iowa Review 10 (Winter 1979): 65.

Unlike endnotes, which are double-spaced throughout and grouped under the title "Notes" at the end of the paper, footnotes appear four spaces below the text. They are single-spaced, with an extra space between notes.

No doubt you will have encountered these documentation methods in your reading. A different style is recommended, however, in the Modern Language Association's *MLA Handbook for Writers of Research Papers,* 6th ed. (2003). The MLA style uses parenthetical references within the text of the paper; these are keyed to an alphabetical list of works cited at the end of the paper. This method is designed to be less distracting for the reader. Unless you are instructed to follow the footnote or endnote style for documentation, use the parenthetical method explained in the next section.

The List of Works Cited

Items in the list of works cited are arranged alphabetically according to the author's last name and indented five spaces after the first line. This allows the reader to locate quickly the complete bibliographic information for the author's name cited within the parenthetical reference in the text. The following are common entries for literature papers and should be used as models. If some of your sources are of a different nature, consult the *MLA Handbook for Writers of Research Papers,* 6th ed. (New York: MLA, 2003); or, for the latest updates, check MLA's Web site at mla.org.

The following entries include examples to follow when citing electronic sources. For electronic sources, include as many of the following elements as apply and as are available:

- Author's name
- Title of work (if it's a book, underline; if it's a short work, such as an article or poem, use quotation marks)
- Title of the site (or of the publication, if you're citing an online periodical, for example), underlined (or italicized)
- Date of publication or last update
- Sponsor of the site (if not named as the author)
- Date you accessed the source
- The URL in angle brackets

A BOOK BY ONE AUTHOR

Hendrickson, Robert. The Literary Life and Other Curiosities. New York: Viking, 1981.

AN ONLINE BOOK

Frost, Robert. A Boy's Will. 1915. Bartleby.com: Great Books Online. 1999. 4 Feb. 2004
   <http://www.bartleby.com/117/>.

PART OF AN ONLINE BOOK

Frost, Robert. "Into My Own." A Boy's Will. 1915. Bartleby.com: Great Books Online.
   1999. 4 Feb. 2004 <http://www.bartleby.com/117/1.html>.

Notice that the author's name is in reverse order. This information, along with the full title, place of publication, publisher, and date, should be taken from the title and copyright pages of the book. The title is underlined to indicate italics and is also followed by a period. If the city of publication is well known, it is unnecessary to include the state. Use the publication date on the title page; if none appears there, use the copyright date (after ©) on the back of the title page.

A BOOK BY TWO AUTHORS

Horton, Rod W., and Herbert W. Edwards. Backgrounds of American Literary Thought. 3rd
   ed. Englewood Cliffs: Prentice, 1974.

Only the first author's name is given in reverse order. The edition number appears after the title.

A BOOK WITH MORE THAN THREE AUTHORS

Gates, Henry Louis, Jr., et al., eds. The Norton Anthology of African American Literature.
New York: Norton, 1997.

(Note: The abbreviation *et al.* means "and others.")

A WORK IN A COLLECTION BY THE SAME AUTHOR

O'Connor, Flannery. "Greenleaf." The Complete Stories. By O'Connor. New York: Farrar,
1971. 311-34.

Page numbers are given because the reference is to only a single story in the collection.

A WORK IN A COLLECTION BY DIFFERENT WRITERS

Frost, Robert. "Design." Poetry: An Introduction. Ed. Michael Meyer. 5th ed. Boston:
Bedford/St. Martin's, 2007. 372.

A TRANSLATED BOOK

Grass, Günter. The Tin Drum. Trans. Ralph Manheim. New York: Vintage-Random, 1962.

AN INTRODUCTION, PREFACE, FOREWORD, OR AFTERWORD

Johnson, Thomas H. Introduction. Final Harvest: Emily Dickinson's Poems. By Emily
Dickinson. Boston: Little, Brown, 1961. vii-xiv.

This cites the introduction by Johnson. Notice that a colon is used between the book's main title and subtitle. To cite a poem in this book use this method:

Dickinson, Emily. "A Tooth upon Our Peace." Final Harvest: Emily Dickinson's Poems. Ed.
Thomas H. Johnson. Boston: Little, Brown, 1961. 110.

AN ENTRY IN AN ENCYCLOPEDIA

"Wordsworth, William." The New Encyclopedia Britannica. 1984 ed.

Because this encyclopedia is organized alphabetically, no page number or other information is given, only the edition number (if available) and date.

AN ARTICLE IN A MAGAZINE

Morrow, Lance. "Scribble, Scribble, Eh, Mr. Toad." Time 24 Feb. 1986: 84.

AN ARTICLE FROM AN ONLINE MAGAZINE

Wasserman, Elizabeth. "The Byron Complex." Atlantic Online 22 Sept. 2002. 4 Feb. 2004
    <http://www.theatlantic.com/unbound/flashbks/byron.htm>.

The citation for an unsigned article would begin with the title and be alphabetized by the first word of the title other than "a," "an," or "the."

AN ARTICLE IN A SCHOLARLY JOURNAL WITH CONTINUOUS
PAGINATION BEYOND A SINGLE ISSUE

Mahar, William J. "Black English in Early Blackface Minstrelsy: A New Interpretation of
    the Sources of Minstrel Show Dialect." American Quarterly 37 (1985): 260-85.

Because this journal uses continuous pagination instead of separate pagination for each issue, it is not necessary to include the month, season, or number of the issue. Only one of the quarterly issues will have pages numbered 260–85. If you are not certain whether a journal's pages are numbered continuously throughout a volume, supply the month, season, or issue number, as in the next entry.

AN ARTICLE IN A SCHOLARLY JOURNAL WITH SEPARATE
PAGINATION FOR EACH ISSUE

Updike, John. "The Cultural Situation of the American Writer." American Studies
    International 15 (Spring 1977): 19-28.

By noting the spring issue, the entry saves a reader looking through each issue of the 1977 volume for the correct article on pages 19 to 28.

AN ARTICLE FROM AN ONLINE SCHOLARLY JOURNAL

Mamet, David. "Secret Names." The Threepenny Review 96 (Winter 2003). 4 Feb. 2004
    <http://www.threepennyreview.com/samples/mamet_w04.html>.

The following citation indicates that the article appears on page 1 of section 7 and continues onto another page.

AN ARTICLE IN A NEWSPAPER

Ziegler, Philip. "The Lure of Gossip, the Rules of History." New York Times 23 Feb. 1986:
    sec. 7: 1+.

AN ARTICLE FROM AN ONLINE NEWSPAPER

Brantley, Ben. "Souls Lost and Doomed Enliven London Stages." New York Times on the
    Web 4 Feb. 2004. 5 Feb. 2004 <http://www.nytimes.com/2004/02/04/arts/theater/
    04BRAN.html>.

A LECTURE

Tilton, Robert. "The Beginnings of American Studies." English 270 class lecture.
    University of Connecticut, Storrs, 12 Mar. 2004.

LETTER, E-MAIL, OR INTERVIEW

Vellenga, Carolyn. Letter to the author. 9 Oct. 1997.

Harter, Stephen P. E-mail to the author. 28 Dec. 1997.

McConagha, Bill. Personal interview.

Following are additional examples for citing electronic sources.

WORK FROM A SUBSCRIPTION SERVICE

Libraries pay for access to databases such as *Lexis-Nexis, ProQuest Direct,* and
Expanded Academic ASAP. When you retrieve an article or other work from a
subscription database, cite your source based on this model:

Vendler, Helen Hennessey. "The Passion of Emily Dickinson." The New Republic 3 Aug.
    1992: 34-38. Expanded Academic ASAP. InfoTrac. Boston Public Lib., MA. 4 Feb.
    2004 <http://infotrac.galegroup.com>.

A DOCUMENT FROM A WEB SITE

When citing sources from the Internet, include as much publication infor-
mation as possible (see guidelines on page 722). In some cases, as in the fol-
lowing example, a date of publication for the document "Dickens in
America" is not available. The entry provides the author, title of document,
title of site, access date, and URL:

Perdue, David. "Dickens in America." David Perdue's Charles Dickens Page. 4 Feb. 2003
    <http://www.fidnet.com/~dap1955/dickens/america.html>.

AN ENTIRE WEB SITE

Perdue, David. David Perdue's Charles Dickens Page. 4 Feb. 2003
    <http://www.fidnet.com/~dap1955/dickens/>.

Treat a CD-ROM as you would any other source, but name the medium before the publication information.

A WORK FROM A CD-ROM

Aaron, Belèn V. "The Death of Theory." Scholarly Book Reviews 4.3 (1997): 146-47. ERIC.

    CD-ROM. SilverPlatter. Dec. 1997.

AN ONLINE POSTING

Kathman, David. "Shakespeare's Literacy--or Lack of." Online posting. 3 Mar. 1998.

    Shakespeare Newsgroup. 4 Feb. 2004 <humanities.lit.authors.shakespeare>.

Parenthetical References

A list of works cited is not an adequate indication of how you have used sources in your paper. You must also provide the precise location of quotations and other information by using parenthetical references within the text of the paper. You do this by citing the author's name (or the source's title if the work is anonymous) and the page number.

> Collins points out that "Nabokov was misunderstood by early reviewers of his work" (28).

or

> Nabokov's first critics misinterpreted his stories (Collins 28).

Either way a reader will find the complete bibliographic entry in the list of works cited under Collins's name and know that the information cited in the paper appears on page 28. Notice that the end punctuation comes after the parentheses.

If you have listed more than one work by the same author, you would add a brief title to the parenthetical reference to distinguish between them. You could also include the full title in your text.

> Nabokov's first critics misinterpreted his stories (Collins "Early Reviews" 28).

or

> Collins points out in "Early Reviews of Nabokov's Fiction" that his early work was misinterpreted by reviewers (28).

There can be many variations on what is included in a parenthetical reference, depending on the nature of the entry in the list of works cited. But the general principle is simple enough: provide enough parenthetical information for a reader to find the work in "Works Cited." Examine the sample research paper for more examples of works cited and strategies for including parenthetical references. If you are puzzled by a given situation, ask your reference librarian to show you the *MLA Handbook*.

Incorporating Secondary Sources

The following questions can help you to incorporate materials from critical or biographical essays into your own writing about a literary work. You may initially feel intimidated by the prospect of responding to the arguments of professional writers in your own paper. However, the process will not defeat you if you have clearly formulated your own response to the literary work and are able to distinguish it from the critics' perspectives. Reading what other people have said about a work can help you to develop your own ideas — perhaps, to cite just two examples, by using them as supporting evidence or by arguing with them in order to clarify or qualify their points about the literary work. As you write and discover how to advance your thesis, you'll find yourself participating in a dialogue with the critics. This sort of conversation will help you to improve your thinking and hone your argument.

Keep in mind that the work of professional critics is a means of enriching your understanding of a literary work rather than a substitution for your own analysis and interpretation of that work. Quoting, paraphrasing, or summarizing someone else's perspective does not relieve you of the obligation of choosing a topic, organizing information, developing a thesis, and arguing your point of view by citing sufficient evidence from the text you are examining. These matters are discussed in further detail in Chapter 26. You should also be familiar with the methods for documenting sources that are explained in this chapter, and keep in mind how important it is to avoid plagiarism.

No doubt you won't find everything you read about a work equally useful: some critics' arguments won't address your own areas of concern; some will be too difficult for you to get a handle on; and some will seem wrongheaded. However, much of the criticism you read will serve to make a literary work more accessible and interesting to you, and disagreeing with others' arguments will often help you to develop your own ideas about a work. When you use the work of critics in your own writing, you should consider the following questions. Responding to these questions will help you to ensure that you have a clear understanding of what a critic is arguing about a work, to what extent you agree with that argument, and how you plan to incorporate and respond to the critic's reading in your own paper. The more questions you can ask yourself in response to this list or as a result of your own reading, the more you'll be able to think critically about how you are approaching both the critics and the literary work under consideration.

Questions for Incorporating Secondary Sources

1. Have you read the poem carefully and taken notes of your own impressions before reading any critical perspectives so that your initial insights are not lost to the arguments made by the critics? Have you articulated your own responses to the work in a journal entry prior to reading the critics?

2. Are you sufficiently familiar with the poem that you can determine the accuracy, fairness, and thoroughness of the critic's use of evidence from the work?

3. Have you read the critic's piece carefully? Try summarizing the critic's argument in a brief paragraph. Do you understand the nature and purpose of the critic's argument? Which passages are especially helpful to you? Which seem unclear? Why?

4. Is the critic's reading of the poem similar to or different from your own reading? Why do you agree or disagree? What generational, historical, cultural, or biographical considerations might help to account for any differences between the critic's responses and your own?

5. How has your reading of the critic influenced your understanding of the poem? Do issues that previously seemed unimportant now seem significant? What are these issues, and how does a consideration of them affect your reading of the work?

6. Are you too quickly revising or even discarding your own reading because the critic's perspective seems so polished and persuasive? Are you making use of your reading notes and the responses in your journal entries?

7. How would you classify the critic's approach? Through what kind of lens does the critic view the poem? Is the critical approach formalist, biographical, psychological, historical, mythological, reader-response, deconstructionist, or some combination of these or possibly other strategies? (For a discussion of these approaches, see Chapter 25.)

8. What biases, if any, can you detect in the critic's approach? How might, for example, a southern critic's reading of "Mending Wall" differ from a northern critic's?

9. Can you determine how other critics have responded to the critic's work? Is the critic's work cited and taken seriously in other critics' books and articles? Is the work dated by having been superseded by subsequent studies?

10. Are any passages or topics that you deem important left out by the critic? Do these omissions qualify or refute the critic's argument?

11. What judgments does the critic seem to make about the work? Is the work regarded, for example, as significant, unified, representative, trivial, inept, or irresponsible? Do you agree with these judgments? If not, can you develop and support a thesis about your difference of opinion?

12. What important disagreements do critics reveal in their approaches to the work? Do you find one perspective more convincing than another? Why? Is there a way of resolving their conflicting views that could serve as a thesis for your paper?

13. Can you extend or qualify the critic's argument to matters in the literary text that are not covered by the critic's perspective? Will this allow you to develop your own topic while acknowledging the critic's useful insights?

14. Have you quoted, paraphrased, or summarized the critic accurately and fairly? Have you avoided misrepresenting the critic's arguments in any way?

15. Are the critic's words, ideas, opinions, and insights adequately acknowledged and documented in the correct format? Do you understand the difference between common knowledge and plagiarism? Have you avoided quoting excessively? Are the quotations smoothly integrated into your own text?

16. Are you certain that your incorporation of the critic's work is for the purpose of developing your paper's thesis rather than for name-dropping or padding your paper? How can you explain to yourself why the critic's work is useful for your argument?

A SAMPLE RESEARCH PAPER

Individuality and Community in Frost's "Mowing" and "Mending Wall"

As you read the paper by Stephanie Tobin on Robert Frost's "Mowing" (p. 357) and "Mending Wall" (p. 359), pay special attention to how she documents outside sources and incorporates other people's ideas into her own argument. How strong do you think her final thesis is? Is it effectively supported by the sources? Has she integrated the sources fully into the paper? How does the paper enhance your understanding of the two poems?

Stephanie's paper follows the format described in the *MLA Handbook for Writers of Research Papers,* 6th ed. This format is discussed in the preceding section on documentation in this chapter (p. 720) and in Chapter 26 in the section on manuscript form (p. 694). Though the sample paper is short, it illustrates many of the techniques and strategies useful for writing an essay that includes secondary sources — including a CD-ROM, a Web site, books, and journals.

Stephanie Tobin

Professor Bass

Poetry 100

November 17, 2006

Individuality and Community in

Frost's "Mowing" and "Mending Wall"

We think of Robert Frost as a poet of New England who provides portraits of the rural landscape and communities. But it was not until Frost's second book, North of Boston (1914), that he truly gave voice to a community--in dramatic monologues, dialogues, and narrative poems. The poems in his first book, A Boy's Will (1913), are mainly personal lyrics in which the poet encounters the world and defines it for himself through the writing of poetry, establishing both an individual perspective and an aesthetic. A poem from the first book, "Mowing," illustrates the theme of individualism, against which a poem from the second book, "Mending Wall," can be seen as a widening of the thematic lens to include other perspectives.

In A Boy's Will, Frost explores the idea of man as a solitary creature, alone, at work in the natural world. Poems such as "Mowing" capture the essence of this perspective in the very first lines: "There was never a sound beside the wood but one, / And that was my long scythe whispering to the ground" (lines 1-2). Jay Parini describes "Mowing" as a poem in which the "poet cultivates a private motion" (121)--the motions both of farm work, done to support oneself, and the motion of the individual mind expressed in the poem as it moves down the page. The sense of privacy and of an individually defined world captured in "Mowing" is central to the book itself.

The dramatic change in perspective evident in North of Boston illustrates Frost's development as a writer. Although the second collection was published just one year later, Frost expresses a different perception and understanding of human nature in North of Boston. W. S. Braithwaite wrote in 1915, in a review of the two books, that A Boy's Will and North of Boston "represent a divergent period of development. The earlier book expresses an individuality, the later interprets a community" (2). The focus on community is best demonstrated by the poem "Mending Wall," which presents the reader with an image of two men, separated literally and metaphorically by a wall, yet joined by their dedication to the task they must undertake and the basic human need for boundaries that compels them. The speaker in "Mending Wall" does not forfeit his own individuality, but rather comes to understand it more fully in the context of the society in which he lives, with its traditions and requirements, some of which he tries to see as a game: "Oh, just another kind of outdoor game, / One on a side" (21-22), while still allowing for deeper implications.

Individuality can be defined by one's differences from others, as well as by the creative work of defining, and self-defining, done in poetry. Frost's own experience of life in New England helped shape the perspectives of both individualism and community exemplified in his first two books. When Frost wrote "Mowing" his perspective on life in New England leaned more toward isolation than community. The first few years of farm life were arduous and lonely, and the stark environment provided an atmosphere far more suitable for self-realization than socialization. Prior to the publication of A Boy's Will, Frost had spent "five years of self-enforced solitude" (Meyers 99). "Mowing," which Frost considered to be the best poem in the collection, exemplifies this feeling of isolation and the need for self-exploration. While the poem is, in the literal sense, about the act of cutting grass in order to make hay, it is metaphorically rooted in the idea that man finds meaning and beauty in the world alone. Parini suggests that the idea that "a man's complete meaning is derived alone, at work . . . is a consistent theme in Frost and one that could be explored at length in all his work" (14).

"Mowing" begins with the speaker's observation of the silence that surrounds him as he works. The only sound is the hushed whisper of his scythe as he mows. He writes, "What was it it whispered? I knew not well myself" (3). The possibility that its meaning could be found in some fanciful imagination of the task is dismissed: "It was no dream of the gift of idle hours, / or easy gold at the hand of fay or elf" (7-8). For Frost, an exaggeration of the action would imply that meaning cannot be found in objective reality, an idea continually argued by his poems.

Instead, this poem asserts a faith in nature as it is, and in the labor necessary to support and define oneself--labor in the natural world, and in the making of poems. This idea is brought forth in the next line: "Anything more than the truth would have seemed too weak / To the earnest love that laid the swale in rows" (9-10). Whether the "fact" that is the "sweetest dream that labour knows" (13) is the actual act of cutting the grass or the verse that is inspired by the simple action, it is something that must be achieved in solitude.

This faith in the work of the individual demonstrated in A Boy's Will is not lost in North of Boston but is redefined. Meyers writes that North of Boston "signaled Frost's change of emphasis from solitary to social beings" (112). In Frost's dedication to his wife he called North of Boston "This Book of People." The poems in this collection demonstrate an understanding of the individual, as well as the community in which he lives. This shift seems a natural development after a book in which Frost so carefully established his sense of self and his particular poetic vision and aims.

"Mending Wall," a poem in North of Boston, illustrates Frost's shift in focus from the solitary individual to the interacting society. In the poem, the speaker and his neighbor set out to perform the annual task of mending a wall that divides their properties. From the very beginning, the speaker's tone--at once humorous and serious--indicates that the real subject of the poem is not the mending of the wall, which he describes almost lightheartedly, but the "mending" of the subtle boundaries between the speaker and his neighbor. The poem begins, "Something there is that doesn't love a wall, / that sends the frozen-ground-swell under it" (1-2), yet this "something," mentioned twice in the poem, refers to more than the seasonal frost that "spills the upper boulders in the sun" (3). Peter Stanlis writes in a commentary on "Mending Wall" that "the central theme falls within the philosophical polarities of the speaker and his neighbor" (1). The man's statement that "good fences make good neighbors" (26) implies his belief that boundaries between people will maintain the peace between them, but the speaker questions this need for boundaries: "Before I built a wall I'd ask to know / What I was walling in or walling out" (31-32). With this he brings the wall into the figurative realm to decipher its meaning.

His neighbor feels no need for such analysis. But while articulating a figurative barrier of noncommunication and different values between the men, the poem is as much about community as individuality; the wall is what connects as well as separates them. Marie Borroff argues that "the story told in the poem is not about a one-man rebellion against wall mending but about an attempt to communicate" (66). However individuated the men may perceive themselves to be, the common task they must undertake and the ethos it represents join them in a particular social community, the assumptions of which Frost articulates in this poem by both participating in and questioning them.

For the speaker, the task of mending the wall provides an opportunity for thought and questioning rather than serving a utilitarian purpose. While the tradition unites the men "by marking their claims to private property through mutual respect," it is still a barrier (Stanlis 3). Both joined and separated by the fence, the two neighbors walk together and alone, isolated by the physical boundary but connected by their maintenance of the relationship and tradition that created it. As James R. Dawes points out, these "men can only interact when reassured by the constructed alienation of the wall" (300). They keep the wall in place, and thereby keep in place their separate senses of self.

While the speaker is explicitly and lightheartedly critical of the ritual, it is he who "insists on the yearly ritual, as if civilization depends upon the collective activity of making barriers . . . . One senses a profound commitment to the act of creating community in the speaker" (Parini 139). Unwilling to placate his neighbor by performing the task in silence, the speaker makes a playful attempt at communication. Explaining that "My apple trees will never get across / And eat the cones under his pines" (24-25), he asks why the wall is necessary. But rather than contemplate the logic behind the boundary, the neighbor rejects the invitation to communicate: "He only says, 'Good fences make good neighbors'" (26). By refusing to think about the speaker's question, and choosing to hide behind his own father's words, he closes any possible window of communication between them (Monteiro 127), not crossing the barrier of the wall literally or psychologically. And even while the speaker jokes about the wall's uselessness, he keeps his deeper questions to himself. Rather than threaten the agreed-upon terms of community, he is complicit in keeping them there in actuality, only privately articulating and upending them, in poetry.

Mark Van Doren wrote in 1951 that Robert Frost's poems "are the work of a man who has never stopped exploring himself" (2); he never stopped exploring the psychology of others, either. "Mowing," which illustrates his initial focus on individualism, was only a starting point in Frost's understanding of his place in the world as a poet. The change of perspective evident in "Mending Wall" demonstrates his enriched idea of man as an individual within a community. Having established a singular voice and his own moral aesthetic--"The fact is the sweetest dream that labour knows" (13)--Frost has the confidence to incorporate different voices into his poems and to allow his "facts" and values to encounter those of others, as the two men in "Mending Wall" do across the wall, each maintaining his own and the other's sense of personal identity.

Tobin 6

Works Cited

Borroff, Marie. "Robert Frost's New Testament: The Uses of Simplicity." Modern
Critical Views: Robert Frost. Ed. Harold Bloom. New York: Chelsea House,
1986. 63-83.

Braithwaite, W. S. "A Poet of New England." The Boston Evening Transcript 28
April 1915. From Robert Frost: Poems, Life, Legacy. CD-ROM. New York:
Holt, 1997.

Dawes, James R. "Masculinity and Transgression in Robert Frost." American
Literature 65 (June 1993): 297-312.

Meyer, Michael. Poetry: An Introduction. 5th ed. Boston: Bedford/St. Martin's,
2007.

Meyers, Jeffrey. Robert Frost: A Biography. New York: Houghton, 1996.

Monteiro, George. Robert Frost and the New England Renaissance. Lexington:
UP of Kentucky, 1988.

Parini, Jay. Robert Frost: A Life. New York: Holt, 1999.

Stanlis, Peter J. "Commentary: 'Mending Wall.'" Robert Frost: Poems, Life,
Legacy. CD-ROM. New York: Holt, 1997.

Van Doren, Mark. "Robert Frost's America." Atlantic Monthly June 1951. Atlantic
Unbound <http://www.theatlantic.com/unbound/poetry/frost/vand.htm>.

28

Taking Essay Examinations

It is the function of the liberal arts education not to give right answers, but to ask right questions.
— CYNTHIA OZICK

By permission of Alfred A. Knopf, Inc.

PREPARING FOR AN ESSAY EXAM

Keep Up with the Reading

The best way to prepare for an examination is to keep up with the reading. If you begin the course with a commitment to completing the reading assignments on time, you will not have to read in a frenzy and cram just days before the test. The readings will be a pleasure, not a frantic ordeal. Moreover, you will find that your instructor's comments and class discussion will make more sense to you and that you'll be able to participate in class discussion. As you prepare for the exam you should be rereading texts rather than reading for the first time. It may not be possible to reread everything, but you'll at least be able to scan a familiar text and reread passages that are particularly important.

Take Notes and Annotate the Text

Don't rely exclusively on your memory. The typical literature class includes a hefty amount of reading, so unless you take notes, annotate the text with your own comments, and underline important passages, you're likely to forget material that could be useful for responding to an examination question (see pp. 679–81 for a discussion of these matters). The more you can retrieve from your reading the more prepared you'll be for reviewing significant material for the exam. Your notes can be used to illustrate points that were made in class. By briefly quoting an important phrase or line from the text, you can provide supporting evidence that will make your argument convincing. Consider, for example, the difference between writing that "Marvell's speaker in 'To His Coy Mistress' says that they won't be able to love after they die" and writing that "the speaker intones that 'The grave's a fine and private place / But none, I think, do there embrace.'" No one expects you to memorize the entire poem, but recalling a few lines here and there can transform a sleepy generality into an illustrative, persuasive argument.

Anticipate Questions

As you review the readings keep in mind the class discussions and the focus provided by your instructor. Very often class discussions and the instructor's emphasis become the basis for essay questions. You may not see the exact same topics on the exam, but you might find that the matters you've discussed in class will serve as a means of responding to an essay question. If, for example, class discussion of Robert Frost's "Mending Wall" (see p. 359) centered on the poem's rural New England setting, you could use that conservative, traditional setting to answer a question such as "Discuss how the conflicts between the speaker and his neighbor are related to the poem's theme." A discussion of the neighbor's rigidity and his firmly entrenched conservative New England attitudes could be connected to his impulse to rebuild the wall between himself and the poem's speaker. The point is that you'll be well prepared for an essay exam when you can shape the material you've studied so that it is responsive to whatever kinds of reasonable questions you encounter on the exam. Reasonable questions? Yes, your instructor is more likely to offer you an opportunity to demonstrate your familiarity with and understanding of the text than to set a trap that, for instance, demands you discuss how Frost's work experience as an adolescent informs the poem when no mention was ever made of that in class or in your reading.

You can also anticipate questions by considering the Questions for Responsive Reading and Writing about poetry (p. 61) and the questions in Arguing about Literature (p. 685), along with the Questions for Writing about an Author in Depth (p. 342). Not all of these questions will necessarily be relevant to every work that you read, but they cover a wide range of concerns that should allow you to organize your reading, note-taking, and reviewing so that you're not taken by surprise during the exam.

Studying with a classmate or a small group from class can be a stimulating and fruitful means of discovering and organizing the course's major topics and themes. This method of brainstorming can be useful not only for studying for exams, but also through the semester as a way to understand and review course readings. And, finally, you needn't be shy about asking your instructor what types of questions might appear on the exam and how best to study for them. You may not get a very specific reply, but almost any information is more useful than none.

TYPES OF EXAMS

Closed-Book versus Open-Book Exams

Closed-book exams require more memorization and recall than open-book exams, which permit you to use your text and perhaps even your notes to answer questions. Obviously, dates, names, definitions, and other details play less of a role in an open-book exam. An open-book exam requires no less preparation, however, because you'll need to be intimately familiar with the texts and the major ideas, themes, and issues that you've studied in order to quickly and efficiently support your points with relevant, specific evidence. Because every student has the same advantage of having access to the text, preparation remains the key to answering the questions. Some students find open-book exams more difficult than closed-book tests, because they risk spending too much time reading, scanning, and searching for material and not enough time writing a response that draws on the knowledge and understanding that their reading and studying has provided them. It's best to limit the time you allow yourself to review the text or notes so that you devote an adequate amount of time to getting your ideas down on paper.

Essay Questions

Essay questions generally fall within one of the following categories. If you can recognize quickly what is being asked of you, you will be able to respond to the question more efficiently.

1. **Explication.** Explication calls for a line-by-line explanation of a passage of poetry or prose that considers, for example, diction, figures of speech, symbolism, sound, form, and theme in an effort to describe how language creates meaning. (For a more detailed discussion of explication, see p. 695.)

2. **Definition.** Defining a term and then applying it to a writer or work is a frequent exam exercise. Consider: "Define *romanticism*. To what extent can Keats's 'Ode on a Grecian Urn' (p. 96) be regarded as a romantic poem?" This sort of question requires that you first describe what constitutes a romantic literary work and then explain how "Ode on a Grecian Urn" does (or doesn't) fit the bill.

3. **Analysis.** An analytical question focuses on a particular part of a literary work. You might be asked, for example, to analyze the significance of images in Sharon Olds's poem "Last Night" (p. 85). This sort of question requires you not only to discuss a specific element of the poem but also to explain how that element contributes to the poem's overall effect. (For a more detailed discussion of analysis, see p. 700.)

4. **Comparison and Contrast.** Comparison and contrast calls for a discussion of the similarities or differences between writers, works, or elements of works. For example: "Compare and contrast the tone of the *carpe diem* arguments made by the speaker in Richard Wilbur's 'A Late Aubade' and in Andrew Marvell's 'To His Coy Mistress.'" Despite the nearly three hundred years that separate these two poems in setting and circumstances, a discussion of the tone of the speakers' arguments reveals some intriguing similarities and differences. (For a more detailed discussion of comparison and contrast, see p. 705.)

5. **Discussion of a Critical Perspective.** A brief quotation by a critic about a work is usually designed to stimulate a response that requires you to agree with, disagree with, or qualify a critic's perspective. Usually it is not so important whether you agree or disagree with the critic; what matters is the quality of your argument. Think about how you might wrestle with this assessment of Robert Frost written by Lionel Trilling: "The manifest America of Mr. Frost's poems may be pastoral; the actual America is tragic." With some qualifications (surely not all of Frost's poems are "tragic"), this could provide a useful way of talking about a poem such as "Mending Wall" (p. 359).

6. **Imaginative Questions.** To a degree, every question requires imagination regardless of whether it's being asked or answered. However, some questions require more imaginative leaps to arrive at the center of an issue than others do. Consider, for example, the intellectual agility needed to respond to this question: "Discuss the speakers' attitudes toward the power of imagination in Emily Dickinson's 'To make a prairie it takes a clover and one bee,' Frost's 'Mending Wall,' and Philip Larkin's 'A Study of Reading Habits.'" As tricky as this thematic triangulation may seem, there is plenty to say about the speakers' varied, complicated, and contradictory attitudes toward the power of an individual's imagination. Or try a simpler but no less interesting version: "How do you think Frost would review Marvell's 'To His Coy Mistress' and Old's 'Last Night'?" Such questions certainly require detailed, reasoned responses, but they also leave room for creativity and even wit.

STRATEGIES FOR WRITING ESSAY EXAMS

Your hands may be sweaty and your heart pounding as you begin the exam, but as long as you're prepared and you keep in mind some basic strategies for writing essay exams, you should be able to respond to questions with confidence and a genuine sense of accomplishment.

1. Before you begin writing, read through the entire exam. If there are choices to be made, make certain you know how many questions must be answered (for instance, only one out of four, not two). Note how many points each question is worth; spend more time on the two worth forty points each and perhaps leave the twenty-point question for last.

2. Budget your time. If there are short-answer questions, do not allow them to absorb you so that you cannot do justice to the longer essay questions. Follow the suggested time limits for each question; if none is offered, then create your own schedule in proportion to the points allotted for each question.

3. Depending on your own sensibilities, you may want to begin with the easiest or hardest questions. It doesn't really matter which you begin with as long as you pace yourself to avoid running out of time.

4. Be sure that you understand the question. Does it ask you to compare or contrast, define, analyze, explicate, or use some other approach? Determine how many elements there are to the question so that you don't inadvertently miss part of the question. Do not spend time copying the question.

5. Make some brief notes about how you plan to answer the question; even a simple list of what you'll need to cover can serve as a useful outline.

6. Address the question; avoid unnecessary summaries or irrelevant asides. Focus on the particular elements enumerated or implied by the question.

7. After beginning the essay, write a clear thesis that describes the major topics you will discuss: "Mending Wall" is typical of Frost's concerns as a writer owing to its treatment of setting, tone, and theme.

8. Support and illustrate your answer with specific, relevant references to the text. The more specificity—the more you demonstrate a familiarity with the text (rather than simply providing a summary)—the better the answer.

9. Don't overlap and repeat responses to questions; your instructor will recognize such padding. If two different questions are about the same work or writer, demonstrate the breadth and depth of your knowledge of the subject.

10. Allow time to proofread and to qualify and to add more supporting material if necessary. At this final stage, too, it's worth remembering that Mark Twain liked to remind his readers that the difference between the right word and the almost right word is the difference between lightning and lightning bug.

Glossary of Literary Terms

Accent The emphasis, or STRESS, given a syllable in pronunciation. We say "*syl*lable" not "syl*la*ble," "*em*phasis" not "em*pha*sis." Accents can also be used to emphasize a particular word in a sentence: *Is* she con*tent* with the *con*tents of the *yel*low *pack*age? See also METER.

Allegory A narration or description usually restricted to a single meaning because its events, actions, characters, settings, and objects represent specific abstractions or ideas. Although the elements in an allegory may be interesting in themselves, the emphasis tends to be on what they ultimately mean. Characters may be given names such as Hope, Pride, Youth, and Charity; they have few if any personal qualities beyond their abstract meanings. These personifications are not symbols because, for instance, the meaning of a character named Charity is precisely that virtue. See also SYMBOL.

Alliteration The repetition of the same consonant sounds in a sequence of words, usually at the beginning of a word or stressed syllable: "*d*escen*d*ing *d*ew *d*rops"; "*l*uscious *l*emons." Alliteration is based on the sounds of letters, rather than the spelling of words; for example, "*k*een" and "*c*ar" alliterate, but "*c*ar" and "*c*ite" do not. Used sparingly, alliteration can intensify ideas by emphasizing key words, but when used too self-consciously, it can be distracting, even ridiculous, rather than effective. See also ASSONANCE, CONSONANCE.

Allusion A brief reference to a person, place, thing, event, or idea in history or literature. Allusions conjure up biblical authority, scenes from Shakespeare's plays, historic figures, wars, great love stories, and anything else that might enrich an author's work. Allusions imply reading and cultural experiences shared by the writer and reader, functioning as a kind of shorthand whereby the recalling of something outside the work supplies an emotional or intellectual context, such as a poem about current racial struggles calling up the memory of Abraham Lincoln.

Ambiguity Allows for two or more simultaneous interpretations of a word, phrase, action, or situation, all of which can be supported by the context of a work. Deliberate ambiguity can contribute to the effectiveness and richness of a work. However, unintentional ambiguity obscures meaning and can confuse readers.

Anagram A word or phrase made from the letters of another word or phrase, as "heart" is an anagram of "earth." Anagrams have often been considered merely an exercise of one's ingenuity, but sometimes writers use anagrams

741

to conceal proper names or veiled messages, or to suggest important connections between words, as in "hated" and "death."

Anapestic meter See FOOT.

Apostrophe An address, either to someone who is absent and therefore cannot hear the speaker or to something nonhuman that cannot comprehend. Apostrophe often provides a speaker the opportunity to think aloud.

Approximate rhyme See RHYME.

Archetype A term used to describe universal symbols that evoke deep and sometimes unconscious responses in a reader. In literature, characters, images, and themes that symbolically embody universal meanings and basic human experiences, regardless of when or where they live, are considered archetypes. Common literary archetypes include stories of quests, initiations, scapegoats, descents to the underworld, and ascents to heaven. See also MYTHOLOGICAL CRITICISM.

Assonance The repetition of internal vowel sounds in nearby words that do not end the same, for example, "asleep under a tree," or "each evening." Similar endings result in rhyme, as in "asleep in the deep." Assonance is a strong means of emphasizing important words in a line. See also ALLITERATION, CONSONANCE.

Ballad Traditionally, a ballad is a song, transmitted orally from generation to generation, that tells a story and that eventually is written down. As such, ballads usually cannot be traced to a particular author or group of authors. Typically, ballads are dramatic, condensed, and impersonal narratives, such as "Bonny Barbara Allan." A **literary ballad** is a narrative poem written in deliberate imitation of the language, form, and spirit of the traditional ballad, such as John Keats's "La Belle Dame sans Merci." See also BALLAD STANZA, QUATRAIN.

Ballad stanza A four-line stanza, known as a QUATRAIN, consisting of alternating eight- and six-syllable lines. Usually only the second and fourth lines rhyme (an *abcb* pattern). Coleridge adopted the ballad stanza in "The Rime of the Ancient Mariner":

All in a hot and copper sky
The bloody Sun, at noon,
Right up above the mast did stand,
No bigger than the Moon.

See also BALLAD, QUATRAIN.

Biographical criticism An approach to literature that suggests that knowledge of the author's life experiences can aid in the understanding of his or her work. While biographical information can sometimes complicate one's interpretation of a work, and some formalist critics (such as the New Critics) disparage the use of the author's biography as a tool for textual interpretation, learning about the life of the author can often enrich a reader's appreciation for that author's work. See also FORMALIST CRITICISM, NEW CRITICISM.

Blank verse Unrhymed iambic pentameter. Blank verse is the English verse form closest to the natural rhythms of English speech and therefore is the most common pattern found in traditional English narrative and dramatic poetry from Shakespeare to the early twentieth century. Shakespeare's plays use blank verse extensively. See also IAMBIC PENTAMETER.

Cacophony Language that is discordant and difficult to pronounce, such as this line from John Updike's "Player Piano": "never my numb plunker fumbles." Cacophony ("bad sound") may be unintentional in the writer's sense of music, or it may be used consciously for deliberate dramatic effect. See also EUPHONY.

Caesura A pause within a line of poetry that contributes to the rhythm of the line. A caesura can occur anywhere within a line and need not be indicated by punctuation. In scanning a line, we indicate caesuras by a double vertical line (‖). See also METER, RHYTHM, SCANSION.

Canon Those works generally considered by scholars, critics, and teachers to be the most important to read and study, which collectively constitute the "masterpieces" of literature. Since the 1960s, the traditional English and American literary canon, consisting mostly of works by white male writers, has been rapidly expanding to include many female writers and writers of varying ethnic backgrounds.

Carpe diem The Latin phrase meaning "seize the day." This is a very common literary theme, especially in lyric poetry, which emphasizes that life is short, time is fleeting, and one should make the most of present pleasures. Robert Herrick's poem "To the Virgins, to Make Much of Time" uses the *carpe diem* theme.

Cliché An idea or expression that has become tired and trite from overuse, its freshness and clarity having worn off. Clichés often anesthetize readers and are usually a sign of weak writing. See also SENTIMENTALITY, STOCK RESPONSES.

Colloquial Refers to a type of informal diction that reflects casual, conversational language and often includes slang expressions. See also DICTION.

Connotation Associations and implications that go beyond a word's literal meaning and deriving from how the word has been commonly used and the associations people make with it. For example, the word *eagle* connotes ideas of liberty and freedom that have little to do with the word's literal meaning. See also DENOTATION.

Consonance A common type of near rhyme that consists of identical consonant sounds preceded by different vowel sounds: *home, same; worth, breath.* See also RHYME.

Contextual symbol See SYMBOL.

Controlling metaphor See METAPHOR.

Convention A characteristic of a literary genre (often unrealistic) that is understood and accepted by readers because it has come, through usage and time, to be recognized as a familiar technique. For example, the use of meter and rhyme are poetic conventions.

Conventional symbol See SYMBOL.

Cosmic irony See IRONY.

Couplet Two consecutive lines of poetry that usually rhyme and have the same meter. A **heroic couplet** is a couplet written in rhymed iambic pentameter.

Cultural criticism An approach to literature that focuses on the historical as well as social, political, and economic contexts of a work. Popular culture — mass-produced and -consumed cultural artifacts ranging from advertising and popular fiction to television to rock music — is given equal emphasis as "high culture." Cultural critics use widely eclectic strategies such as new historicism, psychology, gender studies, and deconstructionism to analyze not only literary texts but everything from radio talk shows, comic strips, calendar art, commercials, to travel guides and baseball cards. See also HISTORICAL CRITICISM, MARXIST CRITICISM, POSTCOLONIAL CRITICISM.

Dactylic meter See FOOT.

Deconstructionism An approach to literature that suggests that literary works do not yield fixed, single meanings, because language can never say exactly what we intend it to mean. Deconstructionism seeks to destabilize meaning by examining the gaps and ambiguities of a text's language. Deconstructionists pay close attention to language in order to discover and describe how a variety of possible readings are generated by the elements of a text. See also NEW CRITICISM.

Denotation The dictionary meaning of a word. See also CONNOTATION.

Dialect A type of informal diction. Dialects are spoken by definable groups of people from a particular geographic region, economic group, or social class. Writers use dialect to contrast and express differences in their characters' educational, class, social, and regional backgrounds. See also DICTION.

Diction A writer's choice of words, phrases, sentence structures, and figurative language, which combine to help create meaning. **Formal diction** consists of a dignified, impersonal, and elevated use of language; it follows the rules of syntax exactly and is often characterized by complex words and lofty tone. **Middle diction** maintains correct language usage but is less elevated than formal diction; it reflects the way most educated people speak. **Informal diction** represents the plain language of everyday use and often includes idiomatic expressions, slang, contractions, and many simple, common words. **Poetic diction** refers to the way poets sometimes use an elevated diction that deviates significantly from the common speech and writing of their time, choosing words for their supposedly inherent poetic qualities. Since the eighteenth century, however, poets have been incorporating all kinds of diction in their work, and so there is no longer an automatic distinction between the language of a poet and the language of everyday speech. See also DIALECT.

Didactic poetry Poetry designed to teach an ethical, moral, or religious lesson. Michael Wigglesworth's Puritan poem *Day of Doom* is an example of didactic poetry.

Doggerel A derogatory term used to describe poetry whose subject is trite and whose rhythm and sounds are monotonously heavy-handed.

Dramatic irony See IRONY.

Dramatic monologue A type of lyric poem in which a character (the speaker) addresses a distinct but silent audience imagined to be present in the poem in such a way as to reveal a dramatic situation and, often unintentionally, some aspect of his or her temperament or personality. See also LYRIC.

Electra complex The female version of the Oedipus complex. *Electra complex* is a term used to describe the psychological conflict of a daughter's unconscious rivalry with her mother for her father's attention. The name comes from the Greek legend of Electra, who avenged the death of her father, Agamemnon, by plotting the death of her mother. See also OEDIPUS COMPLEX, PSYCHOLOGICAL CRITICISM.

Elegy A mournful, contemplative lyric poem written to commemorate someone who is dead, often ending in a consolation. Tennyson's *In Memoriam,* written on the death of Arthur Hallam, is an elegy. *Elegy* may also refer to a serious meditative poem produced to express the speaker's melancholy thoughts. See also LYRIC.

End rhyme See RHYME.

End-stopped line A poetic line that has a pause at the end. End-stopped lines reflect normal speech patterns and are often marked by punctuation. The first line of John Keats's "Endymion" is an example of an end-stopped line; the natural pause coincides with the end of the line and is marked by a period:

A thing of beauty is a joy forever.

English sonnet See SONNET.

Enjambment In poetry, when one line ends without a pause and continues into the next line for its meaning. This is also called a **run-on line.** The transition between the first two lines of William Wordsworth's "My Heart Leaps Up" demonstrates enjambment:

My heart leaps up when I behold
　A rainbow in the sky:

Envoy See SESTINA.

Epic A long narrative poem, told in a formal, elevated style, that focuses on a serious subject and chronicles heroic deeds and events important to a culture or nation. John Milton's *Paradise Lost,* which attempts to "justify the ways of God to man," is an epic. See also NARRATIVE POEM.

Epigram A brief, pointed, and witty poem that usually makes a satiric or humorous point. Epigrams are most often written in couplets but take no prescribed form.

Euphony *Euphony* ("good sound") refers to language that is smooth and musically pleasant to the ear. See also CACOPHONY.

Exact rhyme See RHYME.

Extended metaphor See METAPHOR.

Eye rhyme See RHYME.

Falling meter See METER.

Feminine rhyme See RHYME.

Feminist criticism An approach to literature that seeks to correct or supplement what may be regarded as a predominantly male-dominated critical perspective with a feminist consciousness. Feminist criticism places literature in a social context and uses a broad range of disciplines, including history, sociology, psychology, and linguistics, to provide a perspective sensitive to feminist issues. Feminist theories also attempt to understand representation from a woman's point of view and to explain women's writing strategies as specific to their social conditions. See also GENDER CRITICISM.

Figures of speech Ways of using language that deviate from the literal, denotative meanings of words in order to suggest additional meanings or effects. Figures of speech say one thing in terms of something else, such as when an eager funeral director is described as a vulture. See also METAPHOR, SIMILE.

Fixed form A poem that may be categorized by the pattern of its lines, meter, rhythm, or stanzas. A sonnet is a fixed form of poetry because by definition it must have fourteen lines. Other fixed forms include LIMERICK, SESTINA, and VILLANELLE. However, poems written in a fixed form may not always fit into categories precisely, because writers sometimes vary traditional forms to create innovative effects. See also OPEN FORM.

Foot The metrical unit by which a line of poetry is measured. A foot usually consists of one stressed and one or two unstressed syllables. An iambic foot, which consists of one unstressed syllable followed by one stressed syllable (ăwáy), is the most common metrical foot in English poetry. A trochaic foot consists of one stressed syllable followed by an unstressed syllable (lóvelў). An anapestic foot is two unstressed syllables followed by one stressed syllable (ŭndĕrstánd). A *dactylic foot* is one stressed syllable followed by two unstressed syllables (déspĕrăte). A spondee is a foot consisting of two stressed syllables (deád sét) but is not a sustained metrical foot and is used mainly for variety or emphasis. See also IAMBIC PENTAMETER, LINE, METER.

Form The overall structure or shape of a work, which frequently follows an established design. Forms may refer to a literary type (narrative form, lyric form) or to patterns of meter, lines, and rhymes (stanza form, verse form). See also FIXED FORM, OPEN FORM.

Formal diction See DICTION.

Formalist criticism An approach to literature that focuses on the formal elements of a work, such as its language, structure, and tone. Formalist critics offer intense examinations of the relationship between form and meaning in a work, emphasizing the subtle complexity in how a work is arranged. Formalists pay special attention to diction, irony, paradox, metaphor, and symbol, as well as larger elements such as plot, characterization, and narrative technique. Formalist critics read literature as an independent work of art rather than as a reflection of the author's state of mind or as a representation of a moment in history. Therefore anything outside of the work, including historical influences and authorial intent, is generally not examined by formalist critics. See also NEW CRITICISM.

Found poem An unintentional poem discovered in a nonpoetic context, such as a conversation, news story, or advertisement. Found poems serve as reminders that everyday language often contains what can be considered poetry, or that poetry is definable as any text read as a poem.

Free verse Also called *open form poetry,* free verse refers to poems characterized by their nonconformity to established patterns of meter, rhyme, and stanza. Free verse uses elements such as speech patterns, grammar, emphasis, and breath pauses to decide line breaks and usually does not rhyme. See OPEN FORM.

Gay and lesbian criticism An approach to literature that focuses on how homosexuals are represented in literature, how they read literature, and whether sexuality, as well as gender, is culturally constructed or innate. See also FEMINIST CRITICISM, GENDER CRITICISM.

Gender criticism An approach to literature that explores how ideas about men and women — what is masculine and feminine — can be regarded as socially constructed by particular cultures. Gender criticism expands categories and definitions of what is masculine or feminine and tends to regard sexuality as more complex than merely masculine or feminine, heterosexual or homosexual. See also FEMINIST CRITICISM, GAY AND LESBIAN CRITICISM.

Genre A French word meaning kind or type. The major genres in literature are poetry, fiction, drama, and essays. Genre can also refer to more specific types of literature such as comedy, tragedy, epic poetry, or science fiction.

Haiku A style of lyric poetry borrowed from the Japanese that typically presents an intense emotion or vivid image of nature, which, traditionally, is designed to lead to a spiritual insight. Haiku is a fixed poetic form, consisting of seventeen syllables organized into three unrhymed lines of five, seven, and five syllables. Today, however, many poets vary the syllabic count in their haiku. See also FIXED FORM.

Heroic couplet See COUPLET.

Historical criticism An approach to literature that uses history as a means of understanding a literary work more clearly. Such criticism moves beyond both the facts of an author's personal life and the text itself in order to examine the social and intellectual currents in which the author composed the work. See also CULTURAL CRITICISM, MARXIST CRITICISM, NEW HISTORICISM, POSTCOLONIAL CRITICISM.

Hyperbole A boldly exaggerated statement that adds emphasis without intending to be literally true, as in the statement "He ate everything in the house." Hyperbole (also called *overstatement*) may be used for serious, comic, or ironic effect. See also FIGURES OF SPEECH.

Iambic meter See FOOT.

Iambic pentameter A metrical pattern in poetry that consists of five iambic feet per line. (An iamb, or iambic foot, consists of one unstressed syllable followed by a stressed syllable.) See also FOOT, METER.

Image A word, phrase, or figure of speech (especially a SIMILE or a METAPHOR) that addresses the senses, suggesting mental pictures of sights, sounds, smells, tastes, feelings, or actions. Images offer sensory impressions to the reader and also convey emotions and moods through their verbal pictures. See also FIGURES OF SPEECH.

Implied metaphor See METAPHOR.

Informal diction See DICTION.

Internal rhyme See RHYME.

Irony A literary device that uses contradictory statements or situations to reveal a reality different from what appears to be true. It is ironic for a firehouse to burn down or for a police station to be burglarized. **Verbal irony** is a figure of speech that occurs when a person says one thing but means the opposite. **Sarcasm** is a strong form of verbal irony that is calculated to hurt someone through, for example, false praise. **Dramatic irony** creates a discrepancy between what a character believes or says and what the reader or audience member knows to be true. **Situational irony** exists when there is an incongruity between what is expected to happen and what actually happens owing to forces beyond human comprehension or control. The suicide of the seemingly successful main character in Edwin Arlington Robinson's poem "Richard Cory" is an example of situational irony. **Cosmic irony** occurs when a writer uses God, destiny, or fate to dash the hopes and expectations of a character or of humankind in general. In cosmic irony, a discrepancy exists between what a character aspires to and what universal forces provide. Stephen Crane's poem "A Man Said to the Universe" is a good example of cosmic irony, because the universe acknowledges no obligation to the man's assertion of his own existence.

Italian sonnet See SONNET.

Limerick A light, humorous style of fixed form poetry. Its usual form consists of five lines with the rhyme scheme *aabba;* lines 1, 2, and 5 contain three feet, while lines 3 and 4 usually contain two feet. Limericks range in subject matter from the silly to the obscene, and since Edward Lear popularized them in the nineteenth century, children and adults have enjoyed these comic poems. See also FIXED FORM.

Line A sequence of words printed as a separate entity on the page. In poetry, lines are usually measured by the number of feet they contain. The names for various line lengths are as follows:

monometer: one foot	pentameter: five feet
dimeter: two feet	hexameter: six feet
trimeter: three feet	heptameter: seven feet
tetrameter: four feet	octameter: eight feet

The number of feet in a line, coupled with the name of the foot, describes the metrical qualities of that line. See also END-STOPPED LINE, ENJAMBMENT, FOOT, METER.

Literary ballad See BALLAD.

Literary symbol See SYMBOL.

Litotes See UNDERSTATEMENT.

Lyric A type of brief poem that expresses the personal emotions and thoughts of a single speaker. It is important to realize, however, that although the lyric is uttered in the first person, the speaker is not necessarily the poet. There are many varieties of lyric poetry, including the DRAMATIC MONOLOGUE, ELEGY, HAIKU, ODE, and SONNET forms.

Marxist criticism An approach to literature that focuses on a work's ideological content — its explicit and implicit assumptions and values about matters such as culture, race, class, and power. Marxist criticism, based largely on the writings of Karl Marx, typically aims at not only revealing and clarifying ideological issues but also correcting social injustices. Some Marxist critics use literature to describe the competing socioeconomic interests that too often advance capitalist interests such as money and power rather than socialist interests such as morality and justice. They argue that literature and literary criticism are essentially political because they either challenge or support economic oppression. Because of this strong emphasis on the political aspects of texts, Marxist criticism focuses more on the content and themes of literature than on its form. See also CULTURAL CRITICISM, HISTORICAL CRITICISM, SOCIOLOGICAL CRITICISM.

Masculine rhyme See RHYME.

Metaphor A metaphor is a figure of speech that makes a comparison between two unlike things without using the words *like* or *as*. Metaphors assert the identity of dissimilar things, as when Macbeth asserts that life *is* a "brief candle." Metaphors can be subtle and powerful and can transform people, places, objects, and ideas into whatever the writer imagines them to be. An **implied metaphor** is a more subtle comparison; the terms being compared are not so specifically explained. For example, to describe a stubborn man unwilling to leave, one could say that he was "a mule standing his ground." This is a fairly explicit metaphor; the man is being compared to a mule. But to say that the man "brayed his refusal to leave" is to create an implied metaphor, because the subject (the man) is never overtly identified as a mule. Braying is associated with the mule, a notoriously stubborn creature, and so the comparison between the stubborn man and the mule is sustained. Implied metaphors can slip by inattentive readers who are not sensitive to such carefully chosen, highly concentrated language. An **extended metaphor** is a sustained comparison in which part or all of a poem consists of a series of related metaphors. Robert Francis's poem "Catch" relies on an extended metaphor that compares poetry to playing catch. A **controlling metaphor** runs through an entire work and determines its form or nature. The controlling metaphor in Anne Bradstreet's poem "The Author to Her Book" likens her book to a child. **Synecdoche** is a kind of metaphor in which a part of something is used to signify the whole, as when a gossip is called a "wagging tongue," or when ten ships are called "ten sails." Sometimes, synecdoche refers to the whole being used to signify the part, as in the phrase "Boston won the baseball game." Clearly, the entire city of Boston did not participate in the game; the whole of Boston is being used to signify the individuals who played and won the game. **Metonymy** is a type of metaphor in which something closely associated with a subject is substituted for it. In this way, we speak of the "silver screen" to mean motion pictures, "the crown" to stand for the king, "the White House" to stand for the activities of the president. See also FIGURES OF SPEECH, PERSONIFICATION, SIMILE.

Meter When a rhythmic pattern of stresses recurs in a poem, it is called *meter.* Metrical patterns are determined by the type and number of feet in a line of verse; combining the name of a line length with the name of a foot concisely describes the meter of the line. **Rising meter** refers to metrical feet that move from unstressed to stressed sounds, such as the iambic foot and the anapestic foot. **Falling meter** refers to metrical feet that move from stressed to unstressed sounds, such as the trochaic foot and the dactylic foot. See also ACCENT, FOOT, IAMBIC PENTAMETER, LINE.

Metonymy See METAPHOR.

Middle diction See DICTION.

Mythological criticism An approach to literature that seeks to identify what in a work creates deep, universal responses in readers, by paying close attention to the hopes, fears, and expectations of entire cultures. Mythological critics (sometimes called *archetypal critics*) analyze literature for underlying, recurrent patterns that reveal universal meanings and basic human experiences for readers regardless of when and where they live. These critics attempt to explain how archetypes (the characters, images, and themes that symbolically embody universal meanings and experiences) are embodied in literary works in order to make larger connections that explain a particular work's lasting appeal. Mythological critics may specialize in areas such as classical literature, philology, anthropology, psychology, and cultural history, but they all emphasize the assumptions and values of various cultures. See also ARCHETYPE.

Narrative poem A poem that tells a story. A narrative poem may be short or long, and the story it relates may be simple or complex. See also BALLAD, EPIC.

Near rhyme See RHYME.

New Criticism An approach to literature made popular between the 1940s and the 1960s that evolved out of formalist criticism. New Critics suggest that detailed analysis of the language of a literary text can uncover important layers of meaning in that work. New Criticism consciously downplays the historical influences, authorial intentions, and social contexts that surround texts in order to focus on explication — extremely close textual analysis. See also FORMALIST CRITICISM.

New historicism An approach to literature that emphasizes the interaction between a work's historical context and a modern reader's understanding and interpretation of the work. New historicists attempt to describe the culture of a period by reading many different kinds of texts and paying close attention to many different dimensions of a culture, including political, economic, social, and aesthetic concerns. They regard texts not simply as a reflection of the culture that produced them but also as productive of that culture playing an active role in the social and political conflicts of an age. New historicism acknowledges and then explores various versions of "history," sensitizing us to the fact that the history on which we choose to focus is colored by being reconstructed from our present circumstances. See also HISTORICAL CRITICISM.

Octave A poetic stanza of eight lines, usually forming one part of a sonnet. See also SONNET, STANZA.

Ode A relatively lengthy lyric poem that often expresses lofty emotions in a dignified style. Odes are characterized by a serious topic, such as truth, art, freedom, justice, or the meaning of life; their tone tends to be formal. There is no prescribed pattern that defines an ode; some odes repeat the same pattern in each stanza, while others introduce a new pattern in each stanza. See also LYRIC.

Oedipus complex A Freudian term derived from Sophocles' tragedy *Oedipus the King*. It describes a psychological complex that is predicated on a boy's unconscious rivalry with his father for his mother's love and his desire to eliminate his father in order to take his father's place with his mother. The female equivalent of this complex is called the *Electra complex*. See also ELECTRA COMPLEX, PSYCHOLOGICAL CRITICISM.

Off rhyme See RHYME.

Onomatopoeia A term referring to the use of a word that resembles the sound it denotes. *Buzz, rattle, bang*, and *sizzle* all reflect onomatopoeia. Onomatopoeia can also consist of more than one word; writers sometimes create lines or whole passages in which the sound of the words helps to convey their meanings.

Open form Sometimes called *free verse*, open form poetry does not conform to established patterns of METER, RHYME, and STANZA. Such poetry derives its rhythmic qualities from the repetition of words, phrases, or grammatical structures; from the arrangement of words on the printed page; or by some other means. The poet E. E. Cummings wrote open form poetry; his poems do not have measurable meters, but they do have RHYTHM. See also FIXED FORM.

Organic form Refers to works whose formal characteristics are not rigidly predetermined but follow the movement of thought or emotion being expressed. Such works are said to grow like living organisms, following their own individual patterns rather than external fixed rules that govern, for example, the form of a SONNET.

Overstatement See HYPERBOLE.

Oxymoron A condensed form of paradox in which two contradictory words are used together, as in "sweet sorrow" or "jumbo shrimp." See also PARADOX.

Paradox A statement that initially appears to be contradictory but then, on closer inspection, turns out to make sense. For example, John Donne ends his sonnet "Death, Be Not Proud" with the paradoxical statement "Death, thou shalt die." To solve the paradox, it is necessary to discover the sense that underlies the statement. Paradox is useful in poetry because it arrests a reader's attention by its seemingly stubborn refusal to make sense.

Paraphrase A prose restatement of the central ideas of a work, in your own language.

Parody A humorous imitation of another, usually serious, work. It can take any fixed or open form, because parodists imitate the tone, language, and shape of the original in order to deflate the subject matter, making the original work seem absurd. Anthony Hecht's poem "Dover Bitch" is a famous parody of Matthew Arnold's well-known "Dover Beach." Parody may also be used as a form of literary criticism to expose the defects in a work. But sometimes parody becomes an affectionate acknowledgment that a well-known work has become both institutionalized in our culture and fair game for some fun. For example, Peter De Vries's "To His Importunate Mistress" gently mocks Andrew Marvell's "To His Coy Mistress."

Persona Literally, a *persona* is a mask. In literature a *persona* is a speaker created by a writer to tell a story or to speak in a poem. A persona is not a character in a story or narrative, nor does a persona necessarily directly reflect the author's personal voice. A persona is a separate self, created by and distinct from the author, through which he or she speaks.

Personification A form of metaphor in which human characteristics are attributed to nonhuman things. Personification offers the writer a way to give the world life and motion by assigning familiar human behaviors and emotions to animals, inanimate objects, and abstract ideas. For example, in John Keats's "Ode on a Grecian Urn" the speaker refers to the urn as an "unravished bride of quietness." See also METAPHOR.

Petrarchan sonnet See SONNET.

Picture poem A type of open form poetry in which the poet arranges the lines of the poem so as to create a particular shape on the page. The shape of the poem embodies its subject; the poem becomes a picture of what the poem is describing. Michael McFee's "In Medias Res" is an example of a picture poem. See also OPEN FORM.

Poetic diction See DICTION.

Postcolonial criticism An approach to literature that focuses on the study of cultural behavior and expression in relationship to the colonized world. Postcolonial criticism refers to the analysis of literary works by writers from countries and cultures that at one time have been controlled by colonizing powers — such as Indian writers during or after British colonial rule. Postcolonial criticism also refers to the analysis of literary works written about colonial cultures by writers from the colonizing country. Many of these kinds of analyses point out how writers from colonial powers sometimes misrepresent colonized cultures by reflecting more their own values. See also CULTURAL CRITICISM, HISTORICAL CRITICISM, MARXIST CRITICISM.

Prose poem A kind of open form poetry that is printed as prose and represents the most clear opposite of fixed form poetry. Prose poems are densely compact and often make use of striking imagery and figures of speech. See also FIXED FORM, OPEN FORM.

Prosody The overall metrical structure of a poem. See also METER.

Psychological criticism An approach to literature that draws on psychoanalytic theories, especially those of Sigmund Freud or Jacques Lacan, to understand more fully the text, the writer, and the reader. The basis of this approach is the idea of the existence of a human unconscious — those impulses, desires, and feelings about which a person is unaware but which influence emotions and behavior. Critics use psychological approaches to explore the motivations of characters and the symbolic meanings of events, while biographers speculate about a writer's own motivations — conscious or unconscious — in a literary work. Psychological approaches are also used to describe and analyze the reader's personal responses to a text.

Pun A play on words that relies on a word's having more than one meaning or sounding like another word. Shakespeare and other writers use puns extensively for serious and comic purposes; in *Romeo and Juliet* (3.2.101) the dying Mercutio puns, "Ask for me tomorrow and you shall find me a grave man." Puns have serious literary uses, but since the eighteenth century they have been used almost purely for humorous effect.

Quatrain A four-line stanza. Quatrains are the most common stanzaic form in the English language; they can have various meters and rhyme schemes. See also METER, RHYME, STANZA.

Reader-response criticism An approach to literature that focuses on the reader rather than the work itself, by attempting to describe what goes on in the reader's mind during the reading of a text. Hence the consciousness of the reader — produced by reading the work — is the actual subject of reader-response criticism. These critics are not after a "correct" reading of the text or what the author presumably intended; instead, they are interested in the reader's individual experience with the text. Thus there is no single definitive reading of a work, because readers create rather than discover absolute meanings in texts. However, this approach is not a rationale for mistaken or bizarre readings but an exploration of the possibilities for a plurality of readings. This kind of strategy calls attention to how we read, what influences our readings, and what that reveals about ourselves.

Rhyme The repetition of identical or similar concluding syllables in different words, most often at the ends of lines. Rhyme is predominantly a function of sound rather than spelling; thus words that end with the same vowel sounds rhyme (for instance, *day, prey, bouquet, weigh*), and words with the same consonant ending rhyme (for instance *vain, feign, rein, lane*). Words do not have to be spelled the same way or look alike to rhyme. In fact, words may look alike but not rhyme at all. This is called **eye rhyme,** as with *bough* and *cough,* or *brow* and *blow.* **End rhyme** is the most common form of rhyme in poetry; the rhyme comes at the end of the lines:

It runs through the reeds
  And away it proceeds,
Through meadow and glade,
  In sun and in shade.

The **rhyme scheme** of a poem describes the pattern of end rhymes. Rhyme schemes are mapped out by noting patterns of rhyme with small letters: the first rhyme sound is designated *a,* the second becomes *b,* the third *c,* and so on. Thus the rhyme scheme of the preceding stanza is *aabb*. **Internal rhyme** places at least one of the rhymed words within the line, as in "Dividing and gliding and sliding" or "In mist or cloud, on mast or shroud." **Masculine rhyme** describes the rhyming of single-syllable words, such as *grade* or *shade.* Masculine rhyme also occurs when rhyming words are of more than one syllable and the same sound occurs in a final stressed syllable, as in *defend* and *contend, betray* and *away.* **Feminine rhyme** consists of a rhymed stressed syllable followed by one or more identical unstressed syllables, as in *butter,* *clutter; gratitude, attitude; quivering, shivering.* All of the examples so far have illustrated **exact rhymes,** because they share the same stressed vowel sounds as well as sharing sounds that follow the vowel. In **near rhyme** (also called **off rhyme, slant rhyme,** and **approximate rhyme**) the sounds are almost but not exactly alike. A common form of near rhyme is CONSONANCE, which consists of identical consonant sounds preceded by different vowel sounds: *home, same; worth, breath.*

Rhyme scheme   See RHYME.

Rhythm   A term used to refer to the recurrence of stressed and unstressed sounds in poetry. Depending on how sounds are arranged, the rhythm of a poem may be fast or slow, choppy or smooth. Poets use rhythm to create pleasurable sound patterns and to reinforce meanings. Rhythm in prose arises from pattern repetitions of sounds and pauses that create looser rhythmic effects. See also METER.

Rising meter   See METER.

Run-on line   See ENJAMBMENT.

Sarcasm   See IRONY.

Satire   The literary art of ridiculing a folly or vice in order to expose or correct it. The object of satire is usually some human frailty; people, institutions, ideas, and things are all fair game for satirists. Satire evokes attitudes of amusement, contempt, scorn, or indignation toward its faulty subject in the hope of somehow improving it. See also IRONY, PARODY.

Scansion   The process of measuring the stresses in a line of verse to determine the metrical pattern of the line. See also LINE, METER.

Sentimentality   A pejorative term used to describe the effort by an author to induce emotional responses in the reader that exceed what the situation warrants. Sentimentality especially pertains to such emotions as pathos and sympathy; it cons readers into falling for the mass murderer who is devoted to stray cats, and it requires that readers do not examine such illogical responses. Clichés and stock responses are the key ingredients of sentimentality in literature. See also CLICHÉ, STOCK RESPONSES.

Sestet   A stanza consisting of exactly six lines. See also STANZA.

Sestina   A type of fixed form poetry consisting of thirty-six lines of any length divided into six sestets and a three-line concluding stanza called an **envoy.** The six words at the end of the first sestet's lines must also appear at the ends of the other five sestets, in varying order. These six words must also appear in the envoy, where they often resonate important themes. An example of this highly demanding form of poetry is Elizabeth Bishop's "Sestina." See also SESTET.

Setting   The physical and social context in which the action of a poem occurs. The major elements of setting are the time, the place, and the social environment that frames the poem. Setting can be used to evoke a mood or atmosphere that will prepare the reader for what is to come, as in Robert Frost's "Home Burial."

Shakespearean sonnet See SONNET.

Simile A common figure of speech that makes an explicit comparison between two things by using words such as *like, as, than, appears,* and *seems:* "A sip of Mrs. Cook's coffee is like a punch in the stomach." The effectiveness of this simile is created by the differences between the two things compared. There would be no simile if the comparison were stated this way: "Mrs. Cook's coffee is as strong as the cafeteria's coffee." This is a literal translation because Mrs. Cook's coffee is compared with something like it — another kind of coffee. See also FIGURES OF SPEECH, METAPHOR.

Situational irony See IRONY.

Slant rhyme See RHYME.

Sociological criticism An approach to literature that examines social groups, relationships, and values as they are manifested in literature. Sociological approaches emphasize the nature and effect of the social forces that shape power relationships between groups or classes of people. Such readings treat literature as either a document reflecting social conditions or a product of those conditions. The former view brings into focus the social milieu; the latter emphasizes the work. Two important forms of sociological criticism are Marxist and feminist approaches. See also FEMINIST CRITICISM, MARXIST CRITICISM.

Sonnet A fixed form of lyric poetry that consists of fourteen lines, usually written in iambic pentameter. There are two basic types of sonnets, the Italian and the English. The **Italian sonnet,** also known as the **Petrarchan sonnet,** is divided into an octave, which typically rhymes *abbaabba,* and a sestet, which may have varying rhyme schemes. Common rhyme patterns in the sestet are *cdecde, cdcdcd,* and *cdccdc.* Very often the octave presents a situation, attitude, or problem that the sestet comments on or resolves, as in John Keats's "On First Looking into Chapman's Homer." The **English sonnet,** also known as the **Shakespearean sonnet,** is organized into three quatrains and a couplet, which typically rhyme *abab cdcd efef gg.* This rhyme scheme is more suited to English poetry because English has fewer rhyming words than Italian. English sonnets, because of their four-part organization, also have more flexibility with respect to where thematic breaks can occur. Frequently, however, the most pronounced break or turn comes with the concluding couplet, as in Shakespeare's "Shall I compare thee to a summer's day?" See also COUPLET, IAMBIC PENTAMETER, LINE, OCTAVE, QUATRAIN, SESTET.

Speaker The voice used by an author to tell a story or speak a poem. The speaker is often a created identity and should not automatically be equated with the author's self. See also PERSONA.

Spondee See FOOT.

Stanza In poetry, *stanza* refers to a grouping of lines, set off by a space, that usually has a set pattern of meter and rhyme. See also LINE, METER, RHYME.

Stock responses Predictable, conventional reactions to language, characters, symbols, or situations. The flag, motherhood, puppies, God, and peace are common objects used to elicit stock responses from unsophisticated audiences. See also CLICHÉ, SENTIMENTALITY.

Stress The emphasis, or ACCENT, given a syllable in pronunciation.

Style The distinctive and unique manner in which a writer arranges words to achieve particular effects. Style essentially combines the idea to be expressed with the author's individuality. These arrangements include individual word choices as well as matters such as the length of sentences, their structure, tone, and use of irony. See also DICTION, IRONY, TONE.

Symbol A person, object, image, word, or event that evokes a range of additional meaning beyond and usually more abstract than its literal significance. Symbols are educational devices for evoking complex ideas without having to resort to painstaking explanations that would make a story more like an essay than an experience. **Conventional symbols** have meanings that are widely recognized by a society or culture. Some conventional symbols are the Christian cross, the Star of David, a swastika, or a nation's flag. Writers use conventional symbols to reinforce meanings. E. E. Cummings, for example, emphasizes the spring setting in "in Just—" as a way of suggesting a renewed sense of life. A **literary** or **contextual symbol** can be a setting, character, action, object, name, or anything else in a work that maintains its literal significance while suggesting other meanings. Such symbols go beyond conventional symbols; they gain their symbolic meaning within the context of a specific story. For example, the urn in John Keats's "Ode on a Grecian Urn" takes on multiple symbolic meanings in the work, but these meanings do not automatically carry over into other poems about urns. The meanings suggested by Keats's urn are specific to that text; therefore it becomes a contextual symbol. See also ALLEGORY.

Synecdoche See METAPHOR.

Syntax The ordering of words into meaningful verbal patterns such as phrases, clauses, and sentences. Poets often manipulate syntax, changing conventional word order, to place certain emphasis on particular words. Emily Dickinson, for instance, writes about being surprised by a snake in her poem "A narrow Fellow in the Grass" and includes this line: "His notice sudden is." In addition to the alliterative hissing *s*-sounds here, Dickinson also effectively manipulates the line's syntax so that the verb *is* appears unexpectedly at the end, making the snake's hissing presence all the more "sudden."

Tercet A three-line stanza. See also STANZA, TRIPLET.

Terza rima An interlocking three-line rhyme scheme: *aba, bcb, cdc, ded,* and so on. Dante's *Divine Comedy* and Robert Frost's "Acquainted with the Night" are written in terza rima. See also RHYME, TERCET.

Theme The central meaning or dominant idea in a literary work. A theme provides a unifying point around which the plot, characters, setting, point of view, symbols, and other elements of a work are organized. It is important not to mistake the theme for the work's actual subject; the theme refers to the abstract concept that is made concrete through the images, characterization, and action of the text. In nonfiction, however, the theme generally refers to the main topic of the discourse.

Thesis The central idea of an essay. The thesis is a complete sentence (although sometimes it may require more than one sentence) that establishes the topic of the essay in clear, unambiguous language.

Tone The author's implicit attitude toward the reader or the people, places, and events in a work as revealed by the elements of the author's style. Tone may be characterized as serious or ironic, sad or happy, private or public, angry or affectionate, bitter or nostalgic, or any other attitudes and feelings that human beings experience. See also STYLE.

Triplet A tercet in which all three lines rhyme. See also TERCET.

Trochaic meter See FOOT.

Understatement The opposite of hyperbole, *understatement* (or litotes) refers to a figure of speech that says less than is intended. Understatement usually has an ironic effect, and it sometimes may be used for comic purposes, as in Mark Twain's statement "The reports of my death are greatly exaggerated." See also HYPERBOLE, IRONY.

Verbal irony See IRONY.

Verse A generic term used to describe poetic lines composed in a measured, rhythmical pattern that are often, but not necessarily, rhymed. See also LINE, METER, RHYME, RHYTHM.

Villanelle A type of fixed form poetry consisting of nineteen lines of any length divided into six stanzas: five tercets and a concluding quatrain. The first and third lines of the initial tercet rhyme; these rhymes are repeated in each subsequent tercet (*aba*) and in the final two lines of the quatrain (*abaa*). Line 1 appears in its entirety as lines 6, 12, and 18, while line 3 reappears as lines 9, 15, and 19. Dylan Thomas's "Do not go gentle into that good night" is a villanelle. See also FIXED FORM, QUATRAIN, RHYME, TERCET.

Helen Chasin. "The Word *Plum*" from *Coming Close and Other Poems* by Helen Chasin. Copyright © 1968 by Yale University Press. Reprinted by permission of Yale University Press.

Kelly Cherry. "Alzheimer's" from *Death and Transfiguration* by Kelly Cherry. Copyright © 1997 by Kelly Cherry. Reprinted by permission of Louisiana State University Press.

David Chinitz. "The Romanticization of Africa in the 1920s" from "Rejuvenation through Joy: Langston Hughes, Primitivism, and Jazz," *American Literary History* (Spring 1997), vol. 9, no. 1, pp. 60–78. Reprinted by permission of the author and Oxford University Press.

John Ciardi. "Suburban" from *For Instance* by John Ciardi. Copyright © 1979 by John Ciardi. Used by permission of W. W. Norton & Company, Inc.

Kate Clanchy. "Spell" from *Samarkand* by Kate Clanchy (Picador, 1999). Copyright © 1999 by Kate Clanchy. Reprinted by permission of Macmillan Publishers Limited.

Lucille Clifton. "this morning (for the girls of eastern high school)" from *Good Woman: Poems and a Memoir 1969–1980.* Copyright © 1987 by Lucille Clifton. Reprinted with the permission of BOA Editions, Ltd.

Judith Ortiz Cofer. "Common Ground" is reprinted with permission from the publisher of *Silent Dancing: A Partial Remembrance of a Puerto Rican Childhood* by Judith Ortiz Cofer (Houston: Arte Público Press — University of Houston, © 1990). "The Game" from *The Latin Deli* by Judith Ortiz Cofer. Copyright © 1993 by Judith Ortiz Cofer. Reprinted by permission of the University of Georgia Press.

Billy Collins. "Introduction to Poetry" from *The Apple That Astonished Paris.* Copyright © 1988 by Billy Collins. Reprinted with the permission of the University of Arkansas Press. "Marginalia" from *Picnic, Lightning* by Billy Collins. Copyright © 1998. Reprinted by permission of the University of Pittsburgh Press.

Edmund Conti. "Pragmatist" from *Light Year '86.* Reprinted by permission of the author.

Wendy Cope. "Lonely Hearts" from *Making Cocoa for Kingsley Amis* by Wendy Cope. Copyright © 1986 by Wendy Cope. Reprinted by permission of Faber & Faber, Ltd.

Sally Croft. "Home-Baked Bread" from *Light Year '86.* Reprinted by permission of the author.

E. E. Cummings. "Buffalo Bill 's," "in Just-," "l(a," "next to of course god america i," "she being Brand," and "since feeling is first" from *Complete Poems: 1904–1962* by E. E. Cummings, edited by George J. Firmage. Copyright 1923, 1925, 1926, 1931, 1935, 1938, 1939, 1940, 1944, 1945, 1946, 1947, 1948, 1949, 1950, 1951, 1952, 1953, 1954, © 1955, 1956, 1957, 1958, 1959, 1960, 1961, 1962, 1963, 1966, 1967, 1968, 1972, 1973, 1974, 1975, 1976, 1977, 1978, 1979, 1980, 1981, 1982, 1983, 1984, 1985, 1986, 1987, 1988, 1989, 1990, 1991 by the Trustees for the E. E. Cummings Trust. Copyright © 1973, 1976, 1978, 1979, 1981, 1983, 1985, 1991 by George James Firmage. Used by permission of Liveright Publishing Corporation.

Mahmoud Darwish. "Identity Card" from *The Music of Human Flesh,* translated by Denys Johnson-Davies (Three Continents Press, 1980). Copyright © 1980 by Denys Johnson-Davies. Reprinted by permission of Denys Johnson-Davies.

Peter De Vries. "To His Importunate Mistress." Reprinted by permission of the Estate of Peter De Vries.

Joanne Diaz. "On My Father's Loss of Hearing," *The Southern Review* 42.3 (Summer 2006). Copyright © 2006 by Joanne Diaz. Reprinted by permission of the author.

Emily Dickinson. "A Bird came down the Walk —," "After great pain a formal feeling comes —," "A Light exists in Spring," "A narrow Fellow in the grass," "A Word dropped careless on a Page," "Because I could not stop for Death —," "'Heaven' — is what I cannot reach!," "'Hope' is the thing with feathers —," "I dwell in Possibility —," "I felt a Cleaving in my Mind —," "If I shouldn't be alive," "I heard a Fly buzz — when I died —," "I like a look of Agony," "I never saw a Moor —," "I reason, Earth is short —," "I took one Draught of Life —," "Much Madness is divinest Sense —," "One need not be a Chamber — to be Haunted —," "Safe in their Alabaster Chambers —," "Success is counted sweetest," "Tell all the Truth but tell it slant —," "There is no Frigate like a Book," "There's a certain Slant of light," "The Soul selects her own Society —," "This was a Poet — It is That," and "What Soft — Cherubic Creatures —." Reprinted by permission of the publishers and the Trustees of Amherst College from *The Poems of Emily Dickinson,* Thomas H. Johnson, ed., Cambridge, Mass.: The Belknap Press of Harvard University Press. Copyright © 1951, 1955, 1979, 1983 by the President and Fellows of Harvard College.

Chitra Banerjee Divakaruni. "Indian Movie, New Jersey" from the *Indiana Review,* 1990. Copyright © by Chitra Banerjee Divakaruni. Reprinted by permission of the author.

Gregory Djanikian. "When I First Saw Snow" reprinted from *Falling Deeply into America* by Gregory Djanikian, by permission of Carnegie Mellon University Press. Copyright © 1989 by Gregory Djanikian.

Stephen Dobyns. "Do They Have a Reason?" from *The Georgia Review* 54.4 (Winter 2000). Copyright © 2000 by Stephen Dobyns. Reprinted by permission of the author.

Mark Doty. "The Embrace" from *Sweet Machine* by Mark Doty. Copyright © 1998 by Mark Doty. Reprinted by permission of HarperCollins Publishers.

Rita Dove. "Fox Trot Fridays" from *American Smooth: Poems* by Rita Dove. Copyright © 2004 by Rita Dove. Used by permission of W. W. Norton & Company, Inc.

Bernard Duyfhuizen. "'To His Coy Mistress': On How a Female Might Respond" excerpted from "Textual Harassment of Marvell's Coy Mistress: The Institutionalization of Masculine Criticism," *College English* (April 1988). Copyright © 1988 by the National Council of Teachers of English. Reprinted with permission.

James A. Emanuel. "Hughes's Attitudes toward Religion" excerpted from "Christ in Alabama: Religion in the Poetry of Langston Hughes" in *Modern Black Poets,* edited by Donald B. Gibson. Reprinted by permission of the author.

Louise Erdrich. "Dear John Wayne" from *Jacklight: Poems* by Louise Erdrich. Copyright © 1984 by Louise Erdrich. Reprinted by permission of The Wylie Agency.

Martín Espada. "Bully" and "Latin Night at the Pawn Shop" from *Rebellion Is the Circle of a Lover's Hands / Re-*

belión es el giro de manos del amante by Martín Espada. Curbstone Press, 1990. Copyright © 1990 by Martín Espada. Reprinted with permission of Curbstone Press. Distributed by Consortium. "The Community College Revises Its Curriculum in Response to Changing Demographics" from *A Mayan Astronomer in Hell's Kitchen* by Martín Espada. Copyright © 2000 by Martín Espada. Used by permission of W. W. Norton & Company, Inc.

Ruth Fainlight. "The Clarinettist." Reprinted by permission from *The Hudson Review* Vol. LV, No. 1 (Spring 2002). Copyright © 2002 by Ruth Fainlight.

Blanche Farley. "The Lover Not Taken" from *Light Year '86*. Reprinted by permission of the author.

Kenneth Fearing. "AD" from *Kenneth Fearing Complete Poems*, edited by Robert Ryely (Orono, ME: National Poetry Foundation, 1997). Copyright © 1938 by Kenneth Fearing, renewed in 1966 by the Estate of Kenneth Fearing. Reprinted by the permission of Russell & Volkening as agents for the author.

Karen Jackson Ford. "Hughes's Aesthetics of Simplicity" excerpted from "Do Right to Write Right: Langston Hughes's Aesthetics of Simplicity," *Twentieth Century Literature* 38.4 (Winter 1992). Reprinted by permission.

Robert Francis. "Catch" and "The Pitcher" from *The Orb Weaver* (Wesleyan University Press, 1953). Copyright © 1953 by Robert Francis. Reprinted by permission of Wesleyan University Press, www.wesleyan.edu/wespress. "On 'Hard' Poetry" reprinted from *The Satirical Rogue on Poetry* by Robert Francis (Amherst: University of Massachusetts Press, 1968), copyright © 1968 by Robert Francis. Used by permission.

Daisy Fried. "Wit's End" from *She Didn't Mean to Do It* by Daisy Fried. Copyright © 2001. Reprinted by permission of the University of Pittsburgh Press.

Robert Frost. "Acquainted with the Night," "A Girl's Garden," "Design," "Fire and Ice," "Neither Out Far nor In Deep," "Nothing Gold Can Stay," "Stopping by Woods on a Snowy Evening," "The Most of It," "The Silken Tent," and "Unharvested," from *The Poetry of Robert Frost*, edited by Edward Connery Lathem. Copyright 1923, 1969 by Henry Holt and Company. Copyright 1936, 1942, 1944, 1951 by Robert Frost. Copyright 1964, 1970 by Lesley Frost Ballantine. Reprinted by permission of Henry Holt and Company, LLC. "On the Figure a Poem Makes" from *The Selected Prose of Robert Frost*, edited by Hyde Cox and Edward Connery Lathem. Copyright 1939, 1967 by Henry Holt and Company. Reprinted by permission of Henry Holt and Company, LLC. "On the Living Part of a Poem" from *A Swinger of Birches: A Portrait of Robert Frost* by Sidney Cox. Copyright © 1957 by New York University Press. Reprinted with permission of New York University Press. "On the Way to Read a Poem" from "Poetry and School" by Robert Frost in *The Atlantic Monthly*, June 1951. Reprinted by permission of the Estate of Robert Frost.

Donald B. Gibson. "The Essential Optimism of Hughes and Whitman" excerpted from "The Good Black Poet and the Good Gray Poet: The Poetry of Hughes and Whitman" in *Langston Hughes—Black Genius: A Critical Evaluation* by Donald B. Gibson. William Morrow, 1971. Reprinted with the permission of the author.

Sandra M. Gilbert. "Mafioso" from *Kissing the Bread: New and Selected Poems, 1969–1999* by Sandra M. Gilbert. Copyright © 1979 by Sandra M. Gilbert. Reprinted by permission of the author.

Sandra M. Gilbert and Susan Gubar. "On Dickinson's White Dress" excerpted from *The Madwoman in the Attic*, Yale University Press, 1979. Reprinted by permission of Yale University Press.

Gary Gildner. "First Practice" from *Blue Like the Heavens: New and Selected Poems* by Gary Gildner. Copyright © 1984. Reprinted by permission of the University of Pittsburgh Press.

Eliza Griswold. "Occupation" from *Wideawake* by Eliza Griswold, forthcoming in 2007 from Farrar, Straus and Giroux, LLC. Copyright © 2006 by Eliza Griswold. Reprinted by permission of Farrar, Straus and Giroux, LLC. Originally published in the *New Yorker*.

H. D. (Hilda Doolittle). "Heat" from *Collected Poems, 1912–1944*. Copyright 1982 by The Estate of Hilda Doolittle. Reprinted by permission of New Directions Publishing Corp.

Rachel Hadas. "The Compact" from *Laws* by Rachel Hadas (Zoo Press, 1994). Copyright © 1994 by Rachel Hadas. Reprinted by permission of the author. "The Red Hat" from *Halfway Down the Hall* (Wesleyan University Press, 1998). Copyright © 1998 by Rachel Hadas. Reprinted by permission of Wesleyan University Press, www.wesleyan.edu/wespress.

Richard Hague. "Directions for Resisting the SAT" from *Ohio Teachers Write* (Ohio Council of Teachers of English, 1996). Copyright © 1996 by Richard Hague. Reprinted by permission of the author.

Mark Halliday. "Graded Paper," *The Michigan Quarterly Review*. Reprinted by permission of the author.

Barbara Hamby. "Ode to American English" from *Babel* by Barbara Hamby. Copyright © 2004. Reprinted by permission of the University of Pittsburgh Press.

Sam Hamill. "Sheepherder Coffee" from *Poems Against the War*, edited by Sam Hamill et al. Copyright © 2003. Appears by permission of the publisher, Nation Books, a division of Avalon Publishing Group, Inc.

Joy Harjo. "The Path to the Milky Way Leads through Los Angeles" from *A Map to the Next World: Poems and Tales* by Joy Harjo. Copyright © 2000 by Joy Harjo. Used by permission of W. W. Norton & Company, Inc.

Jeffrey Harrison. "Fork" from *Incomplete Knowledge* by Jeffrey Harrison (Four Way Books, 2006), copyright © 2006 by Jeffrey Harrison, used with the permission of the author. "On 'Fork' as a Work of Fiction," used with the permission of the author. "Horseshoe Contest" from *Feeding the Fire* by Jeffrey Harrison (Louisville: Sarabande Books, 2001), copyright © 2001 by Jeffrey Harrison, used with the permission of the author.

Robert Hass. "A Story about the Body" from *Human Wishes* by Robert Hass. Copyright © 1989 by Robert Hass. Reprinted by permission of HarperCollins Publishers.

William Hathaway. "Oh, Oh" from *Light Year '86*. This poem was originally published in *The Cincinnati Poetry Review*. Reprinted by permission of the author.

Robert Hayden. "Those Winter Sundays," copyright © 1966 by Robert Hayden, from *Angle of Ascent: New and Selected Poems* by Robert Hayden. Used by permission of Liveright Publishing Corporation.

Seamus Heaney. "The Forge" from *Opened Ground: Selected Poems 1966–1996* by Seamus Heaney, copyright © 1998 by Seamus Heaney. Reprinted by permission of Farrar, Straus and Giroux, LLC. Also from *Door into the Dark* by Seamus Heaney, copyright © 1969 by Seamus Heaney. Reprinted by permission of Faber & Faber, Ltd.

Anthony Hecht. "The Dover Bitch" from *Collected Earlier Poems* by Anthony Hecht. Copyright © 1990 by Anthony Hecht. Used by permission of Alfred A. Knopf, a division of Random House, Inc.

Judy Page Heitzman. "The Schoolroom on the Second Floor of the Knitting Mill." Copyright © 1991 by Judy Page Heitzman. Originally appeared in *The New Yorker,* December 2, 1992, p. 102. Reprinted by permission of the author.

William Heyen. "The Trains" from *The Host: Selected Poems 1965–1990* by William Heyen. Copyright © 1994 by Time Being Press. Reprinted by permission of Time Being Books. All rights reserved.

Bob Hicok. "Making it in poetry," copyright © 2004 by Bob Hicok, first appeared in the *Georgia Review* 58.2 and is reprinted here with the acknowledgment of the editors and the permission of the author. "Spam leaves an aftertaste," copyright © 2001 by Bob Hicok, first appeared in the *Gettysburg Review* 15.1 and is reprinted here with the acknowledgment of the editors and the permission of the author.

Conrad Hilberry. "The Calvinist" from *Player Piano: Poems* by Conrad Hilberry. Copyright © 1999 by Conrad Hilberry. Reprinted by permission of Louisiana State University Press.

Jane Hirshfield. "August Day" from *Given Sugar, Given Salt: Poems* by Jane Hirshfield. Copyright © 2001 by Jane Hirshfield. Reprinted by permission of HarperCollins Publishers.

Tony Hoagland. "America," copyright © 2003 by Tony Hoagland. Reprinted from *What Narcissism Means to Me* with the permission of Graywolf Press, Saint Paul, Minnesota.

M. Carl Holman. "Mr. Z." Reprinted by permission of the Estate of M. Carl Holman.

Carolina Hospital. "The Hyphenated Man" is reprinted with permission from the publisher of *The Child of Exile: A Poetry Memoir* by Carolina Hospital (Houston: Arte Público Press — University of Houston, © 2004).

Andrew Hudgins. "Elegy for My Father, Who Is Not Dead" and "Seventeen" from *The Glass Hammer* by Andrew Hudgins. Copyright © 1994 by Andrew Hudgins. Reprinted by permission of Houghton Mifflin Company. All rights reserved.

Langston Hughes. "125th Street," "Ballad of the Landlord," "Cross," "Danse Africaine," "Dinner Guest: Me," "doorknobs," "Dream Boogie," "Dream Variations," "Drum," "Esthete in Harlem," "Formula," "Frederick Douglass: 1817–1895," "Harlem," "I, Too," "Jazzonia," "Lenox Avenue: Midnight," "Morning After," "Mother to Son," "Negro," "Old Walt," "Park Bench," "Red Silk Stockings," "Rent-Party Shout: For a Lady Dancer," "Song for a Dark Girl," "The Negro Speaks of Rivers," "The Weary Blues," "Theme for English B," and "Un-American Investigators," from *The Collected Poems of Langston Hughes* by Langston Hughes. Copyright © 1994 by the Estate of Langston Hughes. Used by permission of Alfred A. Knopf, a division of Random House, Inc. Excerpt from "When the Negro Was in Vogue" from *The Big Sea* by Langston Hughes. Copyright © 1940 by Langston Hughes. Copyright renewed © 1968 by Arna Bontemps and George Houston Bass. Reprinted by permission of Hill and Wang, a division of Farrar, Straus and Giroux, LLC.

Paul Humphrey. "Blow" from *Light Year '86.* Reprinted with the permission of Eleanor Humphrey.

Colette Inez. "Back When All Was Continuous Chuckles." Reprinted by permission from *The Hudson Review* Vol. LVII, No. 3 (Autumn 2004). Copyright © 2004 by Colette Inez.

Mark Jarman. "Unholy Sonnet" from *Questions for Ecclesiastes* by Mark Jarman (Story Line Press, 1997). Copyright © 1997 by Mark Jarman. Reprinted with permission of the author.

Randall Jarrell. "The Death of the Ball Turret Gunner" from *The Complete Poems* by Randall Jarrell. Copyright © 1969, renewed 1997 by Mary von S. Jarrell. Reprinted by permission of Farrar, Straus and Giroux, LLC.

Louis Jenkins. "The Prose Poem" from *The Winter Road.* Copyright © 2000 by Louis Jenkins. Reprinted with the permission of Holy Cow! Press, www.holycowpress.org.

Kelli Lyon Johnson. "Mapping an Identity" excerpted from *Julia Alvarez: Writing a New Place on the Map* by Kelli Lyon Johnson. Copyright © 2005 by Kelli Lyon Johnson. Reprinted by permission of the University of New Mexico Press.

Alice Jones. "The Foot" and "The Larynx" from *Anatomy* by Alice Jones (San Francisco: Bullnettle Press, 1997). Copyright © 1997 by Alice Jones. Reprinted by permission of the author.

June Jordan. "The Reception" from *Naming Our Destiny: New and Selected Poems* by June Jordan. Copyright © 1991. Appears by permission of the publisher, Thunder's Mouth Press, a division of Avalon Publishing Group, Inc.

Donald Justice. "Order in the Streets" from *Loser Weepers: Poems Found Practically Everywhere*, edited by George Hitchcock. Reprinted by permission of the Estate of Donald Justice.

Katherine Kearns. "On the Symbolic Setting of 'Home Burial'" excerpted from "The Place Is the Asylum: Women and Nature in Robert Frost's Poetry" in *American Literature* 59.2 (May 1987), pp. 190–210. Copyright © 1987 by Duke University Press. All rights reserved. Used by permission of the publisher.

X. J. Kennedy. "A Visit from St. Sigmund." Copyright © 1993 by X. J. Kennedy. Originally published in *Light, The Quarterly of Light Verse.* Reprinted by permission of the author and *Light.*

Jane Kenyon. "Surprise," "The Blue Bowl," and "Trouble with Math in a One-Room Country School," copyright 1996 by Jane Kenyon, reprinted from *Otherwise: New & Selected Poems* with the permission of Graywolf Press, Saint Paul, Minnesota. "The Shirt" from *From Room to Room,* copyright © 1978 by Jane Kenyon, reprinted with the permission of Alice James Books.

Maxine Hong Kingston. "Restaurant" from *The Iowa Review* 12 (Spring/Summer 1981). Reprinted by permission of the author.

Galway Kinnell. "After Making Love, We Hear Footsteps" and "Blackberry Eating" from *Three Books* by Galway Kinnell. Copyright © 1993 by Galway Kinnell. Reprinted by permission of Houghton Mifflin Company. All rights reserved.

Carolyn Kizer. "After Bashō" from *Cool, Calm & Collected: Poems 1960–2000.* Copyright © 2001 by Carolyn Kizer. Reprinted with the permission of Copper Canyon Press, P.O. Box 271, Port Townsend, WA 98368-0271.

Yusef Komunyakaa. "Slam, Dunk, & Hook" from *Magic City* (Wesleyan University Press, 1992). Copyright © 1992 by Yusef Komunyakaa. Reprinted by permission of Wesleyan University Press, www.wesleyan.edu/wespress.

Ted Kooser. "A Death at the Office" from *Flying at Night: Poems, 1965–1985.* Copyright © 1980, 1985. Reprinted by permission of the University of Pittsburgh Press.

Philip Larkin. "A Study of Reading Habits" from *Collected Poems* by Philip Larkin. Copyright © 1988, 1989 by the Estate of Philip Larkin. Reprinted by permission of Farrar, Straus and Giroux, LLC. Also from *The Whitson Weddings.* Copyright © 1964 by Philip Larkin. Reprinted by permission of Faber and Faber, Ltd.

Ann Lauinger. "Marvell Noir." First appeared in *Parnassus: Poetry in Review*, vol. 28, no. 1 & 2 (2005). Copyright © 2005 by Ann Lauinger. Reprinted by permission of the author.

Tato Laviera. "AmeRícan" is reprinted with permission from the publisher of *AmeRícan* by Tato Laviera (Houston: Arte Público Press – University of Houston, © 1985).

David Lenson. "On the Contemporary Use of Rhyme" from *The Chronicle of Higher Education* (February 24, 1988). Reprinted by permission of the author.

Phillis Levin. "End of April" from *The Afterimage.* Copyright © 1996 by Phillis Levin. Used by permission of Copper Beech Press.

J. Patrick Lewis. "The Unkindest Cut" from *Light 5* (Spring 1993). Reprinted with permission of the author and *Light.*

Richard Warren Lewis. "From an Interview with John Wayne" from the *Playboy Interview: John Wayne, Playboy* magazine (May 1971). Copyright © 1971, 1999 by Playboy. Reprinted with permission. All rights reserved.

Li Ho. "A Beautiful Girl Combs Her Hair," translated by David Young, from *Five T'ang Poets,* FIELD Translation Series #15. Copyright © 1990 by Oberlin College Press. Reprinted by permission of Oberlin College Press.

Rachel Loden. "Locked Ward: Newtown, Connecticut." Copyright © 2005 by Rachel Loden. Reprinted by permission of the author.

Thomas Lux. "Commercial Leech Farming Today," "Onomatopoeia," and "The Voice You Hear When You Read Silently," from *New and Selected Poems, 1975–1995* by Thomas Lux. Copyright © 1997 by Thomas Lux. Reprinted by permission of Houghton Mifflin Company. All rights reserved.

Thomas Lynch. "Liberty" from *Still Life in Milford* by Thomas Lynch. Copyright © 1998 by Thomas Lynch. Used by permission of W. W. Norton & Company, Inc.

Katharyn Howd Machan. "Hazel Tells LaVerne" from *Light Year '85.* Reprinted by permission of the author.

Haki R. Madhubuti. "The B Network" from *HeartLove: Wedding and Love Poems* by Haki R. Madhubuti. Copyright © 1998 by Haki R. Madhubuti. Reprinted by permission of Third World Press Inc., Chicago, IL.

Elaine Magarell. "The Joy of Cooking" from *Sometime the Cow Kick Your Head: Light Year 88/89.* Reprinted with permission of the author.

Julio Marzán. "Ethnic Poetry" and "The Translator at the Reception for Latin American Writers" are reprinted by permission of the author. "Ethnic Poetry" originally appeared in *Parnassus: Poetry in Review.*

Florence Cassen Mayers. "All-American Sestina," © 1996 Florence Cassen Mayers, as first published in *The Atlantic Monthly.* Reprinted with permission of the author.

David McCord. "Epitaph on a Waiter" from *Odds without Ends,* copyright © 1954 by David T. W. McCord. Reprinted by permission of Arthur B. Page, executor of the estate of David McCord.

Michael McFee. "In Medias Res" from *Colander* by Michael McFee. Copyright © 1996 by Michael McFee. Reprinted by permission of the author.

Rennie McQuilkin. "The Lighters." Reprinted by permission from *The Hudson Review*, Vol. LII, No. 3 (Autumn 1999). Copyright © 1999 by Rennie McQuilkin.

Peter Meinke. "The ABC of Aerobics" from *Night Watch on the Chesapeake* by Peter Meinke, copyright © 1987 by Peter Meinke. "(Untitled)" from *Liquid Paper: New and Selected Poems* by Peter Meinke, copyright © 1991. Reprinted by permission of the University of Pittsburgh Press.

James Merrill. "Casual Wear" from *Selected Poems, 1946–1985* by James Merrill. Copyright © 1992 by James Merrill. Used by permission of Alfred A. Knopf, a division of Random House, Inc.

W. S. Merwin. "When You Go Away" from *The Lice* by W. S. Merwin. Copyright © 1993 by W. S. Merwin. Reprinted by permission of The Wylie Agency.

Edna St. Vincent Millay. "I will put Chaos into fourteen lines" from *Collected Poems,* HarperCollins. Copyright © 1954, 1982 by Norma Millay Ellis. All rights reserved. Reprinted by permission of Elizabeth Barnett, literary executor.

Susan Minot. "My Husband's Back." Copyright © 2005 by Susan Minot. Originally appeared in *The New Yorker* (August 22, 2005). Reprinted by permission of Georges Borchardt, Inc., on behalf of the author.

Janice Mirikitani. "Recipe" reprinted by permission from *Shedding Silence* by Janice Mirikitani. Copyright © 1987 by Janice Mirikitani, Celestial Arts, a division of Ten Speed Press, Berkeley, CA, www.tenspeed.com.

Elaine Mitchell. "Form" from *Light 9* (Spring 1994). Reprinted by permission of the author.

John Mitchum and Howard Barnes. "The Hyphen." Copyright © 1973 DeVere Music Corporation (ASCAP), Batjac Music Company (ASCAP). Reprinted by permission of Cindy Mitchum Azbill.

N. Scott Momaday. "Crows in a Winter Composition" from *In the Presence of the Sun: Stories & Poems* by N. Scott Momaday. Copyright © 1993 by N. Scott Momaday. Reprinted by permission of St. Martin's Press, LLC.

Janice Townley Moore. "To a Wasp" first appeared in *Light Year,* Bits Press. Reprinted by permission of the author.

Lenard D. Moore. "Black Girl Tap Dancing" from *Furious Flower: African American Poetry from the Black Arts Movement,* edited by Joanne V. Gabin. Copyright © 1994 by Lenard D. Moore. Reprinted by permission of the author.

Pat Mora. "Legal Alien" is reprinted with permission from the publisher of *Chants* by Pat Mora (Houston: Arte Público Press — University of Houston, © 1985).

Robert Morgan. "Fever Wit" from *Topsoil Road: Poems* by Robert Morgan, copyright © 2000 by Robert Morgan, reprinted by permission of Louisiana State University Press. "Mountain Graveyard" and "Overalls" from *Sigodlin* (Wesleyan University Press, 1990), copyright © 1990 by Robert Morgan, reprinted by permission of Wesleyan University Press, www.wesleyan.edu/wespress. "On the Shape of a Poem" from *Epoch* (Fall/Winter 1983), reprinted by permission of the author.

Thylias Moss. "Interpretation of a Poem by Frost" from *Rainbow Remnants in Rock Bottom Ghetto Sky* by Thylias Moss. Copyright © 1991 by Thylias Moss. Reprinted by permission of Persea Books, Inc., NY.

Joan Murray. "Play-by-Play" reprinted by permission from *The Hudson Review*, Vol. XLIX, No. 4 (Winter 1997). Copyright © 1997 by Joan Murray.

Taslima Nasrin. "At the Back of Progress . . . ," translated by Carolyne Wright and Mohammad Nurul Huda, from *The Game in Reverse: Poems* by Taslima Nasrin. Copyright © 1995 by Taslima Nasrin. English translation © 1995 by Carolyne Wright. Reprinted with the permission of George Braziller Inc.

Howard Nemerov. "Because You Asked about the Line between Prose and Poetry" from *Sentences* by Howard Nemerov, copyright © 1980. "Walking the Dog" from *Trying Conclusions: New and Selected Poems 1961–1991* by Howard Nemerov, copyright © 1991. Reprinted by permission.

Pablo Neruda. "The United Fruit Co." from *Neruda & Vallejo: Selected Poems*, edited and translated by Robert Bly. Reprinted with the permission of Robert Bly. "Verb" (translated by Ilan Stavans) from *The Poetry of Pablo Neruda*. Copyright © 2003 by Pablo Neruda and Fundacíon Pablo Neruda. Introduction and notes copyright © 2003 by Ilan Stavans. "Verbo" (original Spanish version) from *Pablo Neruda: Five Decades: A Selection (Poems, 1925–1970)*, edited and translated by Ben Belitt (New York: Grove Press, 1974). Reprinted by permission of Carmen Balcells Literary Agency, Barcelona, Spain, on behalf of the Pablo Neruda Foundation of Chile. "Word" (translated by Ben Belitt) from *Pablo Neruda: Five Decades: A Selection (Poems, 1925–1970)*, edited and translated by Ben Belitt. Copyright © 1974 by Grove Press. Used by permission of Grove/Atlantic, Inc. "Word" (translated by Kristin Linklater and Gilda Orlandi-Sanchez) from *Freeing Shakespeare's Voice: The Actor's Guide to Talking the Text* by Kristin Linklater. Copyright © 1992. Used by permission of Theatre Communications Group.

John Frederick Nims. "Love Poem" from *Selected Poems*. Copyright © 1982 by the University of Chicago. Reprinted by permission of the University of Chicago Press.

Alden Nowlan. "The Bull Moose" from *Alden Nowlan: Selected Poems* by Alden Nowlan. Copyight © 1967 by Irwin Publishing Inc. Reprinted by permission of House of Anansi Press, Toronto.

Adrian Oktenberg. "Memory in 'The Negro Speaks of Rivers'" excerpted from "From the Bottom Up: Three Radicals of the Thirties" in *A Gift of Tongues: Critical Challenges in Contemporary American Poetry*, edited by Marie Harris and Kathleen Aguero. Copyright © 1987. Reprinted by permission of the University of Georgia Press.

Sharon Olds. "Last Night" from *The Wellspring* by Sharon Olds, copyright © 1996 by Sharon Olds. "Rite of Passage" and "Sex without Love" from *The Dead and the Living* by Sharon Olds, copyright © 1987 by Sharon Olds. Used by permission of Alfred A. Knopf, a division of Random House, Inc.

Mary Oliver. "Mindful" from *Why I Wake Early* by Mary Oliver. Copyright © 2004 by Mary Oliver. Reprinted by permission of Beacon Press, Boston.

Eric Ormsby. "Nose" from *For a Modest God*, copyright © 1997. Reprinted by permission of ECW Press.

Lisa Parker. "Snapping Beans" from *Parnassus* 23.2 (1998). Copyright © 1998 by Lisa Parker. Reprinted by permission of the author.

Linda Pastan. "Jump Cabling" from *Light Year: The Quarterly of Light Verse*. Copyright © 1984 by Linda Pastan. Reprinted by permission of Jean V. Naggar Literary Agency, Inc. "Marks" from *PM/AM: New and Selected Poems* by Linda Pastan. Copyright © 1978 by Linda Pastan. Used by permission of W. W. Norton & Company, Inc. "Pass/Fail" from *Aspects of Eve* by Linda Pastan. Copyright © 1970, 1971, 1972, 1973, 1974, 1975 by Linda Pastan. Used by permission of Liveright Publishing Corporation.

Octavio Paz. "The Street" from *Early Poems 1935–1955*. Reprinted with permission of Indiana University Press.

Molly Peacock. "Desire" from *Cornucopia: New and Selected Poems* by Molly Peacock. Copyright © 2002 by Molly Peacock. Used by permission of W. W. Norton & Company, Inc.

Laurence Perrine. "The limerick's never averse." Reprinted by permission of Catherine Perrine.

Marge Piercy. "For the Young Who Want To" and "The Secretary Chant" from *Circles on the Water* by Marge Piercy, copyright © 1982 by Marge Piercy. Used by permission of Alfred A. Knopf, a division of Random House, Inc.

Sylvia Plath. "Mirror" from *Crossing the Water* by Sylvia Plath, copyright © 1963 by Ted Hughes, reprinted by permission of HarperCollins Publishers, Inc. Originally appeared in *The New Yorker*. Also from *The Collected Poems* by Sylvia Plath, edited by Ted Hughes, reprinted by permission of Faber & Faber, Ltd.

Peter D. Poland. "On 'Neither Out Far nor In Deep'" from *The Explicator* 52.2 (Winter 1994). Reprinted with permission of the Helen Dwight Reid Educational Foundation. Published by Heldref Publications, 1319 Eighteenth Street, NW, Washington, DC, 20036-1802. Copyright © 1994.

Ezra Pound. "In a Station of the Metro" from *Personae*. Copyright © 1926 by Ezra Pound. Reprinted by permission of New Directions Publishing Corp.

Arnold Rampersad. "On the Persona in 'The Negro Speaks of Rivers'" excerpted from "The Origins of Poetry in Langston Hughes," *Southern Review* 21.3 (1985), pp. 703-4. Copyright © 1985 by Arnold Rampersad. Reprinted by permission of the author.

Henry Reed. "Lessons of the War" (1. Naming of Parts) from *Henry Reed: Collected Poems*, edited by Jon Stallworthy. Copyright © 1991 by the Executor of Henry Reed's Estate. Reprinted by permission of Oxford University Press.

Marny Requa. "From an Interview with Julia Alvarez" excerpted from "The Politics of Fiction," *Frontera* 5 (1997). 29 Jan. 1997 <http://www.fronteramag.com/issue5/Alvarez/index.htm>. Reprinted with the permission of Marny Requa.

David S. Reynolds. "Popular Literature and 'Wild Nights — Wild Nights!'" from *Beneath the American Renaissance* by David S. Reynolds. Copyright © 1988 by David S. Reynolds. Used by permission of Random House, Inc.

Rainer Maria Rilke. "The Panther" from *The Selected Poetry of Rainer Maria Rilke* by Rainer Maria Rilke, translated by Stephen Mitchell. Copyright © 1982 by Stephen Mitchell. Used by permission of Random House, Inc.

Alberto Ríos. "The Gathering Evening" from *The Smallest Muscle in the Human Body.* Copyright © 2002 by Alberto Ríos. Reprinted with the permission of Copper Canyon Press, P.O. Box 271, Port Townsend, WA 98368-0271. "Seniors" from *Five Indiscretions.* Copyright © 1985 by Alberto Ríos. Reprinted by permission of the author.

Theodore Roethke. "Elegy for Jane," copyright © 1950 by Theodore Roethke. "My Papa's Waltz," copyright 1942 by Hearst Magazines, Inc. "Root Cellar," copyright 1943 by Modern Poetry Association, Inc. From *The Collected Poems of Theodore Roethke* by Theodore Roethke. Used by permission of Doubleday, a division of Random House, Inc.

Frederik L. Rusch. "Society and Character in 'The Love Song of J. Alfred Prufrock'" excerpted from "Approaching Literature through the Social Psychology of Erich Fromm" in *Psychological Perspectives on Literature: Freudian Dissidents and Non-Freudians,* edited by Joseph Natoli. Copyright © 1984. Reprinted by permission of the author.

Yousif al-Sa'igh. "An Iraqi Evening," translated by Saadi A Simawe, Ralph Savarese, and Chuck Miller, from *Iraqi Poetry Today,* edited by Saadi A Simawe (Modern Poetry in Translation, 2003). Copyright © 2003 by Modern Poetry in Translation. Reprinted by permission of Modern Poetry in Translation.

Mary Jo Salter. "Home Movies: A Sort of Ode" from *A Kiss in Space: Poems* by Mary Jo Salter. Copyright © 1999 by Mary Jo Salter. Used by permission of Alfred A. Knopf, a division of Random House, Inc.

Sonia Sanchez. "c'mon man hold me" from *Like the Singing Coming Off the Drums: Love Poems* by Sonia Sanchez. Copyright © 1998 by Sonia Sanchez. Reprinted by permission of Beacon Press, Boston.

Sappho. "Artfully adorned Aphrodite, deathless" from *Sappho A Garland: The Poems and Fragments of Sappho,* translated by Jim Powell. Copyright © 1993 by Jim Powell. Reprinted by permission of the author. "Prayer to my lady of Paphos" [Fragment #38] from *Sappho: A New Translation* by Mary Barnard. Copyright © 1958 by the Regents of the University of California, renewed © 1986 by Mary Barnard. Reprinted by permission of the Regents of the University of California and the publisher, the University of California Press.

Peter Schmitt. "Friends with Numbers" from *Hazard Duty.* Copyright © 1995 by Peter Schmitt. Used by permission of Copper Beech Press.

Elisabeth Schneider. "Hints of Eliot in Prufrock." Reprinted by permission of the Modern Language Association of America from "Prufrock and After: The Theme of Change," *PMLA* 87 (1982): 1103-17.

Léopold Sédar Senghor. "Totem" from *The Collected Poetry of Léopold Sédar Senghor,* edited and translated by Melvin Dixon (Charlottesville: U Virginia Press, 1991). Copyright © 1991. Reprinted with permission of the University of Virginia Press.

S. Pearl Sharp. "It's the Law: A Rap Poem" from *Typing in the Dark* (Writers and Readers Publishing, Inc., 1991), Reprinted in *African American Literature* 1998. Used by permission of the author.

Shu Ting. "O Motherland, Dear Motherland" (translated by Fang Dai, Dennis Ding, and Edward Morin) from *The Red Azalea: Chinese Poetry Since the Cultural Revolution,* edited by Edward Morin (Honolulu: U Hawai'i Press, 1990). Reprinted by permission of the University of Hawai'i Press.

Charles Simic. "To the One Upstairs" from *Jackstraws* by Charles Simic. Copyright © 1999 by Charles Simic. Reprinted by permission of Charles Simic and Harcourt, Inc.

Louis Simpson. "In the Suburbs" from *At the End of the Open Road* by Louis Simpson. Wesleyan UP, 1963. Reprinted by permission of the author.

David R. Slavitt. "Height" from *Falling from Silence: Poems* by David R. Slavitt, copyright © 2001 by David Slavitt. "Titanic" from *Change of Address: Poems New and Selected* by David R. Slavitt, copyright © 2005 by David R. Slavitt. Reprinted by permission of Louisiana State University Press.

Ernest Slyman. "Lightning Bugs" from *Sometime the Cow Kick Your Head: Light Year 88/89.* Reprinted by permission of the author.

Patricia Smith. "What It's Like to Be a Black Girl (for Those of You Who Aren't)" from *Life According to Motown* by Patricia Smith. Copyright © 1991 by Patricia Smith. Reprinted by permission of the author.

Gary Snyder. "How Poetry Comes to Me" from *No Nature: New and Selected Poems* by Gary Snyder. Copyright © 1992 by Gary Snyder. Used by permission of Pantheon Books, a division of Random House, Inc.

David Solway. "Windsurfing." Reprinted by permission of the author.

Cathy Song. "A Poet in the House" from *The Land of Bliss* by Cathy Song. Copyright © 2001. Reprinted by permission of the University of Pittsburgh Press. "Sunworshippers" from *School Figures* by Cathy Song. Copyright © 1994. Reprinted by permission of the University of Pittsburgh Press. "The White Porch" and "The Youngest Daughter" from *Picture Bride.* Copyright © 1983 by Yale University Press. Reprinted by permission of Yale University Press.

Gary Soto. "Behind Grandma's House" and "Mexicans Begin Jogging" from *New and Selected Poems* by Gary Soto. Copyright © 1995. Used with permission of Chronicle Books, LLC, San Francisco. Visit www.chroniclebooks.com.

Wole Soyinka. "Telephone Conversation" from *Ibadan* 10 (November 1960). Copyright © 1962, 1990 by Wole Soyinka. Reprinted by permission of the author.

Bruce Springsteen. "You're Missing." Copyright © 2002 by Bruce Springsteen. Reprinted by permission. International copyright secured. All rights reserved.

William Stafford. "Traveling through the Dark," copyright © 1962, 1998 by the Estate of William Stafford. Reprinted from *The Way It Is: New & Selected Poems* with the permission of Graywolf Press, Saint Paul, Minnesota.

Timothy Steele. "Waiting for the Storm" from *Sapphics and Uncertainties: Poems, 1970–1986* by Timothy Steele. Copyright © 1986 by Timothy Steele. Reprinted with the permission of the University of Arkansas Press.

Jim Stevens. "Schizophrenia." Originally appeared in *Light: The Quarterly of Light Verse* (Spring 1992). Copyright © 1992 by Jim Stevens. Reprinted by permission of Edith Stevens.

Wallace Stevens. "Anecdote of the Jar" and "The Emperor of Ice-Cream," copyright © 1923 by Wallace Stevens and renewed 1982 by Holly Stevens, copyright © 1954 by Wallace Stevens and renewed 1951 by Wallace Stevens, from *The Collected Poems of Wallace Stevens* by Wallace Stevens. Used by permission of Alfred A. Knopf, a division of Random House, Inc.

Norman Stock. "What I Said" from *Poetry After 9/11: An Anthology of New York Poets*, edited by Dennis Loy Johnson and Valerie Merians. Copyright © 2002 by Norman Stock. Grateful acknowledgment is made to Melville House Publishing and the author for permission to reprint this poem.

Robert Sward. "A Personal Analysis of 'The Love Song of J. Alfred Prufrock'" from *Touchstones: American Poets on a Favorite Poem*, eds. Robert Pack and Jay Parini, Middlebury College Press, published by UP New England. Copyright © 1995, 1997, 2000 by Robert Sward. Reprinted by permission of the author.

May Swenson. "A Nosty Fright" from *In Other Words* by May Swenson, 1987. Copyright © 1984 by May Swenson. Used with permission of the Literary Estate of May Swenson.

Wisława Szymborska. "Nothing's a Gift" from *View with a Grain of Sand*, copyright © 1993 by Wisława Szymborska. English translation by Stanisław Barańczak and Clare Cavanaugh, copyright © 1995 by Harcourt, Inc. Reprinted by permission of the publisher.

Dylan Thomas. "Do Not Go Gentle into That Good Night," copyright © 1952 by Dylan Thomas, "Fern Hill," copyright © 1945 by The Trustees for the Copyrights of Dylan Thomas, and "The Hand That Signed the Paper," copyright © 1939 by New Directions Publishing Corporation, from *The Poems of Dylan Thomas*. Reprinted by permission of New Directions Publishing Corp and David Higham Associates Limited. "On the Words in Poetry" from *Early Prose Writings* by Dylan Thomas. Copyright © 1972 by The Trustees for the Copyrights of Dylan Thomas. Reprinted by permission of Harold Ober Associates Incorporated.

Mabel Loomis Todd. "The *Character* of Amherst" from *The Years and Hours of Emily Dickinson*, volume 2, by Jay Leda. Copyright © 1960 by Yale University Press. Reprinted by permission of Yale University Press.

Tomas Tranströmer. "April and Silence," translated by Robin Fulton, from *New Collected Poems* (Bloodaxe Books, 1997). Copyright © 1997 by Robin Fulton and Bloodaxe Books. Reprinted by permission of Bloodaxe Books Ltd.

Natasha Trethewey. "Domestic Work, 1937," copyright © 2000 by Natasha Trethewey. Reprinted from *Domestic Work* with the permission of Graywolf Press, Saint Paul, Minnesota.

William Trowbridge. "Poets' Corner," *Georgia Review* 53.1 (Spring 1999). Copyright © 1999 by The University of Georgia. Reprinted by permission of *The Georgia Review* and William Trowbridge.

John Updike. "Dog's Death" from *Midpoint and Other Poems* by John Updike. Copyright © 1969 and renewed 1997 by John Updike. "Player Piano" from *Collected Poems, 1953–1993* by John Updike. Copyright © 1993 by John Updike. Used by permission of Alfred A. Knopf, a division of Random House, Inc.

Richard Wakefield. "In a Poetry Workshop," *Light* (Winter 1999). Reprinted with permission of the author and *Light*.

Derek Walcott. Excerpt from "The Road Taken" from *Homage to Robert Frost* by Joseph Brodsky, Seamus Heaney, and Derek Walcott. Copyright © 1996 by the Estate of Joseph Brodsky. Reprinted by permission of Farrar, Straus and Giroux, LLC.

Ronald Wallace. "Building an Outhouse" from *The Making of Happiness* by Ronald Wallace, copyright © 1991. "Dogs (1)" from *The Uses of Adversity* by Ronald Wallace, copyright © 1998. "Miss Goff" from "Teachers: A Primer," from *Time's Fancy* by Ronald Wallace, copyright © 1994. Reprinted by permission of the University of Pittsburgh Press. "In a Rut" from *The Best American Poetry 2003*, edited by Yusef Komunyakaa, copyright © 2003, reprinted by permission of the author.

Marilyn Nelson Waniek. "Emily Dickinson's Defunct" from *For the Body: Poems* by Marilyn Nelson Waniek. Copyright © 1978 by Marilyn Nelson Waniek. Reprinted by permission of the author and Louisiana State University Press.

Tom Wayman. "Did I Miss Anything?" from *Did I Miss Anything?* by Tom Wayman. Copyright © 1993. Reprinted by permission of Harbour Publishing.

Richard Wilbur. "A Late Aubade" from *Walking to Sleep: New Poems and Translations*. Copyright © 1968 by Richard Wilbur and renewed 1996 by Richard Wilbur, reprinted by permission of Harcourt, Inc. Originally published in *The New Yorker*. "Love Calls Us to the Things of This World" from *Things of This World*. Copyright © 1956 and renewed 1984 by Richard Wilbur, reprinted by permission of Harcourt, Inc.

Miller Williams. "Thinking about Bill, Dead of AIDS" from *Living on the Surface: New and Selected Poems* by Miller Williams. Copyright © 1972, 1975, 1976, 1979, 1980, 1987, 1988, 1989 by Miller Williams. Reprinted by permission of the author.

William Carlos Williams. "Poem," copyright © 1953 by William Carlos Williams. "Spring and All," "The Red Wheelbarrow," and "This Is Just to Say," copyright © 1938 by New Directions Publishing Corp. From *Collected Poems: 1909–1939*, Volume I. Reprinted by permission of New Directions Publishing Corp.

Terry Wilson. "On Hollywood Indians" excerpted from "Celluloid Sovereignty: Hollywood's 'History' of Native Americans" in *Legal Realism: Movies as Legal Texts*, edited by John Denvir. Copyright © 1996 by Board of Trustees of the University of Illinois. Used with permission of the University of Illinois Press.

CRITICAL PERSPECTIVES

Index of First Lines

Index of Authors and Titles

Related to explication —
Ch 11 - p288
        p695

list of Qs - pp 61-62
    - Go over end of 2nd class - 6/2